BRITPOP!

Also by John Harris

Dark Side of the Moon:
The Making of Pink Floyd's Masterpiece
(forthcoming)

BRITPOP!

COOL BRITANNIA AND THE
SPECTACULAR DEMISE OF
ENGLISH ROCK

JOHN HARRIS

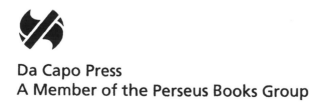

Da Capo Press
A Member of the Perseus Books Group

Cataloging-in-Publication data for this book is available from the Library of Congress.

First Da Capo Press edition 2004
This Da Capo paperback edition of *Britpop!* is a republication of the English-language edition first published in 2003 in the United Kingdom by Fourth Estate as *The Last Party*. It is reprinted by arrangement with HarperCollins UK.
ISBN 0-306-81367-X

Published by Da Capo Press
A Member of the Perseus Books Group
http://www.dacapopress.com

Da Capo Press books are available at special discounts for bulk purchases in the U.S. by corporations, institutions, and other organizations. For more information, please contact the Special Markets Department at the Perseus Books Group, 11 Cambridge Center, Cambridge, MA 02142, or call (800) 255-1514 or (617) 252-5298, or e-mail special.markets@perseusbooks.com.

Contents

PART T H R E E

Author's note: on a small handful of occasions, the text makes reference to episodes – interviews, chiefly – in which I was directly involved. I trust that the few people who recognise them will understand that I have decided to avoid the words 'I' and 'me' and report them in the same terms as other incidents.

Music seems crazy
Bands start up
Each and every day
I saw another one, just the other day
A special new band . . .

Pavement, Cut Your Hair

For my Dad, a hero in an age of none

Preface to the Da Capo Edition

At the tail-end of 1995, a song entitled Wonderwall arrived in the Billboard Hot 100. On first hearing, it was not the most obvious of hit records: its vocal line, sung in bellowing tones that allowed for no hint of light or shade, was built around only a handful of notes; its lyrics often tumbled into impenetrable doggerel; and its musical backing seemed dangerously close to falling into droning monotony. And yet, each time the chorus ascended to its redemptive first line – 'Maybe, you're gonna be the one that saves me' – its shortcomings seem to recede into irrelevance. In terms of giving vent to a sense of hard-fought optimism, Wonderwall spoke a very potent language indeed. 'It's not over anybody's head,' said one Lewis Largent, the Vice-President of Music at MTV and sometime host of *120 Minutes.* 'It's very direct. Lyrically, it's very touching in a simple way, like I Second That Emotion and I Want To Hold Your Hand.'

The song was the work of Oasis, a British quintet whose American profile had been slowly rising over the previous year. Whereas it had long been fashionable for British rock bands to express nonchalance about the idea of American success and commit themselves to only the most cursory transatlantic trips, Oasis had diligently toured the United States on half a dozen occasions, visiting both the big cities and the obligatory 'secondary markets.' Their diligence, however, would have been nothing without the straight-ahead populism of their music: stuff that brazenly pushed some of rock's most well-worn buttons, seemingly on the basis that the oldest tricks are usually the most effective.

Many of their British contemporaries placed an emphasis on avoiding musical cliche as well as lyrics that were founded on the notion of somehow reflecting their time. In the view of Noel Gallagher, Oasis's guitarist and songwriter, they were thereby relegating themselves to irrelevance. 'With Oasis,' he said, 'it's the bottom line: here's a guitar, here's the songs, you have them. We're not preaching about our sexuality, we're not telling kids how to act. You want to write about shagging and taking drugs and being in a band. It's just about a feeling, you just get up and play it.'

If such a rejection of artifice and intellect would soon result in Oasis's music becoming woefully formulaic, for now, the band was buoyed by two factors. First, though his music plundered the rock canon, the cream of Noel's initial run of songs pulsed with an energy that managed to make his debt to the past an irrelevance. The slow-paced likes of Wonderwall may have been his most commercial compositions, but his best work was altogether more adrenalised. Finesse and musical sophistication were nowhere to be heard, but in the likes of Bring It On Down, Rock'n'Roll Star, Acquiesce and Morning Glory, one heard a mixture that was age-old and intoxicating: brutally fuzztoned guitars melding with vocals that somehow expressed the desperate desire for escape. On the latter score, Oasis's key asset was Noel's younger brother, Liam, a swaggering, impossibly arrogant figure who managed to couch much of what he sang in a palpable sense of menace. When the synthesis of his brother's rock classicism and his own snarling belligerence came off, one heard a compelling mixture of melody and punk-rock attitude: not for nothing did one overexcited critic term Oasis 'The Sex Beatles.'

Thanks partly to such qualities, the album from which Wonderwall was taken, the strangely titled *(What's The Story) Morning Glory?*, was soon resting in the top five of Billboard's albums chart, and Oasis were briefly allowed into the upper reaches of the rock hierarchy. By that spring, they had been booked into 20,000-capacity American arenas, and encouraged to think of their first burst of US success as a concrete sign of imminent global domination.

The group's most enthusiastic champion – aside from the Gallaghers themselves – was Alan McGee, the self-styled President of Creation, their British record label. McGee had managed the cliched music business masterstroke of 'discovering' Oasis in a tiny Scottish venue in May 1993. Now, after re-emerging from a drug-fuelled breakdown and a long spell in rehab, he was expressing his belief in their music in downright evangelical terms. 'They are the best British band since The Clash,' he said. 'The first time I heard Wonderwall, within eight seconds I knew it was great. It's Noel's songs, Liam's voice, Liam's sex appeal. They've got the lot. In time, they'll be the biggest band in the world.'

Naturally enough, it didn't quite work out like that, but anyway . . .

In the States, Oasis stood pretty much alone, one of the few British successes in a country that had long since learned the art of musical self-sufficiency. Back in their home territory, however, their US success was portrayed as the crowning glory of a cultural moment that took in an array of rock groups. The Gallagher Brothers, according to some accounts, were the ambassadors of a musical wave that had decisively taken root in 1994 and had been accorded a term that soon passed into ubiquity: Britpop.

In Britpop's three-year genesis, Oasis were relative latecomers. The first stirrings of Britpop came in 1992, when a London-based group called Suede* accompanied their first records with showy statements about their proud sense of place. They emerged mere months after Smells Like Teen Spirit had heralded Nirvana's domination of the UK's left-field rock milieu and the international phenomenon known as Grunge – and craftily tapped into the British music press's eternal liking for following one development with an announcement of the arrival of its polar opposite.

While *Nevermind* blared from every college campus and all around was Pearl Jam, Stone Temple Pilots and Alice In Chains, Suede expressed their fondness for such archetypal British icons as David Bowie and Morrissey, and voiced a haughty disdain for the US. 'I'm not anti-American by any means,' said their singer, Brett Anderson, 'but I've never been impressed by it. Claustrophobic Englishness is conducive to great art. In America, there's no tragedy, no failure, no impotence, no premature ejaculation.' By way of underlining his rather blinkered rhetoric, Anderson delivered a clutch of Suede's songs in a mewling London accent and sprinkled his lyrics with arcane English slang.

Anderson had formed the band – and forged much of Suede's worldview – with his one-time girlfriend, Justine Frischmann, who had

---

* In the USA, Suede were forced to rename themselves The London Suede after legal action from an obscure lounge singer who traded under the same name.

initially been Suede's rhythm guitarist. Splitting from both her boyfriend and the band, she had gone on to become the partner of Damon Albarn, the singer and chief songwriter for Blur, who had enjoyed a brief flurry of British success before falling into the kind of creative crisis that was reflective of a distinct lack of ideas. Under Frischmann's influence, however, Albarn soon became the advocate of an agenda similar to Suede's, pushing Blur's music towards such influences as Bowie, The Kinks and XTC, and ensuring that his songs were founded in his adopted hometown of London.

In Albarn's hands, moreover, the emphasis on Englishness came to form the basis of a kind of cultural-political campaign. Blur's second album, *Modern Life Is Rubbish,* released in 1993, came close to being titled *England Vs America.* In his interviews, he claimed that Blur alone were placed to slough off the hegemony of Nirvana and their ilk. 'If punk was getting rid of hippies, then I'm getting rid of grunge,' he grandly declared. 'People should smarten up, be a bit more energetic. They're walking around like hippies again – they're stooped, they've got greasy hair, there's no difference. Whether they like it or not, they're listening to Black Sabbath again. It irritates me.'

For all the stridency of his pronouncements, Blur's relatively lowly commercial success meant that – in the short-term at least – they couldn't acquire the cultural clout to which Albarn aspired. Throughout 1993, Suede – much to Albarn's disgust – remained much the more successful band; but by the following year, Blur had reversed their respective positions. *Parklife,* fortuitously released mere weeks after Kurt Cobain's suicide in April 1994, soon achieved British sales that dwarfed Suede's achievements and belatedly took Albarn's Anglo-centric standpoint to the centre of the mainstream. By the following summer, Blur would be among the most famous people in the UK, and effusive tributes to Britpop would be filling the country's newsstands.

By that point, thanks partly to a shared generational experience that took in such British rock staples as The Jam, The Smiths and the Specials, Blur had been joined by a host of like minds, most of whom have long since been lost to history. At the time, however, the arrival of Sleeper, Supergrass, Menswear, Gene, Shed Seven, The Boo Radleys and Echobelly – along with Pulp, whose creative feats were as accomplished as those managed by any of the senior Britpop bands – suggested a real musical renaissance, and was celebrated as a pop-cultural moment akin to the one that had taken hold in the Britain of the mid-

1960s. No matter that most of the groups concerned could not hold a candle to The Beatles, Stones, Kinks, Who et al., or that the inability of most of them to spread their influence beyond the UK meant this was an altogether more parochial upsurge; that part of the British national psyche that will forever refer back to the era of *Revolver, My Generation* and Swinging London could not be held back.

Given the no-less insatiable British appetite for soap opera, the success of Elastica – founded by Justine Frischmann, and among Britpop's most accomplished bands – only made the coverage of Britpop more hysterical. Quite apart from the appeal of both their artful punk-pop and convention-trouncing three-quarters female line-up, her former bond with Brett Anderson gave her ascent a mouthwatering subtext of romantic intrigue. Moreover, now she was with Damon Albarn, Britpop surely had its own ruling couple.

'In public,' said one newspaper profile written in 1995, 'Damon grins from the covers of trendy magazines. In private, he lives in a smart London home with Justine Frischmann, lead singer of Elastica, a band already tipped to clean up in 1996. The couple are well on their way to becoming the King and Queen of British pop.'

Blur, Suede, Pulp and Elastica – along with some of their more lowly contemporaries – were tied together by social ties forged in London's pubs and clubs, particularly those in and around Camden Town, a grimy enclave in the city's North that served as its bohemian equivalent of Greenwich Village. They were also united by a broad affinity with the strand of British rock rooted in the art-schools of the 60s and 70s, whereby musical norms were always to be cleverly subverted, and any notion of authenticity was sidelined by the pre-eminence of contrivance and experiment. To this clique, Ray Davies was a way more magnetic figure than Keith Richards; when it came to punk rock, their most oft-quoted influence was Wire, the avant-garde iconoclasts who lived in a very different universe to that of The Sex Pistols and The Clash.

In that sense, the appearance of Oasis at the end of 1993 suggested the sudden appearance of gatecrashers at a party. Though both Gallagher Brothers eventually relocated to London, they were proud products of the Northern British city of Manchester – as evidenced by the likes of the Buzzcocks, Joy Division and The Smiths, arguably the UK's most fertile music city. Moreover, as against the London bands' fondness for art-pop, Oasis were proletarian rock'n'rollers, seemingly set on tapping British music into the eternal verities of cranked-up amplifiers and the three-chord trick.

Strangely, however, they were seamlessly incorporated into the Brit-pop moment. Their vociferous love of The Beatles, whose influence was reflected in only the crudest of outlines, squared with the afore-mentioned comparisons with the 1960s; the Gallaghers' eventual pres-ence on the same social circuit as their contemporaries meant that they were portrayed as part of the same 'in' crowd. In time, moreover, they played up to the Britpop stereotype: by 1996, Noel Gallagher was in the habit of playing a guitar emblazoned with the British flag.

Equally important, however, was their place on the roster of Cre-ation Records and the simple fact of their subsequent success. Quite apart from its sense of place and shared list of influences, Britpop was an outgrowth of British indie-rock: the stuff that, in the wake of punk, had sought to express its ongoing hostility to the mainstream by set-ting up what amounted to an alternative musical universe. In terms of both their listening habits and early experiences as musicians, a good deal of the Britpop generation had cut their teeth in the indie world – but whereas their predecessors had seemed to view mass-market suc-cess as a pollutant of artistic purity, now it was almost seen as a duty.

'I'd always felt compartmentalised and ghettoised,' said Pulp's Jarvis Cocker, who would briefly suffer the malign effects of being a House-hold Name, 'so to get the chance to take part in the mainstream was exciting to me.' The abiding idea, it seemed, was the invasion of the UK's pop culture by those previously kept to the margins – but like so many revolutionaries, a number of the bands quickly discovered that life with power and influence fell short of their expectations and fatally polluted their ideals.

All this was dramatised in the summer of 1995, when Blur decided to schedule the British release of a single entitled Country House for Monday August 14: the same day that Oasis were putting out their own Roll With It. Both had been destined for the top of the charts, but were now locked in a race – and the result, given the summer's usual dearth of hard news, was an outpouring of coverage and comment that turned Britpop into an inflated caricature of itself. The comparisons with the 60s were stretched to breaking point by claims that the con-test was somehow a reflection of the relations between The Beatles and Stones (who, in actual fact, had always co-operated to ensure their sin-gles never clashed). Britpop's in-built emphasis on the importance of filling the charts with something more substantial than manufactured pap was sidelined in favour of the empty fetishisation of the Number One position. To cap it all, the two songs were among both groups' worst work to date.

Thanks in part to marketing chicanery, Blur won out – but the cost to their internal bond was huge. Their guitarist, Graham Coxon, had always exuded a stereotypical indie-rock queasiness about their snowballing success; in the wake of his band's much-hyped 'victory', he pronounced those behind the stunt as a 'circle of freaks' and began to distance himself from his colleagues. He was pulled back to the group on the proviso that they left Britpop behind and went back to an altogether more angular, left-field approach (though, when he finally split from Blur in 2002, the sense of unhealed wounds was clear).

Oasis, by contrast, embraced their ever-increasing fame with no qualms whatsoever. Their associations with the indie-rock ethic had only ever amounted to a Flag of Convenience; now, they were revealed as proud merchants of *de facto* stadium rock. They may have finished second in the race with Blur, but by the time they released *(What's The Story) Morning Glory?*, they were the British public's unchallenged favourites. By the following year, they would be playing two shows at a vast country estate called Knebworth Park, the previous setting for shows by Led Zeppelin, Queen and The Rolling Stones, and living the lives of newly-rich millionaires, with credit card bills and cocaine habits to match. Fuelled by such refreshment, they would also express an ugly dislike for their former rivals, which reached a hideous climax when Noel Gallagher expressed the hope that Damon Albarn and the Blur bassist Alex James might 'catch AIDS and die'.

Though they had long expressed sneering disdain for the term, by 1996, Britpop meant Oasis. Moreover, if part of Britpop's narrative was based on the idea of avenging the dominance of America, Oasis helped the cause by fleetingly becoming the only rock band of their generation to make a substantial commercial impact in the US. As Wonderwall worked its strange magic, they seemed all-conquering, and their strength was thrown into sharper relief by the decline of many of their Britpop contemporaries into self-doubt and commercial decline.

Just as Britpop's credibility, integrity and simple well-being began to slide, however, it was apparently elevated to new levels of influence. This was not simply a matter of Oasis's seemingly unstoppable success, or their having encouraged the success of a second wave of Britpop bands, largely modelled in their own image; it was also down to the spectacle of musicians and their associates being welcomed into unimaginably lofty places.

These days, Prime Minister Tony Blair is chiefly renowned for his habit of couching the Bush Administration's more reckless foreign policies in terms of statesmanlike respectability. Back then, however, he was merely the Leader of the Parliamentary Opposition – all but guaranteed to win the next British General Election, but free of the kind of demands that come with power. Moreover, he moved in a political world that, by modern standards, seems unspeakably innocent: 9/11 was half a decade away, and the UK's politicians often seemed happy to concern themselves with seeming ephemera. In the Labour Party, for example, there was a brief spasm of excitement about the concept of 'Cool Britannia', later translated into a brief political project known as 'the re-branding of Britain'.

The idea, embodied in a celebrated *Vanity Fair* feature published in early 1997, was founded on the fact that Britpop's embodiment of a kind of national cultural renewal had seemingly spread into all kinds of areas: art, books, fashion, movies, architecture and politics. 'Parliament is undergoing a youthquake of its own!' raved the magazine's camped-up text. 'Say hello to shirtsleeved, smiling Tony Blair, the leader of the ascendant Labour Party. The Right Honourable Tony is just 43 years old and has an outlook to match. Change is in the air in London, and the kids, as their idol Liam Gallagher is wont to say, are mad for it!'

Just as Bill Clinton had announced the arrival of a new political generation by blowing into his saxophone and staging inauguration celebrations featuring Michael Stipe, Bob Dylan and LL Cool J, so Blair and his colleagues were keen to ally themselves with the figureheads of the supposed new, vibrant country that Britpop exemplified. Among those who entered his orbit were Damon Albarn, Creation Records' Alan McGee, and Noel Gallagher. Albarn sipped gin and tonic with Blair at the Houses Of Parliament in the summer of 1995, toyed with the idea of some kind of public political involvement, and then shied away. McGee, in keeping with his post-rehab portrayal as a sharp-minded entrepreneur, donated money to Blair's campaign funds and became a Labour Party adviser. Noel Gallagher, meanwhile, accompanied McGee to one of the Britpop era's most celebrated events.

In August 1997, three months after Blair had become Prime Minister, he held a party at 10 Downing Street – the British equivalent of the White House – for an array of stars from sports, entertainment and the arts. Noel, dressed in a nondescript suit and happily humbled by his surroundings, looked more like a soccer player than a rock musician. He and the Prime Minister were photographed in animated conversation; as it later turned out, Blair had made a rather ill-advised joke about Noel's cocaine use.

Within weeks, unfortunately, both Blair and Britpop were sliding out of fashion, sped on their way by, on the one hand, the erosion of Blair's youthful allure by the grim realities of government; and, on the other, the fact that Oasis's *Be Here Now,* the most feverishly anticipated record of the Britpop era, had turned out to be a depressingly tawdry document of the deleterious effects of sudden wealth – or, more specifically, profligate drug habits – on raw talent.

Both the Downing Street party and *Be Here Now* seemed all too emblematic of where Britpop had gone wrong. By 1997, British musicians seemed to have replaced the imperative for innovation and iconoclasm with the worship of wealth and success. Whereas the most notable British music had long been countercultural, its new incarnation seemed to be striking the opposite stance, drawing much of its energy from being included in the mainstream, celebrated in the UK's tabloid newspapers and entertained by the government. The result, which has yet to be reversed, was simple: British rock music lost a great deal of the excitement, experimentalism and artful defiance – in essence, the *otherness* – that had always characterised its best moments.

Ironically enough, much of Britpop's final act was enacted against an American backdrop. Prior to the Downing Street party and the release of *Be Here Now,* Oasis's fall from grace had been symbolised by their premature return from a North American tour, which had ended, among raised voices and flying fists, in North Carolina. Six months later, Blur's ever-increasing distance from what remained of Britpop was amply demonstrated by their sudden success in the States, thanks chiefly to Song 2, a single that betrayed, of all things, the influence of Nirvana.

And then there was Elastica. Against even their own expectations, their admirably intelligent, feminised music had brought them success in the UK – and, much to their amazement, the USA. By the summer of 1995, they had been enlisted to take part in Lollapalooza, an engagement that looked likely to consolidate their American popularity but was wracked by the problems that came from the band's use of heroin. Their experiences on that tour marked their decisive passage into torpor and dysfunction; from thereon in, their story represents a pointed example of how that drug can corrode even the most shining talent.

This book is the story of Britpop: the people who comprised the bands, their closest sponsors and advisers, and the wider cultural moment they created. It is a tale bound up with relationships, rivalries, victories and disappointments – and also, as with so many tales based around rock music, drink and drugs, and their inevitably disorientating effects.

It is also, lest we forget, a story that takes in some truly brilliant music. To grasp the era's early air of excitement, one need only go back to its most energised records. Blur's Popscene marked the beginning of the Britpop period by reawakening the ghost of English New Wave and rerouting its rage towards a very modern kind of cultural wash-out. Suede's Metal Mickey and Animal Nitrate combined the most simple of pop virtues with the underlying sense that the music was drilling towards something shadowy and complex. Elastica's Stutter, by contrast, was as thrillingly primal as could be imagined: little more than two minutes of buzzsaw punk underpinning a snarling treatise on impotence. Its musical economy was startling; its lyrics sounded like a punch thrown at what was left of rock's macho piety.

Oasis, of course, would eventually restore that particular tradition to the rudest of health. All that apart, they, too, initially oozed an adrenalised kind of excitement, dispensing scuffed, distorted rock that bled with a righteous belligerence. Britpop may have gone on to become the music of mainstream vapidity, but all these records prove one thing beyond question: initially, it affected to speak as visceral a language as any of the rock music that preceded it.

Yet Britpop could also edge into altogether more profound territory. Part of its aim, after all, was to restore the links between British rock and its social context; to soundtrack its time. Pulp's Common People, still the period's most elegantly angry record, remains one of music's most accomplished treatments of the British class system; Blur's The Universal identified a condition of tranquillised (and very British) denial as the illness of the modern age. On This Is A Low, meanwhile, the same group managed to infuse both the UK's climate and landscape with a drama as affecting as any of the myths surrounding America. By some distance, it remains the Britpop period's most dizzying single achievement.

As for the albums, to grasp Britpop's rise and fall, one need only listen to three of its most accomplished works. Among its other feats,

Parklife revived the notion of groups finding endless fascination in the failure, delusion and farce that still underlies British life. Five months later, *Definitely Maybe,* thanks to intuition rather than any carefully formulated plan, succeeded in accomplishing similar feats with the long-dormant notion of English rock'n'roll. Though both records decisively began a period of spend-happy giddiness, three and a half years later – after Elastica, *(What's The Story) Morning Glory?* and Blur's *The Great Escape* – came Pulp's heart-stopping *This Is Hardcore:* a compelling distillation of the experiences – panic, self-loathing, burn-out – that, as a simple matter of logic, would materialise the morning after.

Listening to these records – and paying particular attention to the kind of songs listed above – it does not take too big a leap of the imagination for one to realise why their authors were held up as the architects of a pop-cultural renaissance. Moreover, the fact that the passage of the Britpop era also gave rise to as much drama, excess and romance as any of rock music's more celebrated epochs only underlines its importance. The British generations born in the 60s and 70s have often looked like the unlucky victims of a historical curse, fated to live in eternal thrall to the pioneers who went before them. As the story that follows proves, for a time at least, some of their number managed to step out of the shadows and create their own legend.

P A R T **O N E**

No expense accounts/Or lunch discounts/Or hyping up the charts . . .
No Consumer Trials/Or AOR/In Hitsville UK . . .

The Clash, Hitsville UK

I'm sick of your smug limey attitude. You British think you're so fucking
great. OK, name me one British band that means shit any more. Name
one! You can't. You're so fucking la-de-dah and you don't mean shit.

Michael 'Flea' Balzary of Red Hot Chili Peppers, 1993

CHAPTER 1

'It seemed correctly anarchistic not to want to be rich.'

For most of the 80s, the UK remained stuck in the same cultural moment. Its one-woman wellspring was in Downing Street from 1979 to 1990; such was the impact of her governments on every fibre of British life that she gave rise not only to an 'ism', but a fully-fledged era.

Of course, the component parts of the Thatcher years were not only formed by her governments, the economic behemoths that supported them, and the millions of voters who repeatedly put her in power. If one is to understand the 80s – and the 90s – one must also look at the story of her opponents.

For those who did well out of Thatcherism, the period was bound up with the indulging of instincts that the post-war period had often held in check: the thrill of climbing the social ladder, conspicuous consumption, the brazen patriotism that reared its head when the Task Force sailed for the South Atlantic. Among the many messages Thatcherism sent forth to its constituency was the assurance that what had been previously snickered at as vulgar and brash should now be celebrated. Thus a million wagon wheels were placed outside freshly bought council houses, Union Jacks were blu-tacked to front-room windows, and Norman Tebbit assured *Sun* readers that the Page Three girl was 'the working man's Venus de Milo'.

Ranged against all this were both those who had been excluded from the Thatcherite dream, and an ever-present constituency of refuseniks. Simple hardship dictated that the former could play no part in the frenzy of consumption. Many of the latter – an ever-present resistance whose worldview was solidified by the miners' strike – expressed their solidarity by affecting a ten-year display of opposition that often took them into the realms of piety.

The donkey jacket was the fashionable left-wing uniform. Vegetarianism was increasingly de rigueur. One's vocabulary was eternally checked for any racist, sexist or homophobic nuances that might betray an unconscious affinity with the enemy. Naturally, the totems of economic success – flash cars, designer clothes – were spurned as a matter of principle. Communal dwellings vibrated to impassioned arguments about South African fruit, free range eggs, and the unacceptable nature of words like 'tits'.

Within the universe of pop music, the battle-lines were as clearly drawn as anywhere else. On one side, led by Duran Duran, stood the denizens of the 'New Pop', whose delight in their new-found wealth was fully in keeping with the Thatcher ethos. The group's most fondly loved album, *Rio*, was promoted by a series of videos filmed in Sri Lanka; in the short that accompanied the title track, they lip-synched, surrounded by models, on a speeding yacht. 'There are plenty of bands catering for people who want to hear about how bad life is,' said Duran Duran's singer, Simon Le Bon, in 1982. 'We're not interested in that.' The journalist whose tape recorder captured the quote then asked him how he'd avoid becoming fat and wealthy. 'We'll buy a gymnasium,' said Le Bon. 'One of the perks of this job is getting rich.'

For most of the Thatcher years, a loose coalition of musicians stood on the opposing side. Their opinions had been forged in the righteous fire of punk rock; the necessity of maintaining one's radical stance was only confirmed by the result of the 1979 election. For many artists, voicing opposition to the government became an in-built part of their aesthetic. By 1986, the leading lights of this tendency – Billy Bragg, Paul Weller's Style Council, the gay duo The Communards – would be briefly grouped within Red Wedge, an ad hoc organisation affiliated to the Labour Party, set on subverting Thatcherism through music. The most coherent work to emerge from this faction was The Style Council's Our Favourite Shop, released in 1985. Paul Weller's lyrical vocabulary had long spurned rock'n'roll cliché; here, he used a vernacular that took him close to journalism: 'Come take a walk among these hills/And see how monetarism kills/Whole communities, even families.'

Others announced their distance from ruling thinking more circumspectly. In the scratchy, shambolic guitar music that defined the 80s left field, there was a clear sense of the rejection of all kinds of dominant cultural norms: the slick commerciality of the 80s mainstream, ambition as defined by sales figures and chart positions, and the swaggering masculinity that united the likes of Simon Le Bon, Spandau Ballet's Tony Hadley and – ironically – Wham!'s George Michael. The Scottish band Orange Juice, whose first chaotic single had appeared in February

1980, nailed this faction's worldview perfectly in a song released four years later: a sweet paean to romantic ineptitude entitled I Guess I'm Just A Little Too Sensitive.

No-one, however, embodied the anti-Thatcherite current as well as Steven Patrick Morrissey, the singer of The Smiths. Between 1983 and 1987, The Smiths' run of peerless albums and singles – just about all of them innovative, poetic and steeped in a profound sense of English-ness – gave rise to a huge and passionate cult. No matter that Morrissey's three colleagues – led by Johnny Marr, the virtuoso guitarist whose talents gave him the perfect platform – were as fond of rock'n'roll excess as any group of young male musicians; it was Morrissey's ascetic lifestyle, every aspect of which seemed imbued with ideological power, that captured the imagination of the group's most hard-bitten fans.

He was a self-proclaimed celibate, near-teetotaller, outspoken veg-etarian, passionate opponent of the Thatcher government, and advo-cate of a lifestyle that seemed to revolve around libraries, box bedrooms and the doctor's surgery. In a 1985 Smiths tour programme, his likes were listed as 'Films, books, moderation, conversation, civility'; the corresponding dislikes took in 'Meat, cigarettes, breakdancing, fads, videos, modern pop stars, cowards, sexism' (his favourite food, for what it was worth, was yoghurt). His disciples, clad in a uniform usually acquired from charity shops, would dance to The Smiths' music using steps that amounted to cartoon gestures of self-pity: hands placed on the heart, eyes cast skywards in the manner of the crucified Christ.

Crucially, The Smiths were signed to Rough Trade, the leader of a community of independent labels whose absence of links to the corpor-ate music industry underwrote the outsider poses of their artists. The existence of the labels – Manchester's Factory, and such London-based imprints as Mute and 4AD – seemed to answer a question that had bugged anti-establishment musicians since punk: did one use the exist-ing means of communication, or accept that they were beyond reform and build a non-corporate alternative?

It is easy to assume that the UK's first independent labels were forged in some righteous left-wing frenzy; that the anti-corporate spirit for which they came to stand was there from the beginning. The truth, however, is a little more complicated.

Initially, issuing an independent single was an expedient way of bringing a group to the attention of a major record label. The artefact widely accepted as the UK's first independent single – the Buzzcocks' Spiral Scratch EP, released on their own New Hormones imprint in January 1977 – proves the point: in its wake, the group signed to United

Artists and had their first taste of the luxuriant life of a big-league act. By 1979, however, the imperative of such a move was beginning to be questioned.

Geoff Travis was then a young, soft-spoken Cambridge graduate, who had completed a philosophy degree in 1975. Soon after, he established a West London record shop called Rough Trade, which specialised in reggae and imports from the USA. Its opening coincided with the back-to-the-roots revolution of punk, whose oft-celebrated DIY ethic led to a regular scenario: from 1976 onwards, Rough Trade was increasingly besieged by musicians carrying boxes of self-funded 7-inch singles. Their usual opening gambit was simple enough: 'Can you sell my record for me?'

Potentially, the request involved a little more than just placing the singles in Rough Trade's racks; Travis was well aware that to do the musicians' work justice, it should be available throughout the UK. Rough Trade was thus the catalyst for the foundation of a nationwide distribution system, known as The Cartel, created in alliance with a chain of like-minded shops. The idea was simple: although Rough Trade was The Cartel's de facto HQ, no one part of the chain took precedence over any other. To access the whole country, groups in Rotherham, Kirkcaldy, Wrexham or Portsmouth need only take their records to their nearest affiliated record store.

'That was a political decision: instead of deciding, "Right, we want to have a distribution system that's *ours*", we thought it would be good to take it away from the capital holding all the power,' says Travis. 'And it worked really well: then, it was possible to plug into the system wherever you were. The Cartel was specifically designed to get rid of that whole thing where you had to come to London, cap in hand, and say, "Please, sir, can you help us out?"'

Travis's vision was at least partly inspired by the New Left ideas that he had soaked up as a student. 'Some of it came from going into places like WH Smith and seeing the narrow range of literature that they would have on sale,' he says. 'Things like *Spare Rib* and *New Left Review* wouldn't be in those shops. There wasn't a fair representation of what was available, culturally. It was all slanted towards the middle of the road: the left wing wasn't represented. We felt the music business was analogous to that.

'If you made a record,' says Travis, 'even if you just pressed a hundred, and even if we only half-liked it, we'd take it on. It wasn't, "Is this a stepping stone to us making a million pounds?" It was, "Yeah, fine – that's a good local thing that you've done, and we want to encourage it."'

Rough Trade's distribution warehouse was situated on Blenheim Crescent, a quiet, semi-residential street off Ladbroke Grove. By the dawn of the 80s – by which time Travis had set up Rough Trade's own label – it had become a clearing-house-cum-hang-out for scores of musicians: a place not only to deliver one's latest work, but also to make contact with like minds. In keeping with the tenor of the times, the set-up was run as a democratic collective, in which wages were equal and all aspects of the company's activities were open to discussion. Plenty of accounts of Rough Trade's progress detail the laborious consequence: meetings about whether a staff member could buy lunch for a professional acquaintance, or if the company would sanction the purchase of a new jacket for an artist's upcoming appearance on *Top of the Pops*. Travis, however, is adamant that the company's egalitarian codes never led it into the realms of absurdity. 'It wasn't like a collective farm, where every morning everybody gets a cup of cold tea and sits around for three hours, debating,' he says. 'We got things done.'

One thing is for certain: during the first phase of its existence, Rough Trade demonstrated its disdain for music industry decadence by refusing to send journalists and radio stations free records. 'We just thought, "These records are so good, they should come and get them themselves,"' says Travis. 'It's very expensive to give away hundreds of records, simple as that. It makes a lot of economic sense to make people come to you.' The principle was also reflected in the non-existence of guest-lists at Rough Trade-related concerts. 'The important people,' says Travis, with an undiminished enthusiasm for the principle, 'were the kids who wanted to get in.'

Up in Manchester, Factory Records had been founded by Tony Wilson, the broadcaster-turned-impresario who had been sufficiently entranced by the mind-bogglingly innovative music made by Joy Division to offer to fund their first release. The initial plan was to release a single, thus affording them a leg-up to a deal with one of the conglomerates. Soon enough, however, the two parties took the relatively unprecedented step of commencing the recording of an album.

In Wilson's recollection, the band's motivation for doing so was not exactly ideological. Their manager, Rob Gretton, expressed his conditional approval of the idea as follows: 'If this shit does work, I don't have to get on a train to London every week and talk to cunts.' So it was that, with the assistance of Rough Trade Distribution, Factory released Joy Division's debut album, *Unknown Pleasures*, in August 1979.

In doing so, Wilson began to understand the wider significance of what he and other independent pioneers were doing. 'It's praxis, isn't it?' he says, with one of his customary allusions to Marxism. 'You learn why you do something by doing it. The Theory Of Independence was discovered in the act of putting out your own records, doing very well, being friends with your artists and not ripping them off. And by 1981, we were all doing it. We were saying, "Fuck the majors, you're all wankers." Suddenly, we were all intoxicated with it.'

At the centre of the independent ideal was an arrangement – pioneered by a deal Geoff Travis made with the Northern Irish punk band Stiff Little Fingers – that quickly became a given: a 50/50 split of both costs and net receipts between label and artist, as opposed to an industry standard that always tilted the balance in the company's favour. In addition, labels like Factory allowed their musicians the rare privilege of owning their recordings, and treated the idea of contracts with a sneering disdain. Underlying all this was a most un-Thatcherite set of principles: a belief that love of the music should always take precedence over the balance sheet, a pronounced distaste for the idea of wealth, and what often appeared to be deliberate economic ineptitude.

'We were being *profoundly* political by not owning our groups,' says Wilson. ' "The company owns nothing, the musicians own their music and everything they do, and all artists have the freedom to fuck off." That was the famous Joy Division contract that I signed in blood. And our other political act, throughout the eighties, was never to have a publishing arm. Because that would have made a lot of money. That's the reason we didn't do it. It seemed correctly anarchistic not to want to be rich.

'The other thing is, in its first two years, Factory had done this non-promotion thing: "We don't promote. No press officers." It was all about not treating the music as a commodity.'

Of course, one could not discern such thinking by simply listening to the records. Throughout the 80s, though none of the now-dominant British music monthlies existed, there were no less than four weeklies: the pre-eminent *NME*, along with *Melody Maker*, *Sounds* and *Record Mirror*. They quizzed, dissected and contextualised rock groups to the point that rhetoric occasionally seemed to take precedence over the music. Those bands allied with independent labels were among the most pored over; thus, through the pages of the press, labels, musicians and sympathetic journalists could pass the message on. The result was a genuine subculture, bound together by the same philosophies that had inspired the founding of Rough Trade and Factory. The polarised atmosphere of the 80s provided the perfect context: once you had come to the perfectly understandable conclusion that Simon Le Bon was part of the same problem as Mrs Thatcher, the world built around the independent labels offered a warm kind of sanctuary. Counterculture is a word one usually only hears in association with the 60s, but the 80s surely had an equal claim to it.

Thanks to the trade magazine *Record Business*, as of 1980, the mainstream charts were shadowed by an equivalent, restricted exclusively to independent labels. The result was that fans of independent music could forget about the mainstream and simply focus their attention on the fortunes of a select coterie of groups. More importantly, the music press shorthand for the chart gave its attendant subculture a name: 'indie'.

The pronouncements of its figureheads – Morrissey was joined by the likes of James's Tim Booth and The Wedding Present's David Gedge – ensured that the indie world oriented itself around much more than music. In addition, one could detect a mixture of political dissent, 'right-on' attitudes, and a spurning of the traditional totems of rock'n'roll: long hair, leather trousers, drugs, and the hoary musical rudiments that were rooted in the blues. Its adherents took in every level of the pop-cultural food-chain, from musicians, through record companies, to journalists on the national music press, venue promoters, specialist shops, and the droves of young *enragés* who kept the whole network in business.

There was a lot more traffic between independent labels and the established record industry than some of the more hard-bitten advocates of the indie ideal would have liked. In 1983, for example, Geoff Travis began combining his work at Rough Trade with a new label called Blanco Y Negro, distributed and funded by Warner Brothers. And just prior to their break-up, The Smiths would sign a deal with EMI. Even the most fiercely anti-corporate music fan had to acknowledge that, sooner or later, their favourite groups would make the leap.

Nonetheless, the indie milieu became a fixed part of the British cultural expanse. Its empowering ethos, however, meant that many of its constituent parts were ever-changing. The pillars of indiedom seemed to be securely in place – the bigger labels, sympathetic elements within the music press, John Peel's eternally left-field Radio One show – but everything else was in flux. Labels might be founded for the simple purpose of putting out a single record. Some would arrive in a polemical flurry, issue a handful of records and then find that the money had run out. When a small player named Creation joined the fray in 1984, there was no reason to suppose that it would be any different.

In line with its anti-establishment poses, the indie world was serviced by a mass of cheaply produced *Samizdat*: fanzines, founded according to the example set by such pioneering punk publications as *Sniffin'*

Glue And Other Rock'n'Roll Habits. Their 'editors' – usually responsible for pictures, words, crude layout and distribution – would sell their wares at the requisite concerts, frequently bumping into one another and sharing the glow of true believers. Among their number were countless aspirant journalists who would eventually abandon Pritt Sticks and typewriters in favour of pursuing their vocation through the organised press.

In 1985, Steve Lamacq – who would eventually become the host of Radio One's Evening Session – and the future magazine editor and publisher James Brown stood shoulder-to-shoulder at a fanzine stall erected at a GLC-sponsored event in London's Brockwell Park. Lamacq was trying to shift copies of *A Pack Of Lies*; Brown was down for the day from Leeds with a new issue of the more colourfully titled *Attack On Bzag*. Their conversation reflected the puritanical life-code that often defined the indie world. 'There was this little community of fanzine writers,' says Lamacq. 'We all believed quite strongly in certain things: we all voted Labour, we were all anti-apartheid, we were pro the miner's strike, we were all anti-major record labels. That day, I can remember James giving me a lecture: "You should give up eating a meal once a day, and the money you would have spent on that meal, you should give straight to the miners."' Lamacq, as thin now as he was then, was bamboozled. 'I said, "James – I only eat one meal a day anyway."'

For both its supporters and opponents, the Thatcher era began to unravel at the tail-end of the 80s. The woman herself was increasingly displaying both regal pretensions – 'We have become a grandmother,' she told reporters in 1989 – and the accompanying delusions of omnipotence that led her into the debacle of the Poll Tax. The Scottish Poll Tax Act was passed in 1987, becoming operational in 1989; as far as England and Wales were concerned, legislation received royal assent in July 1988, leaving the first tax to be collected on 1 April 1990.

The day before, London was engulfed by riots that duly passed into history oozing all the swashbuckling righteousness of the popular revolts held dear by the British left. As its opponents were fond of repeating, the last time a poll tax had been attempted, the populace had responded with the Peasants' Revolt of 1381; there was much rejoicing at the fact that, even after eleven years of Thatcherism, thousands of people had instinctively tapped into the same insurrectionary tradition.

Within the 80s counterculture, a similarly unexpected development had taken root. What came to be known as Acid House had begun to seep into the UK in the autumn of 1987 – fortuitously at around exactly the time that The Smiths broke up. It arrived in the wake of Margaret Thatcher's third election victory, at the point when the UK's recovery from the recession of the early 80s was peaking.

Its geographical origin was Ibiza, where a clutch of London scenesters had both immersed themselves in locally-run clubs, and started to bring their own entrepreneurial nous to the island. As important was the phenomenon's pharmaceutical root: ecstasy, which had arrived in Ibiza via such diverse locales as Texas and Sydney. Ecstasy was not unknown in the UK: it had caused ripples among a select group of Londoners in the mid-80s. But when the drug reached Britain en masse, it wasn't difficult to discern a striking socio-political subtext: the 'loved-up' E high represented as clean a break with the individualistic mores of Thatcherism as could be imagined.

In Ibiza, the clubs played a pot-pourri of music – including songs by artists as unlikely as Carly Simon – that went under the catch-all banner of 'Balearic Beat'. Back in the UK, however, E-taking became almost exclusively coupled with house music, the four-on-the-floor, trance-inducing form that had been pioneered in Chicago and popularised in the gay clubs of New York. Thus, a new drug was melded to trailblazing music, and a subculture as innovative and pivotal as punk was born.

The celebratory worldview that Acid House fostered dealt a fatal blow to the earnest, self-denying ways of indie-land. The mere fact that a psychotropic drug was in vogue represented a threat to a world in which a surfeit of Newcastle Brown and the odd spliff were just about the only acceptable form of mind-expansion. The anti-Thatcherite culture of complaint was sidelined by the upbeat mindset that would become known as 'positivity'. Acid House's all-embracing hedonism also began to undermine the eternal tendency to fret about one's lifestyle and vocabulary: in the context of frantic hedonism, there was no time to fret about what was alleged to be unsound.

'Once Rave Culture started happening,' says Steve Lamacq, who was by then liberated from fanzines and starving for the miners, and had arrived at the newsdesk of the *NME*, 'you were very aware that something was going on – but it was completely anathema to people like me. You'd see these people coming back with eyes that had been buried in the back of their head, going, "It's just brilliant, man." Right. Well, first you're saying "man", like a hippy, which for someone who was a teenage punk rocker feels a bit uncomfortable – but also, what is the appeal of standing in a huge crowd, off your tits? I really didn't see it. At the time, it looked like they were renouncing the real world.

11

You had a choice: you either tried to understand it, or you sat there like King Canute saying, "I reject this." My King Canute period probably lasted until 1991.'

In the post-Britpop age, when any new aspect of the youth-cultural patchwork seems to be co-opted into the mainstream and rendered harmless at dizzying speed, the suggestion that Acid House terrified both the British press and the country's politicans might seem rather overblown. But it did: by late 1988, illicit mass raves had become the source of a tabloid-led panic, which only served to confirm their cultural importance. It was a gift to the newspapers – and the Tory MPs who increasingly joined their crusade – that the new wave became known as Acid House. The origins of the term are cloudy, but in the context of mass ecstasy use, the apparent allusion to LSD seemed rather misplaced. It hardly bothered the journalists at *The Sun*: acres of space were devoted to the idea that it was acid, rather than ecstasy, that lay at the root of this new scourge.

The paper's headlines from the period represented tabloid hysteria in excelsis: 'Shoot These Evil Acid Barons – Mum In Fury At Girl's Drug Death', 'Mr Big Of Acid Parties – I'll Hurt *Sun* Man And Hurt Him Real Bad', 'Spaced Out! 11,000 People Go Drug Crazy At Britain's Biggest-Ever Acid Party'. The copy underneath tended to be positively hysterical: 'The screaming teenager jerked like a demented doll as the LSD he swallowed earlier took its terrible toll . . . The boy had been sucked into the hellish nightmare engulfing thousands as the Acid House scourge sweeps Britain. Callous organisers simply looked on and LAUGHED.' In response, the police waded in: in October 1989, an Acid House squad – called the Pay Party Unit – was formed in Kent, and by the end of the year, complaints about police brutality were coming thick and fast. Here was Acid House's position vis-à-vis the body politic made flesh: the goggle-eyed representatives of a new Britain hounded and clubbed by an alliance of press, police and politicians.

Scanning back-copies of Hansard from the period, one can sense the hysteria. In November, Teddy Taylor, the Tory MP for Southend, asked the Minister of Agriculture if he would initiate discussions with the National Farmers Union on procedures to prevent farming land being let for 'acid house parties'. Even Labour MPs added their voices to the tumult: the same month, while voicing misgivings about proposals to control 'large gatherings' on the Isle of Wight, one Martin Redmond, the MP for Don Valley, assured the House of Commons that 'I am opposed to acid house parties. That youngsters want to attend such parties is a terrible indictment of our nation. We should provide better means to keep those youngsters away from such parties.'

In December of that year, responding to pressure from the government, Graham Bright, the MP for Aldershot, introduced a Private Members Bill containing proposals to fine rave promoters up to £140,000 and allow the option of up to six months imprisonment, along with the confiscation of profits and seizure of sound equipment. This was Thatcherite enemy-within politics, focused on a new target and underpinned by a mixture of anger and bafflement, as if the government viewed the Acid hordes as positive heretics. How *dare* they?

Acid House had two British centres: London and Manchester. Argument has long raged about the importance of each, but the way the phenomenon played itself out in each city was broadly similar: city centre clubs represented its heart, but with the onset of summer, droves of people were drawn to vast events in the green belt. In London, the M25 became a byword for illicit outdoor gatherings; in the North West, the countryside around Rochdale and Blackburn became the backdrop for ever-larger parties – and increasingly ugly confrontations with the authorities.

Manchester had one key asset: a club whose sheer size meant that the Acid House experience – drug-taking aside – could be played out within the law. The Haçienda had been opened in 1982 by Factory Records; set on giving Manchester its own equivalent of New York clubs like the Danceteria, they acquired a dry dock in one of the city's more threadbare corners, furnished it in a minimal, post-industrial style, and quickly realised that they were a few years ahead of their time. The enterprise initially floundered, caught between being a sparsely-attended nightspot and a far-from-satisfactory rock venue (the sound, musicians complained, was always lousy). As of 1986, however, the UK's burgeoning dance culture gave it a raison d'être, and DJs like Mike Pickering, Graeme Park and Dave Haslam were instrumental in turning the Haçienda into something of a national landmark.

In the context of an age when clubs tended to be low-ceilinged, pokey places, the Haçienda seemed truly vast: a three-floor, 1,500-capacity place whose dimensions suggested those of an aircraft hangar. With the arrival of Acid House, it provided the perfect location for the requisite club nights, and the playing out of its influence on all kinds of curious minds.

Such was the setting for Manchester's changing-of-the-guard: the jettisoning of the ascetic pose personified by Morrissey, and its replacement by something altogether more colourful. 'It was, "Here's the drugs, here's the dance, let's fucking go,"' says Tony Wilson. 'You could take any human being, of any sort, to the Haçienda from mid-'89 onwards and they would just love it. Human beings love fun and happiness and exuberance, and it was the epitome of that. There were no moral questions: it was the politics of joy. There was no possibility of having qualms or quibbles, or wondering what had happened to your right-on principles. It didn't even occur.'

Acid House was bound to impact on British rock culture, and the Haçienda was a cipher for that process. Given its link to Factory Records, it bridged the world of guitar groups and the newer universe of house music and ecstasy tablets, something embodied by the regular presence of Mancunian rock musicians. Among them were the two groups who were part of the city's countercultural aristocracy: Happy Mondays and The Stone Roses.

What passes for rock history has long since suffused the stories of the two groups with misapprehension and cliché. In some accounts, they seem to become melded into a joint entity – 'the Mondays'n'Roses' – as if their music was interchangeable. Moreover, the extent to which dance music impacted on their output has long been misunderstood. By 1989, the two bands were being heralded as the pioneers of some-thing called 'the indie/dance crossover' – as if they had bought drum machines, switched them to the 'house' setting and then played their old songs over the top. The reality, needless to say, was altogether more complex. If the hallmark of great rock groups is a synthesis of influences so unique as to be almost alchemical, then both groups – and Happy Mondays in particular – had the right stuff.

Happy Mondays came from Little Hulton, a grim settlement mid-way between Manchester and Wigan. Their background represented the stuff of proletarian outsiderdom: the rejection of school, life on the dole, aborted marriages, petty crime, drug habits and run-ins with the police (their name, according to legend, was chosen on account of its encapsulation of the benefits of the dole-ite lifestyle). When they signed to Factory Records in 1986, their presence seemed anomalous indeed: given that the label was an integral part of indie culture, Happy Mon-days simply didn't fit – an impression only furthered by the fact that one of their number, Mark 'Bez' Berry, was employed to simply stand onstage and dance.

Their first album, *Squirrel And G-Man Twenty Four Party People Plastic Face Carnt Smile (White Out)*, encapsulated their incongruity: sparse and scratchy-sounding, with singer Shaun Ryder's gob-bledygook lyrics and half-shouted vocals, it sounded oddly cautious – as if, having pulled off the rare feat of defying any generic straitjacket, the group had precious little idea of where they should be heading. Only on one occasion did they decisively find their feet: on Twenty

Four Hour Party People, a nod to the Northern Soul nights that the group had experienced as adolescents, they managed to fuse as a locked-tight groove with an infectious sense of goggle-eyed abandonment. In that sense – as with a stand-alone Mondays single released in 1986 entitled Freaky Dancin' – the track was a portent of what was to come.

Ecstasy changed Happy Mondays. In the wake of the album's release – and muted reception – Ryder, whose drug predilections had already resulted in an on-off heroin habit, spent several months in Amsterdam, where he all but gorged himself on the drug. Bez, meanwhile, became an associate of New Order, freshly returned from Ibiza, where they had been recording *Technique* and sampling the burgeoning culture of Acid House. By 1988, Ryder and Bez were in the habit of selling ecstasy at the Haçienda, marking out a territory that the club's DJs knew as 'Acid Corner'.

Consequently, when the group came together to record their second album, something was in the air. By this time, Ryder had cut down his E habit to a meagre three tablets a day; Bez, meanwhile, was fond of telling those new to the drug that the best way to avoid the comedown was to grit your teeth, close your eyes and have another pill. The album's producer was Martin Hannett, who had supervised Joy Division's pioneering music, and was famed for his nihilistic drinking. Ryder surmised that the best way of warding him off alcohol was to introduce him to E.

The result was *Bummed*. Its sound seemed vast, something apparently down to the fact that, peaking on ecstasy, Hannett and the group had simply turned everything – treble, bass, reverb – up to the maximum. It also contained Wrote For Luck, the group's first true masterpiece. Over an unspeakably dense six minutes, it somehow skewed the aesthetics of dance music out of all recognition – as if the group had read about house music without having heard any, then resolved to reproduce it using standard rock instruments. In terms of its influences, it was impossible to pin down, a quality only heightened by its almost indecipherable words. 'Our sound's all sorts, really,' said Ryder, when asked to clarify exactly where his group was coming from. 'Funkadelic, One Nation Under A Groove being eaten by a giant sandwich . . . that was fucking top, that . . . Northern Soul . . . punk rock . . . Jimi Hendrix . . . fucking Captain Beefheart. And a lot of drugs on top of that.'

Wrote For Luck was released as a single a month before the album. For the first time, Happy Mondays started to turn heads, and the consequent music press coverage allowed their incongruity to come to the fore.

There had never been a group like Happy Mondays: utterly unaffec-
ted; free of any of the pretensions of 'image'; blessed with the sought-
after – and much-faked – quality known as 'working class authenticity',
but free of any idea that it represented anything politically significant.
'Everybody on this stagecoach likes robbin' and bashin'/Big blags
abroad and smoking large amounts of hash,' Ryder had sung on a track
called Olive Oil, from *Squirrel And G-Man*. This was rock music's
eternal outlaw spirit taken somewhere new – and besides, nothing
impresses the average music journalist like a bit of rough.

The contrast between Happy Mondays' worldview and the right-on
mores of the indie world could not have been more pronounced. When
the *NME* met the group on the verge of *Bummed*'s release, comment
was passed on the fact that Ryder spent the first part of the interview
eating a huge plate of meat. 'Vegetarian? Me? Animals just exist to be
fucking chopped up and eaten, pal,' he barked back. 'Especially cows.
I fucking hate cows. They freak me out.'

'They didn't give a shit about that stuff,' says Tony Wilson. 'Even
with Thatcher, the Mondays were very open: "Yeah, she's alright.
She's a heavy dude."'

In 1989, Shaun Ryder was quizzed about the fact that, for all their
drug-related transgressions, his group really did seem to be archetypal
Thatcherites; they seemed not to care about anything but themselves.
'I don't think we do really,' said Ryder. 'I mean, we won't knock things,
we won't go against things. There's a lot of things happening that
shouldn't be happening . . . but there's only one thing you can do
practically: when you've got more money than every other fucker, just
give a big load to somebody else.'

Throughout the next twelve months, Happy Mondays' reputation
snowballed – and in November 1989, they released the record that
would not only mark their apex thus far, but add a new buzzword to
the national consciousness. The *Madchester Rave On EP* took its title
from Factory Records' 1988 Christmas Card ('Happy Christmas from
Madchester'), and instantly propagated the notion that a city once
synonymous with damp weather and post-industrial grime had mutated
into a hedonistic, technicolour paradise. Most crucially of all, it allowed
Happy Mondays to appear on *Top of the Pops*. The same night saw
the debut of The Stone Roses.

To some extent, The Stone Roses were Happy Mondays' opposites.
They were from South Manchester; the Mondays hailed from the more
threadbare North. While the Mondays were largely uneducated casualties of the comprehensive system, the Roses' two core members, Ian
Brown and John Squire, were grammar school boys (Trafford, the

South Mancunian borough in which they lived, had retained selection despite the lion's share of the UK embracing comprehensivisation). They were not averse to discussing history, literature and art; in a music press questionnaire completed in May 1989, they listed their favourite books as Georges Bataille's *Story of the Eye*, Luke Reinhart's *The Dice Man*, and Camus's *The Fall* and *A Happy Death*.

Moreover, while the Mondays were a craggy-faced gang of scruffs, as far from the outward orthodoxy of rock image as could be imagined, The Roses took their lead from beat-group archetypes: floppy fringes, pouts, and an apparent wish to look pretty much identical. Their music, too, was cut from altogether more orthodox cloth than the Mondays' off-beam oeuvre: by 1988, they were playing chiming, melodic guitar-pop that frequently brought to mind The Beatles and The Byrds.

But there was a little more to them than such comparisons would imply, as proved by their debut album, released in April 1989. The lyrics, sung by Ian Brown in a voice that somehow fused soft-spokenness with a swaggering brio, captured the same euphoria that was coursing around the minds of Acid House enthusiasts: 'Kiss me where the sun don't shine,' went She Bangs The Drums, 'The past was yours but the future's mine'. The music also frequently threw up comparisons with dance culture, as with the mesmeric throb of Water-fall, and the frenetic coda of the album's finale, entitled – with no audible sense of irony – I Am The Resurrection.

The album gradually found its audience over the next year, while the group forwent standard rock etiquette. They toured the UK only once, in late 1988. By the summer of 1989, they had opted instead for one-off events, clearly aimed at replicating the communality of the archetypal rave. In August, they played at Blackpool's 4,000-capacity Empress Ballroom. Three months later, they took the stage at London's Alexandra Palace in front of a crowd of 7,000. The venues were emblematic of the group's ambitions: while their peers took refuge in the anti-commercialism that was synonymous with the indie ideal, The Stone Roses saw themselves as people whose duty was to crash-land in the mainstream.

Commercial success wasn't to be spurned; there was an almost moral imperative to embrace it. 'We should be on *Top of the Pops*,' said Brown. 'I like seeing our record go up and Kylie and Phil Collins go down. There's no point moaning about them. You've got to get in there and stamp them out. Because I believe that we have more worth.'

In keeping with all this, the group had little time for the ethic of independent labels. In 1990, Brown was asked if, were the group to sign with a major record company, their music would be altered. 'I don't think you change your music or your attitude,' he replied, evidently unimpressed by the question. 'I don't see the difference between independents and majors. They're all into making money, aren't they? That's what it's about. They all hire pluggers, they all go through the business. And your music doesn't change just 'cos so-and-so's paying for your tape instead of . . . y'know . . . Squirrel Records. The independent scene's a joke, isn't it? No good music's come out of it.'

The Stone Roses' apex lasted from late 1989 to the summer of 1990. In November '89, they released Fool's Gold, a nine-minute single that represented the most perfection fusion of orthodox instruments and dance aesthetics that any of the past-Acid House rock groups had managed. Over a drum-loop purloined from an album of hip-hop breakbeats, the group wove fluid, bubbling music while Brown flipped between opaque storytelling and his trademark statements of self-belief. It went to number eight in the singles charts and prompted the appearance on *Top of the Pops*. It was here that Ian Brown came into his own. Making a mockery of the programme's insistence on miming, he held the microphone way above his head, using it as little more than a prop. His demeanour represented a classic rock gambit: wearing an expression of hard-faced composure, he walked the line between narcissistic cool and outright absurdity. As far as countless Stone Roses disciples were concerned, he was the one to watch.

Early the following year, the group announced that they would be staging a one-off outdoor event the following May, at Spike Island, a nature reserve near Widnes, Cheshire. The intended audience would number 30,000. This was audacious indeed: as far from the indie-rock 'toilet' circuit as could be imagined, beyond even the indoor arenas that British guitar groups had long assumed were out of their reach. To experience the pleasures of playing to huge outdoor crowds, bands had got used to seeking strength in numbers and joining the bill at multi-faceted festivals. The Stone Roses, by contrast, were Spike Island's sole attraction.

Still in keeping with the Acid House emphasis on communality, the band insisted – surely disingenuously – that they were merely one part of a democratic spectacle. 'I'm not performing,' said Brown. 'I'm participating.'

In March 1990, Happy Mondays had risen to number five in the charts with an unprecedentedly commercial single entitled Step On – a reinterpretation of a 70s hit by a long-lost South African called John Kongos. It was their first single to be comprehensively backed by Radio One, who played it well into the summer.

By then, as far as British rock music was concerned, the Mondays and The Stone Roses had become paradigmatic; in their wake came an array of groups who took their lead from one or both. By way of a generic bracket into which to squeeze them, the music press flipped between the painfully naff terms 'indie-dance', and 'baggy'.

The latter was a tribute to the Acid House-inspired fashion for unbelievably voluminous trousers, which came in two varieties: flares, finally allowed back into popular culture after being exiled by the punks ('like trousers, like brain,' The Clash's Joe Strummer had said in 1977); and 'parallels', trousers whose width went from top to bottom. With the right apparel, one could give off the appearance of being triangular, though the look's progenitors were keen to inform their public of where to draw the line. 'People have got to realise that you can't wear anything wider than twenty-one-inch bottoms,' said Ian Brown, helpfully. 'Anything more looks ridiculous.'

Aside from its two kingpins, the new wave's most celebrated sons were Inspiral Carpets, natives of Oldham and fans of 60s garage rock, who craftily managed to group themselves with the Mondays and Roses despite an absence of any dance influence whatsoever. From the Midlands came The Charlatans, transparently in thrall to 60s R'n'B, but linked to the new wave via Tim Burgess, a disciple of Ian Brown, who hailed from just outside the Mancunian sprawl, in Cheshire.

Manchester produced a welter of wannabe heirs: among them, Paris Angels, a knobby-faced gang who took their lead from Happy Mondays and had the rare distinction of being even more ugly; and Northside, signed to Factory Records in a welter of predictions about their imminent success. Their first single featured a clod-hopping ode to the joys of LSD entitled Shall We Take A Trip. It hardly augured well for their future.

London finally caught up and gave the world Flowered Up, a cut-price Mondays in every detail: backgrounds in drug dealing, a creeping air of proletarian menace, and an onstage dancer who called himself Barry Mooncult. Leeds had The Bridewell Taxis, football toughs who took their name from a local minicab firm, boasted – of all things – a trombone player, and achieved their fifteen minutes of fame via a cover of Blue Oyster Cult's Don't Fear The Reaper. Liverpool, meanwhile, was represented by The Farm: one-time merchants of punked-up, politicised music, who duly adopted the right drumbeats and opted for a clumsy populism. In November 1990, they released the baggy Christmas record, All Together Now, written about the legendary Christmas in 1914 when German and British soldiers had momentarily desisted from shooting each other and played football (the tale was given a link to the ecstasy era by an in-vogue myth: given that E had first been synthesised in 1912 by the German Merck pharmaceutical company, the story went round that the German soldiers' friendliness was E-inspired). Eighteen months later, All Together Now was adopted as the Labour Party's anthem for the 1992 election campaign.

The routing of post-Acid House rock music into such a crassly populist place spoke volumes about its rapid decline. In the wake of Spike Island, The Stone Roses had vanished, tangled up in a legal struggle to extricate themselves from their contract with the Silvertone label. The case was settled in their favour in May 1991, and a new deal with the Geffen label – who had paid their legal expenses – was announced. Their pockets bulging with the advance, they took off on a spree of high-living, celebrating their new-found wealth by fleeing to the south of France. Their new wealth sapped their momentum: no new Stone Roses music would appear until the end of 1994.

Happy Mondays released another masterful album, *Pills'n'Thrills And Bellyaches*, in October 1990. Recorded in Los Angeles, it was an altogether slicker record than *Bummed*: whereas that album had expressed its affinity with Acid House almost unconsciously, the new record made the link explicit. The sound mixed guitar and bass with precise and pristine keyboard sounds; the drums were as crisp as on any house record. It was also gloriously commercial: as if to prove that the group continued to walk on water, Kinky Afro, the album's lead-off single, equalled the performance of Step On by reaching number five.

By then, Happy Mondays were becoming used to the high life. In the wake of their first success, their scruffiness had been superseded by a liking for upmarket labels, and Armani in particular: on one trip to New York, Shaun Ryder had flitted around an Armani shop and quickly spent £1,000. Their faces, once as pinched as the dole-ite lifestyle implied, were filling out – aside from that of Bez, whose pharmaceutical intake presumably kept him trim. And their ports of call were proving ever-more exotic: in January 1991, they flew to Brazil to play at the Rock In Rio festival, where they had the obligatory barbecue with Ronnie Biggs and enjoyed a mountain of ludicrously cheap cocaine.

That September, Ryder and Bez were invited to act as 'guest editors' of *Penthouse* magazine. Among the reconstructed elements of the music press, the move served to confirm what some had suspected all along: that the Mondays were boorish oafs. Irrespective of its sexual-political connotations, the stunt – commemorated by photographs of the pair sitting in a jacuzzi with three topless models – looked not a little tawdry.

They at least created one piece of brilliant music out of the drama that the scenario implied: Judge Fudge, released in November 1991.

Its lyrics were as topsy-turvy as ever, but its subtext was the anxiety that comes with sudden wealth. Indeed, thanks to a combination of claustrophobic music and Ryder's hoarse, half-sung vocal, it sounded ever-so-slightly desperate. On *Pills'n'Thrills*, the Mondays had embraced a new sun-kissed commerciality; this song seemed to be the sound of a sudden paranoid comedown. It was not the most marketable of singles.

To promote Judge Fudge, the group were interviewed in the *NME*. The journalist, Steven Wells, exposed the Mondays' unreconstructedness to close and forceful scrutiny for the first time. He had an easy tool with which to perform the task: a clutch of questions surrounding an incident that had occurred a few months earlier, when Ryder had found a flippant comment made in a TV interview jumped on by the *News of the World*.

On MTV, he had joked about 'selling his body' in Manchester's red-light district; within days, a story appeared with the headline 'I Was Rent Boy Says Happy Mondays Star'. Ryder was enraged, venting his fury by storming into a Manchester bar and destroying a mirror with the aid of – worryingly enough – a Magnum shotgun. When the *NME* interview took place, the incident was still an issue. 'Lads who come from where I come from don't like being called a fuckin' faggot,' said Ryder. 'I've got nothing against them, but I have my rights and I ain't a fuckin' faggot and that's it . . . where I come from, that's probably the worst thing you could call somebody . . . I don't suck dick.'

If the language sounded ill-chosen, Bez then pushed the conversation into the realms of extreme ugliness. 'I hate faggots. Anyone who's straight finds them disgusting. Faggots might find shagging pussy disgusting, but we find shagging a bloke not right. The majority of people in Britain aren't gay, are they?'

This was ill-advised behaviour for a group on the cover of the *NME*. Despite their chart positions, their coverage in the tabloids and their new-found place on the arena circuit, Happy Mondays' profile was still driven by the kind of people who formed the core, indie-loving readership of the music press. If the *Penthouse* episode had suggested that the alliance of student record-buyers and licentious ex-drug dealers couldn't last, the *NME* interview confirmed it. Judge Fudge went no higher than number twenty-four and marked the start of Happy Mondays' descent; to this day, the group's associates acknowledge that Steven Wells' interview contributed to their decline.

Their fate reflected that of the upsurge on which they had fed. By early 1991, Acid House was tumbling into crisis. Bedevilled by the gang violence that was a concomitant part of the drugs trade, the

Haçienda had been forced to close for six months. Illicit raves had been squashed by the successful passage of Graham Bright's bill and the ever-hostile stance of the UK's police. Even when they found a bolt-hole and continued the fun, Acid House disciples were discovering the drawbacks of incessant E-taking. What was once euphoric and transcendent had turned ugly and dystopic; though dance culture was now a fixed part of the British patchwork, its initial period of innocence was over.

Britain in 1991 was a remarkably different country to the one that had been dragged through the 1980s. Adding to the sense of a new era, it also sat in the midst of a radically changed world: with the fall of the Iron Curtain, the rigid certainties that had defined the previous half-decade were suddenly rendered obsolete.

Mrs Thatcher had been toppled in November 1990, shoved out of office by a palace coup that, for all the celebrations that followed her demise, deprived her opponents of the thrill of watching her defeat at the hands of the electorate. Her replacement was a sometime bank clerk, whose complete lack of charisma suggested that the only way to follow the Thatcher era was with a period of benign political boredom. Not that the initial phase of John Major's premiership was without drama: within weeks of his accession to power, the UK was engaged in the military operation that would eject Iraqi forces from Kuwait. It was some token of changed times that, despite ripples of protest, the coalition of pop-cultural dissidents that had bemoaned Mrs Thatcher's every move was nowhere to be seen. There were no benefit concerts, few voices raised in the *NME*, no rush-released single aimed at catalysing opposition.

The Labour Party's third consecutive election defeat had marked a watershed for the 80s counterculture. Red Wedge, founded with the 1987 campaign in mind, had spluttered to a halt soon afterwards, unsure of exactly how to respond to the dashing of its hopes. Paul Weller's Style Council, having moved along a downward career trajectory and ditched their political aspect, made an album of house music that their record label refused to release, and decided that the game was up. Even Billy Bragg, the left's musical cheerleader, had paused for thought and recorded *Workers Playtime*, an album of love songs.

In tandem with all this came the effects of Acid House – as perfect a reflection of the new world as could be imagined (as one or two of its enthusiasts were heard to comment, the scenes played out atop the Berlin Wall looked hilariously similar to the archetypal rave). In the midst of its goggle-eyed lunacy, which had touched even the most orthodox rock groups, the fixed sneer of dissent that had been held in place since punk rock had been lost; the sense that one's art had to be consciously positioned against the status quo now seemed rather old-fashioned.

Inevitably, the notion that record labels were important players in some ideological war duly faded. The Stone Roses' defection to Geffen spoke volumes: the notion of 'indie credibility' was rendered irrelevant by the sense that they were now about to realise their big-league aspirations. Besides, by the start of the 90s, the old battle-lines were becoming more blurred than ever. Companies like Dedicated and Hut, though superficially as countercultural as Factory, Mute et al, were offshoots of major labels, and for a time, bands made the most of their appealing mixture of indie aesthetics and corporate budgets.

As if to bring final confirmation that an era was drawing to a close, after months of financial mishap, Rough Trade – encompassing both the company's label and distribution wing – went into administration in May 1991. Its emphasis on workers' democracy and no free records had long since been crushed by music business realpolitik, but the company's disappearance was still deeply significant: without its long-established backbone, what remained of the indie milieu suddenly looked alarmingly vulnerable.

All told, the British rock bands that emerged in the early 1990s were forced to adjust to a world in which a great deal of what had underpinned left-field music had vanished. The result, for a while at least, was a slew of groups who had very little to say for themselves.

Happy Mondays, The Stone Roses and their ilk were succeeded by two kinds of British groups. On one side were a clutch of bands whose raison d'être seemed simply to revel in rock's more basic pleasures – volume, alcoholic excess, the gig ritual – with very little thought of anything else. Their names betrayed their lack of substance: Ned's Atomic Dustbin, Mega City Four, the Senseless Things. They were known as 'T-shirt bands', in apparent recognition of the fact that their prodigious sales of merchandise represented the most interesting thing about them.

The other pre-eminent camp favoured an altogether more serene approach. Following the example set by My Bloody Valentine – the Anglo-Irish group whose neo-psychedelic masterpiece, *Loveless*, was released in April 1991 – they peddled a rock equivalent of abstract art: music in which any sense of personality was swamped by a wash of guitar effects, hushed vocals and opaque lyrics. Slowdive and Chapterhouse, both of whom hailed from Reading, were among this wave's leading lights. One need only scan the titles of the latter's first releases, beginning in 1990, to understand their amorphous aesthetic: Freefall was succeeded by Sunburst, which was followed by Pearl and then Whirlpool. Inevitably, the music they played was hardy the stuff of wild abandon; in honour of their static approach to performance, the *NME* christened them 'shoegazers'.

Now that The Stone Roses had disappeared, their sense of strident ambition was out of the frame. Coverage in the music papers simply guaranteed more coverage in the music papers. A gig at one of London's bigger venues suggested nothing more earth-shattering than the possibility of another. Were a band to trouble the charts, they would probably repeat the trick another couple of times. Each of the new groups ascended to their own plateau of underachievement, and seemed to be mutedly content.

Making one's way around the London indie circuit at this point was a depressing experience. At the Islington Powerhaus, Kentish Town's Bull And Gate, the Camden Falcon or Harlesden's Mean Fiddler, you could spend each night of the week taking in the kind of musicians who would prompt a momentary spasm of attention – a few music press articles, a fleeting chase by a pack of record company talent scouts – before everyone came to their senses and moved on. No-one was ever going to be enraptured by Swineherd, Rollerskate Skinny, Mint 400 or Bivouac. The names said it all: this was music built on lowly aspiration, singularly lacking in any of the qualities – style, articulacy, artful innovation – that had long been British rock's hallmark.

In the midst of such mediocrity, however, there lurked one group who aimed to create music of an altogether higher stripe. At its core were two architecture students named Brett Anderson and Justine Frischmann.

CHAPTER 2

'What's wrong with your mouth?'

The Austrian town of Raiding was once known as Doborjan, before the frenzy of cartographical amendment that followed the First World War took it out of Hungary and placed it within the borders of a new, non-imperial Austria. The Hungarian population of the town thus shrank to 8 per cent, although one emblem of its Magyar heritage remained: the grave of Franz Liszt.

Each year, on 22 October, a bedraggled Morris Traveller would draw into the town, carrying a father-of-two from West Sussex. No matter that its driver was used to an existence spent flitting between dead-end jobs, or that his family's holidays were restricted to trips to Dorset: Peter Anderson's devotion to Liszt meant that this annual pilgrimage, timed to mark the composer's birthday, was a matter of duty. He would save the petrol money over months, steel himself for the inevitable breakdowns, and set off with all the fervour of a religious zealot. So as to bring some of Raiding's magic home with him, he would often return with a jar of soil, gathered from the grave's surroundings.

Anderson and his wife Sandra were the kind of economically blighted bohemians that orthodox class categories could not possibly describe. His working life included spells as an ice-cream man, window-cleaner and swimming pool attendant, until he eventually settled into minicab driving. His family's house was rented from the local council. Yet if the superficial picture just painted suggests a pinched life spent peril-ously close to the *lumpenproletariat*, with all the cultural deprivation that implies, the details evoke something far more exotic.

Aside from the worship of Liszt – and Hector Berlioz – Peter Ander-son was a lifelong admirer of Admiral Nelson, and he marked Trafalgar Day by hanging out a Union Jack. Sandra, meanwhile, was an art school graduate, who festooned the family home with her own canvases and reproductions of works by Gustav Klimt. The names they chose for their children were in keeping with all that: a daughter was born in 1963 and named Blondine, after Liszt's daughter; when her brother arrived in 1967, the couple stepped away from the vogueish torrent of Jasons and Matthews and Pauls and called him Brett. He shared his birthday with Nelson; not unreasonably, he remains convinced that his father – with whom he shares his fox-like features and slim-hipped build – arranged his conception accordingly.

The family home – in which a portrait of Liszt was hung next to a huge painting of Brett eating crisps – was in Lindfield, a village adjacent to Haywards Heath, the dormitory town that lies mid-way between Brighton and London. 'When people say "village",' says Anderson, 'that usually implies some pretty, beautiful, chocolate-box kind of place. But my dad's house, where he still lives, is next to a tip. Lorries were coming and dumping refuse right next to our garden. When we were kids, it'd be like *Stig of the Dump*: we'd go and sort through other people's garbage and take it home.'

The notion of a rural idyll spoiled by incursions from the nearby town was expressed by the infant Brett in a school essay. 'I like living in Lindfield because it has lots of trees,' he wrote. 'I like Lindfield very much because it has lots of farms and on one of them there are some goats. I think some people should be put in prison because they break down trees and it is all done by teenagers because they think they are so great.' With no less righteousness, he went on: 'Lorries make Lindfield look horrid because they are so big and smoky and smelly.' The essay, penned in handwriting whose 'f's were sufficiently ornate to suggest cello holes, won second prize in a competition organised by the Society for the Preservation of Lindfield. Such achievements aside, Brett Anderson's life was characterised by an ever-present want. 'We used to pick our own food,' he says. 'We used to go and pick onions and mushrooms to make into soup. Nicking stuff off farmers' fields. We'd almost be scavengers. It sounds ridiculous but it's true.

'And we'd come home, and my dad would be obsessed with Hector Berlioz and Franz Liszt. And my mum would cover the house with all these paintings. There was a strange . . . *duality*.'

At secondary school, Brett Anderson befriended Mat Osman, a slightly better-off resident of Haywards Heath. By then, his head had been turned by the sound of The Sex Pistols, heard by chance booming from Blondine's record player. No matter that the group had long since split up: Anderson hurled himself into his formative musical obsession, moving on from the Pistols to the 'anarcho-punk' pioneers Crass.

Membership of the requisite playground tribe, he discovered, was not nearly as daunting as it first appeared. 'All you needed,' he recalls with no little amusement, 'was a Nagasaki Nightmare patch, and you were a punk.'

His burgeoning interest in music was founded on the key promise it held: within the slashing chords and barked vocals, and the copies of the music papers he devoured on Wednesday mornings, Anderson could sense an altogether more exciting reality – and the possibility of escape. 'Everything's wrong about Haywards Heath,' he says. 'You get none of the facilities of the city, and none of the beauty of the country-side. There was never any question of staying there. I used to go to the railway station and just look up the tracks to where London was. That was the only place to go.' The words suggest a character from some monochrome 60s drama, gazing down the line at a bright-lights metropolis whose sheer distance makes it seem unspeakably allur-ing; handily for Brett, London was a tantalising forty-five minutes away.

By their mid-teens, Anderson and Osman had alighted on The Smiths. From there, they moved on to The Fall, fellow Mancunians whose equally subversive take on the world was couched in a far more impenetrable – and therefore fascinating – vocabulary. Accompanying both interests was a growing love of David Bowie, in homage to whom Anderson would repeatedly spurn his school uniform and arrive at school wearing a white suit, only to be sent home and feel his coun-tercultural fires glowing yet brighter. The pursuit of new music infused his and Osman's every waking moment. 'It was like arcane knowledge,' says Osman.

Strangely, considering his upbringing, his increasingly outré take on the world – and, perhaps most importantly, he and Osman's fleeting spell in a school band called Geoff, followed by his formation of the more promising Suave And Elegant – Anderson opted to study for his A-levels in among the strait-laced souls who had taken physics, chemis-try and maths. The combination often denotes the aspiration to be a doctor; in Anderson's case, although he displayed a clear aptitude for all three, it was largely a consequence of finding nothing better to do.

A watershed soon occurred, when the time came to decide how he would spend the three years between eighteen and twenty-one. His parents' break-up when he was sixteen may have played a part in waking him from a compliant slumber. 'I suddenly achieved conscious-ness at about seventeen,' he says. 'You're on autopilot up until then, and suddenly, you wake up as a thinking human being. All of a sudden I was doing science. I thought, "Fucking hell." The only thing I could do as a degree that wasn't physics, chemistry or maths or something as boring as that, was this thing Town Planning.'

Thanks to The Fall and The Smiths, and despite his fixation with London, Anderson chose Manchester University. He was billeted to Owens Park, a huge hall of residence whose outward appearance suggested something from the old Eastern Bloc, and whose corridors hosted the standard student mixture of high-jinks, dirty laundry and a complete lack of privacy. The mind raised among paintings and classical music was suitably appalled; lectures about the design of bypasses and zones of workers' housing hardly provided much relief.

'The fact that I hated the whole student thing was magnified a million times by somewhere like Owens Park,' he says. 'That was my first taste of student life, and it was all fucking Rag balls; people going to that fucking Rocky Horror thing. All that crap people do. All those wankers running around. I hated it.'

He dropped out during his second term, but decided to stay in Manchester, living in the student enclave of Chorlton-on-Medlock. For a while, he DJ'd at a shabby city-centre bar called The Cyprus Tavern, splitting his slots between Motown, 80s soul music and his beloved Smiths. In between, he took in the nocturnal life of a city that – thanks in part to the Haçienda – was evolving into a self-confident pop-cultural hub, and prepared for a different version of the Academic Life.

This time, his mind was fixed on what lay at the end of the Haywards Heath railway line. His old friend Mat Osman had since enrolled at the LSE; now, in October 1988, Brett Anderson was going to London.

The first words Anderson spoke to Justine Frischmann were hardly the stuff of romance. 'What's wrong with your mouth?' he asked, thinking she had a speech impediment.

'I wasn't sure if he was a girl or a boy when I first saw him,' says Frischmann. 'He had a bob haircut, two earrings in and a handbag. I didn't speak to him for ages, and then I finally got my guts up. He smiled at me and I went to talk to him. He thought I had a speech impediment because I was so nervous. Someone asked him what his dad did and he said he was a taxi driver, and I said I thought that was really romantic, which he thought was really funny. And then we started becoming friends.

'I'd been mixing with rich kids until I got to university; he was probably one of the first people I got to know really well who didn't have a well-off background. And I guess for me that was quite exotic.'

Frischmann's own background was hardly drab. Her mother, born Sylvia Elvey, was the daughter of Russian-Jewish parents who had arrived in Scotland in 1908, after a sudden spate of pogroms gave them little choice but to emigrate. 'The legend,' she says, 'is that they got off the boat at Glasgow, and thought it was New York, because there's a statue similar to the Statue of Liberty there. It took them three years to find out that they weren't in America because no-one around them spoke English. They were living in a ghetto.'

Her Hungarian father Wilem arrived in the UK in yet more dramatic circumstances, as a fourteen-year-old orphaned survivor of Auschwitz. He was educated at Bunce Court, a country house that sits in Kent's North Downs. Originally owned by one James Bunce, a royalist Sheriff of London imprisoned in the Tower by Oliver Cromwell, it was purchased in September 1933 by Anna Essinger, a refugee from Nazi Germany who set up a school for Jewish children, sent there by anxious parents. Among its alumni were the humorist Gerard Hoffnung and the artist Frank Auerbach, names in keeping with Bunce Court's emphasis on the creative arts. Wilem Frischmann's talents, however, lay elsewhere: in the altogether more precise, practical world of Civil Engineering.

His progress in the wake of his arrival suggests an up-by-the-bootstraps mobility that – even in the spurt of embourgeoisement that occurred in the wake of the Butler Education Act – the British class system should have rendered all but impossible. In 1958, he began working for the CJ Pell company, a firm of engineering consultants; three years later, he became a partner. The company duly mutated into the Pell Frischmann group, while Frischmann became enviably wealthy. One only need gaze at the central London skyline to understand what a big noise he had become: Centre Point – that vast, increasingly kitsch-looking obelisk that marks the junction of Oxford Street, Charing Cross Road and Tottenham Court Road – and the City's Nat-West Tower were built according to blueprints that had passed across his desk. He has occasionally aimed even higher: among the publications listed in his *Who's Who* entry is a paper entitled 'Two Mile High Vertical City'.

Justine was born in 1968, some eight years after Richard, her older brother ('I don't think my parents were planning on having a second kid. It was kind of a shock'). The family lived in Twickenham, in a purpose-built house constructed to her father's designs. As she discovered when she enrolled at her secondary school, the Frischmann home was emblematic of their arriviste status; that fact, in tandem with a very English kind of anti-semitism – vague frostiness and mumbled quips, rather than any outright hostility – gave her the sneaking feeling that she didn't quite fit in.

'Out of a year of sixty there were probably three or four Jewish girls,' she says. 'And there were an awful lot of snobby families sending their kids there, so I was aware of not being quite the ticket. We were definitely New Money. My dad had built himself this really wild-looking modern house in Twickenham, and all these people lived in Kensington in huge old family heirlooms. I remember having birthday parties and people coming to pick their children up, and looking around, really not very keen.'

St Paul's, Hammersmith, is a fee-paying girls' day school, whose alumni tend to have one key advantage over those who have been packed off to more famous rural establishments: along with the straight-backed self-reliance that English Independent education has long managed to hone to near-perfection, many of them ooze the easy-going urbanity that comes from an adolescence spent in the midst of a city. By the time she reached university, Justine Frischmann was a perfect case in point.

Having excelled in the school art room, she had wanted to take her fondness for brushes and canvas one step further – only to find her father nudging her elsewhere. His concerns were typical of the high-achieving immigrant; better, he thought, to be versed in a practical profession than the potentially ruinous ways of bohemia. 'I wanted to go to art college and he convinced me that it was too easy a way out,' says Frischmann. 'He thought I'd end up doing nothing.' Reluctantly, she agreed to read Architecture at University College, London.

As with his abortive spell in Manchester, Brett Anderson was embroiled in a Town Planning degree at UCL. The requisite department was grouped with Architecture in the college's Faculty of the Built Environment, based on Gordon Street. So it was that he crossed paths with Justine Frischmann. They became a couple soon afterwards; she recalls a key marker of their early relationship being the occasion when, prior to a field trip to Milton Keynes, she dutifully made him sandwiches. Most importantly, she managed to convince him that a life spent fretting about imaginary bypasses was no life at all – so Anderson switched courses to Architecture.

The pairing of the taxi's driver's son with the millionaire's daughter might suggest some novelistic, across-the-divide melodrama. According to Frischmann, however, the two met on completely level ground. 'When I was hanging out with Brett and Mat and their mates,' she says, 'my background was never, ever a point of discussion. It was totally irrelevant. I was treated as a creative being and it was interesting to see what I'd come up with.'

Nonetheless, the world from whence she came had given her the kind of wide horizons that, back in Haywards Heath, had apparently been beyond Brett Anderson's grasp. Frischmann's confident sense of opportunity – to call it ambition would be to rather overstate the case – duly oozed into the mind of her new boyfriend.

'Just the fact that he was doing Town Planning shows how little he expected from his life when he first went to university,' she says. 'I think he was a little bit clueless about what the future held; I don't think he was brought up to expect much for himself. He's very sweet about it: he always says that that's something that changed when he met me, because I really believed in him. I guess I'd been brought up to believe that there were opportunities in life, and if you really wanted something, you could have it. I think it was good for him to be around that. It rubbed off on him.'

Music, somewhat inevitably, informed a great deal of their lives. Anderson arrived at UCL with the tastes born in Lindfield taken into new, exploratory places: among his favourite records of the period was Happy Mondays' *Bummed*, released one month after he enrolled. 'When I first met Justine,' he says, 'she hadn't heard of any of the bands that I was really into. The first time she ever heard The Fall and The Smiths and even The Sex Pistols was when I played them to her. She was listening to Joni Mitchell and Van Morrison. One of her favourite records was by Astrud Gilberto and Stan Getz. I can remember saying to her, "We're not listening to this rubbish; *this* is what we're listening to." I used to stick on *Bummed* all the time. I loved that record: it was so dirty and noisy.'

Happy Mondays were the walking embodiment of the effects of ecstasy on rock music, with a flamboyantly hedonistic lifestyle to match, yet there were those who used the drug in an altogether more private fashion. Among them were Justine Frischmann, Brett Anderson and their circle of friends. Frischmann had first taken the drug the year before: 'the first time I did it was in 1987, when it was still legal. I knew someone who'd brought a load back from America and had walked through Customs with it. They were a quid each. I was seventeen, in a room full of people telling each other they loved one another.'

She and Anderson were not the kind of people who were going to drive out to the M25 and patiently wait for directions to that week's field. 'We tended to do E and stay in and talk shit, rather than going out,' she says. 'It was good therapy.' Soon enough, Anderson would become a keen ecstasy user, enthusing about its catalysing effect on his creativity; for now, their social circle provided living proof that, among close friends, controlled ecstasy use could deepen bonds and foster a particularly impenetrable kind of intimacy.

Anderson, Frischmann and Mat Osman were now living on Wilberforce Road, in the none-too-upmarket neighbourhood of Finsbury Park. 'We had a great winter together,' she says. 'It was '88, '89: an absolutely beautiful cold, blue winter. I just remember going to college together in the morning, all wrapped up, staying in this house with him [Brett] and Mat and their friends. It was a really romantic time: I felt like I was seeing London for the first time; seeing it almost through Brett's eyes. He always had a very romantic view of the world and the city.'

In the context of Anderson's starry-eyed mindset, he and Osman's eternal desire to decisively escape the drab ways of West Sussex, and the pair's teenage dalliances with guitars, it was perhaps inevitable that someone would suggest that they should form a group. Justine Frischmann, who had begun to play the guitar during her adolescence, proposed as much when Anderson bashfully played her some of the musical sketches he'd worked on in Lindfield. 'I forced him to play me his old demo tapes,' says Frischmann. 'He was really embarrassed to play them: he was like, "I used to think I could sing," and I said, "Well I bet you can – go on." But they were really good.'

Frischmann, Anderson and Osman soon came to the conclusion that they had the core of a band, though their initial musical experiments did not suggest the stuff of imminent acclaim. Initially, with Osman plunking out bass parts on an acoustic guitar and his two friends gamely strumming along, they spent hours rifling through Smiths, David Bowie and Beatles songbooks. In Justine Frischmann's recollection, the song of which they were the most fond was a chunk of black humour that had been released by The Smiths in 1987: for a while, the walls of the house vibrated to little more significant than clumsy renditions of Girlfriend In A Coma.

When the trio decided to cautiously up their game, there was one glaring snag: they quickly surmised that neither Anderson nor Frischmann had the technical expertise to play lead guitar. An advert was duly placed in the classifieds column of the NME, with the de rigueur sprinkling of musical reference points: The Smiths, David Bowie, the 80s singer-songwriter Lloyd Cole and the Pet Shop Boys. The ad ended with a rather ostentatious twist on a standard kiss-off: 'No musos, please. Some things are more important than ability.'

By the time a reply came forth, the base of the group's operations had moved West: Brett Anderson was living on Highlever Road, near Wormwood Scrubs, while Justine Frischmann flitted between that address and a townhouse, owned by her father, just off Kensington High Street. Bernard Butler, a sometime History undergraduate at

Queen Mary College, who had failed his first year and was marking time working in the Goodge Street branch of Rymans, was duly summoned to Anderson's new flat, where he came face to face with the kind of people who could not help but fill him with a creeping nervousness. 'They were very cool,' he later recalled, 'and I wasn't.'

'He was incredibly quiet,' says Justine Frischmann. 'He said he'd been reading the ads in the back of the music papers for five years, and this was the first one that had said the right things. There was some talk of calling him Laughing Boy, because his face didn't crack once, and he hardly spoke. Incredibly shy: didn't seem to move or speak or have any animation at all until he had a guitar in his hands. And he looked really young.'

The third son of a warehouse manager for Ever-Ready Batteries – who, like Butler's mother, was a native of Dunleary, Ireland – Butler was born in Tottenham, and had moved to Potters Bar at the age of fourteen. As well as dodging the more belligerent locals, he spent his adolescence teaching himself the guitar and falling in love with The Smiths. One of Butler's two elder brothers earned a nefarious living recording rock concerts; having travelled to and from some far-off British metropolis on National Express Coaches, he would return to their shared room in the dead of night bearing his latest tape. Thanks to The Smiths' fondness for introducing new material via their performances, it was thus Bernard Butler's good fortune to learn the guitar parts for Frankly, Mr Shankly, There Is A Light That Never Goes Out and Cemetry Gates long before their official release.

His audition piece was in keeping with his teenage obsessions: displaying a dexterity at which Anderson and Frischmann could only marvel, Butler delivered a rendition of What Difference Does It Make? while trying to make sense of his company. 'I thought they were really posh,' he says. 'Very well-spoken. And they seemed very, very mature. I didn't really believe they were only a couple of years older than me. They were really sociable: they'd shake your hand, give you a kiss on the cheek when you said goodbye. Girls didn't kiss you on the cheek where I came from, unless you were marrying them.'

For all his gaucheness, Butler's talents were obvious – so, after the most cursory of discussions, he was in. At nineteen, he was a little younger than his new friends: when told of their ages, he momentarily forgot his bashfulness and issued what bordered on a challenge. 'Well,' he said, 'you'd better get a move on, hadn't you?'

Initially, as he tried to fathom out how the group might work, he was puzzled by the presence of Justine Frischmann. 'I thought that Justine was just Brett's girlfriend,' he says. 'That's incredibly sexist –

but she did just sit there. I had to ask Brett, "What's the story? Is she in the band?" But gradually, she became more and more involved. I think it was a case of – and this is typical Justine – not getting involved unless something was going on. She waited to see if we were happening first and then she joined in.'

Once her role was cemented, Butler began to draw a very pleasing kind of solace from the time he spent with the group. 'I was very young-looking, and I was very skinny. And they were the first people I'd met who thought they were good things. That helped me warm to them: they encouraged me to be who I was. I didn't have to wear four jumpers to cover up my bones any more. Within two or three meetings, they said I was good-looking. No-one had said anything like that before.

'They'd take me to Justine's flat after rehearsal,' he says. 'We'd smoke dope, which was another thing I'd never done. That was revolutionary. They'd do things like getting pizzas from Pizza Express. That was like, "Wooah – that's a *restaurant*." She and Brett were a very warm, very beautiful couple – it was kind of understood that they were going to get married – and that extended to everyone around them. It was very idyllic: like going to Posh and Becks' house. They had a big telly, an open fire, a big sofa, two beautiful cats. It was a beautiful place. My brothers and my friends thought they were wankers; pretentious toffs. But I loved it. And they liked me. I think they thought I was some kind of spring, waiting to uncoil, and they were going to be the ones to do it. I really felt that. And I really enjoyed being uncoiled.'

By way of confirming their new bond and sense of purpose, the group now had a name. Having toyed with the flatly dreadful idea of calling themselves The Perfect, they were now named Suede, not least because the word simply looked good. Brett Anderson had begun to glue his lyrics to the music that, to the group's delight, Bernard Butler was composing at an admirably prolific rate. Equally importantly, Justine Frischmann and Mat Osman had managed to secure at least occasional custody of the kind of guitars that had to be plugged in.

'They had a song called Deflowered,' says Bernard Butler. 'I remember asking them what deflowered meant – whether it was something to do with gardening. They said, "No – it's to do with losing your virginity." They probably thought that was really funny.' In Butler's recollection, among the group's other early compositions were songs called The World Needs A Father, Break The Law and Carry Me, Marry Me. 'They were pretty,' he says, 'but they had no emotional aspect; no gusto.'

For the moment, the group's lack of a drummer was offset by their use of a cheap drum machine. Frischmann was their de facto manager, making calls and dropping off demo tapes at record companies, in the hope that her repeated appearance in reception areas might, out of politeness alone, facilitate the meeting that could hold the key. One A&R man remembers 'this beautiful girl – quite a hippy chick, quite laid back in the extreme, very, very chilled out. But really lovely.' In the main, and despite her more valiant efforts, their manoeuvres were restricted to the small-scale venues that, thanks to one of the quirks of London's commercial geography, were concentrated in or around Camden Town.

They first performed at a long-defunct indie club called The Sausage Machine. It was here that Justine Frischmann began to get the feeling that somewhere in Brett Anderson's psyche, a latent talent was stirring. 'I was absolutely terrified. I was so nervous I couldn't speak or sing. My palms were sweating so much that I couldn't really play. I was just amazed that Brett had some presence and knew what to do, and knew how to function onstage. It was, "Shit – he knows what he's doing."'

On 6 June 1990, Suede were bottom of the bill – beneath the sometime singer of Altered Images, Clare Grogan, and the beautifully named troupe The Arguments – at the Bull & Gate, the Kentish Town pub that booked groups to play in a black, sticky-floored anteroom whose dimensions rather suggested the inside of a huge truck. A photograph exists of that night, capturing all of Suede's early awkwardness: Butler, ruddy-cheeked and studious, staring intently at his guitar neck; Anderson, dressed in a stripy Katherine Hamnett T-shirt and baggy jeans, his face obscured by his fringe; Osman and Frischmann, the latter dressed in a rather ill-advised second-hand tracksuit, gamely playing along but unable to completely disguise her unease. A reporter from the *Melody Maker* was in the audience that night, and the opening lines of his review perhaps said it all: 'I was told to expect a popped-up version of The Stone Roses played by glamour-pusses. Instead, I encounter four would-be presenters for *Blue Peter*.'

The review caused the group no little upset. 'We were really hurt by that,' says Bernard Butler. 'We thought, "We'll probably have to lie low for a year now, till it all dies down."' Beneath the gawkiness, T-shirts and tracksuits, however, something was starting to cohere. Bernard Butler's guitar parts were starting to take on a slashing, brutal quality, partly derived from his hero Johnny Marr, but imbued with a trebly aggression that was all his own. Better still, Brett Anderson's lyrics were creeping into an even more singular universe. 'I used to read them and go, "Ooh, that's pretty good; that's pretty clever,"' says

Frischmann. 'His words started to get quite twisted sexually; kind of ambiguous. Lots of references to hips. "Jump on my bones." Quite dark-sounding. Definitely the shivering white indie male in his vest and his socks, sitting at the end of the bed, having filthy thoughts. They didn't sound as glamorous as Bowie. And there were elements of The Smiths, but it wasn't as romantic. It was darker.'

Moreover, in Anderson's use of arcane English slang, his evident fascination with London's more grimy aspects, and his propensity for singing in his own accent, there was an implied contrast with just about all of his peers. 'I definitely had the sense that we wanted to go against the grain,' he says. 'I thought the contemporary music scene was dead, and we were starting to do something that was really exciting. We actually reflected our own culture. We talked about what was real to me: being born in a council house, talking about things that were relevant to my world and how I was brought up. We were the first band for ages to talk about these things; to celebrate our own culture.

'You're hit head-on in this world by this huge rush of Americana. The whole world is culturally devoured by America. Even what was happening in the British music scene was basically people trying to update The Byrds. And I never wanted anything to do with that.'

Suede's first drummer was a teenage native of Nuneaton named Justin Welch, who played in a clipped, incisive style that seemed ideally suited to Anderson and Butler's songs. Unfortunately, after six weeks with the group, he was lured away by a superficially promising outfit from Crawley named Spitfire, briefly notorious in the *NME* for loudly extolling the wonders of groupies and employing two onstage go-go dancers.

Upon his departure, Suede placed yet another advert in the 'Musicians Wanted' columns. Once again, they made reference to the influence of The Smiths, whereupon a call came from the outskirts of Manchester. To their delirious surprise, Mike Joyce – The Smiths' one-time drummer, no less – had been in touch. 'Brett walked into this class at college and wrote me a note: "Mike Joyce has just left a message on my answering machine,"' says Justine Frischmann. 'We went up to see him on the train. It was absolutely unbelievable. And of course, it ended up with Bernard playing Smiths songs while Mike Joyce played the drums. But he was absolutely lovely; very flattered that we were so excited.'

Despite Joyce's instant sense that he was rather overqualified for the job, he assisted them with the recording of two songs, Art and Be My God. Thanks to a fleeting arrangement with a company called RML Records – whose heartwarming corporate motto, according to Bernard

Butler, was 'Where music is a way of life' – the songs were placed on either side of a 7-inch single. Five hundred copies were pressed, but the record fell some way short of the group's hopes. The lion's share of the pressing was swiftly hurled into a council skip.

In due course, Suede's prospects seemed to improve. In June 1990, they finally appointed a drummer who assured them he would stick around. Simon Gilbert came from Stratford-upon-Avon: after moving to London, he had divided his time between selling concert tickets at the University of London Students Union and seeking a full-time job as a musician. His outward appearance – Dr Martens, cropped hair, charity-shop attire – suggested that he was cut from the standard indie cloth, though his CV contained one incongruity. For all their right-on liberalism, there were not many indie groups with members who were openly gay. 'That was the thing that swung it,' says Bernard Butler. 'I can remember sitting in Brett's flat with Alan, his flatmate. Alan asked Simon if he was gay and he said, "Yeah." When he said that, Alan and Brett looked at each other and smiled. They loved Simon after that. He was different.'

Gilbert's arrival coincided with a slew of Anderson/Butler songs that represented a genuine watershed. In the likes of The Drowners, Moving and He's Dead, Suede reached a new, startling peak; a feat made all the more remarkable by the fact that it had been little more than eighteen months since the arrival of Bernard Butler. In retrospect, it seems incredible that songs of such merit did not instantly grab the attention of the gaggle of talent scouts and journalists who spent their evenings in London's more dingy venues; their attentions still seemed to be focused on aspirant shoegazers, and the fag-end of the boom that had originated in Manchester. Such, in the short term at least, was the price to be paid for proudly going against the grain.

'I was pretty aware that we were out of sync,' says Justine Frischmann. 'I was horribly sensitive about the fact that a lot of people thought we were shit. Who? *Everyone*. I didn't really believe anything was going to come of it. We'd been doing it for so long, it was quite well formed – and we still couldn't get arrested. It was still hard to get gigs, to scrape together the money for rehearsals.'

She was not the only member of Suede with misgivings. In Frischmann's recollection, as the year wound on, Bernard Butler became increasingly prone to causing tense scenes at rehearsals – though his ire was more a matter of aesthetics than career prospects. 'He wasn't a fantastic communicator,' says Frischmann. 'It seemed like he didn't really know how to get his opinion across in a non-aggressive way. I remember when Bernard turned up, he said that the band he

37

was in before was called The Foundry, and his whole thing was that he wanted to be really ordinary; he was into the working-class, salt of the earth thing. And it became increasingly obvious that Brett's vision was a little more twisted than that. I think Bernard was profoundly uncomfortable with all the sexual ambiguity.'

Thankfully, Suede's increasing musical potency was more than enough to keep Butler in place. Frischmann, however, found that her doubts were only growing deeper. 'I had a really horrible moment, just thinking, "This just isn't going to happen." Brett's always had this kind of tragic romanticism – and it's really lovely, it makes you think Trellick Tower and the Westway are beautiful. That whole decaying London thing is great as a vision, but it occurred to me that all the doomed romanticism was going to be part of the history of the group. We were never going to get anywhere, despite being really great. Nobody seemed to get it.'

As the year drew to a close, her sense of inertia began to extend into her relationship with Anderson. 'Because we were both at college,' she says, 'we were spending every second of every day together. And we hit the year-and-a-half stage that every romance hits – the honeymoon period's over, and it's got to move on or die. It got to the point where we weren't sure if we'd said certain things or just thought them. We thought we might be telepathic. We were spending so much time together that it actually started getting a bit weird.

'Nothing was happening with the band. It was becoming increasingly obvious that we were both going to fail third year at college, because we weren't very interested. And I remember Brett saying, "It'll be really great when we've finished here, and you get a job at an architects', and I stay at home and do the hoovering and make dinner for you when you get home." I had this vision of me working and Brett being at home with a pinny on, cooking vegetarian pizza – and I just thought, "I can't let this happen. This isn't working." If you could put the end of a relationship down to one comment, that was it. It was, "*That's* what this has all been about? *That's* how it's going to end up?"'

So it was that in February 1991, she agreed to go out with a musician who had been pursuing her for a few months. His name was Damon Albarn.

CHAPTER 3

Falling over a lot

Goldsmiths College was founded in 1891. Plonked in the midst of New Cross, a corner of South London famed for precious little save the threatening proximity of Millwall Football Club, it nonetheless managed to carve out an enviable academic reputation, embodied in its long list of ex-students: Bridget Riley, Lucien Freud, Mary Quant, John Cale, Malcolm McLaren.

Alex James went to Goldsmiths to study French in October 1988, arriving in the customary flurry of anxious parents and their equally terrified late adolescent offspring. The James family car had come from Bournemouth, where Alex was known as Steven. It is one of the unwritten rules of University Life that one is permitted to forge a new outward identity; James took his chance and adopted his middle name.

His upbringing had been as middle-English as could be imagined. After a spell in the navy, his father – who speaks with the optimistic plumminess often found in ex-servicemen – had worked as a sales rep for a forklift truck company with the bizarre name of Coventry Climax, before the family inherited a large guest-house in the town centre. An abortive spell as seaside hoteliers suggested that miniature butter portions and family fortnights were not the James's forte: Mr James founded a rubbish compacting company, while his family – Alex was joined by a sister, Deborah, in 1970 – belatedly enjoyed the full run of their new home. Thus, when Alex bought a bass guitar and joined the first of a run of local groups, their rehearsals took place in the guest-house's basement, an arrangement that prevailed despite his mother's horror at his friends' swearing.

While some of his peers stood on either side of the fault-line that divided 80s music, James's teenage tastes were relatively catholic. 'I was a New Order freak,' he says. 'And I liked The Smiths. But there was such a variety of music in the 80s. There was something quite nice about Wham! and Duran Duran, too. The pop stuff was a lot more colourful than it is now: ridiculous people wearing ridiculous things. You had that – the *Smash Hits* axis – and an enormous amount of underground music being made. I suppose I liked both.'

Academically, he was no slouch: at sixteen, he found himself with thirteen O-levels. Tumbling into the sixth form, he took the incongruous combination of French, physics and chemistry, before finding that his scholarly instincts were being corroded by a combination of alcohol and female company. He flunked all three of his A-levels, though salvation was provided by an unconditional offer to read French at Goldsmiths. He opted for deferred entry, and a year out spent in Charminster, doing precious little of any consequence. His musical interests found a focus of sorts in Mr Pang's Big Bangs, an enterprise named after his landlord which also featured his housemate, one Charlie Bloor. Betraying a lack of serious intent, their keynote composition was a purposefully cacophonous song entitled The Neighbours Are Coming Around.

James thus arrived at Goldsmiths after twelve months spent sleep-walking. 'I fluked it, I suppose,' he says. 'I just walked in there. I often wonder what would have happened if I'd gone anywhere else.'

When the family car pulled into his hall of residence, James beheld a similar scene being played out nearby. 'Graham Coxon was the first person I saw when I got out of my parents' car at the hall of residence,' he says. 'As soon as I saw him I thought, "You'll be a big part of my life." And we ended up feeling like we were in the coolest gang in the world.'

Coxon was the son of an army bandsman, and his early life fulfilled the itinerant archetype of the forces child. He was born in West Berlin: the family spent his early years living mere yards from the prison that housed Rudolph Hess. At the age of six, he briefly lived with his grandfather in Derby, on account of his father's on-off postings to Ulster. In the late 70s, however, the family settled in Colchester: leaving army life behind, Bob Coxon had become a conductor for the Essex Constabulary Band, and a part-time music teacher.

The Coxon home was thus very musical indeed. Moreover, the family stereo took in an eclectic selection of music: though his father was a Beethoven enthusiast, Coxon also spent his childhood listening to The Beatles. Like countless curious minds, his enjoyment of The Beatles' albums was only heightened by the discovery that, on their early recordings, the primitive use of stereo meant that one could switch between vocals on one channel, and the backing track on the other. 'They had this real stereophonic geography,' he would later recall, with no little wonder.

An evident talent for art was thus accompanied by a passion for music. Having begun to learn the saxophone, Coxon was given his first guitar at the age of twelve. Coloured by his love of such groups as The Jam and The Specials, his skill at the latter instrument was self-taught, although his formal studies of music extended to an O-level, which joined human biology, English and art on his GCE certificate. From this relatively flimsy base, he elected to stay at Colchester's Stanway Comprehensive and study for A-levels. His spell in the sixth form was short-lived: finding himself particularly exasperated with the arid theory that came with studying A-level music, he began a two-year Foundation course at North Essex School of Art. In turn, a door was opened that would lead him to a degree in Fine Art at Goldsmiths.

It was Coxon, along with a compadre named Paul Hodgson, who allowed Alex James to forget about the fact that he was a Languages student, and step into the intellectual whirl that surrounded Goldsmiths' Art department. 'It was all very cool,' says James. 'There were people building weird catapult machines, and paint everywhere . . . it was a good place to be. It was two years talking about Franz Klein and trying to learn how to throw cigarettes into your mouth. A lot of cool people dressing weirdly and drinking a lot. Staying up all night and talking about the colour blue. It was a big art school, really. And there was this sort of "We are it" feeling. It was a brilliant playground.'

'Graham would get up in the morning and put a telephone in a washing-up bowl, then go to the Students Union bar. I'd go and listen to Voltaire's ideas on optimism and go to the bar. And then everyone else would arrive at the bar, and it was down to who won at pool. We always used to take the piss and say, "There's a fucking lot of geniuses walking around here," 'cos everybody used to reckon themselves – but a lot of them were.'

Coxon and James were well-placed to further their interest in music. A short walk from Goldsmiths was the Venue, an insalubrious place where they could frequently clap eyes on the latest thing they had been told about by the *NME* or heard on John Peel's radio show. Failing that, there was the option of a trip north. Here, Coxon led the way: among his favourite groups were a gang of misfits from Oxford called Talulah Gosh, as well as The Pastels, a no-less angular band from Glasgow. Both fitted the non-conformist 80s indie mould to perfection: in the case of the Pastels' singer, Stephen McRobbie, his disdain for mainstream convention was such that he seemed to affect the look of someone who was mentally ill.

The arrival of Coxon and James at Goldsmiths coincided with a highpoint in the college's history. Two years above them lurked Damien Hirst and Sam Taylor-Wood – for a while, Coxon's workspace was adjacent to Hirst's. In 1988 Hirst curated Freeze, named after his cow-and-formaldehyde piece, in the abandoned South East London Port Authority Building. The exhibition decisively began the ascent of both Hirst and fellow Goldsmiths student Sarah Lucas; soon enough, the period stretching between the late 80s and early 90s would come to be seen as Goldsmiths' golden age.

By way of allying themselves with such developments, Coxon and James – along with the aforementioned Hodgson and one Jason Brownlee – decided to glorify their late-night conversations by forming an alcohol-soaked salon-cum-art movement. In deference to the German talent for The Big Idea, they called it *Nichtkunst*. 'Was it serious?' James considers. 'Yeah. You're never more serious about what things mean than when you're nineteen, twenty. I don't think we knew what we were after: we were just up all night trying to work out who we were. Which you have to do. It's like a three-year French exchange, going to college, isn't it?' History records little of what *Nichtkunst* was trying to achieve, aside from a vague idea of Coxon's about 'dropping scaffolding from a height into an enclosed hall.' Very often, its members would spend the evenings playing Ludo.

When talking to those whose lives have felt Damon Albarn's impact, one thing rapidly becomes clear: he does not excel in the art of first impressions. So it proved in early 1989, when he and Alex James were introduced. 'I thought he was an idiot,' says James. 'A pompous, big-headed fucking moron with a shit band. But Damon does do that: he's so rumbustious and bombastic when you meet him. He's got this confrontational thing going on. He can come across as a total cunt.'

James had been invited to meet Albarn by Graham Coxon. The latter pair, friends since their days at Stanway Comprehensive, had recently collaborated on a batch of music recorded at The Beat Factory, a recording studio within spitting distance of Euston Station. James was played a representative sample, by which he was underwhelmed. With a candour fine-honed by *Nichtkunst* evenings, he articulated his swingeing judgement to the music's chief author. 'To be fair,' he says, 'I did tell Damon I thought he was a wanker, about an hour after first meeting him. He said, "What do you think of the music, then?" I said, "Well, I think it's shit."'

Albarn and Coxon's new project was called Circus. Their work in the studio had been facilitated by the fact that Albarn had been taken under the wing of the studio's management, and given the job of tea-boy; in between shifts, he worked at the nearby Euston branch of Le Croissant Shop.

Albarn was a child of 60s bohemia. His father, Keith, was an alumnus of the creative upsurge that had gripped London as of around 1965: among other episodes, he had staged Yoko Ono's first London exhibition, enjoyed a brief period as a presenter of the BBC's Arts programme *Late Night Line Up*, and gone on to manage the jazz-rock group Soft Machine. Adding to the sense of lives spent on the creative cutting-edge, his wife Hazel was a stage designer at the Theatre Royal, Stratford East. Thus, the counterculture was but one of the creative whirls of which the Albarns had experience: when she became pregnant with Damon, Hazel Albarn was working on *Mrs Wilson's Diary*, John Wells and Richard Ingrams' artful poke at the Labour government.

The Albarns lived in Leytonstone, in a Victorian terrace decorated according to their cutting-edge tastes: the living room was painted silver, and a huge fibreglass sculpture stood in the garden. Damon and his elder sister, Jessica, born in 1965, were brought up in the empowering, attentive atmosphere common to the more forward-looking households of the time: encouraged to voice their opinions and allowed to commune with the grown-ups as equals. Consequently, Albarn has long claimed to have never begrudged his mother and father much at all. 'I always thought my parents were absolutely dead right,' he said later. 'I went against the grain in a weird way, by continually following them.'

In 1978, Keith Albarn decided to take up a post as the head of North Essex School of Art, in Colchester. The family was thereby uprooted, and plunged into a climate where silver living rooms and jazz-rock were rather more anomalous than they had been in London. They set up home in Aldham, a hamlet set among the undulating hills to Colchester's west. Their house was a converted shop that backed on to open country, set in a corner of Essex that has much more in common with Suffolk than the dormitory belt that takes in the likes of Chelmsford and Harlow. The local accent has an archetypally East Anglian burr; when Albarn enrolled at the local comprehensive school, he rubbed shoulders with the children of agricultural workers. Essex's education system had one peculiar quirk: the county had retained the practice of selection, although entry for the eleven-plus was a matter of choice. Secondary education was thus split between grammar schools and comprehensives, the latter populated by a mixture of those who had failed to make the grade, and the children of parents who had chosen not to put their offspring through such a trauma. When Damon Albarn reached the end of his primary school years, his parents – for reasons that doubtless had an ideological element – took the latter decision.

Albarn duly enrolled at Stanway Comprehensive, where, assisted by increasingly evident good looks, he became quite the celebrity. Stanway's strengths lay in the creative arts, which meant that Albarn was in his element. Thanks to his evident combination of talents both dramatic and musical – and the tutelage of Nigel Hildreth, Stanway's Head of Music – he took leading roles in productions of *The Boyfriend*, *Orpheus In The Underworld* and *Guys And Dolls*.

In the meantime, he kept his schoolyard cool intact by being one of a small gang of non-conformists who would congregate in the music block. It was here that he befriended Graham Coxon, an occasional participant in Nigel Hildreth's productions who was in the year below him. In keeping with the upright dress-code of someone partial to The Jam, Coxon had taken to wearing a pair of brogues; Albarn had similar, though more upmarket footwear. The audacity that would mark much of his adult life was present even then: Albarn's first words to Coxon were 'Your brogues are crap, mate. Look, mine are the proper sort.'

Coxon recovered from the slight, and the two soon enjoyed the kind of bond that forms the fulcrum of many a male adolescence, underpinned by the quirks of the class system. Coxon, a member of that part of the middle-class with no bohemian pretensions whatsoever, would spend hours at the Albarns' house, fascinated by an environment in which art, politics and theatre were discussed so freely.

More importantly, there was music. The pair moved from The Jam and The Specials to a shared love of The Smiths. Running between all three the notion of music being used to shine a light on England's backwaters. Their most culturally specific songs were bound up with precisely the kind of environment that Colchester represented: afternoon tea in the Lite-a-Bite, the eternal necessity of evading some closing-time ruck, the faceless thousands speaking – to use Paul Weller's memorable phrase – in 'bingo accents'. Such themes were also reflected in the films of which Albarn and Coxon were the most fond: *Quadrophenia*, the film that melded 60s nostalgia with a very English sense of claustrophobia, and Mike Leigh's *Meantime*.

Albarn could play both violin and piano; Coxon had his guitar and saxophone. Moreover, encouraged by Nigel Hildreth's Music department, Albarn had begun to add self-written compositions to school revues. The pair duly passed through a small handful of ad hoc groups, whose existence teetered between the concrete and purely imaginary, before a group called Real Lives finally took them into the rarefied world of public performance.

Like most school bands, it was laid to rest when its members took divergent paths. Encouraged by Keith Albarn, Coxon exited the sixth form and took a place at North Essex College of Art. Damon, meanwhile, plodded on. Having decided that formal music study was not for him, he applied to be a drama student at the East 15 Acting School in Debden. They accepted him with no insistence on A-level passes: he wilfully failed music A-level, and emerged with a D in English and an E in history.

Most accounts of Albarn's life return, time and again, to the fact that he has long oozed a quite remarkable drive. The next two years, however, rather suggest a mind at a loss as to what to do with itself. In Debden, he rubbed up against a regime that emphasised Method Acting. At one point, his tutors instructed Albarn to spend two months living as a tramp. He left at the end of his first year.

In the midst of a sudden – and atypical – period of self-doubt, he moved back to Aldham. Coxon was newly in love with the life of the art student, which only served to deepen Albarn's sense of crisis. Sensing that his friend's move to London might somehow hold the key, he enrolled for a part-time music course at Goldsmiths. Between lectures, there was his work at The Beat Factory and Le Croissant Shop. For a time, he also worked at the Portobello Hotel, a discreet London establishment through which the likes of Tina Turner and U2 would swish, paying no mind to the young barman who would eavesdrop on their conversations. 'One night Bono was rude to me and I've never really forgiven him,' he later reflected. 'The Edge, on the other hand, was always really polite.'

The Beat Factory's owners, Graeme Holdaway and Maryke Bergkamp, detected Albarn's musical talent: they offered to oversee his progress and did their best to introduce him to like minds. The upshot was an enterprise called Two's A Crowd, consisting of Albarn and another Beat Factory client, Sam Vamplew. Pictures of the pair rather suggest some far-flung 80s synthesiser duo; the partnership was mercifully short-lived. Circus, however, was a little more promising. Albarn formed the group in league with a friend from his drama school period called Eddie Deedigan. In October 1988, just as Coxon and James were arriving at Goldsmiths, they acquired a drummer from Colchester called Dave Rowntree.

Rowntree was four years older than Albarn. Like Coxon, he came from a home in which music was a given: his father worked as a sound engineer at Broadcasting House, while his mother was a former professional viola player. He and Coxon had fleetingly collaborated in a short-lived – and woefully named – Colchester group called Hazel Dean And The Carp Eaters From Hell, a partnership which in turn led him to Albarn. His arrival in the ranks of Circus marked the beginning of intensive rehearsals, polishing songs that touched on such 80s staples as The Smiths, Talking Heads and the Pet Shop Boys, while remaining isolated from the sharp end of musical developments: Circus were not an identifiably indie group, nor had their world been touched by Acid House.

In time, Coxon was summoned to The Beat Factory in the wake of the sudden resignation of Circus's guitarist. The music duly changed, taking on the skewed, distorted sounds that Coxon loved in his favourite indie groups – whereupon Alex James visited the studio and issued his damning verdict. Whether or not his words immediately hit home is unclear. In the short term, Circus persevered. By December 1988, however, two members of the band had been fired and Alex James was in the same group as Damon Albarn, Graham Coxon and Dave Rowntree.

'The first time we played music together we wrote our first single,' says James. 'It all clicked from there. There was a bond.'

The new group was almost called The Beads, before they thought better of it and named themselves Seymour. The name was taken from the central character of the thirteen short stories that sit next to *The Catcher In The Rye* in the slim canon of published literature by JD Salinger. The idea, doubtless given the rubber-stamp at some unspeakably late, booze-drenched hour, came from James and Coxon's *Nichtkunst* ally Paul Hodgson.

Largely by accident, the group were representative of all kinds of long-running strands within British music. The art-school background of Coxon – and, by association, James – was reflective of the seam that had produced John Lennon, Ray Davies, Pete Townshend and half of The Clash. Albarn had the parental link to the 60s counterculture, while his fleeting link with drama resulted in one of the group's more remarkable aspects. He was fond of telling anyone who'd listen about Antonin Artaud's notion of the Theatre of Cruelty: in a nutshell, the idea of exploding bourgeois norms by laying on a particularly confrontational spectacle. As far as Seymour were concerned, it seemed to mean that they fell over a lot.

The music they made was suitably chaotic: at first, Alex James recalls, their rehearsals gave rise to 'three-hour-long performance art pieces:

snapping strings and breaking things.' Eventually, they arrived at prickly, rather discordant songs – all staccato bass, breakneck guitar riffs and breathless vocals – that would hurtle between tempos and keys, seemingly on a whim. Their key influence was The Cardiacs, a cult attraction from Surrey who had spent the 80s combining punk and psychedelia with a very obtuse kind of comedy. Seymour were similarly inclined: listening back to the small body of work they put to tape, it often becomes difficult to discern whether they were earnestly trying to tear up the musical rule book or playing it for laughs.

Seymour's first performance took place that summer at the East Anglian Railway Museum in Chappel, just down the road from the Albarn family home. The occasion was a party organised to mark both Keith Albarn's fiftieth birthday and his son's twenty-first. The audience, numbering around 100, sat in a tube train carriage; lighting effects were provided by a 60s strobe. Alex James was amazed to hear Damon Albarn addressing his parents by their Christian names.

Soon after, they were booked to appear at the celebrations marking the passing-out of Goldsmiths' third years, already sprinkled with the aforementioned celebrities. The occasion provided Coxon and James with their first meaningful meeting with Damien Hirst. With no little understatement, Goldsmiths' most-likely-to student told them that, in his estimation, they were the best group since The Beatles.

Their day-to-day existence, unfortunately, was hardly the stuff of dreams. Though the excitement afforded by the group offset such privations, James and Coxon entered their first summer as Goldsmiths students with precious little money and – in James's case – nowhere to live. Salvation of a particularly shabby kind came in the shape of a vacant building on New Cross Road. In 1989, taking unauthorised possession of vacant property remained a civil rather than a criminal offence; squatting was a practice that underpinned a good deal of London's creative demi-monde.

'Oh God, it was horrible,' says James. 'We discovered that one flat was free: someone who'd left college gave the keys to one of Graham's friends, and then we gradually discovered that the whole building was free, and the whole block was free. It gradually became full of all kinds of undesirable nineteen- to twenty-three-year-olds who just wanted to do hot knives and listen to Talulah Gosh. Somebody would drive off to Blackburn and come back with a million magic mushrooms. It was *Withnail and I* without the Jag and Uncle Monty. Or Withnail.

'You couldn't really lock our flat door. The only thing that kept us safe was the fact that we had nothing of any value. A lot of slugs used to come in. Water wouldn't get hot enough for a bath, and the bath would take all day to run. It was really filthy. Mad Paul would come round at night, this bloke who ended up being a male prostitute, and he was living in this flat upstairs that had no electricity. We'd send him off to bed with a candle. It terrified my parents.'

Squatting did not represent the only governmental loophole through which an aspirant musician could jump. Though the Thatcher government had begun to tighten up, the dole was still freely available to anyone clever enough to dodge the state's attempts to squeeze them into work. While Albarn split his time between The Beat Factory and Le Croissant Shop, and Rowntree held down a job as a computer programmer in Colchester, James and Coxon made the requisite fortnightly visit to the DHSS. The welfare state's munificence kept them at subsistence level, though their poverty bit hard. 'It was a real hand to mouth thing,' says James. 'We got our clothes from Deptford Market. Some days, we'd get up, go down there and drink Tennents Super with the tramps.'

In February 1988, Food Records had stepped over the crevice that divided British rock music. They had begun life as an independent label, issuing a small handful of records, before surmising that outside help – in terms of finance alone – was necessary. They thus became a near-autonomous wing of EMI, and were rather demonised. No matter that anyone stepping into their office would have instantly recognised the garden-shed modus operandi common to indie-land, or that Food's budgets were dwarfed by the clout of the bigger independents; the fact that they took money from EMI and used the company's distribution network meant that they were pariahs. Such was life in the ideologised battlefield of the 80s.

'When we did the deal with EMI,' says Andy Ross, 'we were lumped in with Satan by the likes of the *NME*. But the whole punk revolution . . . that bubble had long since burst. We felt it was essential, to pay the bills, to get money from someone. So we went to a major label.' The result was exclusion from the independent charts, the sealed-off hierarchy still pored over by the music papers, whose machinations rather suggested some British version of what Americans call Affirmative Action. 'Those labels had their own agenda,' says Ross. 'It was, "Our records are independently distributed, there's a chart in the *NME* every week which is only for independently distributed labels, and our records are in it every week. We don't want to let those fuckers in." It seemed to boil down to the fact that our distribution vans were a different colour. I was banging my head against the wall. It was pitiful.'

Ross was a freelance music writer and sometime tax clerk, who had fleetingly experienced life under the spotlight in a late 70s group called The Disco Zombies. He had since fallen into the round of lager, cab rides and tinnitus that defined a loosely-bound London clique – A&R men and journalists, chiefly – eternally in search of music's next step. In 1988, he had been offered 25 per cent of the Food label in return for his input; the man who made the offer was a Liverpudlian called David Balfe.

Balfe had come closer than most to life as an accredited star. Between 1979 and 1983, he was the keyboard player with The Teardrop Explodes, the Liverpool group fronted by Julian Cope. Their commercial highpoint was Reward: a stampeding hybrid of rock and 60s soul that reached number six in January 1981. Its keynote element was its beautifully effective horn part, put there at Balfe's insistence. Food – whose roster, by 1989, included such far-flung names as Voice Of The Beehive, Crazyhead and Diesel Park West – was his domain: though, in London's rat-hutch venues, Andy Ross often represented the label's public face, it was his senior partner who was in command.

In early 1990, Food was preparing to launch Jesus Jones, pioneers of a breed of technology-enhanced rock that would bring them a spurt of success in America. Within a remit that aimed at the signing of one group a year, Andy Ross was out and about. So it was that, in the last week of November 1989, he paid one of his regular visits to the Powerhaus, the Islington venue near Angel tube station that subscribed to the standard indie decor rules by being done out in matt black and giving off an odour of stale cider and refried beans. Handily, it was also built to an 'L' shape, meaning that, should the night's attractions turn out to be a disaster, the clientele could get quietly drunk round the corner.

That night, Seymour were playing. 'They were a fucking shambles,' says Ross. 'But exciting, definitely. I'd had a tape beforehand, which had She's So High on it. There were two good songs, and two rubbishy, indulgent, hippy, backwards guitar, Syd Barrett-type songs: I wouldn't go as far as to say that side of them was unlistenable, but they were the antithesis of commercial. Their live show was a combination of all that. And Dave Rowntree was wearing pyjama trousers. I thought, "Hmmm. Maybe a punkier version of Talking Heads or something." They were art-rock, I thought. Were they an indie group? Yeah. Definitely. No major in its right mind would have touched them.

'I thought Damon was very good-looking, and had a lot of presence onstage. A lot of jumping up and down. But it was the whole package. They all had individual characters: there was Graham, jumping up and down and falling over, but he was a brilliant guitar player; and Alex, who was off on his Oscar Wilde thing, with his fag in his mouth. They had all that, pretty much from the outset. I had this "Get in there quick and sign them" feeling.'

Ross dragged Balfe to a succession of Seymour concerts – at the Ladyowen Arms in Islington, Kennington's Cricketers Arms and the Camden Falcon, where Blur knowingly packed the pub's back room with their friends and acquaintances. By this time – as tended to happen within the village-like confines of the London scene – interest in Seymour had begun to spread to other companies. Balfe's hand was forced; though his interest had initially been counterbalanced by scepticism, he agreed to begin serious talks.

As it turned out, Food had one particular problem with Seymour: their name. Over dinner, Ross told them he thought it was a 'gay indie anorak name', before apologising profusely, lest any member of the group turned out to be gay themselves. His point, reluctantly, was taken: the group, in tandem with Balfe and Ross, began groping around for alternatives.

A cynically vogueish list drawn up by Food included Sensitize and Whirlpool: names that dripped with the lysergic connotations that Acid House had made fashionable. The group also chewed over The Shining Path, and – arguably best of all – The Government. Finally, they agreed on another name from Food's list, and Seymour became Blur. Under Ross and Balfe's tutelage, the change of name began to bleed through into the music. Seymour's more chaotic instincts were reined in, their once-fierce desire to trample every convention into the dust now restricted to Coxon's more unhinged guitar lines, the odd B-side and their unshakeable urge to bump into one another onstage.

They signed to Food in March 1990. Ross and Balfe did not think it necessary to tap EMI for some mind-boggling advance, and the group were handed a cheque for a mere £7,000. In one of his darker moments, Dave Rowntree once claimed it was 'one of the worst record deals in history.'

Alex James and Graham Coxon instantly quit their courses at Goldsmiths. The latter was pleased to discover that the Art department's air of anything-goes grooviness extended to such trifles as sudden exits: he was wished good luck, and told that if things hadn't worked out within a year, he was more than welcome to come back.

Before any records were released, Blur were instructed to clamber into a van and familiarise themselves with the United Kingdom. They were placed in the care of Gimpo, a friend of Dave Balfe's who had seen active service in the Falkland Islands. Aside from the simple business of getting them from Leicester to Leeds and on to Newcastle, he also ensured they had an occasional supply of LSD. It was a more easily available drug, however, that powered them around the country: as everyone who met them quickly surmised, Blur were fond of the kind of drinking best described as 'reckless'.

Into the midst of all this came Justine Frischmann. A few months before the release of their first single, Blur performed at Brighton's Zap Club, supported – thanks to Frischmann's diligent canvassing of the club's promoter – by Suede. The first exchanges between the two camps suggested an age-old rock archetype: the frosty one-upmanship that often runs between the headline band and the act who are propping up the bill. 'I asked Damon for a Blur poster,' says Frischmann, 'and he was really rude to me – "Fucking buy it then." And I remember him coming down and lecturing us, saying, "We've got the biggest dressing room and you've got the little one, but you have to pay your dues." Just being a real arsehole, lecturing us like a real bigwig.'

Albarn had seen Suede before – as he later recalled, he was cajoled into attendance by a simple enough enticement: 'Do you want to go and see this band tonight? One of them's a public schoolgirl and she brings all her really nice friends along.' On that occasion, he had been all but indifferent. In Brighton, however, his belligerence belied the fact that, as he watched Suede play, he could not take his eyes off their second guitar player. 'After that, he took it upon himself to track me down,' says Frischmann. 'I'd never been pursued like that. Brett and I were breaking up at the time anyway – and Damon didn't stop phoning me.'

Early the following year, Frischmann finally acquiesced. 'I agreed to go out for a drink with him. He phoned up on the basis of offering us a gig, and he announced that I was the one, and we would be married and I had no choice in the matter. I was fairly bowled over; no-one had done that to me before. I was quite intrigued. He was really cute then; a really cute twenty-one-year-old. Enormous blue eyes.'

Once she had recovered from the shock of having the rest of her life signed, sealed and delivered, the couple talked about music. Frischmann, whose record-buying was little short of voracious, was shocked to discover that Albarn owned no records whatsoever. 'He had about three tapes,' she says. 'One of them was Janis Joplin. He didn't have a clue; he didn't buy records.'

In due course, she was introduced to the rest of Blur. 'I thought they were a bit weird,' she says. 'I found them quite hard to get on with. I thought they were a bit retarded. They were like children. Bernard Butler had been a bit odd, but Mat and Brett were really cool: very bright, very easy-going. And Blur weren't. Childish, drunk. Not scary, just pathetic.

'I loved Graham's guitar playing, but I thought he was a prat. But Damon was sufficiently interesting to keep me going. I thought the band were really good; I thought they were more musically gifted than Suede. I thought the songs were stronger, the guitar playing was better, the harmonies were there.'

For all her travails with Suede, and her consequent empathy with the kind of life into which Blur had been plunged, Albarn's colleagues sensed the arrival of an impressively sophisticated presence. 'We were very impressed with how rich she was,' says Alex James. 'We were all living in squats, eating grass – and she was wealthy beyond the dreams of avarice. Spectacularly so. She was a posh bird, man. I mean, Damon's posh – his dad ran an Art department. But they were *cash rich*.' James also claims to have had slightly more cynical thoughts. 'I think she had an agenda, possibly. I don't want to rattle any cages. But I think she thought Damon could help her with her career, shall we say.'

Justine Frischmann was also responsible for introducing Albarn to one of the few human beings to have shaken his usually perfect composure. 'Her dad was the only person I've ever known him be apprehensive about meeting,' says James. 'Damon's not scared of anybody. But he was a little bit nervous about him.'

Despite Albarn's rapid declaration of his and Frischmann's perfect fit, he expected their coupling to leave room for the odd brief tryst; the fact that so much of his life was spent on the road apparently made the arrangement inevitable. 'We had quite an unusual relationship,' says Frischmann. 'We saw ourselves as being quite modern, and not affected by the same rules as everyone else. The open thing does nothing for me, but there was no choice. If you're with Damon you're going to be in an open relationship.'

By the spring of 1991, Albarn and Frischmann were a confirmed item, and – after a period of co-habitational purgatory – Brett Anderson moved out of the flat in Kensington that was owned by her father. Thus commenced one of the darker chapters of Anderson's progress, in which he suffered both the pangs of separation and the privations of being broke. 'It was pretty frightening for him – that sense that the security net wasn't going to be there,' says Frischmann. 'And the band didn't look like it was going to work out, he was just about to fail his third year at college, he had no money . . . it was a really horrible time for him. But I had total faith in Brett – that he wouldn't sink, he would swim.'

In retrospect, Frischmann believes that, for all his distress, it was her split from Anderson that gave him the fierce motivation that he had apparently lacked. 'It wasn't until all the ugliness happened and I ran off with Damon that he got enough of a demon in him; a reason to get his own back on the world. He was quite a stable, happy person when we were together – probably a bit too blissfully happy for his own good.'

After their months spent hawking themselves around the UK – and the first stirrings of attention from the press – it was decided that October marked the best time to release Blur's first single. Its two sides had been recorded at Battery Studios in Willesden, soon after Food's first cheque had come their way. She's So High was a sleepy, creepingly psychedelic piece, moulded from a chord sequence improvised by Alex James and lyrics – giving the vaguest suggestion of boy-girl lust – by Graham Coxon. I Know, meanwhile, sounded like a cynical xerox of the kind of lopsided funk that had reared its head on The Stone Roses' Fools Gold. It was intended as a double-feature, though the former song was taken by most of the record's listeners to be the A-side.

As it turned out, the music quickly threatened to be overshadowed by a set of incidents that, in retrospect, cast Blur as the unwitting harbingers of a new era. The sleeve of the single was based around a painting by the Californian pop artist Mel Ramos, a man who had long specialised in the garish portrayal of female nudes, usually set against either consumer ephemera or wild animals. Blur's single featured an image of a smiling nubile, replete with pendulous breasts and bare buttocks, riding a hippopotamus. The piece – also reproduced on a run of T-shirts – was hardly pornographic: its air of irony alone placed it in an altogether more playful place.

Like any freshly launched group, Blur promoted the single via a series of performances at Students Unions, then a particularly feisty part of the world that defined itself against the conservative mainstream. In buildings named after Steve Biko and Nelson Mandela, their ruling councils maintained a particularly pedantic kind of vigilance against the usual bogeypeople: racism, sexism and homophobia. Pop-art irony, it was safe to say, was not a language they were equipped to translate.

The tour to promote She's So High was thereby peppered with a run of gloriously farcical episodes. At Liverpool Polytechnic, the Union was picketed. In Coventry, with a righteous ferocity that would have befitted Mao's Red Guards, it was decided that anyone wearing a Mel Ramos T-shirt in the Steve Biko bar would be forcibly ejected. At nearby Warwick University, the approach was a little less heavy-handed, though no less strange. 'They had a little trestle table set up, opposite the T-shirt stand,' says Alex James. 'There were all these leaflets and signs saying "Don't buy one". It was stupid. We went into it innocently: we just thought, "Fucking hell, that's wacko." It wasn't conceived to annoy. Tits with a hippopotamus just looked new. But we were going, "Fucking great – we're in the press." '

Thanks to the fact that the UK had three weekly music papers, such trifling controversies had long been relayed to tens of thousands of people. Blur's clash with the anti-sexist resistance thus worked the requisite wonders in *Sounds*, *NME* and *Melody Maker*, though it fell some distance short of making them instant stars. Upon its release, She's So High spent three weeks in the singles chart, managing to get as high as number forty-eight.

It was Blur's second single that did it. There was a six-month lull after She's So High, during which they continued to tour, in between grappling with the vexed business of a next record. Initial attempts – on songs entitled Bad Day and Close – didn't amount to much. It wasn't until they were paired with a producer called Stephen Street that decisive progress was made. Street had worked with The Smiths on three of their four albums; that fact alone endeared him to the group.

Blur and Street set to work on two songs: a splenetic, fast-paced piece called Come Together, and an inconsequential sketch brought to the sessions by Damon Albarn. In the studio, thanks to its lolloping rhythm, it began to harden into a song reminiscent of The Stone Roses; when Dave Balfe and Andy Ross heard it, they were delighted. 'They delivered this track There's No Other Way as a demo,' says Ross. 'They said, "Well, that's the B-side sorted." And I said, "What are you talking about? That's an A-side!" "No, it's not." They didn't know they'd written a hit record, that's for sure. We bullied them into that being put out.'

There's No Other Way had many appealing aspects: Graham Coxon's spidery guitar part, Albarn's weary, disaffected lyrics – bemoaning some unspecified source of boredom, while never summoning the energy to say quite what it was – and its drums, bolstered by the use of a sampled beat taken from Run DMC. 'I never thought it was a single,' concedes Alex James. 'But it all made sense when that big heavy drum loop went on it.'

Its video also marked the first occasion when Blur began to define their future aesthetic universe. The idea was simple: a caricatured middle-English family – whose mother was played by an actress from *Grange Hill* – sat down with the group for Sunday lunch. Coxon, James and Rowntree obediently passed the gravy boat and helped Father to potatoes; Albarn, lip-synching his vocal line, fixed the camera with a stare that looked positively hateful.

There's No Other Way arrived in the singles chart at number twenty, one place below a Mike And The Mechanics song that had begun to slip. One week later, it leapt above a record featuring Bart Simpson and landed at eleven. It subsequently moved to ten, before being finally nudged to eight. Blur thus came to rest just below Paul Young and Zucchero's Senza Una Donna: the kind of place that heavy-drinking left-field rock groups weren't really meant to go.

Their success took Blur on to *Top of the Pops*. In honour of the occasion, Dave Balfe slipped each member of the group an ecstasy tablet, allowing them to peer into the UK's living rooms through noticeably dilated pupils.

CHAPTER 4

Pathetic rebellion

In May 1991, Blur were pop stars. They appeared on children's TV and were featured in *Smash Hits*, taking their place alongside Chesney Hawkes, Kylie Minogue and Jason Donovan. Their looks meant that their presence was not nearly as incongruous as it might seem, although the magazine had noticeable difficulty making them fit. 'There's Damon, lead singer, big blue eyeballs and remarkable confidence,' went their first *Smash Hits* feature. 'There's Alex, bass player, "the mad one", always going on about the amoebas in the stratosphere or whatever it is with a permanent foolish grin. There's Graham, guitar, big brown eyeballs, gets "panic attacks" in the street for no reason whatsoever. And then there's Dave. And he's always in the pub.'

In the company of journalists who were in search of something a little deeper, Albarn in particular seemed to have his pitch worked out. Its most notable aspect was an apparent belief that his success was somehow fated. 'It was inevitable we'd end up in the top ten,' he said. 'I'd been brought up in an off-centre way, so I understood the whole machinery. We're early eighties nuclear children, a product of our time. And our time is now.'

In person, an ever-present smirk lent his more sky-scraping claims an air of knowing jest, though it rarely translated well in bald print. 'I've always known I'm incredibly special,' he told one journalist. 'All my life. It's not a big deal. Sorry.'

On a couple of occasions, Blur escorted journalists to Colchester, sketching out their creative motivation in terms of an adolescence spent as eternal outsiders. Not surprisingly, Stanway Comprehensive's Music department and lead roles in *Orpheus In The Underworld* weren't mentioned; their cool was better served by an account of an escape from both closing-time fists and the suffocating embrace of the ordinary. So keen were they to couch their tale in such terms that at a show at nearby Essex University, within deliberate earshot of one reporter, Albarn toyed with the idea of greeting the crowd with the words: 'Hello, we're from London.'

Steve Lamacq, an Essex native himself, based the group's inaugural *NME* feature on a return home. 'Why we did the interview in Colchester, I really don't know,' he says. 'None of us liked the place. I suppose you had to find an angle to sell it to the *NME*. But Damon seemed to have rehearsed for this for a while. He was particularly anti-Colchester. He said something like, "I don't know anyone there any more. I had to move out 'cos it was so terrible. No-one understands alternative lifestyles; that's why we had to leave. I never got on with anyone." We got off the train at Colchester station, walked out to get a cab, and some girl had just parked up her mini in the car park. She went, "Oi, Damon! Alright?"'

Blur were recurrently portrayed as the main players in a weekly London ritual that all but defined the weekly papers' gossip columns. Syndrome was a Thursday night club located at the east end of Oxford Street, where the city's consumer hubbub gives way to shabby tourist shops and unlicensed taxi touts. It was established in early 1990, with the aim of servicing the indie-ish corner of the record business; as the musicians who attended soon discovered, one of its main selling points was the fact that Neal Handley and Jared Pepall, the DJs, would happily play the freshly pressed work of their clientele.

Blur thus rubbed shoulders with a coterie of shoegazers – Lush, Chapterhouse, Slowdive – along with members of such fleetingly vogueish groups as Five Thirty, The Senseless Things and Swervedriver. In honour of the club's founding spirit of mutual support – which churlish minds interpreted as smugness – the *Melody Maker* gave the Syndrome clique a name that quickly stuck. Week in, week out, it was affectionately mocked as The Scene That Celebrates Itself.

'To the outside eye,' says Alex James, 'it was probably awful and we probably had enough for three drinks each. And that's probably why it was good – 'cos nobody could get filthy drunk like they do now. As far as I could tell, it was the first sense of London starting to have a scene of its own. You'd go in and there'd be Lush over there, Chapterhouse over there, The House Of Love here. I was probably there every week.

'It was a deliberate attempt to bring the weekend one day forward. There'd always be a few Japanese people who'd always buy the bands they liked drinks. Jared would play everybody who was there's record, and you'd check out who was dancing: you knew they were your mates if they danced to your record.'

'Nothing much had happened in London for ten years,' says Andy Ross. 'It had all been about Leeds or Manchester. And when Syndrome started, it was just a magnet. We were Johnny Come Latelys: we didn't start going until at least three months in. But I went down with Blur every single week, without fail. They were having a whale of a time: a band that's just been on *Top of the Pops*, straight down to Syndrome.'

In among the warm cans of Red Stripe, the occasional ecstasy tablet, and the endless in-jokes – one week, the Blur party arrived at the 'Universal Riff', a musical figure that could be laughingly parped over whatever indie record the DJs chose to play – Blur and their associates got a cut-price taste of the kind of elitist pleasures that had coloured the lives of their rock star antecedents. 'I did like Syndrome,' says Justine Frischmann. 'Damon went through a phase of snogging boys, so it was really exciting. Girls snogging girls and boys snogging boys. It was pathetic rebellion, really – when you think what Mick and Marianne were up to at the same age, what we were doing was very tame. But they played everyone's records, and everyone was drunk. It was a laugh.'

Unfortunately, Blur's spell as Oxford Street viscounts did not last long. On 29 July, they attempted to repeat the success of There's No Other Way by releasing a new single entitled Bang. The former's resemblance to the post-Acid House Mancunian bands was at least partly transcended by Coxon's wondrous guitar lines; on the new record, they sounded like opportunists, plain and simple. Worse still, Albarn's delivery of his whimsical lyrics – another rather shallow meditation on life's emptiness, beginning with a mention of tube trains – made him sound a little like he was delivering a children's TV item on life in the city.

It entered the singles chart at number twenty-six, whereupon the group turned in another *Top of the Pops* appearance. Albarn, in homage to the single's sleeve art, waved around an effigy of a chicken. Such muted thrills pushed the record up another two places, before it started to slide. The sound of *Smash Hits* pushing the door closed was faintly audible, but Blur had probably asked for it: the single, it later transpired, had been written in fifteen minutes flat.

Behind such disappointments lurked a creeping tension. Andy Ross and David Balfe were convinced that aping the Mancunian groups was still the most advisable course: such, in fact, was the former's enthusiasm for this approach that the group began calling him 'the Andy/Dance Rossover'. Blur, though perhaps not quite as savvy as their later accounts suggest, attempted to pull free, both on account of their suspicion of market-chasing, and an instinctive affinity with more difficult music. Graham Coxon, in particular, was never going to be moulded into some diffusion-line Stone Rose: in 1991, he was besotted with the mind-bending, neo-psychedelic music that My Bloody Valentine had minted on their 1988 album *Isn't Anything*, and would decisively define with that year's *Loveless*.

For want of a truly solid aesthetic, however, Blur were rudderless enough to be cast in several directions at once. The result was a first album that scotched much of their early promise. Having been passed through the supervision of four different producers, *Leisure* emerged in September, suggesting that its authors had already run out of ideas. Albarn later confessed that an inordinate number of his lyrics had been scribbled down in the studio, as the group was waiting for his vocals: in such pressed circumstances, he tended to simply remould the deliberate banality that had defined There's No Other Way. 'Try, try, try,' went the chorus of Repetition, suggesting that its author fancied doing anything but. 'All things remain the same/So why try again?' Relative to the album's more dreary moments, the scratchy lunacy of Seymour seemed much the better option.

The cover of *Leisure* featured an image of a lipsticked female swimmer, taken from the Hulton Picture Library, in keeping with the title but suggestive of no more depth than a flyer for a provincial indie disco. As if to suggest that Blur couldn't quite believe that they had got there, its list of Thank You credits contained seventy-eight names, including dedications to 'the scene that celebrates itself at the Syndrome Youth Club', eight different journalists and 'Marks and Sparks for thermals'.

Some groups craft first albums that are intended as definitive statements of intent. More ambitious souls, having spent years thinking about it, aim at the creation of a masterpiece. *Leisure* felt like it had merely been rushed to the shops in the vague hope that it might maintain Blur's success. There was but one ray of hope: an eerie, almost avant-garde piece called Sing, recorded and produced by members of Blur alone. It lay so far from standard guitar-rock as to sound downright visionary; in the context of the album, it seemed to be the work of a different group.

Leisure entered the album chart at number seven, but it could not shake off the odour of anti-climax. Still, if the album's flimsiness seemed to mark Blur down as the authors of their own fate, they could at least take comfort from the fact that even the most sterling record would probably have proved quickly obsolescent. In November 1991, the

New Thing arrived – when the abiding feeling of musical sleepiness that had already entered journalistic parlance as 'the post-Acid House comedown' was effectively curtailed by three Americans and a brutally powerful single called Smells Like Teen Spirit.

Nirvana were a trio from Seattle who stood at the end of a decade-long heritage of American indie-rock. Having initially been supported by the independent label Sub Pop, they were freshly signed to Geffen Records, a move that had brought on a huge amount of controversy. If the anti-corporate standpoint that united British indiedom seemed hard-bitten, its American equivalent was positively fundamentalist. Moreover, having made the switch, Nirvana themselves seemed eternally troubled by the constant accusations of sell-out. The drama was focused on the tousled head of their singer, Kurt Cobain, a man so locked in to the contradictions of his own success that his three-year spell as a star was built on a compelling Catch 22: the more successful he became, the more troubled he seemed; the more troubled he seemed, the more people seemed to identify with him, and the more the success increased.

In the USA, the single would quickly power Nirvana's ascent from cultdom to the very heart of the mainstream: in January 1992, *Nevermind* knocked Michael Jackson's *Dangerous* from the summit of the US charts. The group's success was fed by Cobain's personality cult, founded not only on his success-related pains – physically manifested in a crippling stomach complaint – but on the scattershot anger that pervaded his every lyric. Little more than a year before, most Americans had equated long-haired rock musicians with bubblegum hedonism: among 1990s big American records were Poison's Unskinny Bop, Aerosmith's Dude (Looks Like A Lady) and Warrant's Cherry Pie. Suddenly, they were assailed by a much more disquieting voice. Much of Nirvana's persona – Cobain's white-trash background, the importance of Seattle to their rise, the fact that their disaffection was so American – made precious little sense in a British context. It mattered little: in the UK, Cobain and his group had enough resonance to give rise to what sociologists call a Paradigm Shift.

Nirvana's success took root from the summer onwards. In August, they performed an afternoon show at the Reading Festival, to a frenetic response. By November, they had played a show at the Astoria, on Charing Cross Road, at which the upstairs balcony had visibly bounced up and down. The same month, they appeared on *The Word*. Smells Like Teen Spirit was duly beamed to the whole of the UK, replete with a spoken introduction to Cobain's fiancée Courtney Love – 'the best fuck in the world' – and a performance so kinetic as to look positively insurrectionary. To an audience suddenly in thrall to this new American noise, aping The Stone Roses or calling your song Freefall was really not enough; as if to announce all this to the London clique, Cobain and Love had already paid a visit to Syndrome.

Nonetheless, one can find affinities between Nirvana and their British competition that, at the time, were overlooked. In his more coherent lyrics, Damon Albarn hamfistedly grappled with the blankness that gripped rock music in the early 1990s: the lack of any real dynamism, the sense that it was becoming uncoupled from its roots in generational revolt, the simple feeling that everything had been done already. Reading through the words of *Nevermind* – In Bloom and Smells Like Teen Spirit are the best examples – one can often discern a similar standpoint: the difference lay in its articulation. Albarn's observations came wrapped in weary sarcasm; Cobain voiced his feelings with a nauseous rage.

On the tour that followed the UK release of *Nevermind*, Cobain was asked by a BBC Bristol reporter if he had heard any good music recently. He sang the chorus of There's No Other Way, in tones of quiet amusement, seemingly tickled that its words could be sung with such apathy. They were lines, after all, that he would have screeched.

In 1991, Suede spent another year as a fringe presence, honing their songs and making occasional appearances in the context of large-scale indifference. Other groups may have let such experiences corrode their motivation; thanks chiefly to Justine Frischmann's new relationship with Damon Albarn, Brett Anderson was powered through their travails by a newborn desire to prove himself.

Certainly, his feelings were angrily poured into a handful of new songs – most notably, Animal Lover and Pantomime Horse – whose lyrics were opaque enough to veil the details, but suffused with enough drama to betray the hurt. Frischmann, initially believing that there might be some means of accommodation, kept her place in Suede for a difficult few months. 'I was in the band when those songs were being written,' she says. 'There was a period of overlap: it was really, really awkward. He was standing there singing, "I'll be gone by the end of the year". That was a line in Pantomime Horse. I was just like, "I've got to get out of this, 'cos I'm just making everyone miserable." And I wasn't really pulling my weight: I was just playing bar chords and muddying up what Bernard was doing.'

'It was really horrible for ages,' says Bernard Butler. 'Before long, she started going on about Damon all the time – while Brett was there, which I thought was really insensitive. He was trying to be mature, just going, "Yeah, yeah" and sucking on his cigarette. She'd turn up late for rehearsals and say the worst thing in the world – "I've been on a Blur video shoot." That was when it ended, really. I think it was the day after she said that that Brett phoned me up and said, "I've kicked her out."'

When asked about his feelings towards Blur – and Albarn in particular – Brett Anderson has almost always feigned complete indifference. Ten years after his split with Frischmann, his schtick remains unshakeable. 'All I can say about them is, I think they've always been obsessed by their career,' he says. 'Suede have always been obsessed by their music. That's the difference.' The sneering disdain with which such words are delivered probably says a great deal more.

Justine Frischmann exited Suede in the early summer of 1991. She reapplied herself to her studies at UCL, though she could not redeem herself sufficiently to avoid repeating her third year; she graduated in 1992 with a 2:1. Suede, meanwhile, discovered that her exit gave rise to a very different group. 'If Justine hadn't left the band,' says Anderson, 'I don't think we'd have got anywhere. It was a combination of being personally motivated, and the chemistry being right once she'd left. She was always someone that confused the issue – which she'd be the first to admit. She was always quite cerebral about music, probably thinking about it a bit too much, and as soon as she left, everything just clicked.'

'More than anything,' says Mat Osman, 'it set Bernard free. As soon as she left, he could let go. Him and Justine was always the weirdest relationship: they were *so* different. I think, up to then, he felt like it was him and these three other people. And suddenly, he and Brett were writing song after song after song.'

Butler's new bond with Brett Anderson was not only based on their creative endeavours. 'Brett was going through it, and I was becoming more and more close to him,' says Butler. 'I felt he was a real friend, which is why we started writing loads of songs. But he was in a really bad way for a long time. There were occasions when I'd meet up with him, and I'd be really worried about him: he'd be going home so miserable and depressed, I'd be like, "I'm getting on the tube with you."'

The two began to dress identically; for a time, they both made a point of smoking perfumed Caravan cigarettes. 'I did truly love Brett,' says Butler. 'We were close, and I felt there was an emotional thing going on, and I felt musically close to someone for the first time. We regarded ourselves, really quickly, like Morrissey and Marr. But it was a really warm relationship. I think those two were much more estranged. But we weren't: we were very similar.'

Against the backcloth of their new closeness, Butler noticed a striking change in Brett Anderson's make-up. Once his distress had subsided, it became clear that Frischmann's departure had not just suffused him with a new resolve; he had also developed a hard-bitten kind of cynicism. 'When I first met him, he was very warm and bubbly. As soon as the Justine thing happened with Damon, he was more aloof. The basic opinion was, "She's gone off with someone more famous than me." That was what Brett thought. And he became harder.'

By now, Suede had grappled with the matter of image. The group's front-line was united by a coherent look, so out of phase with abiding fashion that it beggared belief. While all around were Day-Glo T-shirts and bowl-cuts, Suede clad themselves in charity-shop 1970s shirts, all unwieldy collars and garish prints. Gilbert apart, their hair was unfashionably long, swept back from their faces like Cromwellian soldiers. The look was born out of their dole-ite circumstances: for a matter of a few pounds, each member could be adequately outfitted. 'We had three shirts each,' says Mat Osman. 'When we got bored, we used to swap them.' The effect was as intended: Suede looked like a group with a self-defined aesthetic. 'The first time I saw them after I left,' says Justine Frischmann, 'they were playing at the Underworld in Camden. They were all wearing those shirts for the first time. I just suddenly thought, "They've got it."' She attended the show with Damon Albarn, who – perhaps inevitably – did not seem quite as convinced of their worth. 'Damon seemed kind of pissed off with me,' she says, 'because I was jumping around, going, "That was amazing – they're going to be the next Smiths."'

'We had this thing: you should stand up, look confident in what you do,' says Bernard Butler. 'And all the things that I had tried to hide when I was a kid were now a good thing: it was good that you had girly hair, and were skinny, and wore clingy clothes. It was all very . . . *poised.*'

Unfortunately, Suede were so out of phase with their peers that they remained on the sidelines. For the first half of the year, they were rendered irrelevant by the Syndrome clique; from the summer onwards, the spell cast by Nirvana had equally malign effects. No amount of demo tapes and telephone calls could elevate them out of a cycle of sporadic shows in North London and endless rehearsals. 'It lasted a year,' says Brett Anderson. 'For the whole of 1991, A&R men wouldn't give us a second look.'

As it turned out, the lack of attention bought Suede time. Anderson and Butler's songs were becoming more and more ambitious. Better still, Anderson had alighted on a performance style that couldn't fail to turn heads: in the midst of exaggerated – and downright effeminate – bumps and grinds, he would mark the moment at which the music took him over by slapping his bottom with the microphone. Relative to the likes of Slowdive and Chapterhouse, it amounted to something as confrontational as arriving at school in a white suit.

Towards the end of the year, their luck began to change. In December, after a trickle of favourable notices, they were booked to appear at the *NME*'s annual 'On' concerts at New Cross Venue: two nights during which eight groups heralded the start of the new year. Suede appeared alongside a rum selection indeed: Adorable, a band founded at Warwick University whose role models were Echo And The Bunnymen; Midway Still, a trio from Bexleyheath whose music fell in with the post-Nirvana wave; and Fabulous, an absurdist punk quartet whose membership included one *NME* journalist and two of the paper's photographers.

It has long been a tradition of the media to mark the first weeks of January with a swell of predictions of that year's great musical hopes: news from the 'On' nights thus rippled outwards, through other music magazines, to the broadsheet newspapers. With the pop-cultural wheel moving as fast as ever, the debate about what would follow Nirvana had begun; Suede, so steeped in English references that they could not have lain further away, seemed to be the ideal British riposte. Quite apart from any transatlantic point-scoring, Brett Anderson also held out a tantalising promise: in his love of David Bowie, his conscious androgyny, and the slap of microphone on buttock, Suede's early champions sensed a return to a tradition that had lain dormant since the more theatrical punks put away their mascara and Bowie released his last decent album, 1980's *Scary Monsters*.

At the end of February, Suede played at the Camden Falcon, supporting a New York group called The Werefrogs. They had performed in the oppressive back room before, balancing their amplifiers on the beer crates, and toiling through their set in the vain hope that someone important might be watching. By this time, however, the futility of the enterprise had gone. That night, the presence of one person alone was enough to confirm it: Morrissey, whose voice had once boomed from Brett Anderson's bedroom in Lindfield, stared intently at the stage, seemingly recognising his offspring.

In the audience at the *NME* show in New Cross, Saul Galpern had watched Suede and come away reeling. He had just exited the corporate music industry, leaving the A&R department at eastwest Records to establish his own independent label, Nude. Suede, for some reason, reminded him of Roxy Music: a sufficiently lofty reference point to convince him that he should get in touch. He was amazed to find that his was the only label that was displaying serious interest: within weeks of their first meeting, he and the group had agreed to put out two singles, without a contract. Their debut would be The Drowners: a song whose chorus, sung by Brett Anderson in a soaring falsetto, served infectious notice of their talent.

Galpern's label was a shoestring operation, so for the moment, penury continued to be Suede's lot. Brett Anderson shared a one-bedroom flat in Moorhouse Road, near Westbourne Grove, with his friend Alan. Thanks to the fact that the area had yet to be turned into the new Chelsea, he paid his share of a mere £100 a week. Mat Osman and Bernard Butler, meanwhile, made do with a shared flat in the slightly less bohemian enclave of Leyton, E15.

The prospect of a first single was enough to force the hand of some of the people who were advocating the Suede cause. On the afternoon of Tuesday 21 April, copies of *Melody Maker* plonked on to central London's news-stands. Among other attractions, its front cover featured four unknown faces and seven striking words: 'Suede: The Best New Band in Britain'.

In February 1992, three members of Blur sat in the shabby foyer of Playground, a rehearsal space on Agar Grove, tucked behind the King's Cross Freight Terminal. Damon Albarn, Graham Coxon and Dave Rowntree were awaiting the arrival of Alex James, who eventually showed up displaying the frazzled after-effects of the previous night's acid trip. He joined the latter two watching satellite television, while Damon Albarn answered a run of questions in his usual bullish style.

'Success for us in America is almost inevitable now. You just get a feeling that it's going to happen. And we've got a very powerful record company behind us . . . I've felt incredibly privileged and in control of my own destiny all my life . . . I've got this real feeling that we're coming to the end of a millennium and everything is getting blocked up. We want to make sure we're with the truly inspired items, moving through into the next era . . . I genuinely think we're the most important band of the nineties. Why? I can't give you a worked-out patter. All I can say is there's a bloody-mindedness about us. We're smarter than anybody else . . .'

The same month, a tape of new Blur songs was circulated to a small circle of associates, who were invited to voice their opinions. There were fourteen new compositions, put to tape at breakneck speed, that sounded like the work of a very different group to the one that had burped out *Leisure*. Where once they had sounded listless, there was a new dynamism; the first album's clean, processed ambience was replaced by something altogether dirtier; Albarn at least sounded like he had been thinking about his lyrics. On one song in particular, everything cohered to impressive effect: a ragged burst of neo-punk entitled Popscene.

Unfortunately, Blur were pushed off course by dramatic news indeed. Though how it happened has long been unclear, £40,000 had gone missing from their accounts, and they were £60,000 in debt. The modest success of *Leisure* had more than recouped its recording costs; by now, its authors should have been at least able to keep themselves in beer and clothes. Instead, they hovered close to ruin. Their predicament demanded a difficult game indeed – skilfully parrying demands from the group's creditors, lest the truth would out and they would be declared bankrupt.

They were escorted into less life-threatening waters by Chris Morrison, a manager whose CV extended back into the mists of the 1970s, and the time he had spent seeing to the affairs of the notoriously accident-prone Thin Lizzy. Morrison had tried to contact Blur about a four-group package tour he was organising at the behest of The Jesus And Mary Chain, the Scots duo who were his most indie-friendly charges. After a one-hour meeting with Damon Albarn, he agreed to take charge of Blur's affairs. Enquiries about the missing thousands were launched, and Blur's place on the tour was confirmed.

The travelling circus on to which they had been co-opted was called Rollercoaster. Inspired by Lollapalooza, an annual American trek that sought to bring a freewheeling rock bohemianism to the USA's football stadia, it had been dreamed up as a crafty method of remarketing The Jesus And Mary Chain, whose stock had steadily fallen since their incendiary 1985 album *Psychocandy*. Its other attractions were the American trio Dinosaur Jr, whose fuzztoned rock had presaged Nirvana, and Graham Coxon's beloved My Bloody Valentine. The latter's current party piece was an interlude known as The Holocaust, placed in the middle of a song called You Made Me Realise, during which they would laugh in the face of health and safety regulations and attempt to use amplified sound to traumatise their audience. On more than a few occasions, they succeeded in making their fans faint.

The average age of the other three groups hovered at around twenty-seven; they had all released their first records in the mid-1980s. Blur, by comparison, were mere apprentices. 'We thought we were on holiday,' says Alex James. 'It was indie dream heaven. "Tonight you'll be going bowling with Dinosaur Jr and The Jesus And Mary Chain and you can have as much booze as you like."' The tour passed in a haze of vodka, nicotine and hero-worship, while Blur adjusted to their new company by playing an angular, discordant set, sprinkled with B-sides. At Brixton Academy, Damon Albarn so far forgot himself as to winch down his trousers and show the crowd his genitals.

Popscene was released just as Rollercoaster began, accompanied by an *NME* interview that oozed both a new sense of purpose and the sense that Blur were distancing themselves from their peers. 'There's a noisy indie group on *Top of the Pops* every week now,' said Albarn, as if surveying the bar queue at Syndrome, 'all looking very satisfied with their number eighteen.'

Yet more striking was a passage in which Albarn explained the metamorphosis that had occurred under Justine Frischmann's influence. 'I hadn't bought a record until a year ago,' he said. 'Then I started going out with my current girlfriend and she had a massive record collection and as I started to buy records, slowly I began to find things out ... I began to see all these little coincidences where we were linked with bands that we worshipped. And I began to realise that, fuck, we are something. We are part of a heritage of British bands, we are somebody.'

Popscene was the brilliant proof. The version on the Food cassette had been inflated into something monstrous; pumped up to the point where it sounded like a musical stampede. In its frantic energy and Albarn's home-counties vowels, one could just about discern the influence of The Jam; the addition of a horn section, unheard on a cutting-edge British rock record for a good decade, harked back to the era of Dexys Midnight Runners. Other minds might have alchemised such influences into something that, to use a Paul Weller phrase, sounded 'clean and hard'. Popscene, however, managed to combine its energy with a churning, seasick quality. The result was a record that approximated the condition of being ragingly drunk. Thanks to Albarn's lyrics, one could not help but assume that much of its ire was focused on the Syndrome clique – and, therefore, on Blur themselves. 'Everyone is a clever clone,' he spat. 'A clone clever clone am I/So in the absence of a way of life, just repeat this again and again ... Hey hey, come out tonight/Hey hey, come out tonight/Popscene – alright!' This, it seemed, was the sound of one Thursday night too many.

'Popscene was the breakthrough,' says Justine Frischmann. 'Everything about it was great. It should have been huge.' Instead, as Rollercoaster drew to a close, Blur were poleaxed to find that it had entered the charts at number thirty-two, one place behind Separate Tables by Chris de Burgh. It had little hope of moving upwards. To add to Blur's woes, the new single by their Syndrome pals the Senseless Things –

the very definition of 'a noisy indie band' – had been released the same week, and flown past them to number nineteen. It was a makeweight song entitled Hold It Down, whose alternation between quiet passages and a no-holds barred chorus betrayed the transparent influence of Nirvana. 'We put ourselves out on a limb to pursue this English ideal,' Damon Albarn later lamented, 'and no-one was interested.'

In cahoots with Food Records, a plan had been hatched to follow Popscene – which, it was assumed, would be a hit – with a song called Never Clever, succeeded in turn by an album composed of the songs on the cassette that had been passed round before Rollercoaster. Popscene's failure rendered the idea obsolete; Blur were thus suspended in limbo. To make things more problematic, their next engagement was a two-month tour of the USA. It could be safely assumed that the American reaction to songs with horn sections that harked back to The Jam would not be much warmer than it had been at home.

For all Blur's problems, in the real world, the spring of 1992 saw altogether graver disasters. The same week that Popscene limped into the charts, the UK went to the polls, enacting a heart-stopping twist to an election campaign that had recurrently pointed to – of all things – a victory for Neil Kinnock's Labour Party. It was by no means fanciful to think that victory was beyond John Major's grasp: at the outset of the campaign, Labour's poll rating stood at 41 per cent, the Tories' at 39, and the Liberal Democrats' at 15 per cent – and up until polling day, the figures would barely change. Even among the staff of 10 Downing Street, a Labour triumph – albeit slim – was viewed as the likely outcome.

Labour, however, was still manacled to all kinds of electoral disadvantages. For a start, Neil Kinnock, despite his dark suits and new-found air of measured statesmanship, remained a tabloid bête noire. As evidenced by Tory billboards spreading terror about 'Labour's Tax Bombshell', he could not shake off the notion that a Labour Chancellor would make up for thirteen lost years by impounding half the nation's wealth. In addition, despite all manner of policy changes – not to mention the end of the Cold War – the Tory heartlands still equated his party with some inarticulable threat to national security; the idea that, within seconds of a Labour victory, some leftist unmentionable like Fidel Castro would be given a guided tour of Whitehall.

Such was one part of Major's campaign strategy. 'I want Britain to be seen as strong – not only in our eyes, but in the eyes of others,' he said at the start of the campaign. 'First and first again – a world leader. That is where I want us to be, and stay.' In the Blair era, the words seem so platitudinous as to be almost meaningless. Back then, in among the owner-occupied council houses and Beefeater restaurants, they had a genuine potency.

So, though the opinion polls suggested otherwise, Major won, taking power with a majority of twenty-one. Neil Kinnock's ashen face that night was not simply in response to his imminent demise as Labour leader; it came from the shock of beholding something that he didn't believe could happen. He had been deluded by those answering the pollsters' questions – for, as the pundits later concluded, the 1992 election had been characterised by a remarkable phenomenon indeed: respondents saying they would vote Labour, on account of the selfishness that a pro-Tory answer would imply, and then guiltily voting Conservative. When the Major government began to unravel, and the Tory heartlands found themselves falling victim to the new scourge of house repossession, Labour voters could not help but allege a certain karmic poetry – this, surely, was the price to be paid for doing something you knew was wrong all along.

Still, if Britain was wracked with guilt and internal division, Major did his best to paint a picture of a gentle, serene kind of nation. Twelve months after winning the election, at a Conservative Group For Europe dinner at London's InterContinental Hotel, it tumbled forth in all its sepia-tinted glory: Major spoke of a 'country of long shadows on country grounds, warm beer, invincible green suburbs, dog lovers and pools fillers, and as George Orwell said, old maids bicycling to communion through the morning mist.' The words were purloined from Orwell's *The Lion And The Unicorn*, written as an attempt to meld radical socialism with an abiding sense of Englishness, though their misplaced source seemed less important than their irrelevance. 'What a load of tosh,' commented the *Independent On Sunday*.

In fairness, however, John Major spoke of the dwindling cultural expanse in which he himself belonged. Born in March 1943, just over a month after George Harrison and three before Mick Jagger, he was one of those war babies who nonetheless managed to seem much older. So, though the likes of Michael Heseltine and Douglas Hurd were his elders by upwards of fifteen years, he fitted the Conservatives to perfection: rooted in the monochrome world before rock'n'roll, wary of – if not venomously hostile towards – the permissive society, a stranger to the increasingly aged households in which Saturday nights were marked by the odd joint and a few plays of *Revolver* and *Exile On Main St.*

When he had appeared on *Desert Island Discs* in January 1992, the one concession to pop music had been The Happening by Diana Ross and The Supremes, which had caught his ear while he was working for Barclays Bank in Nigeria. Lest anyone take this as evidence of some long-hidden grooviness, it was succeeded by a BBC recording of John Arlott's cricket commentary, Elgar's Pomp And Circumstance March No. 1 and The Best Is Yet To Come by Frank Sinatra. Even among a swathe of his own generation, Major was little short of a throwback; to millions of people under thirty, he was an occupant of a completely different universe.

In the wake of Neil Kinnock's resignation, John Smith's election as Labour leader took the Labour Party into a similar place. The days of consulting musicians on matters of policy and allowing electric guitars into party political broadcasts seemed further away than ever, not least because the 1992 campaign had convinced many Labour strategists that mixing campaigning and pop culture was always dangerous. One of the factors in the 1992 defeat, it was widely believed, was a vast rally staged at Sheffield Arena on 1 April, where Neil Kinnock had taken his place among musicians and actors, and got sufficiently carried away to briefly yell encouragement in the style of a gospel preacher. 'We're all right!' he yelped. 'We're all right!'

It was not a terribly edifying spectacle. 'Image throttled intellect and a quiet voice in every reporter present whispered that there was something disgusting about the occasion,' wrote Matthew Parris in the following day's *Times*. 'These voices will grow.' And so it proved: on Smith's watch, the Labour Party never repeated the mistake. In keeping with the new leader's strengths, managerial competence was the new image; glitz, spectacle and trendiness were thought to be ballot-box poison. It would be a while before anyone suggested a revival of Labour's bond with British musicians.

In May, Blur set off for the USA. 'We probably went to more American cities than 99.9 per cent of Americans do in their lives,' says Alex James. 'Forty-four cities. The idea was to take it to the next level, and it was patently obvious that that wasn't going to happen.'

Blur had been to America once before: in November 1991, when they had turned in the customary toe-in-the-water tour around the so-called Metro cities: Boston, Chicago, New York, LA. Their Manhattan experience in particular had been a joy: 'We got there in a limo with a phone in and there were skinny, beautiful girls everywhere,' said Alex James. He and Albarn had celebrated their arrival in New York by tumbling through the audience gathered for their performance and drunkenly French-kissing each other.

This, however, was very different. They now had to travel to what the US record industry called Secondary Markets: places far removed from America's urban dazzle, where an appetite for visiting British eccentrics was virtually non-existent.

On account of their debts, Blur's key task was to sell as many T-shirts as possible. That said, their American record company, SBK, saw an opportunity to market *Leisure* anew, and came up with a new wheeze: an EP with the unspeakably witty title *Blur-tigo*, containing a new mix of Bang, put together without the knowledge of the group themselves. They were confronted by this unexpected artefact upon their arrival in New York, where the tour began. Alex James recalls that, in response to such artistic vandalism, they returned to their hotel in tears.

Twelve months before, British groups had felt a frisson of optimism about their chances of – to use the music business parlance – 'breaking' America. A window of opportunity had briefly opened in the summer of 1991, when Jesus Jones and EMF – two not-dissimilar bands, linked by their vogueish combination of guitars and dance beats – had found themselves allowed into the US mainstream. Owing to some transatlantic misunderstanding, both groups were trumpeted as the harbingers of The Manchester Sound; an ironic twist indeed, given that Happy Mondays' attempts to succeed in America had come to nought.

Jesus Jones, as it turned out, were a motley assortment of southerners, from such diverse locales as Carshalton and Devizes. Their making had been Right Here, Right Now: a song written about the fall of the Iron Curtain, that had been taken up as an anthem by bomber pilots during the Gulf War. EMF, meanwhile, hailed from the Forest of Dean, and were accorded their fifteen minutes on account of Unbelievable, a near-perfect party soundtrack that had risen to number one in the US singles chart.

Any sense that they might blaze a trail, however, had gone; Kurt Cobain and his disciples had seen to that. America was now in thrall to what was known as 'grunge': a musical genre-cum-generational mindset that emphasised mewling disaffection and the rejection of soap (the derivation of the term has long been unclear: a likely source is the Led Zeppelin song The Crunge, a suitably dirty-sounding track from *Houses Of The Holy*). 'The youth had found its voice,' says Alex James, 'and we were just wrong, wrong, wrong.'

In the two-and-a-half months it took to complete their itinerary, Blur flew to the edges of psychosis. Touring was not simply a matter of playing each night's show. Like any visiting group, they were expected – if not ordered – to visit a string of local radio stations and field questions from DJs who sincerely believed that they were Mancunian. On top of that, there was the occasional indignity of the 'in-store' – an afternoon spent in a record shop, being nice to the few people who sought their autographs. In Atlanta, the gloom was momentarily lifted by the news that their fellow EMI artists The Beastie Boys were staying in the same hotel. Blur telephoned their suite, in anticipation of a night's revelry. The Beastie Boys, unfortunately, told Blur to fuck off.

Most of their frustrations were vented on each other. At one point, Graham Coxon decided to smash every pane of glass on their tourbus. Later, the level of intra-band brawling reached such depths that each member of the group simultaneously had a black eye. 'That was a side effect of being completely steeped in alcohol,' says Alex James. 'We were all getting up in the morning and drinking beer. We'd go out, trashing everything.

'Club Babyhead is the one place that sticks out,' he continues. 'It was in Providence, Rhode Island. A really nasty, sticky place that smelled of vomit. Going into a nightclub during the day is never very nice. You'd wake up, and the bus would have arrived, and you'd be in a nightclub, so you'd have another drink.'

This was not the kind of behaviour to which those supervising the tour were accustomed. Even the most snotty aspirant star would usually comply with the endless cycle of promotional demands; four people who seemed more keen on becoming paralytic and fighting each other represented a very unwelcome kind of novelty. 'They like their pop stars quite Mickey Mouse in America,' says James. 'You've got to be squeaky clean, and you've got to play ball. You've really got to shake their hands and kiss their arses. And we were slung out of radio stations for swearing and being drunk.'

In the midst of the hell, homesickness inevitably afflicted them. As far as Damon Albarn was concerned, the yearning was not some vague, indefinable longing for home comforts. His two months in the USA stirred the same latent sense of identity that had been tweaked by Justine Frischmann's record collection. This time, however, it was not just a matter of allying himself with new-found musical influences; his American experience awakened something far more deep-seated.

His expression of all this was strangely redolent of John Major's 'Old maids bicycling through the mist' speech, though Albarn's totems of Britishness were mercifully free of backward-looking sentimentality. 'I just started to miss really simple things,' he said. 'I missed people queuing up in shops. I missed people saying "goodnight" on the BBC. I missed having at least fifteen minutes between commercial breaks. And I missed people having respect for my geographical roots, because Americans don't care if you're from Inverness or Land's End. I missed everything about England.'

'We spent two months there,' says Alex James, 'and when you're alone and unwanted, all the annoying things about a place are *really* annoying – like people saying, "Have a nice day." Quite acceptable Americanisms become absolutely painful: everything turns into this bullshit blizzard. We became quite embittered.'

The tour ended in July. Blur, whose time in America had been punctuated by a mere two rest days, were in a wracked, dazed state – 'like soldiers coming back from Waterloo,' according to one friend – yet they could at least return to the land of Radio Four, ad-free television and Chocolate Digestives. Upon their arrival at Heathrow, however, a new, domestically-bred irritant was awaiting them.

'When we got back, Suede were on all the front covers,' says Alex James. 'These little pricks from fucking UCL.'

CHAPTER 5

For Tomorrow

For much of 1992, Suede – and Brett Anderson in particular – took up residence in Damon Albarn's head. Having strode into the top 10 and fleetingly been the leaders of their peer group, Blur were now huddled with the rest of their underachieving friends at Syndrome. Worse still, the source of their decline was his girlfriend's former boy-friend. 'They were incredibly competitive with each other,' says Justine Frischmann. 'Even now, you can't mention Damon in front of Brett. Boys will be boys.'

Just as Albarn's relationship with Justine Frischmann had provided Brett Anderson with his decisive spurt of motivation, so Suede's sudden ubiquity fired Albarn. From the outside, one would have perhaps assumed that the fact he had got the girl might diminish his lust for revenge, but his pronouncements suggest that the Justine factor fired him up all the more. The manner in which this has since been explained has frequently been striking. In 1994, Albarn was quoted in a French magazine as follows: 'I knew that my moment for vengeance would come. Public vengeance and personal vengeance. I wanted to prove to myself that I could dethrone Brett and his group of cretins.' When the words got back to Britain, via two sets of translation that presumably lent them that Olivier-esque air of camp menace, Albarn could only fall back on the limp complaint that they had been taken 'out of context'.

On top of the personal venom, there was also an aesthetic clash. Blur, whose music was much informed by Graham Coxon's angular tastes – as well as the iconoclastic mindset fostered at Goldsmiths – were still an indie group: irreverent, terrified of cliché, scornful of anything 'classic'. Suede, by contrast, represented a more orthodox proposition: a rock group, transparently in love with the 70s canon.

'Bernard Butler was just annoying, wasn't he?' says Alex James. 'It was all long hair and cowboy boots. Guitar solos. I've never been a big fan of guitar solos. I had to go and see them, out of courtesy. There was something embarrassing about the way he [Brett] was flinging himself around. There was a lot of prancing. And waving arms. And there was that Bowie kind of axis: Damon became a big Bowie fan, but I haven't got any Bowie records and nor's Graham.'

To complicate matters yet further, Blur were fond of putting round a particularly scurrilous rumour. Despite her split with Brett Anderson, Justine Frischmann remained on good terms with Bernard Butler; at some time during the winter of 1991–2, he and his girlfriend house-sat while she and Albarn went on holiday. Alex James still alleges that Butler rifled through Blur's current demo tapes and quickly learned some stylistic lessons. If the Suede music of the period had any similarities to Blur in the wake of *Leisure*, the story might be convincing; in the absence of any, it is difficult not to detect the odour of sour grapes.

In their disdain for Suede, Blur seemed to be in a minority of four. That summer, it was difficult to find any occupant of the London indie milieu who did not concur with the idea that Suede had come to save them. As if to prove their brilliance, The Drowners came with two B-sides that broke from the normal practice of fobbing off one's audience with some makeweight afterthought. Far from being the usual dashed-off leftovers, To The Birds and My Insatiable One were, in their own way, as good as the main feature; better still, they showcased the epic, swooping side of Suede that had flowered after Justine Frischmann's departure. In tandem with The Drowners, they laid out Suede's aesthetic universe in an impressively expansive fashion: the single seemed as rich with fascination as any album.

To Brett Anderson's amazement, My Insatiable One would soon be played live by Morrissey. 'I went to Portobello Market,' he says, 'and this guy, who was selling bootleg cassettes, said, "Have you heard this?" I took it home, and there was Morrissey singing it. That was a headfuck, to say the least.'

Such was one token of Anderson's changed existence. More problematically, as his group's profile snowballed, he was discovering the price to be paid for both the accolades thrown their way, and his brazen displays of flamboyance. 'I used to get threatened in the street,' he says. 'Lots of times, people would come up to me and tell me that unless I moved out of where I was living, they were going to come round and smash my windows. People really hated us. It was a really strange time: half the people would be coming up and trying to kiss my feet, and half the people wanted to thump me.'

When Suede ventured on tour, their tendency to polarise their audiences became glaringly evident. At a Newcastle Riverside show broadcast on Radio One, listeners were treated to a massed display of Geordie wit: 'You're a bunch of gays,' chorused a section of the audience. When they reached Sunderland, Bernard Butler spent much of their performance simultaneously dodging volleys of spit, and gleefully stoking up the crowd's hostility. 'It was, "Look at you: You're a rugby player, in Sunderland,"' he says. 'And, "Look at me: I'm on the stage."' In the Scottish town of Greenock, the vast majority of the crowd stood, unimpressed, at the back of the venue; only one hardy soul dared to make his way to the front. After the show, Mat Osman recalls being asked, with no little menace, if he knew where any of Suede were. He managed to blurt out his reply in a Scottish accent before bolting for the exit.

As far as their more Neanderthal audiences were concerned, Brett Anderson was pressing some very ill-advised buttons indeed. The Drowners and My Insatiable One departed from rock etiquette by seemingly referring to trysts with men: in replace of the usual 'she' and 'her' came mentions of 'him' and 'he'. The thinking behind all this was unclear: on occasion, Anderson talked about wilfully extending the reach of his words to take in both heterosexual women and gay men; in some instances, it was difficult to avoid the conclusion that the words had been tweaked to camouflage the fact that they concerned Justine Frischmann.

Sensing a minor journalistic coup, an interviewer named Philip Millo followed his questions about Anderson's androgyny with a remarkable enquiry. In the context of some of his lyrics, Millo made the suggestion that Anderson might be a bisexual man who had never had a homosexual experience. 'I suppose I am really,' he replied. No matter that it was Millo who had coined the phrase: for the next year, 'I'm a bisexual man who's never had a homosexual experience,' became Anderson's defining quote, to be hurled back at him whenever he was in the vicinity of a tape recorder.

'From that point on, he seemed to get more and more distant,' says Bernard Butler. 'He was more and more aware that people wanted to talk to him, and were picking up on any craziness he was talking about. He presented himself to the public in a way that he never presented himself to us. I'd read interviews and think, "What's he going on about?" I'd no idea. But I suppose Brett was very aware of being androgynous, and being a Byron-esque character. And there was all this stuff about *quintessential Englishness*. I didn't get that at all: the way that everybody made the fact that we were English into an extraordinary thing.'

Such was another strand to Suede's initial portrayal by the press, centred around the idea that they were avenging some transatlantic musical imbalance. Despite Butler's misgivings, when they sat for their first substantial feature in the *NME*, Anderson and Mat Osman were only happy to add fuel to the fire, letting rip with a series of quotes that seemed to embody a new kind of patriotism.

'It pisses me off immensely that America has kidnapped British music, and I find the idea of British bands singing in American accents horrifying. All great British pop artists from The Beatles to The Fall have celebrated Britain in some way. Whereas to me, America is exemplified by some dullard like Bruce Springsteen ... Let's face it, The Beatles were a huge one-nil. I'm not anti-American but I've never been impressed by it. I'm not remotely attracted by New York. I mean, all the streets are laid out in a grid. Doesn't that say everything? In Britain, it takes this convoluted, arcane knowledge to get from one bus-stop to the next. That claustrophobic, stifled Englishness is conducive to great art. Compare an American cop show to a Mike Leigh film or an Alan Ayckbourn play ... In America, there's no tragedy, no failure, no impotence, no premature ejaculation.'

Damon Albarn, still smarting from his American experience, presumably agreed with every word. Reading Suede's pronouncements, he must also have realised that he had been beaten to the punch.

Blur's cultural crusade, kick-started by Popscene and hardened by their American experience, had got off to a more hesitant start. Their wardrobe had begun to change: whereas once they had bought their baggy T-shirts from a shop called Passenger on Newburgh Street, W1, they had now moved round the corner to Sherry's and Merc, two outlets that sold cut-price versions of 60s mod couture. Thus, when Damon Albarn took the stage at that year's Glastonbury, he was wearing a burgundy three-button suit and Dr Martens. He also led the group through a song called Sunday Sunday: a camped-up salute to an age-old British ritual – the tabloids, roast beef and Yorkshire pudding, the obligation to 'eat enough to sleep' – that betrayed the influence of Madness and The Kinks.

One month later, Blur and Suede crash-landed on the same concert bill. The occasion was a concert in aid of the homeless charity Shelter at the Town and Country Club in Kentish Town, organised by the *NME*. The two groups shared the bill with Mega City Four and a long-forgotten group of no-hopers called Three And A Half Minutes. Blur were chosen to go on last; Suede were scheduled to arrive onstage second.

That afternoon, Albarn, Alex James and Graham Coxon had decided to acquaint themselves with a string of Camden pubs. Dave Rowntree was at home, dutifully washing a shirt down which Albarn had spilled red wine. When he arrived, he found his colleagues in an advanced state of disrepair, and saw no option but to attempt to catch them up. Such was the build-up to a face-off with a group who, in Albarn's mind at least, were little short of their nemesis. 'I don't know what we were doing,' says Alex James. 'I think it was, "Everybody will see that they're idiots and we're far superior." We were convinced of our genius – that belief you have when you're twenty-three and in the best band in the world. It's totally unrealistic, but that's what drove us. We thought we were Godlike.'

That night, Blur were anything but. Staggering onstage, Damon Albarn at least had the courtesy to warn the audience of what they were in for. 'We're so shit you might as well go home,' he barked. There followed a performance so shambolic that it teetered into comedy; Albarn's early fondness for the Theatre of Cruelty redirected into the realms of drunken farce. 'At any gig, no matter how it went, you'd always get some yes-man coming in the dressing room afterwards and saying, "Well done, lads, it was great!,"' Dave Rowntree later reflected. 'Except for that gig.'

Mike Smith was then twenty-six. In 1991, he had been responsible for Blur's publishing deal with MCA; he had since left for EMI Music Publishing and a new office on Charing Cross Road, but had remained one of the group's inner circle of confidantes. He arrived in Kentish Town with a date, looking forward to introducing her to his talented friends. Instead, he beheld the lowest moment of their progress so far.

'The punchline was that Suede had delivered an absolutely blinding performance,' he says. 'It was like turning up pissed at your ex-girlfriend's wedding to someone really rich and handsome and delightful: you're the former boyfriend standing there with your tie over here and your hair over there and vomit on the front of your trousers.'

The next day, an incensed David Balfe summoned Blur to Food's offices in Camden Town. He told his charges that what with the failure of Popscene, the American fiasco and now this, they were perilously close to being dropped from the label. In any case, he said, their career was probably over.

In addition to bringing girlfriends to career-ending Blur performances, Mike Smith was in the habit of occasionally meeting Damon Albarn for weekday breakfasts on Portobello Road. A Politics graduate from Manchester University who had considered going to art school, Smith was some distance from the kind of jargon-spewing hot-shot who crops up in the more idiotic corners of the music business. To Blur, he had proved to be a treasured sounding board. So it was that over the summer, Smith was let in on Albarn's new vision. 'It was all bound up with the vehemence of his reaction against grunge,' he says, 'and the fact that everyone was only interested in the music that was coming out of Seattle, and the need for a British response to that.'

The realignment begun by Popscene had been turned into a crusade by Blur's increasing sense of marginalisation; Albarn's zealousness betrayed not only the cast-iron confidence of a twenty-four-year-old, but the fact that voices tend to rise when the odds are stacked against them. 'They [Blur] came out with a real manifesto, wanting to create something very strongly British, something that was the equal if not the better of American music,' says Mike Smith. 'It was a massive statement: "We are different, we are together and we are strong and we are not going to take this shit, we are ambitious, and we are proud to be British and fuck America, fuck all your music."'

Graham Coxon, Alex James and Dave Rowntree were not Albarn's only comrades-in-arms: much of his rhetoric had been fine-tuned with the assistance of Justine Frischmann. 'A plan was hatched,' she says. 'Damon and I felt like we were in the thick of it at that point. We were both fairly obsessional about the idea of the zeitgeist. He'd been brought up by artistic parents who were interested in the way culture works, and we talked about it a lot. And somewhere along the line, it occurred to us that Nirvana were out there, and people were very interested in American music, and there should be some sort of manifesto for the return of Britishness. We didn't think Nirvana said anything to us about our lives. I wasn't remotely interested. That's where the manifesto came from.'

Just as Albarn had changed his wardrobe, so Frischmann's appearance changed. She cut her hair into the kind of crude bob once favoured by licentious inter-war aristocrats, and in collaboration with Graham Coxon's girlfriend – a native of Worthing and Goldsmiths alumnus named Jane Oliver – took to wearing Fred Perry shirts and Dr Martens. Blur's immediate social circle thus took on the appearance of some trend-defying cult. 'No-one else was wearing clothes like that,' says Mike Smith. 'It was as rebellious as walking down the street in a binliner in 1976.'

Frischmann's centrality to Albarn's new thinking also embodied a beautiful irony. As their recent interviews suggested, Albarn perhaps had more in common with Suede than he cared to mention; his relationship with Justine suggested that this was hardly an accident. 'I think a lot of it came from Brett, actually,' says Frischmann. 'I think the whole

Suede thing was very much to do with Britishness, and I carried that scene on to Damon and told him about it, and he took it a step further. But he was more playful: he put on a mask and played a part.'

Playfulness did not mark the only difference between Suede's aesthetic and the approach that Albarn was adopting. The former group's Englishness was a matter of implication: allusions within their lyrics, the fact that their music harked back to a time when British rock had tapped into an ambition and sophistication that seemed beyond America's ken. Albarn, by contrast, envisaged something much more overt; for a while, he toyed with the idea of naming Blur's next album *England Vs America*.

And all this from the leader of a group so blighted that even their own record company had served notice of their demise. Compounding the sense of ludicrous ambition, Albarn did not only want to change his own group. He envisaged Blur's turnabout as the start of a process that, in doing away with plaid shirts, lank hair and songs about self-loathing, would alter the whole of popular culture.

'Of the two of us, Damon was probably the most up for having a spoken, predetermined manifesto,' says Justine Frischmann, 'partly so he could decide what he was going to do. If you left it to instinct with him, he wouldn't have a clue. But he was always very ambitious. And that excited me: the idea of sitting in the bath, coming out with grand concepts, running the music business from our bedroom. And in our own arrogant world, that's what we thought we were doing.'

The idea, in part, was to reconnect the UK to the tradition that Albarn had briefly fallen into as an adolescent. Blur's new direction might have been forged in response to their recent experience, and partly thanks to the backhanded influence of Suede, but lurking behind their mission were experiences from a decade ago: brogues, the Specials and furtive smoking behind Stanway Comprehensive's music block.

If Blur's aims sounded innocent enough, that summer saw an episode that underlined how queasy the indie world still felt about the coupling of rock music and brazen celebrations of nationhood. On 8 August 1992, Morrissey – who had just released a widely acclaimed album entitled *Your Arsenal* – appeared at Finsbury Park, on a bill headlined by those most pantomimic of Englishmen, Madness. His performance took place in front of a backdrop featuring a monochrome photograph of two skinheads; he also decided to spend part of the show dancing, Matador-like, with a Union Jack. In tandem with a run of songs that had alluded, both ambiguously and rather insensitively, to the politics of race – Asian Rut, Bengali In Platforms, the National Front Disco – the Finsbury Park performance was enough to persuade the *NME* to run a finger-pointing cover story. Its strapline was in keeping with the leftist fondness for asking provocative but transparently rhetorical questions: 'Flying the flag or flirting with disaster?'

Food Records' pessimism had at least been allayed by the institution of a new Blur rule: the group now promised to restrict their pre-performance drinking to half an hour before showtime. Nonetheless, Andy Ross and David Balfe remained anxious about their charges' progress, vetting their ideas and constantly voicing concerns about the group's commercial potential. If Blur had assumed that life with a label like Food would afford them artistic empowerment – 'Complete Control,' as The Clash once barked – their experiences in 1992 suggested otherwise.

With furrowed brows, Balfe and Ross sanctioned the recording of their second album. Balfe in particular was deeply sceptical about Albarn's new Anglo-centric rhetoric, and yet he gave his assent to the group's first choice of producer: Andy Partridge, the singer and chief creative mind behind XTC. The fact that Partridge squared with the group's intended new direction was proved beyond doubt by Damon Albarn's first visit to his home. Having been ushered through the front door, he was thrilled to have to pick his way through Partridge's vast collection of model soldiers.

At their commercial peak, between 1979 and 1983, XTC had set the kind of template at which Blur were now aiming. Their music was both angular and melodic, rerouting the iconoclasm of punk away from artless rage to an altogether more reflective place. Moreover, their songs were imbued with a beguiling sense of place. Very often, they went beyond sounding simply English, and managed to evoke the place from whence they came: Swindon, the industrial town that borders the chalk downs of Wiltshire. 'I can't write mid-Atlantic airport lounge music,' Partridge said in 1987. 'I can't talk about my hot babe with her leather and whip, or meeting my cocaine dealer. I like to write about what's going on around the town.' In addition, XTC's music often came with a jarring sense of something not being quite right. Partridge was its source: having been inducted into a dependence on tranquillisers at the age of eleven, he had since fallen victim to stage fright so severe that in 1982 his group had given up live performance.

He and Blur began work at The Church, Dave Stewart's opulent studio in Crouch End. Unfortunately, the expected creative heaven failed to materialise. 'It was a bit of a disaster,' says Alex James. 'It started off well, but he wouldn't let us smoke in the control room. He was very schoolmasterly. And it just sounded a bit stilted. As it was all being put together, they were all good parts, but it just wasn't . . . sexy. He was an incredible character: a raconteur, a joker – just immensely intelligent, to the point of being *mental*. But being in the studio with the wrong producer is the worst thing that can possibly happen. You think you're shit, and then you realise what it is. It's not that the producer's wrong, and it's not that you're wrong: it's just that . . . it's like inviting someone into the band.'

On reflection, Blur rather feared that they were losing control of their own album. They had successfully recorded four songs, to an appreciative response from their associates, yet the prospect of repeating the exercise filled them with dread. 'I didn't want to be playing on an Andy Partridge record,' says James.

If their decision to curtail the sessions suggested a deepening of the crisis that had started earlier in the year, they were saved from yet another disaster by a chance meeting with Stephen Street, the producer who had worked such wonders on There's No Other Way. His work with The Smiths perhaps hinted that he was the ideal mind to oversee Blur's headlong charge into a new Englishness, and so it proved. The sessions, split between the cream of the music written immediately after *Leisure* and a new crop that had stemmed from the American tour, resulted in a stream of inspired music: on one song in particular, Star Shaped, Albarn's new vision was beautifully realised. Its first verse – 'Wash with new soap, behind the collar/Keeps a clear mental state' – brought to mind George Bowling, the suburban anti-hero of Orwell's *Coming Up For Air*, and the inclusion of a passage played by an oboe only heightened the air of leafy serenity. The masterstroke was the sudden entry of one of Graham Coxon's most incendiary guitar solos, as if the privet hedges were suddenly being torched in a fit of rage.

The group were justifiably thrilled with what they had recorded. The opinion of their overlords, unfortunately, was a little less positive. Dave Balfe visited them in the studio, where they were keenly awaiting his verdict; having heard the music, he told them they were committing artistic suicide. 'Balfe just couldn't see it,' says Alex James. 'He was going, "Look – everything in the papers is American and you're trying to do exactly the opposite." We were like, "*Yeah.*"' In the wake of the disaster at the Town and Country Club, Balfe had told them that they were close to being cast off the Food roster; that afternoon, that fate suddenly looked more imminent than ever.

Though crushed, they plodded on, handing Food a completed album in December. Not entirely surprisingly, they were told that it was unfit for release. At the very least, they were instructed to fatten up the record with a couple of potential singles.

It is one of the crueller aspects of musicians' lives that times of soul-destroying despondency often coincide with the moment at which producing their best work becomes imperative. That Christmas, Damon Albarn surely felt the weight of that contradiction. He went home to Colchester; falling into a very English ritual, he spent Christmas Eve getting drunk. Early on Christmas morning, Keith Albarn was woken by the sound of his son writing a song at the family piano. Somewhere from behind the hangover, its lyrics wound the existentialist notion of nausea around a panoramic picture of London that managed to be both beautiful and unsettling; its melody, built around chords that betrayed an enviable compositional talent, fitted the picture to perfection.

There was little doubt that this was the best thing Damon Albarn had ever written. Using up his last droplets of optimism, he called it For Tomorrow.

Suede's rise, meanwhile, showed no signs of slowing. In August, they had released Metal Mickey, a ferocious single – in some part, a showcase for the talents of Bernard Butler – that entered the singles chart at number seventeen. It took them on to *Top of the Pops*, where, allowed the rare privilege of performing in front of their own logo, they turned in a debut performance of quite remarkable power. Brett Anderson's performance style was thus mulled over in millions of sitting rooms. 'Interesting use of the microphone stand there,' burbled the presenter.

As the new year arrived, one began to sense that their lives were starting to move at a mind-boggling pace, catalysed by the effects of media coverage that beggared belief. In February, they released their third single, entitled Animal Nitrate, which contained Brett Anderson's most risqué lyrics to date: as their author concurred, the song was partly about a rather violent kind of gay sex.

By way of titillating his public yet further, to his pronouncements about such topics, Anderson now added breezy admissions of his narcotic habits. 'The idea of Animal Nitrate,' he said, 'came from when I was going through a period when drugs were taking the place of people . . . sex was a just a hollow, vacuous thing which was made full and three-dimensional by the fact that I was taking a huge amount of drugs . . . lots of coke and ecstasy and things.'

Given that the single allowed Suede to finally broach the gleaming gates of the top 10, it wasn't hard to predict where all this would take him. So it proved on 2 March, when the *Daily Star*'s 'Rave' column bowed to the inevitable. 'Brett Snorts Up A Storm!' ran its main headline. 'Self-confessed drug user Brett Anderson, of Suede, is facing a massive backlash over his habit. Parents are afraid their kids will start experimenting with cocaine and ecstasy, just to be like him.' Suede's PRs, filing their cuttings in a dossier that would soon have the approximate dimensions of a large telephone book, could only smile, rub their hands, and put in another call.

At least one of Suede felt a creeping unease about both Brett Anderson's more outré habits, and his apparent fondness for explaining them to journalists. 'Everyone did coke,' says Bernard Butler, 'but not in the way he did. I think he just accelerated the experience. By that point, he was off in the clouds. It wasn't that I was a prude about it; I just thought it was the ultimate pointless rock star drug. And anyone who wants to take coke and tell everyone about it is just a tosser. That's what I felt at the time.'

Animal Nitrate was sent on its way by a very telling engagement. The Brit Awards had a long-standing reputation for honouring the music industry's more anodyne aspects; that year's run of nominations seemed more drab than ever. Aside from a solitary sop to Nirvana, the names were redolent of that part of the music market based around cassette stalls in motorway service stations and local radio: George Michael, Annie Lennox, Enya, Genesis, Curtis Stigers. The ceremony – for some reason hosted by Richard O'Brien of *Rocky Horror Show* fame – was scheduled to include a performance by Peter Gabriel, a duet featuring kd lang and Erasure's Andy Bell, and a show-closing set by Rod Stewart and a re-formed Faces. Given that their bass player, Ronnie Lane, had long been incapacitated by multiple sclerosis, they had drafted in a replacement. As if to underscore the ceremony's all-pervading air of senility, his place was taken by Bill Wyman.

In the weeks leading up to the Brits, the *NME* had led the charge against all this, eventually publishing its own list of alternative nominations. Belatedly, the BPI took the point: two weeks before the ceremony, they contacted Nude Records and invited Suede to perform. After initial doubts, Mat Osman, Bernard Butler and Simon Gilbert agreed. Even on the day, Brett Anderson's misgivings were such that he practically had to be dragged from his bed in Notting Hill.

The organisers thought that, were Suede to open the show, they would cause an unprecedented switch-off on the part of ITV viewers. They thus performed mid-way through proceedings. Their performance was as head-turning as the spot on *Top of the Pops*; it ended with a cut-away shot of the assembled crowd of music business dignitaries, looking absolutely bamboozled. Once Suede had flounced off, Bernard Butler marked their triumph by being violently sick.

'That really felt like crashing the party,' says Brett Anderson. 'We felt like terrorists. We suddenly had started to become pretty popular, and the kind of band we were didn't get to do things like that. That was rare. At the Brits, it was hysterical: all these old music business tits, idiots like Cher – and us. We were really snotty. It was very, "What the fuck was that?" There we were amid all this really choreographed, spineless rubbish.'

If anyone needed further proof of Suede's arrival in a new, strange world, it came the following month. In an interview with *The Face,* Anderson had talked about his experience of meeting Morrissey – whose influence on that year's musical developments rather suggested a Thatcher-esque talent for wreaking minor havoc, despite an evident loss of clout – and his consequent sense of disappointment. 'I didn't really like him,' said Anderson. With surprising irreverence, he went on: 'He's so ridiculously shy, it's boring, not charming. He's like some kind of useless teenager.' These were not the words of some callow fan; Brett Anderson seemed to be standing on a new, self-carved pedestal.

Morrissey soon bit back. 'Suede are . . . a group with all reference points so tightly packed that it consequently leaves no room whatsoever for originality, should any be lurking,' he wrote. 'Despite his claims to the contrary, I have never met Brett and wouldn't wish to; he seems like a deeply boring young man with Mr Kipling crumbs in his bed. He'll never forgive God for not making him Angie Bowie.' The change in Anderson's status was also betrayed by Morrissey's response: his words oozed a disdain he usually reserved for those he viewed as true adversaries.

The same month, as if to make up for that fall-out, Brett Anderson met David Bowie. The summit, at a recording studio in Camden Town, was organised by his friends at the *NME.* As often happens when musician meets musician, free from the usual obligation to answer questions formed in a spirit of journalistic investigation, the conversation threw up pretty muted thrills. Bowie commented that Anderson looked like the young Jimmy Page and complimented him on the Suede music he had heard thus far; Anderson, doubtless with his own habits in mind, marvelled at how prolific Bowie had been while in the midst of his drug years. The text, however, was hardly the point. The photographs – consciously modelled by Bowie on his 1973 meeting with William Burroughs – sent out the right signals: the torch, it seemed, was being ceremonially passed from sorcerer to apprentice.

In the wake of all that came Suede's first album. Its cover was so emblematic of Brett Anderson's endless appetite for the risqué as to almost stray into parody: the cover photograph, by an American named Tee Corinne who had also published a 1975 work entitled *Cunt*

Coloring Book, featured two women locked in a lesbian kiss. As it turned out, Anderson had been permitted to only use a detail of the original, in which both figures were sitting in wheelchairs. In tandem with the song titles printed on the reverse – Animal Nitrate, Sleeping Pills, Animal Lover – the image held out the promise of admittance to a colourful universe indeed. Somewhere within its cover, there even lurked the possibility of parental outrage, that countercultural staple that had been lost at some point during the 1980s. The week of its release, *Suede* – sprinkled with the songs Anderson had written about Justine Frischmann – sold well over 100,000 copies. For a group drawn from the world built around the music press and night-time radio, this was almost unprecedented. At a stroke, Suede were elevated into an enclosure that, in recent memory, had only been opened to The Stone Roses.

What was particularly striking was that whereas the latter group had talked of wiping out Phil Collins and Kylie Minogue, Suede's impact was often characterised in terms of its purgative effects on their own constituency. Indeed, to listen to some people, it seemed as if they were indulging in a spurt of internecine warfare. The first casualties to be claimed were a group called Kingmaker, an indie-ish trio from Hull who had scored one top 30 hit before finding that the *Melody Maker* believed them to be the standard-bearers of everything Suede had come to avenge. The naming of the next scalps must have brought Brett Anderson at least a twinge of sadistic pleasure. 'Do you feel no guilt about the bands whose careers you're widely held to have ended?' asked one journalist. 'Blur and Kingmaker are the names who come to mind easiest, bands whose audiences have been all but swept away in the storm . . .'

One of the most curious aspects of the build-up to *Suede* had arrived the previous month, when the magazine *Select* had used Brett Anderson to flag up one of the theme-based issues that defined its difference from the *NME*. Thanks to the wonders of photo-manipulation – and in a clear bid to incur the wrath of the same right-on elements who, only eight months before, had pilloried Morrissey – he was placed against the Union Jack. 'Yanks Go Home!' read the cover line. Suede, it was claimed, were now leading the decisive charge in 'The Battle For Britain'.

CHAPTER 6

'I'm getting rid of grunge.'

Select's patriotic clarion call was spread over eleven pages, given over to a demolition of the grunge aesthetic – 'talentless', 'mumbling', 'witless' – and a celebration of five groups and the overarching British approach to pop music. Its opening spread featured a *Dad's Army*-esque map of the UK and the headline, 'Who Do You Think You Are Kidding, Mr Cobain?', thus displaying that rather unfortunate British tic that leads to most statements of national self-belief being wrapped in the imagery of the Second World War.

Aside from Suede, the magazine gave space to the arch trio St Etienne, the rather aged art-pop project Denim, Luke Haines of The Auteurs, and one Jarvis Cocker, the thirty-year-old leader of Pulp, then toiling in that purgatorial space that lies between acclaim from the press and popular recognition. Cocker, posed next to an array of washing powder packets, delivered the kind of quotes the magazine was doubtless lusting after, making reference to 'Chips, the Peak District and cul-de-sacs'. 'When British pop is great,' he said, 'it's great because of the personality in the music. The sense of the romantic in the everyday. Ray Davies finding the poetic in the sun going down over Waterloo Station. You don't get that much in American rock.'

Accompanying the groups' interviews was a 2,000-word editorial, written by Stuart Maconie, which served as the issue's manifesto. 'Pop doesn't have to be two-faced and superficial,' it went, 'but the best always remembers that we're dealing in artifice and pose. The new English pop groups are as passionate as any amount of chest-beating rockers . . . what none of them are is earnest, petulant, self-serving or dull.'

Brett Anderson was reportedly furious about the magazine's unauthorised use of the Union Jack with his photograph. *Select*, however, evidently thought that it was time to break from the consensus that equated flag-waving with racism and thuggery. The use of the Union Jack was stoutly defended in a small piece written by the magazine's editor, Andrew Harrison: 'A flag should represent the best in a country . . . tolerance, pride without hatred, humour, openness, tenacity, democracy, decency, optimism, invention and above all community spirit – a sense of your own history.' He went on to rail against 'dogma from the gurus of right-on – they could never understand that you can be proud to be British without wanting a return to the days of the Raj.'

The words were printed in a quarter-page sidebar on page sixty-seven of a monthly music magazine. They could easily have been drawn from a Tony Blair speech made three or four years later, when all around was Union Jack guitars, statements of national pride and 'the re-branding of Britain'.

Blur were not featured in Select's patriotic splurge, yet they were enthusiastic advocates of the same cause, apparently furious that the UK's most fashionable music was a primal racket authored by an American, whose wardrobe suggested that he had reclaimed his clothes from a corporation skip. The contrast between the grunge upsurge and Britain's pop-cultural heritage informed Damon Albarn's rhetoric for the next eighteen months. 'It was, "Hang on, we have such a deep, rich musical tradition in this country, we've got something that goes back to the Victorian period,"' says Mike Smith. 'He wanted to bring all that into what Blur did, and combine it with the music of the sixties and come up with an articulate response to what had come from America.'

Modern Life Is Rubbish was Blur's answer. Finally released in May 1993, it was packaged in a sleeve that instantly served notice of where the group had arrived: on the front sat a painting of the Mallard Locomotive, of the kind usually used for boys' birthday cards; the reverse side featured a painting of the four members of Blur sitting on a District Line train, attired in their three-button jackets and Dr Martens.

Its title had been taken from a stencilled graffito on Bayswater Road, put there by one of the anarchist *groupuscules* whose slogans had long been etched on to the capital's walls. In Albarn's mind, however, it transcended being a rabble-rousing statement of a world gone to pot, and expressed the heart of the late 20th-century condition. 'Modern life is the rubbish of the past,' he explained. 'We all live on the rubbish:

it dictates our thoughts. And because it's all built up over such a long time, there's no necessity for originality any more. There are so many old things to splice together in infinite permutations that there is absolutely no need to create anything new.

'I think,' he said, with his customary humility, 'that that phrase is the most significant comment on popular culture since Anarchy In The UK.'

The music the album contained was not quite as thematically coherent as later accounts have perhaps suggested. Its central pieces – For Tomorrow, Star Shaped, Chemical World, Blue Jeans, Advert – were expressions of the group's new thinking, though there was also a handful of throwbacks to late 1991, when they were fumbling towards nothing more codified than what Albarn had called 'a noisy, emotional mess'. In truth, it hardly mattered: the group's interviews, coupled with the record's presentation, meant that *Modern Life Is Rubbish* was taken as an album with a strident agenda.

The announcement of its release was mailed to the press with a new black and white photograph: the group, clad in a hybrid of skinhead and mod attire, posing in front of a wall bearing the words 'British Image Number One'. In front of them lurked a suitably threatening-looking dog. At the *NME*, there was a momentary shudder of disquiet, and similar murmurs to those that had greeted Morrissey's flag-waving the previous year. Damon Albarn countered them by claiming that his new look was pilfered from the multi-racial 2-tone groups of the early 80s (as if to allay any remaining fears, they eventually came up with 'British Image Number Two', a camp restaging of a pre-war aristocratic tea party).

In April, *Modern Life Is Rubbish* was trailered by the release of For Tomorrow. Thanks in part to Stephen Street, what had emerged from the Albarns' piano on Christmas morning had been turned into something breathtaking: a sumptuous, dramatic song that – thanks to Albarn's references to being 'lost on the Westway' – evoked a twilit world of flyovers, snaking dual carriageways and orange-lit streets. One of its B-sides was a retooled version, the 'Visit To Primrose Hill Extended', whose coda featured an ever-circling Graham Coxon guitar figure: this treatment in particular captured the lyrics' mixture of dystopia and romance to near perfection.

To promote the single, Blur had arranged an outing for an *NME* journalist and photographer, aimed at fleshing out the group's vision. In cahoots with their press officer, they hit upon the idea of driving to the Essex Coast in a pair of hired vintage cars, while feasting on Fortnum and Mason's picnic hampers. All was going well until each of the cars broke down; the jaunt was thus leant a filmic aspect by the fact that the Blur party had to think on its feet and make it to Clacton on £45.

The glitch worked to Albarn's advantage: momentarily stranded on the hard shoulder of the A12, a stone's throw from the ever-increasing expanse of bowling alleys and hangar-like hardware stores, he was afforded the perfect backdrop to his explanation of the album's concerns – not least when it came to Colin Zeal, the Kinks-esque character who had his own song, but whose presence apparently infused many of Albarn's new lyrics. 'He's got cable television, he goes to see the WWF wrestling . . . he represents this huge wave of sanitisation which is undoubtedly linked to America,' he said. 'I'm talking about bubble culture: people feeling content in these huge domes that have one temperature and are filled with this lobotomised music.'

There was an even more pointed aspect to what he said that day, which amounted to the New Blur's mission statement. 'If punk was about getting rid of hippies,' he said, 'then I'm getting rid of grunge. It's the same sort of feeling: people should smarten up, be a bit more energetic. They're walking around like hippies again – they're stooped, they've got greasy hair, there's no difference. Whether they like it or not, they're listening to Black Sabbath again. It irritates me.'

When the party finally arrived in Clacton, already half-drunk on their Fortnum's champagne, Albarn's belief in the truth of his new album's title was proved beyond doubt. In the toilets of a town-centre pub, he sprayed 'Modern Life Is Rubbish' all over the Gents, emerging to tell his dumbfounded colleagues that it was probably time to drink up and leave. Less than an hour later, while the journalist kept watch, the group posed for pictures by the sea wall as Albarn once again reached for his aerosol can. The upshot, aside from the *NME* feature, was an irate article in the *Colchester Evening Gazette*.

If Blur were hoping that such antics – along with the small matter of For Tomorrow's brilliance – would speed them to the upper reaches of the charts and thus launch their crusade, they were to be disappointed. It charted at number twenty-eight, one place above the new single by Big Country. Luckily, they had at least breached the all-important top 30; enough to mean that they could be confident, for the moment at least, of remaining on Food Records' payroll.

That summer, in fact, one could sense them gaining ground. On 13 June, Albarn and Coxon made a brief appearance at Great Xpectations, a concert organised by way of a lobbying exercise for XFM, the proposed London radio station that was attempting to acquire a licence. Its pitch was based around the fact that it would be London's only indie station; the bill that day was thus stuffed with the likes of Kingmaker, the

Catherine Wheel, Carter The Unstoppable Sex Machine and Blur's old friends the Senseless Things (such, by then, was the contorted nature of the indie milieu that all five were signed to major labels).

The pair took the stage mid-way through a gloriously sunny afternoon. 'This is a London song,' said Albarn – and they played a pared-down version of For Tomorrow. In among the discarded lager cups, within sight of North London's tower blocks, the song sounded nigh-on perfect. More importantly, in the context of the groups who made up the bill, it revealed that Blur were now dwelling in very rarefied territory indeed. 'For me, that was the turnaround,' says Mike Smith. 'I remember being with a mate and looking at each other and going, "Fuck me, this is going to be huge." The penny dropped. From that moment forward everything went right.'

At the end of August, Blur were booked to play at the Reading Festival. Since 1991, Reading's main stage had been supplemented by a 5,000-capacity big top. Blur headlined its Sunday evening bill, while The The – a prime example of British art-rock turned unbearably pompous – played the main stage. Two things conspired in Blur's favour: a crowd haemorrhaging towards the big top, and a performance of quite startling confidence.

'Everyone knew: this is it,' Albarn later reflected. 'You know when the gig's yours.' In Dave Rowntree's rather colourful estimation, the experience was akin to 'an hour-and-a-half-long orgasm'.

That night, as Reading etiquette dictated, the assembled groups, their aides, and members of the music press made merry at the nearby Ramada Hotel. In among the standard scenes of drunken tomfoolery, Albarn was amused to find himself sitting in between the editors of *NME* and *Melody Maker*, wearing a very wide grin. 'He must have been like the devil,' said Graham Coxon.

Also sitting in the Ramada that night, dressed in a charity-shop jacket and Dr Martens, was a twenty-three-year-old from Newport, Gwent, named Donna Matthews, a new friend and associate of Justine Frischmann. Her demeanour that night was a little hesitant, but also devoid of the usual goggle-eyed awe of those new to the music business. Watching her movements, one got the impression that Donna Matthews knew how to look after herself.

Her history certainly suggested as much. Matthews had decided to give up on school at fourteen, after her father, Donald, had been released from a six-year prison sentence for cannabis trafficking. Dodging the local truancy officers, she lived in a bedsit, until the authorities finally found her. For the three months leading up to her sixteenth birthday, she was placed in a so-called Special Needs Unit, where non-attendance would be punishable by a spell in council care.

In addition to his more nefarious enterprises, Donald Matthews was acquainted with the music business. During the 1970s, he had been the part owner of a London rehearsal space called Point Studios; among its more noteworthy clients, when they were in town, were Blondie. Prior to that, he had a hand in the management of Middle Of The Road, the short-lived early 70s sensations whose brief run of hits commenced with Chirpy Chirpy Cheep Cheep. In that context, it was not wholly surprising that one of his three daughters taught herself the guitar, and discovered the pleasures of busking in Newport's town centre.

Matthews endured a spell in a handful of local groups, frustrated to find that the only role for her seemed to be as some acoustic-strumming Pre-Raphaelite, ordinarily shoved to the back of the stage. Then, at the Reading Festival, she saw an all-female American group called the Lunachicks. 'I just thought, "That's what I do,"' she says. '"I play guitar like that, I don't play it like Suzanne Vega." It was, "There *must* be more girls who play like that." So I moved to London.'

Matthews knew a native of Newport called Jon Lee*, an aspiring drummer who was renting a flat in Cricklewood. She turned up at his door with nothing more than a rucksack and her electric guitar, and asked if she could stay on the floor. Soon after, she began going through the back of the *Melody Maker*, poring over the 'Musicians Wanted' adverts. Among the dozens around which she biro'd a circle was one that read 'Guitarist wanted – influences: The Fall, The Stranglers, Wire'. The fact that she was only familiar with the middle group did not hold her back.

In late September 1992, she duly arrived at the Premises rehearsal studio in Hackney to keep an appointment with Justine Frischmann and her new group. 'It was quite shambolic,' says Matthews. 'I remember thinking, "Fucking hell – you're not very good." But I liked the way Justine looked, and I liked her attitude. She had a brown velvet flared suit on, and foppish hair and Doc Martens. She looked really like she was in Suede. I was impressed with her straight away.'

Since her exit from Suede, Frischmann had been plotting the formation of a band. The central idea, initially formulated in cahoots with her friend Jane Oliver, was to specialise in the polar opposite of the epic, sweeping compositions that had played a role in her departure. 'It was a reaction to Suede's drama,' she says. 'I was sick of the whole

---

* Lee went on to find success as the drummer with the rock trio Feeder. In January 2002, he committed suicide at his home in Florida.

"love and poison of London" thing. I thought life didn't have to be that dramatic. When I broke up with Brett, that whole atmospheric, romantic London thing hurt me. It reminded me of being with him, so I didn't want to go anywhere near that. Plus, I had just discovered Wire, and rediscovered The Stranglers, and Adam And The Ants were very important: I found their Peel Sessions album, which was virtually a manifesto. The lyrics were funny, which was very important. Great, really angular guitar. At that point, it seemed perfect.'

In the summer of 1992, Frischmann began rehearsing with Justin Welch, the drummer who had played with Suede for six weeks back in 1990, and who was currently Mat Osman's flatmate. In the absence of extra personnel, she cajoled Damon Albarn – who had just returned from Blur's American nightmare – to play the bass. Three weeks later, they found Annie Holland, a guitarist from Brighton who seemed willing to switch to four strings, whereupon the idea of Elastica being built around an all-female front-line began to enter Frischmann's head. The arrival of Donna Matthews made the notion concrete.

As with her relationship with Brett Anderson, the new alliance with Donna Matthews represented a superficially unlikely combination: the St Paul's Girl and Architecture graduate, collaborating with a self-sufficient stray who had left school in her teens. 'Donna was obsessed with ways around the dole: how to make your fiver stretch further,' says Frischmann. 'She used to walk around with this bag of change. I always remember her counting out all these 2ps to pay for her food or her tea and coffee. We used to split the money for rehearsal, and she would count out her two pound fifty in two pounds and 5ps.'

'I didn't really understand what the difference between us was at the time,' says Matthews. 'I didn't even *think* that she would have had a completely different upbringing to me. I accepted that she was from a wealthy family, but I didn't know anyone who was really rich then. Now, I can see how differently you grow up. But I felt that we were similar in loads of ways. Justine wanted to be more working class, and I wanted to have more money. We kind of met halfway.'

Matthews moved in to a flat in Camden Town with Jane Oliver, thus entering the orbit of Graham Coxon. In this new whirl of people, all attired in similar clothes, and dropping the same musical reference points, she sensed a loosely-bound clique. 'Immediately,' she says, 'there was like ... this *scene*. Justin lived a hundred yards down the road with Mat from Suede. Steve Mackey from Pulp and him became friends, so you had them involved. And obviously, Justine was going out with Damon. Suede, Blur, Pulp and us – all these little sort of gangs started to happen.'

To keep it in the family, Elastica were given their first run of a studio by Mike Smith. 'I thought Donna was incredible,' he says. 'She was this total counterpoint to Justine, who was this incredibly worldly, articulate, wealthy, beautiful girl who lived in Kensington. And Donna was a doe-eyed street kid who'd been living on her wits, coming up out of dire poverty in South Wales. The combination of those two was incredible.'

Alex James was duly introduced to this new, rather exotic addition to the gang. 'Donna was made out of one hundred per cent rock'n'roll fibre,' he says. 'A good time girl. Sweet. Talented, as well. But she was fucking far out.'

The new group's music instantly separated them from their contemporaries. They played staccato, angular songs, so compact that they could rattle through a large handful within quarter of an hour. The lyrics, sung by Frischmann in a beguilingly deep voice, had the capacity to be both irreverent and risqué: among the first songs they worked up was a minute-long musical joke called Vaseline. It was the group's key achievement to constantly avoid sounding serious, while making music that was admirably artful; in the days when Kurt Cobain was still exercising his angst-wracked hegemony – and Suede hardly specialised in humour – this was no mean feat.

Having played their first gig in Windsor as Onk – calculated to sound so unpromising that they could make their debut quietly – they sorely needed a name. They toyed with Dad, and Kirby Grip: a Mancunian name for a particularly nasty fighting move. For a while, they considered calling themselves Spastics Society. That name eventually morphed into Elastica, which may or may not have tied into Wilem Frischmann's work as an engineer: the Elastica Principle refers to the tendency of structures, when forced out of their initial shape, to move through a period of distortion before assuming a new form.

The summer of 1993 formed the backdrop to Elastica's first spurt of progress: performances in such unlikely backwaters as Bath, Bedford and Aldershot; their first visit to the BBC; the night in August when Mike Smith signed them to EMI Music Publishing on top of Primrose Hill. From then until the end of the year, they appeared to play a clever game: dodging attention lest they should fall into the same frantic place into which Suede had tumbled the year before, while gently tickling a palpable sense of expectation. When they played at the Falcon in Camden on 19 June, a queue spiralled around the block.

'I knew from the first month in the band that we were going to be successful, 'cos of who Justine knew and *what* she knew from Blur and Suede,' says Donna Matthews. 'I trusted her with the business side of it: for me, it was more about "Hey – rock'n'roll," living the lifestyle, than it was about creating art. Justine had more of the art school side of it, whereas for me it was about sex, drugs and rock'n'roll. I was totally infatuated with bands. I'd read all those biographies: *Wonderland Avenue, Heroes And Villains*, Rolling Stones books.'

Thanks to such touchstones, Matthews' appearance began to change. When she arrived in London, she had both long hair and chubby cheeks; by the autumn of 1993, she had managed to cultivate both razor-like cheekbones and the kind of haircut last seen atop the head of Keith Richards in 1966. Her chemical habits – shared by Justin Welch and, in her own quiet way, Annie Holland – had yet to exert much of an attraction on Frischmann. 'Justine was spending a lot of time with Damon,' she says. 'We didn't really hang out over at hers. Me and Justin were mad drugheads, and she had this quiet family life. She'd occasionally invite us to dinner, which we'd never do for her. We didn't eat.'

As if to add yet more colour to the group's internal relations, Matthews and Justin Welch had begun a romantic entanglement. For the moment, it only seemed to confirm that a group put together via tangential acquaintances and music paper small ads had been blessed with a remarkably tight-knit chemistry. Certainly, Frischmann and Holland saw no cause for alarm: when informed of their drummer and guitarist's new sleeping arrangements, they expressed nothing more than benign amusement.

Elastica's inaugural single was released on 1 November. Entitled Stutter, it was a treble-heavy piece of melodic punk, aimed somewhere between the Ramones, Blondie and My Perfect Cousin by The Undertones. More remarkably, its lyrics concerned Frischmann's frustration with the occasional problem of drunken male impotence. If the grunge bands had converted punk rock into a coruscating expression of dysfunction, it was this record's achievement to remind its listeners that its traditions could be appropriated with both poise and guile.

In line with Justine Frischmann's love of the more difficult, anti-commercial end of the musical spectrum – not to mention the ongoing management of expectations – it was restricted to 5,000 copies, all pressed on 7-inch vinyl. The enterprise was cooked up in collaboration with Steve Lamacq: having left the *NME* and begun presenting Radio One's *Evening Session*, he was also a partner in a new independent label named Deceptive, whose aesthetics reflected his background in the slipstream of punk. Stutter's accompanying video only heightened the air of no-frills frugality: shot in a single take, it featured the group simply miming in front of a bright white backdrop.

Such was the context for their first substantial interview in the *NME*, conducted as they toured the UK with the ubiquitous Kingmaker. Here, with a knowing smirk, Frischmann delivered a veritable pearl: 'I can't think of anything better than sixteen-year-old boys wanking and looking at a poster of me. But don't quote me on that 'cos I'll kick your head in.'

During the summer of 1993, Suede had sealed their place as Britain's most admired rock group. When they headlined the second stage at that year's Glastonbury Festival, whispers began to spread through the hospitality area that David Bowie had decided to pay the festival – or rather, Suede – a royal visit. That Saturday night, as Brett Anderson and Bernard Butler closed the group's performance by performing a new song called Still Life, there he was, watching from the wings with his new wife, Iman. Pointedly, Suede did not linger, forsaking the customary lap of honour around the backstage bar and a round with the Senseless Things. They were now moving in an altogether loftier orbit.

On the occasions when they permitted more up-close scrutiny, it was clear that Suede had changed. Eighteen months of life as the Next Big Thing had exacted its toll on Brett Anderson: he now approached the interview ritual wearily, dutifully tossing forth the requisite number of soundbites, but giving the impression of absolute nonchalance. Moreover, the agenda of a year before – their passionate advocation of a new Anglo-centric music – had all but disappeared. One began to wonder, in fact, whether Brett Anderson had believed any of it in the first place. Such, in retrospect, was the upshot of his rhetorical territory being invaded by Damon Albarn.

'From seeing the world, you get a lot more perspective,' he said. 'And now, I have a lot less time for the English way of things . . . I feel absolutely no connection with Britain whatsoever. I mean, this spurious British "scene" that sprang up . . . we happen to be British people, so we make music that's inspired by this country. But to stand Britain up as this paragon of virtue that everyone should try and emulate is nothing but a load of bullshit . . . I'd like to live in America. I love it there – the West Coast in particular, and I don't have much desire to live in Britain much longer. I'd like to be somewhere else within a couple of years.'

Blur's English crusade, by contrast, became more brazen than ever. In October, they plucked Sunday Sunday from *Modern Life Is Rubbish* and released it as a single. It was the most transparently English of the songs on the album, and therefore the ideal full stop to its promotion.

There was but one snag: thanks to the music business's fondness for 'multi-formatting' – releasing as many different versions of a single as possible, so as to encourage hard-bitten fans to buy them all, and thereby send the record hurtling into the chart – Blur had to come up with seven different B-sides. They were used to the practice, but with their reserves of material drying up, they were forced to rummage through the dustier corners of their own archive.

What they found made for strange listening indeed. Across one of two CDs and a 12-inch single, they spread five songs from their days as Seymour, whose bug-eyed lunacy sounded like it had been beamed in from another plane. Even more remarkably, they titled a second edition *The Popular Community Song CD* and included two music-hall staples, Daisy Bell and Let's All Go Down The Strand. They were recorded one Sunday afternoon, in the company of a crowd that included Mike Smith and Justine Frischmann: Damon Albarn led the ad hoc choir in a tremulous, stagy voice that rather suggested a dress rehearsal at Stanway Comprehensive.

Owing to their pinched financial position, Blur were already back in the studio with Stephen Street, recording songs for a third album. On the tour that accompanied Sunday Sunday, they allowed one new composition to creep into their set: a manic, bouncealong song called Parklife, in which Albarn delivered a series of spoken verses inspired by Martin Amis's novel *London Fields*, punctuated by a chorus that represented his most populist trick to date. More remarkable still, according to their inner circle, was Girls And Boys: a gurgling synthesis of punk and disco that was, it was said, almost bound to be a hit.

If Blur had spent 1992 as blighted loners, they could now take heart from the fact that, in London at least, *Modern Life Is Rubbish* had inspired its own small cult. Somewhat inevitably, its gathering ground was Camden Town. From Monday to Friday, the tribe frequented The Good Mixer, a threadbare Irish pub tucked behind Camden High Street that had become Graham Coxon's second home. He was not the only individual from the music business who had become a regular: thanks to the close proximity of both Food Records' offices and the HQ of the PR firm Savage & Best – whose clients included Elastica, Suede, The Verve and The Auteurs – it soon teemed with musicians, their associates, and a slowly increasing gaggle of camp-followers.

'It had a vinyl jukebox,' says Andy Ross. 'Tom Jones, Nancy Sinatra. No people, two pool tables and a decent pint of bitter. We thought, "This is great. We'll go in there, it's a bit shabby, the musicians'll love it." There was one time I went in with Damon, and it was absolutely empty, apart from three members of Madness, and Morrissey at the bar. I just thought, "This is fucking surreal." But as soon as it started getting written about in the gossip columns, next thing you know, there's two hundred people in there. That transformation took less than a couple of months.'

Such changes were quickly decried, not least by the literary titans who lived nearby. 'When us lot moved in to the Mixer, [the novelist] Beryl Bainbridge used to drink in there, quite regularly,' says Ross. 'She wasn't happy; we became the pariahs of the Gloucester Crescent set. Alan Bennett was even more angry, apparently. You could see The Mixer from his house, and he got very uppity about the fact that all these young, noisy people were bringing a blight on this idyll.'

On Saturday nights, many of the Good Mixer crowd would gather at Blow Up, a club-night held at a back-street gay pub called The Laurel Tree. On the ground floor, the crowd was serenaded by obscure 60s soul; upstairs, the DJs played a more abrasive mixture of 60s rock, British punk and the kind of latter-day groups that *Select* had lionised back in March. Among the on-off clientele were members of Blur, Pulp and Elastica.

Increasingly, those groups were not the only ones united by a common Anglo-centric cause. In the same rat-hutch venues that had provided their launch-pad, one could increasingly come across bands who were similarly keen to reactivate a world that had recently seemed all but lost: Echobelly, whose closest musical comparison was The Smiths; Sleeper, who harked back to Blondie and The Pretenders; These Animal Men, whose camp macho poses were redolent of The Clash; and S*M*A*S*H, a righteous neo-punk trio who hailed from Welwyn Garden City. In homage to a supposed common fondness for the more iconic end of British punk rock – and with its tongue lodged in its cheek – in September 1993, the *NME* deemed them harbingers of something called 'The New Wave Of New Wave'.

In the eyes of the world at large, however, there were far bigger stories on which to focus. During 1993, Nirvana had ascended to new heights: on *In Utero*, the album they released that September, Kurt Cobain had grappled with his demons on songs that made much of *Nevermind* sound tame and restrained. The result, inevitably, was an album that fed his myth yet further.

Behind them came a raft of American bands. Pearl Jam's singer Eddie Vedder converted his pain into piety; in place of Kurt Cobain's scattershot rage, he offered his audience a very earnest kind of communion. Soundgarden and Alice In Chains represented the upsurge's more orthodox wing, swerving clear of any punk rock nuances and thereby attracting an audience reared on old-style heavy metal. As far as the international rock audience was concerned, such groups defined the contemporary musical map: their music blared from the student bars and squats of most of the industrial world.

There was but one British voice to be heard in the midst of it all: over the summer, a group from Oxford called Radiohead had scored a surprise US hit with a song called Creep. The song delivered its message in a potent kind of esperanto: a lyric about unbearable self-loathing, and a winning mixture of quiet verses and a fuzztoned chorus. There was a brief flurry of excitement about the possibility that it might have opened a door for other British groups; as it turned out, even Radiohead themselves found it all but impossible to capitalise on the song's success. All told, at the end of 1993, British music seemed to be something that was pretty much exclusive to Britons themselves.

To the more clued-in elements of the UK music industry, however, the prospect of exciting domestic developments – quite apart from any home-grown US successes – seemed enough. As Christmas approached, Mike Smith had some sense of the race that would define the first few months of the following year. Suede had recorded Stay Together, a stand-alone single that was scheduled to come out in February. It had been piloted by Bernard Butler, reportedly trying to come to terms with the recent death of his father by pouring his grief into this new composition. The finished song was eight-and-a-half minutes long; by way of falling in with such ostentation, Brett Anderson contributed lyrics that walked the thin line between poetic invention and absurd pretentiousness.

Primal Scream, meanwhile, were about to finally unveil the successor to their 1991 album *Screamadelica,* the record that had stood as the summation of the group's immersion in Acid House. Though that album had been built on a melange of dance influences and rock attitude, the new record was an altogether more orthodox affair: the group, it was rumoured, were trying to reinvent themselves as successors to the early 70s Rolling Stones.

And then there was the dark horse: the prospect of a first single by a Mancunian band called Oasis, whom Smith had been attempting to sign to a publishing deal since the autumn. 'It was really funny,' says Alex James. 'We went into his office at EMI: me and Graham and Damon. He played us Suede's new single, we played him Girls And Boys, and he played Primal Scream's new single, Rocks. We were like, "Come on then – who's going to have the biggest hit?" He said, "Oh, by the way – these are some guys from Manchester; they're all ugly apart from the singer." And he played us Supersonic, a really rough thing, and we just said, "No, don't sign them – they're shit."'

Justine Frischmann had heard a snatch of Oasis music a couple of months before. 'I thought they were dreadful,' she says. 'Mike Smith played me and Damon the Cigarettes And Alcohol demo. He said, "Do you think I should carry on bidding?" And we both said, "This is pathetic shit baggy rubbish. Do *not* pay for it." They looked crap, sounded really uninteresting. I thought Supersonic had a couple of good lines and that was it. One of them was *bald*. It was, "How could anyone think this is good?" It didn't seem like a threat.'

PART T W O

Rock'n'roll is not just an important part of our culture, it's an important part of our way of life.

Tony Blair, 1994

Please don't put your life in the hands/Of a rock'n'roll band/Who'll throw it all away . . .

Oasis, Don't Look Back In Anger, 1995

CHAPTER 7

Swab the nose and punch the liver

At 4.31am on Monday 17 January, 1994, an earthquake hit the San Fernando Valley in northern Los Angeles. It measured 6.7 on the Richter Scale: enough to cause fifty-seven deaths and at least 1,500 serious injuries. In among the buckled roads and shattered glass, 9,000 homes and businesses found themselves without electricity; over 48,000 were cut off from the water supply. The aftershocks – some measuring as high as 5.0 – continued for well over a fortnight.

Among those who felt the earthquake's effects were Alan McGee and Tim Abbot, two thirds of the ruling triumvirate of Creation Records. They were in California to play their part in the final work on Primal Scream's fourth album, and billeted to the Mondrian Hotel on Sunset Strip. They had finally returned to their beds in the wee hours, having spent the night in the company of George Drakoulias – the American producer who had been brought in to buff up Primal Scream's recordings – and Rick Rubin, the much-admired mind who had brought the world the Beastie Boys. As was McGee and Abbot's way, they had propelled themselves through the night by shovelling a large volume of cocaine up their noses.

'I was on the tenth floor, Alan was on the second,' says Abbot. 'The earthquake lasted for about a minute. And I went out on to the corridor, and this rap band were on my floor. We were all like, "What do we do?" We got downstairs, out into the car park. And I looked around, going, "Where's McGee?" I managed to get a torch and I went back in. I went down to Alan's room, and for some reason, me and him got into bed, freaking out, just going, "Fucking unreal!"

'There were no lights in LA, 'cos all the electricity had gone. And me and him watched the sun coming up, still on gear – we'd been beaked up all night – and we went through till about twelve. Next thing you know, George Drakoulias came by: "Hey, shall we go and look at some damage?" I was like, "Great." But McGee was saying, "Abbot, you're not taking this seriously." He was very, very shaken up.'

Such was the surreality of McGee's schedule that he flew straight from Los Angeles to Tokyo, where he was one of the star attractions at an international conference organised by the Sony corporation. Thus, while Abbot returned to London, frantically recounting his earthquake experience to anyone who would listen, McGee found himself in a place where even the most rudimentary conversation recurrently proved to be impossible.

In addition, there were other problems. As any globally itinerant drug addict will testify, for anyone halfway dependent on illicit substances, Japan is not the most satisfactory place to be. Moreover, the kind of experience that McGee was about to endure was only going to make things worse. The centrepiece of his visit, after all, was a brief meeting with Sony's most famous – and notorious – star turn: a man not exactly known for putting his guests at ease.

'McGee phoned me from Japan, saying, "I'm going out of my mind,"' says Abbot. 'He said, "I've just met Michael Jackson. And Bubbles. He's got Bubbles in a cage." That's how batty it was. They had Bubbles in a royal enclosure, and McGee said he was a horrible, old, mangy chimp. He wasn't a PG Tips chimp: he was an angry, fucked-up chimp.'

The circumstances of McGee's meeting with Jackson and his pet must have heightened his sense of disorientation to the point of absurdity. In Abbot's recollection, McGee told the story as follows: 'There are all these little Japs around him, all five foot two. And he'd met the head of Sony, who had gone, "How is Joe Strummer?" These guys thought he was the manager of The Clash. And then they took him to meet Michael Jackson. He was in the queue with all these Japs, and they go, "Introducing Aran McGree!" They pull this screen back, and he's standing there: this big ginger Scottish fella. I don't know who was more shocked: Michael Jackson or him.'

While in LA, McGee had entertained Keith Cameron, a journalist with the *NME*. He was there to interview McGee for the paper's celebration of Creation's impending tenth anniversary: an occasion to be marked by a front cover, a giveaway compilation cassette, and a two-part trawl through the label's history. Abbot escorted Cameron from London to LA: before their departure, he gleefully informed him that they were about to 'swab the nose and punch the liver'. Cameron's three-day stay fitted the bill; it also indicated that Alan McGee was living in a perilous place indeed.

'I'd never seen cocaine delivered to a room in a big polythene bag before,' says Cameron. 'McGee would make a call and two hours later there'd be a knock at the door, and . . . well, there never seemed to be a shortage, put it that way.

'It dawned on me over the course of those three days that, okay, for me this was a holiday, but I got the impression that for McGee, this was his life. At certain points I'd start to become quite concerned about him. He gave this impression of being fairly indestructible, but I was thinking, "There is no way that I could do this, this is ridiculous." He wouldn't really eat very much, he'd maybe have one meal a day, he had diet pills, and he'd take Night Nurse. He was living life at a very fast, some might say dangerous pace.

'But you have to remember that at that point there was quite a lot of mystique built up around McGee – by people in the press largely; we were complicit in it. And I think, by that point, the myth of McGee had become the reality.'

Whether the Alan McGee of 1980 would have recognised the 1994 model is a moot point. A native of Glasgow, he had marked the dawn of a new decade by moving to London, where he began his second stint as a British Rail clerk. His day job, however, was hardly the reason for his move: accompanied by his friends Andrew Innes and Jack Reilly, he had come to the capital to grapple with the more adventurous end of the music industry.

McGee was one of three siblings, born in 1959 and raised in Glasgow's Mount Florida area. His father, John, was a panel-beater. His adolescence had been enacted against a backdrop of regular truancy – he left school at sixteen with one O-level – and rock music. McGee's first objects of affection were such glam-rock pioneers as David Bowie and Marc Bolan, before he moved on to long-haired purveyors of heavy rock like Deep Purple. Finally – and most crucially – he had been converted by the incendiary roar of punk rock.

Inspired by punk's emphasis on do-it-yourself emancipation, he bought a bass guitar and joined a Glasgow group called H$_2$O. His tenure, which peaked with an appearance at an outdoor CND festival, was relatively brief: tortured by the eternal punk worry that he was in the company of careerists, he quit, taking one Andrew Innes – whom McGee had brought in as guitarist – with him.

The pair then recruited Jack Reilly as drummer and, in rather clichéd homage to Orwell's *1984*, called themselves Newspeak. A move to London was intended to lay the foundations of their big break; unfortunately, Reilly decided that he missed Glasgow and returned within weeks. McGee and Innes were undeterred. In partnership with a drummer from Croydon named Mark Jardim, they formed a new group called The Laughing Apple. The same Glaswegian contact who had put H_2O on the CND festival eventually offered to lend them £500 to release their first single, on the condition that CND were mentioned on the sleeve. So it was that Alan McGee made his first curious trip to Rough Trade Distribution's London warehouse, hodding a box of the EP he had entitled Ha Ha Hee Hee. Among the piles of records that lined its walls, McGee could sense the possibility of his punk-inspired ideas being taken to some new, unforeseen level.

He was fired by two factors. The idea that punk rock's effects on music were being overturned and nullified was common currency in the early 80s: voiced in dozens of diatribes in the music papers, reflected in the fact that such concerns formed the raison d'être of countless fanzines, and most publicly dramatised by the 24-year-old Paul Weller's sudden dissolution of The Jam, lest they betray his ideals. McGee shared the worry, expressing it with a ferocity that suggested his concerns were in danger of turning neurotic. Fused with all this, meanwhile, was a burgeoning love of British rock from the 60s: music which, McGee believed, oozed virtues that the ugly mores of the 80s had long since ruled out.

On a Saturday night in early 1983, he staged the first night of a weekly club named The Living Room, based upstairs at a pub called The Adams Arms, close to the Post Office Tower. Its capacity was little more than sixty; nonetheless, it became a magnet for a coterie of fanzine writers, indie enthusiasts and groups who shared McGee's belief in some righteous rearguard action against an impossibly large host of enemies: the treacherous punks who had turned into 'New Hippies', the decadent leaders of the New Pop – when it came down to it, just about every representative of the musical mainstream.

'By then,' says McGee, 'music had become so manufactured, like it is now. We'd just talk about all the stuff we hated: "I hate this, I hate this, I hate this, I hate that." Then I started this fanzine, probably more of a hatezine. It was called *Communication Blur*. And it was just pure fucking bile. We wanted to do things like water-bombing pop stars as they were coming out of their record companies.'

In late 1983, McGee uncoupled himself from British Rail. Like so many of the era's counterculturalists, he accepted the munificence of the Thatcher Government, and signed up to the Enterprise Allowance Scheme. The resultant £40 a week facilitated the decisive start of his next plan: a record label. He had already issued one single – authored by a Living Room ally named Jerry Thackray, aka The Legend! –

entitled 73 In 83, only to find its distinctly home-made aesthetics greeted by either indifference or ridicule. Now, however, he had plans for a run of superior records, by such bands as The Jasmine Minks, Revolving Paint Dream, and his own freshly-formed group, Biff Bang Pow! Better still, his new venture had a clearly defined aesthetic.

In homage to The Creation – the short-lived 60s group who, like The Who, had fused hard-faced aggression with an avant-garde inventiveness and had posthumously caught McGee's imagination – 73 In 83 had been issued by a label called Creation Artifact. To mark the label's official birth, this was now shortened to one word. 'What I was trying to do with Creation,' he says, 'was to merge psychedelia with punk rock. I was obsessed with Syd Barrett and Pink Floyd, The Creation, The Small Faces – but I was always into punk, and Joy Division and Public Image and stuff like that. They were the two sides of the vision.'

Creation's first real splash came in November 1984, with the release of a single called Upside Down. Its creators were a gang of dysfunctional iconoclasts from East Kilbride – later to escort Blur around the UK on the Rollercoaster tour – called The Jesus And Mary Chain. They fitted McGee's worldview to perfection: such reference points as Phil Spector and the Hamburg-era Beatles were fused with a love of brain-crushing feedback, and a gloriously nihilistic wish to antagonise their audiences to breaking point. In the pursuit of the latter aim, The Jesus And Mary Chain had one trump card: much to Alan McGee's delight, they could hardly play their instruments.

In addition to releasing their debut single, McGee became their manager. Suggesting that the strict indie purism that often seemed to define The Living Room had since been superseded by a rather more Machiavellian set of values, he quickly steered them into a £75,000 record deal with Blanco Y Negro, the left-field offshoot of Warner Brothers headed by Geoff Travis. By now, McGee was fantasising about turning himself into a successor to Malcolm McLaren. Events duly played into his hands: in March 1985, after the usual mixture of screeching amplifiers, minimal stagecraft and a wilfully brief performance, a section of the crowd at North London Polytechnic invaded the stage, toppled the PA system, and set about breaking most anything that lay in their path. The episode – quickly etched into indie folklore as 'the Jesus And Mary Chain riot' – did its work, wrapping the group in a very sexy kind of notoriety. *Psychocandy*, their first album, breached the top 40; in July 1986, a single entitled Some Candy Talking reached number thirteen.

In August 1985, Creation moved into its first proper office, at 83 Clerkenwell Road, EC1. Within two years, McGee appeared to have repeated his most celebrated trick, steering The House Of Love through a string of releases on his own label, before masterminding their signing to Phonogram for £250,000. The notion that, within *NME*-world, he was now as much of a star as his groups was only furthered by his public uniform: leather jacket, black drainpipe jeans, classic 50s sunglasses that never seemed to leave his nose, and that shock of ginger hair. Feeding the image was the knowledge that McGee had an increasingly wreckless approach to his own internal chemistry; thus arose the classically rock'n'roll idea that all his manoeuvring was accomplished in between slurps, tokes and snorts.

His contemporaries in the left-field corners of the music industry had begun to arrive at the conclusion that, despite Creation's place in the indie firmament, McGee did not share its abiding sense of common cause: compared to the likes of Geoff Travis, 4AD's Ivo Watts-Russell, Mute's Daniel Miller, and Martin Mills of Beggars Banquet, he was an altogether more self-centred kind of operator. 'You think of Alan doing his own thing – as opposed to how you would think about Daniel or Martin Mills or Ivo, where you did feel there was some kind of ideology – some kind of ethical morality – linking what you were all doing,' says Travis. 'You wouldn't try and poach each other's groups: it'd be, "Well, I saw them first." That didn't really come into play with Alan: I can recall him going after a couple of my things. He had a much more Alex Ferguson mentality than the rest of us: "I don't care about anyone else – this is what I'm going to do."'

McGee's drug use skyrocketed thanks to Acid House. He was not one of the scene's inner circle, nor did much of the music find its way into Creation's output, but it redefined both his chemical habits – McGee became an ecstasy zealot – and his wider life: for a while, he split his time between his new base in Brighton and Manchester, where he was a regular at the Haçienda. Belatedly, however, the label reflected this new upsurge, when, in February 1990, Creation released a single called Loaded.

Its authors, Primal Scream, had become Creation's core group. They were commanded by two of McGee's oldest friends: the aforementioned Andrew Innes and another Glaswegian, Bobby Gillespie, whose bond with McGee dated back to his teens. Their first album, 1987's *Sonic Flower Groove* – to all intents and purposes, a clumsy attempt at the sound that The Stone Roses were already perfecting* – had been

---

* Ironically, The Stone Roses took at least passing inspiration from this phase of Primal Scream's career: Made Of Stone, released as a single in March 1989, betrays the influence of Velocity Girl, a 1986 Primal Scream B-side.

a rather limp homage to 60s American psychedelia; the follow-up, released in September 1989, found them in thrall to the more scabrous approach of The Stooges and MC5. With Acid House and the Mancunian groups who had fallen under its spell defining music's left-field, it was not likely to find much of an audience: history records no chart position for either the album or its first single. Despite its failure, the album – simply entitled *Primal Scream* – contained one undeniable masterstroke: an aching ballad entitled I'm Losing More Than I'll Ever Have. Word got back to the group that its merits had been recognised by one Andy Weatherall, a DJ at such pivotal Acid House clubs as Shoom and The Trip, and one of the founders of the much-respected fanzine *Boy's Own*. At the instigation of Andrew Innes – and with their perilous commercial position in mind – tapes of the song were handed to Weatherall for a possible remix. Looping the song's three-chord coda and importing a beautiful percussion sample from the American singer/songwriter Edie Brickell, he managed to turn the track into a mesmeric instrumental, strongly evocative of The Rolling Stones' Sympathy For The Devil.

If its mid-paced tempo and use of piano and brass placed it light years from Acid House, its link to the subculture was ensured by its use of dialogue from *The Wild Angels*, much of which was spoken by Peter Fonda: 'We wanna be free, to do what we wanna do . . . And we wanna get loaded . . . and we wanna have a good time . . . and that's what we're gonna do . . . We're gonna have a good time . . . We're gonna have a party.' With both policemen and MPs still in the midst of Acid House hysteria – only two months beforehand, Graham Bright MP had introduced his clumsy anti-rave bill – the words sounded as timely as could be imagined. Sped on its way by daytime exposure on Radio One, Loaded reached number thirteen and thereby inaugurated a new era for Creation and Alan McGee. All that apart, it remains as evocative a reminder of the early 1990s as any Happy Mondays or Stone Roses single.

By now, Creation had relocated to new premises in Hackney. They shared the building with a sweatshop commanded by a Turkish Cypriot named Oz, who made his living through the manufacture of cheap anoraks. McGee and Dick Green – the long-standing ally who co-owned Creation, played guitar in Biff Bang Pow!, and saw to the logistical matters to which McGee was perhaps unsuited – shared a windowless ground-floor space that quickly became known as The Bunker; their colleagues worked upstairs, in among half-opened crates of records and the frequently realised threat of burglary. These were not the kind of headquarters to impress most visitors. 'When I used to imagine being on Creation Records,' said one of the label's musicians, 'I used to think the offices would be this huge skyscraper in the middle of London with a red star above them or something. Then I get there and it's this dilapidated heap in the East End of London that's really difficult to get to.'

Despite the offices' shabbiness, the stakes for the label had long since been raised above the small-time concerns of the average small indie label. McGee now sat in a web of international licensing agreements, distribution deals and outstanding debts. Long-term planning was hardly Creation's forte; more often than not, McGee managed to keep the company afloat through his talent for hawking Creation music to foreign labels whenever things looked grim.

'There was glory in those years,' he says. 'Someone said to me recently, "I never knew, from week to week, if we'd have a job." It was that on the edge. Every time it looked as if we were going down, I'd do a deal, get another two hundred grand in and we'd be alright for another two months. I remember I used to fly to America, going to get money, and I used to look at my diary and it would say, Week fourteen. I'd see we had a Primals record coming out Week thirty-four. And I'd go, "I wonder if we're going to keep it together." I just thought "Fuck – imagine if I pull through the next twenty weeks."'

To insulate himself from such stresses, he ingested just about everything that came to hand. 'I was living on uppers and downers: anything that'd get me through it,' says McGee. 'I was self-medicating. But instead of taking tranquillisers, I was taking speed and downers.'

Into this maelstrom came Tim Abbot. He had spent most of the 1980s as – in his own words – 'a champagne-drinking, cocaine-sniffing, archetypal yuppie prick', working as a freelance marketing consultant for the likes of Pernod and Levi's. His Acid House experiences prompted an existential re-evaluation: he spent nine months in Thailand and grew his hair. Upon his return, he began to promote a club in his native Birmingham called The Better Way. A night spent in McGee's company in the wake of a St Etienne concert had resulted in an open invite to the club; McGee eventually turned up without warning.

'I hadn't seen him for a while,' says Abbot. 'There was a knock on the door in the VIP bit: one of the door guys said, "There's a bloke out there, dribbling, saying he's your best mate." And it was Alan. We let him in, and he traipsed through the club. His glasses were actually steamed up. I couldn't work out how he could see. There was a big curd of E flotsam round his mouth. And he was going round with a bag of pills going, "Alright, mate: do you want an E?" Everyone thought he was drug squad.'

Inevitably, McGee talked to Abbot about Creation: its £2 million turnover, the fact that the money never seemed to be enough. Abbot's command of business logistics impressed him – not least because he had a grasp of matters that had long seemed to be the preserve of straight-backed squares. The pair soon arrived at a plan: Abbot would do a consultancy job for Creation, studying the company's workings and making the kind of recommendations that might drag it away from the ongoing threat of penury.

For two or three days each week, Abbot sat in The Bunker, attempting to make sense of Creation's own brand of managed anarchy. His eventual recommendations included such unprecedented innovations as contracts of employment and job descriptions. 'People would just amble in and amble out,' says Abbot. 'And my thing was, "Alan, you pay these people decent wages – it's a sign of respect that they should come in and do an eight-hour day for you." He was like, "Great! You can see what I want to do in this company!"'

Abbot was no square: though he had arrived at Creation in his standard business uniform of Daks blazer and slacks, his musical knowledge and hyperactive demeanour – not to mention his chemical predilections – made him ideal Creation material. He duly put his own mark on the mass of pictures that Green and McGee had blu-tacked to The Bunker's walls: to the cut-outs of rock icons and supermodels, he added what he called 'Mondo' images: pictures of all manner of horrors, often torn from the German magazine *Stern*. So it was that Johnny Rotten and Kate Moss sat within inches of a picture of corpses in a Brazilian prison and rats surrounding an Indian beggar.

McGee provided another, no less grisly kind of entertainment. 'He'd come back from America with over-the-counter speed,' says Abbot. 'Ephedrine, which as anybody from speed culture knows, is the lowest sort there is: it has the most side-effects. He'd come in and go, "Do you want some of these?" I would never do gear at work, until we'd had the official word: "The Day Is Now Over." That sometimes would be at one o'clock. But Alan would use this stuff while he worked, as his way of getting through. He'd offer pills to the girls, 'cos the girls were always slimming. And I would judge how many he'd had, and find a reason to go up the West End or something, 'cos I knew that by three or four o'clock he'd be ready for an eruption.'

McGee's 'eruptions', in Abbot's recollection, were often focused on Brendan O'Donahue, Creation's accounts manager. 'He'd see the monthly bank figures, and it'd be, "Get Brendan down!" Lovely guy, Brendan; did his best. But Alan would spot a figure that was out, and that was it. "I don't know why I employ you, no-one would fuckin' employ you, you don't respect me, I look after you and what do you do? You fuckin' cunt." He'd come out with these really aggressive torrents, and they would become incredibly personalised.

'Just about everyone got it. He'd go on the tannoy and ask for six people to come down to The Bunker. Then he'd stand them in a line and fly at them: "I don't think you believe in what I'm doing. I don't think you respect me. Why do I pay you money?" And they'd just *take it*.' One of McGee's most oft-used rhetorical flourishes was 'this is not a democracy – it's a Fascist dictatorship'. 'The other one,' says Abbot, 'was, "You lot could learn a lot from Margaret Thatcher. She was great." He'd say it to wind up the lefties.'

The fate of Creation during 1991 was some token of the fact that it tended to stand at ninety degrees to the rest of the music industry. Though British rock music was hardly in rude health – squeezed by Nirvana and their ilk, unsure what to do in the wake of Acid House – the label managed to release three landmark albums: Primal Scream's *Screamadelica*, Teenage Fanclub's *Bandwagonesque* and My Bloody Valentine's *Loveless*. If Blur and the Syndrome clique were characterised by laziness and underachievement, these albums pointed a way out of the mire. In that sense, they conspired to couch Creation in visionary terms.

Screamadelica had built on the example of Loaded, melding the Primal Scream classic-rock approach to the music of clubland. In doing so, it both wired dance music into a decades-old tradition, and rendered old-school, Rolling Stones-esque rock newly exciting; the latter, in particular, was no mean feat. By way of a contrast, *Bandwagonesque* was an orthodox guitar record – but rather than being hoary and reverential, if fused its traditionalism with an overwhelming sense of wit, warmth and soul.

Loveless, meanwhile, extended My Bloody Valentine's abstract rock to a place that their followers considered nothing less than visionary – most spectacularly, on a track called Soon, they managed a perfect evocation of the more lysergic side of the Ecstasy experience. There was but one drawback: behind the creation of *Loveless* lay a three-year saga of perfectionism, periods of creative paralysis and profligate expenditure. 'Fifteen thousand for a guitar loop,' tuts Tim Abbot. By the time it was completed, the album had cost Creation £270,000.

Such was one of the factors behind a jarring irony indeed: for all the label's artistic health, it was in deep financial trouble. Tim Abbot's innovations had brought a modicum of order, but his advice did not extend to Creation's books. Having employed an outside firm of accountants to peer inside, they received news that was not exactly unexpected. Creation were £1.3 million in debt. This time, it seemed unlikely that licensing chicanery and ephedrine tablets would pull them through.

News of Creation's predicament soon reached one Derek Green, the owner of an independent label called China, then responsible for The Levellers. In cahoots with one Brian Lane – the manager of the 70s prog-rock group Yes – he began talks with Creation about a partial buy-out. The idea, as Tim Abbot recalls, was to create an 'uber-independent', capable of finally delivering a cherished indie dream: the ability to confidently compete with the major labels, while holding fast to such indie totems as complete control for musicians and an adventurous policy towards new music. McGee's unease about the proposal was crystallised by his horrified discovery that Derek Green had been responsible for severing The Sex Pistols' fleeting contract with A&M Records in 1977. There was enough punk *esprit de corps* left in McGee to thus mark Green down as the enemy.

In the wake of that revelation, McGee resumed contact with Paul Russell, the chairman of the international, distinctly non-indie, not-exactly-punk-rock Sony Music. McGee had bumped into him in February 1992 at Heathrow Airport, and bemoaned Creation's per-formance in that week's singles chart; though Primal Scream's *Dixie Narco* EP had crash-landed at number twelve, Teenage Fanclub's What You Do To Me had stumbled to a halt twenty places lower. McGee, not entirely reasonably, blamed Pinnacle, the company charged with the distribution of Creation's records.

'My bands used to get really pissed off with me,' says McGee, ''cos I always used to release their records on the same day. I wanted two of my bands on *Top of the Pops* like the Roses and the Mondays. But all that used to happen was, the Creation audience used to go and buy one of the records and not buy the other. I was complaining, going, "Fucking Pinnacle." In retrospect, it wasn't Pinnacle's fault at all; it was just bad management by me. But Paul Russell said, "Well, you know *we'd* do a deal with you."'

Six months later, in full knowledge of the fact that the label was technically insolvent, Sony paid £2.5 million pounds for 49 per cent of Creation Records. 'The assets, primarily, were Primal Scream – flagship band – and Alan McGee – might find us another big band,' says McGee. To some, the sum that was handed over beggared belief; only a few months beforehand, the indie label One Little Indian had offered McGee £400,000 for the whole of the company. Now, however, McGee had joined the ranks of the wealthy. 'The afternoon he was driving back from Sony,' says Tim Abbot, 'he said, "Abbot, I'm a millionaire! I'm just going in the Rolls Royce showroom."'

'The anxiety disappeared,' says McGee. 'And I had money in my bank account for the first time in my life. One minute I had two thousand pounds, the next minute I had two-and-a-half million pounds.'

If Creation's new stability suggested that McGee could now cut down on his ongoing programme of self-medication, the reverse quickly proved to be true. In particular, his fresh riches underwrote a stepped-up fondness for cocaine. 'Did my drug habits escalate?' he considers. 'Yeah. They went up from one gramme to seven grammes. A day? Yeah. But I wasn't doing all seven grammes; I was probably giving away three-and-a-half of them.'

McGee was fleetingly concerned about hostility from the music press, expecting a slew of accusations that he had nullified his maverick status and sold out. As it turned out, the deal with Sony seemed to be accepted as an inevitable reflection of new music business realities. After all, the battle-lines of yore were becoming hard to map: Virgin and RCA had already founded independently distributed offshoots, while on the independent side, in early 1992, the increasingly battle-worn Factory label – once the very embodiment of art-driven indie ethics – had engaged in serious talks with Polygram. To use Andy Ross's phrase, the differences between indies and majors increasingly did seem to revolve around such trifles as the colour of their distribution vans.

Nonetheless, there were still enough pockets of indie fundamentalism to remind McGee what the old Living Room regulars might have made of his latest manoeuvre. Soon after the deal was finalised, he and Tim Abbot visited the Camden Palace, whose Tuesday nights were given over to indie-rock. 'Smells Like Teen Spirit was still a big record,' says Abbot. 'Me and him were looking over the balcony, saying, "Isn't it great when you hear a tune, and inside the first four bars people are just like, Waaargh!" We were like, "*That's* what it's about. That's the magic of rock'n'roll." We were on a high. And some guy came up and said, "Alan McGee?" He said, "Yeah." He said, "You fucking turncoat cunt," and spat at him. Alan was *so* freaked by it. We went back to his flat in Rotherhithe, and he was really, really freaked. I spent the night with him going. "This kid's a wanker. Why are you taking all this on board?" He was like, "What have I done, man?" It was as if someone had challenged him.'

Despite such barbs, it was hardly likely that McGee would quickly turn into a compliant part of the corporate machine. In the wake of the Sony deal, one of his first meetings with Creation's benefactors found his more insurrectionary instincts bursting forth within little more than an hour.

'Once the Sony deal was done,' says Tim Abbot, 'we had a meeting with them: me, Dick and Alan. Alan said, "I'm not being spoken to like this by these fucking cunts: we're going to stage a walk-out. If we don't get action on these three points, I'm going to kick you under the table, and we get up and walk out." We went in there, showed them the new videos, talked about the international side of things, and McGee went, "Right – I need another three hundred thousand pounds." There was a bit of toing and froing and then, "That's it!" Dick put his rucksack on, I got up, and out we went.

'I was like, "What a bluff that was." We got back to the office, and they'd been on the phone: "I think we can do it." It seemed to be, "Keep on feeding it, and he's going to strike gold." And McGee *did*. The crazy thing is, he got Oasis.'

CHAPTER 8

The Burnage Hillbillies

More often than not, those who have documented the early lives of Noel and Liam Gallagher have tumbled into the recounting of a myth that comes with all the poverty, tragedy and eventual redemption of a Dickens story. The place in which they spent the lion's share of their childhood has been portrayed accordingly. The semi-official Oasis biography, *Getting High*, by Paolo Hewitt, makes reference to the Gallaghers' roots among 'motorways, concrete and high-rises'. In a VH1 documentary screened in 1999, the narrator talks of a mother 'struggling to make a home for her teenage boys in the projects of Manchester', conjuring up images of some North-Western version of the Bronx.

Burnage, where the brothers spent most of their childhood, lies some distance from all this. A patchwork of residential streets and avenues to Manchester's south, it sits on the west side of Kingsway, the arterial road that links the city with the neatly trimmed Cheshire suburbs. Burnage borders the Heatons – middle-class enclaves of Stockport – and Didsbury, the Mancunian equivalent of Hampstead. Ashburn Avenue, the cul-de-sac where the Gallaghers grew up, is one of those inter-war municipal developments, conceived long before Britain's planners considered cramming families into functional boxes, where each house has a garden and the residents can luxuriate in a reasonable degree of privacy. Tellingly, it lies within walking distance of two golf courses.

Still, though Burnage does not quite fit the more fanciful accounts of the Gallaghers' history, one can understand why those surveying the tale have gone in for the stuff of tragedy-laden romance. The family's roots in rural Ireland are suffused with a genuine sense of struggle. Moreover, the cruelty that coursed around the Gallagher family home lent their lives a genuinely hellish aspect. If some of the best human stories are based on narratives of escape, Ashburn Avenue held plenty from which to flee.

Peggy Sweeney was born in Swinford, County Mayo, in June 1943, the fourth of eleven siblings. Her father was a labourer, employed by the local council, whose wage packet could hardly stretch to the wants of his ever-increasing brood. The girls in the family slept six to a bed. Their diet tended to be founded on such staples as milk, bread and potatoes. During the winter months, their footwear consisted of nothing more dressy than wellington boots; in the summer, they went barefoot. When Peggy was seven, her father left the family home, never to be seen again. Her mother couldn't cope: Peggy and her siblings thus spent six-and-a-half years in the care of the Sisters at a convent in Ballaghaderreen.

Peggy Sweeney left school at thirteen; her first job was as a nanny to the O'Hara family, who owned a local confectionery shop. Five years later, she travelled to Manchester, taking her place in a wave of Irish immigration that had been kick-started by post-war reconstruction. Initially, she worked as an orderly at the city's Central Station, before fleetingly returning to Swinford on account of her mother's ill health. When she went back to Manchester, she took a low-ranking clerical job with a mail-order company, and fell back into her noticeably quiet life. Though Manchester's Irish diaspora offered no end of bawdy nights out, Peggy Sweeney preferred to forgo such temptations and spend her evenings at home.

One Saturday night in 1964, she was spending a rare evening at the Astoria club, an Irish ballroom on Plymouth Grove. She fell into conversation with a builder from County Meath named Tommy Gallagher, a quiet man whose gentlemanliness seemed to be underlined by the fact that he was teetotal. They courted for nine months, and were married at the Holy Name Church on Oxford Road in March 1965. Perhaps indicating that there was something not quite right about their union, the bride's guests numbered well over thirty. Tommy Gallagher brought along only a best man, who in turn was accompanied by his girlfriend.

By May 1967, the couple had two sons, Paul, born in January 1966, and Noel, who followed sixteen months later. They lived in Longsight, an urban neighbourhood a stone's throw from where they had first met. It soon became clear that Tommy Gallagher was not best suited to family life: in addition to the fits of violence he visited on his wife, he treated his offspring with a capriciousness that lent their days a constant sense of anxiety. The merest transgression might be avenged with a beating; worse still, his family had to tolerate the tyrannical moralism of a father whose own conduct endlessly went against his own rhetoric. 'He'd give me a hard time for not going to school and robbing shops, and he's just beaten me mam up,' Noel Gallagher later reflected. 'Hello? Is there anybody there?' Such was the unease he spread in his wake that both of his sons developed stammers, only cured after lengthy spells of speech therapy.

A third son, christened William and swiftly renamed Liam, arrived in September 1972, whereupon the family relocated to Burnage. Liam had notably softer features than his brothers, a difference underlined by the age-gap that divided them. To some extent, he lived the life of an only child – something perhaps reflected in his recurrent wish to be the centre of attention. In his primary school nativity plays, he managed to secure the roles of one of the three wise men, Joseph and King Herod. In Peggy Gallagher's remembrance of the latter part, the fact that he forgot his lines was craftily obscured by a spontaneous impression of Elvis Presley.

Soon after Liam's birth, Tommy Gallagher established a concreting business, and fared well enough to afford the hitherto-unimaginable luxury of a family car. Unfortunately, his new-found success did not improve the atmosphere within the Gallagher household: with her husband ever-more distant from the business of family life, and his paltry engagement with his wife and children characterised by the usual explosions of violence, Peggy Gallagher surmised that she had reached the end of her tether.

'He'd be in a mood, come in, smash the glass in the door, and when he'd upset everyone he'd get dressed up to the nines and go out the door, head up in the air, not a bother on him, get in his car, and you wouldn't see him again for two or three days,' she later recalled, when all the disruption and endless hurt was a mercifully distant memory. 'Then he'd come back again at the usual time on Monday morning, looking for his breakfast as if he wasn't doing a thing wrong.' Unfortunately, with the cautionary warnings of the Catholic church echoing around her, it took Peggy Gallagher until 1976 to acquire a legal notice of separation, and a further six years to finally lead her sons to a new home.

By then, the effects of the family's fractured home life on the Gallagher children were becoming clear. Paul was a nervous, bashful youth, whose lack of self-esteem was only heightened by a portliness that arrived in adolescence. Liam, long used to a domestic set-up that frequently teetered into riotous disorder, was proving increasingly uncontrollable. Noel's disquiet manifested itself in a moodiness and propensity for solitude that peaked during the early part of his teens. Nonetheless, with the family's exit from Tommy Gallagher's immediate orbit, he became the de facto head of the household.

The Gallaghers were not the kind of family whose progress was likely to be marked by high academic achievement. Besides, any chance of educational progress had been rather offset by their father's habit of dragging his sons to week-night card games, where they would stand sentry with a glass of Coca-Cola until the wee hours. Within a couple of years of enrolling at St Mark's, an all-male Catholic comprehensive, Noel Gallagher was falling into the ways of the habitual truant; when his mother took a job as one of the school's dinner ladies, he altered his daily routine to include a brief lunchtime visit to school, so as to assure her that he was remaining on the straight and narrow. As it increasingly became clear, however, he was frequently up to no good: his teens saw two appearances before a juvenile court, on charges of both shoplifting and minor burglary.

Like Paul Gallagher, Noel left school unencumbered by qualifications. His only immediate option was to follow his elder brother into the kind of manual labour that had been the lot of his father; upward social mobility, the dream that even a pessimistic parent cannot help but project on to their children, was a faint hope indeed. As he sat in the family's new living room, staring into a future that seemed to offer nothing much at all, Peggy Gallagher asked him that most rhetorical of parental questions: '*What* is going to become of you?'

Despite their split from Tommy Gallagher, his sons maintained contact with their father, if only because his work within the construction trade offered them an easy route to casual earnings. The family's troubled history, however, inevitably impacted on their work. 'We'd turn up in this yellow transit van, all sat in the back,' said Noel. 'Because we were always arguing we'd still be working at nine o'clock every night. Then we'd argue about whose fault it was we were late and then, when we got home, Mam had had the dinner in the oven for hours and she'd start kicking off. Years of just rowing. We were the Clampetts, the Burnage Hillbillies.'

As well as several lifetimes' worth of seething resentment, Tommy Gallagher had bequeathed his son one item of potential use: an acoustic guitar, bought on a whim and left to gather dust until Noel tentatively began to master its rudiments during his mid-teens. Among the first pieces he successfully performed was House Of The Rising Sun, whose succession of arpeggios has long been used by aspirant virtuosos to prove that they are au fait with a little more than the three-chord trick. It did not take long for his efforts to extend into the writing of songs, scrawled on to scraps of paper that increasingly littered the floor of the bedroom he shared with Liam. His first composition was based around the chords of G, E minor, C and D. Its chorus, perhaps betraying an early fondness for the kind of homespun wisdom that verges on cliché, went, 'And life goes on, but the world will never change.'

In November 1983, Noel's ambitions were decisively catalysed by a striking arrival on the weekly TV show that has put a rocket under so many teenage lives. 'When The Smiths came on *Top of the Pops* for the first time, that was it for me,' he later reflected. That night's per-formance – of This Charming Man, their second single – is still cited by many Smiths disciples as a watershed moment, but most accounts focus on the compelling presence of Morrissey. Noel, however, was transfixed by the figure to his left: the stick-thin embodiment of rock'n'roll cool who was the group's guitar player and Morrissey's co-songwriter. 'From that day on I was . . . I wouldn't say . . . Yes, I probably would say, I wanted to *be* Johnny Marr,' he said. The aspir-ation was not as unlikely as it sounded: with the exception of their drummer, Mike Joyce, The Smiths were working-class South Mancuni-ans of Irish extraction.

It was Noel Gallagher's good fortune to be a young resident of Manchester just as it moved through a musical phase of quite unprece-dented fertility. To no little heartbreak, The Smiths broke up in Sep-tember 1987, but by the spring of the following year, the first stirrings of their successors were becoming audible. Happy Mondays were about to record *Bummed*; The Stone Roses would soon release a single entitled Elephant Stone and decisively begin their ascent. The mood of height-ened excitement was only furthered by the frantic scenes being played out at the Haçienda: for any young Mancunian hovering around their teens or early twenties, one visit would usually be enough to convince them that they were in exactly the right place at precisely the right time.

In May 1988, Noel – accompanied by his younger brother – went to see The Stone Roses play at the International 2 Club, the ballroom-turned-rock venue once known as the Astoria, in which their mother had shared her first conversation with Tommy Gallagher. Perhaps proving that the politicised mores of the 80s indie milieu had also seeped into the culture that superseded it, the event – headlined by the Manchester-based group James – was organised to raise funds for the campaign against Clause 28, the startling item of Conservative legisla-tion aimed at outlawing the 'promotion' of homosexuality by local councils.

In among the crowd was a figure Noel thought he recognised, furtively taping the group's performance. Fortified by a pocketful of amphetamine sulphate, Noel asked him if he would consider making him a copy of his illicit recording. As it turned out, the name of the small-time bootlegger was Graham Lambert: he was the guitarist with a group called Inspiral Carpets.

Inspiral Carpets were from Oldham. Their geographical distance from cutting-edge developments in Manchester was reflected in their music: rough-hewn, 60s-influenced stuff, inspired by such cultish purveyors of American garage-rock as The Seeds and? And The Mysterians. However, by simple dint of the timing of their arrival – along with the fact that their songs had a slight psychedelic aspect – they were already being included in the moment inaugurated by the Roses and Mondays.

At the end of the year, Noel caught word of an unexpected opportunity. Inspiral Carpets' vocalist, one Steve Holt, was about to leave the group; via his acquaintance with Graham Lambert, Noel applied for the job. 'He'd been to a lot of our gigs by then,' says Clint Boon, the group's keyboard player and senior member. 'We knew him as one of our keenest fans. Even when he broke his leg, he turned up to gigs with his leg in plaster. He came to us and said, "Look, I've heard you're looking for a singer – I want to audition." That didn't make a lot of sense, 'cos we saw him as a fan. He was just this guy that we knew: a scally with a broken leg and funny eyebrows.'

Despite Boon's bafflement, Noel's audition was scheduled for the evening of 21st December, soon to enter history as the night of the Lockerbie air disaster. He arrived at The Mill, the group's rehearsal room in Ashton-Under-Lyne, and was handed a sheaf of the group's lyrics. If the group expected some callow applicant, grateful simply to be given a try, his demeanour suggested an altogether more irreverent approach. 'He was laughing, taking the piss out of my words,' says Clint Boon. 'We had this song called Whiskey: it just listed the bizarre things that boys do when they go out. He started going, "Who the fuck wrote this?"' Noel's most noteworthy performance that night was on the group's cover of The Rolling Stones' Gimme Shelter, slowed down to the point of unrecognisability, over which he attempted to ape the bellowing vocal style of Shaun Ryder.

This was not what Inspiral Carpets were after. 'What we were looking for was almost like a crooner,' says Clint Boon. 'The previous singer had a big voice.' The successful candidate was one Tom Hingley, the son of an Oxford academic who sang with a long-lost indie group called Too Much Texas, and possessed the required tremulous baritone. Thanks to his air of unshakeable cockiness, however, Noel Gallagher remained in Inspiral Carpets' thoughts. So it was that in May 1989, he climbed into the group's van and travelled with them to an engagement in Leeds. He was now on their payroll as the group's only roadie.

For any group who aspired to inclusion in the same bracket as Happy Mondays and The Stone Roses, it was de rigueur to have one or more associate members, there to roll the spliffs, throw their penneth into group discussions and hover in the wings. Happy Mondays' entourage included a figure named Muzzer, a lifelong friend of Shaun Ryder who acted as the group's fixer and confidante; The Roses travelled with one Steve Cresser, who would advise them about trouser widths, dance at the back of the stage and occasionally be allowed into their photographs. The Mancunian groups were built on the idea of the band-as-gang: the inclusion of such people in their number seemed to underwrite their aesthetic.

In his own way, Noel Gallagher – whom the group nicknamed 'Monobrow' – became Inspiral Carpets' equivalent. 'He was a vital part of us,' says Clint Boon. 'I can honestly say he was an inspiration to the band. Just in the type of person he was: a total Manchester dude, more than any of us lot. He knew what was going on. Some bands would call that person a guru, wouldn't they? In terms of the spirit of what Manchester was at that time, I felt like I fed off Noel.'

Noel's integral role with the Inspirals – not to mention the £350 they eventually paid him each week – allowed him to be at the centre of Mancunian developments. With his girlfriend Louise Jones, he lived in a converted warehouse on Whitworth Street – close to the Haçienda, where he became an enthusiastic regular. He was also a recurrent presence at gigs by those groups who were seeking to follow in Happy Mondays and The Stone Roses' esteemed footsteps: one Manchester musician remembers occasional conversations with 'this dead friendly, smiley bloke who looked like John Noakes'.

The rising Mancunian wave soon transported Inspiral Carpets to the kind of places that most of their peers could only dream about. In early 1990, they had their first hit: an unbelievably solemn ode to small-town ennui entitled This Is How It Feels, which reached Number fourteen. That summer, they were one of the headline acts at the Reading Festival, laying on an admirably ostentatious spectacle that climaxed with an appearance by a troupe of drum majorettes. By then, Inspiral Carpets' retinue had expanded to the point that Noel Gallagher could delegate a great deal of the more unpleasant aspects of his job. 'He wasn't the hardest working roadie in the world,' says Boon. 'You'd very rarely see him sweating. But we didn't really want that. We weren't Dire Straits.'

On one occasion, Noel departed from his brief in no little style. An aspirant writer named Stella Blackburn came to an Inspirals show at a Swindon venue named the Oasis, hoping to interview the group, only to have her approaches turned down flat. Suggesting that his self-image was a few notches above his place in the group's hierarchy, Noel suggested that she interview him ('If I was in a band, I'd do an interview with any cunt,' she was warmly assured). Her first question concerned the current state of UK music; the answer included a passing tribute to a London-based group who were then enjoying their first fleeting taste of success. 'Current charts?' he mused. 'Chesney Hawkes – bag of shit, right, but Gary Clail and that, Inspirals, Happy Mondays, Ride, Blur and all them lot, it's good that they're all in the charts. Very, very, very healthy indeed.'

Both on and off the road, Noel tended to keep the company of one Mark Coyle, another second-generation Irish Mancunian, who was employed as Inspiral Carpets' monitor engineer. Coyle was an accomplished guitarist and small-time curator of the music of the 60s, with a pronounced fondness for the early work of the Bee Gees, along with an enviable knowledge of The Beatles. It was Coyle, via a stream of home-made compilation tapes, who stirred his friend's memories of the latter group – surely latent within every British mind – and began to flesh out his understanding of their music. The two would spend time at Inspiral Carpets soundchecks, indulging in elongated readings of Lennon-McCartney songs, endlessly trying to unpick their magic.

They also developed a fondness for the kind of stimulants that have long powered those who spend their lives seeing to the needs of rock groups: chiefly, cocaine. 'I was a party animal in a different sort of way from them,' says Clint Boon. 'I wasn't into the same substances. I was a fucking alkie. They were very rock'n'roll. Towards the end, that was one of the reasons why things changed: his use of it and our non-use of it. That was an issue. When you're on it, you're beautiful, aren't you? But when you're off it, and you're in the middle of Eastern Europe and you can't find any, you become a gargoyle.' Unbeknownst to Boon, Coyle and Noel regularly hid their supplies in the casing of his organ.

Inspiral Carpets were sufficiently successful to enable them to travel to the kind of places that lay several light years from the UK's workaday concert circuit. On one occasion, the group played with Paul Simon at the River Plate Stadium in Buenos Aires; on another, they found themselves on the bill for an outdoor event in the freshly liberated Republic of Estonia, then marking its new-found freedom by staging outdoor events featuring deeply unlikely combinations of British rock acts.

'That was a big festival,' says Clint Boon. 'Bob Geldof was finishing on one stage, and we were due to start on the other stage. And he was going a bit over time. So Noel got on the mike and started shouting, "Geldof! Fuck off! It's time for the Inspirals! Come on! Make it your last one!" He was doing it in between songs: Bob Geldof would say, "This is a new song" and Noel would go, "Come on, you cunt! Knock it on the head!"'

Noel Gallagher was in the USA when he heard that his younger brother was about to make his first public appearance as a vocalist. His group were scheduled to play the Boardwalk – the venue that provided the backdrop to just about every Mancunian group's first steps – on 11 August 1991. Their name was taken from an Inspiral Carpets poster that had been blu-tacked on Liam's bedroom wall: thanks to the afore-mentioned engagement in Swindon, his band was called Oasis.

Three-quarters of the membership was drawn from a group who had been known as The Rain. They had made sporadic performances at the kind of venues that could not help but put a cap on any sky-scraping aspirations: their first show took place in the unspeakably rock'n'roll environs of Withington Bridge Club. Their singer and lyricist was a Burnage local named Chris Hutton: history records that his most not-able work was a song written in tribute to those involved in the Strange-ways Prison Riot of April 1990. In an admirable attempt to link the disorder with the Acid House upsurge, the composition was called Rooftop Rave. Its lyrics were no less inventive: 'See Paul Taylor on the roof/Playing a tune on his guitar/What about the rest of the boys?/ They're having a rave on the roof.'

For much of his adolescence, Liam Gallagher had displayed precious little interest in rock music, preferring to listen to hip hop and indulge in the associated rituals: for a time, he would occasionally display his breakdancing talent outside the Burnage branch of Kwik Save. His mind was changed by the arrival of The Stone Roses, and Ian Brown in particular. The night Liam accompanied his brother to the Inter-national 2 marked his induction into the Roses' cult: in May 1990, he was one of the 30,000 disciples who made their way to Spike Island, portrayed by at least one over-excited journalist as 'the Woodstock of a new generation'. The essence of Brown's persona was the magnifying of a very Mancunian identity into a deeply theatrical style of perform-ance. His feet-out swagger and air of arrogance – not to mention his predilection for flared trousers – were common currency among the city's young men, but Brown was the first to take the package on to the national stage. He was also the first rock vocalist to stake a claim for the Manchester accent. As proved by his performance on *The Stone Roses*, against formidable odds, he managed to make it sound unimpeachably cool.

None of this was lost on Liam Gallagher. If rock music had hitherto represented an arcane, alien world, Ian Brown's success fired a sudden desire to follow him on to the stage – and The Rain, made up of people with whom he shared a nodding local acquaintance, came to represent a possible focus for his ambitions. Having seen them play at a venue named Times Square in Didsbury, Liam began showing up at their rehearsals. In the Mancunian vernacular, Chris Hutton thought he was little more than a 'Klingon': one of those blighted strays who makes an art of repeatedly turning up uninvited.

The Rain's senior member was Paul Arthurs, long known as Bonehead on account of his childhood predilection for brutally cropped haircuts (though the name was given renewed aptness by his rapidly receding hairline). Increasingly convinced that the group's future should not include Chris Hutton, he soon auditioned Liam in the front room of a house he shared with his girlfriend in Fallowfield, asking him to improvise lyrics to an instrumental piece that blared from his stereo. Liam managed two lines, 'She always comes up smiling/And playing with her hair', delivering them with enough brio to land him the job. 'I always thought those words had a blow job connection,' says Arthurs. 'He could sing, anyway. My girlfriend said he sounded like a nightingale.'

Liam Gallagher duly took his place alongside Arthurs, Paul McGuigan, – the group's taciturn bass player – and a just-about-competent drummer named Tony McCarroll. On and off, the quartet rehearsed for four months, managing to come up with no more than four songs. Their best was Take Me, an energised if rather monotonous composition whose lyrics – 'Take me while I'm young and true/Was it me or was it you?' – managed to suggest an unwitting ode to gay sex. Liam Gallagher sang such lines in the same disaffected whine that Ian Brown brought to The Stone Roses; the few awkward movements that formed his performance style were cribbed from the same source.

The show at the Boardwalk, supporting a fleetingly feted band called Sweet Jesus, was the group's debut. Noel turned up with Louise Jones and the lion's share of the Inspiral Carpets to behold a band who prompted little more than nods of muted appreciation. 'It was good, but there was no indication of what they'd turn into,' says Clint Boon. 'They were A Good Local Band Inspired By Ian Brown. None of us came away thinking they were brilliant.' Noel, however, saw the faint possibility of something more promising.

The songs he had been scribbling down since his first experiments with Tommy Gallagher's acoustic guitar were now spilling out at speed, though he had no outlet for them aside from his snatched moments at Inspiral Carpets soundchecks. Over the next week, the idea began to crystallise; soon enough, Noel Gallagher suggested to his brother that he might join the group. 'I said, "Right, if I join this band – and I mean it, right – you fucking belong to me seven days a week and we're going for it big time,"' Noel later recalled. If his pitch sounded so tyrannical as to cast the members of his brother's group as rehearsal-room serfs, none of them voiced any objections.

'He had loads of stuff written,' says Paul Arthurs. 'When he walked in, we were a band making a racket with four tunes. All of a sudden, there were loads of ideas. Very quickly, you could hear it: "Something'll happen with this."'

A reel exists of early Oasis material, recorded not long after they became a quintet. Contrary to the cartoon-strip version of their early progress – that Noel joined, enforced his leadership, and had them playing classic pop songs in no time – it suggests that there was a period of awkward transition, during which the group were still creatively treading water. Though the songs are all competently arranged, Noel's compositions – Colour My Life, See The Sun, I Will Show You – are scarcely more accomplished than those authored before his arrival. Moreover, at least two pre-Noel songs evidently remained in the group's repertoire: the aforementioned Take Me, and an utterly dismal ballad entitled Life In Vain, to which he added a desultory guitar solo. Its lyrics, sung by Liam in a voice so flat as to be almost unlistenable, are downright strange: 'A better life is all I need/To free me from this naughty league.'

The group's first show with Noel – again, at The Boardwalk – took place on 15 January 1992. This was hardly the best time for a Mancunian group to be setting out its wares. That month, Happy Mondays set off for Barbados, to begin work on an album that would be all but ruined by Shaun Ryder's discovery of the island's abundant supply of crack cocaine. *Yes Please* cost Factory Records in excess of £300,000, and promptly stiffed; by the autumn, the label was sliding towards a bankruptcy that would finally be declared in November. Factory's one reliable asset, The Haçienda, was plagued by both the activities of Manchester's drug gangs and the indifference of the city's police: in desperation, it paid close to £400,000 to one gang – protection money, in all but name – to man the door. To cap it all, The Stone Roses had disappeared, beginning a hiatus that would finally be broken in late 1994. Little more than eighteen months after it had been declared a Day-Glo countercultural Eden, Manchester seemed to be in the grip of a particularly traumatic hangover.

Had Oasis made their public debut when the city was at the height of its musical potency, they might well have signed a record contract within months. As it was, the London-based labels who had sent droves of A&R people to buy up any groups with the requisite accents had long since called them home. Neither did the local music industry offer much hope: Phil Saxe, Factory's chief talent scout, fleetingly considered recruiting Oasis to the label, only to be told that the money had run out. They were not the only group that Saxe had to drop from his thoughts: he had also been interested in a group from Sheffield called Pulp.

If Noel Gallagher needed decisive confirmation that his home city was in decline, the fate of Inspiral Carpets perhaps said it all. By 1992, the days of headlining British festivals and wowing the Estonians were an increasingly distant memory; these days, they were adjusting to their re-entry to the British college circuit, and paring back their outflows. On the eve of a trip to the USA, it was decided to excise their senior roadie from the payroll. 'We had to break it to Noel that he wasn't coming to America with us,' says Clint Boon. 'Part of the reason was the gap between us to do with substances, but the band wasn't at its peak then: we were having to cut corners. Oasis were rehearsing down-stairs from us at The Boardwalk. The rest of them had gone home: Noel was there on his own, working, and we went to see him. It was fucking sad. He was really cut up.'

In between trips to the DHSS, Noel's sole focus was now his group. They stuck to a diligent rehearsal regime, eventually meeting at The Boardwalk's rehearsal room five nights a week. By now, they were starting to play songs that occupied a more rarefied place than their early material: their repertoire included two new adrenalised songs entitled Rock'n'Roll Star and Bring It On Down, and they had begun work on a soaring, untypically anthemic composition entitled Live Forever. Moreover, Noel had now turned his new colleagues' beginners-level technique to their advantage.

Under Noel's tutelage, Oasis adopted a musical approach of brutal simplicity: Paul Arthurs was instructed to stick to bar chords, meaning that his fingers need never alter their basic configuration; Paul McGuigan's bass played little more adventurous than root notes; Tony McCarroll took comfort from the fact that his basic 4/4 rhythms were seemingly all that was required. When the group's amplifiers were turned up to the point of distortion, the resulting din was positively monolithic: a sound so devoid of finesse and complexity that it came out sounding pretty much unstoppable.

Between Noel's first performance and the summer of 1993, Oasis played only twelve shows, all in the North West, aside from one incongruous booking at Dartford Polytechnic. That May, however, they were offered the tantalising prospect of a show at Glasgow's King Tut's Wah Wah Hut. The approach came from a three-quarters female band called Sister Lovers, with whom they shared their rehearsal space at The Boardwalk: they suggested Oasis make up the numbers at a gig headlined by 18 Wheeler, four young Scots who had just signed to August, an offshoot of Creation Records. There was but one drawback: in the flurry of excitement preceding the engagement, no-one thought to inform the venue's management that Oasis were coming.

Upon arrival, they were told that an appearance that night, however brief, was out of the question. In the Gallaghers' more colourful accounts of the episode, they responded to the news with a series of threats to lay waste to the club, and the staff swiftly gave way. The notion of Glasgow's pre-eminent rock venue being so easily manipulated rather beggars belief; in fact, their co-operation was secured by a mixture of pressure from the other groups on the bill, and an eventual spurt of sympathy.

'There was a big scene when we got there,' says Paul Arthurs. 'The promoter was saying, "Who the fuck are you?" "Well, we were told we could come up and do a quick support." He was like, "Fucking *no*." There was loads of argument: "Come on – we've come all this way, let us do four songs." And the geezer was like, "Go on then – get on." I don't remember it being a particularly good gig. We were on double early; there was no-one in there. But after we came off, Noel said, "See that geezer there? That's Alan McGee. He's just asked me, 'Have you got a record deal? Do you want one?'"'

McGee was in Glasgow visiting his sister Susan, and was planning to return to London the following day. The presence of 18 Wheeler at King Tut's must have been a key factor in his visit to the venue – he was, after all, President of the label who financed them – but he has also made mention of the fact that he was in pursuit of a possible female conquest. He was a friend of one Debbie Turner, a member of Sister Lovers who first made his acquaintance in 1989. What is certain is that he effectively entered King Tut's by mistake: he expected the headline act to take the stage at 9pm, little realising that they now had a late licence.

As a result, he clapped eyes on Liam Gallagher – a magnetic presence who, McGee later claimed, reminded him of the young Paul Weller – and then watched as he took the stage. Oasis played a mere four songs: Rock'n'Roll Star, Bring It On Down, Up In The Sky, and their new, gloriously scabrous version of I Am The Walrus, placed in the set as a very public demonstration of the Beatles-worship that had by now spread from Noel to his colleagues. This, in McGee's telling, was enough to convince him that he should sign the group to Creation. Mark Coyle was responsible for the sound that night: in response to McGee's enquiries about whether Oasis had a manager, he pointed him in the direction of Noel Gallagher. McGee came away with a ten-song demo cassette and a Manchester telephone number.

'He phoned us up that night, off his nut, from Sauchiehall Street,' says Tim Abbot. 'He was with a load of people from his Glasgow clan, and they were all going absolutely mental. He said, "We've got to get together tomorrow; I've got this fucking amazing band." It was the next day that he told me what they were all about. He played me the stuff and it was just amazing. The most attack ever, on any music you'll ever hear. It was like, "Fuck!" Ride were recording in Oxford that week: we drove out to see them, and we were playing these demos and rocking the car, banging the roof, going, "Punk rock! Rock 'n' roll!"'

Four days after their meeting in Glasgow, Noel, Liam and Paul Arthurs travelled to the offices of Creation Records. 'There was just this chaos: loads of people, no sense of order anywhere,' says Arthurs. 'It was, "Fuck me – what's this *about*?" We expected a big mahogany table and some big proposal.'

The kind of powdered hospitality that was de rigueur at Creation was duly offered up – and enthusiastically accepted, at least by the Gallagher brothers – before the Oasis party were further entertained. 'We just sat with McGee and Tim Abbot and talked about music,' says Arthurs. 'Then they took us round the corner to the warehouse: carrier bag each, full of stuff. We were like, "Free CDs!" We sold them as soon as we got home.'

'I was very intrigued by Liam,' says Abbot. 'He looked fucking amazing. He looked like what I'd like to think I looked like when I was sixteen: this great feathercut, a green kagoul.' If the younger Gallagher seemed to fit Abbot's idea of the archetypal young gunslinger, his behaviour only confirmed it: when a passing Creation staff member enquired about the design on the cover of the Oasis demo – the colours of the Union Jack arranged in a vortex, as if being sucked down the plughole – Liam dispensed a snarling reply. His words, in the right-on days of 1993, must have sounded striking indeed. 'It's the greatest flag in the world and it's going down the shitter,' he said. 'We're here to do something about it.'

In the wake of his first trip to Creation, Noel Gallagher made a return visit in the company of Mark Coyle. This time, he was quickly acquainted with the kind of lunacy that frequently coursed around the label's headquarters. That afternoon's episode concerned Momus, the Scots solo artist whose 1987 Creation album *Tender Pervert* is described in *The Great Alternative & Indie Discography* as 'a compelling set of narratives centering on such cheery topics as incest, paedophilia and bestiality'.

'Momus had run off with this sixteen-year-old Sikh girl,' says Tim Abbot. 'The family found out: he was this twenty-nine-year-old, writing songs about bestiality and buggery and teenage girls. We had six hockey-stick-wielding, tooled-up vigilantes come round, going, "You know where he is." It's like, "*No, we don't.*" So we were having this row, shitting ourselves, and Noel and Coyley just walked in.' Once things had calmed down, the conversation that followed drew Oasis ever nearer to Creation. This time, however, Alan McGee's enthusiasm was accompanied by one item of hard-headed advice: if Oasis were going to make any progress, they needed a manager.

It was now that fate played Noel Gallagher an ace. Around the time of the Glasgow show, he had passed an Oasis tape to one Ian Marr, the actor brother of Johnny, in the hope that his one-time hero might give it his attention. To his awe-struck surprise, he heard from an enthusiastic Johnny Marr soon after: having fallen into a conversation about guitars, the two set out on a trip to a music shop in Doncaster, where Noel witnessed one of the benefits of Marr's enviable wealth. 'I'm skint and on the dole,' he later marvelled, 'and I'm stood behind Johnny Marr at the counter, who's spending nine-and-a-half thousand pounds on guitars. And I'm thinking, "This is what it's about! This is what it fucking means! Sooner or later this is what I've got to be!"' When the pair chewed over Oasis's aspirations, Noel told Marr about the absence of a manager: Marr duly alerted Marcus Russell, the chief of a management company called Ignition.

Russell was a native of Ebbw Vale, who had spent a sizeable portion of his working life as an Economics teacher in Harlow. His first musical charges as a manager were a group called Latin Quarter, a stereotypically 80s attraction whose biggest British hit was a treatise on Third World strife called Radio Africa, released in 1986. In the wake of the demise of The Smiths, Russell had begun managing Marr, which in turn led to the same role with the latter's sometime collaborators The

The. Soft-spoken and often keen to deflate the music industry's more cloudbusting rhetoric, Russell had a reputation for caution rather than braggadocio. 'He's not a Peter Grant or a Robert Stigwood,' says one ex-associate. 'He hasn't got this big world vision. With him, it's kind of a fortnight ahead, a month ahead. He relies on the skills of the people that he's cut the deal with.' In June, Marr took him to see Oasis at Manchester University, where they were supporting the London-based trio Dodgy. It did not take long for Russell to make up his mind: within days, he had offered to fill the Oasis camp's most pressing vacancy.

So it was that he began to work through the group's affairs. Though his role was confirmed via a handshake, the first months after his appointment saw the formalisation of all manner of details: it was this period, according to Paul Arthurs, that saw a legal agreement that decreed that should the band split up, the rights to the name Oasis would be exclusively held by Noel and Liam. Though happy to work on the assumption that the group would sign to Creation, Russell also began to solicit interest from American labels, eventually surmising that they should sign with the US branch of Epic, part of the ever-expanding Sony Music group.

There was only one problem. Though Creation were financially dependent on Sony, thanks to one of the myriad international deals that Alan McGee had signed in an attempt to keep his company afloat, the label was committed to an American firm called SBK – coincidentally, the same set-up who had played a sizeable role in Blur's American nightmare in 1992 – who had first refusal on the American release of Creation's output. The upshot was simple: the contracts Oasis wanted to sign for the US and UK were mutually incompatible.

The eventual way out of the impasse was as convoluted as the web of McGee's overseas agreements. Oasis signed a worldwide contract with Sony's Licensed Repertoire Division, thus committing them to the US wing of Epic. Sony then licensed them to Creation for the UK. They were the first British act to end up on Creation's roster via such an expedient, though this intriguing technicality was never mentioned during the first phase of their progress. (When rumours of the arrangement began to surface in 1995, the music industry's customary vulnerability to Chinese whispers led to altogether more scandalous stories. According to one particularly churlish theory, the whole King Tut's story had been fabricated, so as to lend Oasis the kind of credibility that a deal with the British arm of Sony would have ruled out. This, it can be safely stated, was nonsense.)

Confirming that Marcus Russell was no hothead, Sony paid Oasis a modest advance of £40,000. The same month, they played another show at The Boardwalk and received their first *NME* review, written by one Emma Morgan, a 17-year-old resident of the South Mancunian suburbs who was the paper's North Western correspondent. 'They're not perfect,' she wrote, 'they might find it hard instinctively to impress, but they still stomp out the kind of terrifyingly memorable tunes that most bands forgot how to make as they blundered around on the periphery of true talent. Sound-wise, they're slightly reminiscent of a drugged-up (ahem) version of The Stone Roses. It's almost as though everyone's favourite stroppily invisible Mancs have grown up and decided to take it slow this time, in the process swapping loon pants and T-shirts for sensible trousers and M&S pullovers.'

Through October, November and December, Oasis toured the UK, as a supporting feature to The Verve, St Etienne, and a typically off-beam Creation act called The BMX Bandits. In Birmingham, they were judged by their second *NME* reviewer, who took the crux of Morgan's praise – that Oasis were following an example set by The Stone Roses – and used it against them. 'If Oasis didn't exist, no-one would want to invent them,' wrote Johnny Cigarettes. 'For a start, they look and sound like they're a long overdue product from a bankrupt scally also-rans factory. Vaguely trippy guitar, almost-tunes with vaguely late 60s rock tendencies, vaguely Ian-Brown-as-Tim-Burgess slob of a frontman, singing in a vaguely tuneless half-whine, vaguely shaking a tambourine, vaguely . . . well you get the picture. . . . They evidently have too few brains to realise that any of the above is true. Sad.'

Perhaps predictably, Liam Gallagher was incensed, publicly threatening to track down Johnny Cigarettes and exact violent retribution. At Creation, however, the article was greeted with a backhanded kind of jubilation. 'That review was great,' says Tim Abbot. 'Just, "Forget it." When that came in, we all went, "Great! Nobody understands them! We've done it!" That was one of Alan's things: sometimes terrible press is great press.'

As the year came to an end, Creation began to distribute the first Oasis record: a limited-edition 12-inch single, featuring a Noel Gallagher composition entitled Columbia. It was passed to Creation staff, journalists and radio programmers, by way of a trailer to the group's intended splashdown the following year. Much to Creation's surprise, Columbia – a menacing, mesmeric song, whose lyric came with a clear drugs subtext – found its most enthusiastic reception when it was delivered to Radio One: in the ensuing fortnight, it was played no less than nineteen times. For a record that was not available in the shops, this was unprecedented. Those who were involved in the plans for Oasis's next move began to feel an expectant sense of excitement.

On 27 January 1994, Oasis were booked to play London's Water Rats, a chintzy pub venue tucked behind the ragged bustle of King's Cross. By now, the patronage of Radio One and reports back from the group's provincial engagements had conspired to make them the subject of feverish music industry whispers: the result was a venue stuffed to capacity, and queues snaking down Gray's Inn Road. To the delight of the crowd, Oasis responded to such scenes with a display of the blank-faced insouciance that defined their style of performance. If that night's show – and the resultant ecstatic notices from the press – marked the decisive start of Oasis's ascent, one of their mentors seemed to be sliding in the opposite direction. Keith Cameron, one of the countless journalists who crowded into the Water Rats, stole a glance at Alan McGee in the taxi that took him from the gig. 'I remember looking in the window of that car and seeing Alan,' he says. 'I just remember thinking, "There's something wrong with him."' He seemed really frail, vulnerable, very helpless. He looked *frightened.*'

In the opening months of 1994, the sense that the musical landscape was shifting was palpable. The change was not merely a matter of new faces: surveying the journalism of the period, one also senses the last traces of past eras being finally consigned to irrelevance. What remained of 'right-on', the neurotic mindset fostered in the 80s, was the most visible casualty, not least when it came to tetchiness about music's new Anglo-centric turn.

One could make out the sea-change in the odd voice of protest. In 1993, the *NME* had passed through a revival of the politicised style that had marked its progress through much of the 1980s – and informed its coverage of Morrissey's flag-waving at Finsbury Park. Its latest prompt had been the election of a British National Party councillor called Derek Beackon on the Isle of Dogs in September 1993; there followed a special Anti-Fascist issue, and the brief lionisation of a handful of hectoring groups – Fun-Da-Mental, Blaggers ITA, the pious anarchist veterans Chumbawamba – who were pledged to the cause.

In January, there was a fleeting attempt to extend the agenda into a broadside against the ideas that had been crystallised by *Select*'s celebration of the renaissance of British music. It was written by Steven Wells, the *NME*'s resident battle-scarred left-winger, someone sufficiently in thrall to the ways of the Old Left to confidently draw a line between racist councillors and pop groups and journalists who were fond of The Kinks. 'Sections of the British rock press spew forth a nauseating mixture of bravado, hysteria and xenophobia,' he raged. 'The kind of sneering, desperate guff that you often hear in ex-imperial nations which refuse to believe that, despite their former power and glory, they simply don't mean jack shit to anyone any more.

'Defining a defendable "British rock music" under such circumstances is at best naive and at worst, casually racist,' he went on. 'Doing so at a time when Nazism and racism are undergoing a Europe-wide renaissance verges on the contemptible.' This rather bizarre blast reads like a last stand; from January onwards, the idea of a new British rock, replete with the 'sense of place' that rapidly became a critical cliché, edged ever closer to the mainstream.

First into the fray were Elastica, whose first widely available single was released on 31 January. Line Up was a brittle joke at the expense of some unnamed starstruck hanger-on, whose life revolved around the parade of groups who passed through the pages of the music papers. Its title came from Justine Frischmann's wry observation that the press was in the ongoing habit of placing groups on its conveyor belt, well knowing that all but a few would quickly topple off. By way of rooting the song in the venues of North London, its chorus found her voice tumbling into estuary vowels, so that 'line' became 'loin'. 'It was a very knowing little ditty,' she says. 'So about the music press, it was a bit stupid.'.

It entered the chart at number twenty, guaranteeing Elastica their inaugural appearance on *Top of the Pops*. The group thus rubbed shoulders with the musical jet-set, despite the fact that two of their number were still living in alarmingly pinched circumstances. 'We still had no money,' says Donna Matthews. 'Me and Justin had to move to a squat in Islington. We were living there when we played *Top of the Pops*. I remember getting ready: the squat we were in was leaking, so there was ice on the stairs. At the top of the stairs there was a door: if you opened it and stepped out, there was nothing there, 'cos the other half of the house had been demolished. It opened out to a fifty-foot drop, down into a pile of rubble.'

Two weeks after Line Up came Suede's new single, Stay Together. If its opulent packaging – like a double album, its vinyl version came in a gatefold sleeve – seemed designed to confirm that the group had left their indie peer group behind, the music it contained made the point explicit. In some part, Stay Together was Bernard Butler's attempt to tap into the same majesty that Phil Spector had managed on The Righteous Brothers' You've Lost That Lovin' Feelin': though its opening three minutes were based on orthodox pop aesthetics, it soon spiralled into music of an altogether more ambitious stripe, stuffed with horns and pianos, finally tumbling to a close after eight-and-a-half minutes. 'I wanted it to be an extraordinary piece of music,' says Butler.

'Like a tunnel, going deeper and deeper.' Brett Anderson sang its words in a croonsome baritone, clearly pitched at oozing a new gravitas. His lyrics were no less head-turning. 'Come to my house tonight,' he boomed. 'We could be together under nuclear skies.'

It split the critical fraternity in two: some were seduced by the sense that Suede had massively advanced their artistic boundaries; others believed, not entirely unreasonably, that they had teetered into absolute ludicrousness. On their *Top of the Pops* appearance, the group mimed on a stage ringed by flaming torches, as if a corner of the studio had been turned into a set from a Hammer House of Horror film. In some quarters, it was alleged that their debt to David Bowie was being superseded by a creeping resemblance to the gothic pomp of 70s-era Queen.

Stay Together entered the charts at number three – but whereas Suede's first run of singles had been concise blasts, perfectly constructed to both scythe through the mainstream and seduce the undecided, it marked the point at which their increasingly grandiose aesthetics uncoupled them from developments, leaving them in a cold and lonely orbit. Playing it next to Line Up – economical where Stay Together is bilious, clipped and witty where Anderson's lyrics are florid and verbose – one can sense the zeitgeist changing hands; that it did so between ex-lovers only heightens the two records' poetic sense of importance. Throw in Blur's Girls And Boys, released six weeks later, and the picture of a changing of the guard is complete.

CHAPTER 9

Planet Stupid

The winter of 1993–4 saw one key change that would decisively propel the likes of Blur, Elastica and Oasis towards the musical mainstream, Radio One, for so long the domain of suntanned 'personality' presenters and the most anodyne kind of pop music, was the subject of fevered discussions at the upper reaches of the BBC, where its close similarity to Britain's commercial networks – not to mention the fact that the average age of its listenership was thirty-one – was causing no end of concern. Quite apart from any statistics, by the start of the 90s, such staples as Simon Bates's Our Tune and Dave Lee Travis's Snooker On The Radio quiz sounded little short of absurd. The resonance of Harry Enfield and Paul Whitehouse's portrayal of Smashie And Nicey – 'Tell you what mate, I like cows: they're like horses . . . in *cow form*' – perhaps told the corporation's senior management much more than any listener survey; at one BBC function, Whitehouse was thanked by John Birt for the skit's impact on Radio One's internal affairs.

The gulf that lay between the station and the cutting-edge of rock music had long informed Britain's musical climate. The indie subculture derived much of its righteous fire from the fact that, though Radio One's night-time programmes – and John Peel's show in particular – were sympathetic, daytime radio remained largely impregnable: while Phil Collins and Jennifer Rush ruled the airwaves, indie would remain the music of outsiders. The schism was the subject of a handful of records that managed to simultaneously bemoan and celebrate it. Though The Smiths' 1986 single Panic implored its listeners to 'burn down the disco', its refrain of 'Hang the DJ' was at least partly aimed at the BBC. In 1989 came a single entitled Who Wants To Be The

Disco King? authored by The Wonder Stuff. Its chorus was snarled: 'Over and over and over/The radio's on, but I don't hear a song.' It reached number twenty-eight in the charts, kept at a predictable distance from the top 10 by its failure to find favour with the likes of Bruno Brookes and Gary Davies.

Steve Lamacq had become acquainted with the inner workings of Radio One in the early 90s, when he had applied to join the station's pool of producers. He was asked to come up with a hypothetical playlist for the station's breakfast show, and rather blotted his copybook by suggesting records by Happy Mondays and St Etienne. Soon enough, however, he began occasional stints on *The Evening Session*, the station's gateway into the more left-field approach of its night-time shows, first as a producer and then as stand-in host. He also got an instructive whiff of the old guard. 'I can remember one day very clearly: we'd been given a new producer, who used to produce DLT, and he was in our little office. I walked in as Travis had just walked out, and the stench of his aftershave was so overpowering, I had to put a handkerchief to my face and walk out.'

Lamacq's key mentor at Radio One was a producer named Jeff Smith, who believed the key to the acceptance of cutting-edge music was the way it was presented. 'In the past,' says Lamacq, 'it had been pretty much down to John Peel to sell new music. And Peel doesn't talk over records: that's not his style. Jeff Smith's argument was that all early rock'n'roll radio had been based on presentation, as much as the records. When rock'n'roll happened, you talked over the intros of records; you made them sound exciting. Jeff thought that was how you did it: you made *The Evening Session* sound like a daytime show, and suddenly this music wasn't alienating any more.'

In October 1993, Radio One appointed a new controller: a native of Sheffield named Matthew Bannister, who had recently worked as the BBC's chief assistant to the director of corporate affairs. The fusty title belied Bannister's rather radical brief: while in the job, he had led a no-holds-barred review of the corporation's every aspect. When he arrived at Radio One, he was clearly in the mood to apply some of his findings. 'Getting the job was an attempt to turn the philosophical argument into reality .., and ultimately change the station dramatically,' he later reflected.

Among his first moves was the awarding of full-time contracts to Lamacq and Jo Whiley, who would present *The Evening Session* as a team. Rather more notably, over the ensuing months, he began to purge the station of its more ridiculous DJs, and shove it away from the obligation to play the role of the cross-generational 'Nation's

Favourite'. As with any revolution, in the short term, the result was a great deal of chaos and uncertainty.

'The confusion at Radio One actually played into a lot of groups' hands,' says Steve Lamacq. 'There was such a mish-mash of producers – the old school hanging in there, along with some new blood coming through. The playlist meetings must have been bizarre: it must have been like the scouts having a meeting with the WI. But there was a debate going on about where Radio One should be going, encouraged by Bannister, so the talk around the Radio One building was, "We should be looking for new music."'

So it was that Oasis's Columbia and Elastica's Line Up blared from the UK's radios, and the delivery of Blur's new music to the station was greeted with delight. Though listener figures quickly tumbled, and Bannister's revolution was characterised by bold leaps forward and apologetic steps back, the change in Radio One's musical approach was rapidly consolidated. Indeed, as 1994 rolled on, Lamacq sensed that the fences dividing the station's night-time and daytime output – and by extension, those between what was deemed 'indie' and 'mainstream' – were being torn down.

'Pretty soon, my biggest problem became staying ahead of the game,' he says. 'You'd get a record or find a band, and you almost wanted to have them to yourselves for six months. But it didn't happen: they started going straight on the main playlist.'

On the rain-lashed evening of 9 February 1994, the *NME* hosted an awards ceremony it elegantly titled the Brats. The idea was born out of hostility to the previous year's Brit Awards: instead of merely publishing a list of alternative nominees and railing against music industry senility, the paper's management had decided to set the agenda – and energise the *NME*'s marketing – by staging its own event. It was a homely, pleasantly cliquey affair, held at The New Empire – a compact ballroom on Tottenham Court Road, usually used for cockney theme evenings – and hosted by Vic Reeves and Bob Mortimer, then at the apogee of their popularity. The statuettes they handed out, rather clumsily emphasising the paper's antagonism towards the music industry, took the form of a clenched fist with a raised middle finger. They were not the kind of ornaments that would be proudly placed on many sideboards.

The requisite array of musicians were duly corralled into attendance. Brett Anderson accepted Suede's award for Best Group with a display of borderline parodic nonchalance that caused giggles to ripple through the crowd (he promptly gave his statuette to his father, who decided that

The passage of the Union Jack from right-on bugbear to ubiquitous fashion statement. From left: Morrissey at Finsbury Park, 1992; Noel Gallagher at Maine Road, 1996; Geri Halliwell at the Brit Awards, 1997.

Top left: Brett Anderson in the days when his mind was split between his studies and music. 'The fact that he was doing Town Planning shows how little he expected from his life when he first went to University.'

Below left: Justine and Brett: 'A very warm, beautiful couple'.

Above right: Anderson — 'the shivering white indie male, having filthy thoughts' — rehearses his poses on a UCL field trip to Dungeness, 1990.

Below: Bernard Butler and Brett Anderson, en route through Camden Town, when Suede had yet to make much headway. 'I did truly love Brett', says Butler.

Left: Justine Frischmann and Donna Matthews — 'an incredible worldly, wealthy, beautiful girl ... and a doe-eyed street kid who'd been living on her wits.'

Below: Frischmann and Damon Albarn on their first holiday together in Majorca, 1992. 'He announced that I was the one, and we would be married and I had no choice in the matter.'

Left: Albarn, perhaps betraying the burn-out of Blur's 1992–3 difficult period.

Below: Albarn, Frischmann and Suede's Bernard Butler at the launch of *Leisure*: for a time, the Suede guitarist was on good terms with his ex-colleague and her new boyfriend.

Brett Anderson — in body-paint — and Bernard Butler, pictured just as their bond was starting to fray. 'He'd decided to see me as the person having his photo taken with his shirt off, whereas he was the serious musician.'

Oasis turn on the menace for their first photo session, Manchester,
November 1993. Left to right: Noel Gallagher, Paul 'Bonehead'
Arthurs, Paul 'Guigsy' McGuigan, Tony McCarroll and Liam
Gallagher.

Oasis earlier the same day, two months before their first big
London performance. 'They didn't seem like a threat ...'

The photograph that announced Blur's new Anglo-centric turn. Left to right: Dave Rowntree, Damon Albarn, Graham Coxon and Alex James. 'It was, "Fuck America, fuck all your music . . ."'

Blur with Keith Allen and Damien Hirst on the set of the Country House video. 'It's become Page 3 and Benny Hill,' Graham Coxon complained.

Albarn, the 'Lager-eater', at *Parklife*'s launch at Walthamstow Dog Track. 'I started out reading Nabokov, and now I'm into football, dog-racing and Essex Girls ...'

Albarn and Phil Daniels. 'If Kurt Cobain had played football,' said Albarn, 'he'd probably be alive today.'

Albarn and Alex James leaving the Groucho Club in 1998, just as Britpop curdled.

Albarn chats to Ray Davies in the summer of 1995. 'I was in love with him for that hour.'

Elastica's first photo session, taken when their unlikely alliance was holding firm. Left to right: Justin Welch, Justine Frischmann, Donna Matthews, Annie Holland.

Right: Matthews exits the Met Bar during the height of her drugs period. 'I was hanging out at glamorous parties and then sitting in crack dens.'

its ugliness condemned it into storage in his garden shed). Radiohead's Thom Yorke, still in the phase of his career that had been inaugurated by the American success of Creep, appeared wearing peroxide-blonde hair extensions and videoing the evening with a rather pathetic air of faux-enigma. Justine Frischmann, meanwhile, remained seated while Donna Matthews and Justin Welch ran to the stage to collect their ornamental fist for Best New Group.

The NME had set its sights on a photograph, destined for the paper's cover, of Yorke, Anderson and Frischmann. The awkwardness involved in pairing up the latter two had perhaps not occurred to those in charge of the coverage; it was only after Frischmann insisted on clearing the idea with Damon Albarn that the picture went ahead. Anderson and Frischmann's facial expressions hardly suggested a moment of long-awaited reconciliation.

Albarn had arrived dressed in his *Modern Life Is Rubbish* regalia, on an evident quest to get as drunk as possible. Blur did not win any *NME* awards, but the slight did not seem to bother him: as those attendees who shared his company discovered, he was brimming with self-belief. When a small pack of journalists, fired up by both alcohol and rather more chemical refreshment, cornered him and began ranting about his responsibility to save British music, he simply grinned. 'We've done it,' he said. 'We really have.'

Those gathered at the Brat Awards were not the only ones to behold his confidence. In print, he had reverted to the same cocky rhetoric he had grinningly dispensed during the *Leisure* period, this time – thankfully – backed up by a clear sense of Blur's cause. 'We are the best group in Britain,' he said. 'I think we are the best British group since The Smiths. Over a period of four years, The Smiths maintained a quality and a standard that no-one else could manage, and that is our aim. Plus, we have the same love-hate relationship with Britain. It annoys me when we're accused of having this nostalgic romance with a mythical lost Britain. Where are these songs about how great the country is? Nearly every one is tempered with cynicism and aggression.'

Blur's new album – which could have been called *Sport* or *Soft Porn*, before the group settled on *Parklife* – was the proof of all this. Though the group were justifiably effusive about its merits, David Balfe, for so long the Blur camp's resident naysayer, passed on the message that he was not much more enamoured with this record than he had been with *Modern Life Is Rubbish*: 'This is a mistake,' he told the group's management. Soon after, he decided to sell Food Records to EMI – thus leaving Andy Ross in charge while snuffing out the label's last claims to independence – and move to rural Hertfordshire. The subsequent success of *Parklife* thus came with a subtext of no little irony, not to mention the pleasing taste of vindication.

Many of its fourteen songs reflected Albarn's claims to a bittersweet take on the UK's human patchwork – on London Loves in particular, they managed to construct a vision of Britain that was both modern and affectingly doom-laden. Aside from all that, there were a handful of pieces that lay in a much more personal place: in To The End, End Of A Century and Badhead, one heard the sound of adolescent recklessness colliding with the encroaching demands of one's mid-twenties. Lest anyone require levity, there was also Tracy Jacks, the tale of some office-trained nobody who freed himself by streaking along the beach at Walton-On-The-Naze, and the road-tested Parklife: a knockabout paean to those who avoided the nine to five grind, narrated by Phil Daniels, transported from adolescent afternoons spent watching *Quadrophenia* to Blur's recording sessions.

Parklife's key masterstroke was used as the record's grand finale. This is A Low had lain as an uncompleted, unspeakably atmospheric instrumental, until Albarn was finally given an eleventh-hour deadline for the writing of his lyrics. He took his inspiration from a handkerchief, given to him by Alex James, that featured a map of the UK's shipping regions; the finished lyric was a fantasia centred around the shipping forecast – that inexplicably calming institution that soundtracks the switching-off of the UK's night-lights – narrated as if its writer was gazing at the whole of the British Isles.

Its music veered between serenity and a surreal tempestuousness, thanks in part to one of Graham Coxon's most dizzying guitar solos; by the song's close, it was clear that Blur had attained something close to perfection. The ensuing three years would see all manner of talk about aiming to equal the artistic achievements of The Beatles. This Is A Low, which imbued the UK with a mystery as potent as any American myth, proves that Blur actually managed the feat before anyone thought to make the comparison.

Girls And Boys, released in March, served rather more gaudy notice of what was to come. Inspired by a 1993 holiday Albarn and Frischmann had taken in Magaluf, Majorca, and centred around a glutinous double-tracked vocal and gurgling keyboards, it managed to sound both camply commercial and sneakingly avant garde – in Andy Ross's estimation, like 'Black Lace meets Public Image'. Its lyrics, meanwhile, found Albarn surveying hordes of vacationing Britons and finding himself fascinated. 'All these blokes and all these girls meeting at the watering hole and then just . . . copulating,' he marvelled. 'My mind's just getting more dirty. I can't help it.'

The song's public premiere came on *The Word*, where Blur turned in a quite brilliant performance. The scabrous guitar that Graham Coxon had scrawled over the record as a counterpoint to its synthetic sheen flew up in the mix; the group collided with one another in throwback to the barely controlled anarchy of the Seymour years. At one point, Albarn gave the camera a triumphant wink, before changing the kiss-off of the chorus to 'Always should be someone you want to fuck'. By the end of their allotted four minutes, it seemed that Blur had bashed down the last fence that stood in their path.

'They were a very bullish band by then,' says Mike Smith. 'I went down to that show. There was a very strong, belligerent side to that performance. I remember Damon having a can of beer and opening it at the end, spraying it across the audience. That time felt very, very confident: I can remember being round Alex's flat – him opening the windows really wide first thing in the morning, putting the speakers in the windows, and turning Girls And Boys really loud, and just standing there, flicking the Vs at the rest of the world. What was strange was that no-one actually knew it was going to be a hit.' The stars soon lined up in Blur's favour. Girls And Boys was endorsed by Radio One, who ensured that it blared from shop windows and car stereos for weeks before its release. On 13 March, it entered the charts at number five.

On 5 April, Kurt Cobain committed suicide. His death came at the end of a wretched month that had begun with an overdose of Rohypnol in Rome on 4 March; back at his Seattle home, he achieved his aim with the aid of one of his collection of guns. Its reporting in the mainstream media represented a jarring juxtaposition: this was the first time in years that anyone associated with outdoor festivals, the *NME* and night-time radio had crash-landed in the strait-laced world of *News At Ten*.

Within Cobain's garbled suicide note, there was the clear statement that his death somehow validated the standpoint of America's indie fundamentalists: major record labels, iconic celebrity and most every other aspect of his recent existence were inherently corrosive of the human spirit. 'All the warnings from the punk rock 101 courses over the years, since my first introduction to the, shall we say, the ethics involved with independence and the embracement of your community has proven to be very true,' he wrote. 'I haven't felt the excitement of listening to as well as creating music along with reading and writing for too many years now. I feel guilty beyond words about these things . . . I don't have the passion anymore, and so remember, it's better to burn out than to fade away.'

'That all got to Damon,' says Alex James. 'It was either him or Kurt on the front of the music papers each week for a little while. And then one of them was dead. That scared him.'

The collision of events, in tandem with Blur's two-year campaign for Anglo-centric musical virtues, gave their sudden success a potent narrative: if they were still seeking to wrest the UK away from the tortured hegemony of grunge, Cobain's suicide, in its own horrific way, surely made their lives immeasurably easier. The entry of *Parklife* at number one in the album charts – on which it remained, at various positions, for no less than ninety weeks – only seemed to confirm it. There was a jarring irony at work, however. Though he had long claimed to have his sights set on success and celebrity, the shock of Albarn's sudden elevation gave rise to a period of genuine trauma. There was not quite the yawning gulf between him and Cobain that most would assume.

'It wasn't obvious that *Parklife* was going to be big,' says Justine Frischmann. 'Elastica were bigger than Blur for a while: getting more press, more popular, more hype. Even though Damon desperately wanted it, no-one knew that Girls And Boys was going to go in at number five. And the week *Parklife* went in at number one, he couldn't stop crying.'

With admirable candour, Albarn wrote about the experience the following year. 'I had been someone who had never in their life felt even faintly depressed or suicidal,' he said. 'They were emotions that were as foreign to me as Japanese. Then, completely out of the blue . . . I woke up depressed. It was like the first day at primary school and a very bad hangover all at once. I found my whole upper body becoming incredibly tense. I had pains in my back and shoulder, panic attacks, and the only relief was to cry. I couldn't rationalise what on earth was going on in my head and I was pissed off with myself for being so weak. Things like this didn't happen to me.'

'He couldn't sleep,' says Justine Frischmann. 'He was getting everything he'd ever wanted, and he was losing the plot. He honestly had a nervous breakdown. He went really weird. I was really worried: I can remember phoning Chris Morrison's office, saying "You *can't* send him to Spain to do press. He's not well." They weren't really listening to me. But he did it. After that, he lost the part of himself that was neurotic and childish and couldn't cope, and actually became able to become a pop star.

'Meanwhile, I'm doing press, and putting records out, and going to the studio every day to make an album. And all of a sudden, I stop being there for him, a bit. He's not well, and I can't help him that much. That was the beginning of the problems.'

'It's very difficult to cope with that kind of attention,' says Alex James. 'I'd walk into a bar with him, and people's jaws would drop. It was a lot to adapt to. Was I worried about him? No, never. I probably should have been more worried about him. I wish he'd felt he could have talked to me about it more. It's scary: all of a sudden he was very, very famous. And eventually you realise, it's never going to stop. You're going to be living on Planet Stupid forever.'

Albarn made his way to Harley Street, where a doctor recommended by the Frischmann family asked him about his drug habits: Albarn explained that he smoked a modicum of dope, drank quite a lot, and had an occasional acquaintance with cocaine. He was told to desist from the latter and given a prescription for anti-depressants. The pills were hardly given a chance – Albarn binned them after a few days, later claiming that they made 'the world appear to be coming out of a transistor radio'. He then tried herbal treatment and acupuncture, before discovering the benefits of an altogether more mundane regime: trips to the gym and a once-weekly game of football.

Nonetheless, his difficulties carried on well into the summer: when To The End, the second single from *Parklife*, took Blur on to *Top of the Pops*, Albarn's thoughts rotated around the prospect of nervous paralysis: in his own words, he thought, 'I can't cope. Please, somebody switch me off.'

In the meantime, Blur had set out on tour, round such palatial venues as Nottingham Rock City, Wolverhampton Civic Hall and Bristol University Anson Rooms. Their support act was Sleeper, then mere foot-soldiers in the new wave of Anglo-centric groups, whose breakthrough was a good twelve months away. On the one occasion they shared Albarn's company, he hardly seemed to be someone fretting about the onset of celebrity.

'Blur were drunk most of the time, and quite abusive with it,' says Louise Wener, Sleeper's vocalist. 'I remember Damon just saying, "All you gotta do is make all the birds wanna shag you and all the blokes wanna be you – that's the secret to this game." That was at an aftershow party. The other thing he said was, "Don't be nice to your road crew because they work for you, they're your employees." He said, "I might not bother to talk to you again on this tour, so that's my one bit of advice." And that was it: he went back into Damon-world.'

In 1894, a Manchester-based music hall composer named Felix McGlennon explained the relation of his music to the two strands of people who formed his public. 'It is not the kid-gloved critics in the stalls, the eminent literary men, who do the trick for you,' he said, 'but the people in the pit and gallery, who are not afraid to shout their approval or disapproval. And they like simple pathos or homely humour – something to do with the wife or mother-in-law, and so on. The main thing is catchiness. I would sacrifice everything – rhyme, reason, sense and sentiment – to catchiness.'

A century later, Noel Gallagher surveyed his peers with an equally clear division in mind. 'Music for me at the moment is dead,' he said. 'It's poncey and serious and everyone's got to make some sort of statement, whether it's about "Parklife" or their feminine side or their politics. But we're a rock'n'roll band . . . everyone's dead into analysing, but don't analyse our band. "That's a good song, that is. What does it mean?" Who gives a fuck what it means?'

Throughout Oasis's first months of exposure, this was Gallagher's constant refrain: his vision, reflective of an age-old British archetype, of Oasis as proletarian sons of the soil, come to avenge music's dependence on intellect and artifice. This emphasis was then turned on his group's forebears, as he merrily rewrote rock history according to his own prejudices.

'Those bands that claim to be punk rock, they've totally missed the point,' said Noel, making reference to 1994's brief spurt of New Wave revivalism. 'They're all going on about The Clash and slogans and taking speed and all that, but they're dead uptight about it. For me, punk rock was about The Sex Pistols, and they were big time *fun*. They covered The Small Faces and Chuck Berry, and Johnny Rotten went on *Desert Island Discs* in 1977 and all he played was Neil Young . . . The Pistols were a fucking laugh, and that's what it's all about.'

He was mistaken on just about all counts. The Pistols' Berry and Small Faces' covers were a fleeting, early part of their repertoire, and had only been released long after their split. On the occasion to which Noel was alluding, Rotten had actually appeared on Capital Radio and brought with him records by Neil Young, Captain Beefheart and Peter Hammill, founder of the terrifyingly cerebral prog rock group Van Der Graaf Generator. Most importantly, The Sex Pistols, motivated by both Malcolm McLaren's desire to tap into a long European tradition of artistic subversion and John Lydon's deep class consciousness, were some distance from being 'a fucking laugh'. It mattered not. Reading Noel's pronouncements, one was taken to the core of his own credo.

It did not take much persuasion for his younger brother to join in, often taking the conversation into a place that was both banal and absurd. When Liam dispensed his take on the group's beloved John Lennon, one could envisage even Noel rolling his eyes: 'He was just an average fuckin' lad from Liverpool with a fuckin' *mad* sense of humour,' said Liam. 'And that was it. He was a comedian more than anything. Not a rock star. He was a fuckin' comedian. Bernard Manning, man.'

In the context of the groups that would eventually appear in their wake, what was remarkable about Oasis was that their rejection of artifice was not manifested in either a dour emphasis on craftsmanship, or the kind of inconsequential party soundtrack that Noel's reading of The Sex Pistols might have suggested. Some of their best songs – Columbia, Bring It On Down, Supersonic – pulsed with a kinetic sense of confrontation; as if, despite the absence of a real agenda, the Gallaghers could not help but vent some deep-seated rage. Liam, in particular, managed to ooze the idea that this was anything but 'big time fun': when he stood onstage, staring out his audience, one was reminded of a twenty-year-old summation of a very pointed kind of incoherence: 'Don't know what I want but I know how to get it.'

Besides all that, one only had to spend a night with Oasis to know that they were hardly dullards. Their early tours were characterised by daily outbreaks of chaos; what lent the debauchery an additional air of hilarity was the fact that it was not conducted with the customary rock'n'roll insouciance, but a goggle-eyed amusement that suggested they couldn't believe they were getting away with it. 'It was bonkers,' says Paul Arthurs. 'Mad. I'd never been to Birmingham in my life; I'd been to London once. And all of a sudden, someone was saying "Here's enough money to fill your transit full of petrol – get down to Salford Van Hire, it's all been sorted out. Here's your little itinerary, this is where you're going. *And* we've booked you a bed and breakfast."'

To use the photographer Pennie Smith's description of touring with The Clash, Oasis's manoeuvres rather suggested 'a commando raid performed by the Bash Street Kids'. Their attire said it all: in the midst of the unpaid bills and splintered wardrobes, Liam Gallagher must have been the only aspirant rock icon ever to be dressed by St Michael.

'He wasn't fashionable,' says Tim Abbot. 'He used to shop in Marks and Spencer: he'd go in there and just pick out the most fantastic garb. I remember Liam taking me into a Clark's shoe shop once and going, "Look at these, Abbot – great shoes." He'd go to Dunn & Co. and pull stuff out.'

In February, the group boarded a ferry to the Netherlands, twenty-four hours before a booking at Amsterdam's Sleep Inn Arena. Sent into the highest of spirits by the prospect of Oasis's first foreign engagement and a lake of duty-free, four of the group managed to antagonise the boat's security staff to the point that one of them attempted to cosh Liam Gallagher. Paul McGuigan promptly decided to put in a pre-emptive punch. He and Liam were duly locked in the brig, and only released once the ferry had returned to the UK. From within his quarters, Liam assailed his captors with the kind of abuse that betrayed the fact that he had never been abroad: Paul Arthurs recalls hearing full-throated cries of 'You German bastards'.

Though they escaped incarceration, Arthurs and Tony McCarroll had their passports confiscated, and faced the same return journey. Only Noel made it to Holland, brimming with ire at his comrades' stupidity. As it turned out, the episode managed to advance Oasis's cause: news of the adventure was relayed to London; the *NME* accompanied its news story with a picture of a lone Noel, scowling in front of a poster for the cancelled show.

The episode inevitably fed its way into their first round of substantial interviews. On 7 April, the night before the discovery of Kurt Cobain's body, the group appeared on a live Radio One broadcast from Glasgow. The occasion was notable not only for the swaggering brio that infused Oasis's performance – 'Good evening, Great Britain,' said Liam, with no little glee – but for the events that would transpire back at the Forte Crest Hotel.

The *NME* had dispatched a journalist and photographer to capture the next chapter of Oasis's progress; lounging in the bar, the group quickly surrounded themselves with empty glasses before the two Gallaghers decided that the time was right for the inquisition that would form their first feature in the paper. In the meantime, word quickly spread that Andrew Roachford, the author of the 1988 hit Cuddly Toy – not exactly the most celebrated single of that decade – was holding court mere yards away. Liam, Paul McGuigan and Paul Arthurs were inexplicably starstruck, and quickly mobbed him. 'Roachford!' Liam yelped. 'Cuddly Toy, man! Tune of the eighties!'

At around midnight, Noel and Liam took their drinks to the room that the latter was sharing with Mark Coyle – Arthurs, McGuigan and McCarroll meekly remained downstairs – and began to hurl their thoughts in the direction of a tape recorder. Their few interviews so far had suggested that the Gallaghers were on some unified crusade to return rock music to its visceral, hedonistic roots, but the ensuing scenes proved that a struggle between brain and groin perhaps divided the brothers themselves.

Via debates about their touchstones – The Beatles, Happy Mondays, The Stone Roses – the two made their respective positions all too clear. Liam celebrated his role as an uncontrollable libertine; Noel, taking issue with his brother's pride in Oasis's high jinx, insisted that attention should be paid to nothing but the music. The resultant stand-off suggested that the endless rows that had apparently defined life in the Gallagher home were not about to stop.

The Gallaghers were first asked about their snowballing reputation for being 'rock'n'roll animals' in the wake of the Amsterdam farrago.

Liam: 'I like the way it's bubbling up. It's reminding me of The Roses all over again. I like that, me. I want to get two thousand people in a nice gaff who are there to see me. I want to be there . . .'

Noel: 'Woah. Hang on a minute. That's not what he's on about.'

Liam: 'He is.'

Noel: 'He's on about a reputation, about getting thrown off fuckin' ferries. Getting thrown off ferries and getting deported is summat that I'm not proud about.'

Liam: 'Well I am, la.'

Noel: 'Alright. Well if you're proud about getting thrown off ferries, why don't you go and support West Ham and get the fuck out of my band and go and be a football hooligan? We're musicians, right? Not football hooligans.'

Liam: 'You're only gutted 'cos you was in bed fuckin' reading your fuckin' books.'

This went on for a good half-hour. 'I'm into it,' said Liam, reflecting on his various debauched transgressions to date. 'I'm into all that fuckin' shit.' He then glanced at Noel with a look that had doubtless been flashed across the lounge of 14 Ashburn Avenue on scores of occasions. 'He's teetotal. He's a fuckin' priest,' he said, summoning the most uptight archetype a Catholic upbringing could provide. 'He was born to be a priest.' And so they continued . . .

Liam: 'You want to be Andrew Lloyd Webber, you do. You fucker.'

Noel: 'Who's Andrew Lloyd Webber?'

Liam: 'I haven't got a clue. He's a golfer or something.'

Noel: 'Right. Shut the fuck up then. What I'm saying is, it's not about saying "We're hard." That's what the Mondays were about. Fucking hell, man . . .'

Liam: 'Sit down, man. You're getting in a state. You've had too many G and Ts. Sit the fuck down. The Mondays were *not* about "We're hard." It was like "We like having loads of Es, being in a band, shagging loads of whores."'

Noel: 'No, *you* like shagging loads of whores.'

Liam: 'Yeah, I do . . . Look, all I've got to say is, I'm having the
crack. It's not doing anyone any harm. That's me. John Lennon
used to fuckin' burn about doing little mad things.'
Noel: 'Do you know John Lennon?'
Liam: 'Do you know him?'
Noel: 'I don't, but do you?'
Liam: 'Yeah.'
Noel: 'Well, you must be pretty old. How old are you?
Twenty-one?'
Liam: 'No. About fuckin' thousand and five fuckin' one.'
Noel: 'You're twenty-two.'
Liam: 'I'm twenty-one.'
Noel: 'Right. And remember, I watched you being born, and I
don't even know John Lennon. So shut the fuck up about know-
ing John Lennon.'

There seemed to be but one inconsistency in the elder Gallagher's
complaints about his brother's boasts. Cigarettes And Alcohol, a song
yet to be properly released, but already included on a giveaway Creation
cassette, contained the line 'you might as well do the white line'. Within
the indie constituency, songs that loudly celebrated cocaine use were
pretty much unprecedented; by dint of those eight words, Noel seemed
to be announcing that he was an advocate of remarkable licentiousness.

The lyrics' author, however, seemed to think the sentiment was
altogether more mundane. Six years hence, when the issue of drug
decriminalisation finally prompted liberal editorials in the broadsheet
press, his answer to that night's question about the song would have been
unremarkable; in 1994, it spoke a rarely acknowledged truth. 'I'm sorry
mate,' he counselled, 'but that is a fact of everyday life. People are sat in
England, right now, in flats across this country, whether it be Glasgow,
Manchester, Birmingham, London, Leeds, Liverpool, Sheffield . . . in
rooms like this. And they've all got the drugs out.' There followed a
perfect soundbite: 'We all snort white lines . . . *every day.*'

In retrospect, one other exchange stands out. Tired of his brother's
censoriousness, and having already compared him to a priest, there
was but one figure from the brothers' past to be brought into play.
'You're like me dad,' moaned Liam.

''Course I'm like your fucking dad,' said Noel. 'It's only fucking
right.'

The Glasgow interview was aimed at promoting their first single.
Alan McGee, seeking an opening statement of intent, had argued for
the release of Bring It On Down, charmed by the punk rock romance

in the opening lines of its chorus: 'You're the outcast/You're the underclass/But you don't care/Because you're living fast.' Noel Gallagher, however, opted for a song called Supersonic: a drawled expression of nothing in particular that used nonsense poetry, distorted guitars and a reined-in tempo to sound appealingly menacing. Within its four-and-a-half minutes, one could discern a love of John Lennon's breed of sneering psychedelia, though its key influence was a little closer to home: more than any other song in the Oasis repertoire, Supersonic was strongly redolent of Happy Mondays.

It was released on 11 April; the following Sunday, it entered the chart at number thirty-one. Creation Records were still in the habit of toasting any of their bands who managed to breach the top 40. To do so with a debut single suggested that Oasis were already walking on water.

The group, meanwhile, continued to make their way up and down the UK's motorways. On 2 May, they arrived in Portsmouth, where they followed their gig with the now-predictable hotel disturbance. The two Gallaghers brawled over an argument about an ex-girlfriend; when he decided to have a swim in the hotel pool, Paul Arthurs found that he was quickly joined by a selection of bar furniture; at 6am, the night porter calmly informed the Oasis party that his shift had ended with a call to the police. 'On the first two British tours, I didn't actually get in a hotel bed the whole time,' said Paul McGuigan some time later. 'I sometimes got carried up to one and put on it, but I didn't ever get *in* one.'

One morning, his head blitzed by yet another grinding hangover, Arthurs informed McGuigan that he couldn't take much more. 'There's no such word as "can't",' McGuigan retorted.

'But I *can't*,' said Arthurs. 'I'm giving up this rock'n'roll business. I'm going to be a Tory MP. Get me a satsuma! Get me a satsuma!'

The reference was to Stephen Milligan, a Conservative parliamentary private secretary whose corpse had been discovered on 7 February. His fate rather suggested some grisly version of the kind of characters that occasionally found their way into Damon Albarn's lyrics: though outwardly the very image of respectability, he had been found wearing women's hosiery and underwear. Stranger still, a piece of cord was tied to his neck from his ankles and a piece of satsuma was found in his mouth. The detailed explanation for the latter was a matter of conjecture: according to some accounts, he had probably sucked the fruit to take away the taste of amyl nitrate; others said it had been soaked in the solvent.

Milligan was the most colourful example of a parade of causes célèbres that had lent political life a recurrent air of absurdity. The run had begun in July 1992, when the *Sunday People* broke the story of David Mellor's affair with a statuesque actress named Antonia De Sancha. There followed a week of progressively more lurid tales, culminating in the claim – fabricated, as it turned out – that Mellor had been partial to having sex while wearing his Chelsea kit.

In October 1993, the swashbuckling transport minister Steven Norris managed to ride out tales of affairs with five women which had resulted in the elegant nickname 'Shagger'. Two months later came news that Tim Yeo, a minister in the Department of the Environment, had fathered a child with his mistress; after the obligatory period of posing for pictures with his hapless spouse and insisting this was purely a personal matter, he resigned. Come the new year, the wife of Lord Caithness, the minister for aviation and shipping, shot herself, giving rise to a spate of stories claiming that he had been about to leave her for another woman. By way of bathos, there quickly followed a storm-in-a-teacup concerning one David Ashby, a Tory backbencher who had dared to spend a night in the same hotel bed as a male friend. The tabloids suspected a gay tryst; Ashby simply insisted that no twin rooms had been available.

Such tales were presented with the tasty subtext of hypocrisy. At the Conservative Conference of October 1993, John Major – who, it later turned out, had himself departed from the Tories' treasured Family Values with the help of Edwina Currie – had announced his intention to lead the country 'back to basics'. The precise upshot of this new crusade was unclear: though the Prime Minister had reportedly intended the emphasis to be placed on the importance of government's core responsibilities – education, public services, the economy – its more florid passages implied a concern with matters of personal morality. Encouraged by Major's aides, the newspapers talked about a 'war on permissiveness' and 'making liberalism as dirty a word as socialism is now'. As any devotee of lobby gossip could have told him, the Prime Minister had set a dependable trap for his own government.

In 1994, moreover, sex scandals were being superseded by the first rumblings of more serious transgressions. In October, Neil Hamilton would issue his ill-fated libel writ against the *Guardian*, who had begun their revelations about questions, cash and brown envelopes. Whispers were spreading about Jeffrey Archer's dealings in Anglia Television shares, and Mark Thatcher's arms trading; Jonathan Aitken's name was associated with looming trouble. Even the Conservatives' most valued supporters could sense the onset of a terminal malaise. 'What fools we were to back John Major,' said *The Sun*.

As far as the Labour Party was concerned, the expected narrative of the next two or three years had already been established: John Smith, whose leadership had seen Labour soaring to poll leads of over twenty percentage points, could be reasonably expected to avenge the hurt of two decades and become the first Labour Prime Minister since James Callaghan. Instead, an unexpected and tragic run of events transpired: Smith suffered a fatal heart attack on 12 May. His death engendered a head-rattling sense of arbitrariness; of history being taken somewhere quite by chance.

The front runner in the contest to replace him was quickly established: a sometime barrister who had spent some of his college years as the vocalist with a rock group fond of songs by The Doobie Brothers and The Rolling Stones. Britain, to hear some people talk, was about to get its first first rock'n'roll Leader of the Opposition.

The Labour Party's last organised dalliance with rock music had been announced to the world on the morning of 21 November 1985. At 11.30am, a crowd of 200 musicians, politicians, trade union officials and journalists gathered in a marquee, pitched on the terrace of the Houses of Parliament. They were served hot punch, and regaled by a speech from Neil Kinnock. The leader was there to place his formal approval on a new wing of the Labour Party's campaign structure: an organisation called Red Wedge. 'Can I first disabuse anyone of the idea that Red Wedge refers to my haircut,' he said, to a smattering of groans.

The name, taken from a Russian propagandist painting entitled Beat The Whites With The Red Wedge, had been suggested by Billy Bragg, who stood with Paul Weller – then in his avowedly political Style Council phase – as the new set-up's most recognisable face. The pair, along with a handful of other musicians, had recurrently bumped into each other on the platforms that often defined the life of the switched-on 80s musician. From there, it was only a short leap to formalising their alliance.

'The key event was the miners' strike,' says Bragg. 'That was the thing that heightened political awareness to such an extent that an initiative like Red Wedge could actually happen. You can't do things like that in an ideological vacuum. Red Wedge came about because we were constantly meeting one another – the same bands on different platforms, for different issues: the miners, Nicaragua, anti-apartheid, anti-racism. It was all the same people.'

Bragg also believes that the generational background of the Labour leader was crucial: without the enthusiasm of someone familiar with rock music, Red Wedge might not have come to life. 'Neil Kinnock was the first leader of any major political party who knew who Gene Vincent was; the first member of the post-war generation to lead a mainstream political party. That was really significant. He was a member of the Gene Vincent fan club, and a big fan of Phil Ochs. He knew that popular music could be used as a vehicle to spread ideas. He was aware of that. And that's really important. If it had been Roy Hattersley, I'm not sure he'd have got it quite so well. Kinnock was a bit of a rocker, in his spare time. I once saw him pick up a guitar and sing Help Me Make It Through The Night. It's a pretty hard song, that. I can't play it. I bet Blair can't play it.'

Precisely what Red Wedge was out to achieve was a little unclear. Certainly, all the musicians – who were eventually joined by a gaggle of comedians – wanted the Thatcher government out and Labour in. But they envisaged themselves as a much more autonomous set-up than the glamorous campaign wing that many had expected. In return for their qualified endorsement of the party, many of the Red Wedge inner circle expected to exercise a modicum of influence on the party's direction – chiefly in the areas of youth and cultural policy. There were even fleeting mutterings about the decriminalisation of cannabis. 'Red Wedge doesn't pretend that the Labour Party is the answer to all our problems,' advised a pamphlet entitled *Move on Up!*. 'In fact, we believe that the Labour Party itself must change and take more notice of young people – the citizens of tomorrow's Britain.'

It was the idea of Red Wedge acting as a cipher for youth opinion that kept many of the musicians' scepticism in check. Paul Weller, in particular, was prone to venting dark thoughts. Three years after the demise of The Jam, he was quite a catch for the politicians, a figure whose words were still pored over by a thousands-strong constituency of suburban malcontents. When he came face-to-face with Labour MPs, he could not help but detect the whiff of cynicism. 'He always did say to me, "You know they're just using us,"' says Bragg. 'And I would say, "Yeah, but we're using them too, Paul."'

Despite their nominal independence, Red Wedge were given an office at Labour Party HQ, then on Walworth Road, in Lambeth. A neighbouring workspace was the domain of Peter Mandelson; Bragg recalls him frequently slipping down the corridor to share his thoughts with whichever youth cultural hot-shots had popped by. In accordance with Labour Party protocol, its meetings were minuted. 'Robert Elms said that all this ideological theorizing about Individualism and Collectivism was a load of bullshit,' read one such document, 'and would be lost on most of the youth we were trying to reach.' The Labour Party's usual bureaucratic vernacular was nowhere to be seen.

In January 1986, a coachload of musicians set out on the first Red Wedge national tour. Weller and Bragg were accompanied by the gay duo The Communards, The Specials' Jerry Dammers, the soul singer Junior Giscombe, and a shifting supporting cast that included Madness, Tom Robinson and – to the evident surprise of many observers – Spandau Ballet's Gary Kemp. The Smiths' Johnny Marr and Andy Rourke tagged along from the show's opening date in Manchester; at Newcastle City Hall, Morrissey was cajoled into attendance, and the band's full membership turned in a performance of legendary ferocity. The gigs frequently managed to communicate a sense of euphoric optimism – Labour was ahead in the opinion polls, and the week of the first show in Manchester, Michael Heseltine resigned from the government over the Westland affair. When Billy Bragg read out a supportive telegram from Tony Benn, his words all but brought the house down.

Such activities – as well as a quarterly magazine entitled *Well Red* – continued up until the ill-starred 1987 election, around which all Red Wedge activity had been oriented. Having organised a tour of key marginal constituencies, the organisation marked 12 June with an election night party at the Mean Fiddler in Harlesden, inevitably transformed into a wake. 'We were gutted,' says Billy Bragg. 'I got drunk and walked home in the bright summer sunshine, feeling terribly, terribly disappointed. And it's a long walk from Harlesden to Chiswick.'

Red Wedge limped on, but it wasn't to be. Having exited Walworth Road, the organisation was wound up in 1988. By then, the tenor of Britain's pop culture was changing: the ideological ferocity of the Thatcher period was giving way to an altogether more apolitical climate. The Stone Roses and Happy Mondays were the vanguard of this; though the former group would happily express left-wing opinions, the two bands' modus operandi was much more bound up with drug consumption, pulling strange faces and sweating over the cut of one's trousers than bringing down the Tories.

'That was the next generation of bands coming through, rejecting what the previous generation had done,' says Bragg. 'And that's what you're supposed to do: we were rejecting what the New Romantics had done. We'd had so much politics for so long, everyone was fucking sick of it. It was, "We're stuck with the Tories, let's just get on with it," whereas before there was a spirit of "We can do this." People didn't want to talk about politics in the *NME* any more – they wanted to talk about "Let's just get out of it." And what was the alternative? To try and get our hopes up again, for 1992? It was hard to motivate people. The momentum had gone. That's what pop's like with ideas: "What's next?"'

In February 1991, Billy Bragg was backstage at an event called The Great British Music Weekend, designed as an appendage to that year's Brit Awards. Put together by that passionate fan of young talent, Jonathan King, it was designed to add a frisson of excitement to the annual Brits hoop-la by showcasing a selection of left-field acts. The bill included such names as Jesus Jones, Ride and The Farm. Thanks to the success of a single entitled Sexuality, Bragg had also been invited.

Mere weeks beforehand, the US had announced the commencement of Operation Desert Storm; Bragg, in line with the habits of the previous decade, set about trying to drum up support for an anti-war benefit. 'I was going round winding people up,' says Bragg. 'Blur were on, and I said to their manager, "Do you mind if I have a word with them about the Gulf War?" He said, "Don't scare 'em." They were like, "Wooooah." They didn't want to know.'

Until the summer of 1971, Tony Blair was a pupil at Fettes College, the Scottish public school used by Ian Fleming to flesh out the early life of James Bond. It was there, during his two years in the sixth form, that Blair opted to forgo trips to the barber's and became noticeably fond of rock music. According to one Hugh Kellett, a Fettes pupil two years below Blair, he came to represent the very acme of subversion: 'Masters were very worried about sex, drugs and rock'n'roll, and Blair looked like all three.' Not that Fettes' masters were so anxious as to completely banish the dreaded rock from the school: in October 1970, at the start of Blair's last year, Fettes hosted a concert featuring Atomic Rooster and Anno Domini, exactly the kind of volume-loving longhairs of which Blair had become fond.

Blair's next stop was London, where he whiled away what was then known as a Year Out. He spent it assisting a friend-of-a-friend named Alan Collenette in the promotion of a run of small-scale concerts. The two formed a self-styled agency named Blair/Collenette Promotions, whose chief asset was a second-hand Ford Thames van. To underline his grooviness, Blair took to dressing in a brown fur coat, and fine-tuning catchphrases that were in line with his love of The Rolling Stones: when he was in the company of females, an oft-heard incantation was 'Let's go, honies.'

Among the groups to benefit from Blair and Collenette's labours was a trio called Jaded, founded by Adam Sieff, the son of Edward Sieff, then chairman of Marks and Spencer. 'We were into the Allman Brothers, Hendrix, Mountain – guitar rock,' says Sieff. Jaded covered such songs as Jimi Hendrix's Who Knows, Mountain's Never In My Life, The Allman Brothers' You Don't Love Me and Moby Grape's

Can't Be So Bad. Sieff went on to be a session guitarist, lending his talent to such songs as Spitting Image's The Chicken Song and the theme to *Whose Line Is It Anyway?* Perhaps more notably, in December 1973, his father survived a gun attack by Ilich Ramirez Sanchez, alias Carlos the Jackal.

'I wasn't even aware that there was something called Blair/Collenette Promotions,' says Sieff, now the head of Jazz and World Music at Sony's UK headquarters. 'We're not talking about great organisation here. It was just a bit of fun. Tony just wanted to do something: "We can set up the van here, we can do the lighting there." He had a positive influence.'

Blair reached his twenties in an era when a great deal of rock music was stepping away from the countercultural baggage of the 1960s. Three years before his arrival in London, he might have felt the ripples from a capital-based scene that was fizzing with anti-authoritarian ideas; five years later, he could have been party to the upsurge of punk rock. For one so wedded to moderation, it was perhaps convenient that he engaged with music during the age of Rock For Rock's Sake. During his second year at university, his beloved Rolling Stones issued a camped-up manifesto for all this: It's Only Rock'n'Roll, the self-parodic single in which Mick Jagger assured the world that his rebellious streak had been tamed.

Three months after it was released, Mark Ellen arrived at Pembroke College, Oxford, to study English. He was an alumnus of Winchester School, where he had formed a short-lived rock group with Adam Sharples, who had arrived at Corpus Christi College the year before. Ellen was a bass guitarist; displaying heartwarming loyalty, Sharples had guaranteed that, if he was able to form a group in Oxford, he would keep the bassist position vacant until his friend arrived.

The promise was kept. Sharples had found a drummer at Pembroke named James Moon – he and Ellen would often attempt to pass him off as the younger brother of The Who's drummer Keith – and with Ellen's recruitment, they had a band. They looked like most aspirant rock musicians of the period. 'I had long, curly hair,' says Ellen. 'A mass of split ends. Horribly unconditioned. A velvet jacket, obviously. And a pair of flared trousers, a big belt, and a pair of Cuban-heeled cowboy boots.'

The group's first engagement involved providing the music for a rock opera based on the legend of Faust, entitled *Faustrock*. Squatting in the orchestra pit of a theatre on the Abingdon Road, making the requisite diabolic noises, they had a fine enough time – but this was not the kind of stuff they truly had in mind. The trio wanted to be in a proper group, the kind that might enable them to perform at college balls, and – in Ellen's words – 'hopefully meet exciting girls in floral-print dresses'.

They had a name, taken from the sleeve of The Grateful Dead's *From The Mars Hotel*, released in the summer of 1974. If the record's cover was held upside down in front of a mirror, an illegible legend was suddenly rendered comprehensible: it read 'Ugly Rumors', which became Dead aficionados' alternative title for the album. By adopting the name, Ellen, Sharples and Moon figured they were sending a coded signal of their hipness to potential fans.

There was but one glaring hole in their plans: none of the trio wanted to take the step of providing lead vocals. A solution arrived when Adam Sharples recalled a fellow longhair at St John's College, who had displayed his vocal talent in a recent musical revue.

Tony Blair – then in his final year, studying Law – duly arrived at Sharples' rooms at Corpus Christi, clutching a sheaf of neatly transcribed lyrics to the songs that formed the group's intended set: Live With Me and Honky Tonk Woman by The Rolling Stones; Jackson Browne's Take It Easy; Black Magic Women by Fleetwood Mac; China Grove and Long Train Running, both by The Doobie Brothers; and Free's All Right Now. These were the days before printed lyrics became an established aspect of record packaging, so Blair's diligence was impressive.

'We sat in this room,' says Mark Ellen. 'I had a bass guitar with no amplification, Jim had a waste paper bin, and Adam Sharples had an acoustic guitar. Tony said, "What do you want me to do?" We had this little microphone that we'd somehow plugged into the stereo: he was kind of mildly amplified. And we ran through the songs, and he was fantastic. He did a few moves. We said, "What kind of stage act can you put on?" At which point he stood up and threw a few shapes. He left, we reconvened the band meeting, and he was unanimously voted in.

'He had a kind of Mick Jagger-esque delivery. Quite high, not enormous volume. But it was coupled with this very entertaining act. He definitely modelled himself on Jagger. There was a lot of "Well alright!"'

His vocals were not Blair's only contribution to the group. Though Sharples, Ellen and Moon had a casual attitude to the matter of musical preparation, Blair proved to be a little more thorough. On their way to their first gig, at Corpus Christi College, Blair insisted that they forgo the pleasures of a pre-performance visit to the pub, and commit themselves to a further twenty minutes of rehearsal. 'We were like,

"Christ – we should be sticking down the pints. We've got beer to drink. What do you mean, *rehearse?*"' says Mark Ellen. 'But he made this speech, the sentiment of which was, "Look, guys – if this is worth doing, it's worth doing really well. We're OK, but we could be really good." This was an extraordinary thing for us, because we'd never thought about the concept of being good. We had no ambition at all, other than to be in a group and meet attractive women. I remember him saying, "We need to work out precisely what the chords are, and there need to be some dynamics: there've got to be loud bits and less loud bits." A basic, rudimentary concept of arrangement was brought in. That was a novelty.'

The group's shows would begin with Live With Me, a hymn to debauchery that hardly sits comfortably with the older Blair's image as an upright advocate of the Christian life. A send-up of the kind of existence that moneyed rock stars were once assumed to enjoy, it finds Mick Jagger inviting a female conquest to move into his mansion. There is a suggestion of a *ménage à trois* involving a 'best friend who shoots water rats and feeds them to his geese'. The hapless children, who have 'earphone heads' and 'dirty necks', are 'locked in the nursery'. In the kitchens, meanwhile, all kinds of rum doings are afoot. 'The servants they're so helpful, dear,' crows Jagger. 'The cook she is a whore/The butler has a place for her/Behind the pantry door.' This, it would be fair to say, is not a very New Labour vision of domestic husbandry.

'The group would go onstage and kick into Live With Me, and keep the intro going – until, obviously, the audience were built into a frenzy of excitement,' says Mark Ellen. 'And then, on the nod, Tony would come out of the wings – in a massive pair of flares and T-shirt that revealed four or five inches of torso – with one hand on his hip, wagging his finger. "Well alright! This is Ugly Rumours!"'

By the group's third show, Blair was in sure command of his role. As it turned out, he needed to be: mid-way through the show, in the dining hall of St John's College, disaster struck. 'We used to nail bits of the drum kit to the floor. But because we were playing in some gorgeous sixteenth-century oak-panelled hall, hung with oil paintings, there was a certain amount of respect as regarded hammering six inch nails into the floorboards. And on the third number, it all started to fall apart.

'I looked over at Jim, and his snare drum had fallen over, the cymbals had gone, and the bass drum just rolled off the stage into the audience. None of us had the presence of mind to know what to do. We were paralysed with fear. And Tony stepped to the mike and went into this monologue. "Hi! We're Ugly Rumours. Hope you're having a fantastic time." He plugged all our dates: "We're playing the Corpus Christi Alternative Ball, 'cos we all feel quite strongly that the prices for the conventional balls are exorbitant." A little bit of politics. And he managed to maintain the attention of all these people, while we cobbled the drums back together. I was very impressed by it: that ability to address a large number of people, under pressure, isn't something that comes naturally when you're that age.'

His confidence brought other benefits. Blair had already proved to be an assured player of the mating game – history records that during his first year, he had a relationship with one Suzie Parsons, apparently renowned as 'one of the most beautiful women in Oxford' – and his performance style reaped similar benefits. 'There were loads of fantastic looking women in Laura Ashley dresses with no shoes, slightly Pre-Raphaelite creatures, all flooding around his microphone,' says Mark Ellen. 'That was slightly irritating, to be fair. I think there may have been dark mutterings about that, behind his back.' In point of fact, his time in Ugly Rumours brought Ellen his share of female attention: it was through Blair that he began dating Anji Hunter, then a student at St Clare's, one of the A-level 'crammer' colleges that dot the city centre's perimeter.

The group's key booking that summer was the aforementioned performance at Corpus Christi's Alternative Ball. Ugly Rumours took to the stage – or rather, the lawn – after performances by an all-female string quartet and a local trad jazz band, dressed in candy-striped jackets and straw boaters. Unbeknown to his colleagues, Blair had the idea of allowing them to join the group in an impromptu celebration of musical togetherness. Such were the first stirrings of what is now known as Blairist inclusivism.

'He did it at the end,' says Mark Ellen. "OK. Listen. *Listen.* This is what we've decided to do, OK? We're gonna get both the support bands back on, and we're gonna get together." He may well have used the word "Jam". It was news to us – totally his idea. And I was a bit panicked by this. But we played Honky Tonk Women, with their horrible bass player doing flashy things that I patently wasn't able to do. Certainly, on Tony's part, there was some suggestion that he liked the idea of some great unity. The string quartet loved it. But I thought it was an affront to the credibility of the Rumours – to be seen onstage with these lamentable old hacks and their straw boaters, who had just been playing Little Brown Jug. I mean, Jesus Christ – we'd just been playing China Grove.'

In their brief spell as Tony Blair's musical collaborators, Ugly Rumours' founders witnessed no signs of his future calling. 'I talked to him a little bit about things outside of music,' says Mark Ellen. 'Not politics, interestingly. He wasn't terribly interested in politics. He wasn't involved in college politics, put it that way. I can remember having that conversation with him: I think he felt that side of it was irrelevant.'

One other aspect of Blair's time with Ugly Rumours merits a mention. His long hair, loon pants, and admiration for Mick Jagger did not denote a fondness for exotically flavoured roll-ups. 'None of us were dope smokers,' says Ellen. 'We were never really involved with it – and he was certainly never involved with it. Not censorious about it; didn't object to anybody else doing it – just decided it wasn't for him. He'd made a lifestyle decision that it wasn't his bag.'

Whatever, Blair was clearly a paid-up member of a generation reared on rock music. Moreover, his enthusiasm did not end when he exited both Oxford and Ugly Rumours and entered the legal profession: in 1994, among his favoured car listening was *Definitely Maybe*. After his visit to the *Q* Awards, it was not entirely surprising that the Labour Party began cultivating the friendship of Britain's newest celebrity musicians. Soon enough, in fact, one of them would be invited to the Palace of Westminster for drinks.

CHAPTER 10

Men who should know better

On 5 May 1994, Graham Coxon was spending an unremarkable week-day evening in his usual surrogate living room, The Good Mixer in Camden Town. Across London in SE1, meanwhile, the Gallagher Brothers were at work, participating in a question-and-answer session with a small crowd of *NME* competition winners. The occasion was part of the build-up to Creation Records' tenth anniversary concert, confirmed for the following month at the Royal Albert Hall, and – thanks to Tim Abbot – given the rib-tickling title 'Undrugged'. The Gallaghers sat next to members of Ride and The Boo Radleys, two other Creation groups who were scheduled to play at the event, and fielded a series of nervously voiced enquiries. Their ease with the ritual – manifested in a series of spontaneous comic set-pieces – quickly made them the stars of the show. At the event's end – and having pilfered at least one microphone – the Gallaghers asked a couple of the journalists present if they fancied taking them to Camden, the nocturnal paradise about which they had read so much. So it was that two cabs made their way across the river and via the West End, in the direction of The Good Mixer.

And, for the first time, Blur's universe was gatecrashed by Oasis. Having arrived at the pub and spotted Coxon, the Gallaghers sprinted towards his table with all the starstruck enthusiasm that had character-ised Liam's meeting with Andrew Roachford. This time, however, their greeting was laced with a noticeable irreverence, as Coxon was bombarded by a stream of backhanded tributes. 'Good band Blur,' said Liam. 'Shit clothes, though.' When the two parties stood next to one another in the Gents, the Gallaghers went in for an age-old jape, jostling Coxon so that he splashed his own trousers.

Understandably rattled, Coxon asked the landlord if he would ensure the Gallaghers were never allowed back in. With such valuable custom at stake – and right undoubtedly on Coxon's side – he could only agree.

The Gallaghers' rather ugly arrival in Camden looked like the dramatisation of Noel's rhetoric: Oasis terrorising London's aesthetes in the name of 'shagging and taking drugs and being in a band'. Yet Oasis's increasing notoriety could be squared with the developments that had been crystallised by *Parklife*: focusing on their debt to The Beatles, the sense that they shared Blur's mission to avenge the hegemony of grunge, and their obvious ease with the idea of huge success, one could surely incorporate them into the same cultural moment. The argument would be advanced with ever-increasing confidence as the year rolled on, and the two groups were proudly wrapped in the same flag.

In addition, Damon Albarn increasingly seemed to aspire to the kind of proletarian swagger that the Gallaghers had off to a tee. The mewling cockney he used for the vocal on Girls And Boys was starting to define his speaking voice; for one reason and another, he took to wearing a chunky silver identity bracelet. 'I've got this real Essex man vibe,' he explained, rather unconvincingly.

All this was reflected in the hoop-la surrounding *Parklife*. In keeping with the photograph of racing greyhounds that adorned its sleeve, it was launched by an evening at Walthamstow Dog Track. Coachloads of invitees were ferried from The Good Mixer to E17, where they nervously moved among the regulars and inexpertly frittered away their money. Albarn arrived in his new uniform: leaving behind the hybrid of mod and skinhead attire that had gone with *Modern Life Is Rubbish*, he was now dressing in the style of an 80s casual, all Sergio Tacchini and Fila tracksuit tops and desirable trainers.

In addition to his Sunday kickabouts, during the previous year, he had begun going regularly to watch Chelsea FC. 'That was when he invented football,' says Andy Ross. 'Damon didn't know much about football before he discovered Chelsea. The Premiership had only just started; he started going to Chelsea because a couple of his mates, people who had worked on Blur's videos, always went. Chelsea are the luvvie football team, aren't they? I suppose Damon may have thought that football was a people's thing; but you go down to Chelsea, and you can't get a more middle-class environment. Realistically, he should have supported Leyton Orient, 'cos he bangs on about how he's from Leytonstone all the time.'

The *NME* was similarly unimpressed. In May, they ran a spoof Albarn interview, in which he enthused about his new passion. 'I've always been a fan of Chelsea and love to see them score lots of goals,' it said. 'My favourite Chelsea players are Eric Cantona and "Gazza". Do you want a fight, mate?' (As if to give such barbs the ring of truth, in August 1995, Albarn told *Just Seventeen* magazine that the greatest football player of all time was Trevor Brooking. 'I don't think it stands up to any argument,' he later explained. 'It's just an emotional thing.')

Charges of affectation apart, the drama-school fop was mutating into something a little more testosterone-fuelled. As if to square the transformation with Blur's cerebral side, Albarn reinvented Thomas De Quincey and came up with the new archetype of the 'lager-eater'. Unfortunately, even some of his closest associates were not convinced. 'I thought Damon was negating a whole side of himself that was much more interesting,' says Justine Frischmann. 'All of a sudden, he was getting really macho. The swing from super-PCness to *Loaded* magazine – which in theory I was in favour of – went too far. It started to get really ugly. I like the idea of no self-censorship, but it seemed to be all about football and being an idiot. That was a completely different Damon to the pre-*Parklife*, pre-breakdown Damon.

'I went with him to Chelsea once,' she says. 'They drew: it was a nil-nil draw. Maybe against Tottenham. Damon had a full-on cockney accent, shouting and screaming. There was a guy behind me shouting really racist remarks at a black guy on the other team. I just found it offensive.'

Neither was Alex James about to buy a season ticket, though he retrospectively expresses his bafflement in more unreconstructed terms: 'It's a big gay bar, football, isn't it?'

The first issue of *Loaded* magazine – tag-lined 'For men who should know better' – appeared in April 1994. By way of laying out its stall, the cover featured Gary Oldman, Eric Cantona and Paul Weller, and the chest-beating headline 'Superlads!' It was the latter four letters that caught the imagination of those who documented *Loaded*'s arrival: from the *Guardian* to the *Mail On Sunday*, via *MediaWeek* and *Campaign*, the Lad – a word that, from thereon in, *Loaded* would purposefully avoid – became the year's most inescapable stereotype: batted between columnists, identified in marketing reports, and used as the fulcrum of countless adverts.

In that context, the arrival of Oasis was perfectly timed. 'They galvanised us,' says Tim Southwell, then *Loaded*'s deputy editor. 'We started off celebrating people who were older than us: Paul Weller, Eric Cantona and those kind of people . . . and suddenly there were these people who were a bit younger. All of the music we loved was in the past: we weren't really enamoured with what was going on. But Oasis gave us a soundtrack: it felt as if the music was being written to coincide with what was going on in the magazine.'

The group's first *Loaded* article materialised in the third issue. They were pictured in the car park at Maine Road, the home of the Gallaghers' beloved Manchester City: Liam seemingly about to treat the camera lens as a football while the other four slouched in the middle distance. 'Sex ain't bad if it's with total strangers,' said Noel. 'But the problem is girls who want to hang around with you. Oh fuckin' hell no, I'll go with you but I don't want to be your mate.'

Later that year, Liam proudly aligned himself with the *Loaded* stereotype, before engaging in one of his increasingly customary rewrites of rock history. 'Being a lad is what I'm about,' he said. 'Define lad? I don't define anything . . . There's no lads in any bands today, end of story. Johnny Marr's a lad. The Stone Roses are lads. Bez and [Shaun] Ryder were lads.' He then paused for thought. 'Although they were a bit too laddy.'

Damon Albarn did his first – and last – *Loaded* interview two months later. His pronouncements were a little less Neanderthal than the Gallaghers': he referred to *The Tin Drum*, Herman Hesse and Karl Marx, and dared even to broach the subject of homosexuality. Here, however, there was a rather familiar subtext. 'I'm more homosexual than Brett Anderson,' he said. 'Always have been. As far as bisexuality goes, I've had a little taste of that particular fruit . . . But I've never been able to get very excited about all that. When you get down to it, you can't beat a good pair of tits.'

He then moved through a two-paragraph exploration of cunnilingus in the context of menstruation, before concluding thus: 'I started out reading Nabokov,' he said, 'and now I'm into football, dog-racing and Essex girls.' Albarn was not the only son of the middle classes to take such a detour: suddenly, greasy spoon cafés and visits to away matches were accorded a new kind of exoticism, as if a spell as a designer prole was an obligatory stop-off on some modern equivalent of The Grand Tour.

For the previous two years, Alan McGee had surely been living out the *Loaded* ideal of international hedonism. Flitting between London, Los Angeles and Tokyo, buoyed by diet pills, cocaine and quadruple measures of bourbon, his legend was only fuelled by the tributes paid by his latest group. 'We gave him Supersonic,' said Noel Gallagher, 'and he was going, "You've not wrote this! You're taking the piss out of me, man." We said, "No, Alan – we wrote it yesterday." . . . At that point, he poured a bottle of Jack Daniel's over his head and said he was going to phone up each and every one of his bands and fire them.'

This rather embellished story – as it turned out, McGee had merely spilled his drink in a spasm of excitement – tumbled out in April 1994, some two months after McGee's appetites had finally led to a horrific breakdown. Gallagher's timing suggests either that he, like most of the music industry, was unaware of the gravity of McGee's condition, or the more likely notion of tales continuing to be told by way of a decoy.

On 19 February, McGee had spent a Friday night in the company of Primal Scream, knowing that he was about to fly to California the following day. The evening passed in a blur of cocaine and alcohol: having forgone sleep, McGee boarded his plane to LA – in the company of his sister Susan – the following morning. 'A few hours into the journey,' he says, 'the world started getting a bit funny. What it really was, essentially, was one almighty panic attack. I'd had panic attacks before, but this was off the Richter Scale. I thought I was going to die. I was four hours into a twelve-hour flight. I basically flipped out, the stewardesses thought I was on acid or something. It was pure psychosis: I thought I could hear people talking to me, twenty feet down the plane; I'd open my eyes and think I was in heaven. It was quite interesting for two or three hours, but not something I'd recommend.'

McGee was met at the airport by paramedics, who told him he was suffering from nervous exhaustion. He was advised to rest, and spent thirty-six hours in bed at the Mondrian Hotel. On Monday, however, he was ready to get back to his own frazzled kind of normality: he went to see Swervedriver, a Creation band, playing at the Roxy club, and gorged himself on Jack Daniel's.

'And then,' McGee continues, 'I woke up the next day, absolutely hungover to fuck – and took some speed pills to get me going. You know that song from *Diamond Dogs*? "As they pulled you out of the oxygen tent, you asked for the latest party"? That was what it was like. I then went down to try and do a Primal Scream movie deal, to get them in some film, with Mo Austin and Lenny Waronker, the people that ran Warner Brothers. And as I was travelling down there, it was all getting really fucking bizarre. I got in there, and the blinds started moving towards me – and at that point, I was just utterly freaked out. I wasn't in control of my body. Or my mind.

'We got back to the hotel, and I thought I had a metal pole in the back of my neck – which, now I know all about drugs, was obviously hypertension. They got the paramedics out, and they said my blood pressure was 172. It's 110 in a normal person. They were worried about a blood clot – so then, suddenly, they put me in a wheelchair, on oxygen. I'm getting taken through the Mondrian Hotel to the van, with seventeen paramedics. I'm laid down, and they're going, "Don't move." That was the point it was over for me and drugs. These people think you could be on your way out, you're on oxygen – what the fuck is this about? Rock'n'roll? Who gives a fuck?'

McGee was taken to the Cedars-Sinai Medical Center in West Hollywood, the huge hospital with wings named after Steven Spielberg and Max Factor, and the unique status as a clearing house for celebrity corpses: Lucille Ball, Danny Kaye, Frank Sinatra, Sammy Davis Jr. Three months before McGee's arrival, its doctors had tried in vain to avert the death of River Phoenix, sped to the emergency ward from The Viper Room, one of McGee's LA haunts. Thankfully, McGee was not in quite such a life-threatening state: he was injected with a sedative and discharged the same day, whereupon he returned to the Mondrian. His stay lasted another ten days: each morning, he was visited by a doctor who gave him booster injections.

When he returned to London, most of the staff at Creation were informed merely that he would be taking some time off. His closest associates, however, quickly became aware of how ill he was. 'I went to see him at his flat in Rotherhithe,' says Tim Abbot. 'We went for a walk: we walked down to this little pond we used to go and have a chat at. And we had to sit down: he was out of breath. And that's when he told me: "This is not a head thing – this is a physical thing. My mind's left my body, my body's left my mind." I got a cab back home and thought, "Shit – he's fucking ill."'

McGee was back in London for a mere seven days. He established contact with Dr Colin Brewer, the medical director of The Stapleford Centre – an addiction clinic based within spitting distance of Buckingham Palace – and surmised that, prior to entering rehab, he needed to 'balance'. At the suggestion of his father, he moved back to the family home in Glasgow, where he made one startling resolution: the LA episode, he decided, had marked the end of his time in the music business.

'I'd given in,' says McGee. 'I was chucking it. I was bitter because I'd been doing everything to please everybody else. The bottom line was, everyone wanted Alan McGee to be out of control, and the only person who got fucked by it was me. I had a couple of million in the bank, and I thought, "Fuck this for a game of soldiers – I don't even want to come back."'

It was some token of the bonds that tied the indie milieu that, though rumours of McGee's state began to swirl around London, no magazine sought to investigate them further. His breakdown was the focus of concern and sympathy rather than prurience; on only a few occasions did a hint of his condition make it to print. One such sentence appeared in an *NME* concert review in June: 'Rumour has it he's in retreat from living the dream too high and fast,' wrote Steve Sutherland, the paper's editor. The subject of the article was the night to which Creation had been building up since the New Year: Undrugged, the tenth birthday celebration at the Albert Hall.

Undrugged took place on 4 June. In addition to the label's founder (who, by way of a replacement, sent his father), notable absentees included most of the groups who had defined Creation's history: The Jesus And Mary Chain, Primal Scream, My Bloody Valentine, Teenage Fanclub. Instead, there was an array of bit-part players, and the rather unsatisfactory spectacle of ordinarily electric musicians dispensing acoustic versions of their songs. 'The idea could have been great,' says Tim Abbot. 'If McGee had still been in power, it would have worked. We would have got The Scream. Alan would have made the calls.'

As if to prove that Undrugged was the victim of some supernatural curse, even the appearance of Creation's new hopes was blighted by bad luck. That night, Liam Gallagher complained of a sore throat: Oasis – introduced as 'the best reason to believe in rock'n'roll in 1994' – were thus represented by Noel Gallagher and Paul Arthurs.

It was the absence of Alan McGee, however, that lent the night its most striking sense of mishap. In the ensuing months, as musicians suddenly found their bank accounts in the black, and fidgeted with ten pound notes and handmirrors to celebrate, he was an implied presence: the embodiment of a cautionary tale to which no-one – for now – was prepared to pay much attention.

Sunday 26 June was the last day of the Glastonbury Festival. These were the days before the mobile phone had become an integral part of human existence; one of the resultant effects was that three days' watching groups in the English countryside was combined with a very pleasurable ignorance of the outside world. Rumours – often involving celebrity deaths – could sweep through the fields at speed. Even when it came to events on-site, information tended to circulate in the form of wildly exaggerated hearsay.

And so it proved that year. By Sunday lunchtime, whispers were doing the rounds about a late-night shooting outside a blanket stall-cum-outdoor rave location called Joe Bananas. Only when the bedraggled hordes went back to the straight world did the facts become clear: five people had indeed been injured by gunfire in an incident that oozed a very potent kind of drama: the festival's licentious paradise, resourced by the kind of people who were intimately acquainted with firearms, had just been confronted by its own dark side.

In the meantime, the crowds had simply got on with the festival. That Sunday, Glastonbury's second stage featured Pulp, Radiohead, Blur and Oasis, all at various stages of their progress, and – with the exception of Blur, who were the day's penultimate act – seemingly scattered through the bill at random. For Noel Gallagher, the running order held one additional source of intrigue: a few places above his group were none other than Inspiral Carpets, playing out the last notes of their nine-year career.

Oasis took the stage mid-way through the afternoon. They were preceded by Echobelly, one of the explicitly British groups who had appeared in the slipstream of *Modern Life Is Rubbish*. As far as Liam Gallagher was concerned, they represented little in the way of competition. 'Are you gonna wake up, then?' he asked the crowd. 'For some real songs?' As usual, Oasis's performance ended with I Am The Walrus; Liam swaggered from the stage while the group whipped up its set-closing cacophony, seemingly secure in the knowledge that they had done what was expected of them.

Blur, meanwhile, took the stage at 8.30. They were to that year's festival what Suede had been in 1993: the year's favoured sons, booked with the expectation that Glastonbury would be the setting for a pivotal performance. Even the fine details of their performance betrayed the fact that they had risen to the occasion: Graham Coxon, much to the audience's mirth, broke sartorial rank from his colleagues by appearing in full Vietnam-era US army uniform. And when it came to the music, they did not disappoint: Phil Daniels turned in his cameo on Parklife, and when Blur played This Is A Low, the sun began to set. Damon Albarn's paean to the mysteries of the British landscape was thus given a perfect backdrop: sitting behind his keyboard, surveying the multitudes as the evening breeze wafted across the stage, he looked both serenely happy and momentarily omnipotent.

That evening, Oasis's second single entered the charts at number eleven. Shakermaker glued the pilfered melody of I'd Like To Teach The World To Sing to that most orthodox of musical undercarriages: a four-minute ramble through a 12-bar blues. As it turned out, however, Oasis managed to make their use of such a hoary old archetype sound engagingly cheeky: thanks also to its nursery-rhyme lyrics and Liam Gallagher's fractured repetition of the song's pay-off – 'Shake along with me' – Shakermaker actually sounded slightly avant-garde. In tandem with Supersonic, it fed the fleeting idea that Oasis, like Happy Mondays, might just be the kind of untutored minds that could push rock music somewhere unforeseen.

The following Thursday, the song took them on to *Top of the Pops*.

They performed in front of a backdrop taken from the cover of their 1993 demo tape: the Union Jack being sucked down a plughole. For the benefit of those who had not made the group's acquaintance, the first seconds of their performance were captioned 'New UK Talent From Manchester'.

Among the audience that night were four other Mancunians, finally working on the follow-up to a debut album that had been released four years before. The Stone Roses gathered round the TV set at Rockfield Studios, near Monmouth, united by curiosity about the group that claimed to be their spiritual offspring. 'We all watched it,' said John Squire. 'I didn't think the tune was that great, but they just looked right. It was like some pristine archive footage of a great sixties band you'd never got round to hearing.'

One month before, Bernard Butler had ceased to be a member of Suede. The group, cloistered in a studio in Kilburn, North London, were mid-way through a second album on which both he and Brett Anderson had sailed to artistic extremes, creating songs that mixed lyrical melodrama with its florid musical equivalent. Stay Together had set the tone for what was to come – both in terms of its overarching air of ostentation, and the fact that its creation saw repeated flashes of tension between its authors.

'Now, I find Stay Together pompous and bombastic,' says Brett Anderson. 'It was one of the few points in our career where hype actually did dictate its success. It was successful, and people saw it as being good, because it was connected with the first album. It was quite a conceited record. And that was the point where a rift started to form between me and Bernard. He seemed to have the impression that I was becoming seduced by the wrong side of it all: by the fame. He'd decided to see me as the person having his photo taken with his shirt off, shooting his mouth off, whereas he was the serious musician.'

Butler's alienation from the group had been furthered by the experience of travelling around the USA in the autumn of 1993, an episode that – as with Blur's 1992 tour – suggested that British indie groups entertained American ambitions at their peril. After a superficially successful round of the USA's major cities during the summer, Suede returned to the States to join a tour with Counting Crows and The Cranberries – hardly the most suitable of road partners. To make things yet more vexed, Butler left the UK knowing that his father was about to die of cancer. 'I spoke about it with my mum and dad,' he says, 'which was the strangest thing: "If you're going to pop your socks, are you going to do it before or after the tour?" But he told me to go and do it. He died two days after we arrived in New York. I went home the next morning, went to the funeral, and went back to America the next day. I was frozen.'

No sooner had the tour begun, than things were further complicated by The Cranberries' sudden US success. Thanks to a sugary single entitled Linger, they became the tour's main draw; their singer, Dolores O'Riordan, commemorated her elevation by using a day off to fly to San Francisco, have a gold tooth fitted, and buy a pair of leather trousers. Suede, meanwhile, grumpily festered at the bottom of the bill, while three-quarters of the group propelled themselves from city to city using a mixture of alcohol, chemicals and sexual profligacy. 'We used to take a load of drugs and get laid all the time,' says Mat Osman. 'That's what touring *was*.'

'Touring America was a non-stop orgy,' says Brett Anderson. 'It was wicked.'

Butler was not only recently bereaved, but also freshly engaged: the combination was hardly likely to nudge him towards the group's more hedonistic exploits. 'They got really resentful of the fact that they were on tour with someone who didn't want to party,' he says. He expressed his separation from his colleagues by travelling with their road crew, and adopting a frazzled work-to-rule policy. 'We'd be going onstage at half nine,' he says. 'I'd plan it so I'd arrive at 9.29, put on this red shirt, which became a uniform, and go on. The rest of the time, I'd just wander around, getting stoned. Every city we went to, I used to go walking: "Which way should I go? *That* way. I wonder how far I'll go before anyone tries to run after me." It became a game. I was completely out of control: getting stoned, and doing charlie in the evening.'

On at least one occasion, Butler walked from the stage during Suede's performance, sat in the wings, and encouraged one of The Cranberries to strum his guitar for him. By the time they reached Boston, the last of Suede's patience had been used up: Simon Gilbert and Saul Galpern were dispatched to Butler's hotel room to pull him back into line. 'They put me in a corner and just said, "You *are* going to get on with Brett, and that's the end of it. Don't give us any more grief. We're not listening to any of your shit any more." I remember just looking at them, laughing, saying, "Fuck you."'

Back in Britain, Butler's distance from his colleagues was hardly helped by Brett Anderson's increasingly off-beam lifestyle. The new album's lyrics had been written in his new home: a rented flat in High-gate that allowed him to distance himself from London's newest musical clique, and formed the backdrop to a period of mind-bending excess.

On the occasions that he collided with past acquaintances, they were struck by how out-there he had become. Driven by the romantic ideal of chemical derangement in pursuit of artistic ambition, Brett Anderson was reportedly sailing into the stratosphere.

'I was dangerously close to becoming a celebrity, which is the last thing I wanted to be,' he says. 'I saw this scene starting, and I thought I'd isolate myself from it as much as I could. This thing that we'd started off had been distorted into something I never wanted it to be, and I wanted to remove myself from it as much as possible. It was, "Let's get away from this Camden Town, Good Mixer bollocks." So I moved up to Highgate.

'I became obsessed with the number sixteen,' he continues. 'I decided that every place I lived in had to have that number. And I randomly found this flat and it was number sixteen. I was living below this sect called the Mennonites. I started to write in a very different way. And I was taking huge amounts of drugs: a lot of acid.'

The Mennonites had been founded in 16th-century Holland, advocating adult baptism, and – with the arrival of industrialism – scepticism about the luxuries of the modern world. A drug-gobbling rock singer, it was fair to say, represented a very incongruous kind of company.

'They'd sing hymns all the time,' says Anderson. 'I liked it, 'cos it created this very surreal environment that I thrived on. The flat was in the basement of this really beautiful, big gothic place. It had this amazing garden. There was a summer house at the bottom: a real kind of mansion-type vibe. And I would be up for a week, tripping off my nuts, and they'd be singing hymns next door. They had no idea what was going on. But they were surprisingly friendly. Especially seeing as I had this slightly insane girlfriend at the time, who used to come round and smash my windows if I wasn't in.'

In between the sounds of breaking glass and Christian worship, Anderson wrote lyrics that had a distinctly theatrical aspect. Some were surreal and dream-like, populated by the ghosts of James Dean and Marilyn Monroe; others sought to shine light on the blighted, dysfunctional side of Britain that Anderson believed was being forgotten. What united them was his belief that he was pushing himself to new heights. He already had a title for the album: *Dog Man Star*, apparently intended as a proud summation of Suede's evolution. 'It was meant to be a record about ambition; what could you make yourself into,' says Anderson. 'The title was meant to reflect the music: I thought it was like onomatopoeia.'

Bernard Butler was similarly minded to push the creative envelope. '*Parklife* had come out by that point,' he says. 'And I was convinced that Girls And Boys was the worst pop song ever made. I thought it was the pinnacle of *funny music*, which I hate. Like, "*Very* funny, very ironic, that horrible synthesiser line is *very* funny." There's no beauty about that record at all, and that really annoyed the fuck out of me. I just thought, "I don't want to make music like that. I want to make something that's beautiful and graceful and poised and sensual and elated" – all those things that The Smiths were, taken a step further.'

In the eyes of his colleagues, unfortunately, many of his ideas proved to be unpalatably ostentatious. According to Mat Osman, he piloted a version of a song called The Asphalt World that was twenty-five minutes long, a musical conceit expansive enough to leave enough room for an eight-minute guitar solo. Butler is adamant that the result-ant piece of music was not only altogether shorter, but that he intended it to be edited to an orthodox length. Nonetheless, his ex-colleagues maintain that the album was headed towards an unbecoming gaudiness. 'Lots of the musical ideas were too much,' says Osman. 'They were being rude to the listener: it was expecting too much of people to listen to them.' Very often, Osman says, he, Anderson and Simon Gilbert began to think that Butler was driven by a desire to simply wind them up.

To make things yet more fractious, Butler was clashing with Suede's producer, Ed Buller, who eventually came to be the focus of most of his frustrations. 'He was telling me all the time, "I don't want you to do this, I don't want you to do that,"' he says. 'And I was just like, "Fuck off – I'm doing it. This is *not* your record."' Feeling he was being backed into a corner, Butler issued the band and their management an ultimatum: either they dispensed with Buller, or Butler left the group. It is perhaps some token of the threadbare state of Suede's internal relations that, claiming that Buller might sue for breach of contract, the group elected to leave their guitarist out in the cold. 'I was utterly amazed that they would go for him rather than me,' he says. 'They called my bluff. And I lost.'

Butler's exit came mere days after his wedding, at which only he and his wife had been present. The rest of Suede, however, interpreted the fact that they hadn't been invited as a snub; decisive evidence, it seemed, that they and Butler were now occupants of completely differ-ent worlds. 'We hadn't spoken for weeks,' says Brett Anderson. 'A lot of *Dog Man Star* was recorded very separately. Bernard would come in, do his guitar parts, work in the day – and I'd come in at night. There wasn't much anyone could do. It had gone beyond the point where anyone could really reason it out.'

'I took my wedding day and the next day off,' says Butler, 'and I came back to the studio, and I wasn't allowed in: the assistant was told that Brett was doing his vocals, and that was that. I was like, "I'm not allowed in? This is a joke, isn't it?" I went back the next day and said, "I want my guitar – I want to do some stuff at home." And they brought it out: through the intercom, they said, "We'll bring it out and put it on the street." It was like, "There you go – fuck off." That was it, really. I didn't leave; I was kicked out. That's really obvious. If I'd just left, no-one would have let me leave, if I'd been wanted.'

As far as the rest of Suede were concerned, the split was a cause for celebration: in cahoots with a horn section, they marked its final confirmation with a joyful rendition of The Girl From Ipanema, captured on video by Simon Gilbert. In the real world, however, their troubles suggested that their fate had suddenly changed: they were now living in a different universe from the one that had seen the sky-scraping triumphs of the previous year.

The group's manager, Charlie Charlton, made one last attempt at a rapprochement. 'He phoned me up and said, "I'm going to put Brett on now,"' says Bernard Butler. 'I was like, "What? Doesn't he dial the phone any more?" I had a conversation along the lines of "This is not what I want, this is not happening, why can't you get it together?" I got more and more angry with him, 'cos it was just one-word answers. In the end I said, "You're acting like a fucking cunt," and the phone went dead. I phoned him back and Charlie answered the phone. He said, "Brett doesn't like being called a cunt." I said, "Well, tell him he is one. Someone should." And that was it. That was the last time I spoke to him.'

Bernard Butler exited the sessions leaving *Dog Man Star* some distance from completion. Brett Anderson had recorded little more than a string of guide vocals; several songs did not have titles; much of the music was still to be embossed with overdubs. Anderson, Mat Osman and Simon Gilbert – along with Ed Buller – succeeded in taking the record to its conclusion, though some of the work they accomplished seemed to belie the idea that they and Bernard Butler had been pulling in different directions: among the eleventh-hour additions was an unspeakably camp orchestral coda on Still Life, the song he and Anderson had premiered at 1993's Glastonbury. Its new arrangement seemed to transfer Suede's spiritual home from London to the more spaghetti-strewn end of the Wild West.

Despite its trouble-strewn creation, with the album's eventual release, the group talked about *Dog Man Star* with a wide-eyed enthusiasm. However, the sense that Suede were now a depleted force would be confirmed by its muted collision with the public. To its lyricist and singer, the album's grandiosity set a new musical standard; what failed to occur to Brett Anderson was that the British mind has long been prone to greet such grand conceits by blowing raspberries. Indeed, in a culture increasingly defined by *Loaded*, Girls And Boys, and Noel Gallagher lyrics about gin and tonic, the response was pretty much inevitable. Suede were about to be eclipsed.

CHAPTER 11

All the people

.

By August 1994, to anyone under thirty, *Parklife* had become inescapable. Its ubiquity was only boosted by the release of its title track as a single, which duly parachuted into the top 10, commencing a month in the charts. Driven along by Phil Daniels' endearingly gruff monologue and a chorus – 'All the people/So many people' – that sounded like some inclusivist clarion call, it managed to hark back to singles that had once acted as a kind of national soundtrack. Madness were the most apposite reference point: within Parklife's knockabout three minutes, there lurked the ghosts of Our House, Baggy Trousers and House Of Fun. As the single worked its wonders, one could detect a remarkable phenomenon indeed: those who thought rock music had left them behind, scuttling to their local HMV to invest in this new, amazingly friendly sound.

If Damon Albarn's traumatised response to the first stirrings of his new audience had suggested that fame might not be for him, he now seemed to suggest that – despite his panic attacks, visits to Harley Street and intimations of imminent collapse – he actually wanted to go further. 'I really want to write music that is more universal,' he said. 'I see so many limitations to what we do. I've got to divorce myself from writing songs that have that semi-detached quality and go for shopping centres. This is the way I think about music and that's why people get confused about us. I want this album to reach that Britannia Book Club level. Y'know, take your trousers down at the Brits and then come back with an album that competes with Garth Brooks but is intelligent. That's the future for me. I can't see any alternative really.'

In retrospect, his words are fascinating. Those indie musicians who had aspired to huge success in the recent past – The Stone Roses are the best example – had always envisaged their music gatecrashing the mainstream with its countercultural purity intact: indeed, in the spectacle of creative defiance mixing with vast success lay the last traces of the punk ideal. Albarn, however, wanted to actively pursue the mass audience: to nip and tuck his music until he was speaking the language of the everyman. 'Intelligence' would presumably represent his one bulwark against the banality that often comes with such knowing commercialism; nonetheless, there was something worryingly Faustian about his aspirations.

Though Noel Gallagher had long implied that Oasis's music poured forth with the kind of frantic speed borne of pure instinct, the recording of their first album had brought them within spitting distance of disaster. They had been billeted to Monnow Valley Studios, near Monmouth, at the start of the year. There, they were to begin work under the tutelage of Dave Batchelor: a contact of Noel Gallagher's from his Inspiral Carpets days. Batchelor was an old hand – a producer whose CV stretched back to his work in the mid-70s with The Sensational Alex Harvey Band. His pairing with a gaggle of young Mancunians, most of whom were still reeling from their first acquaintance with The Road, was always going to be incongruous.

And so it proved. 'It wasn't happening,' says Paul Arthurs. 'He was the wrong person for the job. A lot older, for a start. Knew Mick Jagger personally. We'd play in this great big room, buzzing to be in this studio, playing like we always played. He'd say, "Come in and have a listen." And we'd be like, "That doesn't sound like it sounded in that room. What's *that*?" It was thin. Weak. Too clean. He had us doing Slide Away for two days, solid. He was like, "Keep doing it, keep doing it." There was no vibe.'

Monnow Valley was no low-budget demo studio. Oasis's labours were costing £800 a day; as it dawned on them that the money was being hurled on to the fire, panic began to spread through the group. 'Behind the scenes,' says Arthurs, 'Noel was frantically on the phone to the management, going, "This ain't working." For it not to be happening was a bit frightening.'

The Batchelor tapes offer decisive proof that a group needs a little more than a stock of impressive songs to ascend to the intended heights. For the most part, Oasis sound like amateurs: Liam Gallagher's vocals are flat and reedy; the guitars, later to be rebuilt into a roaring cacophony, seem uncomfortably slight. Were anyone to be played them with no knowledge of the authors' identity, they might very well assume they were listening to a callow covers band.

Mindful of the money that had been spent, Noel Gallagher attempted to rescue the music they had recorded. The tapes were dragged around a couple of London studios, while the group's associates were alerted to what had gone wrong. 'I visited them in Chiswick,' says Tim Abbot. 'Batchelor had been fucked off and they were trying to mend the tapes. McGee, Noel, me and various people had a great sesh, and we listened to it over and over again. And all I could think was, "It ain't got the attack." There was no immediacy.'

Forty-eight hours after the Amsterdam episode – and on the same day Alan McGee boarded his fateful flight to Los Angeles – the group found themselves in Cornwall. They had resolved to re-record the album at Sawmills, a beautifully located studio on the western bank of the River Fowey. It was located in a private tidal creek: among the delights of the group's stay was a nightly boat-ride back from the nearest pub. Photographs taken during the sessions also record the deeply unlikely spectacle of Oasis attempting to learn how to canoe.

This time, the music was produced by Noel Gallagher and Mark Coyle. The usual studio convention of ensuring that each instrument is soundproofed against the others was gleefully flouted; the group recorded en masse, convinced that the only option was to replicate the noise that they made onstage. In addition, Noel had decided to use one brutally simple weapon. 'There were *loads* of guitars,' says Paul Arthurs. 'That was Noel's favourite trick: get the drums, bass and rhythm guitar down, and then he'd *cane* it. "Less is more" didn't really work then.'

Even then, the results failed to measure up to the group's expectations. By now, there was little chance of a third recording; what had been put to tape in Cornwall had to somehow be transformed. In desperation, Marcus Russell contacted Owen Morris, an engineer-turned-producer whom he had met through Johnny Marr. Morris was duly played the Sawmills recordings; his verdict was uncomfortably redolent of Tim Abbot's misgivings about the Batchelor tapes. 'I just thought, "They've messed up here,"' he said, 'and I guessed at that stage that Noel was completely fucked off. Marcus was like, "You can do what you want with it – literally, whatever you want."' Among Morris's first actions was the stripping down of Noel Gallagher's piled-on guitar tracks.

Morris did his final mix on May bank holiday weekend. The miracle was that music that had passed through so many hands sounded so dynamic: the guitar-heavy stew that Morris had inherited had been remoulded into something positively piledriving. When the songs were placed in sequence, his achievement was made explicit. *Definitely*

Maybe opened with Rock 'n' Roll Star: as steely and frenetic an opening statement as could be imagined. Somehow, Oasis had done it.

On 8 August, *Definitely Maybe* was trailed by Oasis's third single: a song that had sat in their live set for nigh-on a year, amassing so many mentions in the group's reviews that its release had long seemed inevitable. It had been written in 1991, when Noel Gallagher had been spurred into action by The Rolling Stones' Shine A Light. The melody of its verses was purloined from Jagger and Richards, though the subject matter of its lyric lay a little closer to home: Live Forever, founded on the simplest of chords, was written in tribute to Peggy Gallagher.

If large chunks of the group's live repertoire suggested a group in thrall to such rock'n'roll staples as brain-crushing volume and instinctive iconoclasm, this song suggested something that was almost their polar opposite: an ability to craft balmy modern anthems with an appeal to all ages. The implicit dedication to Noel and Liam's mum said it all – while Damon Albarn was wondering how to cease being 'semi-detached' and push his songs into Britain's shopping centres, Noel Gallagher sounded like he'd already got the knack. By way of proving the potency of such an idea, Live Forever entered the singles chart at number ten.

Two months before, Creation Records had nearly disappeared from the map. Sony's munificence in 1992 had only proved to be a temporary plug in an ever-swelling financial hole. By the summer of 1994, the label was £2 million in debt; powerful voices within Sony were heard to wonder whether it might be time to withdraw their help, and abandon them to the receivers. Alan McGee's absence – not to mention the confusion that surrounded the prospect of his return – hardly helped Creation's cause.

Thanks in part to Oasis's snowballing success, the crisis was ridden out. A handful of Creation staff were made redundant, while such long-lost talents as The Telescopes, Medalark 11, Adorable and Dreadzone were excised from the label's roster. In addition, Tim Abbot discovered that he was now being allotted the princely sum of £60,000 to cover the marketing of *Definitely Maybe*. Within such tight limits, there was no chance of metaphorical blanket-bombing; Abbot had to choose his targets carefully.

The resultant campaign spoke volumes about where Oasis – and, indeed, British rock music – were heading. 'I'd go back to the Midlands every couple of weeks,' says Abbot, 'and people I knew would say, "Oasis are great. This is what we listen to." And I'd be thinking, "Well, you lot don't buy singles. You don't read the *NME*. You don't read *Q*. How do we get to people like you?" It was about getting momentum going. I was thinking, "I wonder if there's people who haven't had a sense of occasion for a long time."'

Abbot resolved to step outside indie etiquette, and establish contact with the kind of publications that had never been approached by Creation. Adverts for *Definitely Maybe* were placed in such football magazines as *Shoot!*, *Match* and *90 Minutes*. Abbot even went so far as to take out space in a handful of match programmes. On top of that, he built bridges to the UK's dance music magazines, booking ads in such publications as *Mixmag* and *Jockey Slut*. His suspicions that Oasis were finding favour in such circles were confirmed when *Mixmag* – who would ordinarily rule out any record founded on a stone-age totem like the guitar – awarded *Definitely Maybe* five stars.

On 4 September, sent on its way by such frenzied reviews, Tim Abbot's marketing campaign and the group's ever-increasing reputation, *Definitely Maybe* entered the album chart at number one. Its nearest competition was *The Three Tenors*, a record that most observers had assumed would leave everything else in the shade. Instead, Oasis outsold Pavarotti, Carreras and Domingo by a factor of 50 per cent, and *Definitely Maybe* registered 100,000 sales in its first four days. Those fond of the hyberbolic use of statistics quickly realised that it was the fastest selling debut album in the history of the British charts.

Alan McGee, meanwhile, was still in Glasgow, all but convinced that he had exited the music industry for good. 'I was single,' he says, 'my girlfriend had left me, and I thought, "Fuck – I'll just stay in Glasgow." I was so low at that time, my ambition was to be well enough that I didn't have to live with my dad. That's how fucked I was, with the drugs. It wasn't, "Let's get back to Creation." It was, "My ambition is to be well enough to have my own house, so I don't have to live with my dad."'

The week that *Definitely Maybe* was released, McGee became sufficiently desperate to pay a visit to a building whose interior he had last seen when he was a boy. 'I'd never been to church in twenty years,' he says. 'And I was so depressed; mortally depressed. There'd been two or three times during that phase when I'd thought about taking my own life. I was strong enough to never let it get on top of me, but I was very down. And I went to church, to see if I could get some . . . whatever, I don't know. I was thirty-three years old, hadn't been to church since I was thirteen, and I went in my old church, and everybody there was eighty-five. They were all coming up to me, going, "I remember you when you were a wee boy, you've done really well." And I was twitching, like Brian Wilson.

'And then I went back home. I knew Oasis were putting their album out that week, but I hadn't even bothered to phone up and find out what was happening, 'cos in my head, I wasn't coming back. And I went home, and Dick [Green] was on the answering machine going, "We've got a number one album! We've got a fucking number one!"'

For Alan McGee, the news had a distinctly bittersweet taste. 'I was happy,' he says, 'but I was also like, "What is the price for a number one record? Did I have to fuck myself so bad?"'

Though Oasis had often seemed to pride themselves on a fondness for hitting the UK's towns and cities and leaving wreckage in their wake, there were occasions that year when the local toughs seemed more than happy to meet them halfway. In mid-August, they paid a visit to Newcastle, where sections of the crowd were evidently in the mood for a ruck. Five songs into Oasis's performance, one particularly fool-hardy oik sprang on to the stage and punched Noel Gallagher in the face, managing to draw blood. Liam and Noel promptly leapt into the crowd in pursuit of his assailant; soon after, it became clear that the show was over.

Some of the audience duly voiced their displeasure. 'Soft as shite,' was one chant; 'Manchester, wank, wank, wank' another. A crowd of 300 quickly gathered outside the venue, breaking windows in the group's van, and causing such panic that Oasis's exit was only accomplished after they had ploughed into a parked car. Liam Gallagher was enraged. 'We've been saying for a year to our record company and our manager that we need more security,' he spat, 'and it's all, "We can't afford it." But does it take someone to lose an eye to get security?' Marcus Russell took the hint: the next morning, he called an acquaintance named Ian Robertson, and invited him into the group's camp as head of security.

Robertson was a thick-set former paratrooper who had seen active service in Northern Ireland. He spoke in the assured, clipped manner of a man who had perhaps been destined for officer rank, until a long-held fondness for music got the better of him. His first taste of life as a rock aide had been with Duran Duran; he had gone on to share the company of such 80s titans as Spandau Ballet, The Sisters Of Mercy and Sigue Sigue Sputnik.

As far as the Oasis camp were concerned, however, there were more pressing matters to discuss. 'When I met Mark Coyle,' says Robertson, 'the first question he asked me was, "Do you drink?" I said, "Yes." "Do you take drugs?" "On occasion." "Fine." Not, "Who have you worked with, what do you do, how do you see this working?" But that was the deal. There was a lot of The Keith Richards Guide To Life

On The Road. It was, "We're going to do these things. I know it's been done before, I know we're not breaking new ground. But it's our turn." You could argue that they could have seized the moment by looking at it as an opportunity to travel the globe and take in a lot of culture. But they seized the moment by saying, "We're going to stay up late, every single night."'

In September, as *Definitely Maybe* stuck fast to the upper reaches of the charts, Oasis paid their second visit that year to Manchester. Poetically, they were playing at the Haçienda: the sometime embodiment of the city's pop-cultural importance at which Noel Gallagher had been a regular. Pummelled by the gang wars that were still being fought out on the city's streets, it had long since fallen from its revered pedestal; by 1994, in fact, it was perilously close to being Just Another Venue.

Noel made his way to the club with Ian Robertson, who innocently enquired as to his feelings about his home city. The reply hinted that the memory of Tommy Gallagher had become synonymous with the Mancunian cityscape. 'We were on our way to the soundcheck in a cab, and I was just interested in how he felt about the place. Liam, Guigsy, Bonehead and Tony were always going back to Manchester, every opportunity they got; and Noel was living in a hotel in London. I was like, "Is this home?" I'm paraphrasing, but the guts of his reply was, "There's an awful lot of pain here." Some of it was girlfriend stuff, but it obviously tracked back into something much deeper.'

Tommy Gallagher was not the only ghoulish figure preying on Noel Gallagher's mind. Some time later, he explained one of the key factors behind his move south: 'I was sick and tired of young crackheads coming up to me in clubs, sticking a screwdriver in my back and saying, "We're doing the merchandising on your next tour" or "We're going to be your security team."'

The scenes that transpired at the Haçienda were a perfect case in point. As the group readied themselves for their performance, the vultures – clad in the usual mixture of upmarket labels and chunky jewellery, and inexplicably allowed into the group's orbit – began to circle. 'It was quite staggering,' says Ian Robertson. 'These brain-dead thugs turned up. And, of course, they ended up backstage. And it was, "How did you people get back here?" And then we had the conversation: "Oh, we're doing Oasis's security." "Really? As a matter of fact, you're not." They thought they were going to be part of the gang. Whenever we did shows in Manchester, I took extra security on the road. I even took one person who was *my* security, because I was pissing people off left, right and centre.'

In addition to Oasis's would-be assistants, there was another menacing presence at the Haçienda that night. Shaun Ryder was in the midst of a three-year retreat that had commenced with the break-up of Happy Mondays; his only recent press coverage had concerned an occasion when he had drunkenly driven his car into a vehicle owned by a Mancunian pastor. Nonetheless, he remained a local dignitary: as Oasis were about to take the stage, he demanded that he and his girlfriend be allowed to watch them from the wings. Ignorant of the local star system, Ian Robertson told him he would have to stand out front. In Robertson's account, Ryder greeted this news in rather bad humour. 'My posse's here and you're a dead man,' said Ryder. 'You won't leave Manchester alive.' Mercifully, Robertson managed to make it to the M6 the following morning.

Three weeks later, Oasis began their first tour of the USA. Americans were not yet sufficiently affected by Oasis to want to punch them, so Ian Robertson was left at home. They had played in the States once already: in June, when Sony had paid for a one-off performance at a pokey New York club called Wetlands Preserve. This time, however, their itinerary stretched into the middle-distance: beginning in Seattle, they were to travel on to San Francisco, Sacramento, Minneapolis . . . and on to Philadelphia, Washington and Hoboken, before a final rematch with New York. All the requisite accoutrements had been hired: eight months after they had made their way to Amsterdam in a hired transit, they were to travel round America in a gleaming silver bus.

On 28 September, they reached LA. Two sources of amusement were awaiting them: Paul Arthurs' brother Martin, a sound engineer who had made his home in California; and crystal methedrine, the unspeakably potent American pick-me-up, beloved of roadworn truckers and recreational drug users with precious little left to lose. The night before their show at the Whisky A Go-Go, the group had made merry at The Viper Room, before the Oasis party repaired to Martin Arthurs' house. Eventually, the revelry was rudely halted by the arrival of the Los Angeles Police Department.

'Martin brought the bag of whatever it was: a binbag full,' says Paul Arthurs. 'I actually didn't take any. But it was chaos. The next day, having been up all night, everyone was wired. The morning of the gig, Liam was caning loads of this gear. I think Noel had had some, too. But onstage, before Liam had even sung a line, he was chopping one up behind an amp. Halfway through a song, he'd have another one. More and more, until two songs in, it just went tits up.'

Oasis managed to hobble through their set, but things repeatedly teetered on the brink of collapse. Displeased by the group's rendition of Shakermaker, Liam decided to cosh Noel with his tambourine. During Live Forever, he changed the lyric to 'I don't wanna know why you pick your nose' and repeatedly turned to his brother and made the masturbatory hand gesture. Well before he had completed the lyric of I Am The Walrus, Liam stalked from the stage. Pictures of the night show his eyeballs expanded to the point that he looks little short of possessed. 'After the gig, there was a fight in the dressing room,' says Paul Arthurs. 'A really big scene. Noel passed me on the stairs, and that was the last I saw of him.'

Noel Gallagher had taken $800 from the tour manager and simply disappeared. 'Nobody knew where he'd gone,' says Arthurs. 'We were all back at the hotel in Marcus's room: we called it the War Bunker. We didn't know what to do: do we go home, or do we hang fire?'

Back in the UK, Tim Abbot's afternoon was interrupted by an unexpected transatlantic phone call. 'Noel phoned me at about 4.30,' he says. 'He said, "What are you doing this weekend? I'll see you Saturday. I'm coming back." I said, "What are you on about?" He said, "I'm coming back. The band's over. I've had a massive ruck with our kid. That's it."'

Abbot swiftly flew out to California, desperate to help avert a crisis that seemed to have drawn the curtain on the group. He was greeted by a forlorn spectacle indeed. 'I got there about six in the evening, their time, and the rest of the band were coming down off a load of methedrine,' he says. 'They'd come back to find Marcus saying, "Great. Well done. Your band's over."'

The rest of Oasis took Russell at his word. 'Me and Guigs walked down Sunset Boulevard to McDonalds,' says Paul Arthurs, 'and we said, "We've blown it. That's it. It's finished. Fucking hell – right on the verge of the big time. What else can we do?" I said, "Do you reckon if we got a transit van and went round fixing ceilings, people would have it?"'

Back in the UK, Elastica were proving to be no less combustible. On 18 October, a week before the release of Connection, their second single, they played a show in Glasgow. Back at the group's hotel, a crowd of a dozen or so – split between the band and their associates – set about getting uncontrollably drunk. That night's favoured drink was the brandy slammer: neat cognac, ignited, and rudely knocked back. Perhaps predictably, once the last of the gang had made their way to bed, the hotel's night staff started to hear the sound of breaking glass, splintering wood and and wrecked fittings.

As it turned out, this was not the standard display of rock'n'roll abandon. Donna Matthews and Justin Welch's relationship – begun the previous December, and hothoused by nine months of living in one another's pockets – was entering its last pain-wracked episode: a tear-up in the small hours that ended with a visit from the police. 'We were just punching the shit out of each other,' Matthews later recalled. To make matters yet more problematic, the pair had to conceal their bruises, board a plane to London, and spend the following afternoon at *Top of the Pops*.

The backcloth to such extremities was not only formed by Elastica's frantic schedule. As any member of the group's London circle well knew, Welch and Matthews' romance had been at least partly built on the pair's prodigious intake of chemicals. Initially, they had been partial to amphetamine sulphate, that cheap'n'cheerful stimulant that is as scuzzily British as cider and blackcurrant. Such, back in 1993, had been Justine Frischmann's introduction to the druggy aspects of her colleagues' universe.

'I really was quite innocent about drugs,' says Frischmann. 'I'd never seen anyone doing heroin; I'd never met a heroin addict. I don't think I'd ever had a line of coke. But I went to rehearsal, and Donna said, "Do you want some speed?" Annie, Donna and Justin were all doing speed, and I was like, "Why would you want to do speed? What's the point?" But they persuaded me to have a line. Speed seemed really fun; it made you gab all night and smoke loads of cigarettes.'

The habits of her colleagues, however, had begun to extend into altogether darker territory. From the late summer onwards, whispers began to circulate that Donna Matthews and Justin Welch were increasingly fond of smoking heroin. Unbeknown to many of the whisperers, they were not the only members of Elastica with experience of brown powder and tinfoil. Annie Holland – the bass player who lived in Brighton, played no part in the group's interviews, and seemed content simply to add her gloriously clockwork basslines to the songs – had a habit that had long since fallen into daily routine.

'My dad was a heroin addict, so I grew up with it,' says Donna Matthews. 'I took drugs all the time from when I was about twelve. And when I joined the band and I found out that Annie did heroin, I was like "Wa-hey!" It was, "Don't tell the others." I wasn't a heroin addict, but Annie was. Annie was a heroin addict from day one. She had to take it every day. She used to take methadone as well. With me, I just took it like I took speed and E. I didn't have a heroin habit for a while. I'd go down to Brighton and stay with her and do heroin. Smoking it.'

While Matthews and Welch were still a couple, the group's financial position had begun to improve. Soon after the release of Line Up, Justine Frischmann's income from songwriting enabled her to pay the other three a weekly wage. Most crucially, in May, Elastica signed a worldwide contract with Geffen Records. In the UK, their records remained the property of Steve Lamacq's Deceptive label, but the Geffen deal ensured that money began to come in. Geffen's move was a consequence of their belief that Elastica could perhaps pull off what countless British groups had failed to: in the group's staccato chords, their welter of punk-era influences and that all-female front-line, they sensed the possibility of success in the USA.

As a consequence of their improved finances, Matthews and Welch had been able to move out of squat-land. Their choice of new neighbourhood was telling: from Islington, they shifted down Pentonville Road to King's Cross. 'We wanted a place where you could get drugs twenty-four hours a day,' says Donna Matthews. 'When we were thinking of a place to move, we thought, "Well, we always end up in King's Cross in the middle of the night trying to score, why don't we move there?" There was a twenty-four-hour alcohol place at the end of the street. That and heroin and crack, and anything you want. We were just like, "Let's move here! Perfect."'

Their rented flat was hardly luxurious. Visitors were waved in to a stereotypical crash-pad: a toilet with no door, a lounge festooned with nothing more elegant than a mattress and a couple of cushions. At the end of another elongated evening, they would emerge, blinking in the dawn light, to make their way home past the addicts and whores who make up King's Cross's human traffic. Nonetheless, even when Welch and Matthews split up, the flat remained Elastica's unofficial HQ. 'Donna had come from this hippy background, where people would come round to wherever she lived,' says Justine Frischmann. 'She was really up for people having parties at hers. We'd always end up back there.'

Though relationship fall-out, illicit drugs and a twenty-four-hour lifestyle might have quickly put paid to Elastica, for the moment they seemed as confident as ever. Connection was a pearl: an impressively raffish pop song that stepped outside the group's usual brand of punk rock, and affixed their guitars to heaving keyboards. One critic was heard to allege that it was a blend of The Knack's My Sharona and the theme from *Are You Being Served?*, references that only served to heighten its arch appeal. Indeed, in October 1994, its two-and-a-quarter minutes seemed like the very essence of cool.

*   *   *

In November, Damon Albarn added his voice to the increasing chatter about musicians' use of heroin – but he was also aiming at an all-too-familiar target. 'I think heroin is shit,' he said, 'and I know for a fact that Brett is doing heroin, and he is a fucking idiot. From Damon to Brett: you're a twat for doing that. Get a life.'

'Was I cross with Damon about that?' considers Justine Frischmann. 'Yeah, I was actually. Very cross. Damon was a real bully, and he had a real problem with Brett, even though Brett hadn't done him any wrong, as far as I could see. But they both seemed to get fired up by the fighting. This is something I've since discovered. Boys love a good scrap.'

Albarn's allegations were not exactly unexpected – quite apart from his belief in the Byronic ideal of stimulating creativity through getting out of one's mind, Brett Anderson had dangled the subject of heroin in front of his public on at least two occasions in the recent past. One of Stay Together's B-sides had been a maudlin song called The Living Dead, based on the predicament of some smack-addicted unfortunate. More celebratedly, there was So Young, the first track on *Suede*, whose chorus swooped to a beguiling kiss-off, crooned in an ecstatic falsetto: 'Let's chase the dragon.'

Anderson was asked about his heroin use on a few occasions that year: his uniform response was to refuse to give anything away and bat the conversation elsewhere. 'It was a difficult thing to talk about,' he says, 'because there's such a huge taboo about it. I tried it, but I wasn't a heroin addict. There was always a fascination with it, but I was talking about it from the perspective of not being an addict.* You have to be careful about it – not just in terms of how you take it, but how you talk about it. I was using it casually, but for some people it dictates their lifestyle.' As to Albarn's accusations, he was as curt as ever: 'I object to arseholes who should know better putting those kind of stories around,' he seethed.

In retrospect, Albarn was indulging in the mean-spirited art of kicking someone while they were down. At the end of 1994, Brett Anderson was not at all happy. 'It was a very hard time for me,' he says. 'It's still difficult to talk about: personally, I was probably the most confused I'd ever been in my life. I'd taken far too many drugs, I'd been in a very strange situation where I'd gone from adulation to extreme criticism – and I felt really fucked up. And I didn't feel like I was capable of

* In 2002, Anderson told *The Observer*: 'I was a crack addict for ages, I was a smack addict for ages.' It remained unclear whether he was referring to this period of his life.

explaining it to anyone. I felt as though we'd made some great music and done some great things, and we weren't getting any kind of respect for it. And we were in this weird limbo: it felt like we were promoting somebody else's records. It was, "Where the fuck are we?"'

Suede had announced Bernard Butler's replacement in September, to a mixture of gasps of incredulity and stifled guffaws. He was a seventeen-year-old from Dorset, plucked from his A-level studies in Classics, French and history, and a brief spell in a group called The Poole Grammar Stompers. Richard Oakes's first gig had been a Suede concert at Poole Arts Centre; his admiration for the group had extended into his note-perfect learning of their songs' guitar parts. His fate was redolent of the far-flung 70s TV show *The Big Time*, an analogy only furthered by some of his interviews. 'It's funny, because my mum never used to like Brett,' he said. 'Whenever he'd come on TV, she'd say, "Oh no, not him again."'

Many of those who beheld Oakes's first manoeuvres with the group could not help but notice his seemingly intentional resemblance to Bernard Butler. This was not simply down to the fact that, for the time being at least, he was expected to replicate Butler's guitar parts; the fact that he seemed to have carefully soaked up his predecessor's performance style lent his recruitment a genuinely surreal aspect. 'I couldn't believe that they were getting away with it,' says Butler. 'They were just getting someone to copy what I did, to copy what I wore . . . he had the same guitar. He was moving the same, shaking his head – but he was shorter and plumper. They got a *lookalike*. But the press went for it. For me, it was like, "I've missed a page here." That was the final kick in the teeth, really.'

In affectionate tribute to Oakes's inexperience, the group nicknamed him 'Mad Dog'. When he played his first show with them, at the Raw Club on Tottenham Court Road, Brett Anderson introduced him in a fashion that rather suggested the arrival of a new character in *Grange Hill*. 'There he is – Richard!' he barked. ''E's my mate!' Oakes's arrival prompted a reshuffle of the group's internal hierarchy: with palpable glee, Mat Osman resumed his role – forged back in Haywards Heath – as Brett Anderson's lieutenant.

Suede's new guitarist had the unenviable task of hawking an album that he had had nothing to do with. *Dog Man Star* was trailed by a single entitled We Are The Pigs, a camply dramatic Anderson/Butler fantasia about urban anarchy that, despite the almost comical pomposity of its lyric and vocal delivery, at least beat a retreat from the excesses of Stay Together. Oakes fleetingly appeared in the video and dutifully mimed to the song on *Top of the Pops*. Unfortunately, all the promotional graft could propel We Are The Pigs no higher than number eighteen. Stay Together, by contrast, had entered the charts at number three.

Dog Man Star emerged three weeks later. By and large, the critics greeted it as the proud step forward at which Brett Anderson had aimed – 'with *Dog Man Star*, the group has vindicated just about every claim that was ever made on their behalf,' said *Q* magazine – but when it collided with the public, it seemed to falter. In the context of Anderson's ornate lyrics, the song's echo-laden arrangements, and the vast orchestral swell that brought the album to a close, only zeitgeist-defining success would have suited *Dog Man Star*. When it failed to materialise, one beheld the strange spectacle of the Greatest Show On Earth being nudged into the wings. Though the album entered the charts at number three, it slid the next week to twelve, then to eighteen, then thirty-one . . . on, through the forties and fifties until, by the end of the year, it sat outside the top 75.

Even the release of The Wild Ones, the glorious ballad that Brett Anderson still thinks may be the best song Suede have ever recorded, did not seem to help: as if to suggest that Suede were the sudden victims of a numerological curse, like We Are The Pigs, it charted at a deeply disappointing number eighteen. '*Dog Man Star* got lost because people saw it as the swansong of a band,' says Brett Anderson. 'And it kind of was. We had a deliberately optimistic, gung-ho point of view, but everyone else saw it as "Suede are over."'

That December, Suede set out on a tour of the UK, with a set composed of nothing but Anderson/Butler material. Anderson's unhappiness was transparently clear: he looked ragged and fatigued, as if the excess and mishap of the last year had belatedly caught up with him. When he was interviewed, his statements were obviously meant to sound bullish and self-assertive; on the printed page, he seemed twitchily defensive.

'It's a load of shit about *Dog Man Star* being over the top. It's another example of people's two-second attention span. It's just the fact that we've actually got the scope to do more than one sort of music, to write more than one fucking type of song . . . People at the moment seem obsessed with the idea of bands being good blokes. And you seem to have to be ironic about *everything*. We've always hated that . . . People enjoy trying to kick us to bits, don't they? That's the way it is. I know I'm a whipping boy for a gang of people who drink down the Good Mixer, because I don't go there, and I've got no interest in any of that.'

Anderson and Mat Osman were speaking in Bradford, the setting for Suede's last performance of 1994, on 21 December. The usual end-of-tour celebrations failed to materialise: before Suede drove back to London, they sat in among a few disciples in their dressing room, killing time before their equipment was stowed away. Seemingly, no-one had thought to bring any music on tour: for want of anything else to listen to, the scene was soundtracked by a fan's copy of *The Head On The Door* by The Cure. Brett Anderson in particular was an awkward presence – slouched in a corner, tugging on a glass of Malibu, occasionally snuffling into a tissue. It seemed a muted way to end the year.

One only had to venture into Bradford's record shops the following morning to be confronted by the source of Suede's malaise. The racks containing *Dog Man Star* were left largely undisturbed. With two shopping days left to Christmas, and the musical map carved up between Blur and Oasis, people were queuing up to buy *Parklife* and *Definitely Maybe*.

The cultural moment inaugurated by Blur and Oasis had one particularly striking set of co-ordinates: the yearly run of British awards ceremonies. Much of punk's key period had been enacted in basement dives and pub backrooms; the Acid House upsurge was largely founded on short-lived club nights and illicit raves. The most notable development of 1994, by contrast, consisted of a new generation of musicians being embraced by the mainstream. In that sense, their arrival in a world of flashbulbs, snatched interviews and metallic statuettes was an integral part of the tale.

Q magazine's annual awards were held on 9 November 1994 at the Park Lane Hotel on Piccadilly. Given that *Q* had established itself as a magazine all but predicated on the importance of success – where the latest crew of upstarts championed by *NME* would only be allowed entry once their commercial clout had been established – admittance to the occasion represented a step upmarket: the trading of a pint with Nigel from Dodgy for a quiet chat with a member of U2.

Blur, accompanied by Justine Frischmann, arrived to accept *Parklife*'s award for Best Album. The accolade came a month after a performance that had confirmed how far they had come: on 7 October, they had performed in among the Victorian finery of Alexandra Palace, to a crowd of 7,000. The last indie group to play there had been The Stone Roses, at a 1990 concert that went down in history as a howling anti-climax. Blur's show, by contrast, was characterised by the press as a gleaming triumph.

Oasis were represented by a lone Noel Gallagher, dressed in a charcoal-grey suit, with his hair newly shorn into a fuzzy crop. After the career-threatening ruckus in Los Angeles, he had been tracked down by Tim Abbot in San Francisco, where the pair began a cocaine-fuelled mini-odyssey that took them to Las Vegas. In among the neon lights and fruit machines, Noel had surmised that Oasis should perhaps carry on after all: after a recording session in Texas and a testy reconciliation with his brother, the group's American tour had resumed in Minneapolis.

And so Oasis's grinding schedule had continued: forty-eight hours before the *Q* Awards, Gallagher had taken his place on the stage of the Theatre Du Moulin, Marseilles. He travelled to London to accept Oasis's award for Best New Act; the suit reflected a clear desire to prove to the assembled crowd that he was not the yob many had expected. His acceptance speech clinched it: 'To the readers,' he said. 'I'd just like to applaud your wisdom. Thanks.' Soon after, he was photographed in animatedly friendly conversation with Damon Albarn.

That year's recipients of *Q*'s Inspiration Award – the annual doffing-of-the-cap to the rock aristocracy – were very well chosen indeed. As if to square the success of Blur and Oasis with the heritage that the magazine held dear, the honour was given to The Kinks. Ray and Dave Davies, the group's eternally warring siblings, sat at different tables, prompting muttered quips about their resemblance to the Gallaghers; the oration that preceded their appearance onstage inevitably mentioned *Parklife*.

Among the ceremony's roll-call, there was one other notable guest. Tony Blair's ascension to the Labour leadership had caused a flurry of interest in his fleeting spell as the singer with Ugly Rumours – which led him to send a postcard to Mark Ellen: 'Looks like Ugly Rumours finally made it,' Blair wrote. Having graduated from Oxford and hung up his bass guitar, Ellen had gone on to be *Q*'s founding editor – and, in that capacity, he invited his old compadre to the awards. Blair arrived with Alastair Campbell and Anji Hunter, the key aide who had once been Mark Ellen's girlfriend. Blair made a quick speech, and stayed long enough to meet a handful of rock royalty – Ray Davies, Bono, Pink Floyd's Dave Gilmour – before it was decided to make a quiet exit and return to the day's political business.

Mark Ellen duly walked Blair up the two flights of stairs that led to the exit, as the latter enthused about how much he had enjoyed himself. In the meantime, Noel Gallagher had made a refreshing visit to a toilet cubicle, in the company of Ian Robertson. He emerged freshly emboldened; the spectacle of the Leader of the Opposition walking towards him presented too good an opportunity to resist.

'There was just Tony and me,' says Mark Ellen. 'I don't think Alastair was there; Anji and someone else were behind us. I was just trying to get him out of the crowd, without him getting too bothered by people. It had gone so well: he'd made a great speech, he'd met lots of people, he'd had a fantastic time – couldn't stop saying what a great time he was having – so as far as I was concerned, we had ninety-nine per cent concluded a very successful day. We had one per cent left. And suddenly, it looked like it all might have gone wrong.'

'We'd just come out of the shithouse, having hoovered up a few quid's worth,' says Ian Robertson. 'We were ready for the party – and as we walked out, Tony had done his speech, and Mark Ellen was pulling him out, and there he was. Noel was just *there*, in a flash. You could see the fear in Mark Ellen's eyes.'

'We were coming up the stairs, and charging down the stairs came Noel Gallagher,' says Mark Ellen. 'The imagination ran riot: he looked a little . . . accelerated. He said something like, "Fuckin' hell! Fuckin' do it for us, man!" He put his arm round him, and he clapped him on the chest: "Fuckin' do it for us, man!" Tony went, "Oh right. OK." And then he said to me, "Noel Gallagher!" And I said, "*Noel Gallagher!*"'

CHAPTER 12

'Do you want to be Tony Blair's mate?'

Tony Blair's *Q* Awards oration had been delivered, without notes, at the ceremony's start. In its opening moments, he neatly established his credentials by making humorous reference to Leslie West, the one-time guitarist with the heavy metal group Mountain. From there, he went on to adopt a slightly more purposeful tone, gently laying claim to a groovier kind of statesmanship than that being practised by John Major. The implication was that, upon his election to the premiership, some of the assembled revellers might just be allowed access to the machinery of government:

> I just want to say two things to you here. First of all, rock'n'roll is not just an important part of our culture, it's an important part of our way of life. It's an important industry; it's an important employer of people; it's immensely important to the future of this country. In Parliament, you can have debates about all sorts of industries and people will think it entirely normal. If you had a debate about the music industry, they'd think it rather strange, but that actually just shows how far Parliament is behind the times . . . The great bands that I used to listen to – The Stones and The Beatles and The Kinks – their records are going to live forever, and the records of today's bands, the records of U2 or The Smiths and Morrissey, will also live on because they're part of a vibrant culture. I think we should be proud in Britain of our record industry and proud that people still think that this is the place to make it.

No matter that he had casually glossed over U2's Irishness, or that The Smiths had split up seven years before: the idea that Blair was a friend of the music industry had been established. Indeed, when he embarked on a managed walkabout – supervised by Mark Ellen – he found nothing but friendliness. It was a *Q* Awards tradition to issue each table with a polaroid camera, so as to provide personal souvenirs: when Blair began to circulate, the flashbulbs went into overdrive. Better still, the musicians to whom he was introduced were happy to make his acquaintance.

'What you can't do, if you're a public figure, is to be seen to be in any way snubbed – as the tabloid journalists milling around the crowd would have it – by anybody,' says Ellen, who checked with each celebrity before introducing them to Blair. 'If their extraction of the day's events was that Tony Blair wanted to talk to Dave Gilmour and Dave Gilmour didn't want to talk to Tony Blair, that might become a headline story. But everybody I asked was absolutely thrilled to meet him.'

What doubtless assisted Blair's cause – aside from the reference to Mountain – was the idea that he had once been intimately familiar with amplifiers, guitar strings and the black art of executing a convincing Mick Jagger impression.

Four months later, Blur took their seats at the 1995 Brit Awards. In Damon Albarn's words, the evening 'changed Blur's lives dramatically, for ever and ever': in the wake of the ceremony's broadcast, they were more famous than any group from the indie world had ever been. 'I don't think my parents' neighbours knew who Blur were until that night,' says Alex James. 'At that point, we became a household name.'

Suede's performance two years before had encapsulated the fact that they were outsiders – grudgingly allowed their three minutes, and then hurried from the stage, so as to allow Annie Lennox, Rod Stewart and Curtis Stigers to get on with the show. With *Parklife* working its expectation-defying wonders, the UK's latest left-field sons were a far more central part of the proceedings. Blur arrived at Alexandra Palace acknowledging that they were likely to win a couple of statuettes; by the close of the show, they had one for each member of the group.

Their four awards – for Best Band, Best Album, Best Single and Best Video – were unprecedented. With each trip to the stage, where they air-kissed the American singer Cyndi Lauper and wrestled Vic Reeves and Bob Mortimer to the ground, they looked ever more bamboozled, though they accepted the awards with an excited kind of grace. Within a year, it would be the cool pose to arrive at such occasions oozing a mixture of apathy and belligerence; Blur, by contrast, entered into the ceremony's spirit. Their irreverence was expressed with admirable wit: when Prince appeared, pursuing his complaint with the record industry by writing 'Slave' on his cheek, Dave Rowntree borrowed an eye pencil and put the word 'Dave' in the same place.

By the time of their final accolade – the Best Band award – Blur were incredulous. 'This is getting very embarrassing,' said Alex James. 'But I've thought of something to say. I never studied an instrument at school – it was really boring doing music. It was all grammar and no conversation. So what I say, kids, is get your Oasis records and get your Blur records and your Eternal records and your East 17 records and take 'em into school and say, "This is industry. Teach me this. This is what I want to know about." '

Damon Albarn then squeezed his way to the microphone. 'I think this should be shared with Oasis,' he said, holding the award aloft.

'Yeah,' Graham Coxon concurred, in a voice that left it unclear whether he was indulging in heartfelt appreciation or withering sarcasm. 'Much love and respect to them.'

'Thanks to everyone who's had blind faith in us, past and present,' Albarn concluded. 'And, er, wake up America.' As if to prove that the Brits could not tolerate a complete revolution, he was followed on to the stage by Elton John, there to accept the obligatory Lifetime Achievement Award.

Mere yards away from Blur sat Oasis, who had received their accolade early on in the ceremony. The Best Newcomer Award had been presented by Ray Davies, who had announced the winner thus: 'Truly wonderful – Oasis.' It was noted that, when Blur took the stage for a performance of Girls And Boys – sung by Damon Albarn in a voice so comically cockney that it sounded like he was inventing a completely new accent – Noel Gallagher ensured that everyone at the Oasis table rose from their seats and danced.

His response to Damon Albarn's tribute only furthered the impression that the two groups shared some common cause. 'If we'd won that,' he said into one of the many microphones thrust in his direction, 'none of our lot would have said what he did. Our lot would have said, "Fuck the lot of you!" What Blur did was a great gesture, and I want to go on record as saying that it's us and them now, against the world.'

The elder Gallagher's sentiments were rather undermined by the conduct of his younger brother. In Liam Gallagher's eternally solipsistic universe, each Blur award seemed to represent nothing more than a slight on his own group. 'I was sitting right next to Liam,' Graham Coxon later recalled, 'who was just being provocative and trying to intimidate us all night. Every time we came back from the stage with another one, he'd glare at me and say, "You fucking look me in the eye and tell me you deserve that award." Then he'd make to hit you

. . . it was a weird enough night without him fucking going on and on.'

Over the next two days – the Brits, as usual, were televised twenty-four hours after they happened – Blur found themselves presented in new, jarringly unfamiliar terms. The more risqué elements of Damon Albarn's *Loaded* interview were gleefully regurgitated; photographs of his performances in Nigel Hildreth's musical productions were exhumed; their past music press interviews were combed for the merest hint of naughtiness. The morning after the ceremony, the ever-imaginative *Sun* ran an article entitled '10 Things You Never Knew About Damon's Demons'. Number two read as follows: 'The four lads strip naked for weird male-bonding sessions and love to party for days. Saucy Damon shocked fans when he tore off his clothes and threw himself into the audience at the end of one concert.'

The next day came a deluge. 'Blur hijacked the Brit Awards last night, winning a record four categories and finally consigning the golden oldies of British rock to a fading memory,' gushed the *Daily Mail*. 'The four-piece band with the carefully-crafted cockney image of greasy caffs and greyhound racing beat legends like The Rolling Stones, Pink Floyd and Tom Jones as the controversial awards at last embraced a new wave of young talent.'

In the now-defunct *Today*, one James Bennett truly excelled himself. For some reason, his article was headlined 'Blurred Vision'. Its strapline read 'Band of hope and glory: How four Essex Lads with a belief in beer and fun set the Brit Awards alight.' And then he got to work. 'Overnight, those four Brits have propelled the Essex Lads – and that's Lads with a capital L – from hotly-tipped alternative band to household name . . . Manager Andy Ross is unconcerned at the Laddish image that goes with it. "They work hard and they deserve it," he says. "I'd rather they had a few beers than got hooked on heroin."'

For the next year, Blur and their inner circle adjusted to a new syndrome: when they forgot themselves, and fell into the old habit of being candid and confessional with the kind of journalists they counted as friends, anything remotely revelatory came back through the tabloids as a garbled echo. At the Brit Awards, Damon Albarn had been persuaded to pose with a copy of *The Sun*; by way of expressing their gratitude, the Bizarre column soon ran a story headlined 'Blur Indoors Dishes The Dirt: Damon "Sex Flop"'. Its source was an interview by Amy Raphael in *The Face*, in which Justine Frischmann had been baited – via rumours of Albarn's promiscuity – into claiming that he had a low sex drive. With enough nipping and tucking, *The Sun* had a story: 'Blur heart-throb Damon Albarn is unfaithful and lousy in bed – says his girlfriend.'

'I suddenly had to watch what I said,' says Frischmann. 'I did this thing with Amy, and we were talking about Damon's sex drive. She was really winding me up about how unfaithful he was meant to be, and I said, "I don't think he's that sexually motivated – he's more attention motivated." That came out of *The Face* and straight into *The Sun*: "Blur star can't get it up." And all of a sudden my days of saying I wanted teenage boys to wank over posters of me were over.'

The morning after the Brit Awards, while most of Britain was blearily reading the papers, Alex James was still wide awake. At Alexandra Palace, he had been introduced to Keith Allen, the actor and gravelly-voiced bon viveur. The pair ended up in Venus, a Soho drinking den located in the basement of a pornographic bookshop.

In the next few weeks, Allen would reintroduce James to Damien Hirst, by then on his way to winning the 1995 Turner Prize and bringing dead animals suspended in formaldehyde – as in Mother And Child Divided and Away From The Flock, the two centerpieces of his Turner Prize exhibit – to the attention of the same kind of people who had just been familiarised with *Parklife*. He and Allen had begun to amass a reputation for smearing their intoxicated presence over the members-only circuit with which Alex James was increasingly becoming acquainted; when the trio bonded, they discovered that they had that most thrilling of human organisations: a gang.

'Damien is a visionary,' says Alex James. 'He defined that period of time, just because he was so bold: able to just go, "Let's move the North Pole. We'll get everyone to send us magnets." Just someone who's not afraid to think big; a real motivator. Someone who's brilliant at getting the best out of people. With me, it was, "Right, you've had a number one – what are you going to do now, you idiot?"

'Winning all those Brit Awards and meeting all your heroes – that was kind of Mission Accomplished. What they made me think was, "This is where you start working." They were always saying, "You have no idea how much power you have at the moment." And they were quite right about that. It was, "Just go for it: do it all."'

The idea, it seemed, was to swan through as many doors as possible – and attempt to boot open those that remained closed. 'There was this collision of lunacy,' says Andy Ross, who watched James enter this new world with no little amusement. 'And it was articulate lunacy, which kind of makes it even more dangerous. You get these smart-arses – interesting smart-arses – dabbling in other spheres. The bass player from Blur, this mad artist and this lunatic actor, all going bonkers together. It was just . . . a maelstrom of insanity.'

*   *   *

Oppositions are altogether more youthful creatures than governments. Whereas a ruling party can spend a huge wage bill on the policy experts of its choosing – and take much of its advice from the ever-present ranks of greying mandarins – those on the opposite political side must rely on a mass of eager rookies. The Parliamentary Labour Party of the mid-90s, staffed by scores of post-graduate research assistants, was a case in point. By 1995, it was their good fortune to be serving a cause that was all but guaranteed to prove successful: the result was that the party's young workers oozed a very heady kind of optimism.

Among their number was Darren Kalynuk. In between an abortive spell at Manchester University and his eventual arrival at Royal Holloway And Bedford College, he had worked in Neil Kinnock's office; even in the midst of his studies, he had found time to assist the Labour Party with a number of events aimed at gently advancing its appeal to the younger part of the electorate. Throughout, he was careful not to replicate the approach that had held sway in the previous decade: his celebrity roll-call was far more Ben Elton than Billy Bragg.

'Red Wedge failed because people had too many opinions, and it turned into a political lobby group, rather than what it should have been, which was a source of support for the leadership and the policies of the party,' he says. 'You would have Paul Weller waxing lyrical about Labour's employment policy. Well, frankly, who cares what Paul Weller thinks?' Such was the curt New Labour take on the musical philanthropists of the 80s.

By 1995, Kalynuk had arrived in John Prescott's office, with instructions to pursue his youth-oriented brief. As far as musicians were concerned, Kalynuk envisaged a very informal approach: cultivating contacts, encouraging them to make the right noises in their interviews, ensuring that word of their sympathies reached the press.

Blur were his first target. At the end of 1994, Damon Albarn had sprinkled a run of interviews with notice of his support for the Labour Party. Among his hopes and ambitions for the new year was 'a Labour government'; elsewhere, for some reason, he expressed the wish that Tony Blair should 'give up politics and join Blur'. In the same interview in which he had clumsily accused Brett Anderson of using heroin, he had cut to the political quick: 'I will vote for a Labour government, definitely,' he said. The fact that the Brit Awards had made Blur familiar to even the fustiest parliamentarians only seemed to confirm Albarn's suitability.

After several phone calls to Chris Morrison's office, it was suggested that Kalynuk visit the filming of *Top of the Pops* on 22 February. This was an auspicious occasion indeed: Albarn was at *Top of the Pops* to both perform with Blur – on a rendition of Jubilee from *Parklife*, designed to underline their Brits achievement – and also appear with Elastica. The latter's new single was entitled Waking Up; Albarn contributed keyboards. As with the appearance of The Stone Roses and Happy Mondays in 1989, the occasion spoke volumes about the arrival of a new musical aristocracy.

'I saw him coming out of the studio at the very end,' says Kalynuk. 'And I called after him: I said, "Damon, I'm from John Prescott's office, can we have a chat?" We walked up the corridor, away from everyone else, and I said, "Look, I see you've been saying some pretty complimentary things about Tony in the press. Are you a Labour supporter?" And he said yes, so I said, "Well, we're just thinking about ways that we can use people like yourself. It's in its very early stages, but would you like to come in and meet Tony and John?" And he said, "Would I? Of course I would. But it won't be Red Wedge, will it?" And I said, "Absolutely not Red Wedge."'

Soon enough, Kalynuk was escorted into the BBC bar and introduced to Blur's inner circle. 'You're quite easy to find when you're number one and you're selling a lot of records,' says Alex James. 'Darren kind of appeared and ingratiated himself all of a sudden. That was quite a carrot to dangle: do you want to come to the Houses of Parliament and be Tony Blair's mate and get out of jail free? Basically, that's what I saw it as. And Darren had a real vitality. What an operator: a man who could drink ten pints of beer and still be on a mission. He really had an agenda. And the level of dedication that he showed: I'd never go that far for music. He was prepared to make an absolute cunt of himself, going on and on and on about why Labour was brilliant.'

Kalynuk was given Albarn's home number, and in the ensuing month, he was readied for a visit to the Houses of Parliament. The run-up to all this had been rather vexed: when Kalynuk suggested the meeting to Blair's coterie, it was vetoed by Peter Mandelson. In the wake of the Brit Awards, *The Daily Telegraph* had run two stories alleging that Blair had been slated to attend, only for him to pull out. The nominal reason was a 'heavy cold', though the *Telegraph* had other suspicions. 'The reason that Tony Blair was not among those present at the Brit Awards, say the whispers, is that he was avoiding association with the pop group Blur,' said one of the pieces. '"Blur" is the nickname that Tory MPs have given Blair because they say he is "soft focus", and he may have thought that the photo-op would backfire on him.' The prospect of further Blur-related barbs was apparently more than Mandelson could bear.

In the end, John Prescott suggested that Mandelson might be over-ruled. 'John said, "Look, this lad's been invited up here. I really want to meet him, Tony should meet him,"' says Kalynuk. With help from Alastair Campbell, Albarn's invitation was finally approved.

Albarn arrived, alone, on a March afternoon, not long after the end of Prime Minister's Question Time. 'We went up to John's office, which was deliberate, so if we were asked if a meeting had taken place in Tony Blair's office, we could say no,' says Kalynuk. 'And that's where everyone met. I'd had a bet with some people before that Tony and Alastair would come up with their jackets off and sleeves rolled up. John poured some drinks, and he's incredibly charming and funny – he really knows how to play it very well – so he put Damon at his ease.' In addition to the display of Prescott's rarely chronicled social skills, Kalynuk recalls Albarn proudly describing Blur's new stage set, built around a number of specially constructed giant hamburgers.

'We had a couple of gin and tonics,' he continues, 'and then Tony and Alastair came up. We sat around and had a little chat, a few more drinks. It was just a very relaxed conversation.'

Albarn's recollection of the meeting, dispensed for the benefit of a Q magazine interviewer in 1999, suggests a slightly more strained ambience. 'They invited me round, appearing to be quite casual but then saying, "If you're as successful as you are now come the election then we can do some business together." . . . Emotionally, there was very little connection. I just felt troubled.'

'The thing about Damon, who I love dearly, is that he has a really selective memory, and that comes into play when he's talking in public,' says Darren Kalynuk. 'Tony had said, "It's really good you're doing so well," but he absolutely did not say anything like that.'

One exchange that undoubtedly did happen formed the meeting's most uncomfortable moment. With his eternally watchful eye on poss-ible future mishap, Alastair Campbell quizzed Albarn in as pointed a fashion as the occasion would allow. 'He said, "This is great, and we're really glad that you might be able to help, and we want to talk to you about that, but what if you turned round and say, 'Tony's a wanker?'"' says Kalynuk. 'Tony bristled at this slightly and smiled, and Damon said, "No, no, no, we'd never do that. Honestly, all the lads in the band have got their heads screwed on. We'll help. We're not stupid. We just wouldn't do that."'

Albarn left the Palace of Westminster in the early evening, and made his way to Alex James's flat in Covent Garden. Albarn couched his report of the event in terms of glowing admiration for Labour's rotund deputy leader; whether he was outwardly 'troubled' remains unclear. 'He said he thought John Prescott was cool,' says James. 'I think.'

In the wake of the Westminster meeting, Kalynuk suggested that he and Albarn should meet up for a drink, and perhaps push the agenda forward. This time, Albarn brought Alex James: they met Kalynuk at Soho House, the members-only den at the bottom of Old Compton Street, much beloved of those who work in the higher echelons of film and television. As if to underline how far away they sat from the era of Red Wedge, by the end of the evening, Kalynuk had been escorted to Stringfellow's, where Albarn nudged him into a seat behind the VIP rope and ordered champagne.

'Alex was pretty agnostic about it all,' says Kalynuk. 'I suspect that the fact that he was there meant that we didn't talk very much politics. We talked about Damon's class a lot . . . Damon still thinks he's working class, and I don't think he is, frankly. But he absolutely did think he was. Alex disagreed. And one of the things Damon felt really strongly about was education. I don't think he agreed with grammar schools at all. Education was certainly one of the issues that he felt made him a Labour supporter.'

Despite Alex James's air of political nonchalance, Kalynuk's next masterstroke was designed to ensure that he did not feel left out. At the end of 1995, well aware that he was now involved in a quest to proudly gain admittance to London's more exclusive clubs, Kalynuk invited him for drinks at the House of Commons, having cajoled the eternally swinging Mo Mowlam into joining them. She was accompanied by her close friend Adam Ingram, the MP for East Kilbride and a front-bench spokesman on trade and industry. 'Alex completely fell in love with her,' says Kalynuk. 'He thought she was amazing. Adam introduced him to various kinds of whisky.'

'There was the usual drunk Scotsman in the corner and a leggy blonde,' says Alex James. 'I kissed Clare Short, which I'd always wanted to do. It was a bit like going to Syndrome, really: "He doesn't like him, and they're a gang, he's got some good ideas." I was there till it closed, as usual. It's easy to make friends when you're top of the charts. I was introduced to loads of people. Did we talk about politics? 'Course we didn't. It's like when you're backstage at the Reading Festival and no-one talks about music.'

Kalynuk remained in Blur's orbit until 1997. He was a close friend of John Prescott's son Dave, then working as a news producer at GMTV; the pair became a familiar presence to Blur associates. 'They started coming to the gigs,' says Mike Smith. 'At all the Blur shows, Darren would be there, usually with John Prescott's son, who looked normal; a really nice chap. But Darren looked like a political animal. He'd wear a suit to the gigs. Just the *wrong* clothes.'

In the course of Kalynuk's visits, there were vague murmurings of taking things further – at one point, the idea of including Labour Party postcards in Blur's singles crossed his mind – but Kalynuk was content with the fact that Blur were perceived to be on-side. Such was the Blairite way: a few mentions in the gossip columns, it seemed, were worth a thousand formal meetings. Better still, as against the strange days of Red Wedge, Blur had no wish to attend meetings and exert an influence on Labour Party policy.

'Darren just wanted us to be something that was associated with New Labour, so that New Labour would look hip,' says Alex James. 'Just like Camel sending me free cigarettes and getting free clothes off Prada. It's the easiest way to sell something: associating it with people who are seen as successful and a bit sexy. And it was obviously something that worked: it was in the *Evening Standard* diary that I was in the House of Commons with Mo Mowlam. By a process of osmosis, it came through that we were associated with them. They didn't want anything more than that. They did a fucking brilliant marketing job. I just wanted to get my beak in there and see how it all worked.

'It was very subtle,' he says. ''Cos nobody wanted Paul Weller doing fucking benefit gigs in Finsbury Park with concept albums about how good left-wing politics are. That was just cack.'

Standing at the bar, holding court with a member of the Shadow Cabinet, surrounded by a crowd of MPs who wanted to make the acquaintance of an exemplar of a new swinging Britain, Alex James could also detect a phenomenon all too familiar to the successful musician. 'There was a bit of a starfucker thing going on there, wasn't there? But they're just like the rest of us. They just want to get pissed and shag famous people. And who can blame them?'

CHAPTER 13

'I said half a million pounds, and no-one laughed.'

As Blur, Oasis and Elastica worked their wonders, a new buzzword began to creep into the press coverage of their progress. In some early accounts, it was split into its two component parts. By the end of 1994, however, it was uniformly used as a single word, soon to be trailed across magazine covers and gleefully splurged on to the airwaves by thousands of DJs: 'Britpop'.

As early as May 1994, *The Face* was paying tribute to Blur's 'passionate view of Brit pop . . . [it] looks like an idea whose time has come.' By September, the *Guardian's* arts pages claimed that, 'We have never had it so good. We are in the middle of a Britpop renaissance.' In the *NME*'s first issue of 1995, there were two uses of the word: in an article looking back on the highlights of the previous year, subtitled 'Ten Great Britpop Moments', and in a review of the new single by the 60s-indebted trio Dodgy, which tentatively aimed at a stylistic definition, praising 'a blissful slice of Britpop, all sweeping melodies, triumphant choruses and a big bursting guitar bit at the end'.

Initially, however, the precise meaning of Britpop was a matter of conjecture. When the *Melody Maker* decided to build a hyperbolic cover story around it, they opted for a rather banal notion: here, Britpop was simply good music of British origin, lent a new air of excitement by the fact that it was allegedly avenging the dominance of the US. In their view, Radiohead – those eternal outsiders whose second album, *The Bends*, sat in an utterly different universe to *Parklife* – were as much a part of the new mood as any of the habitués of The Good Mixer.

Elsewhere, the word quickly became a signifier for a slightly more coherent set of ideas. By and large, Britpop was music that accorded with Damon Albarn's two-year-old wish to reacquaint domestic rock music with a heritage that took in music hall, the upper end of the 60s canon, and the more cerebral aspects of punk. Its lyrics were expected to ooze an inescapable sense of Englishness – a quality that would, at speed, become a hoary cliché – and preferably combine even the saltiest observations with an overarching air of camp. There was a requisite look, of sorts: cropped hair, charity-shop clothing that took in either 60s fashions or decade-old sportswear. Once suitably attired, a Britpop group could reasonably be expected to pose for their publicity shots in a greasy spoon caff, and ensure that any journalistic visitor caught glimpses of their cans of Vimto and packets of B&H.

But Britpop also denoted a moment: the short-lived era of – to borrow the words of *The Independent* – 'British indie-pop bands magpieing the past and enjoying mainstream success.' There was an almost moral point implied in this change: if The Stone Roses had talked about launching an attack on the mainstream 'because we have more worth', much of the rhetoric surrounding Britpop suggested that reinforcements had belatedly arrived. Oasis, having landed at Creation Records and begun shouting about their own inevitable success, had arguably originated much of this: thus, with the added factor of their Beatles fixation – and despite the fact that *Definitely Maybe* had precious little in common with *Parklife* – they were included in Britpop's vanguard.

The Independent's reference to Britpop's plundering of the rock canon was equally significant. Some of the UK's most notable genres-cum-youthquakes had been founded on pop culture's in-built tendency for iconoclasm: The Clash nailed punk's year zero essence with the declaration 'No Elvis, Beatles or Rolling Stones in 1977'; the fact that Acid House was built on electronic music inherently cut it off from thirty-five years of rock history. This latest upsurge, by contrast, spoke an altogether more reverent language. The fact that Damon Albarn talked so admiringly of a British musical heritage spoke volumes: in Blur's respect for The Kinks, Elastica's fondness for art-punk, and Oasis's wide-eyed Beatles-worship, there was a clear sense of the arrival of a generation steeped in a new classicism – what came to be maligned as 'retro'.

What was particularly striking was the music press's enthusiasm for the term. 'Brit', after all, tended to signify a rather more strident sense of nationhood than the simple use of the word 'British'; thanks to a million 'True Brit' tabloid headlines, the word was forever bound up with a heroic sense of derring-do, all trips to the North Pole and against-the-odds Olympic triumphs. As far as the *NME* and *Melody Maker* were concerned, however, the old leftist worries about the politics of patriotism – last voiced in early 1994 – seemed to be completely forgotten. Layouts were now set in red, white and blue, and writers infused their reports with a newly acceptable kind of patriotism.

For musicians, the term caused a little more queasiness. It is standard music business form for those grouped in generic brackets to object to them; with Britpop, the hostility seemed more pronounced than ever. 'As soon as that name existed, everybody had a problem with it,' says Justine Frischmann. 'Nobody liked it. We knew it was trouble.'

Regardless, as of the new year, there seemed to be no shortage of Britpop foot soldiers. In the first week of January, Sleeper – Blur's one-time support act, who had quickly morphed from a rather gothy indie group into an exemplar of music's new Anglo-centric turn – released a single called Inbetweener. Its words dealt with the outer London expanse from which Louise Wener, the group's singer and lyricist, came; the accompanying video, as if to hammer the point home, featured that most suburban of icons, Dale Winton, cavorting around the set of *Supermarket Sweep*. Sleeper's previous efforts had got nowhere near the top 40: this one, sped on its way by the patronage of Radio One, reached number sixteen.

The following month, a young Oxford group called Supergrass released their second single. Their first, released in October 1994, had pushed all the Britpop buttons: a supercharged composition entitled Caught By The Fuzz ('when I was still on a buzz'), it smirkingly told the tale of a teenage arrest for dope smoking, replete with a visit to the police station by an irate parent ('Here comes my mum/She knows what I've done'). Its successor, Mansize Rooster, only continued the fun, fusing the group's fondness for punk rock with the oompah-oompah stomp that Blur had minted with 1993's Sunday Sunday. Better still, its words were enunciated in a mewling estuary accent by a singer whose name – seemingly confirming that British music was newly reconnected to the world of *Grange Hill*, *Graham's Gang* and *Murphy's Mob* – was Gaz Coombes.

Further down the Britpop hierarchy lurked a mass of groups who had evidently sighted their chance, gathered up their possessions and begun sprinting after the bandwagon. The same edition of the *NME* that saw the paper's first references to Britpop contained a live review of a new London group called Pimlico. At around the same time, a female-fronted quartet called Powder began to prowl around North London's music venues, peddling a see-through approximation of the wiry neo-punk pioneered by Elastica. The punchline to all this was provided by a transparently opportunistic trio called Thurman, whose debut single was entitled English Tea. 'Oh, what a lavvly day, to drink some English tea,' they sang, 'and talk about the wevvah/Isn't it lahvly?' Rumours rapidly spread that mere months before, they had been a heavy metal group called To Die For.

To some of those who had consciously pioneered British aesthetics in the days when they were greeted with disdain, such developments were bound to prompt imperious sneers. 'We had started this thing,' says Brett Anderson, 'and it got distorted and made less special and commercialised, in the form of Britpop. When we started, it was edgy: it wasn't this big gang of people all slapping each other on the back and drinking lager.' For the next two years, such haughtiness would all but define Anderson's public persona.

'You started hearing songs about chip shops,' sniffs Mat Osman. 'It's a very strange feeling, to see the cartoon of yourself, especially when the cartoon seems to be doing pretty well. You see the superficial side of what you're doing, which always seems to be the easiest one to sell.'

In a backhanded fashion, those charged with nudging new talent into the offices of the major record labels seemed to agree. The success of *Parklife* had convinced the music industry that Britpop was the thing to get, and money was the surest way of securing it – and no-one illustrated the new atmosphere of hysterical munificence better than a hastily assembled group called Menswear.

Simon White was a native of Birmingham, who had spent a couple of his teenage years in an indie group called Cooler Than Jesus. Convinced that a move to London held the key to a step upward, he bagged a place on a Social Studies course at North London Polytechnic through the clearing system. He arrived in the capital in October 1994, just as Camden Town was enshrined as the nerve-centre of ongoing musical developments. His introduction to the N1 whirl came via a visit to the Saturday night club that had been a favoured haunt of indie musicians since the previous year.

'I'd bought a load of speed with me from Birmingham,' says White, 'because I knew I'd be skint, and I thought the one thing I could do was sell some drugs. This girl took me down to Blow Up, and I brought all this speed with me. It was really strong: I didn't cut it with anything, 'cos I didn't have much experience in drug-dealing. I sold speed to everyone in Blow Up. I did so much selling that night that I kind of became a face. And I ended up in Holloway Road, outside my halls of residence, at three in the morning, puking my guts up, with all that beer and speed I'd had, thinking, "Welcome To London."'

At Blow Up, White had been introduced to a clique who were already becoming faintly notorious. It was centred around Johnny Dean and

Chris Gentry, a couple of emigrés from Southend, who were among Blur's most celebrated fans, honoured with an appearance in a *Select* article that celebrated an alleged London-centred mod revival, and identified Graham Coxon as its leader. The piece made fleeting reference to their group, a 'top new unsigned band' called Menswear, an enterprise that existed chiefly in its members' imaginations.

White met Gentry – the band's supposed guitarist – in slightly more sober circumstances a few weeks after his first visit to Blow Up. The pair discovered they had similar musical taste; not long after, White was invited to join the group – only to discover that Gentry had not run the idea past his colleagues. By way of a compromise, he was invited to prove his worth at a rehearsal in Leyton. This did not prove difficult: Menswear had only one song, a piece inspired by Elastica's more robotic compositions, built around the novel expedient of having no chord changes whatsoever. 'The only song that they had at the time, was this thing Daydreamer,' says White. 'They were desperately trying to write four songs for this gig that was coming up in four weeks.' White threw in a self-written song called I'll Manage Somehow. Having thus increased the size of the group's repertoire by 100 per cent, he was in.

The show for which the group was rehearsing was due to take place at Smashing, a Friday night club that had become Menswear's home-from-home. It was located in a basement on Regent Street called Eve's, whose decor and fittings oozed a very faded kind of glitz: as well as an abundance of plastic shrubbery and a handful of velvet-lined booths, Eve's was built around a *Saturday Night Fever*-esque flashing dance-floor. In addition to music by the new crop of British rock groups, Smashing's DJs played a pot pourri of 60s and 70s pop, a good deal of it seemingly selected for reasons of rib-tickling irony. In that context, Eve's was the perfect location.

The club had begun in November 1991, at an equally kitsch venue called Maximus on Leicester Square. 'We wanted to get away from the whole E club culture thing: people going out and necking loads of pills and hugging each other,' says Adrian Webb, the small-time impresario who formed a quarter of Smashing's ruling council. 'The idea was to create an environment in which you'd get dressed up, go out, get pissed and fall over.'

Smashing soon relocated to the Gaslight of St James, a hostess club that was licensed to hold no more than twenty-five, but was quickly stuffed with upwards of 100. By now, the clientele included members of Blur, Pulp and Elastica; with their snowballing success, everything came together. 'When we got the white label of Girls And Boys, it was *so* along the lines of what we were doing at the club,' says Webb. 'The dancefloor went insane. We played it three times in a row.' In essence, Smashing had become the successor to Syndrome, the indie honeypot whose rise and fall had been played out no more than a quarter of a mile away.

Smashing arrived at Eve's in the wake of the release of *Parklife*, soon after which Chris Gentry and Johnny Dean became regulars. They were spotted by Adrian Webb at a backstage soirée held after a Blur show at Shepherd's Bush Empire. 'I remember having a huge discussion about whether Chris was a boy or a girl. That lasted two months: "Is that a boy or a girl? I can't tell." We headhunted them for the club: "You're cool. You should come."' When the pair began to talk about forming a group and staging their coming-out performance at Smashing, it was all but inevitable that, despite a complete absence of experience, Webb would be their manager.

'I remember driving to the first rehearsal and saying, "I hope they're good,"' he says, 'and then thinking, "Well, fuck it – we can always do a Frankie Goes To Hollywood." Even the most wily managerial scamster is nothing without a receptive music industry; conveniently for Adrian Webb, the dawn of Britpop meant that plenty of record labels were ready to be fleeced.

Menswear's Smashing gig was preceded by a warm-up show at the Amersham Arms in New Cross. A few days later, Adrian Webb escorted the group to a Hammersmith charity shop, where they bought the stagewear for the imminent performance at Smashing. The sartorial aspect was crucial, for the crowd was to be stuffed with the kind of people who needed to be impressed: no less than thirty-six A&R people from London's record labels, and journalists from each of the weekly music papers.

'When it came to the gig, I was shitting it,' says White. 'We all went down on the Tube. We got to Smashing and went in the back entrance, and I remember thinking, "We're going to go and blow the world up today." It was bursting to the rafters. I remember someone taking a shit in the corner, because he couldn't hold it in. Everyone was just *shaking.*'

Thanks to poor amplification, Menswear still had no idea if Johnny Dean, their lead singer, was actually up to the job. By now, their set-list had swelled to four songs. It mattered not: according to White, the goodwill of the man from the *Melody Maker* was secured via the provision of some cocaine, while the *NME*'s correspondent, the sixteen-year-old wunderkind Emma Forrest, wrote a review that bursted with enthusiasm. 'Menswear are like a Tarantino movie,' she wrote. 'Totally derivative, completely superficial, shamelessly glossy and frequently brilliant.' (There was a lot of this around: as of late 1994, borderline oxymoronic praise was a regular feature of the music papers' Britpop coverage. By the spring of 1995, the *NME* would honour the aforementioned Thurman with the epithet 'Brilliantly rubbish'.)

Such tributes only intensified the record labels' frantic interest in Menswear – although a rather disastrous third performance at the Garage on Highbury Corner convinced a large handful of prospective bidders that they should bow out. 'That night was dreadful,' says Adrian Webb. 'I was just sitting there thinking, "It's over." I think the nerves kicked in at that stage. But it did us a favour. It halved the ridiculous number of people we had to go and see.'

Eventually, Menswear were left with two options: Blanco Y Negro, the offshoot of Warner Brothers headed by Geoff Travis, the indie veteran who had founded Rough Trade; and Laurel, a new faux-indie funded and distributed by the London label. 'It turned into a bidding war between the two of them,' says Simon White, 'so Adrian said, "The band want to go to America and try to be a big British band over there, and we want to go and look at the American side of the operation." London paid for the flights, and Warners paid for the hotels.'

White, a sensitive soul who was by now wondering whether Menswear had bitten off more than they could chew, elected to stay at home, while his colleagues – luxuriating in the achievement of having written their seventh song – went to New York. 'London had given us a chauffeur-driven limo and all the vintage champagne we could drink,' says Adrian Webb. 'At one stage on that trip, we were driving through the East Village in a chauffeur-driven limo, drinking vintage Dom Perignon, listening to Smells Like Teen Spirit. I was thinking, "This car could crash now, and I'd be happy, because I've done it."'

Mid-way through their second day, Menswear were nudged towards a deal with London by an event of quite startling mundanity. 'Geoff Travis made us pay for our own pizza,' says Webb. 'We had lunch in one of those dollar-a-pizza places. We all expected him to pick up the tab. We hadn't paid for anything for about six weeks. And he paid for his slice and walked out. We were like, "What the fuck?"' In some small way, Travis had perhaps stayed true to the no-frills ethics of the heyday of indie; Menswear, by contrast, expected the platinum credit card treatment.

'They came back,' says Simon White, 'saying, "Well, London took us out to loads of restaurants, and we went for a pizza with Geoff Travis, and he made us pay. So we're going to sign to London."' Such were the economics of Britpop.

At the last minute, one other label re-entered the chase. In early December, the night before they were due to formally sign with London, Indolent, a sub-section of the BMG group, sent the group a case of champagne, and relayed a mind-boggling message: if Menswear deferred their decision, they would fly them anywhere in the world. By now, however, like sated aristocrats, the group were growing tired of the music industry's generosity.

So it was that Menswear signed a two-album contract with London, via the Laurel label, for a £90,000 advance. If the initial pay-out seemed surprisingly moderate, Adrian Webb's craftiness was reflected in the group's royalty rate. The industry standard was 16 per cent of gross revenues; Madonna's contract with Warner Brothers gave her 18 per cent; Menswear managed 18.5. 'We pushed that,' says Adrian Webb. 'I wanted nineteen and they said no, so we walked out. Then they came up to us and said, "We can't give you nineteen because that's our profit margin."'

In the wake of the signing of the London deal, Adrian Webb began a tour of London's music publishers, where the conversations became positively surreal. 'In a meeting at EMI Publishing,' he says, 'they said, "How much do you want?" I said, jokingly, "Half a million pounds," and no-one laughed. I was drunk: I'd been out to lunch. It just came out of my mouth. But I thought, "OK, let's stick with that figure then. You're obviously taking it seriously."' Soon enough, Menswear signed to Island Publishing for exactly the figure that Webb had blurted out. Thanks to their pocket-sized repertoire, that worked out at around £70,000 per song.

In their first spate of interviews – usually conducted in The Good Mixer – Menswear were continually quizzed about the spend-happy hysteria that surrounded them, usually greeting such questions with nonchalant shrugs. 'They'd never been involved in the industry before,' says Webb, 'and this was kind of how they'd dreamt it would be. The fact that it was like that didn't phase them: I think they thought it was like that for everyone.'

They also managed to mark themselves down as the vanguard of a new musical generation; graduates of the indie milieu who betrayed precious little sympathy with its countercultural roots. On occasion, their pronouncements seemed to hark back to the days of Duran Duran and Spandau Ballet. 'At the end of the day,' said Simon White, as yet another tape recorder whirred, 'vast financial gain has got to be your main motive. I want a helicopter.'

When they were asked about the Anglo-centric aesthetics that seemed to lie at the heart of their approach – I'll Manage Somehow remains the only rock song in history to contain the phrase 'trying jolly hard' – the sense of a break with the past was only furthered. 'There's people who'll go on about Englishness and then the next minute they'll say they want the heads of the Royal Family on the gates of Buckingham Palace,' said Johnny Dean, who managed to combine a peacock-like dress sense with the earnest demeanour of a nervous sixth-former. 'What's the point of going on about Englishness and hating the Royal Family? They're an integral part of Englishness.'

If Menswear appeared to be callow bandwagon-jumpers, their acceptance by the Britpop inner circle went some way to underwriting their credibility. By the end of 1994, Chris Gentry – by now confirmed as the group's pretty-boy pin-up, who looked all of fifteen – was going out with Donna Matthews, and his colleagues were regular visitors to her house in King's Cross. For a time, after Menswear took precedence over Social Studies and he was ejected from his halls of residence, Simon White was a resident, though his brief tenure was marked by uneasiness about the crowd that would regularly return there once the pubs had closed.

'I always thought they were a bunch of vampires,' he says. 'William Burroughs once said that if you ever walk into a room and feel like you've lost a pint of blood, then avoid those people. And that's kind of how I felt. Donna was always really nice, really cool. And she was genuinely into music. It was just the people who surrounded her. People sort of gravitated towards her, because she was for real.'

There was also the small matter of regular rituals with tin foil and brown powder. 'It was obviously going on, and I remember being very shocked at first that there were people doing heroin,' says White. 'For me, it always had this stigma: I remember dirty junkies in Birmingham, and what they used to get up to, and having my house robbed, and I always equated it with that. And yet, here were all these posh, well-heeled, cultured people doing it for fun. I found it a bit distasteful and decadent.

'I think the bottom line was that they had this snobbish thing, like, "No-one understands our little heroin scene, because we can just do it, and take it, and we're not addicts or anything." I think they thought about themselves like that. I was ashamed of myself that I'd even bothered to try it, just the one time. I did see some horrible sights round there. Some very fucked-up people.'

For the moment, Elastica managed to combine their more reckless instincts with a schedule that might have rattled even the most disciplined minds. As of February 1995, their commitments stretched into the distance, as they reluctantly gave up the cautious approach that had defined their first manoeuvres, and began hawking themselves around the globe. Geffen Records, the US label to whom they had signed the previous summer, expected nothing less. That month, they turned in their first American performances, beginning with a show in New York. In among the 300 people crammed into the Mercury Lounge on East Houston Street were Iggy Pop and Debbie Harry; the latter was sufficiently impressed to dance to the whole of Elastica's set. Whereas Blur and Suede had travelled to the States and found themselves viewed as little more than curios, Elastica sensed that they were putting down roots; the proof was a never-ending stream of admirers, gushingly announcing that they were the season's hippest thing.

To Justine Frischmann, who had started the group aiming at nothing more earth-shaking than a handful of singles and the odd appearance in the *NME*, the result was the jarring feeling that comes from life taking a very unexpected turn indeed. 'On that first trip to America,' she says, 'it occurred to me: "This is getting silly." It all sat really incongruously with what we were doing. But it was thrilling, too. How could you not want that?'

Donna Matthews, meanwhile, was still enjoying the fun in the manner of a girl guide on a picnic. Twelve months before, she had been living in a squat and saving up enough change for a trip to the laundrette; now, she was being hoisted into the high life. 'It all felt very glamorous,' she says. 'We'd be on planes, taking drugs in the toilet. We'd be taken by a limo to where we were going. Get taken to someone's mansion, sit round the pool taking drugs. Then we'd go out partying: we'd be run here, run there, running up a three thousand pound bill. We'd all be in hotel suites, off our nuts. Everyone wanted to meet us. We'd go to New York and meet Debbie Harry and Iggy Pop; we'd go to LA and get put on the guest-list for The Viper Room. All the places we'd read about, we were being invited to. Suddenly everyone wanted to come backstage to meet us. I'd always be meeting people I was really nervous about.'

Elastica released their debut album on 13 March. Wrapped in a monochrome sleeve that was consciously in keeping with Justine Frischmann's love of punk, it contained fifteen songs: the group's four singles, along with a collection of tracks that had been amassed over the previous two years. Just about all of them fused the brittle wit and musical economy that had become the group's calling cards: on Car Song, Frischmann camply celebrated the pleasures of sex on the back seat; during the frantic seventy seconds of Annie, Elastica even paid humour-laden tribute to one of their own number. The album's best song, however, broke with the template, sounding a note of genuinely affecting candour.

Never Here was Justine Frischmann's concise, mournful treatise on her relationship with Brett Anderson. It stands as Elastica's most compelling song: three minutes in which Frischmann's recurrent smirk was sidelined in favour of a brutal honesty. As against Anderson's songs about her, there was nothing by way of a poetic veil: this was a blunt remembrance of a relationship in which wide horizons had eventually been fogged by a comfortable kind of inertia: 'I moved straight into your shoes/I took up your cause and answered your phone/I couldn't really imagine/What life was like when I was alone/Then I started to worry/I thought of our lives left on the shelf/Too much TV and curry/ Too much time spent on ourselves'. Quite what Brett Anderson made of it remained a mystery.

Upon its release, *Elastica* provided further proof of the shift in public taste that had been heralded by *Parklife*. In its first six days on sale, it managed to surpass even the gargantuan sales tally managed by *Definitely Maybe*: Elastica were thus awarded the unwieldy honour of having released the fastest selling debut album of all time. In among the celebrations, the accolade surely marked the end of Justine Frischmann's idea of the group managing to hang on to the cultishness to which she had initially aimed. She had bemoaned 'all this neurotic stuff about chart positions' mere weeks before the album was released. 'I really don't believe you have to go through that to be in a band,' she went on. 'I'd be quite happy to just have a cult following. I want to be underground.' Her group's success dashed such hopes at a stroke; in the music business parlance, Elastica had Crossed Over.

In March, they toured the UK. Throughout April and May, they trekked around Europe. By the early summer, Elastica were back in the States, on a twenty-date tour that took them through the staple US stop-offs, along with such unlikely places as Tempe, Arizona and Salt Lake City, Utah. For Justine Frischmann, the frenzied pace of their itinerary had one upshot: for the next eighteen months, her relationship with Damon Albarn became a matter of long-distance phone calls and the odd snatched weekend.

With the help of her father, the pair had bought a new house in Kensington Park Road, W11, already celebrated in the tabloid newspapers as their '£350,000 love nest'. Frischmann's possessions were moved in in her absence. Albarn, preoccupied with the recording of Blur's fourth album, did not find time to begin home-making. 'Damon was there for six months on his own,' says Frischmann, 'and he didn't buy a chair to sit on. There was a telly on a box, loads of newspaper, an ashtray and a bed. And that was it.'

On Sunday 30 April, as Elastica made their way between Amsterdam and Rennes, Oasis achieved their first number one single. Some Might Say had been written in 1993, when Noel Gallagher heard Suede's Animal Nitrate on the radio and promptly attempted to equal it. His efforts were largely in vain: its lyric was based on little more than a chain of clichés, while its production saw the return of his beloved multi-tracked guitars, so densely layered that the backing track sounded positively stodgy. Fortunately, enough of Oasis's winning qualities – encapsulated by Liam's swaggering delivery of the vocal line – remained for the song to endear itself to their public; and besides, its supporting features were good enough to make debate about the A-side all but academic.

As on Suede's early singles, Noel Gallagher was now brazenly showing off his talent by using some of his best compositions as B-sides. Oasis were in the habit of turning each single into what used to be known as an EP, so Some Might Say came with three extra songs: Talk Tonight, a hushed account of his disappearance on the 1994 American tour; Headshrinker, a chunk of spittle-flecked belligerence on which Liam Gallagher turned in an unprecedentedly ferocious vocal performance; and a composition called Acquiesce. It was this song that truly nudged Some Might Say into the shade. The title was used merely because Noel Gallagher liked the sound of the word; by way of explanation, the Creation Press Office claimed that its use was aimed at stopping 'people like Damon out of Blur saying Oasis aren't intelligent'.

Fortuitously, however, it fitted the song, simply by dint of a musical power that offered the listener little option but to surrender. Its brutally constructed verses, though they soon tumbled into doggerel, initially gave Liam lines that not only nailed what made him such a compelling presence, but identified him with an unspeakably potent archetype: the same Dionysian menace who had reared his head on such milestones as Jumpin' Jack Flash and Anarchy In The UK. Then, just as the lyrics' aggression threatened to turn in on the song itself, Noel sang a chorus that – although he denied any such conscious intent – sounded like a heartfelt acknowledgement of the Gallaghers' mutual dependence: 'Because we need each other/We believe in one another . . .' As with Live Forever, the words dealt in an unmistakably sentimental language, but the Gallaghers' sheer conviction meant that they managed to avoid sounding cheap.

Not long after the single's release, Radio One issued a short promotional film in which the DJ Mark Radcliffe was shown listening to Acquiesce and frantically drumming along, and marvelling at how good it was. His question was simple enough: 'Why didn't they release this as the A-side?'

Over the previous five months, the vistas opened up by the success of *Definitely Maybe* had only seemed to grow wider. On 21 November 1994, in the hours after a performance at Hamburg's Markthalle, Noel Gallagher had instructed his colleagues to listen to a clutch of his latest compositions. 'We were sat on the bus,' says Paul Arthurs. 'He said, "Come in the back lounge, I'm going to play the next album for you on an acoustic guitar." He just sat and played it: pretty much the whole thing. It pickled my head. It was just like, "Fucking, *yeah* – how did you do *that*?"' By Arthurs' own admission, he was sufficiently awed by the new songs to weep openly.

One month later, Oasis released their Christmas single. Whatever had lain in Noel Gallagher's stock of songs since the group's beginnings, long envisaged as the kind of tune that demanded a sizeable budget. Now, it could have one: its strait-laced chords and pretty much meaningless lyrics were frosted with a part for strings that sounded like the yuletide season incarnate. The sounding of such a populist note had the desired effect: Whatever entered the chart at number three, just behind Mariah Carey's All I Want For Christmas Is You and East 17's dirge-like Stay Another Day. When the single arrived at the *NME*, the paper's staff gathered around the office stereo in a circle. The paper's traditions of irreverence and prickliness quickly melted into insignificance: 'You can almost see the snow falling,' cooed one sub-editor.

On 28 January, Oasis were due to fly back to America, to begin their most extensive American tour thus far. In preparation, one of their aides was dispatched to the American Embassy to snip through the last obstructive length of red tape. 'One of my most powerful memories is of getting an American visa for Liam,' says Ian Robertson. 'It was at fairly short notice: I had to go down to the embassy and pull a couple of shimmies. And I was putting Liam's visa into his passport, the photograph of Liam when he got the passport was this blue-eyed, clean-shaven, extraordinarily beautiful teenager. And the photograph that was on the visa, taken not an awfully long time later was . . . he was *lost*. It looked like ten years had passed. He was unshaven, the eyes were hooded. All of us look like that on occasion, but at that point, it was kind of the norm. I still find that quite moving.'

As Oasis pinballed from San Diego to Mesa, Arizona, and on through Utah and Colorado to Texas, it became ever more obvious that Tony McCarroll – the sprig-haired drummer who always sat hunched over his kit, as if anxiously guarding it – was being shoved ever closer to redundancy. He had long been the subject of very public barbs that, in any sphere of activity, would have had his colleagues accused of lamentable unprofessionalism (when asked if he was looking forward to Oasis's acoustic performance at Creation Undrugged, Liam Gallagher had responded, 'Our set's going to be great, 'cos our drummer's not doing it.'). By now, as McCarroll's colleagues decisively reached the conclusion that his distinctly basic technique could not possibly do the next album any kind of justice, the cruelty – most often dispensed by Liam – had reached quite spectacular depths.

'There's always somebody who gets the kicking on any tour, but it's not usually somebody in the band,' says Ian Robertson. 'Tony was even considered fair game for the crew. In terms of the hierarchy, it was Noel, Liam, Mark Coyle, Bonehead and Guigsy, Marcus, me . . . and Tony was somewhere way down the list. It was, "You're a fucking shit drummer, I'm going to sack you, You're going to be back on the dole before you know it, What the fucking hell are you wearing that shirt for?, Why are you shagging her?" Just *everything*.

'There wasn't a single part of his universe that wasn't shredded. But it kind of bounced off him. We were chatting on the tourbus one night, and he said, "I can hack it, because I'm in the band. I am the drummer with this fucking group. The rest of it is incidental." He genuinely believed that that would always be the case. He never saw the hammer drop.'

On this tour, McCarroll's predicament was hardly eased by the fact that most of his free time was devoted to a new friend he had met during the tour's opening engagements. On the few occasions when Ian Robertson conveyed an invitation to join his colleagues in some hotel bar or downtown restaurant, he recalls McCarroll answering his hotel room door clad in a bath-towel, bashfully claiming to be otherwise engaged.

'She was from Florida: a good-looking, very horny groupie,' says Ian Robertson.'And Tony didn't see it. Everybody else did. The rule is, Fuck 'em and forget 'em. And Tony didn't. He fucked her and fell in love. That was another stick to beat him with: "You idiot. Can you not see why she's shagging you? Don't you *get it?*"'

Oasis returned from the US to begin the seven-day build-up to a huge show at Sheffield's Arena, in front of 12,000 people. Marcus Russell's initial mooting of the event had been greeted by his charges with gasps of incredulity, but it quickly became apparent that *Definitely Maybe* had easily levered them into such territory. The occasion, long since relegated to the margins of the Oasis story on account of their later triumphs in football stadiums and provincial fields, sits in a pivotal place within the group's history: for as well as marking the apex of their popularity thus far, it also saw the last performance by Oasis's original membership.

Having accompanied the group to such a spectacular pinnacle, Tony McCarroll was finally told that his services were no longer required. A few months later, Paul Arthurs gave voice to the group's feelings about their departed colleague, using a typically poetic metaphor. 'There's no guilt,' he said. 'If the five of us owned a fish and chip shop, and he wasn't putting enough batter on the fish or he weren't frying 'em right or he was burning the chips, it'd be, "Right, you're sacked."'

McCarroll's replacement was one Alan White, the brother of Paul Weller's drummer Steve, recruited after a meeting with Oasis's leader that, Noel Gallagher later claimed, had been largely set up as a means of checking that the new recruit wasn't fat. White was from Eltham, South London: in a flurry of reports about the improbability of the group's new member being a Charlton Athletic supporter, his new job was duly announced to Oasis's public.

As Tony McCarroll trudged back to Burnage, another new face entered Oasis's world. On the few occasions when he paused between tours, Noel Gallagher had kept the company of a couple of London-based females: a music journalist named Lisa Verrico, and Rebecca De Ruvo, who was both an aspirant solo singer and a presenter on MTV Europe. Through the latter, Noel had been introduced to her flatmate, one Meg Mathews: prior to their departure for the States, the pair had seen in the New Year at The Landmark Hotel on Marylebone Road. Upon his return, it became obvious that she and Noel were now an item. As if to confirm that Camden Town was London's most swinging neighbourhood, he had moved into her flat on Albert Street, mere yards from The Good Mixer.

Mathews – born in Guernsey, and brought up in Durban, South Africa – was the occupant of a world that had been cemented by Acid House, where the catwalk, the music industry, and the London club scene collided: a place in which one's female friends were habitually addressed as 'babe', the designer label was king, and nights out were usually predicated on which friend-of-a-friend could work the requisite wonders on a guest-list. She had worked at the L'Equipe Anglaise club on Duke Street, W1, and Ministry Of Sound, and spent a year as the personal assistant to Betty Boo, the short-lived early 90s pop sensation. These days, Mathews was attempting to make a go of running a DJ-booking agency, while studiously keeping abreast of the correct length of cutting-edge hemlines.

'When they first met,' says Tim Abbot, 'she was a very well-connected, fashionable person, and Noel was a bit of a cloth-cap, down-from-the-North bloke. She was very happy now she'd got this name guy who was on the up. And he was absolutely besotted with her. She moved in and ran things for him, and I think he liked it like that. She looked after his social diary, dressed him ... and they went out and shopped for England. Where Oasis had an M&S style, and an intrinsic knowledge of Fred Perry and Lacoste, she took it the next stage further, to Gucci and Prada.' A little too hard-faced to fit the stereotype of the trophy girlfriend, Mathews gleefully assumed the job of leading her new partner to his other glittering prizes.

This new injection of urbanity into Oasis's world was perhaps reflected in the location for the party thrown to celebrate the success of Some Might Say. It was held at the Mars Bar in Covent Garden, one of Alex James's favourite haunts. Not entirely unexpectedly, he and Damon Albarn made an appearance, intending to strike the same note of mutual support that they had sounded at the Brit Awards.

As it turned out, their welcome to the event came wrapped in a triumphal kind of belligerence. The opportunity to wave Oasis's achievement in Blur's faces was hardly something Liam Gallagher was likely to pass up; not long after James and Albarn's arrival, temptation got the better of him. 'I went to their celebration party, you know, just to say "Well done,"' Albarn recalled. 'And Liam came over and, like he is, he goes, "Number fuckin' one," right in my face. So I thought, "OK, we'll see . . ."'

While Oasis's success led them into Bond Street boutiques, Blur's triumphs often seemed to be accompanied by deliberate steps down-market. Although Alex James was enthusiastically flitting around the more rarefied corners of the West End, Graham Coxon and Damon Albarn seemed keener than ever to ooze what James – with a sneaking irony – refers to as a 'street vibe'.

In June 1994, Coxon was interviewed by *Select* magazine at his flat on Holloway Road, North London, hardly one of the capital's more upmarket thoroughfares. The journalist noted that he had no cooker, and only one chair. 'I was watching a telly report about crime,' he said, 'and it showed all the areas in Britain marked from yellow to red to indicate differing levels of lawlessness. I'm living in a red area. It means there's always a kebab shop open, and you get a sense of the nitty gritty.' Six months later, Damon Albarn explained his fondness for Walthamstow Dog Track in not-dissimilar terms. 'You get the ooze of life there,' he told the *Guardian*.

In the context of rock music, there was nothing all that new about such poses: Albarn and Coxon were merely indulging in their own version of the eternal bohemian fondness for anything that gives off the odour of proletarian authenticity. In the mid-90s, however, the notion of slumming it seemed nearer to the core of British pop culture than ever. Thanks to a tangled web that took in *Loaded*, the all-pervading emphasis on avenging the pieties of the 80s, and a new-found fondness for a cartoonish Britishness built around football and fried breakfasts, many a bourgeois was frantically learning the art of the glottal stop, scanning *Loot* for a suitably rootsy abode, and memorising their chosen team's terrace chants.

The most memorable hit single of 1995 was a righteous blast against all this. Common People was the work of Pulp, the natives of Sheffield who had become members of the same London clique as Blur and Elastica. 'It seemed to be in the air, that kind of patronising social voyeurism, slumming it, the idea that there's a glamour about low-rent, low-life,' said their singer and lyricist, Jarvis Cocker. 'I felt that off *Parklife*, for example . . . there's that noble savage notion. But if you walk round a council estate, there's plenty of savagery and not much nobility going on.'

Cocker, born in 1963, came from a similar background to Brett Anderson. His mother, Christine, had been to art school; his father, Mack, was a sometime jazz trombonist. The latter exited the family home when his son was seven, leaving his wife to raise Jarvis and his younger sister Saskia alone; for a time, she earned a living emptying fruit machines. The family lived in Intake, a glamorously named enclave of Sheffield, where children with such irregular Christian names were bound to stick out. Their incongruity was only heightened by Jarvis's appearance: 'I was the only kid on the block with long hair,' he once recalled, 'which my mum wouldn't cut. Long hair and skinny-rib jumpers with really short shorts: she made her own clothes, so it would look like a jumper dress.' For a while, thanks to the generosity of a German relative, a mortified Cocker went to school in lederhosen.

In his mid-teens, Cocker formed a group called Arabicus Pulp, who were sufficiently in thrall to the iconoclastic ways of indiedom to have a drum kit fashioned from a burglar alarm and pocket calculator. With their name shortened to one word, they caught the attention of John Peel, and were invited to London to record a session for his Radio One programme. The precocity implied by such an achievement did not go unnoticed: Pulp were given a front-page story in the *Sheffield Star*.

Unfortunately, the fun did not last. Various incarnations of Cocker's group hobbled through the next decade in fits and starts, dispensing the kind of rickety, home-baked music that tended to find favour with small pockets of *NME* readers and John Peel listeners, but remarkably few others. Listening to a song like Dogs Are Everywhere, a single released by the group in 1986, one is reminded of a very common source of confusion in the 1980s: what with Cocker's voice (which rather suggests a self-conscious foghorn), his clumsy attempts at lyrical gravitas ('Sometimes I have to wonder about the dog in me') and the group's audibly shaky grasp of their chosen instruments, one begins to wonder whether they were playing it for laughs.

Throughout this period, Cocker could not help but feel cheated of his rightful destiny. 'I resent the eighties,' he later reflected. 'In all walks of life, it was like, "You've had your fun, let's get back to Victorian values." I'd been born in the sixties, and you'd see stuff on telly about how great it was, and by the time it comes to your formative years where you're thinking, "Come on then, let's have a bit of that," it's all going in the opposite direction. I often said I wanted a refund on my adolescence.' The decade at least saw one fillip to Cocker's morale: in 1984, he met Russell Senior, the violinist and guitarist who became almost as integral a part of the group as Cocker himself.

In 1988, the same year that Alex James and Graham Coxon arrived at Goldsmiths and Justine Frischmann and Brett Anderson began their courses at UCL, Cocker took a place at Central St Martins College of Art and Design, studying for a degree in film-making. Like so many aspirant musicians, he spent some time living in squats, in both Mile End and Camberwell. His arrival in London coincided with the decisive advent of Acid House: he later recalled visiting an M25 rave with his hair tied in bunches, looking 'like some demented Girl Guide instructress'.

Gradually, a new line-up of Pulp began to make headway. My Legendary Girlfriend, a single released in September 1990, was the *NME*'s Single Of The Week, and Pulp's London bookings became increasingly frequent. Word began to spread about the group with the singer who sounded like a cut-price Scott Walker, with a performance style that rather suggested one of the more flamboyant turns on a 70s variety show. Nonetheless, Pulp's progress was still frustratingly slow.

By the autumn of 1993, however, the group were signed to Island Records. Their aesthetic had now been fine-honed: thanks to the fact that Cocker's lyrics were recurrently rooted in a world of grimy sexual intrigue and endlessly frustrated hopes, one tended to be reminded of The Smiths – although Pulp were a very different proposition indeed. Whereas The Smiths' visual sense was predominantly built on the iconography of the 1950s and early 60s, Pulp – not least in their charity-shop attire – drew on the 1970s. Moreover, if The Smiths derived much of their power from Johnny Marr's rock classicism, Pulp dealt in an altogether more off-beam musical vocabulary, partly founded on Candida Doyle's gurgling synthesisers and Russell Senior's fondness for the violin. On occasion, they sounded as if they were aspiring to some deep-pile artistic sophistication without quite the means to achieve it. Given the subject matter of Cocker's lyrics, such a musical backdrop was nigh-on perfect.

Their first major label album, *His'n'Hers*, was released in August 1994. It reached number nine in the charts, though Pulp's singles – whose quality peaked that year with the tragi-comic Do You Remember The First Time? – got no higher than the lower end of the top 20. For a time, those who recognised Cocker's unquestionable charisma allowed him to ride above his station, cajoling him into television appearances that, as much as any of Pulp's records, fed the idea that a breakthrough was imminent.

In July, he presented *Top of the Pops*. That October, he turned in a glorious performance on BBC1's *Pop Quiz*, in which he initially maintained a quiet presence, before finding his metier in the show-closing buzzer round: to gasps of admiration, he correctly answered every one of Chris Tarrant's rapid-fire questions. By February, when he made a brief appearance at the Brit Awards, it was telling that Chris Evans was referring to him simply by his Christian name. Given Pulp's eleven-year history of ignominious indie slog, his new ubiquity was surely the Britpop narrative in excelcis.

Common People was released on 28 May 1995. Its lyric took Cocker's discomfort about the notion of slumming it back to an encounter with one of his fellow students at St Martin's: a female Greek emigré who had expressed the wish to spend a season in the company of the British working classes (although he rather embroidered the memory; contrary to the lyric, she had not expressed the desire to sleep with him). By the end of its second verse, however, Cocker had abandoned any pretence at storytelling, and fallen into an amazingly articulate tirade against those who, for all their 'street' poses, 'will never understand how it feels to live your life with no meaning or control'. For a group who were commonly held to deal in knowing irony, this was startling stuff: one of the few records of the period that brimmed with a splenetic sense of rage. Thankfully, it also had a fantastically infectious chorus.

'Common People was a pivotal record, because everybody desperately wanted Pulp to have a hit,' says Steve Lamacq. 'I was DJing at

Nottingham Rock City on the Saturday before the chart was announced: it felt like Britpop's election; the landslide victory. If the chart the next day had been televised, you'd have had the other five records on a podium and Jarvis making a victory speech.' Common People was that week's highest-charting new release, entering the chart at number two, to sit just behind Robson & Jerome's interpretation of Unchained Melody. The fact that such a big hit had been scored by a group of proud misfits with an average age of thirty – not to mention Common People's subject matter – suggested that the mainstream had now been blown wide open.

If the song's lyric had at least been partly aimed at Blur, animosity was soon flowing in the opposite direction. For the previous year, Pulp's most enthusiastic social gadflys had been Cocker and Steve Mackey, the bass player who had joined Pulp in 1988. The latter shared a house in King's Cross with Justin Welch; by dint of that fact alone, Pulp were now a central part of the same social universe as both Blur and Elastica. Perhaps inevitably, the bonds that tied that clique together were occasionally taken to the next tempting level. 'Everybody shagged everybody else,' says Alex James. 'Especially round at Donna's house. [Affects Welsh accent] "We're having an orgy." Hahahahahaha.'

At this point, James's relationship with Justine Andrew – his girlfriend since his late teens – was going through a rough patch. Word reached him that Steve Mackey, Pulp's bassist, had seized his chance. To make life yet more complicated, Mackey was also rumoured to have spent the night with Justine Frischmann.

'We felt a common cause with Pulp at first,' says Alex James. 'We really supported them. But in a lot of ways, they were even bigger cunts than Oasis. They were in our birds' knickers: devious little fuckers. We definitely tried to help them; we thought they were cool. But they never had a kind word for us. Steve Mackey was shagging my bird, the cunt. That's all they wanted to do. I mean, Cheers. I thought they had a bigger agenda than shagging our birds. I was a bit disappointed. I kind of object to them more than Oasis, actually. At least Oasis said, "We're going to shag your bird." There was something a bit snidey about Pulp. And they still took the support slots.'

While Alex James fumed, Common People began a two-month spell as the soundtrack to the first part of the British summer. Within a couple of months, however, it would be drowned out by two new singles, and an outpouring of media hysteria that was little short of deafening.

CHAPTER 14

The well-oiled German war machine

The British summer has long been famed as the season when the notion of Hard News is temporarily put to bed, and the press and broadcast media are stuffed with all manner of frippery. On account of Parliament's most lengthy recess, the period between the end of July and the middle of October tends to be given over to a cabinet of curiosities: beasts on Bodmin Moor, the annual glut of corn circles, the presence of killer turtles in the Thames.

The summer of 1995 would later be confirmed as one of the warmest and driest since records began. In July, Glaswegian hospitals were reporting cases of serious sunburn, and meteorological stations in Worcester and Rickmansworth registered temperatures of 34 degrees. The following month, sunshine totals were 60 per cent above normal. For the people of Yorkshire, the effects were grim indeed: thanks in part to the shortcomings of utility privatisation, by the end of the summer, many of them depended on tanker deliveries of water. As far as slightly more fortunate Britons were concerned, afternoons drifted into long, humid evenings, and beer gardens echoed to quips about the benefits of global warming.

The good weather was not the year's only rare occurrence: in August, it was the good fortune of the British Fourth Estate to be handed a story that offered its journalists something a little more mouthwatering than the usual off-beam nonsense that marks out the warm months. Its foundation was the simultaneous release of two pop singles – seemingly as trivial an event as any of the usual silly season staples. Fortunately, however, the story bulged with subtexts: the enduring importance of class, the age-old North/South divide, the nation's long-standing affection for the 1960s. No columnist was too haughty to dispense their opinion; even the most upmarket leader-writers seemed quite happy to explain their paper's standpoint on this most pressing of matters.

Monday 14 August, 1995 marked the beginning of Blur Versus Oasis Week. In the ensuing seven days, the two groups achieved an unprecedented level of ubiquity: one only need glance at the image of John Humphrys, that most un-swinging of broadcasters, sitting ashen-faced in front of both group's logos on the BBC's *Six O'Clock News*, to appreciate that the story crash-landed in places to which neither band had ever been admitted.

Such was Britpop's highpoint. For Blur, it also came to represent the start of a season of nightmares.

Since the New Year, Blur had been working on their new album. Other groups in their position might have surmised that London held too many distractions, temptations and sources of harassment, but Blur gave such arguments short shrift. Like *Parklife* and *Modern Life Is Rubbish*, the new album was recorded with Stephen Street at Maison Rouge studios in Fulham, while the more colourful scenarios bound up with their celebrity – the walkover at the Brit Awards, Damon Albarn's visit to the Palace of Westminster, Alex James's endless circuits of Soho – were played out. 'There was no break between *Parklife* and *The Great Escape*,' says James. 'Even the day after we won all those Brits, we went to the studio. It was being recorded over the period when everything snowballed.'

On occasion, Blur's lives outside the studio took on the pleasantly surreal glow that came from the sudden easiness of wish-fulfilment. In March, Albarn duetted with Ray Davies on a new TV show called *The White Room*: the pair sang alternate verses on an endearingly tender version of Waterloo Sunset, after which Davies improvised a few choruses of Parklife, as if to even matters up. 'That's a good song,' said Davies, perhaps aware that from his mouth, such faint praise would be taken as the most fulsome of tributes. 'I was in love with him for that hour,' Albarn later commented. His affection found its way into one of Blur's works in progress, a piano ballad Albarn entitled Dear Ray.

In the summer, with echoes of Brett Anderson's long-lost summit with David Bowie, the two met one Friday morning in Wandsworth Park, while a journalist from *Mojo* magazine operated a tape recorder. As with Anderson and Bowie, their conversation threw up little of any consequence, save for a telling exchange prompted by Davies' remembrance of the reception given to The Kinks' Sunny Afternoon. A one-time believer in the sanctity of the generation gap faced someone who seemed to believe he was duty-bound to transcend it; the resulting exchange shone light on one of the most striking differences between the 60s generation and their successors.

'I remember the record coming out,' said Davies, 'and I walked into a British Legion . . . All these people, old soldiers and things, singing it. I was twenty-three years old. I said, "Wow, all these old people really like it." And this old guy came up and said, "You young guys . . . this is the sort of music we can relate to!" I thought, "Wow, this is it. It's the end."'

'But it's not, is it?' Albarn replied. 'I love it when my gran likes anything I've done.'

Blur's new familiarity to Britons of all ages was proving to have its drawbacks – chiefly, the fact that in the wake of the Brit Awards, the UK's tabloid newspapers needed only the flimsiest of pretexts to run Blur stories. When Albarn took his cat to the vet in a cab, a photographer was waiting for him: the resulting picture appeared in *The Sun*, with the caption 'Blur's frontman may be pop's hottest name, but he still has time for his small furry fans.' One week earlier, the ever-enthusiastic *Today* ran a photograph of Albarn making his way uphill on a mountain bike. 'He's spent eight years getting to the top,' wrote an unnamed sub editor, 'and now Blur singer Damon Albarn looks like he wants a rest. Surely the dizzy heights of pop stardom can't be as tiring as climbing this hill by pedal power.'

On the morning of 3 March, *Today* truly excelled themselves. The previous evening, Graham Coxon had been making his way home from a Dolce & Gabbana party in Hampstead, when he suffered a minor collision with a Rover saloon car. One of the attendant paparazzi recorded the accident in a set of ghoulish photographs: Coxon, pale and clearly shaken, being helped from the tarmac as the flashbulb did its work. 'Pop pin-up Graham Coxon was left dazed and confused after he was hit by a car as he left a showbiz party last night,' ran the attendant copy. The incident was reported in terms of drunken hi-jinks; Coxon's appearance suggested a very heart-rending kind of distress.

As they ricocheted between parties, pubs and members' clubs, and found the most mundane aspects of their lives splurged back at them in italics and bold print, much of the music Blur were creating took a queasy, seasick aspect. The abiding feeling of something not being quite right was only furthered by the slew of third-person characters who featured in Albarn's new lyrics. On *Parklife*, contrary to its reputation, there had been only three such creations: Tracy Jacks, the harried commuter who exorcised his pain by demolishing his own house; Bill Barrett, the British dreamer who lay at the heart of Magic America;

and the anti-hero of Jubilee, a throwaway ode to the pre-millennial teenager. Albarn's new material, by contrast, bulged with them: in Charmless Man, Top Man, Stereotypes, Ernold Same and Mr Robinson's Quango, there lay a menagerie of wife-swappers, cross-dressers, odious braggarts and crushing bores.

'It was all more elaborate, more orchestral, more theatrical, and the lyrics were even more twisted,' says Alex James. 'It had gone from a cartoon into a horror movie. There wasn't one nice person in there, was there? It was all dysfunctional, misfit characters fucking up.'

On 17 June, Blur broke cover to perform a huge show at Mile End Stadium, in front of 18,000. The occasion, announced two months before, appeared to be as perfect a summation of Britpop as anyone had yet managed, not only in terms of the bill – which included such mid-table Britpop attractions as Dodgy and The Boo Radleys – but also on account of its audience. In Albarn's estimation, Mile End represented 'the first time that lads and indie kids went to a gig together'. In addition, the fact that the location was a rather shabby sports ground in E14 added to the sense of a neat fit – given that music was newly suffused with affected cockney accents, a bit of East End authenticity was surely part of the fun. As if to confirm it, the encore featured Blur's reading of Daisy Bell, throatily accompanied by the crowd.

Perhaps equally significantly, Mile End saw the public premiere of a new Blur song entitled Country House, greeted with a completely unexpected outbreak of the kind of massed swaying usually seen only when middle-of-the-road balladeers perform on *Top of the Pops*. Its joyous reception sealed a question that had been buzzing around the Blur camp for weeks. Country House would be their new single.

Its lyric was founded on a sarcastic nod to Blur's old overlord David Balfe, and his move to Hertfordshire ('He had a croquet lawn and there were lots of rabbits,' says Andy Ross). In truth, however, the song also dealt, albeit vaguely, with Damon Albarn's travails over the last year: what with a reference to Prozac, and its crestfallen middle section – 'Blow, blow me out/I am so sad I don't know why' – it was not difficult to discern a sense of personal disquiet, though at the time, few people seemed to notice. Country House, after all, was a lolloping example of what Graham Coxon would later term 'the Blur stomp': a chunk of vaudevillian camp whose chorus oozed all the simplicity of a terrace chant. Lyrical nuances apart, it was little more than a lightweight burlesque; nonetheless, the group scheduled it to come out in mid-August, three weeks before the new album.

Tony Wadsworth, the managing director of the Parlophone label, was a friend of Marcus Russell: the two had kept in touch throughout the spring, aiming to ensure that the new Blur and Oasis albums were released sufficiently far apart to allow each party a clear run. The requisite messages were relayed to Food Records' offices in Camden Town. 'We were very, very careful about the release dates of the albums,' says Andy Ross. 'It was always, "If there are any changes of the release plans for either record, keep us posted." That dialogue went on, in a fairly casual manner, once a month or so. And we reached the point where everyone got quite relaxed about the fact that there wasn't going to be a problem.' The initiative seemed to work: Blur scheduled theirs to appear in September, while Oasis settled for October.

'You aim for a number one single,' explains Ross, 'and number one singles then develop a momentum of their own, and have a big chance of being number one for a second week. Then you drop – that's the music business word – the album in week three or whatever, and the album goes in at number one. So we thought, "We'll be doing that, followed by a similar pattern by Oasis. Everyone'll be happy, cheers." That's what we assumed.'

Then came very bad news indeed. Though Blur and their associates had assumed that Oasis would follow standard music business protocol, releasing a single three weeks or so before their album, word reached them that the gap would be more like a month and a half. Oasis, in fact, were aiming at putting out their new single seven days before Country House.

The information sent the Blur camp into a spin. 'We thought they were being mad,' says Ross. 'But the thing is, a number one record tends to have a better-than-evens chance of being one the week after, just because it's on *Top of the Pops*, and all the kids hear it. So had Oasis released their single before Blur, they would have had a number one, and by that logic, they would have had an extremely good chance of staying there the next week, even if Blur had a good crack at it.

'We *had* to move the release date. We could have pushed it back a week or two and delayed the album. But when you get locked into a release, you've got all the advertising booked, posters done up with the release dates. You can't muck around with stuff like that. It's like the well-oiled German war machine. You can't say, "Well, hang about. Stop it." Also, that would have looked like we were chickening out.'

Given the fact that the Gallagher brothers needed little persuasion to indulge in the kind of self-celebration that was usually accompanied by a sneaking nastiness, this latter prospect was too much to bear. 'The Oasis lot were – as had become clear – slightly vocal,' says Andy Ross. 'There would have been no end of it: "Soft southern puffs duck out of fight with Oasis."'

One sun-soaked June afternoon, Ross, Chris Morrison and Damon Albarn sat outside The Westmoreland Arms, a Marylebone pub. It did not take long for them to surmise that they should release Country House the same week as the Oasis single. It was not hard to fathom what had pushed them towards their conclusion. Albarn's encounter with Liam Gallagher at the Mars Bar had reawakened the ferociously competitive streak that, back in the dark days of 1992, had defined his view of Suede. The head-to-head scenario offered Blur the chance of a victory tinged with *Schadenfreude*: for Albarn, it was surely the perfect outcome.

By the time of Tony McCarroll's ejection from Oasis, seven months had passed since Noel Gallagher had flown out from Los Angeles and fleetingly decided to call time on the group. Even with the appointment of their new drummer, however, it quickly became clear that Oasis's internal affairs were as fractious as ever. No matter that they had just achieved their first number one, and taken their first dizzying steps onto the kind of stages reserved for accredited rock stars: Oasis remained enviably skilled at kicking the wheels off their own wagon.

In May, they began recording their second album at Rockfield Studios, near Monmouth, in the company of Owen Morris. The songs Noel had played to his colleagues in Hamburg were initially put to tape at a breakneck pace: during their first spurt of work, the group came close to averaging one song every twenty-four hours.

The new material included two slow songs: a stately ballad written in tribute to Meg Mathews that Noel had named Wonderwall, after a long-lost 60s art film scored by George Harrison; and Don't Look Back In Anger, a more florid composition that shared its chord structure and abiding air of wilful populism with Whatever. Their author informed his younger brother that he wanted to sing lead vocals on one of them, which was not the kind of news that Liam Gallagher wanted to hear. As far as Liam was concerned, such a prospect amounted to temporary exile from his own group.

For the moment, the issue was submerged: to an appreciative response from his brother, Liam added his vocals to Wonderwall. Matters became strained, however, when the group were recording a song entitled Champagne Supernova. Thanks to his fondness for lager and B&H, Liam was audibly straining for the song's high notes. Tension began to seep into the studio; it was hardly eased by Noel's decision to move on to the song on which he was to take the lead vocal.

While Noel stepped up to the microphone, Liam passed the time in a local pub, sharing the company of a crowd of locals, and slowly working himself into a state of alcohol-assisted testiness. Much to his brother's annoyance, he returned to Rockfield with a quickly assembled retinue, evidently intending to call time on any recording and commence an impromptu party. The eventual result was a particularly ugly brawl, which saw Liam making his point with the aid of the studio's furniture. Noel, meanwhile, repeatedly bashed his younger brother with a cricket bat.

'It was a proper fight,' says Paul Arthurs. 'Noel said to Alan White, "Have you got a driving licence?" He said, "Yeah." Noel goes, "Right, Bonehead – give him the hire car keys. Drive me to London, we're out of here." This was at four in the morning. Alan had had a few pints: there was a wheel spin, cloud of dust, *gone*. The whole place was trashed.' Arthurs had wisely decided to lock away a clutch of air rifles brought to the studio by Paul McGuigan, in case the younger Gallagher suddenly decided to try his hand at the art of marksmanship.

'I rang Ignition at seven that morning,' says Arthurs. ' "It's Bonehead." "Yeah, what's up?" "Erm . . . the album's off. Noel's gone home. I need a train ticket." They hung up; they didn't believe me.' As the group's management quickly discovered, the scenario was real enough: Noel was back in his Camden Town flat, vowing – once again – that this was it.

His colleagues, however, were perhaps less rattled than he would have liked. 'Owen Morris was gutted,' says Arthurs. 'In the control room the next day, he was like, "What happened?" We were like, "Noel's gone home. We've got to go." He was going, "Do you think that's it?" I said, "It'll be alright. Give him a week at home." By then it was just, "Oh – *another* fight." '

The Gallaghers were reunited three weeks later. The terms of their reconciliation would surely have been familiar to any expert in the finer points of human relationships: 'I was a cunt and he was a cunt and it had to be dealt with,' said Liam. After a final fortnight's work – to be followed by a spurt of post-production in London – Oasis emerged into the sunlight with their chests out. 'This album will wipe the field with any competition,' said Owen Morris. 'It's astonishing. It's the bollocks for this decade. It's a piece of piss recording with Oasis. We only spent fifteen days recording it.'

The group's first key engagement of the summer was a Friday night performance on the main stage of the Glastonbury Festival. They arrived at the site that afternoon: Noel Gallagher, seemingly mindful of his surroundings, was dressed in a tweed jacket that looked like it had been ordered from the back pages of *Country Life*, replete with leather elbow-patches. Furthering the sense that he was striking the pose of a gracious local squire, he made a flying visit to the festival's VIP tent, greeting those who had made his acquaintance as if welcoming them to his annual fete.

Tim Abbot was now in the habit of recording Oasis's progress with his camcorder. He filmed Oasis immediately before they took the stage, expectantly hovering outside their portakabin, waiting for their call. His footage has an innocent, familial ambience: Ian Robertson, a deeply incongruous presence, dressed in a cricket jumper and issuing instructions in his officer-class accent; Marcus Russell, bidding the group an early farewell as he sets off to watch the show from the crowd; Alan White, about to play his second gig with his new group, cutting a figure of surprising composure, betraying his nerves only in repeated requests for chewing gum.

There was also a new addition to the Oasis entourage: Robbie Williams, then still shackled to Take That. He arrived at Glastonbury alone, but managed – via an acquaintance with Meg Mathews – to slip into Oasis's inner sanctum. Abbot's camera finds him ingratiating himself via the simple expedient of being the class clown, dispensing endless approximations of the Manchester accent, attempting to find comic potential in even the most mundane aspects of his surroundings. At one point, he and Liam Gallagher enjoy a fleeting conversation with Jonathan King, loitering by the bridge that separates the festival's dressing rooms from the main stage. 'Are you going to do a good show tonight?' asks King, rather nervously. 'Oh, I think so,' says Liam.

Unfortunately, Glastonbury '95 was hardly Oasis's finest hour. They opened their set not with one of their incendiary calls-to-arms, but with The Swamp Song, a one-chord instrumental that had been recorded for the new album. It sailed far over the audience's heads: four minutes of screeching guitar solos from which Liam was bafflingly absent. In its anti-climactic wake, it took Oasis at least half their allotted time to find their feet. The moment at which they rallied was perhaps marked when, during Oasis's rendition of Shakermaker, Robbie Williams loafed on to the stage at Liam Gallagher's invitation, turning in thirty seconds of camped-up dancing before he returned to the wings. Tim Abbot's camcorder footage captures him continuing to sing along: as proved by a number of close-ups, Williams didn't know the words.

Though his appearance grabbed no end of tabloid headlines, it was hardly enough to make Oasis the unquestioned hit of the weekend. That honour would go to Pulp, awarded the following night's headline slot when The Stone Roses – who had intended to use Glastonbury to mark their return to the British stage – cancelled at the eleventh hour. Their performance peaked with a reading of Common People whose reception verged on the orgasmic; adding to the sense of a righteous triumph, they had decided to demonstrate their allegiance to the festival spirit by camping backstage.

Among the songs Oasis played at Glastonbury was the first song they had recorded at Rockfield. Roll With It was not among the cream of the new material: an attempt to ape the trebly energy of the early Beatles, it fell instead into the kind of banal rhythm and blues that once found its spiritual home in the backrooms of provincial pubs. Its lyrics were not much better: as had happened on Whatever, Noel Gallagher revealed a dearth of inspiration by penning words that meant very little at all. It was curious that, when his brain was switched off, he fell into doggerel that marked him down as a stereotypical child of the 80s: certainly, Roll With It was based on the kind of glib slogans of self-empowerment – 'say what you say', 'don't let anybody get in your way' – that were that decade's pop-cultural *lingua franca*. Had Roll With It been called Go For It – which would hardly have changed the thrust of its words – the sense of déjà vu would have been complete.

For one reason and another, Roll With It was scheduled to be Oasis's new single. For all Andy Ross's bafflement, the fact that it was to be released a good six weeks before the group's new album was not considered remarkable by any of the Oasis camp. 'It wasn't meant aggressively, put it that way,' says Tim Abbot. 'That's the way Creation worked, I suppose. It was, "Well, if it's ready – we'll put it out."'

So began what the *NME*, with no little subtlety, called 'The Britpop Heavyweight Championship'. Such was the hysteria generated by this most compelling of battles, that even those global titans Madonna and Michael Jackson, whose new singles were also released that Monday, were shoved into the shade.

'I'm going on holiday that week,' Damon Albarn told an interviewer. 'I'm not getting involved. And I'm going to leave specific instructions that if I come back on Sunday and we're not number one, someone is going to suffer some sort of grievous bodily harm.'

His few explicit pronouncements on the looming battle were infused with the sense that if – or rather, when – Blur were handed victory, justice would be done. 'We haven't had a number one . . . they [Oasis] wouldn't be having them if we hadn't got the whole ball rolling in the first place,' he said. 'Because I know the environment when we put out *Modern Life Is Rubbish* and how anti- the whole idea of Britpop this country was.'

Before he went away, Albarn committed one last act of provocation. On Friday 28 July, just over a fortnight before the crucial week, he appeared on Chris Evans' Radio One Breakfast Show. Down the phone line, Evans played him Roll With It. Albarn responded by singing a handful of lines from Status Quo's not-dissimilar version of Rockin' All Over The World.

So it was that, with a sighing predictability, the gloves came off. Soon after Albarn's Radio One spot, Noel Gallagher described Blur as 'a bunch of middle-class wankers trying to play hardball with a bunch of working-class heroes'. Johnny Hopkins, the group's PR, offered the opinion that 'Blur are the Chas & Dave of pop. It's no contest. They're not in the same league as Oasis.' He went on to make the rather unlikely suggestion that Graham Coxon had faked his recent road accident in pursuit of publicity. And then Owen Morris joined in. 'I don't like Blur,' said the producer. 'They're not even cockneys. They're from Cheltenham or something. The Oasis camp are just laughing at them.'

To every last one of the UK's mainstream newspapers, this was glorious news indeed. The most ubiquitous editorial line was the parroting of Noel Gallagher's belief that Blur and Oasis were enacting the latest instalment of the class war. It had been nearly five years since John Major expressed the aspiration of ridding the UK of such divisions and building a classless society; the press's view of Blur and Oasis suggested that it was a vain hope indeed. To anyone familiar with British rock's internal dialectic, the subtext was all too familiar: here, it seemed, was a re-enactment of Roger Daltrey's tiffs with Pete Townshend, The Faces' polar opposition to Roxy Music, Sham 69's disdain for the more upmarket end of punk.

The *Guardian* headlined its first story 'Working Class Heroes Lead Art School Trendies'. To *Today*, Blur were 'Clean-cut middle-class southern boys', battling a group of 'Rebellious working-class northern lads'. The man from the *Daily Express* got rather more carried away: 'On the one hand,' wrote the impressively named York Membery, 'you have Blur – the sensitive art school popsters, slipping references to French authors into their songs . . . on the other you have Oasis, hard-drinking lads who boast about drug-taking, and seem to spend just as much time fighting as writing . . . It's not just a conflict of attitude, image and style. It's a conflict of "pitbull v poodle, squat vs mansion and armpit v deodorant", to quote one wit.'

The other endlessly repeated opinion, dispensed by everyone from the *Guardian* to the *Doncaster Free Press*, was that the war had parallels with the Beatles' relations with The Rolling Stones. The nod to the 60s fitted the Britpop aesthetic, but it was ludicrously misplaced: as any student of the two earlier groups well knew, it was their shared policy to consult one another about imminent release dates and studiously avoid any clashes. Equally ill-advised was the extension of the analogy to the personae of the groups themselves: Blur certainly had some of the same spirit of wilful reinvention as The Beatles, but most of the comparisons between Oasis and The Stones – both seen as 'bad boy rockers', or similar – took matters into the realms of stupidity. Noel Gallagher's group were unlikely to consider trips to Morocco in the company of London art dealers, or compose songs about Lucifer that took their lead from Russian novels. Oasis, as they proudly said, didn't even read books.

By the Wednesday of the crucial week, the race was on to find some new, unforeseen angle. With their customary brio, *The Sun* managed to trounce all competition, telling the thrillingly unlikely tale of Richard and Mandy Vivian-Thomas, a couple from Redcliff, near Bristol. 'Oasis-mad Mandy and Blur fan Richard have waged a war at home as the bands battle to be number one,' read a news story headlined 'You Blur-ty Rat'. 'Mandy, 24, was so angry at Richard constantly playing new Blur disc Country House that she went on a nookie-strike and banished him to the sofa and threw his Blur CD collection out of a window.' Her husband, it was claimed, wrought his revenge by putting her CDs in a microwave oven and 'brazenly wearing a Blur T-shirt round the house'.

As far as the more upmarket end of the newsagents was concerned, an army of leader-writers and columnists performed the customary broadsheet trick of attempting to wryly comment on all the fuss while betraying the fact that they were as worked-up as everyone else. In a *Sunday Times* piece headlined 'It's A Blur For Tired Old Hacks', the venerable Julie Burchill proved to be no exception, taking aim at anyone over thirty who had written about Blur and Oasis, while stumbling upon sufficient inspiration to pen a good 700 words herself. Curiously, she saw fit to also mention a group who the week's hyperbole had shoved even further towards the margins. 'Blur and Oasis have made it so big mainly because both bands have lead singers who look literally edible. They are not in the same league – Liam Gallagher of Oasis is a raving beauty who could turn a gay girl straight with one gaze from those swimming-pool eyes, while Damon Albarn is a shameless cutie who appeals to girls a little too old for horses and a little too young for men – but prime cuts they most certainly are.

'They are, respectively, the filet mignon and sirloin of modern pop; Suede, who the mandarins of rock originally put their shirts on, fell at the final hurdle because nobody really wanted to go the Whole Hog with Brett Anderson, a preening piece of overdone scrag-end.'

Two years after their popularity had reached its apex, Suede's position in the summer of 1995 seemed to underline the cruel speed at which the pop-cultural wheel could rotate. While they bravely played out the last notes of the purgatorial campaign around *Dog Man Star*, Bernard Butler had returned in the company of a gay, falsetto-voiced singer named David McAlmont. The pair's first single, simply entitled Yes, was a beautifully euphoric song of self-confidence that fulfilled Butler's long-standing aspiration to create epic, ostentatious music while avoiding any of the overcooked showiness that had bedevilled him in the recent past. It sounded like a joyous leap from Suede's gothic shadows; to Butler's evident delight, Yes reached number eight in the singles chart.

In July, Butler's old colleagues appeared at the Phoenix Festival, an ill-fated attempt to steal some of Reading and Glastonbury's thunder. The event was staged at a threadbare airfield near Stratford-upon-Avon; the resulting spectacle rather suggested a refugee camp with the added bonus of both live entertainment and a traditional British funfair. Inclement weather ensured that Suede's performance was the perfect metaphor for their embattled position. For most of their set, as the waltzers and ghost trains flashed away in the middle distance, they played into a torrential cloudburst, but Brett Anderson entertained Phoenix's scattered, sodden crowd with a performance of quite remarkable ferocity. He looked for all the world like a man who was embroiled in the most important performance of his life.

One could froth about class, The Beatles and The Stones, and the two groups' respective quotients of sex appeal, but the Blur/Oasis battle was chiefly the province of their two record companies, and the marketing chicanery on which, since the turn of the decade, the singles market had increasingly been based.

Country House was, to all intents and purposes, an EMI single, funded and distributed by a company whose workforce numbered well over a thousand. Creation's payroll, by contrast, included only nineteen names. Any romantic notions of some David vs Goliath stand-off, however, were offset not only by Creation's partnership with Sony, but by the revival of company fortunes that had occurred in the wake of *Definitely Maybe*. The days of taking on the competition using five-figure budgets were gone: one only had to flick through the requisite magazines to see that the advertising spend on Roll With It was pretty much equal to that devoted to Country House.

According to the chart rules that prevailed in 1995, any single could be released on up to three formats. Since 1993, Blur had sought to take full advantage of the consequent openings: five of their singles had been released on two different CDs, in the hope that the group's more hard-bitten disciples might purchase both, and thereby lever them yet further up the singles chart. In keeping with their determination to reach number one, they reverted to the same practice.

Country House was released on two different CD singles, one featuring the standard couple of B-sides, the other a selection of recordings from Mile End. Yet more cannily, Blur's third format was a cassette single: an invention about to slip towards extinction, but still popular with cash-strapped adolescents. 'I always hated the format nonsense,' says Andy Ross. 'It's like an arms race. But ultimately, if its "Do we want a number one or not" and the gloves are off, you use the maximum amount of arms at your disposal.'

Creation, by contrast, stuck to their established ways. Like every Oasis single since Supersonic, Roll With It was released on the stone-age formats of 7- and 12-inch vinyl, and compact disc. With the purchase of the latter format alone, one had possession of all of the songs on offer; there was precious little marketing magic, save for the standard knock-down pricing that meant that the CD would retail at £2.99. Blur, by contrast, subsidised the first CD of Country House to the point that it would sell for a pound less.

To this day, Andy Ross is unrepentant. 'I would have thought that Oasis, if they wanted to, could have put out one CD, priced it at £3.99 and said, "We're not participating in this contest,"' he says. 'But they wanted, and Sony wanted, a number one. If it came down to who had the best marketing people, then fair enough.'

Then there were the singles' videos. The impression that Oasis were sticking to their usual modus operandi was only reinforced by the clip that accompanied Roll With It: a standard faux-concert job which, like all their previous videos, suggested that performing for the camera was one of the many pretensions at which they sneered. Blur, however, approached the making of their video with something slightly more remarkable in mind, seemingly conceived at the tail-end of a night at the Groucho club.

The video for Country House was directed by Damien Hirst, with the assistance of a production company run by Keith Allen's wife. Allen himself starred as the song's anti-hero, plunged into a gaudy rustic pantomime. In among an abundance of haystacks and livestock – Alex James, for one reason and another, was required to ride a pig – the cast was also swelled by a handful of women, seemingly awarded their roles on account of their cleavages. They included Joanne Guest, a graduate of the gynaecological world of the top shelf who had gone on to become *Loaded's* poster-girl, and Sara Stockbridge, who had recently starred in a film with the gut-busting comedian Roy 'Chubby' Brown.

'I can't believe this video,' Stockbridge marvelled, as she paused between takes. 'Every time you look round, there's some girl getting her tits out or bending over in a short skirt.' The result was a collision of Carry On and *Loaded* magazine: three minutes so in tune with the spirit of the age that it both dominated the airwaves and dated at speed.

'Damien now thinks it's a really good video,' says Alex James. 'It got played a lot on the telly. I can't think of anything that would have worked better for that song. That was the only way out we had: to be camp and light-hearted. When they're talking about your fucking band on the ten o'clock news, what are you supposed to do? You can't start being earnest. You have to go the other way. It was very Damien: tits and arse and visual jokes.'

Mike Smith paid a visit to the set on the second day of shooting. 'Damien was sitting on the side, very much enjoying being a director, and Keith was marching round in a suit,' he says. 'And Alex and Damon were having the time of their lives, running around with a bunch of glamour models: basically, a bunch of very game girls, up for a laugh. And everyone piled into town afterwards and had a night out with them.' Even in the two-dimensional media, the video did its work: *The Sun* ran a series of stills, in which Blur were dwarfed by a photo of Sara Stockbridge, headlined 'May Bust Men Win'.

To cap the sense that Blur were – to use Menswear's phrase – trying jolly hard, on Wednesday 16 August, BBC2 screened a one-off programme entitled *Britpop Now*. It was a product of the same department as Jools Holland's *Later*: a no-frills succession of live performances – all rather stifled by the lack of a studio audience – from the likes of Blur, Elastica, Pulp, Supergrass, Menswear, Sleeper, The Boo Radleys and Powder (and the incongruously non-Britpop PJ Harvey). Oasis were asked to appear but turned the approach down; Blur were thus the show's de facto headliners.

Their pre-eminent billing was secured when Damon Albarn suggested to the show's producers that he might take the role of presenter. The job involved no more than four links, but Albarn dispensed a little more than the standard pleasantries. His introduction was given over to a crisply phrased statement of the Britpop narrative, illustrated with a backwards look at one of Blur's legendarily miserable experiences.

'Three years ago in the spring of 1992,' he said, 'Blur had embarked on their second tour of America. We'd been there the previous autumn and had been very well received, but this time it was very different. In short, Nirvana, Nirvana – everywhere Nirvana. America had found a voice, and face capable of expressing its anxiety and self-loathing: an angelic face amongst the shopping malls. If America felt like this, then the whole world had to feel the same way. In short, if you were in a band that was not Nirvana or a diet Nirvana, you were nothing.

'Well, I think all that's changed now. British bands are no longer embarrassed to sing about where they come from; they've found their voice.' Such was Albarn's wish to demonstrate all this that he led Blur through their performance of Country House dressed in plus-fours and a deerstalker hat.

As the week went on, such efforts – along with EMI's marketing strategy – began to work their wonders. Thanks to Radio One's marginally greater fondness for Roll With It, initial predictions had pointed to success for Oasis; on the Wednesday, William Hill still had Blur as second favourites, at odds of 6–4. At lunchtime on Sunday 20 August, however, it was Blur's telephones that trilled with the good news. Country House had sold 274,000 to Roll With It's 216,000. To the music industry's delight, it was also reported that the overall singles market was up by 41 per cent. This, it seemed, was the kind of outcome that the occupants of corporate boardrooms tend to term 'win-win'.

That said, the face-off had one rather cruel upshot. Within the spectacle of two groups – both, in the broadest terms, drawn from the indie constituency – battling for number one, there lurked the idea that lamely paddling in the chart's lower reaches was no longer good enough. 'That's something we were partly responsible for, with Oasis and that stupid pantomime,' says Alex James. 'Suddenly sales did become the yardstick for success. Something did change then. At some point after that summer, it wasn't good enough to have your single go in at number eighteen. Indie bands had to be selling.'

It was perhaps telling that at the party to celebrate Blur's success, Graham Coxon had considered jumping out of the window. It was held on the Sunday evening at Soho House, the members' club a mere stone's throw from the Groucho where Damon Albarn and Alex James had entertained Darren Kalynuk. Invitations were limited to around twenty-five friends and associates, although the intended intimacy did little to assuage Coxon's snowballing disquiet, brought to the surface that night by a surfeit of free wine.

'I think Graham just thought, "Oh My God, this isn't what I wanted when I was listening to the Pixies and Pete Townshend. I didn't want to be sitting in a poncey Soho club with an oompah record at number one. What I have I done?"' says Alex James. 'Graham was very disillusioned at that point. He wanted to be in The Smiths; I wanted to be in Duran Duran. Damon was Buttons.'

In the autumn of 1994, Coxon – long the member of Blur most wedded to indie ideals – had begun a relationship with one Jo Johnson, the sometime guitarist with a briefly notorious band named Huggy Bear. Their fifteen minutes had arrived in 1993, when they crash-landed in the music press bearing an esoteric manifesto centred around opposition to 'boy-rock'. The idea – embodied by the group's occasional habit of playing women-only concerts, though they had two male members – had come via such American bands as Bikini Kill and Bratmobile, pioneers of a movement known as 'riot grrrl'. Huggy Bear's home-made aesthetic and charity-shop dress-code gave them the air of a throwback to the 80s heyday of indie, which was in keeping with their agenda: in essence, the indie world's traditional disdain for rock machismo taken to a new, crusading pitch. Not that such subtleties meant much to some of those monitoring Blur's progress. 'Big boozer Graham Coxon is dating bloke-bashing punk Jo of Huggy Bear,' revealed *The Daily Star*.

'Graham had very much set his stall out when he started seeing Jo,' says Mike Smith. 'She was working in a bookshop in Croydon. If you contrast that with what Alex was doing, you see the difference. It caused problems. She'd turn up with a number of her mates, and Alex would be his usual charming self, and they'd take great offence, and so would Graham. Jo was never going to approve of Alex and his lifestyle. And Alex knew that; he'd ham it up.'

'Graham was suffering a bit from right-onness at that point,' says James. 'His girlfriend really didn't like me very much at all. She'd come to gigs and do the Harry Enfield thing. Like, "You don't want to do that. You're a cunt." Really nasty. But I could see where she was coming from.'

Two days after he was persuaded not to jump from the Soho House window, Coxon was interviewed by Keith Cameron of the *NME*. As if to defiantly demonstrate that Britpop hysteria was not going to alter his long-established habits, the pair met in The Good Mixer – from which, thanks to a sudden flood of Britpop tourists, the 'in' crowd had recently fled. Coxon, whose unease was amply demonstrated by a headline that read 'I'm At Complete Odds With Everything', did not need much persuasion to express his doubts about the place at which Blur had so recently arrived.

'I came back from holiday and I was shown a video of all the news items broadcast on one day,' he said, 'and it was people in HMV with huge Blur versus Oasis placards. I went into a state of shock and I don't think I've got out of it. It's a circle of freaks and I don't want to be involved.' He claimed to have toyed with the idea of publicly buying 300 copies of both Roll With It and Country House, so that charges of chart manipulation would have been levelled and the contest declared void.

He seemed particularly pained about Country House's video. 'I like the song,' he said, 'but . . . it's become Page Three and Benny Hill, and I don't think I had the sense to complain about it, which is my fault. I didn't realise what dirty minds Damien Hirst and Keith Allen had. They're from an area I don't want to associate myself with any more.'

The chief problem, however, was the public image that had been constructed by Damon Albarn since the release of *Parklife*, along with Alex James's endless – and very public – West End roistering. 'The thing is,' said Coxon, 'if he [Albarn] wants to go on about football and Page Three girls that means we all get associated with it, 'cos none of us have ever really said we hate football or we hate anything to do with Page Three girls. *I* hate football and *I* hate anything to do with Page Three girls. But people always want to hear Damon's opinion . . . I don't want Blur to become some fucking football band. And I don't want it to become "John Taylor [bass player of Duran Duran] was seen getting wrecked in Stringfellows with a load of white powder up his nose." . . . And I don't want it to be "Guitarist goes to live at his mother's and has gone a bit funny." Because that, in the classic Spinal Tap tradition, is the way we're going.'

Such was the upshot of two eras colliding within one group: Coxon's devotion to the 80s indie counterculture clashing with the hedonistic life-code that had all but superseded it in the 90s. For the moment, there seemed little chance of any detente – for while Coxon loudly expressed his unease, the success of Country House seemed to turn Damon Albarn into little short of a caricature. His latest *NME* inquisition took place during the same week as Coxon's, and tumbled, somewhat predictably, towards the topic of football. His key prompt was the interviewer's claim that football gave one 'a clear sense of achievement', whereupon Albarn said this: 'I know it's a very flippant thing to say, but if Kurt Cobain had played football, he'd probably be alive today. I know it sounds the most ridiculous thing, but if you play football you'll know what that means . . . I find it increasingly hard to find things that it can't solve. To do with love, maybe. It doesn't solve anything between men and women, but I think it can solve most things between men and men.'

If the announcement of Country House's success could have been expected to lower the curtain on the rivalry between Blur and Oasis, any such notion was soon scuppered. On 12 September, Blur were due to begin an eight-date tour of British seaside resorts, taking them round such compact and bijou venues as Pier 39 in Cleethorpes and Clacton Oscar's. It was an exercise predicated on the prospect of having some fun rather than the business of hard-faced promotion, an impression only furthered by the pseudonyms under which the group checked into their hotels. Damon Albarn was 'Bert Hammond', Graham Coxon 'Carmen Guinness', and Alex James 'Reginald Chumfatty'. In tribute to the golden era of 1970s *Blue Peter*, Dave Rowntree was to be registered as 'Joey Deacon'.

By a diabolic coincidence, Blur were booked to play Bournemouth's Showbar the same night that Oasis performed at the town's International Arena, some 200 yards away. *The Sun* had already worked itself into a lather over the scenario, running a news story headlined 'The Gig Fight'. In his *NME* interview, Damon Albarn joined in the fun: seemingly giddy with both alcohol and the euphoria of victory, he suggested that Blur would both fly a huge inflatable number one over their venue, and project their logo on to the International Arena's outside walls.

The response to such talk from the Oasis camp was a very righteous kind of outrage. They were perhaps more familiar than Blur's overlords with the belligerence that can surface when young men are filled with alcohol; the fact that both gigs would take place against the backdrop of the seaside – always the perfect place for a very British kind of ruck – only served to heighten their ire.

'That whole Blur versus Oasis thing was fuelled entirely – *entirely* – by the Blur management team,' says Ian Robertson. 'Marcus Russell and I were sitting by a swimming pool in Tokyo, and he was writing a letter to their management to say, "What are you doing?" Marcus was saying, "Potentially, we have problems here, 'cos the kids are taking sides. It's Mods and Rockers." It was, "Pull the show. We booked ours first. Don't allow this to happen. We're not interested in this marketing exercise. We don't want to play. Drop it."'

On 11 September, Blur released the album they had decided to title *The Great Escape*. The name had been suggested by Alex James, apropos of very little at all, but it caught Damon Albarn's imagination on account of its accidental fit with the abundance of character-based songs he brought to the sessions. 'All my characters have always been escaping or trying to become somebody else or returning to the fold after being out of it,' he explained. He was also keen to inform his public that his new work represented the last of a chapter inaugurated by *Modern Life Is Rubbish*. *The Great Escape* was intended as the third part of the so-called Life Trilogy, tied together by Albarn's Anglo-centric lyrics and the group's original intention to include the word 'life' in each of the three album titles.

The reviews of *The Great Escape* brimmed with ecstasy, as if the success of Country House had propelled the critics into a state of credulous excitement. 'This is a thing of great beauty, humour and insight,' said *The Daily Mail*. 'There's no doubt that *The Great Escape* sees Blur at the peak of their form,' advised *The Sunday Telegraph*. 'It's polished, richly textured, expertly played and streets ahead of its predecessor.' '*The Great Escape* is a spectacularly accomplished, sumptuous, heart-stopping and inspirational album,' mused the ever-understated *NME*.

Its musical scope was certainly impressive, bolstered further by the sense that, more than ever, Graham Coxon was still using his guitar to battle with the group's in-built melodic instincts. But there was something very cold about *The Great Escape*. The gloopy, theatrical arrangements accorded to songs like Top Man, Dan Abnormal and Mr Robinson's Quango suggested music that aimed at a kind of whimsical ugliness, hardly the most endearing of musical qualities. When Alex James – who remains bullish about the album's merits – says that its abiding feeling is that 'nothing is quite right', he perhaps nails one of *The Great Escape*'s overarching flaws: that in seeking to convey a world of creeping dysfunction, partly based on Blur's recent experience, it frequently sounded as unpleasant as much of its inspiration.

Its key weakness, however, lay in Damon Albarn's lyrics. Though *Parklife* subsequently acquired the reputation of a garish cartoon set to music, some of its best songs – Badhead, End Of A Century, To The End – were rooted in his own life. Here, however, any sense of Albarn's interior universe tended to be hidden beneath songs recurrently sung in the third person. Even when he wrote about the trials of sustaining his relationship with Justine Frischmann across different continents, he opted to bury his hurt under a song about two harried Japanese lovers entitled Yuko And Hiro.

Much of *The Great Escape* was spent acquainting its listeners with an array of suburbanites whose lives were – rather predictably – going nowhere fast. Dear Ray had by now mutated into a piece founded on the popular obsession with The National Lottery entitled It Could Be You. Fade Away was based on the fate of a couple who 'settled in a brand new town/With people from the same background'. On Ernold Same, Ken Livingstone – then the MP for Brent East – narrated the yet-more-uneventful tale of a hapless commuter whose life endlessly repeated itself; the song would perhaps have been a little more successful if its lyric had aimed higher than the vocabulary of a nursery rhyme.

Running through them all was the rather empty sneer of the bourgeois bohemian, passing predictably withering judgement on sad little people living sad little lives.

'The strange thing about Damon's songs,' said an incongruously critical article in the *Guardian* by Jim Shelley, 'is that, unlike a writer such as Morrissey or Ian Dury, he has no sympathy for his characters. Instead of Madness's quirky warmth or [Paul] Weller's outright hostility, Albarn's attitude to his characters is totally uncharitable, a kind of snide contempt.' In Stereotypes, a fairly dismal piece about suburban wife-swapping, Albarn wearily droned out a chorus that went, 'Oh, they're stereotypes/There must be more to life'. He perhaps should have reflected on the fact that his lyrics might also have benefited from focusing on something more substantial than thin fictional conceits.

'I was away when Damon was making *The Great Escape*,' says Justine Frischmann. 'That was the first record apart from *Leisure* that he made without me around. I hated it. I thought it was terrible. Awful. I remember Graham having a nervous breakdown because he thought it was so awful. But they had to put it out. They were going to call it London, and I persuaded Damon not to – I thought it would be so sad if that was the album called London, because it was so shit. It was fake, soulless, irritating.'

If a good deal of *The Great Escape* misfired, there were three compositions that shared the same rarefied air as the best bits of *Parklife*. He Thought Of Cars had come to Albarn on the road, in the midst of a grinding hangover. Both its music and words managed to ooze an atmosphere of murky inertia, capturing an alluring sense of both twilight and gridlock. Despite an ill-advised opening reference to Bow Bells, Best Days surveyed the London expanse with a sighing poetry; in its chorus, Albarn seemed to movingly allude to his unexpectedly tormented reaction to Blur's success. And then there was The Universal: the beautifully poised song that took its title from an imagined successor to Prozac, seemingly used to sedate any suspicion that things had taken a wrong turn. In that sense, it mapped out a future Utopia founded on that most modern of conditions: denial. 'When the days they seem to fall through you/Well, just let them go,' sang Albarn. Its closing passage managed to crystallise all this in a triumphal fanfare that also managed to suggest a fatalistic kind of sadness. Here, Albarn's wish to shine unflattering light on the contemporary world bore wonderful fruit; would that the trick could have been repeated.

Justine Frischmann, however, was not even convinced by that song. 'The Universal's one of the worst songs on *The Great Escape*,' she says, rather perplexingly. ' "It really really really could happen." Disgusting.

Terrible lyric. Really lazy. It's almost as bad as "D'you know what I mean, yeah yeah yeah." It's awful.'

Frischmann claims that she was not the only one who had doubts about *The Great Escape*. 'Damon didn't like it,' she says. 'Graham hated it. But Damon felt like they didn't have time to do it again like they did with *Modern Life*: they had to get another one out, so he just went with it. None of us liked it. It was like a cheesy shadow of *Parklife*: *Parklife* without the soul or the intellect or the balls. It made our relationship difficult. But it was difficult anyway by that point.'

For the moment, no-one seemed to share her sense of *The Great Escape*'s shortcomings. It sold close to half a million in its first month, proving that the party inaugurated by *Parklife* had hardly slowed.

Besides, the summer had surely generated enough momentum to extend the mood of celebration long into the winter months. Car stereos still boomed with the warm season's hits: Pulp's Common People, Roll With It and Country House, Dodgy's Staying Out For The Summer, the songs assembled on *Elastica*. There was also Supergrass's Alright, the knockabout anthem to youth that had risen to number two in July. It has often been rock music's habit to couch such declarations of vivacity in terms of an ageist sneer of exclusion. It surely suited the Britpop moment that in Alright's barrelhouse piano and music-hall nuances, there lay the reassuring promise of Fun For All The Family.

Much of the excitement, after all, was bound up with the joy of finally *belonging*. In begetting Britpop, indie music was divested of its last remaining pretensions to countercultural subversion: led by apostates like Damon Albarn and the Gallaghers, the Britpop groups learned to love the idea of appealing to just about everybody. 'Who wants to be a sad little indie noise-freak who alienates everyone?' said Albarn. Like teenagers finding that life is more pleasant if you talk to your parents and don't purposefully leave muddy footprints on the carpet, many of the Britpop musicians represented a hitherto difficult aspect of the UK's cultural life, newly rendered polite and well-adjusted.

As if to acknowledge that some national epiphany had been reached, some of those who had inspired the Britpop groups were suddenly back. Shaun Ryder had returned in May with a new group called Black Grape, whose music rerouted the sprawling lunacy of Happy Mondays towards gleaming commerciality. Six months before that, The Stone Roses had finally broken cover, issuing an album of booming hard rock, and eventually setting out – after their no-show at Glastonbury – on the path that would lead them to a triumphant tour of the UK at the end of 1995. Strangest of all, a new single by The Beatles – *The Beatles*! – was sitting in the vaults, awaiting release in December.

In response to Britpop's endless delights, the writing in the music press took on a new aspect: an air of frantic celebration, as if its staff had been instructed to become journalistic cheerleaders. In July, the *NME* nominated the debut single by a Liverpudlian group called Cast as its Single Of The Week. By simple dint of being British and clearly in love with the rock music of the 60s, the group were swiftly allowed entry to the party. 'Life is great,' read the review. 'Blur, Oasis, Dodgy, Elastica, The Bluetones, and now Cast, yet more fab mates for discerning stereos everywhere.' This was hardly the most erudite critical vocabulary. There again, as the Britpop moment unfurled, who wanted to be critical?

As far as the media were concerned, celebration had supplanted the usual cynicism. The capital, after all, was festooned with the perfect drug: for £60, one could purchase a gramme of cocaine, share it with one's fellow Britpop enthusiasts and gabble excitedly about how great everything was. Rock groups were not the only topic of such conversation: it did not take much to project Britpop euphoria in the direction of the Palace of Westminster, and the party leader whose much-trumpeted brand values – youth, a clear belief that ideals were nothing without popular success – seemed to be of a piece with those of the country's newest musical celebrities.

Moreover, his prospects seemed to be following a similarly triumphant trajectory to Britpop's leading lights. In June 1995, John Major had announced his resignation as leader of the Conservatives, and launched the 'Back Me or Sack Me' ruse, intended to silence his critics and thereby re-establish his authority. The immediate effect, inevitably, was simply to suggest that his weakness had reached a new, dramatic depth; without having to lift a finger, Tony Blair entered high summer looking more like the Prime Minister Designate than ever.

In July, the BPI – the umbrella group that included most of the UK's record labels – had held its Annual General Meeting. The occasion saw a telling photo opportunity: the presentation of an electric guitar to the Leader of the Opposition, who also addressed the assembled delegates. Blair wowed them: having compared him to Kennedy, Paul Conroy, the managing director of Virgin Records, went on to pay tribute to Blair's enviable pop-cultural nous. 'He knows what a Fender guitar is,' he gushed. 'And he knows the difference between Motorhead and Enya.'

And so the joy went on. In the wake of the mass of comparisons drawn between Blur and Oasis and The Beatles and The Stones – and now with Blair included in the Britpop moment – the analogies with the sixties did not stop. Looking through squinted eyes, those charged with documenting Britpop had seemingly managed to glimpse an update of the kind of scenes beautifully portrayed in Philip Norman's Beatles biography *Shout!*, in which, during the baking summer of 1966, a new breed of tourist came to London . . .

> They were teenagers, besotted by all British pop music, who came flooding into Carnaby Street and the King's Road, hopeful of glimpsing their idols . . . among the frill-shirted baronets and debutante shopgirls, in the shops, bistros, bric-a-brac markets and artificially-aged pubs. Such was the demand, the product could not help but materialise. London, by some alchemy of hot weather and warm money, burst like a conjurer's bouquet into riotous new fashion, new colours . . . new match-thin, long-legged girls, new slow-burning, strange-smelling aromas.

A generation who had grown up in the wake of the sixties, forever both entranced and crushed by its wonders, had finally come up with its own shining equivalent. It was true: if one whirled around the dance-floor at Smashing in the company of two Pulps and three Menswears, or spent a fuzzy afternoon in the pubs of Camden Town on the off-chance that one might clap eyes on Graham or Damon, or wended one's way to Glastonbury to share the air breathed by Liam and Noel and shout along to Cigarettes And Alcohol, there was the evidence. It really, really, really had happened. Hadn't it?

PART THREE

'It looked more like a backstage party than a gathering at Number 10 . . .'

The Daily Mail, **Thursday 31 July, 1997**

'The death of a party came as no surprise.'

Blur, Death Of A Party

CHAPTER 15

'I wouldn't carry a horrible little pissed brat around.'

By the end of 1994, Alan McGee's darkest thoughts had begun to recede. His inclination to declare himself retired and leave the music business – not to mention the occasional consideration of suicide – had been superseded by the gradual realisation that he should resume his role at Creation Records. 'I thought, "I've got to do something with my life: I can't just retire at thirty-three,"' he says. 'So I came back to London.'

McGee spent six weeks in the Charter Nightingale Clinic on Lisson Grove, NW1, a centre for the care of 'psychological disorders, eating disorders and addictions', under the dual care of Colin Brewer and Keith Stoll: the former the addiction specialist with whom he made contact after his breakdown in Los Angeles, the latter a Harley Street psychologist. In the course of therapy, McGee discovered at least one cause of his crash: in the eyes of his doctors, he had fallen into the trap of being a 'facilitator' – someone whose every thought was tailored to the needs of others. From here on in, McGee would be an altogether more self-assertive embodiment of one of the recovery process's universal maxims: 'Me is enough'.

Having ended his time at Charter Nightingale – and stopped taking prescribed tranquillisers – McGee moved back to his flat in Rotherhithe. This, however, was not the most sensible of moves. 'I was on my own and I lasted about two days before I started feeling terrible again,' he later reflected. He quickly decided to take up residence at The Landmark Hotel on Marylebone Road: the impressively opulent establishment whose luxurious rooms and gargantuan atrium have long attracted visiting rock royalty. At a charge of £200 per day, he stayed for a little over two months.

It was from here that McGee began the tentative process of

re-entering the music industry. At first, he spent one day a week at Creation, lending an ear to forthcoming releases and mooted new signings. He also began to adjust to the strange business of socialising without the aid of ephedrine tablets, bourbon and cocaine. In their place came a new interest, fully in line with modern cultural currents: trips to see Chelsea at Stamford Bridge, where McGee eventually bought an executive box.

In his avoidance of chemicals, he was assisted by a handful of close friends. 'I had my sponsors,' he says. 'They were there to stop me taking drugs, but little did they know, the last thing on my mind was drugs. I was *so* not going to take drugs. I'd looked over the edge of insanity a couple of times, I'd been suicidal two or three times – the last thing I wanted was a line of coke. But you couldn't tell that to the Gallagher brothers or Bobby Gillespie – they still thought, "Total drug monster." So I was getting shepherded about.'

When it came to his trips to Creation's offices, the imperative for McGee to be chaperoned was not quite as pressing. In preparation for his return, Dick Green – McGee's senior ally, and the most long-suffering of Creation's upper hierarchy – had orchestrated a comprehensive clean-up. The days when powders and pills would be used to brighten up office life's more drab moments were shoved into history; from now on, Creation was outwardly a drug-free enterprise.

'We'd got rid of the drugs, 'cos Dick had cleared out most of the offenders,' says McGee. 'Those people went for one reason and another: some of them went because it just wasn't right; some went because me and Dick had spoken and I'd said, "If I come back, we can't be doing lines in the office. It's not fair. I'm not wanting to take drugs, but if you show me people taking drugs, I'm not going to be able to deal with it." So we had to have a rule: no drugs in the office. Not that people weren't allowed to *take* drugs: you're not going to stop kids taking drugs. But there were no drugs in the office – or, if they were getting done, they weren't getting done in front of me. That was the main difference.'

As if to underwrite this revolutionary transition, in April 1995, Creation moved its offices. The company left behind the sweatshop in Hackney and moved to 109 Regent's Park Road, a set of offices in Primrose Hill, housed in a converted Victorian school chapel. Though the interior was a low-ceilinged warren rather than some gleaming corporate dreamland, the setting spoke volumes about the label's new-found opulence: in place of Hackney's kebab shops and minicab bureaux, Creation now sat in among fusion restaurants, gastropubs and chi-chi bookstores. 'The move said it all,' says Tim Abbot. Hackney to Primrose Hill: warm bitter to chilled Evian water. Perhaps more importantly, Creation's new HQ was a stone's throw from Camden Town.

Tim Abbot did not make the journey. In the first stages of McGee's retreat, their once impenetrable partnership had come to grief over McGee's purported promise to formally co-opt him into Creation's upper echelon and award him shares in the company; fearing an imminent buy-out by Sony Music, Abbot had attempted to finalise such plans, only for McGee to accuse him of taking advantage of his breakdown and cut off all communication. In ever more strained circumstances, Abbot stayed at Creation until late 1994, before setting up as an independent consultant near Baker Street. He continued to play a central role in Oasis's marketing campaigns, and maintained his place within the group's inner circle.

Despite his exit, Creation continued to move along the trajectory that had been established when Abbot arrived in Hackney bearing flip-charts, new model contracts and marketing plans. 'When I got back,' says McGee, 'we suddenly had a marketing department. And I don't mean this to sound horrible, but the beginning of the end, or the start of the future, a necessary evil, or the saviour of our finances – was the marketing department. Creation up to '93 was an A&R label – it was utterly driven by my whims. And Creation after '93 was a marketing label . . . It killed something. It makes people like me pragmatic. Marketing people reason everything out, and unfortunately, if you let them go the full way down the line, they suffocate what was good about your company.'

Certainly, Creation – perhaps shown the way by the success-driven Gallaghers – did seem newly attuned to the business of getting its records into the charts. In February 1995, the label had its first post-Oasis Britpop hit: The Boo Radleys' Wake Up Boo!, a sun-kissed pop song that endeared itself to dozens of radio stations and entered the charts at number nine. The group's guitarist and songwriter Martin Carr later described the single as 'the most cynical thing I've ever done'. That May, Teenage Fanclub, the Scots group who were seen by many as Creation's most talented songwriters, released a fantastically accomplished album entitled *Grand Prix*, whose supporting singles used the hitherto taboo ploy of multi-formatting. And in July, Creation released the first single by Heavy Stereo: a troupe of London-based musicians whose testosterone-fuelled, 70s-esque rock was clearly envisaged as the label's crafty follow-up to the music made by Oasis.

If McGee found some of Creation's new hard-headedness a little difficult to take, when he heard the keynote song from Oasis's second album, he too seemed to translate the sound tumbling from the speakers into sales targets and profit forecasts. 'The minute I heard Wonderwall,' he says, 'I thought, "We can sell ten million records."'

Noel Gallagher prepared for the release of the album with the customary flurry of interviews. Among the first was with *The Observer*, who had chosen to reflect Oasis's ever-increasing clout by honouring them with the cover of *Life* magazine. The article was written by Miranda Sawyer, who had initially been promised time with both Gallagher brothers. Liam, however, proved frustratingly elusive, so Sawyer was offered two separate interviews with his elder brother. The first took place in a Portakabin at Irvine Beach in Ayrshire, the setting for two frantically received Oasis performances in July; the second was conducted in August, via a phone line, while Noel Gallagher was in Japan.

It was during Oasis's trip to the Far East that news reached them of Blur's plans to play in Bournemouth on the same night that Oasis were booked to play the town's International Arena. In the context of the resultant ire, it was not that surprising that Noel Gallagher's response to a question about his feelings for his supposed rivals was ugly in the extreme. 'The guitarist I've got a lot of time for,' he said. 'The drummer I've never met – I hear he's a nice guy. The bass player and singer – I hope the pair of them catch AIDS and die because I fucking hate them two.'

The article appeared on 17 September. Blur were mid-way through their tour of minuscule seaside venues; that morning, some of the group were still in the midst of the revels that had followed their performance at Eastbourne's Floral Hall. Alex James heard the news from their PR, Karen Johnson. 'I was on the beach,' he says. 'Karen was going, "Oh *no*!" We were just going, "What a fool. He's in trouble." He sounded like a desperate idiot to me.'

A much more worrying kind of censure came from Burnage. 'The first person on the phone was me mam saying, "I didn't raise you to say things like that,"' said Noel Gallagher, some four months after the event. 'My whole world came crashing in on me then.'

Those charged with overseeing Oasis's progress were quickly plunged into a frantic rearguard action. 'I had to sit with Noel when he got back from Japan,' says Tim Abbot. 'He said, "They've really bolted me up here." I said, "Tell me, first and foremost, did you actually say it?" "Yes – but I didn't mean it in the context it's come out in. I know it was a cuntish thing to say." I said, "This is your 'Bigger than Jesus Christ' thing. You're mimicking The Beatles a bit too much now."' Abbot composed a letter that evening to the Terrence

Higgins Trust, which went to Marcus Russell for his approval. 'It was a damage limitation exercise,' says Abbot. 'Noel was very upset. Tearful? No. They don't get tearful.'

A statement signed by Noel duly found its way into the music papers and the letters page of *The Observer*. 'I would like to apologise to all concerned who took offence at my comments about Damon Albarn and Alex James,' it said. 'The off-the-cuff remark was made last month at the height of a "war of words" between both bands, and it must have been the fiftieth time during that interview that I was pressed to give an opinion of Blur. As soon as I said it, I realised it was an insensitive thing to say as AIDS is no joking matter and immediately retracted the comment, but was horrified to pick up *The Observer* and find that the journalist concerned chose to still run with it.'

As proved by Sawyer's original tape, Noel's central claim – that Sawyer had ignored the retraction of his most obnoxious comment – is simply not true. Thanks to *The Observer*'s anxious legal advisers, yet more off-colour remarks had been excised from her article. The last five minutes of her interview began as follows:

> MS: 'Do you like Blur? I mean as people . . .'
> NG: 'Erm . . .'
> MS: 'You must have met them enough times now.'
> NG: 'The guitarist . . . I've got a lot of time for the guitarist. The drummer: I've never met him.'
> MS: 'Yeah, he never goes out though [laughs].'
> NG: 'I hear he's a nice guy. The bass player and singer, I hope the pair of them catch AIDS and die, 'cos I fuckin' hate them two. I really hate Damon. For what he's said, not even in public, but some of the snidey things that I've heard he's said about us, it's like . . . the guy is asking for a smack in the fuckin' mouth, big time.'
> MS: 'I thought you got on with him. I thought there was a phase when you used to get on with him . . .'
> NG: 'That was when we gave him the benefit of the doubt and we thought, "Well, alright, you said a few nice things about the group at the Brits, you're not a bad guy." But, you know, he's shown his true colours, you know what I mean? He thinks we're thick northerners because he wanted to write for the theatre when he was sixteen and we were football hooligans. He thinks all our fans are thick northerners and he thinks everyone that buys our records are, like, idiots because they don't know the difference between Balzac and Prozac or whatever he's going

on about. I don't like him. And the bass player's a closet faggot
who wants his nose smacking in.'
MS: '[Laughing] Mince your words there then, Noel. Pull your
punches.'
NG: 'He pinched my arse – proper pinched it when I was out. I
turned round and said, "What do you think you're doing?" And
he went, "Alright mate?" I'll give you Alright, you twat. But
apart from that, I like 'em [laughs].'
MS: 'Do you ever feel like you're out of control? Everything's
changed so much in a year . . .'
NG: 'Yeah. I don't want to be in control. When you've been in
control, you want get out of control. We're on a rollercoaster,
a white-knuckle ride, and we're just hanging on seeing when
the rollercoaster comes to a stop.'

Thanks to *The Observer*'s lawyers, Noel Gallagher had actually got
off lightly. After all, the last time the word 'faggot' had been used in
an interview by high-profile Mancunian musicians had been November
1991, when Shaun Ryder and Mark 'Bez' Berry vented their spleens
in the *NME* and subsequently watched their stock plummet.

By way of making Oasis's lives yet more troubled, less than a week
after *The Observer* story, the wires throbbed with even more bad news.
On their return from Japan, the group had managed to leave four weeks
free of any concerts; then, just as they were about to begin a fresh
spate of rehearsals, it was announced that Paul McGuigan – whose life
seemed to contain nothing more vexatious than his play-in-a-day bass
parts and a prodigious marijuana habit – was incapacitated. 'At first,'
he said, 'I couldn't even get out of bed; couldn't stand up or nothing.
I was fucked. My body was fucked and my head was gone. Nervous
breakdown, me crumbling . . . whatever you want to call it.'

Such was the Oasis camp's party line. According to Ian Robertson,
however, McGuigan's problems – portrayed in reports of his exit as
something close to the chimeric rock ailment known as 'nervous exhau-
sion' – stemmed from his increasingly dysfunctional relationship with
Liam Gallagher.

As Oasis's success increased, Liam's propensity for bursts of truly
hateful invective – often aimed at his colleagues – only seemed to
increase. 'Guigs was so solid: the classic bass player,' says Robertson.
'But actually, it was all going in. He was feeling it. Think about it: how
could the experience of being in this group not be fun? But there were
occasions when Liam would kick off, and it *wasn't* fun. There were
some really scabrous personal taunts. Everybody got a little bit of Liam

– and most people went, "Oh fuck it – it's just him." But Guigsy actually got really hurt. Looking back, I think he felt every single assault.' Certainly, it is a matter of record that, just before his crash, McGuigan was the victim of a particularly vicious tirade at the end of a day spent doing interviews in Paris; he was sufficiently crushed by the experience to publicly wonder whether he had any future in the group, and to insist on travelling home alone.

In McGuigan's own account, his doctor prescribed both beta blockers and a course of Temazepam, before his patient decided to stick with more familiar medication. 'Fucking no thank you,' McGuigan later recalled. 'A spliff and a beer'll do me.' Most importantly, McGuigan – doubtless to his own relief – was ordered to suspend his membership of the group, and rest. His retreat had at least one positive upshot for the band: the looming engagement in Bournemouth, envisaged as the setting for a fight to the death between Blur and Oasis supporters, was postponed until October.

With admirable speed, the group quickly announced a temporary replacement: one Scott McLeod, a native of Chadderton, near Oldham, who had been poached from a group called The Ya-Yas. He travelled to London with Liam Gallagher and Paul Arthurs, emerging from the Manchester train to be faced by the inevitable phalanx of paparazzi. 'Scott was getting freaked out by the cameras,' said Noel Gallagher. 'He said, "Is this what it's like?" I said, "No, it gets much worse."' In a picture reproduced in the press, McLeod stood next to a typically bellicose Liam Gallagher, who was raising his fist as if to declare that Oasis had survived yet another crisis. McLeod's face, by contrast, captured a mixture of excitement and anxiety that gave him the appearance of a stowaway.

By then, copies of Oasis's second album had been sent out to the press. The punctuation-defying *(What's The Story) Morning Glory?* was initially heard on a promotional cassette, wrapped in a cover that featured only the group's logo. With a head-spinning sense of expectation, it was placed in dozens of office stereos, as the media class wondered what changes had been wrought on the proud roar that had so defined *Definitely Maybe*. The first play, however, seemed to reveal little more inspired than a string of musical hand-me-downs. Hello, the album's opening track, lifted the chorus of Gary Glitter's Hello, Hello I'm Back Again. Don't Look Back In Anger had the same chiming piano introduction as John Lennon's Imagine. She's Electric stole both the TV theme for the 1970s children's programme *You And Me* and the coda of The Beatles' With A Little Help From My Friends, and Morning Glory was founded on the same pummelling guitar riff as REM's

The One I Love. One song, Step Out, bore such a resemblance to Stevie Wonder's Uptight that it was eventually withdrawn from the album under threat of legal action.

Then there was the matter of Noel Gallagher's lyrics. 'They scan; they fill a hole; end of story,' said *Q* magazine's David Cavanagh, whose review made a compelling case for the album's inferiority to *Definitely Maybe*. 'There's no phrase as strange or as hypnotic as Up In The Sky's "It's just a case of never breathing out before you're breathing in"; no brazen rhymes of the "supersonic/gin and tonic" sort; nothing much about anything, in fact.' As if to unwittingly back him up, Noel Gallagher revealed that in Champagne Supernova, his sumptuous evocation of yet another early-morning comedown, the flatly strange couplet 'Slowly walking down the hall/Faster than a cannonball' had been inspired by a distant memory of Brackett, the butler from the children's programme *Chigley*.

Though the opinions of the daily newspapers struck an altogether more encouraging tone, *Q* magazine was not alone: *Melody Maker* ran a one-page review that ended with a withering observation indeed: 'They sound knackered.' The result, for the few days in between the reviews and the album's release, seemed to be a momentary outbreak of panic. When Noel Gallagher turned up at a birthday party thrown in King's Cross by James Brown, the editor of *Loaded*, he seemed to make a point of seeking reassurance from a handful of the journalists present. 'What,' he asked, 'do *you* think of my album?'

His anxiety was misplaced. The album was released on 2 October; the following morning, the *Daily Express* announced that central London HMV shops had been selling copies of *What's The Story* at the rate of two every minute. 'It has sold more in a day than Blur sold in a week,' gasped one of the store's PR staff. 'It has been astonishing.' After seven days, the album had managed sales of 346,000. There followed the inevitable announcement of a sky-scraping statistic: *What's The Story*, it was claimed, was the fastest-selling album since Michael Jackson's *Bad*.

Such was the massed enactment of Noel Gallagher's long-standing insistence that those who fussed about music's more artful aspects were missing the point. While some writers had bemoaned his reliance on second-hand music, the fact that his songs contained so many musical echoes seemed to couch the album in an air of homely reassurance. The fact that some of *What's The Story* – Hey Now, Roll With It, the throwaway She's Electric – seemed so ordinary turned out to be part of its deeply populist appeal. 'When we hear Liam's voice,' marvelled Pete Townshend the following year, 'it's *our* voice. It's *everyone's* voice.'

All that apart, the album did contain a clutch of masterstrokes. Its best songs were seemingly built on a compelling contradiction, encapsulated by Hello, the opening song. Though Noel's words betrayed a weary, questioning response to the group's ascent, Liam's bulgy-veined delivery suggested that he had no such misgivings: if the group were ever to slow down, it would not be his foot on the brake. One could hear the same dialectic in the beautifully adrenalised Morning Glory; only on the balmy, faintly other-wordly Champagne Supernova did it reach a fairly glorious kind of resolution.*

In September, Oasis announced one show at London's Earl's Court, the gargantuan indoor venue whose musical aspect had long been synonymous with the rock aristocracy of the 1970s: The Rolling Stones, Pink Floyd, David Bowie. It did not take long for the music papers to make much of the fact that the expected crowd of 20,000 was 2,000 more than Blur had entertained at Mile End Sports Stadium. 'You can't compare it to Mile End,' counselled an Oasis spokesman. 'It's much bigger. It's taking things to a completely different level.' As it turned out, he was not wrong: within weeks, surpassing even their own expectations, the group had added a second night.

In the meantime, Oasis – replete with Scott McLeod – had begun a nine-date American tour. They began in Baltimore, before passing through New York, Danbury in Connecticut, Boston and Pittsburgh – whereupon their new bass player decided to repeat the trick played by Noel Gallagher the previous year. Finding that his new life was not to his taste, McLeod did a midnight flit and returned to Manchester. With Paul Arthurs playing bass, the group managed to honour a booking on David Letterman's chat show, before they cancelled the remaining four shows, returned home and contacted Paul McGuigan. He dutifully returned to rehearsals, though his comeback seemed distinctly premature: puffy-eyed, overweight and seemingly even quieter than usual, he did not look at all well.

Nonetheless, he took his place on the stage at Earl's Court for the two concerts that marked Oasis's elevation to a very rarefied place indeed. As if to underline the achievement, the building's exterior was hung with two huge portraits of each of the Gallagher brothers. The guest-list bulged with new, striking names: U2, George Michael, Elton John. By way of commemorating the occasion, Noel Gallagher arranged for the delivery of five Italian scooters, on which, during the afternoon,

---

* The author owes this point to a brilliant review of (What's The Story) Morning Glory? by the NME's John Robinson. Of the Gallaghers, he wrote: 'One is beginning to try to come to terms with the possible downside of the rock'n'roll dream, the other is still intent on hurtling unchecked into the uncharted.'

he and his colleagues performed repeated laps of honour. In private footage shot backstage, Noel sits astride his own model, theatrically staring at his reflection in one of its mirrors. With the look of scrunch-eyed pride that he would wear for the next eighteen months, he camply asks the camera a question: 'Where did it all go right?'

Loitering in the background of such scenes was Robbie Williams. In the wake of his revels at Glastonbury, he had exited Take That in July, to a deluge of tabloid headlines and the sound of pre-pubescent weeping. His place in the Oasis clique was underwritten by the fact that he was now managed by Tim Abbot and his brother Chris; to prove the wonders that such associations could work, Noel Gallagher had already offered to write him a song. For the moment, however, he was stranded in a contractual no-man's land, as the Abbots tried to extricate him from his deal with the Bertelsmann Corporation. There was little to do but drink, ingest a steady supply of chemicals, and eat.

'He wanted to let off some steam,' says Tim Abbot. 'And quite rightly: he'd had four years of heavy working out. He danced four times a week. But you see photos of him as a kid, and he's naturally got a high fat content. He could eat for England: that was his thing. He had no concept of diet. Me and our kid used to just laugh: Jackie, his girlfriend at the time, would often cook us all a Sunday lunch – and if there were a few spuds on the side of your plate, he'd be, "Hey – have you finished with those?" We were amazed at what he could consume. And he'd always be looking at his watch, going, "Oh, eleven o'clock – can we stop for coffee and cake?" He ran his day by food.'

Williams fell victim to one of the curses of the hanger-on: though any rock group can stuff their faces and drink the bar dry, secure in the knowledge that the strains of each night's performance will maintain their svelte physiques, those who clutch their coat-tails are subject to the same metabolic laws as any other mortal. By the summer of 1996, Williams had ballooned, and Oasis were growing tired of him: like so many occupants of dressing rooms and hotel bars, it was his unlucky fate to be picked up like a petrol-station novelty, bent out of all recognisable shape, and then chucked from the tourbus.

The morning after the second Earl's Court show, Oasis released the single whose strains had already convinced Alan McGee of their latest album's vast commercial potential. For both of the weekend's concerts, Wonderwall had been sung by Noel Gallagher, accompanied only by his acoustic guitar: it was some token of the song's resonance that, far from bemoaning Liam's absence, the audience sang along as if that was how it had been recorded. When it reached its redemptive chorus, it was clearer than ever that this song, more than any of Noel's compositions, was working a quite unprecedented kind of magic.

Wonderwall went on sale on 5 November. At the end of the year, it was still in the top 10, joined by a novelty version – the work of The Mike Flowers Pops, the mercifully short-lived leaders of an easy listening revival – of which Noel Gallagher, perhaps mindful of his skyrocketing composer's royalties, had quickly expressed approval. In the meantime, sent ever higher by the song's ubiquity, the sales total for *(What's The Story) Morning Glory?* edged ever closer to a figure of two million.

Thus began Oasis's imperial phase.* For Noel Gallagher, their new-found regality was reflected in an endless parade of interview microphones, a rapidly expanding guitar collection, and the fact that his aspirations to equal the achievements of The Beatles could now be voiced without fear of any cynical giggling. His brother, meanwhile, had fallen into some of the more unbecoming habits of the freshly successful. 'There were occasions when Liam's behaviour was ... *shabby*,' says Ian Robertson. 'Remembering where he comes from, there were occasions when he would abuse bar staff, waiters, porters, doormen, bellhops – which I found very difficult to get my head round.' If such behaviour clashed with the frequent claim that Oasis were somehow a 'people's band' – made by their more vociferous champions in the press, and usually given the royal assent by Noel – Liam did not seem bothered by the contradiction.

The younger Gallagher also discovered that the group's status had pleasingly carnal benefits, mostly to be found on his occasional circuits of London. This was the time when, according to Tim Abbot, 'Liam could just walk into Brown's and pull the top bird there.'

At least one of the capital's notable women, however, remained beyond his grasp. At the Mercury Music Prize ceremony in September, he sought to sustain the Blur/Oasis feud via an incident involving Justine Frischmann. That year's award would go to Portishead for *Dummy*; Oasis were nominated for *Definitely Maybe*, while Elastica's first album had also made the shortlist (*Parklife* had been a contender in 1994, when to gasps of surprise, it had lost out to M People's *Elegant Slumming*).

In June, Justine Frischmann had been interviewed by the *NME* in New York. Among her more noteworthy comments – in apparent

---

* With reference to music, this phrase was first coined by the Pet Shop Boys' Neil Tennant: 'All very successful pop groups go through an imperial phase.'

contravention of her new rule to be careful with her words, lest the tabloids distort them – was the following: 'I would pose for *Playboy*, I have to say. It's very weird. It seems like when women get to a certain point of fame they have this unconscious desire to shed their clothes. And I can see the attraction of that.'

That night, the quote gave Liam the pretext he needed. 'He shouted, "Get your tits out," and I was offended by it,' says Frischmann. 'It got quite ugly. That night, he just grabbed hold of me and wouldn't let go. And a journalist I knew saved me; he dragged me away and told him to go away. It was really quite unpleasant.'

Some days later, Liam reflected on the episode in an interview. 'I was double rude to her the other night, going, "Go and get your tits out,"' he said. 'It's her boyfriend, innit, 'cos I love getting him at it 'cos he's a dick. If anyone said that to my bird I'd chin the cunt. But I fancy her big time. I'm mad for her . . . if she sat down and talked to me she'd understand. I'd take her out for a meal any day. I'd go, "Come on, let's go for a meal, let's chill."

'But you know how she said she wouldn't mind getting her tits out for *Playboy*? Right. The other night I said, "'Ere Justine, get your tits out, come on you slag." Don't say that, though. 'Cos I'm mad for her and that'd fuck it right up.'

'I had this romantic idea at one point that it was Britpop against the world,' said Damon Albarn, a mere four months after he had presented *Britpop Now*. 'But of course it was every man for himself. It's all over now, though. As far as I'm concerned, we killed Britpop, chopped it up and put it under the patio long ago.' His words suggest a belief that Blur remained as culturally potent as ever, able to redirect the onward march of music with a couple of well-timed signals – and yet they were uttered at a point when his group was perilously close to collapse. In truth, Blur had to try and kill Britpop before it killed them.

The sense that Oasis had risen from the defeat of the summer, writing off the battle but decisively winning the war, informed Blur's woes. The Gallaghers were not the only ones who seemed to turn sadistically on Blur – and Damon Albarn in particular – once *What's The Story* worked its wonders; much to Albarn's dismay, members of the public seemed only too happy to join in. 'The end of that year was the Wonderwall Christmas, wasn't it?' says Alex James. 'I remember Damon coming round to my flat one evening, with real fear in his eyes. I think he'd been told he was a wanker and thumped six times on his way round. He was the uncoolest man in Britain at that point.'

Worse still, Graham Coxon's unease with the place at which the group had arrived had only seemed to increase. He was now making a point of listening to the most discordant, ragged kind of American college-rock: Britpop's polar opposite, if not the very kind of music the Britpop groups had come to avenge. His commitment to the group seemed to be sliding: in November, when Blur were filming the video to accompany the release of The Universal – an ornate take-off of *A Clockwork Orange* – he reportedly arrived on the set several hours late and informed his colleagues that he was planning on being there for no more than sixty minutes. 'We didn't think Graham was going to turn up,' says Alex James. 'In most of that video, all the long shots that Graham's in, it's not actually him.'

In December, Blur set out on a tour of Britain's arenas. The experience was hardly likely to assuage Coxon's anxieties: in addition to the obligation to play a slew of songs from *The Great Escape*, he had to make himself heard above the massed pubescent screams that had begun to be heard in the wake of *Parklife*. To cap it all, there was the prospect of a fortnight spent in the close company of Alex James, whose flamboyant displays of champagne-soused urbanity now tweaked the rawest of Coxon's nerves. 'I hate a lot of the things Alex stands for,' he explained, for what seemed like the 200th time. 'I don't want people to think it's what this band is about. All that Groucho Club bollocks and him going on about birds and boozing all the time. I hate that.'

Mid-way through the tour, the Blur party arrived in Bournemouth, where Alex James's family were issued with the requisite credentials and ushered backstage. 'It's always nice to go back there,' he said. 'We try and slip in a show every couple of years. It's what you dream of doing when you grow up: returning triumphant.' Unfortunately, what transpired that night was a little less celebratory than James perhaps envisaged.

By now, Blur's retinue had been swelled by the writer Adrian Deevoy and photographer Andy Earl, there to piece together a cover story for *Q* magazine. 'We were on the tourbus in Bournemouth,' says Deevoy, 'and there was obviously a problem with Graham: he was drunk to a worrying degree. Damon kept looking at me as if to say, "Ignore him. This is embarrassing." I was talking to Graham about the American music he was into, and he suddenly blacked out – but before he did it, he lunged forward and bit my leg, really hard. It was painful: he almost drew blood.

'Damon was trying to pull him off. He had this kind of "Here we go again" look on his face, and Graham didn't know what was happening. It wasn't funny. I remember saying to Graham, although he was too pissed to take it in, "If you're blacking out like this, you're going to get into a lot of trouble. This is problem drinking." But he got worse and worse.'

As the pain in Deevoy's leg subsided, he found himself at a compact aftershow soirée, apparently thrown in the James family's honour. 'That was when Graham tried to twat Andy Earl,' says Deevoy. 'Andy's pretty hard to take exception to, but Graham took a really irrational dislike to him. He was chucking champagne around. And there was this awful moment when he went to lob a glass of champagne at Andy Earl – and Andy stepped out of the way, and you could see it heading towards Alex's mum. It just missed her. Their minder guy, Smoggy, picked Graham up by the waist and started carrying him out of the room. And as he was doing it, Graham hit him, so fucking hard, on the side of the face. I remember thinking, "I wouldn't do that for a living – carry a horrible little pissed brat around."'

Deevoy, Andy Earl and Smoggy were not the only victims of Coxon's scattershot temper that night. Prior to his enforced exit, Coxon had also seen fit to punch Andy Ross, who had to be quickly talked out of retaliating. Not entirely surprisingly, the party did not last much longer. 'Everyone just disbanded,' says Deevoy. 'It was like someone kicking off at a wedding.'

The following morning, Deevoy sat in the breakfast lounge of his hotel, where he was unexpectedly joined by Damon Albarn. 'Very diplomatically, he said, "Can we make some sort of arrangement so you don't write about that in the piece?" He said, "There is a problem, but Graham's trying to deal with it. It's not going to help if you write about it. At the moment, he's flipping out: he's under a lot of pressure, he hates this tour."' Consequently, Deevoy excised the most alarming facets of Coxon's behaviour from his notes.

When the circus reached London, where Blur were booked to play two nights at the notoriously soulless Wembley Arena, Justine Frischmann – along with Jarvis Cocker, Keith Allen, Damien Hirst and just about every other member of London's new cultural elite – was in attendance. Aside from any backstage discord, she instantly divined the group's tensions from their performance. 'Graham was hiding behind his amp,' she says. 'It was just sad. They weren't any good any more. I remember saying to Damon, "This is shit." And he said, "It doesn't matter – people can't tell."'

Adrian Deevoy's article appeared early the following year. Despite his concordat with Damon Albarn, his piece served notice that Blur were hovering close to what *Q*'s sub-editors called 'a nervous break-up'. When Graham Coxon was asked what could conceivably tear the group apart, his printed reply was as follows: 'Death. Or if we made another *Parklife*. And I don't think we could carry on if one of us left . . . unless it was Alex.'

Damon Albarn's most remarkable pronouncement concerned the crisp layer of white powder that had descended on London over the previous year. When the tape recorder was switched off, he had alerted Deevoy to the apparent effects of cocaine on Alex James. 'I remember Damon saying, "Look at him with his fucking cokey confidence,"' says Deevoy. '"He even *walks* differently."' In print, however, his observations were seemingly focused on the entire Britpop milieu.

'Everyone is taking drugs apart from Graham and me,' he said. 'We are virtually the only exceptions on the entire scene. He drinks too much; I drink a lot but not as much as him and I smoke a bit of dope but that's it. There's a fucking blizzard of cocaine in London at the moment and I hate it. It's stupid. Everyone's become so blasé, thinking they're so ironic and witty and wandering around with this stupid fucking cokey confidence.'

Though the words suggest some loud, righteous tirade, Deevoy recalls him issuing them in a crestfallen whisper. 'He sounded kind of wistful,' he says. 'He was really beaten down at that point. I think he thought the band was going to split up.'

One other striking quote lurked earlier in the piece, when Albarn considered his relationship with the group who had so defined his experience of the last twelve months. 'The only thing we've really got in common with Oasis,' he said, 'is the fact that we're both doing shit in America.'

It was perhaps unfortunate that by the time the article appeared, Wonderwall had climbed into the upper reaches of the US singles charts.

Word that Oasis were on their way to achieving such a feat had reached the UK at the end of 1995. *(What's The Story) Morning Glory?* was averaging weekly American sales of around 200,000; Wonderwall endeared itself to American radio stations as surely as it had pulled off the trick in the UK. If the Britpop moment was bound up with rejecting the dominance of the American grunge groups, the fact that Oasis had apparently managed to take the fight to their home turf surely represented a new, dizzying phase of the story. 'If you take a kid from Brixton and the Bronx,' said Noel Gallagher, 'probably the one thing they've got in common is they both own a copy of *What's The Story*.' In fact, the record-buyers who were pushing Oasis up the US rankings were drawn from the bourgeois ranks of America's white college students, but such trifles hardly mattered; the sheer fact that Oasis were selling was suffused with more than enough romance.

Since the days of punk rock, with the exception of the odd freak hit, the groups who were so frenziedly championed by the UK's music papers had always had one Achilles heel: though they and their journalistic sponsors might talk excitedly about imminent world domination, just about all of them seemed incapable of re-enacting one of British rock's founding myths – the arrival at JFK in a storm of flashbulbs, the sell-out shows at Madison Square Garden, the coast-to-coast tour, leaving chaos and carnage in its wake. The best that could be hoped for was cult success on the East and West Coast; any musician who dared to think any bigger could usually be dismissed as a deluded fantasist. In appearing to break from all this, for a while at least, Oasis were considered almost superhuman.

Swiftly, they were packed off to play a string of the seasonal radio spectaculars that characterise the tail-end of the USA's musical year. Oasis dutifully played for Seattle's KNDD, Washington's WHFS, Chicago's Q101, and Los Angeles's KROQ, while Wonderwall worked its wonders via the airwaves. No matter that their statuesque stage presence contravened the American requirement to Give Good Show, that they sneered at some of the US music industry's eternally schmooze-laden etiquette, or that their accents rendered much of what they said incomprehensible; Oasis seemed to be making a very lucrative kind of virtue of their incongruity.

Upon their return to the UK, they were handed their invitations to the Creation Records Christmas Party. In seeming recognition of the label's new-found clout, Alan McGee had decided to hold it at the Halcyon Hotel in Holland Park, the secluded establishment favoured by those who require shielding from the attentions of the paparazzi. That night, Creation's payroll, along with a clutch of hangers-on, watched McGee hand Oasis their Christmas presents. Liam Gallagher, Paul Arthurs, Alan White and Paul McGuigan were handed all manner of delights: Rolex watches, guitars, designer clothes. Noel Gallagher, meanwhile, was instructed to follow McGee outside.

In one of his early interviews, he had mentioned an ongoing fantasy about owning a chocolate brown Rolls Royce. With evident delight, McGee handed him a set of keys and led him towards a Silver Shadow of the appropriate hue. The fact that Noel could not drive only added to the abiding impression of undreamed-of munificence. In fact, the gift was not quite as bounteous as it appeared. 'It was second-hand,' says Tim Abbot. 'An old knacker. There was about forty grand on the clock. It cost about twelve grand. It was an M or a P, last time round:

'77 or something. A Silver Shadow Mark Two. But the gesture was everything: "Creation buy Rolls Royce."'

Aside from their new toys, one could gauge Oasis's pre-eminence by their snowballing influence on wider musical developments. If, throughout 1994, many of the groups who had caught the imaginations of journalists and talent scouts had cast themselves in Blur's image, it was Oasis who were now paradigmatic. That summer, *Select* magazine had caught the new mood in a two-page spread headlined 'Supersonic Youth', in which the likes of Cast, Smaller, Pusherman, Coast and Creation's Heavy Stereo were profiled and quizzed about their 'Oasisness'. The article's upshot was clear enough: if a group were fond of high-street casualwear, endowed with a swaggering machismo, in thrall to The Beatles, and fond of the word 'top', they were in with a shout.

One of *Select*'s tips perhaps said it all. Northern Uproar were a teenage quartet from Heald Green, an unremarkable outpost of the Mancunian sprawl that sits close to the city's airport. They aspired to replicate Oasis's magic, but were devoid of either Liam's swashbuckling charisma or Noel's melodic knack. In the absence of such qualities, they could only dispense workaday approximations of the kind of energised rock that had characterised *Definitely Maybe*, and issue proclamations that sounded like a *Spitting Image* parody of the Gallaghers. In their first big *NME* feature, they were asked how they might spend the untold millions that would soon come their way. Their drummer, one Keith Chadwick, leapt straight in. 'I'll buy me own fuckin' casino,' he said, like the South Mancunian spawn of Simon Le Bon. 'An' a pub. I'll be watching people lose money while I'm linin' me pocket and I'll be sat there eating me dinner off me belly.'

As 1995 ended, the UK's season of awards ceremonies got off to its usual pre-Christmas start. On 7 November, *Q* magazine hosted its annual bunfight at the Park Lane Hotel on Piccadilly, welcoming the likes of Eric Clapton, Cher, Bob Geldof, David Bowie and Van Morrison. Blur expressed thanks for their Best Album award – given to *The Great Escape*, in apparent defiance of their zeitgeist's lurch towards Oasis – via a video filmed in Paris. The Gallagher brothers, perhaps mindful of the fact that the ceremony took place the same week Wonderwall went to market, dutifully turned up to accept a cursory honour for Best Live Act, and belatedly express their displeasure at *Q*'s review of *What's The Story*. 'I'd like to accept this on behalf of a shit album with shit lyrics,' said a po-faced Noel Gallagher, who did not behave nearly as sociably as some people would have liked.

Mid-way through the ceremony, a familiar figure made his way to the stage. For the second year in succession, Tony Blair had accepted an invitation, arriving with Anji Hunter and Alastair Campbell for the forty-five minutes that his schedule would allow. In the kind of unwitting nod to the old ways of the Labour Party that might set off dozens of parliamentary pagers, Blair's walk-up music was Curtis Mayfield's Move On Up, the song used as a show-closing rallying call on the Red Wedge tour of 1986. Once it was faded out, he announced the winner of the Best Compilation award: an album entitled *Help*, released that September. Its purpose had been to raise money for War Child, the charity founded to help victims of the bloody strife that was besetting the former Yugoslavia. Consequently, Blair could subtly couch his tribute to *Help* in familiar New Labour themes: a gentle kind of all-hands-to-the-pump communitarianism, and his fleeting belief in an ethical foreign policy. Lest anyone accuse him of scoring vulgar political points, however, he was also crafty enough to indulge in an audience-pleasing spurt of self-deprecation.

'This is a remarkable album,' he said. 'A whole lot of people came together, left their egos behind, put aside self-interest, thought about the common good ... so why you've got a *politician* presenting this award I don't know! At a time when there was a danger of the West turning its back on the war in Bosnia, it helped put it back in the headlines and reactivate public interest. It helped us be aware of our responsibilities to other people.'

Help had indeed been an impressive exercise. Conceived by Tony Crean and Andy McDonald – the latter the founder of the Go! Discs label, the former the company's senior marketing staffer – it had been predicated on an idea that quickly caught the imagination of Britain's media: the setting-aside of one day – 4 September, three weeks after the Blur/Oasis conflict – on which an array of acts would enter a studio and record a song for inclusion on the album, to be released a week later. *Help* was not a Britpop record – the presence of the likes of Massive Attack, Stereo MCs and Portishead ensured that its scope extended elsewhere – and yet it was accepted as further proof of the UK's new-found musical fecundity; a manifestation of the ambition and brio that had taken root in the previous eighteen months.

Blur rather scored a PR own-goal by contributing an unremarkable instrumental in-joke entitled Eine Kleine Lift Musik. Suede managed to claw back some lost goodwill by recording a delicate version of Shipbuilding, the song written by Elvis Costello at the time of the Falklands War. The album's most remarkable rock track, however, was the work of a group who had played no part in either Britpop's genesis or its much-celebrated fruition. Radiohead's poised, impossibly affecting Lucky served notice of an artistic coup de grâce that would materialise two years later with *OK Computer*; here, though too few people seemed to be listening, was the sound of a world beyond Camden Town.

Noel Gallagher, meanwhile, was sufficiently enthused by *Help*'s concept to manage two contributions. Firstly, there was a sighing version of the old Oasis B-side Fade Away, featuring guitar-playing by the group's new friend Johnny Depp, on which Noel risked the wrath of his younger brother by taking the lead vocal. Yet more notably, he had assisted Paul Weller with his version of The Beatles' Come Together. Noel was not the only outside help that Weller recruited; in among the song's growly three minutes was an electric piano part played by Paul McCartney.

It was McCartney's presence that nailed *Help* as a quintessential Britpop artefact. With consciously romantic intent, Weller had chosen to record Come Together in Abbey Road's Studio Two, the holy-of-holies in which The Beatles had worked most of their magic. When McCartney made his entrance, some of Britpop's most lofty promises – of an age-defying world in which musicians could collaborate with the deities who had so inspired them, and the reconnection of Britain to its own shining musical heritage – seemed to be made flesh.

Two months later, an even greater miracle came to pass. In November, the three surviving Beatles announced the imminent release of three compilations of unreleased material and an eight-part television series – both entitled *Anthology* – via the unveiling of a song they had been working on since 1994: a balmy hymn of redemption entitled Free As A Bird. Thanks to the cutting-edge of modern recording technology, the song had been constructed around a discarded demo tape recorded by John Lennon in 1977. His fragile, nigh-on indecipherable vocal drifted through the music with the kind of distracted grace that led reviewers to coin words like 'ghostly'.

Fortuitously, Free As A Bird was of a piece with the more contemplative end of the UK's current rock music of choice; indeed, one could play it next to Wonderwall, Don't Look Back In Anger or The Universal and barely notice the join. It was almost as if its author had heard the songs blaring from Britain's radios and decided to abscond from the afterlife; as though Britpop, in its final act of wonderment, had woken the dead.

CHAPTER 16

Is this the way they say the future's meant to feel?

Elastica's schedule for 1995 and the first part of 1996 still beggars belief. In less than twelve months, they performed no less than 102 shows, across the UK, Europe, the USA and Australia. The resultant transcontinental grind was made yet more vexing by one of rock music's more unfortunate commonplaces: Donna Matthews, Justin Welch and Annie Holland had fallen victim to the random cycle of occasional fix and ongoing withdrawal that is the lot of the travelling heroin user.

'I wasn't really aware of the whole cold turkey scenario,' says Justine Frischmann. 'I just thought people were being very bad-tempered; really grumpy and fucked-up all the time. And there was big-time denial going on with me. They were extremely furtive. It was like, "Don't tell teacher." I used to get called the Führer. They called me that to my face.'

The fact that three of Elastica were bonded by their drug travails inevitably impacted on the one member who, in the users' parlance, remained clean. Throughout 1995, Justine Frischmann sensed that she was the focus of snowballing resentment about the group's never-ending itinerary, cast in the role of demanding school ma'am by colleagues who increasingly equated the group's commitments with illness and worry. 'I remember one night in America, Donna saying to me, "You're just a cunt. I'm going to end up like you – just a cunt." I was like, "What are you talking about?" She said, "You're like a robot. How can you get onstage, and do all these interviews, and say how great everything is? You're like a machine, you're not human." I was like, "Well, *cheers*."

'I thought Donna and Annie were my best friends,' she says, 'and over the course of touring it became obvious that they actually weren't

Menswear in 1995, camping it up as latter-day Lord
Fauntleroys. Left to right: Stuart Black, Johnny Dean, Matt
Everitt, Chris Gentry and Simon White.

Menswear Mk II in 1999, with Darren Tudgay (second left)
and Paul Fletcher (far right). 'I looked at them and
thought, "You don't look like you want to sell records. You
look like you don't give a fuck."'

Justine

JOHNNY.

MAT.

mnie

LIAM

Donna

Bernard

UP YOURS!
(Graham)

DAMON.

Chris.

Simon.

Mr. JARVIS COCKER

Britpop's central players. Eleven of the pictures are taken from the wall of Savage & Best, the Camden-based publicists for Suede, Elastica, Pulp and Menswear; Liam Gallagher was photographed at the 1996 Q Awards.

The pathologically sociable Jarvis Cocker at the launch of the new Action Man in 1996. 'He is coming to resemble Christopher Biggins,' said the *Evening Standard*, 'and that is a national tragedy.'

Pulp in 1994, just before they became Britpop's most unlikely success story. Left to right: Steve Mackey, Candida Doyle, Nick Banks, Jarvis Cocker, Rusell Senior.

Noel Gallagher, Jarvis Cocker and Justine Frischmann review 1994's singles for the *NME*. 'At one point it was Britpop against the world ...'

Damon Albarn and Liam Gallagher, squaring up at the annual celebrity Soccer Six tournament in 1996.

A briefly reunited Justine Frischmann and Brett Anderson, with the bizarrely-coiffed Thom Yorke playing gooseberry, at the Brat Awards, February 1994.

Albarn and Noel Gallagher at the 1994 *Q* Awards, in the days before cordiality had given way to loathing.

Oasis at their Knebworth photo-call, proving that glamour was one of Britpop's more expendable elements.

A duffel-coated Liam at the photo session for the sleeve of Roll With It. 'He used to shop in Marks and Spencer; he'd go to Dunn & Co.'

Liam and Patsy Kensit at the 1996 Brit Awards. 'Are we alike?' pondered Liam. 'I think so. We're both moody bastards.'

Noel exits the Belsize townhouse where he played out his imperial phase among a sea of hangers-on. 'It was, "Hello, who the fuck are you?"'

Noel and Meg Mathews in their *Be Here Now*-era pomp. According to her *Sunday Times* column, she dyed her hair platinum blonde to match her credit card.

Noel and Tony Blair at the Downing Street reception, perhaps caught at the moment when Noel mentioned the Liverpool dockers. '[Blair's] words were, "We'll look into it". And I said, "Yes, you probably will, won't you?"'

Alan McGee, with Tony and Cherie Blair at the Labour Party's 1996 Youth Experience rally, and (inset) McGee in 1993, when his prevailing interests were pharmaceutical rather than political.

very keen on me. I'd become a kind of authority figure, forcing them to go on tour, making them do interviews. It was very unfair really, because I actually didn't make them do that much. I did most of it.'

In July, the group turned in their first six performances on Lollapalooza, the travelling carnival whose bill provided a simple index of who the American alt-rock fraternity considered to be hip. Having played in such glamorous settings as New York's Downing Stadium and Charles Town Racetrack, West Virginia, they returned to the UK for a sprinkling of dates in Scotland and Ireland, with a commitment to return to the States soon after – whereupon, to no-one's great surprise, Holland announced that she wanted out. Despite a flurry of last-ditch conversations, she could not be persuaded to stay; news duly reached the press of both 'tour fatigue' and tendonitis.

The main factor, according to Donna Matthews, was more simple. 'Annie left because of heroin, really,' she says. 'We were on tour for so long that we'd stopped being able to always get it. So she just got fucking miserable; sick of it. I think she wanted to go home and . . . take heroin.'

'The moment that Annie left, we should have had a break,' says Justine Frischmann. 'But I didn't feel I had any choice in the matter. And to be fair, if I'd been offered the choice I probably wouldn't have taken it. I didn't realise how fucked-up we all were at that point. But our management should have realised it, and the record company should have realised it. You shouldn't be in a position where your bass player leaves and they tell you to get back on the next plane. That's nuts.'

With amazing haste, the group announced that, for the moment, her place would be taken by one Abby Travis, the bass player in the backing band used by Beck. The group thus went back to the US and resumed their place on the Lollapalooza running-order, and Donna Matthews and Justin Welch's troubles – chiefly, the ever-present imminence of going cold turkey, or 'clucking' – continued. 'I started getting a lot of fear,' says Matthews. 'I'd be taking drugs, but it would be really desperate. I remember feeling, "I've got to take more drugs to get rid of this feeling." There wasn't a break: I was on valium as a prescription; also methadone, 'cos we'd always be withdrawing. Coming away from London, on tour, we'd take a certain amount of heroin with us, but it'd be gone. We'd be clucking; we'd be really ill. So then people would go off and try to get more heroin for us, and it'd get desperate. We'd all be pretending we didn't have any.

'There was a time when we all used to share our drugs. Then it got to the point that Justin would be like, "Oh god, I'm clucking – I can't go onstage tonight." And I'd be saying, "Oh, I feel dreadful for you, Jus – but I just haven't got anything." And he'd *know* I did, because I wasn't ill. That's when it started getting bad: we'd go on tour, and we'd be lying to each other, constantly. Even when the other person knew you were lying, it didn't matter. If you saw them really in pain, you were just thinking, "There's no way I can let them even know I've got *that* much, because they'll take it off me." We'd all be doing our drugs secretly.'

In addition to the recurrent deceit, Donna Matthews' year was punctuated by desperate visits to the kind of places that touring British musicians were best advised to avoid. 'I remember being in dodgy, dangerous situations loads of times. When we were in New Orleans trying to score, we got taken to this crackhouse, not knowing whether we were going to get ripped off. I got beaten up in Hamburg, on the Reeperbahn. We ran, and we just pulled this car up, and just got in the car. The guy ran after us with a brick, threw it and smashed the back window of the car. Things like that used to happen all the time. I had to do a whole American tour with my face a mess, because I got beaten up trying to score. I had to have injections in my face because it was so swollen. Everything became about drugs.'

Lollapalooza ended with a show at the Shoreline Amphitheatre in Mountain View, California. Elastica were billeted to a hotel in San Francisco; it was here that Donna Matthews finally confided in Justine Frischmann. 'I remember crying to Justine,' she says, 'saying, "I'm scared to go home, because I know I can't stop doing heroin." The only time I'd stop doing it was when we were away. And she said, "Oh, Donna, don't be stupid – of course you'll never become a heroin addict." She laughed at it. She said, "I'll never let you become a heroin addict."

'Three months later, I went to the doctor for the first time and said, "I've got a problem with heroin." And he said, "You're going to have to go into rehab." I said, "I haven't got time – I'm going on tour again." It took me another five years to get clean.'

Elastica's commitments finally came to a close on 4 February 1996, when they played at the Big Day Out in Perth. The sudden prospect of a life outside the tourbus could reasonably be expected to prompt euphoric celebration; instead, Donna Matthews returned home with a genuine sense of dread. 'It started to get really desperate then,' she says. 'Everyone was doing loads of crack, loads of heroin. I got into hitting up, which separated me even more from the group. I started hanging round with street junkies; hanging out in crackhouses.'

By early 1996, the use of heroin by musicians and their acolytes had extended way beyond the clique who congregated at Matthews' King's Cross house. Within the same London circles in which cocaine and ecstasy were a given, the drug was becoming increasingly fashionable: indeed, if one had binged on fast drugs, it was increasingly de rigueur to ease the comedown with the aid of tinfoil and brown powder.

Mike Smith was Elastica's music publisher; for him, the next phase of their progress was particularly important, given that they were expected to spend a good deal of the next year working on new songs. He too observed the London scene's transition from cocaine-assisted hyperactivity to the introversion and sleepiness that comes with heroin use. 'I'd read enough books about the music business before I started working in it to know that drugs, and cocaine in particular, featured incredibly heavily,' he says. 'When I first started as a talent scout at MCA on eight grand a year, I didn't see any drugs, really. I was going to the Bull and Gate, the Falcon: the grim end of the indie world. Cocaine only became a complete accessory when people had the money to afford it. Around the time of *Parklife*, it seemed as if everyone in London was doing it.'

Less than two years on, things had markedly changed. 'There was a lot of heroin around by that time. That was making things a lot darker and more dangerous. That was prevalent. People think of it as this very upbeat, frivolous period but there were an awful lot of very serious drugs being taken. A lot of people went from alcohol to cocaine to heroin. Or so it seemed. It was a shame, because whereas alcohol and cocaine were about people going out and having a good time and being very vibrant and extremely in-your-face in the media, with the advent of heroin, it pushed a lot of people back into their homes. Suddenly, the whole scene pretty much collapsed.'

For the moment, no-one seemed to notice. Indeed, as gouching out behind closed curtains became a fashionable leisure option, the celebration of the Britpop milieu seemed to reach a new pitch; as if, for fear of the party reaching its inevitable end, its observers felt duty-bound to shout all the louder.

The increasing vogueishness of heroin placed yet more distance between Oasis and many of their London-based peers. During the first part of her interview for *The Observer*, Miranda Sawyer had asked Noel Gallagher what drugs he had never tried. 'Heroin, crack, ketamine, Prozac,' he replied. 'I don't really think that I'm going to be tricked into taking them. I don't smoke pot, I don't do trips, I don't take speed. It's usually Ecstasy and cocaine and serious amounts of drinking.'

She then asked him whether he thought there were now more people doing heroin than in the pre-Britpop period – 'Absolutely,' he said, before he tumbled into an illustrative anecdote. 'I had a do one night at this little place where I was living,' he said. 'There were some seriously famous people there, and they were all just like . . . I didn't get it for about two or three hours, but they were going to the bogs in twos and all that, and their eyes were like pins. In the end, I was like, "I'm not having them in my fucking house – you've got to go."'

With no little venom, he rose to his righteous conclusion. 'I hate all that trendy Portobello Road smackhead fucking bollocks. I wouldn't mind if they admitted that they took it, but it's like . . . I could name thirty people in the biggest bands in this country, and I have fucking seen them do it . . . they all take heroin. They're all at it. Horrible.'

For now, Oasis's chemical intake apparently posed no threat to their momentum: the white lines of which both Gallagher brothers were fond seemed to act as nothing more career-threatening than a very potent kind of fuel. Indeed, if they were increasingly expected to fulfil their public's stereotyped expectations – that Liam would affect his swaggering arrogance, while Noel dispensed endless proclamations of the group's majesty – cocaine was surely the ideal drug. That said, after the mention of coke in Cigarettes And Alcohol, the new album contained yet another reference – only this time it seemed to be far more of a vexed admission than a licentious clarion-call. 'All your dreams are made/When you're chained to the mirror and the razor blade' – in Morning Glory's opening couplet, set to a piledriving backdrop, there lurked the sense that perhaps the powder would eventually have to be put away.

By early 1996, Oasis's immediate circle was visibly different. Ian Robertson, the imposing ex-soldier with the incongruously plummy accent, had been let go in September 1995, when his impatience with an all-but-uncontrollable Liam Gallagher had led him – perhaps not unreasonably – to land his charge with a punch. 'There were only three people at that stage who would say no to Liam,' he says. 'One of them was Noel, one of them was Marcus and one of them was me. But Liam had got to a place where he didn't want to hear no. By then, he was a rock star.'

In the wake of Robertson's exit, the group were usually shadowed by personal security men provided by a firm called Topguard. Noel's favoured human shield had the unlikely name of Kevin Camp; Liam's more volatile nature was perhaps betrayed by the recruitment of one Terry Neill, a man-mountain whose zen-like composure, no matter how extreme the scenario, never seemed to be under threat.

It was some token of Meg Mathews' clout that she had been given a job as the head of 'Artist Liaison' at Creation Records. At the music industry's larger labels, the job denotes an endless grind of meeting acts at Heathrow, escorting them to West End musicals and ensuring that they are provided with macrobiotic meals at five in the morning. Mathews, by contrast, had one key responsibility: the organisation of the label's parties.

Her first brief was the launch of (*What's The Story) Morning Glory?*. Rather than the usual music business gambit of hiring some West End dive and ensuring the gathered throng could drink and drug until the wee hours, she put on a Sunday brunch, at which the album was rendered by a string quartet, while revellers gazed in wonder at an ice sculpture of the Oasis logo. Those who had greeted news of her appointment with stifled scepticism were impressed; nonetheless, there were still whispers about the fact that, all of a sudden, questioning any aspect of Oasis's activities at Creation's HQ seemed off-puttingly awkward.

'She became pivotal,' says Tim Abbot. 'She lived with the talent. She had his ear, twenty-four-seven. So somebody who was really a party organiser-cum-cloakroom attendant, with a good sense of spin – and nice, don't get me wrong – was suddenly very important.'

After two years of carousing – and to the evident delight of the tabloid newspapers – Liam Gallagher was now going out with Patsy Kensit, the actress-turned-singer-turned-actress who had perhaps served notice of the two poles between which she would bounce by making a childhood appearance in a Bird's Eye peas advert, and quickly going on to a role in *The Great Gatsby*. When she and Liam met, she was married to Jim Kerr, the lead singer of the increasingly irrelevant Simple Minds; Liam, by contrast, transported her to the very heart of cutting-edge developments. If the coupling seemed hilariously incongruous, both parties were at pains to insist that they were a perfect fit. 'Are we alike?' pondered an evidently lovestruck Liam. 'Me and Pats? I think so. We're both moody bastards.'

On 19 February 1996, Oasis – and friends – took their seats around two tables at the Brit Awards. If the 1993 ceremony had seen Suede's decisive arrival in the UK's living rooms, and 1995 marked the corporate coronation of Blur, this year belonged to the Gallaghers. By way of expressing his disdain for the assembled members of the music industry, Liam Gallagher had seemingly forgone both washing and shaving for the occasion: wrapped in a voluminous fur-lined leather coat, with the rather more fragrant Kensit by his side, he wore a five-day beard that made him look like Grover from *Sesame Street*. By some

271

feat of subterfuge, he appeared to have brought his own alcohol supply: though the beer slurped by his fellow revellers came in bottles, Liam was equipped with endless cans of Red Stripe. 'He was very edgy that night,' says Tim Abbot. 'Growly. That was the cocaine.'

Liam's air of dishevellment seemed to be in keeping with the ceremony's abiding atmosphere. If the previous year had seemed to dramatise the sudden arrival of indie-rock in the mainstream, with all the surprise that the scenario implied, 1996 was the year that some of those present affected a pose of arrogant indifference, as if they expected nothing less. The impression extended even to the ceremony's compere: in 1995, Chris Evans had dressed in his full *Don't Forget Your Toothbrush* pomp: an electric-coloured suit, garish tie, and carefully gelled quiff. This year, his shirt was worn outside his waistband, his hair had been given the merest brush, and he too had mislaid his razor.

Moreover, whereas Blur had accepted their 1995 awards with a visible pleasure, the group who had wrested the zeitgeist away from them affected a display of oafish belligerence. Oasis were first called to the stage to accept the award for Best Video, given to the clip that had accompanied Wonderwall. 'I've got nowt to say except I'm extremely rich and you lot aren't,' said Noel Gallagher. He then looked over at Michael Hutchence, who had announced their win. 'Has beens,' said Noel, 'shouldn't present fuckin' awards to gonna-bes.' Hutchence looked unconcerned; according to accounts of the episode that appeared after his death, he was actually deeply hurt.

Oasis's next award was for Best Album, given – to no-one's great surprise – to *What's The Story*. They stepped up to the rostrum with a handful of associates, before the ever-enthusiastic Owen Morris exhorted the group's entire retinue to join them. Then, to the organisers' disquiet, Liam decided that they were all going to stay put. 'Before we go any further, right, surely the security in this place can send up more than fuckin' Ginger Bollocks to throw us off the stage. A ginger geezer cannot throw Oasis off the stage.' The barb was directed at Evans, though the equally ginger Alan McGee looked no less uncomfortable. Mercifully, after pretending to stick the group's latest statuette up his bum, Liam was eventually persuaded to return to his table.

Oasis's last award, presented by Pete Townshend, was for Best Group. By now, their sneering hostility was begging one question: if they were that dismissive of the ceremony, why had they not opted for the infinitely more stylish option of simply not turning up at all? 'It's all a fake,' Liam drawled. 'We knew we were going to do it and that is it.' As if to offer a slightly more polite oration, the usually emollient

Alan White stepped up to the microphone. Unfortunately, he was apparently too drunk to speak.

Then Noel Gallagher thought of something. Seizing on the presence of the Leader of Her Majesty's Opposition, he was about to issue five sentences that combined drug-fuelled hubris – by his own admission, Noel was under the influence of both Ecstasy and cocaine – with the cultural and political optimism that was one of the hallmarks of the Britpop era. 'There are seven people in this room who are giving a little bit of hope to young people in this country,' he said, steadying himself on his feet. 'That is me, our kid, Bonehead, Guigs, Alan White, Alan McGee and Tony Blair. And if you've all got anything about you, you'll go up there and you'll shake Tony Blair's hand, man. He's the man! Power to the people!'

Eighteen months later, when quizzed about this very frazzled endorsement, Noel simply shrugged. 'We were off our heads that night,' he said. 'We were talking some right bullshit.'

Blair, accompanied by his wife Cherie and their seven-year-old daughter Kathryn, was there to present an Outstanding Contribution Award to David Bowie: a timely recipient, given that his influence, from Suede onwards, had pervaded the Britpop moment as much as any of the 60s acts who were currently in fashion. After Blair's presence at two *Q* Awards ceremonies and his photo-opportunity at the BPI's Annual General Meeting, his appearance at the Brits appeared to put the final gloss on his self-portrayal as a new, hip kind of politician. Indeed, his speech not only paid tribute to Britpop's success and acknowledged its debts to the past, but extended Blair's musical appreciation into new, unforeseen areas. In under a minute, he became the first aspiring Prime Minister to pay tribute to both punk rock and the Mancunian groups of the late 80s:

> It's been a great year for British music. A year of creativity, vitality, energy. British bands storming the charts. British music back once again in its right place, at the top of the world. And at least part of the reason for that has been the inspiration that today's bands can draw from those that have gone before. Bands in my generation like The Beatles and The Stones and The Kinks. Of a later generation: The Clash, The Smiths, Stone Roses. But there is one man who spans the generations, who has been a source of inspiration to everybody. He's always on the cutting edge, he's an innovator, he's pushed the frontiers back, he's a man not afraid to go up the hill backwards. He is now in his fourth decade of music, and here are some of the highlights . . .

There followed a two-minute flit through Bowie's career history, before Blair reached for his statuette. Now, he had to utter little more than a dozen words – but an unforeseen trap awaited him.

There are those who say 'Bowie' with the same first vowel sound as 'showy'. Others, for one reason or another, prefer a pronunciation that rhymes with 'Wowee'.* Blair had obviously not considered this: when it came to the requisite two words, a look of panic flashed across his face. 'The award for outstanding contribution to British music,' he said, 'goes to . . .' There was the merest of stumbles, before Blairite logic kicked in. Somehow, he managed to masterfully incorporate both pronunciations and thereby alienate no-one: 'David Bow-oh-ie!' said Blair, just as the walk-up music boomed from the speakers and the man himself ran on to the stage.

Bowie performed Hallo Spaceboy with the Pet Shop Boys, and thereby closed the ceremony. Thus commenced the usual two hours of mutual congratulation and table-hopping. Inevitably, the Oasis party exerted a magnetic spell on the gathered multitudes: Noel Gallagher, in particular, seemed to take a great delight in holding court.

The Blair family duly made their way over to say hello: a well-placed paparazzo captured Noel signing an autograph for Kathryn, watched by her father. Noel appeared to be as full of beans as he had been all night; Blair's expression was a little more troubled. 'They were very sheepish,' says Paul Arthurs. 'Cherie Blair was like, "Would you mind awfully signing something for my kids – they're very big fans." We just went, "Waaaaargh." We were fucked.' Such was one possible source of the Blairs' unease, bound up with the occupational hazards of fraternising with rock musicians. 'There were literally *ounces* of cocaine,' says Tim Abbot, 'just a couple of feet away from them.'

If the Gallaghers' behaviour suggested that Britpop's vindicatory narrative – the entry of outsiders into the mainstream, avenging the music industry's more idiotic aspects as they came – was becoming swamped by a very ugly kind of arrogance, Jarvis Cocker managed to spectacularly redress the balance. That night, he single-handedly revived the idea that success could come with an almost moral subtext. In that sense, the 1996 Brit Awards represented Britpop's last proud stand.

The success of Common People had propelled Pulp to within spitting distance of the roped-off enclosure occupied by Oasis and Blur – but if their achievement of enviable commercial success might be expected

---

* The correct pronunciation, as with the inventor of the hunting knife, is the former.

to quash the notion that they were prickly outsiders, the ensuing months would suggest that the group's countercultural instincts remained intact. In September, they released two songs as a double A-sided single. Mis-Shapes was the group's against-the-odds ascent set to music: a ferocious clarion-call to those who identified with their unlikely exit from the cultural margins. The real masterstroke, however, was Sorted For E's And Wizz, which queasily evoked Cocker's trips to M25 raves in the far-flung days of Acid House: 'Is this the way they say the future's meant to feel/Or just 20,000 people standing in a field?'

In keeping with the demands of their record company's marketing department, the single's compact disc format was available in two versions. The packaging of the one devoted to Mis-Shapes was founded on a very Pulp-esque parody of a 60s sewing pattern; when it came to Sorted For E's And Wizz, the group's designers had chosen to base the sleeve art around a wrap, an example of street-level origami in which the UK's drug users tend to carry their refreshments. Inside the CD booklet, though there was no mention of its usual application, there was a nine-point guide to a wrap's construction.

Though the tabloid newspapers had spent the last year clutching Britpop to their bosom, this – for the *Daily Mirror*, at least – was too much to take. 'BAN THIS SICK STUNT: Chart stars sell CD with DIY kids' drugs guide,' roared the paper's front page. In tribute to the principles of Athenian democracy, the *Mirror* opened the obligatory free phone-line, asking their readers whether the single should be banned; to help them make up their minds, the paper canvassed the expert opinion of the Capital Radio DJ Neil 'Doctor' Fox. 'Drugs kill, it's that simple,' he said. 'And the scale of the problem we have with drugs in Britain is frightening enough without this kind of encouragement.'

Whatever was actually entailed by the idea of 'banning' the single, 2112 *Mirror* voters favoured such a course of action, while 770 thought that Pulp should be left alone. The same day as the poll's result was revealed, Island Records announced that – to the great delight of the UK's pun-crazed tabloid sub-editors – all copies of the offending CD booklet were being pulped. 'Following the *Daily Mirror's* accusations, there is now the possibility the booklet will be misinterpreted as an endorsement of drug use,' read the label's statement.

Two weeks later came an album entitled *Different Class*. Much of it had been written in the wake of Common People, whose success had solidified Cocker's hunch that he should take his abiding interest in the British class system to new heights. In that sense, it continued many of the themes of His'n'Hers, but infused them with a new, confident sense of confrontation. One heard it in Mis-Shapes and Common People, but it came to its most startling peak during I Spy, which found Cocker wreaking a very pointed kind of revenge on the bourgeoisie by sleeping with some middle-class unfortunate's wife: 'Smoking your cigarettes, drinking your brandy, messing up the bed you chose together . . . Take your Year in Provence and stick it up your ass,' he hissed.

To listen to some journalists, in terms of the album's depiction of the contemporary English expanse, it seemed that even the wonders of *Parklife* had been surpassed. '*Different Class* is Pulp's masterpiece,' wrote the venerable Tony Parsons in *The Daily Telegraph*, 'a class-concious concept album populated by posh girls looking for a bit of rough, gorgeous single mums and poor boys made good . . . The greatest living Yorkshireman sings of love behind the net curtains and the ennui behind the bright lights.'

Its success was underpinned by a very British tradition. Proving that tabloid outrage remained the very best kind of advertising, *Different Class* entered the charts at number one.

At the Brit Awards, immediately prior to Oasis's contretemps with Michael Hutchence, Pulp performed Sorted For Es And Wizz, surrounded by dancers dressed in Acid House attire. The choice of song was clearly intended to demonstrate that, despite the tabloid brouhaha, the group had not been cowed. Twenty minutes later, Chris Evans introduced a performance from Michael Jackson, and thus began an episode that would make the previous year's media storm looking positively trifling.

In 1993, Jackson's alleged status as the 'King of Pop' had been rather shaken by allegations of child sex abuse, made by the parents of a thirteen-year-old boy named Jordy Chandler. The family withdrew their allegations in exchange for a $26 million dollar settlement, whereupon Jackson began recording an album entitled *HIStory*, aimed at protesting his innocence and thereby re-establishing his career. To promote it, his British record company had decided to sail a huge plaster statue of Jackson down the River Thames.

If that stunt had fallen rather flat, his Brits appearance was obviously intended to restore Jackson to his throne. It was to be followed by his acceptance of a one-off award for being the 'Artist of a Generation', handed to him by Bob Geldof, who had written a tribute to Jackson that rather beggared belief. 'When Michael Jackson sings,' he would gush, 'it is with the voice of angels, and when his feet move, you can see God dancing.' Here, it seemed, was the music business at its addled, insensitive worst.

Jackson was to mime to Earth Song, a pious moan about the state of the planet that, against all kinds of odds, had topped the British charts at the end of 1995. Its staging involved a supporting cast dressed in rags, a huge pyramid, and a simulation of a full moon, on to which were projected pictures of endangered wildlife. At the song's end, he was to slip out of his black body-suit to reveal robes of virginal white, and throw a crucifix pose, while a succession of children embraced him, before adult representatives of the world's races and religions followed suit. Tellingly, the procession would end with a rabbi. Not even Jesus had convinced the Jews of his credentials: Michael Jackson seemed to be anxious to tell the world that, far from being an alleged paedophile with a mis-sculpted face, he was actually the Messiah.

It was Jarvis Cocker's good fortune to be standing at the side of the stage during Jackson's performance, his neck draped with an Access All Areas pass, having consumed enough alcohol to put him in the mood for a small-scale adventure. Towards the end, as Jackson was lifted high above the stage on a cherry-picker platform, Cocker sprinted on to the stage, dodged the wailing hordes, and shot Jackson a look of caricatured disapproval. He then bent over with his backside to the crowd, and performed the kind of hand gestures that signify farting. Finally, he managed to ascend the pyramid at the back of the stage, pausing in front of the illuminated moon. For some reason, he camply lifted his shirt, before scampering away. Given the scale of the Jackson production, precious few of the assembled revellers were aware of what Cocker had done. Indeed, Pulp blithely carried on with their evening, before Cocker was approached by two police officers, and arrested on suspicion of causing Actual Bodily Harm.

He was driven to Kensington Police Station and held until 3am, when he was released and instructed to reappear for questioning on 11 March. 'The police weren't bad, actually,' he said. 'In fact, I felt very happy that this happened in England rather than America. I think if it had happened in America, I'd really be in trouble . . . It weren't a bad cell. It even had a bit of padding on the bench. From what I've heard of police cells, it was apparently quite a luxury one.' It soon became clear that the allegations he faced were centred on the notion that, while he was on the stage, Cocker had caused injury to some of the more diminutive members of Jackson's supporting cast. Ironically enough, he was being accused of the mistreatment of children.

In the next two days, Cocker was pilloried. Once again, the *Mirror* sounded one of the shrillest voices: 'Jacko Pulps Lout Cocker', read its front-page headline. 'A furious mum threatened to sue Pulp star Jarvis Cocker yesterday after the singer brought terror to her 12-year-old daughter,' wrote Matthew Wright, the paper's showbiz figurehead. 'Budding dancer Ashley Moore and three young boys were hurt when loutish Cocker crashed Michael Jackson's star turn at the Brit Awards ceremony.' *The Daily Mail*, meanwhile, ran a story headlined 'The Night Our Young Dreams Were Pulped', in which Moore's mother recounted the heartwarming story of Jackson phoning the family home to make sure her daughter was alright.

As the week wound on, however, it became steadily clear that the newspapers had misjudged their public. News of Cocker's antics – not to mention his arrest – had stirred a very British reaction, imbued with both sympathy for the underdog, and repulsion at Michael Jackson's antics. Among a handful of people whose letters were printed by the *Guardian* – including Bernard Butler and Brian Eno – was one Desmond Mason of Penarth, who sounded the kind of patriotic note that was usually the preserve of the tabloids. 'Thank heavens for Jarvis Cocker,' he wrote. 'Jackson's deification of himself was the most lunatic display of posturing vanity that the King of Pop has achieved so far. What made it even worse was the connivance in his self-adulation by Saint Bob Geldof . . . Jarvis makes me proud to be British.'

So it was that the *Daily Mirror* performed the kind of volte-face that punctuates the pages of *1984*. Jarvis Cocker was innocent; he had always been innocent. Beginning on Thursday 20 February, Matthew Wright spearheaded the paper's 'Justice For Jarvis' campaign, cajoling an array of celebrities – Yasmin Le Bon, Zoe Ball, Barbara Windsor, Patsy Kensit – into wearing specially manufactured T-shirts. Wright claimed that a viewing of unseen footage from the Brits had scotched any notion of Cocker's guilt; if anyone had been reckless about the children's welfare, it had been the security operatives whom Wright referred to as 'Jacko's goons'.

On Monday 11 March, Cocker was once again interviewed by police before the charge was formally dropped, and he made his way to a press conference. 'It wasn't very nice to have people thinking that you're the type of person who goes round punching children,' he said. 'It's one of the worst things you can be accused of.' Now that the dust had cleared, one fact was indisputable: Jarvis Cocker was more famous than ever.

By way of proof, on 7 April, a make-up artist named Sarah Reygate opened her heart to the *News of the World* about a recent tryst with Britain's new housewives' favourite. 'I know he looks like a skinny trainspotter,' she said. 'He kept his shirt buttoned up every time we made love. It was drip-dry bri-nylon and there was lots of static.'

★   ★   ★

Though the Brit Awards ceremony only seemed to further Britpop's abiding sense of celebratory hysteria – with no little restraint, ITV's broadcast claimed it had been 'one of the most memorable evenings in living memory' – it was telling that many of those who had set the ball rolling were absent. The four members of Blur had seemingly resigned themselves to the evening being turned into a coronation for Oasis and decided to stay away. Besides, the event – quite apart from the presence of their one-time rivals – was surely the embodiment of everything that had served to set Blur against one another.

Elastica, meanwhile, had been back in the UK for no more than a fortnight, after the final stretch of their twelve-month tour of the globe. Inevitably, they were suffering from what rock lore terms Decompression Syndrome – and for Justine Frischmann, the pains seemed particularly severe. 'I think looking back on it, I had a nervous breakdown,' she says. 'We came back, finally, and I just felt like everything that had made me feel like me no longer existed. I'd been away from my mates and my family, I was living in this huge house with no furniture in it. I got home and didn't have a clue who I was. I didn't want to go out. When the doorbell rang I was scared to answer it.'

In Britpop's first stirrings, Frischmann had sensed a reclamation of some of British music's more cerebral aspects; now, on her return, with Noel Gallagher's songs enshrined as the national soundtrack and the new post-Oasis groups apparently in the ascendant, she found that that agenda had been nudged to the margins. 'A lot of people had said to me, "Oh, punk rock was great after all; intelligent music is worthwhile," ' she says. 'And then all of a sudden they loved Oasis. That seemed really hypocritical.'

When she re-entered London's hedonistic social whirl, her sense of disorientation was compounded. The drug that her colleagues had attempted to hide from her was suddenly everywhere, treated with a nonchalance that belied its more malign effects. It was the year of *Trainspotting*, the film that managed to tie itself into the Britpop moment via both a soundtrack that included songs by Blur, Elastica, Pulp and Sleeper, and the sense that it was the work of ascendant homegrown talent. Unbeknown to most of the media, its sense of timeliness was only deepened by the fact that snowballing numbers of London's Bright Young Things were learning the rituals so beloved of Renton, Spud, Sick Boy et al.

'Heroin seemed to get fashionable,' says Frischmann. 'People would be doing Es, and at the end of the evening, it would come out on a bit of tinfoil. No-one was jacking it up; everyone was smoking it. It was being passed round like, "Ooh – try this, it's mellow and nice." So under those circumstances, it was in my immediate vicinity.'

It did not take that long for her curiosity to finally get the better of her. Donna Matthews dates Frischmann's first experience of heroin to before Annie Holland left Elastica; her own recollection is that she began using the drug in early 1996.

Whatever, rumours were quickly eddying around London that a musician renowned for her hard-headed drive, who had once baulked at her colleagues' fondness for amphetamine sulphate, whose boyfriend had so railed at Brett Anderson for experimenting with heroin – and whose father had insisted that she spurn art and study architecture, lest she fall into the lethargic ways of bohemia – was living the torpid life of a drug addict.

CHAPTER 17

'What am I doing? This is ridiculous.'

For the moment, Elastica's troubles remained a matter of conjecture: with no records scheduled for release, they were able to retreat behind closed doors. Besides, in the opening months of 1996, the British press had another story to chase: that, with the Gallagher brothers triumphant, Blur were spiralling towards a very messy demise.

Alex James remains of the opinion that, in the context of Oasis's ever-increasing success, even the most trivial wobble within the Blur camp was trumped up to the point that it looked like some life-threatening catastrophe. 'The battle of Britpop had been fought and won,' he says. 'Everything had to go right for the winner, and everything had to be going totally wrong for the loser.'

Blur's predicament was hardly eased by the fact that, despite their alleged fall from grace, they were still shadowed by a constant stream of observers sent by the British media. The run of promotion for *The Great Escape* extended into the spring of 1996; as Adrian Deevoy had discovered, the result was that Blur's more fractious moments were effectively played out in public.

'At the time, we were Big Brother contestants, really,' says Alex James. 'There wasn't a moment of our lives that wasn't being broadcast, filmed, or written about. There was always a journalist there. And when you're on the road, you go from almost having a punch up to very tender moments. It all happens every day. So it was very easy to say, "Graham calls Alex a wanker," because we would call each other a wanker – and mean it – a dozen times a day. But there was never any question that it would ever be anything other than the four of us. That was immutable. I certainly don't think anything else occurred to me. I don't know ... maybe everybody else hated me and I was within a hair's breadth of being thrown out of the band.'

Whatever the gap between the public perception of Blur's affairs and their actual state, the group's experiences in the first four months of 1996 certainly suggested a band that was reaching the end of its tether. In late February, they were booked to appear at the San Remo Festival – a syndicated TV bunfight, long a fixture of British groups' promotional schedules, which required little more of its guests than a few days spent in a faded Italian seaside resort and a willingness to mime to their latest hit.

Only Damon Albarn and Dave Rowntree made the trip. Graham Coxon had sent advance word that he would not be coming; Alex James overslept after yet another night of Soho roistering and missed the plane. Blur thus performed with a cardboard cut-out of Coxon, and the ever-dutiful Smoggy approximating James's bass part. News quickly reached the *NME*, where the story was put in a rather inevitable context. 'Blur last week fuelled rumours that they are about to split,' said the resulting report.

Six weeks later, by way of supporting the release of Charmless Man as a single, the group appeared on Chris Evans's *TFI Friday*: the garish, irony-caked TV show that was now enshrined, for better or worse, as Britpop's equivalent of *Ready Steady Go*. Looking forward to an evening's drinking, Mike Smith visited them on the set, only to find that Graham Coxon had once again gone missing. 'We were trying to find Graham all day,' he says, 'going round to his house and shouting through his letterbox, not knowing whether he'd turn up. They'd already done that show in Italy that Graham and Alex hadn't turned up for. At that time, there was definitely a sense of "This is not great."'

By then, thankfully, Damon Albarn had begun to plot the course that would allow his group to escape a great deal of what was corroding their morale. His plan – based on an alteration of both the group's aesthetic and their commercial horizons – was explained to Smith over one of their occasional Portobello Road breakfasts. 'Damon had realised the error of his ways,' says Smith. 'He sat down with me at the beginning of 1996, and said, "Bollocks to the arenas, bollocks to being as big as Bon Jovi, it's got to be about the music – about the art. I want to be taken seriously."'

In essence, Albarn was aiming at escaping Britpop. To accomplish such an aim, there was little doubt that – for a period at least – he would have to find a bolthole far away from London. By now, he and Justine Frischmann had started to equate the capital with the more unpalatable aspects of their success. They could still not venture out of their front door without fear of a paparazzo snapping even their most mundane movements; in early 1996, Frischmann watched, horrified, as their rubbish was stolen. The couple talked about buying a property in southern Europe, before Albarn decided that he wanted to fly north.

'He literally woke up one morning and said he'd been dreaming of windswept tundra, and said, "I must go to Iceland,"' says Justine Frischmann. 'And that was it. It was a real turning point for him. The cliché is finding a place in the sun. For him it wasn't exactly that, but it was a place where he didn't feel quite so hemmed in. I went a few times. I don't like cold; I felt like I was going in the wrong direction on the aeroplane. I wasn't that keen. I saw it as a slightly aggressive move, because we had been talking about Spain or France or Turkey; somewhere to have a flat where you could escape.'

'He met a nice Icelandic girl in Los Angeles, which I think made it even more alluring,' says Alex James. 'And he went out there. And about three days into his trip, I got a message on my answerphone: a voice of infinite calm saying, "Alex . . . it's . . . really . . . really . . . good . . . here." Which it really, really was.'

James would travel to Iceland later that year. 'It's a small, dynamic, outward-looking, exciting, resilient, poetic place,' he says, with no little enthusiasm. 'Somebody once said that everywhere you look in Iceland, you can see a distant horizon, 'cos it's mainly quite flat. That brings out the poetry in people: it's a land of two hundred and fifty thousand poets. And because it's very small, it's kind of ideal democracy size. You'll be in a bar getting absolutely pissed, talking to the bloke next to you, and he'll turn out to be the minister of finance. Everyone's got two jobs. Very modern. A lot less of the bullshit you get in big cities like London. There didn't seem many uncool people. Everybody seemed to be up for having a good time, and talking about horizons and poetry. And pixies.'

Through the spring, Albarn came to the conclusion that Iceland should become his second home. 'It changed my life,' he later reflected. 'It really is amazing. But I hope everyone doesn't go there now, 'cos it would turn into Ibiza, which would be terrible.' By the following year, encouraged by Albarn's pronouncements, parties of pop-cultural tourists would indeed be flocking to Reykjavik. For the moment, he was able to luxuriate in Iceland's serenity and work on a slew of new songs.

Unfortunately, if Albarn thought that Blur could make a clean break from Britpop, the summer brought rather unwelcome news. In April, thanks to a request from Damien Hirst for music that would soundtrack a short film, Alex James had recorded three songs with an ad hoc group called Me Me Me. He was joined by his friend Stephen Duffy (formerly the singer with an embryonic Duran Duran, who by now was a Britpop-affiliated singer-songwriter), Elastica's Justin Welch, and his one-time Charminster flatmate Charlie Bloor, who now worked for Westminster Council. The quartet soon decided to release their work on a single: when it came to choosing the A-side, the obvious candidate was a knockabout musical joke entitled Hanging Around.

Built from a hilariously banal lyric ('So he said how do you do/She said, talk about things/He said, he said, What do you do?/She said, I do anything'), a supercharged take on Britpop's stereotypical ooompah-oompah arrangement, and parping brass, Hanging Around was a work of very timely musical satire. Entirely deservedly, when it was released in August, its cause was taken up by Radio One, and it entered the charts at number nineteen.

In the meantime, Damon Albarn had attempted to veto the enterprise, via the group's old confidante Mike Smith. He had a professional stake in their world once again, having lured them to EMI's publishing wing with a contract reputed to be worth £4 million; as a result, he reluctantly found himself cast in the role of Albarn's last-ditch envoy. 'I was driving up the motorway, and I got Damon on the phone, going "You've got to stop Alex,"' he says. 'I had him on the phone for about an hour. You can imagine Damon's frustration: he's trying to get the band taken really seriously, he's moving away from the media and the frivolity and Cool Britannia. All that, and then Alex puts out Me Me Me. It's called Me Me Me, it had a beautiful, bright pop video – Alex, Stephen and Justin queening like mad, and having a great time. It was a celebration of all that was utterly ridiculous and absurd and great about pop music. You could see why that was at odds with where Damon wanted to go.'

'I suppose it was, wasn't it?' considers Alex James. 'That's what you get when you're in a band. It's the same as "Oh god, Dave's wearing those trousers again." It doesn't stop. You're always fighting your corner. I knew Damon hated that song, but that was the only track of the three that was going to get played on the radio. He was going, "Don't fucking release that, you cunt – release one of the other ones." I said, "I'm doing one bit of press and one TV show – it'll be fine."'

Me Me Me duly disbanded after a triumphant appearance on *Top of the Pops*. Talking to Alex James, it is difficult to avoid the conclusion that Albarn got off lightly: among James's other mooted projects at the time was a song called Proper Girls, which was to be recorded by 'a band with 100 women in it'. For one reason or another, the enterprise never got further than a handful of champagne-assisted conversations.

In truth, Albarn's flight from Britpop was complicated by at least one of his own commitments. Later that year, he would play a support-ing role – as a getaway driver named Jason – in a British film entitled *Face*, an East End gangster thriller starring Robert Carlyle and Ray Winstone. 'I've been getting back to my roots,' he explained, which rather sounded like the Damon Albarn of the previous year. None of his new songs were designed to be sung in his old faux-cockney accent; moreover, the prospect of minor movie stardom seemed to clash with Albarn's desire to reassert the fact that Blur were musicians.

Albarn was well aware of such contradictions. Unfortunately, his creeping unease about the project came up against the simple fact that he was legally bound to fulfil his obligations. 'I think he'd woken up and gone, "I'm trying to get the band taken really seriously, I'm really focused – and I'm about to appear in an East End gangster movie,"' says Mike Smith. 'He desperately wanted to get out of that project: it was like Sting. It was, "What am I doing? This is ridiculous." But he couldn't get out of it. Film contracts are very, very severe.'

In the early summer, Blur began to regroup. As with *Modern Life Is Rubbish*, *Parklife* and *The Great Escape*, the new album would be pro-duced by Stephen Street, who began his labours by attempting to unravel the group's ongoing wrangles. Inevitably, it was Graham Coxon who required the most attention: he and Street met for a drink in Camden Town, after which the latter reported back. His diagnosis, based in particular on Coxon's malign feelings towards Alex James, was hardly encouraging: 'I've done what I can but you'll have to tread carefully.'

Coxon's lingering resentments were at least partly allayed by a brief postal correspondence with Damon Albarn, suggested as a means of addressing some of the tension without the threat of raised voices or pregnant silence: 'You're braver when you're writing letters,' said Coxon. By way of making the process of rapprochement that bit easier, in June, Coxon decided to quit drinking, filling his suddenly vacant evenings by reviving his talent for painting. Meanwhile, he took increas-ing heart from the fact that Albarn had begun to share his listening habits.

Contrary to Britpop's in-built insistence on uniquely British in-fluences – which Albarn had so loudly advocated – he was now a vociferous fan of such US acts as Beck and Pavement, the Californian group whose music had moved from an angular approximation of the more avant-garde end of British indie-rock – and The Fall in par-ticular – to a broad palette that mixed irreverent wit, humorous warmth, and ramshackle musicianship to often wonderful effect. That year, their singer, Stephen Malkmus, was a house-guest of Albarn and

Frischmann; among Blur's inner circle, only Alex James seemed to be unwilling to embrace their influence. 'I didn't like that archness; pretending to be bad musicians,' he says. 'They sounded like a sixth form band to me.'

When Blur gathered in the recording studio, such misgivings were initially focused on the group's new material. Albarn and Coxon were clearly aiming at music that would nudge Blur into music's left-field; James thought they could play to rather more populist strengths. 'I thought we could still win a battle on the same battleground as before,' he says. 'But it was, "Cut to the quick! Back to the art-school roots! Retreat!" My only problem was that it felt a bit like scuffing up new trainers, and I'd be inclined to say, "They're just fucking new trainers – it'll be alright." The music was deliberately unprettified. Positively, pro-actively made less pretty. Not just done and left as an unpolished thing, but done and scuffed up. Things were being done to make the songs less like pop songs. Which, in hindsight, made people think we had depth.

'We'd worked so hard to get ourselves in that position – where if we had a single coming out, it was on the news. And suddenly we were making this music that was going to deliberately alienate a lot of people. But I suppose we had to make that turn. Damon was absolutely right.'

The abiding tone had perhaps been established at the outset of the sessions. 'Graham said, "I want to tune my guitars once at the beginning and that's it. Then I'm just going to leave them,"' says James. 'He was giving Stephen Street heart attacks. Streety used to go in at night and tune them.'

Among the first compositions Blur recorded was a song entitled Beetlebum. Its music was at least partly inspired by the sound The Beatles had minted on some of the tracks on the so-called *White Album* – on John Lennon songs like I'm So Tired and Happiness Is A Warm Gun, one can hear the same mix of a pared-down, percussive arrangement, and an underlying air of emotional intimacy. As with the former song, Beetlebum's music possessed a languid, resigned quality, which was in keeping with its lyrics. 'She turns me on/All my violence is gone,' Albarn sang, in a fragile falsetto. 'Nothing is wrong/I just slip away/And I am gone.' During its gloriously soporific coda, Albarn chorused a three-word refrain: 'He's on/He's on/He's on it.'

'I thought it was about Justine Frischmann,' says Alex James. 'It's a drug song, isn't it? All great pop songs are about love or drugs. And all really great pop songs are about both.'

Beetlebum would be released early in 1997. It was perhaps remarkable that a lyric so transparently about heroin did not attract more attention. Yet to those close to the London rumour-mill, it served decisive notice that the drug had entered Damon Albarn's immediate orbit. Indeed, owing to Justine Frischmann's heroin use, its soporific effects had started to define the terms of the couple's relationship. The tensions caused by her ongoing absence during 1995 – not to mention her scathing view of *The Great Escape* – seemed to ebb away; heroin rendered her an altogether more accommodating partner than her outspoken, trenchant nature might have suggested.

'I think it prolonged things,' she says. 'Because it made me more passive. It's something that you share with your partner, and it makes problems go away. You don't confront anything. You don't have problems if you're half asleep whenever you're together.'

Blur and Elastica's progress rather suggested an inescapable cycle: a big hit single launching eighteen months of ubiquity, before the more malign aspects of success forced either a retreat, an artistic rethink, or both. In time, the experiences of the other Britpop groups would confirm that only the most talented minds could successfully navigate all this: in many cases, the basic chapters of most careers – aspiration, achievement and rapid decline – were enacted over little more than three years.

Menswear, the group whose fate was umbilically linked to the waxing and waning of Britpop, appeared to be no exception – but one key aspect of their fate set them apart: it was their creditable achievement to cram the whole process into little more than twelve months.

Their first single, I'll Manage Somehow, had been released in April 1995. By the summer, Daydreamer – the churning, Wire-inspired, one-chord composition that sounded not unlike an Elastica cast-off – had breached the top 20. And, though the weekly music press recurrently viewed them with a rather sniffy disdain, Menswear could take heart from the fact that the demographic represented by *Smash Hits* seemed to be obediently falling into line. Certainly, the scenes that were soon played out at their live shows said as much. 'Seventy-five per cent of our audience was fifteen-year-old girls,' says Simon White. 'There was a lot of screaming at our gigs. Especially the London shows. When we played at Shepherd's Bush Empire, it was just deafening. My dad came down for it, and he just couldn't believe it. I actually found it totally embarrassing.'

Adrian Webb, the manager who had steered the group's progress using a mixture of cheek and ludicrous bravado, drew rather more comfort from the adolescent screeches; for him, they provided welcome proof that everything was falling into place. 'Shepherd's Bush was like you would imagine a Bay City Rollers gig to have been,' he says. 'But that was the market we set out to take. The idea was to be the indie Take That.'

For all Simon White's discomfort, his new-found celebrity seemed to have plenty of benefits. In Camden Town, the members of Menswear took great delight in carrying themselves with all the regal swagger of young aristocrats. Much of their fanmail was sent to The Good Mixer, where they proudly held court; beholding all five members playing pool, at least one observer was heard to wonder if they were doing so at their record company's insistence. When the deluge of pop-cultural tourists became too much, Menswear moved to the rather more plush Spread Eagle on Camden Parkway. As if to confirm their cultural potency, most of the North London in-crowd quickly followed them.

Better still, on the frequent occasions that the group crossed paths with their rather more experienced peers, they tended to find nothing but goodwill. On one occasion, Noel Gallagher cornered the group at Stringfellows and graciously told them that if Oasis were the new Beatles, he figured that Menswear had a claim to being The Faces. 'He was going on about how there was room for everyone,' says Simon White. 'I think he was on an E that night.

'I'd met all the bands that I really liked,' says White, 'and I was going to a lot of parties and clubs. I was taking a lot of drugs: a lot of E, cocaine, and smoking draw constantly. Drinking all the time. We didn't have to pay for drinks at most places. Most people would give us drugs, give us drinks . . . there was always somewhere to blag into. Because we were well-known then, kind of famous, we could go to these clueless media parties, and they would let us in and be impressed by the fact that we were there.'

Over the summer of 1995, the group recorded their debut album. Their repertoire had now been fattened up to the point that they had well over a dozen songs: the result was a record that, though it regularly betrayed the group's inexperience, at least held out the prospect of more hit singles.

They decided to title it *Nuisance*; it was released in October. 'I must admit that as soon as it came out, I started to get the feeling that a black cloud was following us around,' says Simon White. 'The longer it went on, the more holes in the whole thing started to appear. Nothing seemed to be very well organised. Sometimes we would end up doing these terrible, crap TV shows, where no-one knew why we were there.'

By now, most of the group had decided to propel themselves through their promotional chores with the aid of all manner of pharmaceuticals. 'When we were in America, we were buying over-the-counter drugs to take,' says White. 'We heard about these 222 codeine pills that you could get in Canada, and so we loaded up with them. And we were buying NiQuil, an opiated cough mixture, because we knew it had active ingredients in it. It was a recreational thing, I suppose. I remember doing the Jack Dee Show, and taking about twenty Codeine pills and drinking half a bottle of wine.'

It was perhaps not surprising that the mixture of chemical excess and a gruelling schedule quickly led at least one of the group towards incapacitation. Like Damon Albarn in 1994, Simon White started to become acquainted with panic attacks. 'My heart would start racing, and I would start getting, like, *rushes*,' he says. 'It felt like I was going to have a heart attack or something.'

In November, Menswear passed through the kind of weekend that might have rattled even the most stable minds. 'We got back from a European tour on a Friday,' says Adrian Webb. 'Saturday, we rehearsed for the *Smash Hits* Poll Winners Party, Sunday we did it, Monday we flew to Japan. And at the airport, Simon was going, "I can't go, I can't go – I can't get on the plane." He was a little bit of a drama queen, so I was saying, "Don't be ridiculous – get on that plane. This is our most important market in the world." They were all prone to throwing rock star strops at that point. They were believing the press.

'I got him on the plane. And we got to Japan, and on the first night there, Simon was wandering the corridors of the hotel in his pyjamas. I said, "Shit, you are seriously ill." He was obviously on the verge of a breakdown; a look of absolute fear in his eyes, not really knowing where he was or why he was there. I booked him a flight, phoned his mother. She was worried, to say the least. I said, "Get him medical help. These are the accountant's details. Any bill will be picked up by us."'

Adrian Webb was little short of terrified, not only of irate Japanese promoters, but by the prospect of the tour's projected profits – no less than £350,000 – falling through the group's hands. One Paul Fletcher, a multi-instrumentalist who had been hired to play keyboards, was rapidly persuaded to learn White's guitar parts, and the group spent a fortnight entertaining arenas full of Japanese fans. Their commercial clout was illustrated by the impossibility of going anywhere without organised security; in Tokyo, Webb recalls being mobbed in a branch of McDonald's, whose staff allowed the group to make a desperate exit through the kitchens.

Simon White – who says, without any hint of melodrama, that he was fearing for his sanity – duly became a patient at a private clinic near Bristol. 'They didn't put me in the drug addiction program, because I'd already really stopped taking drugs,' he says. 'They said I was suffering from exhaustion, and they recommended I do nothing. They put me in a ward with anorexics and manic depressives. I had to eat five meals a day, and wasn't allowed to do anything, apart from exercise.

'I got felt up by a big fat old nurse the first day, which was a bit depressing. I stayed there about two weeks, and then just thought, "I can't deal with this anymore." ' White returned to his family home over Christmas, re-emerging with a new-found resolve to avoid drugs, an anxiety even about excessive drinking, and a fondness for physical exercise. He also took to wearing elastic bands on his arms, having discovered that snapping them against his wrists was a reliable way of staving off panic attacks.

Within months, Johnny Dean, the singer whose demeanour managed to combine preening narcissism with an evident insecurity, had also plunged into psychological trauma. His episode occurred when the group were on tour in Spain.

'That was due to cocaine,' says Adrian Webb, 'and a very inept security guard. We were in Barcelona. We got to the venue, and it was the usual question: "Mr manager, can you get us some drugs?" I was with – how can I put this – a representative of our agency, who procured the drugs from the promoter. Chris and I did a line each and just went, "*Fucking hell* – this is the purest cocaine we've ever taken in our lives." There were two wraps, one of which kept me and two friends going for four days. I gave the other gram to the security guy and said, "Do not, on any account, let any one member of the band stay up with this. Let them have a line each after the gig tomorrow." He then proceeded to let Johnny do the entire gram himself.

'It was total cocaine psychosis. He thought John Lennon was talking to him, telling him not to play the gig, so he didn't. The band did a set of instrumentals, with Simon doing vocals as and when he could remember the words. We were very lucky; we had no comeback from the promoter, because he'd supplied us with the cocaine in the first place. How was the gig? I don't know. I wasn't there.'

Despite such horrors, the early months of 1996 represented Menswear's apex. In March, Being Brave – the group's obligatory string-laden ballad – entered the singles chart at number ten. Better still, they seemed to have the perfect follow-up: a version of the old Easy Listening standard Can't Smile Without You, recorded for a charity album to be released by Island Records. Island were keen to pair the song with Pulp's version of Thin Lizzy's Whiskey In The Jar and release a double A-sided single; Adrian Webb believed that the idea held the promise of Menswear's biggest hit to date. Led by Simon White, however, the group refused to entertain the idea. 'It was, "We don't want to release Can't Smile Without You, we don't want to be a pop band, we want to be a serious group." I just thought, "You *can't* be."'

By now, however, White's discomfort with the universe of *Smash Hits* was dominating Menswear's thinking. Matt Everitt, the drummer who had seemed both perfectly happy to be a member of the indie Take That and opinionated enough to challenge White's standpoint, was fired in the spring; Adrian Webb saw the move as another shift away from Menswear's stock-in-trade. 'He was acting like a bit of a twat, I suppose. But we all were. When you have record companies throwing money at you and telling you you're set to be the new Beatles, you do become a bit of an arsehole. He was very skilfully manipulated out.'

As the year progressed, Menswear's internal politics changed yet further. By now, they had six members: White, Johnny Dean, Chris Gentry, Stuart Black, a replacement drummer named Darren Tudgay and the aforementioned Paul Fletcher, given a full-time position on account of his heroic efforts in Japan. In the wake of his Spanish episode, Dean was publicly wondering whether pop stardom represented quite the glamorous nirvana that he had expected, and stepping back from the group's creative core. More seriously, Chris Gentry was now a resident of the same lethargic world as Elastica.

He had started going out with Donna Matthews in late 1994; though she had spent the lion's share of 1995 on tour, the two had resumed their relationship on her return. By early 1996, Gentry was living at her increasingly notorious King's Cross abode, and dabbling with heroin.

'Donna's place was like Mick Jagger's house in *Performance*,' says Adrian Webb. 'It was quite frightening. And that's how Chris got into heroin – which is basically what destroyed the prospects for Menswear's second album. He lost interest. He'd written most of the music on *Nuisance*, but you were now left with Simon, Stuart and Darren Tudgay as principal songwriters, and they decided to take Menswear in a West Coast rock direction. It wasn't the wisest move. A nineteen-year-old boy student isn't going to suddenly turn round and go, "Oh, actually, I like Menswear." They're going to say, "Fuck off – you're that pop band that my fourteen-year-old sister likes."'

Webb paid a few visits to the King's Cross house. 'In some ways it was very, very decadent,' he says, 'but it was also quite boring.' On one occasion, he recalls entering what he calls 'the inner sanctum' and finding Gentry, Matthews and a couple of members of another successful Britpop group gouched out around the table. 'They were all doing heroin and all dressed in black,' he says. 'And I just thought, "This is something of a cliché, actually."'

'I did talk to Chris,' says Webb, 'but with people doing drugs, the more you tell them not to do it, the more they're likely to go ahead and do it. It was a very difficult situation to be in – trying to get Chris interested in the band again. And at the same time, I had to cover him with the record company. They had always said, "If any of the band get into heroin, we'll drop them immediately." They would say, "How's Chris?", and I'd be like, "Fine, fine! Absolutely fine!", while inwardly going, "*Shit.*"'

In August, the group unveiled their new single. We Love You was a fairly flimsy attempt to capture the Californian joie de vivre of The Beach Boys; as if to serve notice that their days as a teen-oriented pop group were numbered, Simon White had also tried to capture the influence of Randy Newman. In addition, the group had a new look: by now, their fondness for suits had been superseded by saggy casualwear, presumably intended to convey the idea that the days of gimmickry and glamour were over. 'It was all going wrong by the time We Love You came out,' says Adrian Webb. 'I looked at them and thought, "You don't look like you want to sell records. You look like you don't give a fuck."'

To Menswear's dismay, the single stalled at number twenty-two. In its wake, they were packed off to Japan to appear in a TV spectacular, and give a handful of interviews. Their approach to such chores betrayed their plummeting enthusiasm. Worse still, to Adrian Webb's horror, they made at least one smirking reference to Britpop's increasing links to heroin.

'The band were being rude to reporters in interviews, which is a big no-no in Japan,' he says. 'Someone asked them about what was going on in London and they said, "You should go to Camden and ask for the brown." It was, "You really don't want this any more, do you? You seem to be doing the most you possibly can to completely sabotage your own career."'

Despite the fact that his world had expanded way beyond the rather parochial concerns of the British music papers, Noel Gallagher still made a point of voraciously reading them each Wednesday. It was through the pages of the *NME* and *Melody Maker* that he received word of Menswear's problems. 'Me and our kid pissed ourselves laughing,' he said. 'We opened the press to find out that poor Johnny and poor Simon from Menswear have had nervous breakdowns . . . It was like, "You want to try being me and this cunt for an afternoon. You'd slit your own fuckin' throat, mate."'

Such was yet another aspect of the Gallaghers' self-trumpeted difference from the groups they tended to see as part of some arty-farty London conspiracy. While Menswear fretted about their schedule, Blur argued about the ethics of success and Justine Frischmann clung nervously to the notion of being 'underground', Oasis's stratospheric success seemed to cause them no angst whatsoever. Liam in particular did not seem to possess even the merest iota of self-doubt: considering his drug intake, the fact that he apparently remained indestructible was no mean feat. 'In 1996, I was doing as much cocaine as anyone you've ever heard of,' he later reflected. The drug's effects are manifested in crushing melancholy as well as swaggering confidence; in public, at least, Liam Gallagher suggested that he was fortunate enough to have avoided the downside completely.

The Gallaghers' fondness for cocaine was underwritten by their snowballing wealth. Given Wonderwall's global ubiquity, Noel Gallagher's authorship of that song alone was enough to make him a fortune; when one factored in the receipts from all his other compositions, it was instantly clear that he had joined the ranks of the super-rich. Though Oasis's junior members were not quite as affluent, from late 1995 onwards, they too had seen their bank balances swell to mind-boggling proportions. 'I was out with a mate once,' says Paul Arthurs. 'I said, "Can we stop at the cash machine?" I pressed "Display balance" and it said, "Your balance is £480,000." He was like, "Is that right?" I said, "Look at *that*! Check it out!"'

In the context of the group's ever-increasing riches, it was perhaps not surprising that one ghost from the Gallaghers' past should make an unwelcome reappearance. On 22 March, Oasis played the first of two shows at Dublin's Point Depot. They were billeted to the Westbury Hotel, off Grafton Street: upon their arrival, a message from one of their fellow guests was delivered to both Gallagher brothers. To Liam and Noel's evident dismay, Tommy Gallagher had decided to join them. The fact that he was aided and abetted by a *News of the World* journalist named Jane Atkinson – who doubtless saw Ireland as a poetic backdrop to the story – perhaps undermined his protestations that his reappearance was caused by a sudden pang of belated obligation.

That weekend was not the best occasion for such events. Peggy Gallagher was travelling with the Oasis party; fortuitously, she avoided much of the fuss, given that she was booked into a different hotel. To complicate matters yet further, Oasis's Irish fans, doubtless aware of the parentage of four-fifths of the group, greeted their arrival in Dublin with a hysteria that meant that the group had to be shepherded around the city in the manner of visiting foreign dignitaries. All that aside, they had to perform in front of two packed houses: the trauma reawakened by Tommy Gallagher's appearance did not seem likely to assist their preparation.

Against not inconsiderable odds, the first of the shows went impressively well. The group duly returned to the Westbury's chintzy lobby bar, where the usual revels began. They were curtailed, however, when Tommy shuffled into eyeshot. 'He turned up at the hotel,' says Paul Arthurs. 'There was a big to-do. We all just sat in the bar while he was sorted out: "Come on – do one. You shouldn't be here." Liam and Noel were very on edge. It was a horrible journalistic stunt; turn up, cause a scene, here's a few quid. Noel was saying to Liam, "Calm down. Chill." And Liam says, "Calm down? I'm going to *kill* him." It freaked them.'

In the wake of the day's events, the *News of the World* evidently thought it had got its money's worth. The resultant article, peppered with the usual human debris of family break-ups – a sick aunt named Kathleen, the Gallaghers' pining paternal grandmother, Annie – claimed that Tommy 'choked back tears of disappointment as he explained how he had made an emotional pilgrimage to Dublin in the hope of ending a bitter 11-year feud.' To add to the fun, tapes of two phone conversations between Liam and Tommy, the result of the delivery of his initial message, were made available on a special phone line: at the bargain rate of 39p a minute, one could hear such words of familial rapprochement as 'If I catch you walking round the lobby in this hotel, you're going to get your legs fucking broke.' From then on, many of those who had been used to sharing Oasis's orbit, striding into dressing rooms and foyers with only the most informal accreditation, discovered that the usual doors had suddenly been locked shut.

As it turned out, Tommy Gallagher posed a relatively minor threat to Oasis's universe. On 27 and 28 April 1996, the group were booked to perform at Maine Road, the home of their beloved Manchester City. The engagement had been conceived with a deliberate romance, holding out the promise of a deeply spectacular homecoming. Unfortunately, if their previous professional visits to Manchester had been characterised by the local hoods attempting to muscle in on their merchandising or security, it was some token of Oasis's new celebrity that this time, some of the city's gangsters had something more ambitious in mind.

'Someone had threatened to kidnap Liam,' says Paul Arthurs. 'And knowing the mentality of some of the gangsters in Manchester . . . I could imagine it. It was taken seriously. The security was really, really on at that gig. Double tight. People were patrolling corridors, constantly.'

The Maine Road concerts proved to be an undoubted triumph, infused with all the prodigal-son magic that Oasis had intended. On both nights, when they flipped out of a defiant plod through The Swamp Song into an impassioned performance of Acquiesce, it was instantly clear that despite all manner of superficial handicaps – chiefly, their statuesque stage presence – Oasis had become confident speakers of the grandiloquent language known as Stadium Rock.

It was at Maine Road that, with an eye on the line that separates mere pictures from iconography, Noel Gallagher played a guitar – first unveiled that February on *Top of the Pops* – resprayed in the colours of the Union Jack. Less than four years before, the *NME* had characterised Morrissey's flag-waving as a provocative dalliance with right-wing imagery; it was some token of Britpop's purging of such anxieties that the paper made its only comment on Gallagher's guitar in a celebratory caption: 'Union Jack The Lad: Noel Gallagher goes Mod for It!' Somewhere, Morrissey must have been angrily chewing his knuckles.

As had happened at Earl's Court, the guest-list contained the odd unlikely name: Alex 'Hurricane' Higgins, Angus Deayton, much of the cast of *Brookside*. In keeping with the fact that the gigs' location lent them the very zeitgeisty sense of rock music colliding with soccer, there was also an abundance of football players; among those who were waved into Maine Road's VIP enclosure were the likes of David Beckham, Ryan Giggs, Gary Neville and Graham Le Saux, along with most of Manchester City's first eleven. These, it was fair to say, were not the kind of people whom the staff of Creation Records were used to entertaining.

In the wake of Maine Road, Oasis's pre-eminence was illustrated by one of the *NME*'s periodic attempts at inventing a new musical genre. As if to inflate Noel Gallagher's self-belief to the point that he drifted off towards the moon, their latest concept was called Noelrock; it was founded on the notion that the older Gallagher was now so powerful that his tastes were dictating the prevailing direction of British rock music. 'If Noel Gallagher, the most successful songwriter of his generation, champions a group,' said the article, 'then said group are guaranteed more kudos and, quite possibly, more sales. And since Noel has taken to championing only five or six groups, then it's a powerful cabal he's promoting.'

Some of the acts featured in the *NME*'s article had appeared in *Select*'s post-Oasis predictions the previous summer. Twelve months on, the list had been swelled by a handful of new names, and the upper end of this New Wave – the Liverpudlian quartet Cast, Birmingham's Ocean Colour Scene – were enjoying enviable success. Among several common bonds, they, Oasis and their other allies seemed to be tied together by a fundamentalism: a dewy-eyed love of the 1960s, a spurning of much beyond rock's most basic ingredients, and a belief in the supremacy of 'real music'. Such a credo had partly underpinned Oasis's feuding with Blur; now, it was starting to define a sizeable portion of the rock mainstream.

Noel Gallagher was not the sole mover behind all this. There was little doubt that his view of ongoing developments was influenced by his new friend Paul Weller, with whom he had habitually shared concert stages and recording studios over the past eighteen months. After a five-year lull, Weller's career had been reawakened by the release of his second solo album *Wild Wood*, a pared-down, pastoral work that emphasised themes of self-doubt and eventual redemption. However, if its lyrics were bound up with an introspective fragility, Weller's interviews suggested that, when it came to the wider world, he knew exactly where he stood: given that it lacked a vital kind of authenticity, most modern music was worthy of little more than withering contempt. 'People come up to me and say, "Listen to this record, it's fucking brilliant,"' he said. 'And I get it home and it's a piece of shit. If you think Elastica or the new whatever-it-is are great, I'd like to play some records to you. I could play you things that'd blow your mind.' By the time of 1995's *Stanley Road*, his worldview – founded on his reverence for many of British music's founding fathers – seemed more unshakeable than ever.

At the age of thirty-seven, after almost twenty years making records, Weller was probably entitled to such a credo. After all, he had spent much of the 80s in thrall to an approach so adventurous that it had frequently prompted loud ridicule. The Style Council, the ever-changing enterprise he had formed in 1983 and disbanded five years later, had attempted to found their progress on an exotic mixture of left-wing politics, a love of jazz, lyrics sung in French and a distinctly bizarre sense of humour. In terms of musical quality, the venture was more successful than many retrospective accounts suggest, but its presentation eventually sealed its fate. By the time they called it quits – after a house-influenced album entitled *Modernism: A New Decade* had been rejected by their record company – The Style Council were rock critics' favourite punch-bag. It was perhaps not surprising that, having had his fingers so comprehensively burned, Weller should retreat behind the eternal verities of technical proficiency and proper songs.

Unfortunately, in the hands of younger musicians, such beliefs were vulgarised into a conservatism that often bordered on the moronic. Whereas Weller had long boasted an impressive knowledge of soul, jazz and 70s funk, the worldview of his new protégés seemed to be a lot more reductive. In February 1996, Noel Gallagher had appeared as a guest DJ on Greater London Radio. Musicians tend to use these occasions to shine light on the more esoteric corners of their record collections; by contrast, most of Noel's selections sounded like a Saturday night session on a pub jukebox. In addition to songs by some of the Noelrock bands, he played The Sex Pistols' Anarchy In The UK, The Stone Roses' I Wanna Be Adored, John Lennon's Imagine, The Who's Anyway, Anyhow, Anywhere and The Kinks' Waterloo Sunset.

It was this approach that one sensed in the crop of British groups who stamped their presence on 1996. In the eyes of the more crass sections of the media, they seemed to be prolonging the fun of Britpop, but since the halcyon days of 1994, the prevailing agenda had been comprehensively rerouted. In place of the artful, multi-faceted approach that had been embodied by *Parklife*, music seemed to be hacked down to its most predictable essence. The change could even be observed in Oasis themselves: whereas Supersonic and Shakermaker had been founded on a quality later summed up by one critic as 'guttersnipe surrealism', the success of Wonderwall seemed to have sealed the idea that their trump-card was Noel Gallagher's talent for crafting populist anthems. It was this aspect of Britpop that would characterise its rather lamentable legacy: the guiding of rock music away from dissent and experimentalism, towards a field full of people holding up their cigarette lighters.

CHAPTER 18

'Is this cool or not cool?'

In the wake of the Maine Road concerts, Oasis announced that on 10 and 11 August, they were on to play two shows at Knebworth Park, Hertfordshire, to a total of 250,000 people. In response, there were 2.6 million applications for tickets: one in twenty-four of the population wanted to go and see them. If Britpop was built on the hope that rock music could tie the UK into a moment of blissful musical unity, such news surely represented its high watermark.

'We could have done sixteen nights at Knebworth,' says Alan McGee. 'That's how mad it was. That's how big Oasis were. Oasis were so fucking big, if Noel Gallagher had stood for Prime Minister, he could probably have got twenty-five per cent of the vote.' The words are suffused with McGee's customary hyperbole, yet they tap into the mind-boggling moment that Knebworth represented. Indeed, having surveyed the statistics and beheld the concerts' endless human expanse, even the most sceptical minds may well have concluded that Oasis had surmounted rock folklore's most impossible obstacle. For that brief moment, they may just have been bigger than The Beatles.

'We have sold more records than The Beatles,' concluded Noel Gallagher, sitting in one of Knebworth's backstage Portakabins. 'We've played bigger gigs than The Beatles. I will say, yeah, we are bigger than The Beatles.' He then paused. 'But you've got to look at it this way, right? If The Beatles had formed in 1991 and started off with *Rubber Soul*, they'd be bigger than us now. They had better songs.'

If the words sounded dangerously close to humility, a moment's reflection suggested otherwise: Noel's rather laboured hypotheses implied that only with their sixth album had The Beatles managed a record as good as *Definitely Maybe*. Besides, his next quote was triumphalism incarnate: 'We are the biggest band in Britain of all time, ever,' he concluded.

If he was right, by the time Oasis prepared for the gigs, they did not exactly look the part. Evidence was provided by a photo-call staged twenty-four hours before the first performance. Paul Arthurs, Alan White and Paul McGuigan had never been expected to fulfil any rock star archetypes – but the Gallaghers did not look much prettier. Having just emerged from a three-month holiday, Noel Gallagher had put on weight. His face was round and jowly; dressed in the kind of coat made for all-weather hiking, his hair cut into its customary mop, he did not exactly cut a dash.

Even Liam, who could usually be relied upon to provide a smidgeon of rock star glamour, faced the cameras dressed in the kind of leather jacket that rather suggested an ill-advised impulse buy at C&A. Those who had conquered Knebworth in the past included The Rolling Stones, Led Zeppelin and Queen – all, in their own way, emblematic of the idea that it was incumbent upon stars to convey a sense of flamboyant otherness. It was Oasis's peculiar achievement to play two gigs in front of 125,000 people looking like they had randomly been drawn from their ranks.

And yet maybe that was the point. Knebworth – preceded by two 30,000-capacity performances at Balloch Castle, near Loch Lomond – was the decisive dramatisation of their myth: the passage of, to use one of Liam's malapropisms, 'average day lads' from roughnecked beginnings to the Top Of The World. When, at the end of each night's performance, they stood at the lip of the stage and applauded the crowd, the sense that they had not forgotten their roots was made explicit.

There were aspects of the weekend, however, that rather jarred against all that. 'I always find VIP bits hilarious, 'cos the whole point of punk rock was to get rid of fucking VIP bits,' says Alan McGee. 'But the Creation hospitality tent was fucking top. It was bigger than most of my bands could *play*.'

Out in the fields, unfortunately, Oasis's public were having a slightly less splendid time. Much to the group's annoyance, the tabloid newspapers' subsequent coverage of Knebworth would zero in on the privations that came from standing in a crowd numbering an eighth of a million. *The Sun* made reference to 'two-hour queues at the beer tent and a 90-minute wait to use the loos'. *The Mirror* invited survivors to send in their complaints: the merits of Oasis's performances were submerged by far more mundane considerations. 'The sound was pretty abysmal,' wrote one fan, 'but my main criticism is that the queues were too big . . . And we paid £4 for chicken nuggets and chips.'

Alan McGee, meanwhile, was discovering that he too was suffering on account of the event's size. 'Three times during the day, they wouldn't let me in my own tent,' he says. 'I had to go and shout and get someone to go, "Oh, it's you." And we had all these sponsorship deals so that we would get drink, and I remember going up, saying, "Can I have a Perrier water?" And they said, "You can only have alcohol." I said, "I don't think you understand." It was so removed from reality.'

On Saturday 10 August, Oasis were flown to Knebworth from Battersea heliport. Soon after his arrival, Noel Gallagher took a bath in Knebworth House, where he was delivered a bottle of champagne by someone he assumed to be a member of the site's staff. By way of underlining his importance, it turned out to be Lord Cobbold, the owner of the estate.

On both days, the group were preceded by a bill that combined a gaggle of post-Oasis bands – Cast, Ocean Colour Scene, the flatly awful 60s revivalists Kula Shaker – with the likes of The Chemical Brothers, Manic Street Preachers and The Prodigy. While the supporting features rattled through their sets, the members of Oasis counted away the hours in five mobile homes, in which – thanks to the logistical difficulties of a quick getaway – they also stayed, with their wives and girlfriends, on the Saturday night. Liam Gallagher was the one exception: at Patsy Kensit's insistence, the couple stayed with the road crew at a hotel in nearby Stevenage.

'It was very Butlins,' says Paul Arthurs. 'Weird, really. Liam said, "Fuck this." And Patsy was being a film star: "I'm not showering in *that*."'

When Oasis took the stage, they could not help but crow about the achievement that Knebworth represented. On the Saturday, Liam Gallagher was first to a microphone, surveying the multitudes and sarcastically mewling the hookline from Blur's *Parklife*: 'All the people, so many people . . .' Twenty-four hours later, his brother was the first to speak, dispensing a rather less comic greeting. 'This is *history*!' yelped Noel, with no little gravitas. 'Right here, right now, this is *history*!' Finding the opportunity to burst his bubble too good to pass up, Liam provided the punchline. 'Really?' he shot back. 'I thought it was Knebworth.'

Each night's set began with Columbia, the menacing song from *Definitely Maybe* whose reappearance in their set threw the crowd a noticeable curveball. From there, however, Oasis joyously piled through an array of crowd-pleasers – Acquiesce, Supersonic, Some Might Say, Roll With It, Cigarettes And Alcohol, Live Forever. They also played two new compositions, My Big Mouth and It's Getting Better (Man!!), whose adrenalised tones seemed to suggest that Noel Gallagher's populist songwriting knack remained intact. On both Saturday and Sunday, their closing renditions of Champagne Supernova and I Am The Walrus featured John Squire – the guitar virtuoso who had announced his exit from The Stone Roses that April; so it was that a member of Oasis's second favourite group added his talents to a song by their first. Once that moment was over, the audience left under a blaze of fireworks, while those on the guest-list made merry until the wee hours in Creation's tent.

By now, although his bond with Noel Gallagher had once formed a crucial ley-line within Oasis's world, Tim Abbot had been nudged out of the inner circle. To his displeasure, he had had to make waves with Ignition Management to secure his desired ticket allocation; rather than partying until daybreak in the inner sanctum, he made his way home in the company of Jarvis Cocker and Steve Mackey from Pulp. 'We went to observe,' he says. 'We drove off in a jeep: it was "Fuck the queues," and we went off-road, through the fields. Everybody was going, "That's it then, isn't it?" Not like, "You can't top that"; more like, "How vulgar was *that*?"'

In time, Noel would appear to share such misgivings. 'We're not doing gigs as big as that any more,' he said the following year. 'I'm not, anyway. They're too big. You do it once and you can't be doing it again.'

Perhaps predictably, his brother was having none of it. 'Why can't you?' Liam implored. 'It was a great day out. Packed lunch, all that: it was a *great day*.'

Knebworth formed one aspect of a summer that saw the UK reaching quite remarkable levels of cultural unanimity. Between June and September, the conclusion that millions of Britons were singing from the same hymn sheet was not simply the stuff of tabloid sentimentalism: walking around the country's towns and cities, leafing through both *The Sun* and the *Guardian*, or flitting through the TV channels, one did get the feeling that any guns still rattling out the divisive battles of the 80s had been silenced.

Much of this was down to those two great examples of social glue, music and sport. But even the fractious world of politics seemed to be held together by a new air of consensual certainty. With the Conservative government rattled by yet another crisis – this time, the scourge of mad cow disease – the prospect of Tony Blair entering 10 Downing Street was looking ever more concrete. By the autumn, he felt sufficiently confident to put himself forward as the focus of a new national unity. 'We're on the same side,' he assured those who had voted Conservative, but were now wavering. 'We're in the same team.'

On 8 June, a match between England and Switzerland began the 1996 European Championships. That they were being held in England on the thirtieth anniversary of the country's illustrious World Cup win over West Germany was hardly going to go unnoticed: just as Oasis and Blur had spent the previous summer compared to The Beatles and The Stones, so the national football team were seen as potential successors to Geoff Hurst, Nobby Stiles et al. It was a seductive vision; if the Welsh and Northern Irish were not included in the party, and the Scots had their own team to support, most of the occupants of England seemed to rise happily to the occasion.

The previous summer, prior to the Blur/Oasis feud, there had been a brief spurt of tabloid speculation about the two groups collaborating on the official Euro '96 anthem. It was a forlorn hope: as it turned out, the job was given to an alliance of The Lightning Seeds, the group-cum-studio project commanded by Ian Broudie, and Frank Skinner and David Baddiel, hosts of the irritatingly smug TV show *Fantasy Football League*. The result was a song entitled Three Lions. If its synthesised arrangement left it some distance from being a Britpop record, it still pushed a lot of Britpop buttons – not only on account of its stomping rhythm, but the fact that its chorus had a distinct Oasis-like aspect.

'We didn't want to do a big patriotic "rah rah rah" song,' said Skinner. 'It's not blindly optimistic, because when people get like that you just think, "Oh God, they're just being stupid." But if we say, "Well, we have been a bit shit, but I think we might actually be getting better" . . . I think people relate to it far more.' For whatever reason, Three Lions did its work to impressive effect: when England defeated Spain on penalties in the quarter finals, much of the home crowd remained on the Wembley stands to euphorically bellow its hookline: 'It's coming home/It's coming home/It's coming/Football's coming home . . .'

With the beer'n'footy culture peddled by *Loaded* magazine – and bolted on to Britpop – at its absolute peak, it was hardly surprising that the build-up to the championships caught the imagination of the UK's musicians. There was a commemorative compilation album entitled *The Beautiful Game*, featuring a clutch of specially recorded songs – of which Black Grape's England's Irie was far and away the best, setting out to sound a note of cheerleading oomph, but embodying the giggly absurdism that comes with heavy marijuana smoking – along with such crowd-pleasing staples as Blur's Parklife.

It was launched by a celebrity-strewn England v Scotland match at Wembley Stadium, in which the likes of Damon Albarn, Phil Daniels, and members of Primal Scream, Supergrass and Massive Attack displayed varying levels of sporting ability. Anyone wondering what had happened to the idea that rock musicians were meant to be wheezing low-lifes could at least take heart from the fact that Gaz Coombes flew the flag of the effete aesthete. 'I had to come off the pitch and throw up,' he gasped. 'I haven't eaten for three days and I started feeling really ill in the middle of the game. The pitch is fucking huge. I can't believe you're meant to run up and down there hundreds of times.'

Once England's fans had recovered from the national team's achingly inevitable ejection at the hands of the Germans – and the courts had dealt with 200 toughs arrested in central London after the defeat – Euro '96 entered the national psyche as something of an epiphany. Certainly, Three Lions quickly became a rabble-rousing standard, working its reliably Pavlovian effects at hundreds of awards ceremonies, company conferences and morale-building awaydays.

On 1 October, Tony Blair made his keynote speech at Labour's conference. To no little fanfare, he set out a ten-point 'performance contract', a series of policy pledges in the rather ill-advised form of vows. He also reiterated one of the central themes of his conference address the previous year – the idea, doubtless inspired by the apparently rude health of the UK's pop culture, that Britain could come to reflect the strident potency of youth. 'I want us to be a young country again,' he said. 'With a common purpose. With ideals we cherish and live up to. Not resting on past glories. Not fighting old battles. Not sitting back, hand in mouth, concealing a yawn of cynicism, but ready for the day's challenge. Ambitious. Idealistic. United.' His speech concluded with a craftily populist rallying call. 'Eighteen years of hurt never stopped us dreaming,' he said, affecting his increasingly familiar approximation of statesmanlike destiny. 'Labour's coming home.'

Three days earlier, Blair had managed to link himself with the summer's other popular phenomenon. On the evening of 28 September, he stepped on to a stage at Blackpool's Norbreck Castle Hotel and was handed a specially inscribed Oasis platinum disc by Alan McGee. The occasion was Labour's oddly-named Youth Experience Rally, sponsored by Creation Records, at which 18 Wheeler, one of the label's minnows, were introduced by Blair as 'Wheeler 18', and Steve Coogan interviewed the Leader of the Opposition in the guise of Alan Partridge.

Throughout this part of the evening, Blair wore a deeply nervous grin, like an over-eager teacher embroiled in a playground snowball fight.

Blair duly paid tribute to McGee's company, though his words betrayed the fact that he was unaware of the glory years of financial ineptitude and ephedrine tablets. With a grandly revisionist sweep, Blair recast Creation as a shining example of hard-headed entrepreneurship.

'It's a great company,' he said. 'We should be really proud of it. Alan's just been telling me he started twelve years ago with a one thousand pound bank loan and now it's got a thirty-four million pound turnover. Now *that's* New Labour.'

Less than a week before, McGee had been contacted by Margaret McDonagh, the key strategist in Blair's watershed abolition of Clause IV, who had gone on to be the Labour Party's general election co-ordinator. As far as McGee could tell, she only had the vaguest of plans for the Youth Experience Rally, whose organisation – despite New Labour's reputation for cool efficiency – seemed to be a matter of eleventh-hour desperation.

The pair met at Creation's offices, where McDonagh was surprised to find that McGee did not work behind a desk. 'I didn't know what to expect,' she says. 'I hadn't been in a lot of record companies. It seemed quite a creative environment. But I was a bit worried I might be a bit out of my depth: they were so trendy and hip and I was so square.'

'She said, "Can you get Noel Gallagher to come up with an acoustic guitar, and do a couple of songs or something?"' says McGee. 'So I phoned Noel up, and he went, "I don't want to go up and do that – I'm fucking shattered. I just need a rest." So me and Marcus Russell spoke, and we went, "Alright: we'll give them an Oasis platinum disc. It'll get in all the papers, and say that Oasis want the Labour Party in and the Tories out."' Their plan had the intended results: several reports of the event in Blackpool featured the headline 'What's The Story? Don't Vote Tory'.

Such was the first public manifestation of a relationship that had been taking root since the summer. In early 1996, McGee had been sent an invitation to a government reception for the music industry by Virginia Bottomley, the sometime Conservative Health Secretary who was now in charge of the Department of Heritage. He ran the prospect by Andy Saunders, Creation's head of communications. Saunders, then thirty, was a family man, settled in St Albans, who cut a rather more grown-up figure than many of his colleagues. He did not work with Oasis, having conspicuously failed to match McGee's enthusiasm for their first demo tape, but his title betrayed the fact that he saw his role as something more high-powered than mere PR. Indeed, such was his insistence on precision and protocol that he had a reputation for almost military efficiency: The Boo Radleys, one of the groups he looked after, nicknamed him Union Jack Jackson after a character in the war comic *Victor*; at the *NME* he was known as 'D.I. Saunders'.

Saunders was a member of the Labour Party. When he was shown Bottomley's letter, he quickly saw an opportunity to extend his and McGee's influence beyond the usual confines of the music scene. 'At one point,' he says, 'Alan was like, "That'd be great, to go there." I said, "Alan – you *can't* go. Even if you were going to be subversive" – which he certainly would, he wouldn't go as an innocent – "you can't. The message that it would send out would be really poor." I said, "If you really want to make a statement, you should write back to Virginia Bottomley, and issue what you've written as a press release, saying 'You're having a laugh, you mad old cow – you've closed down so many hospitals, I don't want to be in the same *room* as you. What are you on about?'" '

Saunders duly shoehorned the story into the news pages of *NME* and *Melody Maker*. Within a few months, he and McGee – partly, it seems, for their own amusement – had come up with an even more adventurous wheeze, and decided to offer their services to the Labour Party. Saunders made contact with Jack Cunningham, the Shadow Heritage Secretary, who agreed to meet them at the Palace of Westminster.

'We were in the taxi saying, "This is mental – what are we doing? Why are they seeing us? We're just a couple of neds," ' says Saunders. 'We got ushered up to Jack Cunningham's offices, with Lewis Moonie there, who was his Private Secretary. He was the more verbose of the two. He was a twenty Marlboros, fourteen pints sort of geezer. Quite punk rock. Hardcore. An ex-dock worker.'

With no prepared script, McGee and Saunders could only offer Moonie and Cunningham the vague promise of contacts within the music industry and advice on snaring the youth vote. After a while, Cunningham grew impatient enough to try and push the conversation towards specifics. 'He said, "Well, okay – have you got any specific ideas?" ' says Saunders. 'And Alan, having not discussed nothing with me, says, "I've got a great idea. It's for a poster. We'll get Damon Albarn on one side, Noel Gallagher on another, staring at each other. And the headline will be, 'The only thing they hate more than each other is the Tories'." Which was brilliant. Genius.'

Moonie and Cunningham eventually surmised that they should put

McGee in touch with Margaret McDonagh. 'At our first proper meeting,' says Saunders, 'she said, "Are you football fans?" And Alan said, "I've got a box at Chelsea – do you want to come?" She was a Wimbledon fan, so she came and hung out with us. She was young, and fairly idealistic – but also very New Labour. She knew that it was about marketing and PR and hitting the right people to get across the right message. She became very close to us. We talked to her a lot.'

The pair's bond with McDonagh was not only down to football. Like so many Blairites, her past contained a record of rather more radical engagement: her initial involvement in the Labour Party had been at least partly prompted by her teenage experience of Rock Against Racism, the leftist umbrella group that aimed to use some of punk rock's scattershot ire to an admirably constructive purpose. Without much persuasion, she will still recount such memories as watching The Clash play an RAR rally in East London's Victoria Park, seeing The Jam and The Stranglers at Camden's Roundhouse, and buying The Sex Pistols' first and only LP. 'I still think *Never Mind The Bollocks* is one of the most near-perfect albums ever made,' she says; the image of such a central New Labour figure pogo-ing to Anarchy In The UK seems even more bizarre than Blair's Mick Jagger impressions.

In the wake of the Youth Experience Rally, McGee, McDonagh and Saunders began to work on their next event: a lunchtime meeting between Tony Blair and a crowd of power-brokers from the British music industry. 'My thinking,' says Saunders, 'was, "It's Tony Blair – he's obviously the next Prime Minister." He'd been to the *Q* Awards, he'd done his rock'n'roll bit. So who from the music industry *wouldn't* want to meet him? No-one was going to pass up the chance to say, "I was hanging out with Tony Blair the other day." At that point, Tony Blair was as big as Oasis. And as sexy.' Though he detected a frisson of resentment about the fact that McGee – still viewed by much of the industry as a hotheaded outsider – had the Labour Party's ear, Saunders' hunch proved correct. 'Of the people we invited,' he says, 'everyone turned up.'

So it was that on Monday 27 January, 1997, around sixty representatives of the music business were herded into the Jubilee Room at the Houses of Parliament. It was there, prior to Blair's appearance, that Andy Saunders met Alastair Campbell, whose opening gambit suggested that football was to the Blairites what funny handshakes were to the Freemasons. 'He was great. He said, "Who the fuck are you? Do you like football?"'

Blair made a short oration, assuring his audience that he backed their concerns in such areas as copyright enforcement, before he took questions from the floor. Though he did not seem to have done much in the way of preparation, he gave what sounded like model answers. 'I thought, "This is incredible,"' says Saunders. '"This guy is such a bullshitter; a genius talker."'

The event was judged to have been a success, which only increased McGee and Saunders' clout with the Blairites. At Margaret McDonagh's suggestion, they began to make occasional visits to Labour's Millbank headquarters; on their first trip, they spent time with Peter Mandelson, then Labour's campaigns chief, and his research assistant, Benjamin Wegg-Prosser. 'We chatted about music,' says Wegg-Prosser. 'But they were very nervous. It was a slightly awkward meeting: no-one could quite work out what they were supposed to be saying to each other.'

As their visits increased, McGee and Saunders began to understand their role: in Saunders' words, they amounted to an ad hoc 'Think Tank for the music industry and the youth vote.' On one occasion, Mandelson and McDonagh showed the pair a campaign video, sound-tracked by D:Ream's Things Can Only Get Better, the euphoric melding of house music and mass-market pop that had been a top 10 hit in early 1994, and would soon become New Labour's election anthem (the only other contender, according to McDonagh, was M People's 1993 single Movin' On Up).

'Me and Alan were going, "This is shit. No-one's going to watch this. Why have you chosen this?"' says Saunders. '"You want Wake Up Boo! by The Boo Radleys. You don't want this nonsense." We were very scathing about it. But there was also a sense of, "This is great! They're asking our opinion!"'

In the days of Red Wedge, the Labour Party's relations with the music industry had been subject to the procedures of minuted meetings and long-standing party rules. This was not the Blairite way, as Saunders quickly discovered. 'You never actually sat down and said, "Let's get down to it." You'd walk out and go "What was that about?" But they'd probably got loads out of us. They asked all the right questions, like "How many are Oasis selling?", but it was never anything overt. I suppose they saw Alan as a point of access to pop culture. Someone they could go to and say, "Is this cool or not cool?"'

Though all was usually cordiality and mutual appreciation, Saunders and McGee occasionally sensed that one particular issue was nagging at their new friends: the possibility of persuading Noel Gallagher to give the party a more marketable endorsement than he had managed at the Brit Awards. Though McGee did not apparently rule it out, he was hamstrung by the fact that Marcus Russell was against the idea; moreover, McGee did not want to make such a fuss that, in line with the Oasis camp's increasing independence, Russell decided to prise them away from Creation.

'Alan's relationship with the band was strong; his relationship with Ignition was cordial, but it was a dance of terror at that point,' says Saunders. 'You had Alan saying, "I don't want to fuck Ignition off, 'cos I don't want them taking the band off me and going to Sony. So I'm not going to go to Noel behind their back, in case it gets back to them and they think I'm trying to stitch them – and then they stitch me." It was quite a difficult situation.'

In the end, McGee's Millbank contacts attempted to solicit the use of a particularly mouthwatering item: Oasis's fan database, the result of their disciples filling in postcards that came with their releases. 'We said, "No – we can't do that,"' says Saunders. 'There were one hundred and thirty thousand names on it. I think it eventually went up to a quarter of a million. But Oasis owned that.'

In March, Saunders was awoken by an early morning phone call from McGee. Although he was used to such disturbances, the hour was sufficiently early to suggest that McGee was either panicking or excitedly formulating some new scheme. 'He went, "Right. I'm going to give fifty grand to the Labour Party. How do I do it?" He also said, "What can we get out of it?" I said, "I don't think you can give fifty grand with strings attached. I don't think we can be as blatant as that: I think you have to think of it as putting favours in a big favour bank, and at some point, when you really need it, you can pull it in. It's a big red button you push once." He said, "Yeah yeah yeah – but how do I *do* it?"'

McGee put one condition on the donation – he wanted it to be used in Scotland. By the opening of office hours, Saunders was in touch with Margaret McDonagh – who swiftly referred him to Alastair Campbell. 'Campbell said, "Why don't we do a piece in the *Daily Record*?" And I said, "How are you so confident?" And he said, "'Cos I'm going to write it." I said, "What do you mean, you're going to *write* it?" "We'll write it, we'll draft it. They're fine, they know me." And I'm like, "Okay ... I wish I could do that."' Naturally enough, Campbell was not bluffing: on 25 March, the story duly appeared, with the headline 'Look Back In Anger: Labour Man McGee Puts His Money Where His Mouth Is'.

The piece took the form of a first-person comment article. Campbell's prose – which gave off the whiff of having been written in mere minutes – was so energised that he managed to make McGee sound slightly unhinged. 'I HATE the Tories. When I vote on May 1, I will be voting Labour ... To misquote one of the biggest-selling Oasis songs – DO look back in anger. Look back in anger at what these Tories have done to the health service. Look back in anger at the hated poll tax ... And when you've looked back, and got angry thinking about it, make sure you vote. Voting to me is a joy. I wish we could do it more often. When you mark that X on the ballot paper, you're doing something positive for once about all your moans and anger ... I have met Tony Blair and I have absolutely no doubt that he has the heart, the strength and the ideas to turn this country round. He is a genuine guy. When Tony Blair says he wants to make Britain great again, I say: "Sign me up." He can do for British politics what Creation Records has done for British music.'

'After that,' says Andy Saunders, 'my phone didn't stop ringing for about two years. Five Live, the *Today* programme ... on any one of about fifteen issues – donations, business reaction to the Labour Party, youth, drugs and the Labour Party – I'd get called, day and night. I spent two years being woken up at five in the morning by the *Today* programme. He worked his balls off. The thing is, Millbank never phoned me up and said, "Can Alan do this, this and this?" They were cleverer than that. They'd unleashed all this media interest, and then they stood back and watched.'

Such was the progress of New Labour's most enthusiastic music business ally. Whereas musicians always carried the threat of some sudden change of heart, if not active treachery, McGee provided a perfect combination: rock'n'roll cred, counterbalanced by the assumed reliability of a drug-free businessman in his late thirties. To his new friends' probable delight, he was recurrently introduced to viewers and listeners as The Man Who Discovered Oasis. He was not a natural media performer – his spoken sentences were always punctuated with nervous nuances like 'sort of like' and 'right' – but his almost familial link with the Gallaghers, coupled with the idea that he was now a New Labour insider, made him a coveted interviewee.

One Friday night, Tim Abbot – by now completely estranged from both Oasis and Creation – came back to his flat after an evening spent in the pub. 'I came in at eleven o'clock, made a cup of tea, looked round – and there were Jeremy Paxman and Alan,' he says. 'He looked so like a fish out of water, in among these professional spinners, who had TV savvy. He was on with Charles Moore. I thought, "What is he trying to achieve here?"'

Abbot is still of the opinion that McGee's sudden high profile was at least partly explained by his need to make up for the eighteen months he had spent away from Creation in the wake of his chance meeting with the Gallaghers. 'He'd missed the glory days of Oasis because of his illness. There was a big self-justification thing when he came back, because there had been all these long nights that Alan should have been part of. And he wasn't. Never since Malcolm McLaren had someone been as associated with that sense of "*I discovered this*".'

Though the Knebworth concerts represented the apex of Oasis's popularity, they were not allowed much time to consider their achievement. Less than a fortnight later, they were ushered on to a transatlantic airliner, in preparation for another American tour. This time, in an attempt to decisively push *(What's The Story) Morning Glory?* into the kind of middle-American homes that denote true mass-market success, they would be stepping outside the usual metropolitan circuit into what the US music business terms 'secondary markets'; so, along with engagements in Philadelphia, Chicago and Atlanta, Oasis were booked to ply their wares in such cutting-edge hotbeds as Bristow, Virginia and Charlotte, North Carolina.

Unfortunately, on 27 August, as their flight was readied for take-off, Liam Gallagher announced that he was staying put. Unbeknown to at least two of his colleagues, who had yet to make it to the gate, he insisted that his luggage was removed from the hold, and he was transported back inside the terminal building.

'You know those golf buggies they have at airports?' says Paul Arthurs. 'The ones with flashing lights? Me and Alan White were legging it to the gate, and one of them came towards us, going in the opposite direction, with Liam on the back. Alan said, "Did you see that? Lazy cunt." I said, "Yeah – but he's going the *wrong way*." We got on the plane and the tour manager's like, "Bad news – Liam's done one. He says he needs to sort his house out." We decided what to do on the plane: Noel said, "I'll sing. Fuck him." That was the attitude: "Fuck him."'

Of late, Liam had been making an art of such unpredictability. Four days before they set off for the States, Oasis had been booked to film a performance for MTV Unplugged at the Royal Festival Hall. As their corporate backers well knew, the show stood as a signifier of the fact that Oasis had now joined the transatlantic rock aristocracy; a good performance would only heighten their standing in the States. Liam, however, gave such thinking short shrift: claiming that he had laryngitis, he left the lead vocals to Noel, and spent the duration of the group's performance sitting in the venue's circle with Patsy Kensit, to whom he had recently announced his engagement, Meg Mathews and Kate

Moss. It was noticed that, despite his alleged ailment, he spent the night smoking a steady succession of B&H.

When it came to his latest flit, however, he could at least logically account for his behaviour. Having successfully sold her St John's Wood townhouse, he and Kensit were scheduled to vacate the premises while he was on tour. For one reason or another, they had not managed to find a replacement love-nest; the result was the prospect of a spell spent living in a London hotel. In the face of such a nightmare, Liam's vaudevillian obligation to his public did not seem to count for much. 'I don't care about the tour,' he said. 'I'm fucking sick of it. I've got to find a place to live . . . I'm not going around touring when I've got nowhere to live. I'm sick of living my life in hotels. I need to be happy.'

If his words were aimed at currying sympathy, they fell rather flat. In the eyes of the tabloid newspapers, Liam had effectively been dragged from the plane by his nagging fiancée. He was, it was implied, not quite the macho libertine of legend. *The Daily Star*'s front-page headline was 'Patsy's Got Him By The Wonderballs'; the *Express* ran a two-page spread, also alluding to her marriage to Jim Kerr, titled 'Is Patsy Kensit Ruining Our Top Bands?'

Though the attention accorded to the story suggested the usual silly season news vacuum, there was actually no shortage of more important material: the day Liam left Heathrow, a Sudanese airliner was flown on to British soil by Iraqi hijackers; at the same time, the divorce of the Prince and Princess of Wales was nearing finalisation. Still, no-one seemed to let such frippery get in the way. In St John's Wood, a brigade of photographers, TV crews and journalists quickly set up camp, though there was nothing much to report. ITN's Ian Glover-James was only able to tell his viewers that, though Liam had arrived looking rather ragged, he had since had a bit of a wash and brush-up. 'Liam is here,' he said. 'His beard has gone.' *Newsnight*'s Jeremy Vine, a man perhaps used to grappling with more substantial intrigue, was dispatched to take the bold step of buzzing Kensit's entryphone. Even the prospect of such upmarket company failed to bring Liam to the door.

Meanwhile, Oasis prepared to play a concert in Rosemont, Illinois. The show's promoter tacked up a number of posters, informing Oasis's audience of the disappointment that awaited them: 'Liam Gallagher is ill and will not perform this evening. Noel Gallagher, songwriter and guitarist/vocalist will be performing all vocals and the show will go on.' The crowd were offered a refund, though precious few decided to go home. Nonetheless, they beheld an Oasis rendered competent and workmanlike rather than brooding and volatile. As the crowd at the

Royal Festival Hall had discovered, Oasis without Liam dispensed a very lukewarm kind of entertainment: Noelrock, in excelsis.

On 30 August, Liam rejoined the group in Auburn Hills, Michigan, where he took the stage in front of 15,000 people. Five days later, Oasis arrived at the annual MTV Awards ceremony, at Radio City Music Hall in New York. If Liam was still feeling a little prickly, this was not the kind of occasion that was going to seal his passage into Oasis's US commitments. Its constituent ingredients seemed to be celebrity piety and simpering gratitude: the tone was set when Alanis Morissette dedicated her award to 'the acknowledgement and under-standing of artistic differences'.

So it was that Liam took on the job of spoiling the party. 'You're all here to have a great time, but you're having a shite time,' he said, as Oasis began their rendition of Champagne Supernova. As the song's opening bars boomed forth, Liam performed the age-old playground conjuring trick whereby a length of phlegm emerged from his mouth, and was slowly dribbled on to the floor. When the song reached its chorus, he changed the lyric to 'a champagne supernova up your bum'. The audience, needless to say, did not seem terribly impressed.

On 7 September, Oasis played two dates at Jones Beach Theatre, Long Island. Liam's mood did not seem to improve: 'Liam Gallagher should have stayed in England to finish his house-hunting,' said the *New York Newsday*. 'The dour-faced younger Gallagher was so busy cultivating his iconoclastic image that he couldn't be bothered with his singing . . . Liam spent the 90-minute set guzzling beer, swearing loudly in a slurred voice, giving fans the finger and repeatedly kicking over his mic stand.'

Oasis reached Charlotte on 11 September. By now, Liam's mixture of irascibility and dejection seemed to be spreading to the rest of the camp; morale was hardly boosted by the news that that night's perform-ance had been moved from the city's 12,000-capacity Independence Arena to the glamour-dripping confines of the Hornets Training Facil-ity, which could easily contain the 3,500 who were expected. 'Every-body was complaining,' said Noel, 'and I just said, "Why don't we go home? . . . There's nothing stopping anyone from getting on a plane and going home." Our kid suddenly gets an attack of the morals and says we can't go home, it ain't right. I said, "You can shut up, you never came in the first place, you cunt" . . . I said, "I'll show you how easy it is to go home." I went to my room, phoned for a taxi and went to the airport and came home. That was it.'

There was little doubt that something slightly more serious had tran-spired – in Liam's belated insistence that the show must go on, there surely lurked the spark for a bout of brotherly fisticuffs. Whatever, Noel made it to New York, bought a Concorde ticket, and sped back to Heathrow. For the third time in as many years, he had seemingly left his own group; by now, it was starting to look like an annual ritual. 'I'm sure it was Noel who wanted to go home, really,' says Paul Arthurs. 'I remember saying at the time, "I haven't gone, you haven't gone; we're all still here. *He's* the one who's gone."' He claims that the remaining quartet considered performing Oasis's four remaining engagements without their leader: 'There was talk of "Let's turn the tables – shall we do it without him?"'

In the meantime, the UK's media had worked itself into a tantrum that made the fuss surrounding Liam's sojourn in St John's Wood look positively trifling. The assumption was that Noel and Liam had been through an apocalyptic bust-up and Oasis had split up. All the TV news bulletins carried speculative reports about the group's future: the likes of John Suchet, Anna Ford, Jon Snow and Julia Somerville gravely outlined a scenario that seemed to be tantamount to some kind of national bereavement. Meanwhile, packs of reporters and photographers patiently waited for both Noel and Liam's return. In Manchester, Peggy Gallagher did her best to assure the country that, although the backdrop to this latest crisis was basketball arenas and Marriott hotels rather than building sites and burned dinners, she had seen her sons' bond survive worse.

Noel arrived back in the UK at 5.20pm on Thursday 12 September, 1996, to be met by his manager. 'I phoned Marcus on his mobile,' he later recalled. 'He was outside, waiting. I asked him, "Is there any press?" He went, "*Is there any press?* Wait till those doors open." The doors opened and it was bedlam. I wanted to go back to America.' With the protective figure of Kevin Camp at his side, Noel solemnly plodded through the arrivals concourse, while dozens of flashbulbs exploded and the waiting reporters barked their questions. His uncharacteristic silence – along with a very portentous facial expression – only added to the suspicion that something had gone horribly wrong.

The idea of carrying on without Noel had come to nought: Liam, accompanied by the other three, arrived at Gatwick twenty-four hours later. In order to give the paparazzi the slip, his security detail had the inspired idea of taking refuge in a nearby cemetery. 'I had an egg and bacon sandwich in a fucking graveyard,' he later recalled. 'It was top.'

At an unspecified rural location, the Gallagher brothers duly met, got drunk, and decided – if it had ever truly been in doubt – that Oasis would carry on. Word reached the press that weekend, whereupon Britain's most popular tabloid excelled itself: 'The Sun Saves Oasis', claimed Saturday's most remarkable front page. The logic was truly gorgeous; in breaking the story, it was claimed, the newspaper had caused such an outbreak of hysteria that Noel and Liam had been reminded of their place in the nation's affections, and had thus decided to carry on.

When the dust had settled, it was clear that – despite official protestations that the group's early return had been all but an irrelevance – the tour had inflicted serious wounds on their prospects in the States. Aside from their early exit, there was an abiding sense that, in the wake of Knebworth, they were striking the kind of regal poses that made little sense to their North American audiences: in Toronto, Noel had instructed the crowd to 'show your appreciation for the best band in the fucking world'. Sceptical eyes saw only four statues and a singer who often seemed to view his public with a sneering contempt. 'Few bands put out so little and expect so much,' was *The New York Times*'s elegantly Churchillian verdict.

Back in the UK, the group could at least seek solace in the home-grown staples of their everyday lives. 'I was mad for it – for beans on toast, man,' said Liam. 'A nice cup of PG Tips. It was top.' So it was that as the bread popped up and the kettle whistled, Oasis began recording their third album: the record that would kill the Britpop dream stone dead.

CHAPTER 19

'Wanting to be the biggest is a weakness.'

In the late summer of 1996, Suede had re-emerged with a new album. In terms of recorded music, they had been silent for the best part of eighteen months: a period so crammed with intrigue – the decisive arrival of Britpop, the Blur/Oasis battle – that they felt like refugees from an altogether different era. Surveying much of what they had missed, Brett Anderson struck a typically haughty pose, making dismissive reference to 'silly little bands singing about rolling out the barrel'.

For all his snootiness, however, he could not help but stake a claim to the credit for a lot of what had transpired. 'It's very easy for bands now to follow our blueprint,' he said, 'but when we started we were trying to play songs about twisted English lives to rooms full of people obsessed with Pearl Jam. We kicked the fucking door in! I wouldn't say we started Britpop because The Beatles, Bowie and The Kinks did that. But I think we were crucial in opening people's ears to British music again.'

Given the sudden profusion of interview microphones, he also sought to decisively settle a matter that had been festering since November 1994, when Damon Albarn had clumsily drawn attention to Anderson's use of heroin. 'It was a boring sidetrack, like reading some piece of fiction . . . I don't give a fuck if anyone thinks I've got my head down a toilet with a needle up my arse, but I object to people attacking me . . . I find that objectionable.' Then came the rather inaccurate punch-line: 'Especially when it's a talentless public schoolboy who's made a career out of being patronising to the working classes.'

Relative to the quartet who had made such waves in the early 1990s, Suede were nigh-on unrecognisable. The last vestiges of Brett

Anderson's sartorial flamboyance were now replaced by an austere dress-code that found all of the group wearing black leather jackets. More importantly, they were now a five-piece, thanks to the recruitment of one Neil Codling: a keyboard player and guitarist who was Simon Gilbert's cousin. Codling, whose enviable bone structure and air of glacial cool would soon push him to the front of Suede's photographs, was a twenty-one-year-old English and Drama graduate. 'He's definitely prettier than Richard,' said Brett Anderson, 'but a year-and-a-half on the road with us will turn anyone into a gargoyle.' The first concert Codling had attended was a Suede gig; given the presence of Richard Oakes, the group thus had two members whose formative musical experiences had involved the band they had joined.

The upshot of this strange circumstance gradually became clear. It is in the nature of the stereotypical fan to cling to a reductive notion of a group, and begrudge them any move away from it: the merest hint of a stylistic makeover, and they will bombard the *NME* with outraged letters and move their affections elsewhere. Certainly, from here on in, Suede seemed more locked than ever in a universe of black attire, 70s influences, and lyrics bound up with urban grime, dashed hopes, and inconclusive sexual encounters. Among Suede's post-1996 B-sides lurk songs called Waterloo, Crackhead and Jumble Sale Mums.

Thanks to Richard Oakes, the working title of their new single had been Pisspot. On account of its chorus, it was retitled Trash, and previewed in July. A knowing, romantic clarion-call to those who saw their experiences reflected in the group's music – the occupants of 'nowhere towns' and 'nothing places', 'the lovers on the streets' – it was so crassly melodic, relentlessly upbeat and intentionally commercial as to land just the right side of absurdity. The semi-operatic croon that Anderson had used on much of *Dog Man Star* had been replaced by his old mewl, this time treated with a studio effect that made it sound like it had been sped up; the arrangement, for some reason, was redolent of Peter Frampton's long-lost mid-70s hit Show Me The Way.

Such, as it turned out, were the abiding qualities of the album that Suede had decided to call *Coming Up*. To prepare for its recording, the group had immersed themselves in T. Rex's 1972 album *The Slider*, and its successor, *Tanx*, whose fuzztoned, bubblegum aesthetics informed Suede's new approach. 'I wanted it to be a complete turnover from the last album, which was very dark and dank,' said Anderson. 'I wanted it to be almost like a Greatest Hits, the sort of album you could listen to at low volume, with pop songs on it that gradually bored their way into your head. The first two albums suffered at certain times from being quite obscure. I wanted it to be communicative and understandable. Pop music generally has to be pretty dumb, I think. And I've had my little affair with the avant-garde. It's not as exciting as pop music.' Given that his new co-writer was the strikingly inexperienced Richard Oakes, this artistic about-turn was probably no bad thing.

In keeping with its title, *Coming Up* had been written while 'sitting around taking a lot of drugs'. Whereas *Dog Man Star* had reflected Anderson's seclusion in Highgate, by now he was resident in the more bustling environs of W11, keeping the company of a small group of friends who lived the post-Acid House lifestyle of weekend binges and Tuesday comedowns. Such were the lyrical themes of Lazy, Saturday Night and The Beautiful Ones: in the latter, Anderson's new compadres were witnessed 'shaking their bits to the hits' (in its first draft, it was 'tits' rather than 'bits'). Though there was one nod to the sweeping balladry of the last album – By The Sea – these songs defined *Coming Up*: in place of its predecessor's gothic portentousness, the new album spoke a language of goggle-eyed hedonism and Day-Glo musical simplicity. 'I was really enjoying the insanity of it all at that time,' says Anderson. 'It was Suede's party album: our lightest, most frivolous record. In my own specific, personal way, I was partying.'

In the reviews of *Coming Up* by the UK's more erudite critics, it was clear what this meant. A great deal of the in-built mystery of the Bernard Butler period – embodied by such songs as My Insatiable One, in which Butler's dramatic guitar line had collided with couplets like 'On the escalator/We shit paracetamol' – had gone. 'Instead,' said the *NME*, 'we get choons: the very stuff of these instant party times.' Though it awarded the album eight out of ten, the paper's review went on to quietly bemoan Suede's sudden accent on a very brash kind of economy: 'Let's face it, it's going to be pretty hard to believe they're the living embodiment of Ziggy [Stardust], The Doors and JG Ballard all rolled into one, eternally trawling London's late night drug underworld, if they never do another number over eight minutes; hard to see them as the spectral outsiders Brett's always eulogising when their music's becoming so *obvious*.'

In as far as it entered the album charts at number one, and contained no less than five top ten singles, *Coming Up* was a triumph. That said, in stripping Suede of all their pretension and floridity, it rather rendered them mundane and prosaic: they were dangerously close to becoming Just Another Band.

In the context of the contemporaries that the band affected to despise, there was also a sweet irony at work. If, to demonstrate his disdain for the era inaugurated by *Parklife*, Mat Osman still expresses horror at the idea of 'songs about chip shops', it should perhaps be noted that Anderson's lyrics were getting alarmingly close: 'Cracked up, stacked up, 22/Psycho for sex and glue/Lost it to Bostik, yeah'; 'Here they come gone 7am/Getting satellite and Sky, getting cable'.

In tandem with the record's proud emphasis on hooklines and hit singles, it all led to one conclusion. In their own spindly, leather-clad, vampiric way, Suede had actually made a Britpop record.

Suede apart, the dominance of Oasis had apparently sealed the idea that the most successful rock music was held together by a profusion of testosterone. As the *Guardian* surmised, this was 'the wrong era to be anything but a red-blooded geezer playing unambiguous geez-rock'.

In that context, Elastica were a more singular presence than ever. This was not simply a matter of the fact that women formed the majority of the group's membership; on *Elastica*, one heard music that staked a claim for exactly the kind of virtues – wit, musical economy, an avoidance of cliché – that were now being smothered by the post-Oasis groups. The fact that the album had been so successful suggested that this was a battle still worth pursuing.

A month after their return to the UK from Australia in February 1996, Elastica began working on new songs. Justine Frischmann and Donna Matthews had agreed on the broad outlines of a new approach: harking back to the fact that they had both been enraptured by New Order's headline performance at the Reading Festival in 1992, they wanted to fuse the group's guitars and drums with the kind of noises made by circuit boards and digital processors. With all that in mind, they recruited Dave Bush, a Mancunian who had briefly been a member of The Fall, the northern iconoclasts of whom Frischmann was so fond, and was a masterful practitioner of the electronic sounds that she and Matthews wanted to graft on to the group's music. Annie Holland's replacement, meanwhile, was Sheila Chipperfield, a daughter of the circus family who followed the terms of her employment to the letter and began a relationship with one of Menswear: by the time the group formally announced her appointment in July, she had started going out with Johnny Dean.

Throughout their time with the group, Bush and Chipperfield expressed no interest in the drug that was starting to sap the group's motivation. Justine Frischmann, unfortunately, had apparently progressed from casual heroin use to a full-blown habit at a rate of knots. 'I can remember her asking me for heroin,' says Donna Matthews, 'and I said no for ages. She was like, "I just want to try it." This was after I said to her, "I think I'm a heroin addict." So she knew *I* had a problem with heroin before she started taking it. And as soon as she started taking it, she became an addict straight away.'

For the moment, Frischmann managed to pursue her habit while fulfilling her obligations to the group. Unfortunately, it did not take long for her heroin use to warp her view of the music Elastica were making. 'I was still going to work every day,' says Frischmann, 'but not getting very much done; thinking everything was shit. You lose your joy of life and you lose your ability to hear things properly. I think if you're clean you can get a spirit from music; you know it's good, just 'cos of the way it makes you feel. If you're doing drugs, it's much harder to get that feel from music. Maybe at the beginning when you do it, everything feels great, but you can't really tell whether something's right or not. It just *muddles* you.'

One member of the group seemed particularly bewildered. The addition of Dave Bush's electronics meant that Justin Welch had to keep time with pre-programmed, rigidly metronomic music. He was thus beholden to the bane of many a drummer's life: the 'click track'; his drug use, unfortunately, made the task pretty troublesome. 'Drummers on heroin are not fun,' says Frischmann. 'It just got tedious. You had Bushy knocking out this four on the floor racket, trying to make everything go techno, which Justin could barely keep up with. It wasn't pretty.'

A great deal of the time, the business of successfully executing the group's new ideas seemed rather a distraction. 'We used to turn up at rehearsal rooms and just take drugs,' says Donna Matthews. 'We'd always be late. We'd sometimes do music, but most of the time we'd take drugs: we all used to sit and just do heroin together. For Dave and Sheila it must have been mad: just three people sat there in the corner, with foil, just doing gear. Then we'd play some songs. The look on Sheila's face sometimes was just, "These people are fucking mad."'

'Poor girl, man,' says Frischmann. 'Clean-living young chick, really up for it. I really felt sorry for her. We weren't very furtive about it. We weren't furtive at all, in fact. But none of us would let her go anywhere near it.'

Occasionally, one or other of the group would decide that their drug habits were corroding Elastica to the point that someone had to take the lead and clean up. 'It did stop a few times,' says Frischmann. 'But it always seemed to go the same way: if you put the five of us together, one person was going to be doing something, and then everyone was, and then it was all over again. If anyone was doing drugs – whatever the drugs, whether it was speed or something the doctor's had given you, like Valium or Temazepam, or *anything* – it'd make other people who were around want to take them.'

It was no small miracle that, in the face of all this, the group actually appeared to be making headway. In July, the new line-up recorded a session for Steve Lamacq's programme on Radio One. The four songs put to tape sounded more than promising.* Justine Frischmann's I Want You – a piledriving rock song that, whether unwittingly or otherwise, shared its chord structure with Robert Palmer's Addicted To Love – sounded like the first draft of a future hit single. Donna Matthews' songs, though no less impressive, were of a rather darker stripe – though the lyric of A Love Like Ours superficially dealt with some all-consuming affair, she was clearly alluding to something else: 'Take a look/Kept in deceit/A love like ours will never die.' The songs were given a live premiere when the group played a four-date club tour and performed at the V96 Festival in August; the resulting press reports were couched in terms of renewed vigour and glowing prospects.

So it was that in November 1996, Elastica finally began recording their second album, overseen by Bruce Lampcov, a one-time associate of Frischmann's beloved Wire. It was now that their problems really began. The world of the habitual heroin user is usually a morass of unfinished business and vain hopes; so it proved when Elastica put their new ideas to tape. 'We came out with loads of intricate music,' says Donna Matthews, 'but because we were out of our heads, we couldn't seem to put it in a cohesive form. There were loads 'of unfinished songs: thousands of pounds' worth of tape, full of them. You could probably have made ten albums on the material we had, but everyone's heads were in different places.'

By now, Matthews had grown fond of music that lay way outside the group's staple influences: the sample-laden output of the Mo'Wax label, American R'n'B icon Missy 'Misdemeanour' Elliott, and Beck. Her colleagues thus beheld the latest in a long line of musical phases: it was perhaps not insignificant that Matthews was on to her fourth hairstyle in two years.

'Donna's a very interesting character: very bright, and totally chameleon-like,' says Frischmann. 'And I didn't have a clue. I totally underestimated her. Her chameleon thing worked for a bit, in terms of her understanding the idea of Elastica and adding to it – but eventu-

---

* Three of the songs from this session – I Want You, Only Human and A Love Like Ours – were released on *Elastica: The Radio One Sessions* in 2001.

ally, she went completely off the rails, changing personalities and changing looks until it got quite frightening.

'I remember her walking into a rehearsal, maybe six months after Sheila had joined, saying, "Oh, I heard the album [*Elastica*] last night. I was round someone's house and they put it on, and I was just *so* embarrassed." She was never that into Elastica as I saw it. Donna was very impressionable about what was going on at the time. She wanted to be Beck when he was doing well . . . she wanted us to be whatever she was into at that point. And I couldn't really keep up.'

'I started getting really egotistical, thinking "I deserve to be writing half the songs,"' says Matthews. 'And that's when it started going wrong. I'd started to become very competitive, which pissed Justine off, because it was her band. She had the direction that made Elastica what it was, and I never appreciated that at the time.'

'The whole balance of power in the band had shifted,' says Frischmann. 'She could play the guitar better than me, and sing better than me, and at that point her songs were working better than my songs.'

In desperation, for a period of three months, Frischmann simply stopped attending recording sessions and rehearsals, taking refuge in she and Albarn's house while she worked out her next move. 'The band carried on without her,' says Matthews. 'I ended up singing; Sheila was doing backing vocals. We did that for a while, and Justine came to one rehearsal and was just like, "What have I fucking done? The band's carrying on without me." And then she banned me from the studio. It all just went mental. It was mad.'

Though precious few people had any idea of how dysfunctional Elastica had become, the immediate result of the group's problems was clear enough: in an increasingly moribund musical landscape, a source of innovative, intelligent music fell silent.

Thankfully, war-hardened reinforcements were on their way. In the first weeks of 1997, Blur prepared for the release of an album that, by way of indicating some kind of creative year-zero, they had simply entitled *Blur*. To prepare the ground, Damon Albarn had given an end-of-year phone interview to the *NME*, in which he announced that his tenure as a merchant of Britpop was over. 'It's quite amusing to me, seeing papers like the *Guardian* rewriting how Britpop started and the key components of it. But I know how unpopular it was, saying it was cool to be British. I feel I have the right to say it's just meaningless now. It sold us all lots of records and made some of us very famous, but apart from a few good records – and I would include *Parklife* – it's been a bad thing. That's how I feel about it. The Beatles became canonised for the wrong reasons. They were always a really bright, adventurous, funny, witty band. But where's the intelligence in this music now?'

Those who shared his company noted that Albarn's voice had changed: though he had once been prone to lapsing into mewling faux-cockney and launching rapid verbal tirades, he now spoke in a deep, hushed timbre, and issued his words at half his previous rate. Nonetheless, his new measured tones were used to dispense all kinds of revelations. 'Wanting to be the biggest is a weakness,' he told *The Sunday Times*. 'I slowly recognised that in myself. It was a flaw in my personality that I wanted to be the most famous, the most loved. I'm on top of that now.' ('Which,' added the journalist, 'is just as well, given the inexorable rise of Oasis.')

In an article he wrote for *The Face*, Albarn announced an equally remarkable volte-face. 'Two years ago I was fervently in favour of New Labour. Now I've got serious doubts about them. If you are going to take a country's population with you on a big political change, then they have to *feel* the reason why they're doing it, as well as understand it, and I don't feel it any more with New Labour. Obviously I'll vote for them, but if I'm being honest it's more for the kind of reasons that I always drink Coke rather than Pepsi; you make your choice and you stick with it.'

The same point was made in a brief exchange published in *Q* magazine. 'Blair has a worryingly conservative streak and he's taken his own personality so far into the arena of appeasement that he's no longer a valid leader of a socialist party,' said Albarn. 'But I will be voting for him, and Labour will get in – just don't expect any changes, that's all. We'd do better with a coalition government.'

These comments, squeezed into a 200-word sidebar, were enough to prompt comment in at least one of the broadsheet newspapers: *The Independent* ran a story headlined 'Blur Turn Against Blair In New Battle Of The Bands'. Though Albarn's language was a little more temperate than expected, the 'Tony's a wanker' scenario envisaged by Alastair Campbell was coming to pass. Blur's old Labour Party associates were discovering that rock musicians are among nature's more capricious creatures.

The first music to be released from *Blur* was Beetlebum. The subject matter of its lyrics was passed over; instead, a great deal of comment was focused on its similarity to the later work of The Beatles. Unbeknown to most observers, a rejected design for its sleeve, based on a skit on the drumskin from the *Sgt. Pepper* sleeve, had made the point explicit, even spelling the song's title 'Beatlebum'. When Damon Albarn was quizzed about all this, however, John, Paul, George and Ringo were accorded noticeably less importance than Noel and Liam Gallagher; this song, it seemed, aimed at striking back at Oasis by showing them how unlike their heroes they actually were. 'I want Noel to listen to Beetlebum and realise that it is . . . *closer*,' said Albarn. In the same interview, he then got down to more emotive business. 'There's still no love lost between us. He wished I'd died of AIDS, and he can go fuck himself basically . . . I don't care if he apologised for it. He never apologised to *me* for it.'

Beetlebum entered the singles chart at number one. Its shadowy, fractured ambience staked a timely claim for the idea that ambitious designs could still be combined with commercial clout, though the single's success only heightened speculation about the rest of the imminent album. All manner of whispers circulated around London: according to particularly hysterical rumours, Blur had fulfilled Graham Coxon's desire, articulated later that year, 'to make a record that nobody likes or understands'. As it turned out, though he and Albarn had evidently gone out of their way to – to use Alex James's term – 'unprettify' the album's songs, the group's melodic aspect remained intact: in Country Sad Ballad Man, On Your Own, Movin' On and M.O.R., one simply heard Blur's talent decisively rerouted to the angular place that they habitually occupied anyway. Besides, within *Blur* lurked the group's biggest single – in financial terms at least – to date.

Song 2 was a ninety-second throwaway, thrown on to tape while the group awaited the delivery of some new equipment. Much of its lyric had been spontaneously improvised; the finished version featured a vocal performance that Damon Albarn assumed would merely serve as a guide. In the fact that it snapped between pared-down verse and splenetic, brain-crushing chorus, one heard – of all things – the influence of Nirvana. This, as far as its commercial prospects were concerned, was no bad thing: when Tony Wadsworth, the head of the Parlophone label and Blur's ultimate boss, came to take stock of their progress, this song alone seemed enough to convince him that they were not about to propel themselves to the margins.

'We said, "We'll just play you this one, it's really short," ' says Alex James. 'And he was just grinning, from that point on. Once you get a big single in the bag, everyone becomes a lot more relaxed.' In time, Song 2 would soundtrack advertising campaigns for the Pentium II Processor and Nike sportswear, as well as accompanying just about any TV footage that reflected its atmosphere of speeding abandon. 'They still use it all the time on the telly,' says Alex James, 'whenever they want to show something going fast.' The receipts from such exposure are said to have earned Blur somewhere in the region of £2 million.

For those who might miss what Graham Coxon once termed 'the Blur stomp', there was but one sliver of consolation: a rather self-conscious song called Look Inside America, pitched somewhere between End Of A Century and For Tomorrow. Though such reference points suggested some stray throwback to everything from which Blur were running, its words – founded on the business of touring the USA, the ritual that had once driven Blur to near-breakdown – suggested that their author could now derive an unforeseen sense of comfort from the American expanse. 'I didn't want that to go on,' says Alex James. 'It was "Fuck off Britpop." That's why it had to be included. Look Inside America is exactly what Britpop was urging you not to do.'

Nevertheless, as *Blur* proved, in freeing themselves from character-songs, cockney accents and their one-time insistence on an all-pervading sense of place, the group had turned in some of their most satisfying, sympathetic music. In many reviews of the album, one could divine a loud sigh of relief, prompted by the impression that the group seemed to be happily returning to the world from whence they came. 'Will all teenage girls please vacate the building in an orderly fashion,' said *Q* magazine. 'You've had your fun. You've had your piece of ass. Take it home, press it, keep it, date it, and move on. The sexy little indie band want the screaming in their ears to stop. They want to move on too.' Screaming adolescents were not the only ones Blur were about to leave behind; *Blur* also served notice that only the cloth-eared would now associate the group with the Gallagher brothers. 'They are now,' said *Q*, 'officially on different planets.'

One track on *Blur* seemed to encapsulate all this. Death Of A Party, an echo-laden nod to the Specials' Ghost Town, had originally been brought to the sessions for *Modern Life Is Rubbish*. Though Albarn's intent had been to write a song about 'the paranoia of sex, the fear of AIDS', both its lyric and abiding ambience suited early 1997 to perfection. Here, it seemed, was the sound of a weary exit from some wee-hours hellhole, where only the truly misguided were left at the bar. In Alex James's recollection, the song had been revived at the suggestion of Andy Ross, who gleefully seized on its fortuitous topicality.

In late 1996, Ross took his finished copy of *Blur* on holiday. 'I was on a beach in the Caribbean, listening to it, thinking "Oh dear – I'm a bit worried about this. This isn't going to sell as many as the last one,"' he says. 'But I remember thinking to myself, really quickly,

"You bastard! Have you deserted to the other side?" I actually felt quite ashamed."'

Like the group he had first beheld in a shabby North London club seven years earlier, Andy Ross had just left Britpop.

Some people, however, were moving in the opposite direction. The same month that *Blur* announced its authors' exit from the party they had started, *Vanity Fair* – that byword for celebrity, glamour and all matters newsworthy on the Upper West Side – contained a twenty-five-page special report that aimed to confirm London as the globe's new pop cultural capital. The cover image featured Liam Gallagher and Pasty Kensit tucked under a Union Jack duvet: she in a translucent black bra, tights and stack-heel boots; he in a white woolly hat with a B&H on the go. Inside lurked a camped-up article, peddling the old Britpop notion that London had reawakened the ghosts of the 1960s: 'Move it along, Granddad [sic], you're getting in the way of the scene! The London scene, that is! From Soho to Notting Hill, from Camberwell to Camden Town, the capital city pulses anew with the vibrations of an epic-scale youthquake! Change is in the air in London, and the kids, as their idol Liam is wont to say, are mad for it!'

The piece – written by David Kamp – soon fell into a rather more strait-laced vocabulary. It touched on food, art, music, football, drugs, design – and politics. 'Tony Blair is, to use the ancient parlance, kind of switched-on, as politicians go,' wrote Kamp. 'He doesn't exactly exude JFK charisma, but he has an informality and shiny nowness about him.' A few paragraphs on, he posed a commendably prescient question, predicated on Blair's expected victory at the imminent general election: 'Will rock stars be welcome at No. 10 Downing Street?'

The initial prompt for *Vanity Fair*'s splurge had come from Toby Young, the London émigré who had begun work for the magazine in the summer of 1995. He had in mind a 400-word article for Vanities, its all-happening bits-and-bobs section, but rapidly found his pitch elevated to something much more extensive. At each stage of his discussions with his superiors, he found that he was expected to make a case for London's importance with progressively more enthusiasm. 'I think I took a few things from other articles: London was becoming an ever more popular destination with the youth of Europe, particularly the French,' he says. 'And Oasis were doing well in America, so I dressed that up in a bit of "They're The Beatles of our era."'

Young's first idea had been based on a spate of coverage that had begun in the summer of 1996. That August, *The Sunday Times* had run a one-page article in its News Focus section, presented with a similar air of camp to *Vanity Fair*'s coverage. The text nestled in a swirl of cod-60s psychedelic graphics; its headline, presented in bubble type, was 'Swinging City'. It began with an encounter with an admirably media literate young Frenchwoman: 'The young Parisienne stepped out into the night air of Europe's most vibrant city and savoured the sense of excitement that seemed to palpitate in the breeze around her. "Ah, London," she smiled. Nadia Gaborit, a twenty-three-year-old secretary, had just arrived on the Eurostar at Waterloo Station, and was eagerly awaiting a weekend of clubbing, cinema-going and culture with her London friends ... "London is taking over as the culture capital of Europe," said Gaborit. "It is a city that is at once funny, crazy, eccentric and exciting ... London is wonderful."'

On 4 November, *Newsweek* ran a cover story headlined 'London Rules'. 'London is a hip compromise between the non-stop newness of Los Angeles and the aspic-preserved beauty of Paris – sharpened to New York's edge,' it claimed. 'In short, this is the coolest city on the planet.' Though its coverage was peppered with references to what remained of Britpop – Noel Gallagher was pictured playing his Union Jack guitar, as was 'rocker Jarvis Cocker' – British rock groups were implicitly accorded the status of minor cultural players: in *Newsweek*'s estimation, London's clubs, fashion designers and art scene were much more worthy of comment. Given the increasingly washed-out state of the UK's music, this was perhaps rather well-advised.

Vanity Fair had something rather more ambitious in mind. Led by Aimee Bell, one of the magazine's senior editors, they set up camp in the Dorchester Hotel in November, and began to corral the capital's cultural aristocracy – restaurateurs, musicians, models, tailors – into posing for their photographers. One of Toby Young's responsibilities was the co-ordination of a photo shoot at the Groucho Club with Damien Hirst, Keith Allen and Alex James, whom *Vanity Fair* had chosen to term 'The Boulevardiers'. He arrived at 11am to find the trio unshaven, unsteady on their feet and smelling 'as if they'd spent the night on the floor of the Coach and Horses, rolling around in dog ends'. The shoot, buoyed by vodka and a rather more illicit intoxicant, took no less than six hours; when Hirst finally agreed to sign a release form, he simply wrote 'Suck my big dick'. Alex James, meanwhile, rather got the sense that the Anglo-American world's most upmarket magazine was winging it. 'I remember them saying, "Who else can we ask? We've run out of ideas. We've got Liam and Patsy, and we've got you three ... can you think of anyone else?"' he says. 'There was a real sense that they were scrabbling around.'

The same afternoon, Young was taxi'd to Park Royal, NW10, to assist with a portrait of the senior staff of *Loaded* magazine – 'The Hedonists' – and a gaggle of models, including the celebrated Sophie Dahl. The photographer was the unspeakably fashionable American conceptualist David LaChapelle, who was aiming, at no little cost, to pay tribute to Stanley Kubrick's *A Clockwork Orange*. Mischievously, he also snapped Toby Young snorting cocaine with James Brown, *Loaded*'s editor. Young spent the next three weeks in a recurrent panic, terrified that the picture would make its way back to his bosses in New York. Upon his return to the USA, however, they were more worried about LaChapelle's commissioned work. 'The *Vanity Fair* staff were a bit shocked when they set eyes on the people from *Loaded*,' says Young. 'It was, "*These* are the most glamorous journalists in London?"'

Damon Albarn was pictured at the Atlantic Bar and Grill, W1, with Phil Daniels, the gravelly-voiced actor who had played precious little role in cutting-edge developments since the release of *Parklife*. Liam Gallagher and Patsy Kensit were photographed by Lorenzio Agius. Their picture was headlined 'The Couple', with a smattering of gushing text: 'The Mick and Marianne for our time . . . he is the lead singer of Oasis, Britain's most beloved band since The Beatles . . . she has been a movie star since the age of 17.' According to Toby Young, Liam's rough-hewn charm managed to set at least one American heart a-flutter. 'Aimee Bell came back from that shoot saying, "He looks like a monkey! He looks like a monkey! But I have a real crush on him!"'

The intended coup de grâce was a re-creation of the cover of The Beatles' *Abbey Road*. Inspired by the version of Come Together that had been recorded for *Help*, *Vanity Fair* aimed at persuading Noel Gallagher, Paul Weller and Paul McCartney to ceremonially walk across the St John's Wood zebra crossing outside EMI's famous studios. Initially, soundings suggested that the idea might come off; for a time, Young even toyed with the idea of re-creating one of British rock's most iconic images with Gallagher, Weller, McCartney – and Tony Blair. Eventually, the idea was ensnared by a predictable mixture of clashing schedules and record company politics, along with the Blair team's wariness.

To get Blair in their London coverage, *Vanity Fair* were reduced to a five-minute shoot at the Palace of Westminster. 'We really wanted him to be in the issue,' says Young. 'I had several conversations with Tim Allan, who worked in Tony Blair's office. They were sceptical. On the one hand, if there was this new spirit, maybe Tony Blair could embody it, and cash in; but on the other hand, if there was this new spirit *right then*, then didn't John Major deserve the credit for it? That's what they were debating.'

Blair's portrait was titled 'The Visionary', with a blurb that made reference to his time with Ugly Rumours. He was photographed in the colour-saturated style that was currently in-vogue in the UK's music magazines. Even a set of House of Commons chairs looked like kitsch props.

Though it was conspicuously absent from their coverage, *Vanity Fair* sealed the vogueishness of a buzz-phrase that had been eddying through the press since the winter. Though it was unclear who had first used it in the context of the mid-to-late 1990s, its original source was a track on the Bonzo Dog Doo-Dah Band's 1967 Album *Gorilla*. Thirty years later, 'Cool Britannia' had become a new media clarion-call: here, it seemed, was Britpop's sense of garish cultural renewal, extended as far as the eye could see.

Though the Blairites had managed to associate themselves with this new agenda, the Conservative government initially seemed keen to stake a claim to it. On 6 November 1996, two days after the publication of the *Newsweek* article, Virginia Bottomley's Heritage Department had issued a press release announcing that August had seen a record-breaking three million overseas visitors. 'London is universally recognised as a centre of style and innovation,' it said. 'Our fashion, music and culture are the envy of our European neighbours. This abundance of talent, together with our rich heritage, makes "Cool Britannia" an obvious choice for visitors from all over the world.' Later the same month, at the Lord Mayor's Guildhall Banquet, John Major reiterated *Newsweek*'s assertion that London was 'the coolest city on the planet'.

Early in 1997, just as *Vanity Fair* hit the news-stands, Bottomley canvassed Major's office about the possibility of holding a Downing Street reception for figures from the so-called Creative Industries, to be held in the wake of the Oscars. He ruled it out. 'John Major was reluctant to look as though he was exploiting celebrity and success,' she says. 'I understood where he was coming from, but I would have liked him to go ahead with it. I think he felt that people might regard it as a cynical gesture.' Soon enough, those in charge of Prime Ministerial engagements would have considerably fewer qualms.

The *Vanity Fair* episode came with one twist. Though London's media class were thrilled by the idea that the city's importance was being loudly announced to the USA, any visitor to America would have noticed that Liam and Patsy and their Union Jack duvet were nowhere to be seen. Suggesting that Britain's new clout was being celebrated chiefly for the benefit of Britons themselves, they were only placed on the cover of the magazine's UK edition. In the States, they were passed over in favour of Julia Louis-Dreyfus from Seinfeld.

CHAPTER 20

The last party

At 1pm on Friday 2 May, 1997, Tony Blair arrived at Downing Street. He was greeted by droves of bussed-in Labour Party workers, on whom he performed his by-now familiar trick – learned from Bill Clinton – of laying-on hands at the rate of at least three people per second. They waved miniature Union Jacks, and sang the anthem that Blair had so craftily rewritten the year before: 'It's coming home, it's coming home, it's coming/Labour's coming home . . .'

If some Millbank insiders had once harboured fantasies of a Britpop element to the 1997 election campaign – Noel Gallagher and Damon Albarn criss-crossing the country dispensing acoustic versions of Roll With It and Country House, while studiously avoiding one another – they had long since given them up. The only musician to appear in a Party Election Broadcast had been Mick Hucknall. When it came to campaigning on the stump, the party fell back on an array of TV personalities: Michelle Collins, Liz Dawn, Ross Kemp, Lily Savage, Stephen Tompkinson, Colin Welland, Jean Boht, Sue Johnston, Clive Dunn and Tony 'Baldrick' Robinson.

On election night, many of them excitedly followed the Conservatives' rout at Labour's official celebration, staged in the Royal Festival Hall. Here, the party's triumph blended with the new, celebrity-crazed London. If *Vanity Fair* had painted a picture of the capital in which every evening was marked by some dizzyingly upmarket soirée, this, surely, was the ultimate invite-only party: the launch, not of a new gallery, or a new album, or a new magazine – but a *new government.*

The Festival Hall crowd was a strange mixture of Labour's traditional celebrity constituency – Brian Glover, John Mortimer – and the kind of names that might cause slightly more of a stir: Jarvis Cocker, the aforementioned Hucknall, George Michael. Alan McGee and Andy Saunders were among them, quietly wondering what surprises lay in store now that their new contacts were moving from Millbank to Whitehall.

Blur, meanwhile, were on tour in the USA. By now, their old associate Darren Kalynuk had departed John Prescott's office and taken a temporary post at Rock The Vote, a nominally apolitical set-up – given much of its profile by the comedian Eddie Izzard – aimed at maximising the number of young people on the electoral register. In line with his new job, he was contacted by a representative of Blur's management mere days before the election; none of the group, it seemed, were registered to vote. This, unfortunately, was the province of London's borough councils rather than Rock The Vote. So it was that, for all his apparent interest in politics, Damon Albarn failed to put a cross in the requisite box.

Noel Gallagher had turned up at his local polling station to find that he was required to produce one more item of identification than he was carrying. 'Do you want me to sing you a fucking song?' he protested, before celebrity eventually got the better of bureaucracy. That night, though the South Bank beckoned, he remained on the sofa. 'I had a ticket for the Labour Party party, but I had that much fun watching Portillo and the others get done over I stayed at home in front of the TV. It was all champagne and cigars round our house. Meg and me got pissed and went out into the garden and played [The Beatles'] Revolution dead loud with the neighbours banging on the walls.'

As those close by had found out, Noel and Meg were now resident in a house on Steele's Road, in the raffish North London neighbourhood of Belsize Park. They had moved from a rented pad in St John's Wood in April, whereupon Noel had decided to commemorate his arrival by giving his new home a new name. Spelled out in stained glass, in letters large enough to be seen from the street, were the words 'Supernova Heights'. As the more hard-bitten elements of his public – not to mention the paparazzi – soon discovered, it made spotting the house a cinch.

At a reported cost of £300,000, the house's interior had been remodelled by a designer named Darren Gayer, who – according to a celebration of his work in a book entitled *London Interiors* – 'convinced Noel and Meg to push their ideas to the limit'. The results included a fourteen-foot, three-and-a-half-ton fish tank set into a wall, a set of leopard-print sofas, pink leather chairs originally designed for the Swedish royal family, and a circular red-white-and-blue 'target bath', built from moulded fibreglass and Venetian tiles. Any connoisseur of the more licentious side of the USA would have recognised the abiding style: thanks to its all-pervading gaudiness, Supernova Heights looked distinctly like a bordello.

Within its walls, Noel and Meg began entertaining the kind of friends who recurrently found themselves wanting to extend their evenings beyond the wee hours. There was a Supernova Heights inner circle – Kate Moss, the sometime soap actress Anna Friel, Sadie Frost and Jude Law, the increasingly ludicrous drum'n'bass figurehead Goldie, with whom Noel would collaborate on a clumsy attempt at musical cross-pollination entitled Temper Temper – along with an endless parade of hangers-on. 'It was, "Hello, who the fuck are you?"' Noel later reflected. 'That wanker DJ Sasha said the scene round my house was "seedy". Well, I didn't see him complaining at the time.'

On one occasion, the gang of West End leftovers who took cabs to Belsize Park included the unlikely figure of Alex James, who managed to put aside the lingering memory of Noel's AIDS comment and spend the early morning suggesting they bury the hatchet by recording in Supernova Heights' studio. 'It was a classic All Back To Mine,' he says. 'I was like, "Are you *sure?*" And then we got there and I was going, "Let's do a tune – come on!" But he wasn't having it. I think he drew the line there.'

Elsewhere, Noel and Meg were occasionally keeping slightly more incongruous company. In June, they turned up at Ronnie Wood's fiftieth birthday party, thrown at his Surrey country pile. Among the guests were Mick Jagger, Marianne Faithfull, Jeff Beck, Frankie Dettori, Tim Rice and the ubiquitous Mick Hucknall. Wood had decreed that his guests should dress in the style of the Wild West. Mathews excelled herself, dressing up as a gold rush saloon wench, replete with tumbling ringlets; Noel turned up in his regulation designer attire. In the photographs of the event, his uneasy countenance rather betrayed the fact that middle-aged rock aristocrats' fancy dress parties were not entirely his scene.

Since Oasis's premature return from the USA the previous autumn, Liam and Patsy Kensit had crash-landed in the tabloid newspapers on what seemed like a daily basis. Their relationship was characterised by recurrent bust-ups and tear-drenched crises; it only took the vaguest word to reach the offices of *The Sun* or *Mirror* for a pack of photographers to roar across London, drooling at the possibility of yet another scoop.

In October 1996, the couple had turned up, along with Noel, at the annual *Q* Awards, where the Gallaghers were to be handed the much-coveted statuette for the Best Act In The World Today (Tony Blair, one of the stars of both the 1994 and '95 ceremonies, was mysteriously absent). If observers of Oasis had started to gauge the chances of Liam misbehaving by his amount of facial hair, they were reassured: he arrived looking clean-shaven and dapper, seemingly the very essence of grace and compliance. By the time he and Noel were given their accolade, however, he was not in quite such a good mood. Liam's acceptance speech was curt indeed: 'Thank you very much. I was about to smash the gaff up anyway if you didn't do it.'

On the way to the stage, he had underlined Oasis's achievement with a show of patricidal disdain for a previous musical generation: as TV footage of the ceremony later proved beyond doubt, Liam had flicked cigarette ash on Mick Jagger's head. 'It was appalling,' says Mark Ellen, who watched Liam from the stage. 'The spotlight followed Liam, so I could see Mick Jagger in the audience. I talked to him beforehand; I'd introduced him to Ian Hislop. And suddenly, up the central aisle, came Liam. He did that "Fucking hell, I'm really surprised it's me" schtick that people pull, got a pack of cigarettes out, lit one, took a big drag, and started the walk, stopped next to Mick Jagger – and in a very, very pronounced way, tapped the ash in his hair. I thought, "This is just awful. This is horrible."'

The day's air of unpleasantness eventually caught up with Liam. Upon his and Kensit's exit from *Q*'s post-ceremony party, they were involved in a testy altercation with a *News of the World* reporter, who showed the couple a photograph of Liam, allegedly in the company of another woman. Seven hours later, after Liam had taken refuge in a West End hotel and then slipped away from his minder, he was arrested in possession of two wraps of cocaine.

'It was top, actually,' he said. 'I was thinking, "They're either going to well do me in or they're going to let me off." As soon as I heard them whistling Roll With It, I thought, "I'm well away." It was all, "Can you sign this for my daughter?", while I was doing my fingerprints. The main sergeant was going, "I daren't wash my hands now, my daughter'll kill me."' A conviction would have threatened the prospect of Oasis touring the USA; to a chorus of hand-wringing from *The Daily Mail* and a handful of Conservative MPs, Liam was eventually let off with a caution.

Having become engaged in August, he and Kensit had scheduled their marriage for the following February. At the eleventh hour, the prospect of the couple making their vows against a cacophony of flashbulbs, mobile phones and motorbike engines led to a sudden cancellation; the pair were eventually married on 7 April 1997 at Marylebone Registry Office. 'It was top. Me, Pats, the builder who's doing me house and her hairdresser,' said Liam. 'Just kept it really small, otherwise we were never going to get it done.' Thankfully, their honeymoon dripped with the fairytale quality that both bride and groom presumably intended. 'We just stayed in a hotel for three days and got off it,' said Liam.

It was against this backdrop of excess and media ubiquity that Oasis recorded their new album. Noel Gallagher had written the lion's share of its songs on the Caribbean island of Mustique, in a house owned by Mick Jagger, where he and Meg Mathews had holidayed with Johnny Depp and Kate Moss. Six months after his return – and having patched up the rift that had exploded in North Carolina – they began work, with the ever-dependable Owen Morris, at EMI's Abbey Road studios. They had booked the mythical Studio Two, seemingly trying to reap whatever spectral magic The Beatles had left in their wake. Unfortunately, Abbey Road's rather oppressive atmosphere, the ever-present paparazzi, and Liam's arrest conspired to curtail their stay prematurely. From there on in, Oasis recorded at Ridge Farm, a studio that sits just south of the M25, near Horsham, West Sussex.

It was there that the Gallaghers began to frenziedly mix work with the kind of pleasure that arrived in small polythene pouches. 'I used to go down to the studio,' says Alan McGee, 'and there was so much cocaine getting done at that point . . . Owen was out of control, and he was the one in charge of it. The music was just *fucking loud.*'

'I would go home at weekends,' says Paul Arthurs. 'It'd get to Friday, and someone would be driving down from London with a big bag. People would be invited. It'd be, "We're having Friday night, Saturday and Sunday off – we'll start work again on Monday. We're going to have it large." Cocaine isn't my scene: I just used to go home. And Owen used to like to go to the pub all day and then start work. Or he'd have to have two bottles of red wine – out of a pint pot – and three hundred Silk Cuts. That's how he'd have to start work, at midday.'

Quite what the world was expecting from the group's third LP was a moot point. In 1996, Noel had collaborated with The Chemical Brothers on a number one single entitled Setting Sun. Given that his Beatles-worship showed no signs of fading, it was perhaps not surprising that the song took its lead from John Lennon's Tomorrow Never Knows. That said, Noel's collaborators were masters of booming electronics rather than blaring guitars – and within the song's incendiary, almost atonal arrangement, some of Oasis's more optimistic champions sensed the possibility of more avant-garde ideas creeping into the group's music. As if to scotch such fantasies, Noel quickly informed an *NME* reporter that the album would contain nothing less than 'the usual pub rock bollocks'.

As it turned out, this was not quite true. As Alan McGee was discovering, the group were changing their game: recording songs that escaped the strictures of orthodox rock composition and regularly clocked in at well over six minutes, and layering on Noel Gallagher's guitars to the point that mere speakers could not hope to contain the racket. When he had remixed *Definitely Maybe*, Owen Morris had worked his magic by stripping back such aural excess; now, he seemed to gleefully encourage it. In Noel's estimation, a track entitled My Big Mouth contained the sound of thirty different guitar tracks.

The album's keynote track had been held back from both *Definitely Maybe* and *What's The Story*, pending the kind of budgets that had only just materialised; so it was that All Around The World was caked in strings, horns, superfluous vocal overdubs, grandiose drum fills and squalling guitar solos, none of which gave up the ghost until the song's ninth minute.* The new watchwords were Bigger, Louder and Longer; here was the moneyed regality of life after Knebworth, put to music.

This, it eventually became clear, was more a matter of pharmaceutical excess than artistic design. 'It was an album mixed on cocaine,' Noel later explained. 'That's why it sounds like it does. Loads and loads of trebly guitars.' Worse still, his bilious musical designs were wrapped around songs that, he later admitted, tended to barely pass muster. 'I wasn't prepared to make things any better,' he rued. 'I'd get to a certain point and go, "Fuck it, that'll do." We made the record to justify the drug habit. I was making records to justify spending fucking thousands on drugs.'

To cap it all, the group's success had kiboshed the possibility of even their close associates voicing much in the way of criticism. 'The record company are hardly going to come round when you've sold twenty-five million albums and tell you that you might want to shorten the arrangements,' said Noel. 'And your manager's not going to say anything 'cos he doesn't want to upset anyone. Everyone's going, "It's brilliant!" And right towards the end, we're doing the mixing and I'm thinking to myself, "Hmmm, I don't know about this now."'

---

* Noel Gallagher had talked up All Around The World in the group's earliest interviews. In April 1994, he described it as 'the song to end all songs . . . Hey Jude by a load of kids from Manchester'. He went on: 'The reason we haven't recorded that song is because there isn't enough money in Creation Records' bank balance to pay for the production.' He also talked about Oasis using the song to enter the Eurovision Song Contest.

For all the sycophancy, there was once voice prepared to echo such doubts. When Noel played the new album to his friend Paul Weller, his response was blunt: 'I'm not having it,' he said. By then, however, it was rather too late.

Noel's master copy of the new album arrived at Supernova Heights on the morning of the general election. It was to be entitled *Be Here Now*, a phrase that lay buried in the arcane fringes of The Beatles' legend. During their infamous visit to India, the Maharishi Mahesh Yogi had told them that these three words formed the essence of his teachings; in the early 1970s, John Lennon claimed this was also the maxim that underpinned all great rock'n'roll, while George Harrison used it for a song on one of his solo albums. It was perhaps a telling summation of the Oasis aesthetic that whereas Harrison and Lennon had been inspired by slightly mystical factors, Noel had simply filched it.

It became increasingly obvious that the Oasis camp – led by Marcus Russell – was gripped by fear about two prospects. Firstly, there was the possibility that – god forbid – the album might be hyped: talked about at such length and with such frenzied anticipation that the group could not possibly hope to match their public's expectations. On top of that, there was snowballing unease about counterfeit copies emerging before the official release date, an anxiety only heightened by the newly popular smugglers' paradise that was the Internet.

As a result, the first focus of their attention was the endless unofficial Oasis websites: the modern equivalent of fanzines, on which droves of hard-bitten fans paid tribute to the group. On 5 May, Ignition Management sent out an e-mail to the hundreds of people responsible, informing them that they had a month to consign 'copyrighted material' – audio and video clips, record sleeves, lyrics, guitar chords, photographs – to their computers' wastebaskets. The resultant press coverage rather suggested a moneyed Goliath wreaking quite unnecessary havoc on a string of defenceless Davids. Stephen Penna, aged fourteen from Redhill, was among the crestfallen disciples who had to remove his work from the web. 'I am still a big Oasis fan,' he said. 'But Ignition and Creation are making a big fuss for nothing.'

Later in the summer, when it came to the album's first exposure on national radio, the sense of borderline panic was only intensified. Much to Radio One's delight, songs from *Be Here Now* were to be premiered on Steve Lamacq's *Evening Session*. Unfortunately, when Lamacq met Oasis's radio plugger, Dylan White, he discovered that things were not going to be quite so simple.

'It was an absolutely ridiculous scenario,' says Lamacq. 'At first, we had the plugger saying, "You can play all the tracks off the album on one show." So we were just about to start trailing that, when it was, "Actually, we're a bit worried about bootlegs creeping out, so you can play four tracks one night and three the next – but you have to talk over the tracks, or put a jingle in the middle." Dylan said to me, "Can't you put a jingle, right in the middle of the track?" I said, "There is *no way* I'm dropping a jingle in the middle of an exclusive new Oasis track. You either run with this, in all good faith, or we don't do it." I said, "Give us the tracks and we'll see what we can do." And we got three tracks.

'We played them,' he continues, 'and we got a call the next day saying, "Steve didn't talk over them enough, so you're not getting the others." So I had to go on air the next night and say, "Sorry, but we're not getting any more tracks." It was just *absurd.* I didn't care about what it looked like for us. It wasn't about our egos. But we'd promised it to the people who wanted to hear it. We started to get e-mails from people saying, "What are they playing at? Why is this going on?" By then, I was sick to the back teeth of the politics. The politics were so bad, I would have cheerfully never played them again.'

Journalists, meanwhile, were no less affected by Ignition's anxieties. *Be Here Now* was to be trailed by a single entitled D'You Know What I Mean; to hear the four tracks that were assembled on the CD, it was necessary to visit Creation's offices in Primrose Hill, where Johnny Hopkins, the group's PR, was in possession of a single copy. For the purposes of revealing its content to the press, he had taken the strange step of hiring a plush saloon car, in which he drove favoured contacts on endless laps of Regent's Park, while the music blared from the audio system.

When it came to the album, the Oasis camp implicitly acknowledged that such measures were simply impractical. The air of neurotic control freakery, however, was maintained by a contract, reproduced under an Ignition Management letterhead, that had to be signed before any reviewer was sent a copy. It read as follows:

> In connection with this Article [i.e the review of the album] you will receive a cassette copy of the album entitled 'Be Here Now' by Oasis ('the Cassette') to listen to. By signing below, you confirm that you will not duplicate the Cassette or any part of it in any medium, nor will you allow any person other than yourself to hear the contents of the Cassette, nor will you discuss the contents of the Cassette with any persons other than those necessary to produce the Article. Further you confirm that neither

you nor [space left for title of publication] will exploit the Article, or any part of it, in any other medium or manner than set out on the following page* and no rights will be granted to any third party to exploit the Article, or any part of it, in any other medium or manner. You further acknowledge that to do any of those acts you have agreed to refrain from doing above may cause substantial and unquantifiable damage to Oasis.

The worldview implied by this passage seemed to suggest a truly surreal kind of paranoia: according to the contract's logic, if any journalist talked about *Be Here Now* in the presence of their partner, family or friends, by some chain of coincidence akin to the Butterfly Effect, the Gallaghers might be forced to give up on their dreams and return to Burnage. 'I got the blame for that,' says Alan McGee. 'I remember opening *The Sunday Times*, the Sunday before *Be Here Now* came out, and it went, "McGee is the new Peter Mandelson." All I can say is, you're looking at a man who never had record contracts until 1990, and I started the label in 1983. Does that sound like the work of a man who, in 1997, is going to be making people sign disclaimers so they won't play the record to their girlfriend?'

When *Be Here Now* had been premiered to the staff of Creation, Ignition's jumpy mindset had been made clear. The album was played at a lunchtime reception held on the first floor of Quo Vadis, the Soho restaurant that was once the site of Karl Marx's home. It was a hot day, so the management had allowed fresh air to circulate. This, unfortunately, left open a truly chilling prospect: some crafty passer-by hearing the music, figuring out what it was, running to one of Tottenham Court Road's hi-fi shops, buying a professional-standard Walkman, shinning up a drainpipe and illicitly taping however much music was left.

This was obviously far too scary to contemplate. Within the album's opening bars, one Creation employee recalls Alec McKinlay, Marcus Russell's right-hand man, sprinting around the room, closing every last window.

On Monday 2 June, Oasis were rehearsing at Music Bank, a plush, air-conditioned facility in Bermondsey, about as far from the backroom of the Manchester Boardwalk as could be imagined. Around them, there was no shortage of evidence of their new easy life: Liam, who had decided not to sing that day, sat on a sofa, dividing his attention

---

* Here, the reviewer was required to enter his or her name, the date the review would be published, the territory their publication served, etc.

between a consignment of designer clothes, a can of Red Stripe, and a catalogue for a forthcoming Christie's auction of Beatles memorabilia. Over the din of an instrumental version of Don't Look Back In Anger, he passed judgement on his colleagues. 'They're good, aren't they?' he shouted. 'Look at them. They're good.'

Noel, meanwhile, talked about the new album. It was notable that whereas in the past, he needed only the slightest shove to proclaim the brilliance of his own work, he suddenly sounded more hesitant. Indeed, among the words he uttered that afternoon, there lurked a pretty concise critique of *Be Here Now*'s failings.

'I'm proud of the songs, but I think me and Owen got a bit lazy in the studio. That's *my* opinion, and I'm allowed to say it – no-one else is. We weren't taking too many risks . . . I'm getting a bit bored of the Roll With It-type song, the Wonderwall song and summat in the middle. That's why I was saying, years ago, about doing three albums and having a big rethink . . . I like the songs, but the production's a bit bland . . . There's a song called I Hope, I Think, I Know, which is a bit [makes fart noise], a bit like Roll With It – pie-in-the-sky fucking shit, really. All Around The World – that's a bit cheesy.'

That Friday, he and Meg Mathews were married in Las Vegas, in a small wedding chapel called The Church of the West. Marcus Russell was the best man; the only other members of the congregation were Mathews' parents. The chapel's organist played versions of The Beatles' This Boy, Yesterday and All My Loving, before giving way to an Elvis impersonator called Ron Decars. It was reported that, by way of a wedding present, Noel bought Meg a set of breast implants, one of which duly slipped its moorings on a transatlantic flight. Mere days after the front pages accorded to the wedding, the mishap secured Oasis another splurge of tabloid coverage, and, in its own grisly way, once again ratcheted up the anticipation surrounding the album.

One month later, during an interview with the *NME*, Noel delivered his pièce de résistance. As those who had taken a ride in Johnny Hopkins' hire car had discovered, D'You Know What I Mean was a rather lumbering would-be epic whose bridge made clumsy reference to meeting the almighty, before its chorus, inspired by Noel's opening proclamation at Knebworth – 'Right here, right now, this is history!' – sounded a note of hubristic confidence.

'The song seems to be pitting your people against God's,' said Ted Kessler. 'Do you think Oasis are more important to the youth of today than God?'

'Now, that's a loaded question,' said Noel, well aware that his inquisitor was leading him towards John Lennon's 1966 claim that The Beatles were bigger than Jesus. Predictably, however, he could not stop himself. 'I would have to say, without a shadow of a doubt, that is true. Yeah. Football is more important to me than religion. Some of the pop stars I like are more important to me than God, so yeah. I would hope we mean more to people than putting money in a church basket and saying ten Hail Marys every Sunday. Has God played Knebworth recently?'

The Daily Mirror swiftly bowed to the inevitable and smeared the story across its front page. The headline, like something taken from the kind of souvenir newspaper one can have printed at Hamleys, read: 'Oasis: We Are Bigger Than God'. The idea that the group amounted to a limp post-modern pantomime loosely based on the career of The Beatles looked more convincing than ever.

The reviews of *Be Here Now* suggested that Noel might not be far wrong. If Ignition Management had intended their tactics to dampen any suspicions that the album was a work of epochal significance, the contracts, radio embargoes and website closures seemed to conspire to suggest the exact opposite: such ludicrous precautions had obviously been put in place to guard Oasis's equivalent of the Ark of the Covenant. By the time the review cassettes were couriered across London, few journalists seemed in any mood to scale down the expectations – and from the second week of August onwards, *Be Here Now* was awarded truly amazing praise.

Once again, The Beatles were an apposite reference point. To find an album that had attracted gushing notices in such profusion, one had to go back thirty years, to the release of *Sergeant Pepper's Lonely Hearts Club Band* – in response to which *The Times* had praised 'sweeping bass figures and hurricane glissandos', *The New York Times Review Of Books* had acclaimed 'a new and golden renaissance of song' and *Newsweek* had so far forgotten itself as to compare John Lennon with TS Eliot.

In the *Guardian*, Caroline Sullivan could only marvel at *Be Here Now*'s excellence: '*Be Here Now* validates most if not all of the Gallaghers' boasts about their greatness. It's not an especially original work, but it proves that old sounds can yield new meanings if pasted together cunningly enough . . . Far from being the "footnote" predicted a year ago by *The Daily Telegraph*, Oasis are writing the history of 1990s pop to suit themselves.'

'*Be Here Now* is a great rock record,' said *The Daily Telegraph*'s Neil McCormick, making up for his paper's previous slip-up. 'It refines the Oasis sound, a potent combination of Beatles-esque song construction and hard-rock delivery, and takes it to the final frontier . . . It captures the moment. Right here and right now, this is the place to be.'

It was *The Observer* that got the most carried away, deciding to run its review – written by the paper's resident rock critic, Neil Spencer – on the front page. Its headline was 'Here At Last. Oasis Break The Drought'. '*Be Here Now* delivers all the necessary excitement and more,' said Spencer, who went on to imply that the album's release would mark little short of a decisive moment for human civilisation. 'Grandly conceived and invested with sensurround production, it pumps up Oasis's mix of scabrous guitars and melodic ballads to an epic scale far beyond their earlier records . . . *Be Here Now* is a triumph. It is also the album that will make Oasis into a global force, insinuating itself into tormented, hopeful young hearts from Indiana to Jakarta and filling arenas full of waving scarves and flaming cigarette lighters across the planet.'

For some reason, *The Daily Express* handed its copy of *Be Here Now* to Terry Major-Ball, the oft-ridiculed brother of the ex-Prime Minister. As well as contravening the terms of the Ignition contract by playing it to his wife, Shirley, he broke from protocol by delivering a rather negative judgement. 'I'm sorry,' he said, 'but my ancient ears are incapable of accommodating the raucous sounds of a modern band . . . I'd rather listen to a dripping tap.'

In the UK's music magazines, the chorus of credulous tributes only got louder. *Q* magazine made up for the three stars it had awarded *What's The Story* by according *Be Here Now* the full complement of five, and giving its gleeful assent to Noel's old contention – conspicuously absent from his latest batch of interviews – that his group shared the same rarefied orbit as The Beatles. 'On the evidence of *Be Here Now*, Oasis don't sound afraid of anything,' wrote the usually level-headed Paul Du Noyer. 'Actually, it's a bad month to be in any band that isn't called Oasis. This is their long-anticipated third album and – sorry, but there's no way around it – *Be Here Now* is the heavy, heavy monster sound of summer 1997 . . . Huge as a planet, *Be Here Now* rolls as slowly as a planet also, and just as unstoppably . . . You have to go back, as Noel so often does, to efforts like The Beatles' *Revolver*, for a set whose every constituent could be spun off into the singles chart . . . Sometimes, there is nothing wrong with being obvious. A trouble shared is a trouble doubled. Oasis are not in the business, right now, of handing out trouble. Instead, they are doing just what The Beatles did in the same phase of their career – they took it as their job, nothing more and nothing less, to cheer up the country.' Even the *NME*, despite voicing plenty of scepticism, were sufficiently convinced of *Be Here Now*'s merits to give it eight out of ten.

Mojo, meanwhile, had given the album to Charles Shaar Murray, the sometime *Oz* and *NME* writer whose byline had enough clout to be run on the magazine's cover. He had nothing but garlands to dispense, working himself into such a frenzy that he lapsed into Jamaican patois. 'This is the Oasis World Domination album,' he wrote. 'Dem a come fe mess up de area seeeeeerious.'

On top of all this, the night before *Be Here Now*'s release, BBC1 screened a thirty-minute programme predictably titled *Right Here, Right Now*. Put together by the team responsible for the music show *Later*, it followed Oasis on a helicopter trip to Manchester, where Noel and Liam climbed into a people-carrier and gave the film's makers a tour of Burnage. The resulting footage was peppered with grainy cutaway shots of urban dereliction – which, as anyone familiar with the Mancunian expanse would have spotted, were actually filmed down the road in Rusholme. Such was the rather patronising subtext of the film: that Oasis had been blighted members of the underclass who had only just managed to escape a truly unthinkable fate.

Mark Cooper, the programme's producer, made the point explicit in an article he wrote for *The Daily Telegraph*: 'The Gallaghers know that people like them aren't meant to have a say,' he wrote. His sympathy had been sufficiently stirred to allow the group thirty minutes of prime-time TV, during which they played pool in a Mancunian pub, performed three songs from their new album, and talked about how great they and the album were.

In all the responses to *Be Here Now*, one could detect an age-old syndrome. Its advocates seemed to be driven not by the album's merits, but by a massed desire to maintain Oasis's myth and thereby prolong the delirious fun that had started three years before. By 1997, however, hyperbole was hurtling away from reality, driven by a force that was all its own. By the end of the year, the praise hurled at Oasis would look deeply misplaced.

It has long been standard music industry practice to release albums at the start of the working week. *Be Here Now*, however, was finally placed on sale on Thursday 21 August. Ignition's seemingly unquenchable anxiety was once again the reason: given that American record companies tend to send merchandise to stores way before release dates, they were worried about the nightmarish prospect of import copies making it over to the UK prematurely. The release date was commemorated on the album's sleeve, thus encouraging the group's fans to believe that to buy a copy on the day it appeared was to participate in some kind of historical event.

In the light of the reviews – not to mention Oasis's inescapable celebrity – it was hardly surprising that *Be Here Now* flew from the shops. Its initial sales were certainly helped by the fact that, thanks to his antics aboard a French yacht with Patsy Kensit and Kate Moss, Liam Gallagher made it on to the front page of every tabloid newspaper on the day of the album's release – but even the most ubiquitous media profile would have fallen short of convincingly accounting for the response. On its first day, *Be Here Now* managed sales figures of over 350,000. By the close of business on Saturday, the number was 696,000. Michael Jackson's *Bad*, for so long the benchmark of first-week success, was now an irrelevance: as far as the UK was concerned, *Be Here Now* was officially the fastest-selling album of all time.

Initial signs suggested that many Oasis fans were happy with their purchase. 'It's the best album I've ever heard,' said Barry Pask, one of many *Sun* readers who had faxed in his judgement. 'It's even better than The Beatles. Just brilliant. Mad for it.' As the weeks rolled on, however, one began to sense the dull thud of anti-climax. It did not take a musicologist to empathise with the sudden feeling of queasy uncertainty that Noel Gallagher had experienced towards the album's conclusion. The fact that bilious arrangements had been draped over thin musical designs made for the feeling that one had fallen victim to an age-old con-trick: short weight being dressed up as ostentatious luxury.

There were a couple of good songs on *Be Here Now*: its swaggering, gonzo-rock title track, and the equally energised It's Getting Better (Man!!), initially mooted as a single. But its failings were manifold. Tellingly, after spending two albums cheekily pilfering from his musical heroes, Noel Gallagher had begun to plagiarise himself. The opening passage of Don't Go Away was eerily similar to Slide Away; the verse of Stand By Me had exactly the same vocal melody as Married With Children. Be Here Now, meanwhile, found Liam lapsing into a 'yeah yeah yeah' coda lifted from Columbia.

One track in particular embodied the album's malaise. Magic Pie was sung by Noel, in the plaintive, slightly whiney voice that usually paled next to his brother's visceral roar. It contained a lift from Tony Blair's millennially-minded Labour Party Conference speech of 1996* – and like large parts of that oration, Noel's words oozed a very clumsy faux-profundity. As an added bonus, however, there were baffling non-sequiturs: 'There are but a thousand days preparing for a thousand

---

* Pointing out that at the time of the next election, there would be around 1,000 days until the end of the 20th century, Blair said that Britain would have 'One thousand days to prepare for one thousand years.'

years/Many minds to educate and people who have disappeared/D'you dig my friends? D'you dig my shoes?/I am like a child with nothing to lose but my mind.' Such borderline nonsense, set to one of Noel's weaker vocal melodies, was stretched over no less than seven minutes.

Be Here Now seemed to be the perfect soundtrack to Oasis's increasingly ludicrous lives. In the album's soulless mulch, one could make out the echoes of Union Jack duvets, fourteen-foot fish tanks, Wild West birthday parties and a mountain of Peruvian flake.

One image evokes the *Be Here Now* period – and the end of Britpop – better than most. Three weeks before the album's release, Noel Gallagher and Meg Mathews had crash-landed on the front of every British newspaper, when, accompanied by Alan McGee and his wife Kate, they sashayed into a reception at 10 Downing Street.

The night before, Gordon Brown had held a reception at Number 11 to celebrate new tax concessions for the UK film industry: his guests had included Kevin Spacey and Sinéad Cusack. The Blair's soirée, however, was an even more star-spangled occasion. It was supposedly thrown to thank some of those who had contributed, in however small a fashion, to Labour's election victory – but as at least one of their music industry allies discovered, there was an equally important qualification for an invite: the simple currency of celebrity.

Despite his many trips to Millbank, Andy Saunders was not invited. 'Alan said, "They've invited us to Downing Street,"' he says. 'I must admit, I was like, "Cool, great – that is punk rock. The bloody Prime Minister's invited you for tea – that's insane." But I was a bit pissed off they didn't invite me, because I'd done a lot. The only people who got to go were sexy, high-profile kind of people. But when I saw who went . . . it was a bit tacky.'

Noel arrived dressed in an unremarkable blue suit and open-neck shirt; all told, his attire was more redolent of a footballer than a musician. He paused outside that most iconic of front doors and held his fist aloft in an old-school socialist salute – a rather incongruous gesture, given the company he was keeping. The Gallaghers and McGees – who had been driven to Downing Street in Noel's second-hand Rolls Royce – were joined by such leftist rabble-rousers as Maureen Lipman, Sir Ian McKellen, Anita Roddick, Simon Mayo, Michael Grade, Lenny Henry, Eddie Izzard, Vivienne Westwood, Tony 'Baldrick' Robinson and Ross Kemp. Mick Hucknall was presumably detained elsewhere.

'That morning, Alastair Campbell phoned me up,' says Alan McGee. 'He said, "Are they going to behave?" I said, "Oh yeah – no problem.

I think he's coming in a Gucci suit. It'll be fine." He said, "No – is he going to *behave?*" I went "Oh *right.*" We got followed around that entire party by Alastair Campbell, the whole way round. He was just on our case, in case Noel or Meg slipped into the toilets for a flyer.'

'I did get followed to the toilets quite a lot,' said Noel. 'I think they were quite concerned that I was going to . . . there were quite a few phone calls going into McGee: "He's not going to misbehave, is he?" And he was going, "No, no, he's not going to misbehave." And in the car, on the way there, McGee was going, "You're not going to misbehave, are you?" I was going, "Well, no, I'm not going to go in and fucking trash the joint; I'm not going to start spraying 'The Sex Pistols' and 'God Save The Queen' everywhere."

'I didn't want to go in there and act like a yobbo and give the press what they wanted. Because I think everyone was expecting me to turn up in jeans and trainers, with a bottle of Stella and cig, standing on the doorstep, like, "Fuck them all." I wanted to go in there and carry myself as . . . an intelligent young man.' The obligation to cut a decorous figure was perhaps sealed by the intervention of Peggy Gallagher. 'I thought we'd get slagged off for going,' said Noel, 'but I rang my mum on Sunday and she said it was a great honour for her to say one of her sons was going to see the Prime Minister. She told me to go.'

In the run-up to the event, the more fusty corners of the press had seen a brief burst of irate comment. Norman Tebbit used his *Mail On Sunday* column to advise Blair to 'keep well clear of this drug-taking megalomaniac who thinks his band is "bigger than God".' In *The Daily Express*, Peter Hitchens raged: 'Tony Blair should admit that he doesn't really care about drugs and has no serious plans to combat the narcotic epidemic which is ruining the lives of millions of young people . . . The only thing that will guard our children from harm when the pushers sidle up and smile, is the knowledge that *it is wrong to take drugs.* How can we tell them this when the Prime Minister allows such guests beneath his roof, within sight of his own sons and daughter?'

Had they been party to Noel and Blair's brief conversation – centred on their very different experiences of election night – Hitchens and Tebbit would have exploded. 'We were chatting away,' said Noel, 'and I said, "Oh, it was brilliant, man, because we stayed up till seven o'clock in the morning to watch you arrive at the headquarters. How did you manage to stay up all night?" And this is his exact words: he leant over and said, "Probably not by the same means as you did." And at that point I knew he was a geezer. I turned to McGee and went, "Did he just say that?" I thought that showed the guy's got a sense of humour.'

Noel managed to squeeze in one more conversational topic, before

Blair flitted elsewhere. Courageously, he brought up the distinctly un-Blairite cause of a group of striking workers who had been dismissed for refusing to cross a picket line in 1995. 'I did ask him about the Liverpool dockers,' he said, 'which probably went in one ear and out the same ear – probably didn't even go in the ear. His words were, "We'll look into it." And I said, "Yes, you probably will, won't you?" And that was the end of that.'

He and Meg had also been given a tour of the ruling family's apartment at Number 11 Downing Street. 'We talked about furniture, pictures and that sort of thing,' said Mathews, before adding, rather ominously, 'Tony said Cherie and I were extremely alike in our tastes.'

Alex James has never been one for righteous indignation. When he glimpsed the pictures of the Downing Street bunfight the following morning, it simply caused a burst of wry amusement. 'A man who wished that I'd died of AIDS, a loud-mouthed drug-taker, going round to the Prime Minister's for drinks,' he marvels. 'It was just another fucking crazy day. Things did get fucking surreal. Being courted by the Labour Party, getting drunk with Mo Mowlam, and then seeing the bloke you've had a fight with in the playground going to the headmaster's office for tea and cakes – it's just a fucking stupid kid's playground.'

As it turned out, despite the sceptical pronouncements he had made earlier in the year, Damon Albarn had been invited to Downing Street. 'I think it was a good job that he didn't go, actually,' says Alex James. 'I'm quite proud of that. I found that all a bit galling, the fact that fucking grotty Meg Mathews went.' Albarn had sent word that he would not be attending in curt terms indeed. 'I left a message at the House of Commons saying, "Dear Tony, I've become a communist. Enjoy the schmooze, comrade. Love, Damon,"' he later recalled. 'I wouldn't have dreamed of going.'*

Looking at the pictures of Noel and Blair, in which Alan McGee hovered in the background, one was assailed by all kinds of questions. Who was more compromised: the politician, whose aspirations to upright statesmanship suddenly seemed swamped by star-struck superficiality; or the musician, whose presence spoke volumes about just how tamed his art form, once built on scattershot dissent, had become? More intriguingly still, who was truly using who?

---

* *3862 Days*, the official Blur biography, states that 'at the horrid triumphalist Number Ten champagne reception . . . a parade of Britain's finest . . . sipped Krug and cosied up to Tony while a block away in the House of Commons, the Labour Government tried to impose legislation to take £10 of benefit away from single mothers. The symbolism was unforgettably sickening.' The parliamentary business to which this passage alludes actually took place on Monday 28 August.

'We're leaving.
The bar's shut.'

Despite the fact that Noel Gallagher's presence at Downing Street suggested that his influence had reached a new peak, 1997 found the zeitgeist edging away from him. In the context of wider musical developments, *Be Here Now*'s songs increasingly sounded as superfluous as its myriad guitar overdubs; as of the summer, rock music began to take on a rather more artful, questioning tenor.

Early notice of all this had arguably been served in April 1996, with the release of a Manic Street Preachers single entitled A Design For Life. The group's first release since the disappearance of their lyricist and nominal guitarist Richey Edwards, it combined a string-laden arrangement, heavy on *Sturm Und Drang*, with a stirring restatement of the group's proletarian origins. In the midst of Oasis's most hegemonic period, the fact that the song's words were couched in terms of education and self-improvement – its opening line was 'Libraries gave us power' – sounded an incongruous note indeed. Strangely, however, as they achieved the success at which they had aimed since the early 90s, the Manics seemed to assent to a semi-detached role in Oasis's new empire. In April, they had been one of the support acts at Maine Road; by September, they were accompanying Oasis on the American tour that crashed to a halt in North Carolina. When asked their opinions of the Gallaghers, they were happy to pay tribute: 'Pop stars can be shining heroes,' said James Dean Bradfield. 'Liam Gallagher wears a suit of armour as far as I'm concerned.'*

---

* Nonetheless, the Manics announced their detachment from music's ruling thinking via one very telling act: in the wake of their success, the group donated money to Arthur Scargill's Socialist Labour Party.

In June 1997, however, Oasis's dominion was palpably weakened by the release of Radiohead's *OK Computer*: the album on which the promise embodied by the latter's contribution to 1995's War Child album was gloriously realised. Its songs captured both the terror and beauty of the contemporary world: Airbag evoked the euphoria of escaping death in a car-wreck; Subterranean Homesick Alien managed to take the most clichéd modern fantasy – abduction by extra-terrestrials – and render it both beautiful and moving. The album's lead-off single had been a six-minute suite entitled Paranoid Android, which – against all expectations – had been enthusiastically championed by Radio One. Its combination of splenetic, almost violent passages and moments of transcendent calm was thus piped into thousands of British workplaces. 'The amount of typing mistakes that must have been going on,' marvelled the group's singer and chief songwriter, Thom Yorke. 'I never imagined it happening.'

Radiohead were now confirmed as standard-bearers of a British tradition that, in the previous year's flurry of so-called Noelrock, had almost been forgotten: the imperative to wreak controlled havoc on music's accepted norms, and in doing so, express a very potent kind of cultural dissent. These were not the kind of minds that were going to get terribly excited about Blair's arrival at Downing Street. 'For three hours when the Labour Party got in, people were nice to each other,' said Yorke. 'That was it. It's been bullshit ever since. I won't be going to Ten Downing Street, put it that way.'

The Verve's *Urban Hymns* was released in September. Having begun to explore an updated kind of psychedelic rock in 1992, they had reached their apogee with an album called *A Northern Soul*, released in 1995. In among its rolling grooves, however, there lurked two accomplished ballads: On Your Own and History. By then, The Verve were close associates of Oasis, and there was little doubt that the latter song had inspired Wonderwall; one only need play them back-to-back to hear it.

Long frustrated by a lack of success, the group had split up in 1995, but had eventually seen fit to reconvene. Now, led by their imperious lead singer Richard Ashcroft, they were trading in elegant, slightly pompous songs that recurrently dealt with themes of futility and loss. Their comeback single, Bitter Sweet Symphony, was all this incarnate: a stately, string-laden piece in which Ashcroft curtly outlined his bleak take on existence: 'You're a slave to money then you die.' That he managed to make such clichéd words sound heart-stoppingly important was probably all part of the achievement.

Urban Hymns and *OK Computer* – along with Spiritualized's *Ladies*

And Gentlemen We Are Floating In Space and Primal Scream's *Vanishing Point* – sounded a far more uncertain note than the Gallaghers' increasingly clumsy anthems. In All Around The World, as the strings crashed into one another, Liam had sung 'I know what I know/It's going to be okay.' When *Blur* was also taken into account, the conclusion was clear: 1997's best rock records seemed to confirm that things had turned out to be a little more complicated.

Elsewhere, a very different kind of music was only underscoring the idea that the Britpop moment was fading fast. When Take That had split up in 1996, there had been some rather premature chatter about rock music's long-anticipated triumph over mere pop. Months later, however, The Spice Girls set about proving that the kind of music that drew on the vaudevillian ways of showbiz rather than The Beatles' White Album was in rude health. Their first piece in the music industry trade magazine *Music Week* was prophetic indeed: 'Just when boys with guitars threaten to rule pop life . . . an all-girl, in-yer-face pop group have arrived with enough sass to burst that rockist bubble.' By the end of the year, their first three singles had all reached number one, and *Smash Hits* was gleefully readjusting to a world in which sour-faced rock musicians could once again be kept off its cover.

Early in 1997, there came decisive proof of a sea-change. As if to confirm that her group had snatched the spirit of the age from those responsible for Britpop, at 1997's Brit Awards, Geri Halliwell wore a minidress emblazoned with the Union Jack.

On 31 August 1997, the UK was plunged into a run of events that gave the summer – whose two key cultural co-ordinates had been Blair's election victory and the release of *Be Here Now* – a very surreal coda indeed. The massed response to the death of Diana, Princess of Wales, took the country somewhere quite unprecedented. The ensuing weeks saw endless talk about the changed realities of 'post-Diana' Britain; all that had perhaps become clear was that the promise of participating in 'History' – whatever that was – was enough to bring the atomised, alienated millions out of their homes, seemingly poleaxed by the fact that they were not alone.

Less than two weeks later, Oasis began the *Be Here Now* tour at Exeter's Westpoint Arena. If anyone was wondering what the Gallagher brothers might have to say about recent developments, an answer arrived halfway through their performance: that night, Live Forever was introduced by Liam as 'Princess, Live Forever'. Noel was reportedly furious; his anger must have only increased when, ten days later, Liam repeated the dedication inside the hallowed walls of Earl's Court.

If the elder Gallagher was concerned about the fading of his group's outlaw reputation, the antics of other members of the Oasis camp should have been even more of a worry. As 1997 rolled into 1998, Meg Mathews became an increasingly central part of the group's coverage in the press. Having left her artist liaison post at Creation Records, she had established a 'party consultancy' company called 2 Active, in cahoots with her oft-photographed best friend Fran Cutler. The pair specialised in the organisation of soirées at which, it seemed, the bigger their fee, the greater chance there was of a handful of Mathews' celebrity acquaintances deigning to appear. 'I work on a very personal level,' said Mathews. 'I can ring up Johnny Depp and Courtney Love, basically because of the friendship, and have a chat rather than just send an invitation.'

As far as the tabloids were concerned, her hard work was rather overshadowed by Mathews' prodigious shopping habit. In November, *The Sun* published a two-page spread, founded on the paper's estimate that she was now spending £27,000 a month on clothes, trips to the gym, facial treatments and beauty products. Rarely a week went by when a lucky paparazzo didn't snap Mathews and her retinue emerging from some Bond Street designer store, carrying enough shopping bags to fill a fleet of black cabs.

'The likes of Fran Cutler – it was like, "*Who?*" All of a sudden, she was being photographed on South Molton Street,' says Tim Abbot. 'I don't know where she got her money from. Meg was getting her card picked up, but I always felt a bit sorry for Fran. She had to try to keep up: "Just a pair of socks for me, but can you put them in a big fucking bag?"

'But it was gratuitous shopping. Everybody liked it at first, but then it was, "You're just a bunch of greedy cunts, aren't you? I'm on the dole in Norwich, I'm paying £12.49 for an Oasis album, and look at you." The circus became bigger than the band.'

To cap it all, at the tail-end of 1998, Mathews began a column, entitled 'Yeah!', in *The Sunday Times' Style* magazine. Her dispatches, doubtless gabbled down the phone to some dutiful sub-editor who may or may not have written them up with slightly mischievous intent, portrayed a life of endless pleasure and unlimited spending. The column revealed that Meg and Noel kept three cats, named Benson, Hedges and Rosie, who were fed on tuna fish and mackerel; that Meg was a keen fan of George Michael; that she – like the designer Alexander McQueen, apparently – was fond of rescuing abandoned dogs; and that Anna Friel was 'today's Julie Christie'.

And so it went on. 'I've dyed my hair platinum blonde again – I feel more co-ordinated when my hair matches my credit card . . . We were so hungover on Sunday that all I could do was call a cab to pick up two roast dinners . . . We had friends over for a takeaway, but unfortunately the pizza was cold and battered by the time we got to it because the poor delivery boy had to use the box to fight his way through the phalanx of paparazzi . . . I'm hoping the dogs will be delighted with the Arran jumpers I have bought them from Paul Smith . . . It's off to Java for three weeks in the New Year. Life's so tough sometimes . . . Over the New Year, former Scary Spice Mel G came round to swap presents. Her mansion is only about 15 minutes away, which comes in handy when I run out of Fendi croissants.'

Rumours suggested that, as the weeks went on, Noel was increasingly unhappy with the column's impact on his credibility: the scenario rather suggested Oasis's version of *Absolutely Fabulous*, with Mathews and Cutler as Edina and Patsy, and Noel in the role of Saffy, stoically sitting at the kitchen table, rolling his eyes as the champagne flowed and another invite popped through the letterbox.

From February 1998 onwards, the promotion of *Be Here Now* had taken Oasis on a tour of foreign territories that included the Far East and Australia. On a Cathay Pacific flight from Hong Kong to Perth, Liam Gallagher became sufficiently unruly to attract the wrath of his fellow passengers and a lifetime ban from the airline. 'Some pilot told me to shut up,' he explained. 'Some pilot who needs stabbing through the head with a fucking pickaxe. If someone tells me to shut up then I'm not going to like that, am I?' In Brisbane, Liam was alleged to have head-butted a twenty-year-old fan named Benjamin Jones. Four years before, such incidents might have looked like the high-jinx of goggle-eyed rookies. Now, they simply seemed oafish.

While on one of his regular trips to Iceland, Damon Albarn had commented that, were Oasis to touch down in Reykjavik, 'they wouldn't leave the hotel bar.' Listening to *Be Here Now* and observing the group's manoeuvres, it was hard not to disagree. For all their globetrotting, Oasis seemed trapped in an ever-smaller world of drugs, drink, craven worship of The Beatles, and increasingly unjustified arrogance. Precious little of their music had ever been recorded outside the UK; on their frequent trips to America, they had not followed the path trodden by The Rolling Stones and U2, and immersed themselves in rock music's ancestry; there seemed little chance of some Beatles-esque pilgrimage to India. It was difficult to think of any group whose career had combined stratospheric success with such stubbornly limited horizons.

At least one of their old allies traces some of the explanation back

350

to Ashburn Avenue, and the father who displayed scant interest in his sons' upbringing. 'Noel was sharp and worldly,' says Tim Abbot, 'but they were both damaged goods. I once found out he couldn't swim. I was like, "Why's that?" He said, "I was never taught." Some of that came from their father. They don't drive, they can't swim – basic things that a dad might have shown them, they didn't have in their vocabulary.'

Their failure to develop only seemed to throw their fall from grace into sharper relief. 'When they're flicking ash on Mick Jagger's head and they're the coolest band in the country, that's fine,' says Alex James. 'But when they're definitely not the coolest band in the country any more, and they're still asking everyone for a fight . . . they've had it, haven't they, really?' By way of confirming that they were no longer untouchable, the tail-end of 1997 had seen Oasis's mantle as people's champions pass to a very unlikely figure indeed: their old groupie Robbie Williams, suddenly transformed from the portly class clown into an altogether more toned-up, self-assured presence. His soaring, showy ballad Angels belatedly ignited his solo career, and proved that Noel was no longer the UK's pre-eminent merchant of populist balladry. In essence, Williams had evicted Wonderwall from its place in the national psyche, though the Gallaghers seemed reluctant to acknowledge the competition – in Noel's eyes, Williams remained 'a fat dancer from Take That'.*

As far as the quality of Oasis's music was concerned, there was but one cause for optimism. In the summer of 1998, while he was watching that year's World Cup, Noel Gallagher – for so long the one Britpop figure whose celebrity, success and drug intake seemed to cause him no disquiet whatsoever – came to the conclusion that he was in trouble.

'Ten past two in the afternoon,' he later recalled, 'I went to the kitchen, straight out of bed, hair all over the place, got a can of lager out of the fridge, chopped a fucking line out – and at that point I thought, "What am I fucking doing?" I worked myself into such a fucking state that I phoned a doctor and said, "Please man, just give me something." And he said, "I can't give you anything, just fucking stop doing it." From that day, I never touched drugs.'

Inevitably, the business of quitting was not nearly as simple as he might have liked. 'I'd wake up in the middle of the night sweating, feeling like I couldn't breathe and I was going to die,' he said. 'It was a difficult time for me . . . all the people around me were still doing

* From here on in, relations between the two camps took on the appearance of a playground feud. At the 2000 Brit Awards, Williams proposed that he and Liam Gallagher should wager £100,000 each on a televised punch-up between the pair, with the proceeds going to charity. Nothing came of his plans.

loads of drugs and it was quite hard for a while. I'd start having a panic attack even if I had a drink . . . It was at that point that I said to the wife, "Get your gear. Put it in the fucking car. We're leaving. The bar's shut."'

So it was that Noel Gallagher and Meg Mathews exited Supernova Heights and began a new life in Chalfont St Giles, a small Buckinghamshire village in the commuter belt. Upon hearing the news, Damon Albarn must have surely sniggered: here, it seemed, was a re-enactment of the song that had so incurred the Gallaghers' ire in the summer of 1995. Caught in the rat race, paying the price of living life at the limit, Noel was moving to a very big house in the country. If Britpop's vexatious history had ever suggested the potential for a film script, this surely marked the moment at which the credits should roll.

Among the records released during Britpop's twilight period, one in particular provided a very apposite soundtrack to all the dysfunction, fall-out and failure. Pulp's *This Is Hardcore* was released in March 1998, two years after Jarvis Cocker's heroic antics at the Brit Awards. It suggested that the notoriety that had arrived in their wake had led to little more than a very paranoid kind of misery.

In Cocker's estimation, 1996 had been 'sick'. After the Brits incident, he had been more visible than ever, showing his face at so many social functions that the *London Evening Standard* ran an article advising him to stay in. 'He haunts the freebie feast like Banquo's ghost,' it said, 'a pale presence at every shoulder, his spectacles permanently fogged by the exhalation of useless chatter. He is taller and undeniably slimmer, but Jarvis Cocker is, in every other respect, coming to resemble Christopher Biggins, and that is a national tragedy.'

By the end of the year, it was all clearly getting to him. Cocker spent that Christmas alone at the Paramount Hotel in New York. 'There were some hairy moments there,' he said. 'You have to go through a crisis point, I think. I did it to get away from everything, and to have a think about what I wanted to do next, or even if I wanted to continue doing it anymore.' His peace of mind can hardly have been helped by the Paramount's notoriously cabin-like rooms; nor by the fact that among the few people who knew his whereabouts was a Labour Party intern named Imogen, who was attempting to ape Darren Kalynuk's fleeting relationship with Blur. 'I told her to fuck off,' said Cocker. 'I don't know how they tracked me down. Nobody was supposed to know I was there.'

In the meantime, as if to prove that Pulp were still an accredited Britpop group, rumours began to swirl around London about Cocker's drug intake: specifically, visits to Donna Matthews' house and his alleged experience of heroin. 'I've heard lots of rumours . . . I don't really want to talk about it,' he said, just before the album's release, 'because if you talk about it, it doesn't really help anything, because one person's experience is going to be completely different from somebody else's. One thing I will say about it is this. I think that what happens is, say you've got a group of ten people who are friends and they all do that kind of thing: everybody eggs everybody else on, but if you talked to each individual person out of that group and said, "Are you really wanting to do that?", they'd probably say, "No, I think I'd be better off without." It's peer pressure. Like when your mum says to you, "If Martin Hunt jumped in some dog dirt, would *you*?" The answer is probably, "Yeah, I would. If he said it were a good laugh, yeah, I'd do it."'

The new album had been created by a different group from the one responsible for *Different Class*. Russell Senior, Cocker's lieutenant since the days of frustration in Sheffield, had announced his departure upon Cocker's return from New York. According to his official statement, he had left the group because: 'It wasn't creatively rewarding to be in Pulp any more.' Whatever the explanation, his exit only reinforced the idea that Pulp were living in a troublesome place indeed.

In keeping with the theme of its doom-laden title track, *This Is Hardcore*'s sleeve art was based around the cold, impersonal aesthetics of American porn, a theme inspired by Cocker's on-tour experiences of piped hotel TV. This, quite apart from the details of the lyrics, couched his observations of celebrity in a distinctly sexual sense of degradation. One track that had not made the cut, entitled The Professional – released as a B-side – was a vomitific screed that found him indulging in something close to self-flagellation. 'Just another song about single mothers & sex . . . OK, you've heard it before/It's nothing special, but it's a living, can't you see?/I'm a professional.'

Though the album did not sail to any similar extremes, one quickly got the sense that very little in Cocker's world was as it should have been. Its most affecting evocation of his woes, however, was The Fear, which snapped between verses that oozed an almost gothic eeriness, and a chorus that sounded like a last-ditch confession. 'This is the sound of someone losing the plot,' he sang. 'Making out they're okay when they're not . . . A monkey's built a house on your back/You can't get anyone to come in the sack/And here comes another panic attack.'

Inevitably, *This Is Hardcore* threw a curveball at both Pulp's audience and many of those who were charged with writing about the album. In the view of one magazine, it was 'about as close as you can get to commercial suicide without actually arriving at the studio with a loaded gun in your mouth.' They were not far wrong: the album sold only a fraction of the figure managed by *Different Class*, and two of its three singles failed to breach the top 20. As of the spring of 1998, Jarvis Cocker no longer played the role of the housewives' favourite.

As if to seal the idea that Pulp were staking a new claim to being pop-cultural dissidents, that summer saw the release of Cocaine Socialism, put out as a B-side of a single called A Little Soul. A reworking of a song from *This Is Hardcore* called Glory Days, its lyrics found Cocker turning up for a meeting in Whitehall to discuss his contribution to 'the nation's heart and soul', signing an album for someone's daughter, and then settling down to rather sleazier business. 'Do you want a line of this?' went its lyric. There followed two sharp sniffs. 'Are you a *socialist?*'

Pulp had at least had the chance to make their post-Britpop album. As 1997 and 1998 ticked by, scores of groups were silenced as the UK's record companies surmised that guitars were now surrounded by the whiff of obsolescence. Those who had followed in the wake of *Parklife* were sent packing; so too were the kagoul-wearing hordes who had popped up after *What's The Story*. The cull's roll-call was seemingly endless: the world would not be hearing again from The Gyres, The Dandys, Thurman, Mantaray, Bawl, Lick, Pimlico, Powder, Salad, Smaller, Octopus, Livingstone, Silver Sun, Straw, Proper and Sussed. It was safe to assume that Keith from Northern Uproar would not be buying a casino.

For those who were acquainted with at least modest commercial success, Britpop's dying moments held out an arguably even more dreadful fate. As Menswear had discovered, because of the all-consuming importance of chart positions, a group could go from being *NME* cover material to dejectedly taking the train back to their hometown within a matter of days. The archetypal chain of events was simple enough: a single release on Monday, a disappointing 'early midweek' chart position by Tuesday, confirmation of its underperformance on Friday, and the final chilling experience of hearing Mark Goodier utter the dread words 'Straight in at number twenty-eight' on the Sunday.

Such was the experience of Sleeper, who had gone from supporting Blur on the 1994 *Parklife* tour to selling well over 300,000 copies of an album entitled *The It Girl* in 1996. They returned the following September with a single called She's A Good Girl, a horn-laden attempt to combine the straight-ahead pop that accounted for their success with the aura of a new creative depth. The *NME* and *Select* tussled for the honour of putting Louise Wener on their covers; Radio One were happy to place the single on their playlist. Unfortunately, She's A Good Girl did not prove to be popular with their public: it entered the charts at number twenty-eight.

'It was over for us when we got the early midweek,' says Wener. 'It was twenty-something, which was totally crap in terms of what it meant for future record company support. I knew we were as good as done for. I can remember walking down Oxford Street, looking at everyone, thinking, "I'm back in the throng." I had no illusions that anything else was going to happen. We did *TFI Friday* that week, when we knew for sure, and I was drinking from midday onwards. Chris Evans then invited us out for a curry, and I was too pissed to carry on eating with him. I was in the men's loos of this curry house, just lying down, puking. There I was, knowing my whole career was over.'

All that was left to savour was the *Schadenfreude* that came from watching her contemporaries succumb to an identical fate. 'It happened to us,' says Wener, 'and we thought we'd be the only ones. But then everyone started to go, so that was kind of satisfying.'

Over in Whitehall, however, it often seemed as if Britpop was only just beginning. In the autumn of 1997, Demos – a think tank stuffed with eager young Blairites – had published a vogueish-looking pamphlet entitled Britain™, the work of a twenty-three-year-old named Mark Leonard. Though it tended to read like an essay written in the last twenty minutes of a General Studies exam – 'Britain is seen as a backward-looking has-been,' he wrote, 'a theme park world of royal pageantry of rolling hills, where draughts blow through people's houses' – it caught the imagination of those responsible for the more ephemeral areas of government policy.

Leonard apparently wished to see the UK's image wrenched away from tea shops, castles and heraldry, and recast in the terms set by the 'London Swings' issue of *Vanity Fair*. Thus was born the mercifully brief exercise known as 'the re-branding of Britain'.

One only need scan the minor headlines of 1998 to see how quickly the idea caught on. In April, the BBC reported that the then-Foreign Secretary Robin Cook had announced the make-up of Panel 2000: a group of people 'chosen to help give Britain a "cool" image abroad'. They included Peter Mandelson, Zeinab Badawi, Stella McCartney, and a former member of the cast of *Gladiators*. Six months later, the British Council unveiled a set of adverts aimed at promoting the UK in the context of 'great traditional successes, but also as a contemporary, forward-looking society'. Their tactic reflected the old Britpop idea that the 90s was somehow analogous to the 60s: the proposed ads included a poster split between images of Michael Owen and Geoff Hurst, and another that featured both Noel Gallagher and John Lennon. Mindful of the idea's air of naffness, Noel sent word from Chalfont St Giles that he did not want his picture to be used.

Virginia Bottomley's successor at the Department of Heritage – which Labour would swiftly rename Culture, Media and Sport – was Chris Smith. Though conversant with rock music, Smith was more familiar with the Royal Opera House than the Hammersmith Odeon. He soon began to sense that the government's apparent fondness for the brasher end of culture was making his new job rather difficult. Seven months after the election, in a speech to key players from the British theatre, he summed up his predicament: 'Judging by our critics, we are a platoon of philistines that have had to boogie to Oasis and applaud *The Full Monty*, but who are totally uninterested in the Royal Shakespeare Company or the British Museum.'

'The Press ran away with the notion that Labour was riding on a bandwagon,' he says. 'I lost count of the number of articles that talked about New Labour being all about Cool Britannia, which is a phrase that I hate, and never consciously used. But a mythology then developed that Labour was just in this for the glitz and the glamour.'

One of the myth's key sources, Smith claims, was a celebrated occasion that had occurred the year before. 'I think the thing that triggered it,' he says, 'was the famous photograph of the Prime Minister with Noel . . . I think that with hindsight, allowing an iconic image of that kind to become common currency was a mistake. If you were having a reception for leading figures in the British music scene, you couldn't not invite Oasis. But perhaps the press organisers should have been more careful about what photographs were taken, and by whom.'

On occasion, Smith hardly helped his own cause. In October 1997, he made a speech in New York, to the Recording Industry Association of America. It still stands as one of the stranger speeches ever made by a British government minister, not just in terms of its simple incongruity, but also its bizarre reading of pop-cultural history. 'Punk rock started as an underground movement in this city,' said Smith, 'spearheaded by groups like the New York Dolls. Their manager Malcolm McLaren brought both the music and fashion back to Britain and went on to manage The Sex Pistols who, together with other British punk bands such as The Clash, influenced American bands like Guns'n' Roses. Reggae was pioneered in the Caribbean, popularised in Britain, and developed into rap in the United States.' Had the speech been reproduced in a music magazine, it would surely have been followed by the words 'That's right, Dad.'

Among the new government's array of associates and advisers was Alan McGee. Soon after the election, he had been appointed to a body named the Creative Industries Task Force, along with David Puttnam, Paul Smith, Richard Branson and Waheed Ali. 'It's weird,' he said. 'Two worlds colliding. I just tell it like it is from the shop floor.' Among the body's proposed offshoots was a Music Industry Task Force, which would include the seemingly inescapable Mick Hucknall. 'Clever bloke, Mick,' said McGee. 'I might not be into his music, but he's not just a drugs-and-women singer. He knows his politics.'

McGee was now one of those eternally newsworthy creatures known as New Labour Insiders. Towards the end of 1997, he and his wife Kate received the ultimate proof of his new influence: an invitation for dinner at Chequers. 'We didn't know what to expect,' he says. 'I was wearing a suit, Kate was dressed up. When we drove up to the house, there were SWAT teams everywhere: guys crawling around on the grass, with guns. He [Blair] answered the door wearing jeans, with a pint in his hand. We went in, and that was when it got totally fucking psychedelic. Judi Dench was there, a guy from Psion computers, that author, John O'Farrell . . . and Jimmy Savile. I introduced him to Kate, and he started kind of sucking her fingers. It was all totally weird.' McGee and Blair discussed the relative merits of the recent albums by Blur and Oasis; towards the evening's end, the pair had an extended conversation about drugs policy.

If McGee symbolised the alliance between the government and the music business, its more irreverent elements were soon to call time on the partnership. For all Blair's rock'n'roll poses, the more orthodox areas of the government's policies were hardly likely to endear them to anyone of a remotely bohemian disposition: what with the imposition of student tuition fees, and the dole-denying strictures of the so-called New Deal, there seemed little doubt that New Labour were not nearly as groovy as some people had hoped. As if to underline the government's fall from grace, when John Prescott turned up at the 1998 Brit Awards, a member of the avowedly anarchist band Chumbawamba emptied an ice bucket over him.

The same month, Damon Albarn made his second visit to the Palace of Westminster. This time, however, he had no intention of drinking gin and tonic with Tony Blair: in cahoots with Ken Livingstone, then the Labour MP for Brent East, he was the star attraction of a press conference aimed at galvanising opposition to New Labour's higher

357

education policies. It was his comments on another subject, however, that grabbed the following morning's headlines. 'I thought that the sort of display when Labour won the election and everyone turned up at Number Ten was pretty disgusting,' he said. 'It was vulgar. I'm not surprised that most young people want to stay well clear of Labour and any of its ideas.'

So it was that on Wednesday 11 March, the *NME* put Tony Blair on its cover, with the headline 'Ever Get The Feeling You've Been Cheated? Rock'n'Roll Takes On The Government'. Inside was a lengthy demolition of the government's youth-cultural credentials – 'New Labour is both taking us for granted and taking the piss,' raged an opening editorial – and an array of interviews with disillusioned musicians, most of which ended with the same question: 'Should pop stars be going to Number Ten?' Of the Britpop elite, only Jarvis Cocker was among the interviewees. Damon Albarn declined to comment, claiming that involvement might complicate his own campaigning; the Gallaghers, to nobody's great surprise, were unavailable.

Nonetheless, as had been intended by its market-watching senior staff, the issue created the *NME*'s biggest impact for years. Its writers were interviewed on national news bulletins; other elements of the printed media were transfixed. 'Such was the ferocity of the assault that there is surely no way back,' wrote Martin Jacques in that week's *Observer*. 'In what amounts to a manifesto, Britpop has severed its links with New Labour less than a year after the election. The event marks the beginning of the end of Cool Britannia.'

'It was seen as being significant,' says Chris Smith. 'But at the same time, there was a general sense that this was something that we couldn't and shouldn't try officiously to do anything about, because that would simply make things worse.'

As it turned out, Alan McGee and Andy Saunders would soon work with the government on at least one measure that would answer some of the *NME*'s criticism. The New Deal decreed that anyone under twenty-five who had been out of work for more than six months would be pushed into full-time education 'on an approved course' or accept employment selected on their behalf, for which they would be paid benefit rates. As McGee had long since realised, for any aspiring young musician, this was grim news indeed.

The previous September, he had been approached to be the keynote speaker at In The City, a music industry convention organised by Tony Wilson, the former chief of Factory Records. As usual, he canvassed the opinion of Andy Saunders. 'Alan said to me, "They've asked me to give a speech. I've never done that in my life. Do you think I should?"' he says. 'I said, "I think you're *capable* of it; you've just got to have something to say. What do you want to say? What's pissing you off?"

'We talked about it, and he said, "You know what really fucks me off? If you're a musician, and you're on the dole, they're not going to let you be a musician; they're going to make you go and work in McDonald's. That's a really crap Tory attitude." He really went off on one. I said, "That's great." And I went away and wrote a twenty-minute speech about that whole thing. It ended with the line, "If we want all the benefits of the music industry, then you have to allow musicians to eat."'

That year, In The City took place in Glasgow. McGee's appearance went down well. He and Saunders then travelled to Brighton, where McGee watched Tony Blair's speech at the Labour Party Conference, and repeated his In The City oration at a Fabian Society fringe meeting. 'He was crap,' says Saunders. 'He knew he was crap, and I knew he was crap. He was nervous, intimidated. It was a much more in-your-face audience. And it wasn't a speech-type affair: you were meant to stand up and ad lib. They hadn't told us that.' Despite the setback, he and Saunders' campaign went on into the following year: part of the *NME*'s anti-Blair splurge was an article in which McGee claimed that when it came to The New Deal, Labour was proving to be worse than the Conservatives.

It was some token of New Labour's sensitivity to media criticism that eight days after the *NME*'s appearance, McGee and Andy Saunders were invited for talks by Andrew Smith, then a minister at the Department of Employment. 'It was, "What can we do for you?"' says Saunders. '"Well, we'd like to change the law please. We've given you fifty grand and done loads of work – now it's payback time." That was essentially the vibe we went in with. Alan said, "We've been very supportive, and we've worked very closely with you, and this is the right thing to do, and you should do it."

'We said, "We think The New Deal is crap, we think it's discriminatory, we think it doesn't offer any flexibility, and we don't understand how you can expect the music industry to support it." We went in on this big moral crusade. And they were like, "Ooh, I'm not sure we can do that." And we said, "Well, you'd better – because if you don't, we're going to raise a big fucking stink about it." By this point, we'd already started to lobby the media. I'd already started to drop a few stories about how we were going to do this, just to get the ball rolling. The one thing we knew the government hated was bad publicity. It brought them out in an allergic reaction.'

Over the ensuing months, Saunders attended a tortuous run of meetings, aimed at amending the government's welfare-to-work programme. The result was unveiled as The New Deal For Musicians in October 1998, and took effect a year later. Its beneficiaries would receive the so-called Jobseekers Allowance for a maximum of thirteen months, on the proviso that they could display evidence of 'talent and commitment'. The Conservatives called it 'a charter for scroungers'; more fusty elements of the press ridiculed the notion of rock'n'dole; even those who viewed the scheme sympathetically were bamboozled by the apparent prospect of demo tapes being exchanged for cash. Nonetheless, the scheme is still in place. It remains the sole example of Britpop legislation.

Towards the end of 1999, Alan McGee had a chance meeting with an erstwhile Britpop musician who had signed up. One of the first to benefit from The New Deal For Musicians was Chris Gentry from Menswear.

As 1998 went on, it was evident that, despite his new clout, Alan McGee was feeling restless. During the summer, Creation issued a very telling press handout, assuring their public that the company was still 'a label of misfits, drug addicts, dysfunctional human beings and out-and-out losers'. That may have been true, but in the wake of Britpop, Creation was an altogether different operation to the freewheeling, chaotic set-up that had made its home above the sweatshop in Hackney. 'These are interesting times,' McGee told a *Q* interviewer, 'but something has to change. Creation is now a big machine – because we have one of the biggest groups in the world – and I'm not a big-machine-type person.'

Now that all the certainties embodied by Oasis's Knebworth concerts had evaporated, Creation was visibly struggling. In 1998, its biggest success had been the first solo album by Bernard Butler, who was now trading in gentle, orthodox rock balladry that, McGee claimed, marked him down as 'our Neil Young'. Its follow-up, *Friends And Lovers*, stiffed. The label's newer recruits were faring equally badly: the world did not make much of a white Rastafarian singer called Mishka, or such rock groups as The Diggers, Toaster and One Lady Owner. In 1999, the label released *My Beauty*, a deeply strange album of cover versions by the ex-Dexys Midnight Runners singer Kevin Rowland. His new image was based around the novel idea of wearing ladies' lingerie. The album was rumoured to have sold under 700 copies.

At the end of November, McGee announced that he and his long-standing partner Dick Green were leaving Creation. Initially, it was unclear whether the label might carry on: within days, however, the improbable notion of Creation continuing without its founder was scotched. After sixteen years, and in the wake of labyrinthine negotiations with Sony, the label was being wound up: suddenly, 109 Regent's Park Road fell silent.

On the afternoon of 2 December, McGee sat in the office he kept over the road from Creation's HQ, tugging on a bottle of San Pellegrino mineral water and slowly making his way through a bag of crisps. He was three hours away from a meeting with a group of investors that would seal his plans for Poptones, the new label whose foundation would be announced early the following year.

'In 1993,' he said, while his mobile phone let out another unwelcome trill, 'it was my gang. And by '99, it was somebody else's gang. Me and Dick used to sit at Creation Christmas parties: there'd be thirty-eight people there, and I'd look round the room and go, "I only like about five of the people in the room." I felt as if I was running Railtrack. I'd nothing in common with any of the people I worked with. What happens is, you get huge: we were doing something like fifty million pounds' worth of business a year. You just need to hire people that can do a professional job for you.

'This is the thing about when I stopped taking drugs,' he said. 'I do not facilitate for other people. I do things for me now. Because I nearly killed myself, I'm going to do it for myself. I've not been happy for two years. People are really pissed off with me 'cos I've chucked it. Sony are pissed off with me, the staff are really pissed off with me, some of the people in some of the bands are pissed off with me ... but the bottom line is, I've got to be happy myself. And if I'm not, then I've got to go.'

For most of 1997, Blur had been on tour, performing in support of an album that, although it was widely characterised as an act of artistic retrenchment, would turn out to be their biggest worldwide-selling record to date. Their manoeuvres took them to the USA – where, much to their delight, they were finally making substantial inroads – along with Australia, the Far East and such unlikely locales as the Faeroe Islands and Greenland. In Bangkok, they played in front of an audience that included the Thai royal family. 'They were sitting on thrones with a two hundred-strong armed guard,' marvelled Alex James. 'It was a new kind of mental.'

Justine Frischmann, meanwhile, was at home, bedevilled by drug-related inertia and the not-unconnected travails of Elastica. With Damon Albarn once again absent, she decided to re-establish contact with someone whose company she had not shared for the best part of six years: Brett Anderson.

'I had a terrible dream about him: that he was dead, and I wasn't invited to the funeral,' she says. 'I was watching the funeral from the other side of some gates. It was horrible. And I realised I hadn't seen him for years, and it was sad, so I called him. He was really nice, straight away. It was the first time I'd seen him in three years. Maybe more. And it was great.'

Thanks to the success of *Coming Up*, Suede had secured top billing on the Sunday night of 1997's Reading Festival. Their performance included a two-minute curio, written well before the group began releasing records, entitled Implement Yeah!. Having rehearsed her part at a warm-up concert in the unlikely environs of Bracknell, Justine Frischmann duly took the stage to provide backing vocals. 'Brett basically organised it so I'd have something to do, so I didn't feel bored and bitter and twisted about the fact that I wasn't onstage,' she says. 'I was only onstage for two minutes. I was completely adrenalined-up for the whole thing, so by the time I came off I couldn't remember what had happened at all. I didn't have a chance to calm down and *be* onstage. It was a real non-experience, basically. I went onstage, jumped up and down and sang incoherently for two minutes and walked off. It wasn't remotely significant.'

Upon Albarn's return, his response to Frischmann's renewed bond with Anderson – which, contrary to a slew of rumours, remained steadfastly platonic – was not altogether surprising. 'I think Damon was a bit pissed off that suddenly, Brett was back, but I think he knew that at some point he would be,' she says. 'He just hated Brett. They loved hating each other. He was just like, "Why is that cunt back on the scene?"'

'I even brought Brett round to say hello to Damon, to try and heal old wounds,' she says. 'He was living round the corner, and I'd got really friendly with his girlfriend, Sam. We were all doing drugs together, and I was like, "Well, look – why don't you just make friends?" Brett was like, "Okay, I'll finally bury the hatchet." They both thought they'd give it a go.

'And it was one of the weirdest, nastiest scenes ever. It was like a cat and dog meeting each other. Just, "*Sssssssss!*" One of them went to shake the other's hand and he didn't look round. I can't remember which way round it was, but it was really weird. I got Brett out of there within two minutes; I realised it just wasn't happening. When they actually had to be in the same space, they still wanted to kill each other. It was so beyond anything to do with me: it had got to a point where

Brett was driven by hating Damon – and Damon's driven by hating *everyone* – so they really needed to hate each other. I think they were scared of not hating each other, because that would have marked the point where they didn't care any more.'

Elastica, meanwhile, were stuck in much the same place that they had occupied during 1996: working on songs that never seemed to approach completion, frequently forgoing rehearsal and recording in favour of chemically-related recreation. In desperation, Frischmann decided that reconvening the group's original line-up might just pull them out of their lethargy. Sheila Chipperfield, the hapless bass player who had been a member of the group for well over a year but played only six gigs, was told she was no longer required, and Frischmann made contact with Annie Holland. Her first rehearsal initially suggested that the hunch had been well-founded, but things rapidly took on the appearance of one of the more farcical scenes from *This Is Spinal Tap*.

'Donna didn't want Annie to come back,' says Frischmann. 'But we had this one rehearsal: the four of us, with Dave Bush, and the old songs suddenly sounded great again. Then we started jamming on new stuff, and Donna just went off, looking for "the note". She spent four hours looking for "the note", while we jammed this one song over and over. She was like, "I just know there's this one note, and if I play it, the whole song'll sound great." She went through all the notes: there's not that many. But she just kept looking for it.

'She'd gone by this point. Totally mental. There was terrible shit going on all the time: total chaos in her house. She had braces fitted, because she wanted to get her teeth sorted out, despite the fact that she was killing herself. She was about six stone.'

'I was blowing four grand a week at one point – on drug bills and hospital bills,' says Matthews. 'We had loads of money. I was getting flights to go away and detox: I'd say, "Right – I'm going to New York for the weekend. Get me a flight." I'd miss the flight. "Get me another flight." I went to the Chelsea Hotel to try and detox, on my own, for the weekend. And I went insane, and took loads of drugs and came home.'

In London, Matthews was pinballing between two social poles, splitting her time between the Met Bar, the Park Lane niterie that was now a gathering ground for the capital's moneyed socialites, and rather more dangerous places. 'I'd think nothing of spending five hundred quid on a night out,' she says. 'A grand on a weekend. There was a scene of people I was hanging around with: people like Rebecca De Ruvo and Kate Moss, Lisa Moorish, Lisa l'Anson . . . girls who were into partying. It was all a bit crap, really. It wasn't very me at all. But I'd lost my sense of who I was. I had to make taking drugs more normal, 'cos all I did from morning to night was take drugs. I was going through a phase of, "As long as it looks alright from the outside, then it must be okay." I was having this extreme double life, hanging out at so-called glamorous parties and being photographed, and then sitting in crack dens. There were quite a few people doing that sort of stuff, but we kept it quiet. We knew it wasn't good.'

Paparazzi pictures of Matthews from this period have a desperate quality: stick-thin, bizarrely dressed, and with a cadaver-like pallor, she was pretty much unrecognisable. As far as Justine Frischmann was concerned, her behaviour only underlined the point.

'The last conversation Donna and I had in the studio,' she says, 'was when she said she wanted to turn a song called Operate into a Missy Elliot song. And I said to her, "Donna, I don't think you want to be a guitarist any more." She said, "No, I just don't want to be the guitarist in Elastica." And she went on to say, "I don't like your voice, your lyrics make me cringe, and the way you play the guitar makes me cringe."'

'I did say that,' says Matthews. 'I was barking mad. Not to say that Justine wasn't, but in my addiction, I was a lot further advanced than she was. I'd gone through ODing, and Justine was nowhere near that. I'd lost it.'

By this time, Matthews had at least tried to kick her drug habit. Initially, she underwent Naltraxone treatment: a method of combating heroin addiction in which implants which block the effects of the drug are sewn into the abdomen. In particularly grisly circumstances, however, Matthews came to the conclusion that this method was not for her.

'I did three implants,' she says. 'None of them worked. Well, they *work*, but you need to sort out why you take heroin. You can't just peel the drugs away: you need to go away and do a lot of therapy. The implants were about six hundred pounds each. It blocks morphine, but you go and cane crack. It lasts for six weeks, and you're a fucking lunatic. I nearly died so many times during that six weeks: I was hitting up crack every day, taking anything I could get my hands on. I was just insane. I was ODing by the end, because I was hitting up smack and it wasn't working. The Naltraxone would wear off, you'd have a hit, and go over, and OD. I'd wake up, someone would call an ambulance, and there'd be paramedics here, trying to get me back to life. I was rushed into emergency so many times. Naltraxone is dangerous.'

At her most desperate, Matthews simply removed the implant from her body. 'I pulled the stitches out, stuck my finger in and gouged it out. But even if you do that, it's still in your system. That's another twenty-four hours before you can take drugs.'

It was perhaps in her best interests that, after one last fractious phone call, Frischmann informed her that she no longer had a role in Elastica. Matthews duly let out her King's Cross house to tenants, and took the M4 out of London. By now, the money had run out: she secured an £8,000 loan, underwent an eight-week rehabilitation programme based around the twelve steps, and spent eight recuperative months in Bristol.

The same weekend that Frischmann ejected Donna Matthews from her life, she called time on her relationship with Damon Albarn. The decision was made in the context of a sudden fit of resolve, bound up with the fact that she had begun to emerge from the narcotic haze into which she had tumbled the previous year. Aside from acknowledging that the first step towards quitting heroin was a visit to a doctor, Frischmann will not be drawn on how she finally accomplished it; whatever, there is little doubt that she distanced herself from Matthews and Albarn during the time that she started to clean up.

In retrospect, she and Albarn had started to separate during 1995, when their bond tended to be maintained via phone conversations across different time zones. Worse still, upon her eventual return from Elastica's year-long world tour, Frischmann found that their respective visions of their lives' next phase were very different indeed. 'Damon was saying to me, "You've given me a run for my money, you've proved that you're just as good as I am, you've had a hit in America – now settle down and let's have kids." He wanted me to stop being in a group, stop touring and have children. I wasn't very happy. In fact I'd say I was suffering from depression, quite seriously. And he kept saying, "The reason you're unhappy is because you really want children but you don't know it." It did throw me: I thought about it quite seriously.'

By 1997, however, Albarn was not exactly behaving like an aspirant family man. 'He was being more and more open about being unfaithful,' says Frischmann. 'He was spending a lot of time in Iceland. I went over there, and I got told that there'd been a local comedy programme that had done a sketch with a load of women with babies and they were all called Damon. That's how out of hand it had got.'

For the moment, however, her suspicion that the relationship had run its course did not lead to any genuine action, due to two factors: the tranquillising effects of her heroin use, and the simple fact that Albarn was on tour. 'There was no point breaking up with him then,' says Frischmann, 'because he wasn't here.'

Upon his return to London, despite Frischmann's evident belief that he should leave, Albarn refused to say die. 'I kept saying I wanted him out, and he kept telling me to go and lie down, because I wasn't feeling well. And I *wasn't*. He'd put too much time in to walk away from it: he wanted children out of it; he wanted something I hadn't given him, and he was going to stick around till he got what he wanted. He was of the opinion that he wasn't going to go anywhere, because he hadn't chosen to. It took a long time to break up.'

Finally, after a last-ditch holiday at the end of 1997, Albarn and Frischmann went their separate ways. She remained in Notting Hill; he moved to a flat in the vicinity of nearby Golborne Road, in the long shadow of the Trellick Tower. It was there that Albarn would write many of the songs that would appear on the album Blur entitled *13*; a sprawling, frequently soul-baring record that was as different from *Blur* as that record had been from *The Great Escape*.

'It had got to its elastic limit,' says Frischmann. 'It snapped. I just couldn't take any more. It had got so beyond the point of being a sensible way to live. There was no discussion any more. It was, "Whatever happens, it can't be worse than this." We'd stopped rowing, which was the scary thing. It was just totally pointless. We weren't sleeping in the same bed, and we hadn't been for a while, put it that way.' Bizarrely, she is still not sure exactly when her decisive break from Albarn occurred. 'I think it was spring time. It was kind of cold and sunny – that kind of weather. It isn't that vivid.'

Close up, the details of their break-up were no different from those of countless relationships. In the minds of those who saw only the broadest of outlines, however, there could be no clearer sign that the era begun by *Parklife* and defined by such records as *Elastica* was now over.

By 1999, its architects were scattered: cloistered in rural piles, hidden away in rehab, or simply sitting at home, anxiously pondering their next move. In Camden Town, the only people drawn to The Good Mixer were either its old regulars, glad to have their pub back, or misinformed tourists, taxi'd to NW1 only to discover that it now offered nothing more exotic than fridge magnets, vegetarian spring rolls and overpriced Dr Martens. At Westminster, some of the Blairites were discovering that there were slightly more pressing matters than the rebranding of Britain; in Milan and New York, journalists were looking for the planet's next hypeworthy city. Britpop's garish colour-scheme had faded – as ever, London was reverting to a cold, damp grey.

Endpiece

Superficially, Britpop had followed patterns that would have been familiar to any student of rock's history. Talent and promise had led to commercial achievement, which had inevitably given way to fall-out and failure; the pleasures of living at the cutting-edge had been superseded by a troubling existence in the moronic inferno of the mainstream; what had initially seemed cool had rapidly given off the odour of yesterday's thing. The role of drugs in the tale only furthered the sense of the re-enactment of eternal archetypes. In the case of Oasis, cocaine had led to disastrous hubris; with Elastica and their associates, heroin had ushered in a period of dozy seclusion. Given Britpop's debt to the past, both stories underline a poetic irony: for all their knowledge of rock history, this generation of musicians were still fated to repeat it.

Relative to its antecedents, however, Britpop had one crucial difference. Compare it to punk, or Acid House, or the 60s subculture known as the 'underground', and it becomes clear: this was the first upsurge in which such a premium was placed on commercial success. By the time the term was coined, one of Britpop's most central notions – the idea of restoring British music's sense of place, along with its traditions of articulacy and intelligence – had started to fall away. From 1995 onwards, one began to get the sense that being an accredited Britpop musician was a simple matter of carrying a guitar, paying lip service to the classic rock canon and – most crucially of all –

making hit records. In that sense, Tony Blair's four-year ride on the bandwagon was no surprise: in Britpop's fetishisation of chart positions, platinum discs and huge crowds, he surely saw the same impulses that informed his own rise to power. Principles, it seemed, were secondary to popularity.

Such was the tenor of the age. Those who drew endless comparisons with the Britain of the 60s rather missed a crucial point: though one could draw lines between the aspects of each era, one was not truly linking like with like. In contrast to such legendary countercultural magazines as *Oz* and *International Times,* the Britpop period's most celebrated publication was the avowedly mass-market *Loaded.* Instead of marching against Vietnam, the 90s generation enjoyed the altogether safer pleasure of watching the Blair election landslide – nice enough, but hardly the stuff of swashbuckling insurrection. The drugs that defined the respective periods perhaps say it all: whereas the 60s were defined by the mind-expanding effects of LSD, much of the Britpop moment was fuelled by cocaine. In that sense, the eventual return of the brutal narcissism of the 80s – as embodied by the Gallaghers circa 1998 – was hardly a surprise.

Ironically, Britpop's roots lay in a subculture that had been founded on the spurning of that decade's worst aspects: indie, which was in turn connected to the far-flung wonders of punk. Both sources were emblematic of one of British rock's central notions: the fact that, because the music was born on the other side of the Atlantic, the brightest British minds were free to experiment with it. From The Beatles, The Kinks and The Who, through David Bowie and Roxy Music, on to The Sex Pistols, past XTC, Wire, Gang Of Four and Joy Division and on to The Smiths and Happy Mondays, one sees the same idea: innovation and iconoclasm were the whole point. Populism, however, is an altogether more corrupting enterprise: though there have been frequent occasions when adventurous minds have achieved huge success, the conscious pursuit of it tends to lead to crushing banality.

Most of those responsible for Britpop had cut their teeth when the mainstream was something to be spurned rather than embraced – and though Britpop's successes initially seemed to thrill them, their old instincts rapidly resurfaced. Alan McGee returned from his breakdown to find, to his horror, that Creation Records was now ruled by its marketing department. Graham Coxon was so repulsed by the time that Blur spent playing to screaming adolescents that, to all intents and purposes, he made an artistic left turn a condition of the group's staying together. Though Jarvis Cocker had initially taken to the life of the celebrity socialite, he soon sprinted for the Exit door.

Oasis were the one exception to all this, and though their lustful pursuit of success and unshakeable self-assurance initially formed part of their appeal, such qualities soon turned out – in the standard of their music, at least – to be their downfall. Only one of the Britpop musicians proved to be confident enough to keep his head, and sufficiently self-aware to know when it was time to move on. One need only listen to Blur, 1999's *13* and Blur's most recent album, *Think Thank,* to understand why Damon Albarn was probably the period's most remarkable talent, both in his musical gift and the pace at which he adapted it.

As the Britpop moment faded, there were fleeting signs that British rock music might be returning to its inventive traditions. Blur's move back to angular, off-beam music certainly set an example. Radiohead's *OK Computer,* along with the envelope-pushing *Kid A* and *Amnesiac,* sounded an even louder clarion call.

As it turned out, however, the period after Britpop cemented the dominance of an altogether more conservative tendency. Britpop's most potent legacy was not *Parklife*'s brazen Englishness, the mixture of rage and guile that one heard in Common People, the wit and economy of *Elastica*, or the audacious panache that oozed from *Suede*. It was the compelling vision of Noel Gallagher, perched alone on a stool, playing Wonderwall while the assembled thousands sang along.

The first post-Britpop group to achieve similar success to Blur and Oasis were Travis, four Scots who had appeared in 1996 and attracted hearty endorsement from Noel Gallagher. Their first album, *Good Feeling,* served promising notice of both talent and intelligence: in U16 Girls and All I Wanna Do Is Rock, one heard an ironic, almost satirical take on the primal rock that had once been the Gallaghers' calling card. By the time of 1999's *The Man Who,* however, they had found a rather less interesting niche, delivering gentle ballads of redemption that seemed tailor-made for a vast, cross-generational audience. As if to acknowledge the example they were following, a single called Writing To Reach You included a wry reference to Wonderwall, and it pilfered the song's chords. It was succeeded by the huge British hit Why Does It Always Rain On Me?, in which Fran Healy sketched out a tale of everyday woe against his band's approximation of a watercolor backdrop. One critic summed up its message as follows: 'Don't get your hopes up, kids.'

Travis were soon joined by others. Starsailor, a quartet from the same Northern English climes as Oasis, were not quite as successful, but their bleeding-heart balladry found a ready audience. In terms of their music and background, they seemed to announce the arrival of a new breed of musician: three of them had met at college, where they had taken courses in the rudiments of pop music and the workings of the record industry.

And then there was Coldplay. Four graduates of University College, London (the same institution at which Justine Frischmann had met Brett Anderson), they dealt in altogether more artful music than the aforementioned names. There again, much of the explanation for their vast success in the UK and USA was down to Chris Martin's talent for writing expansive, anthemic songs – Yellow, Trouble, In My Place, Clocks – that, for all their appeal, betrayed a noticeable musical con-servatism. They were widely portrayed as the band who had capi-talised on Radiohead's flight towards music's left field by writing songs akin to Thom Yorke's few stabs at stadium balladry: High And Dry, Fake Plastic Trees, Street Spirit (Fade Out). There was something to that argument, but Coldplay's rise could also be understood in the context of what might be termed The Wonderwall Effect.

If, to varying degrees, these groups were Oasis's progeny, Noel and Liam Gallagher's rhetoric often suggested otherwise. They recognised British rock's decline, partly blamed the UK's record com-panies, and implicitly denied a role in what had happened. In 2001, the reliably erudite Noel summed up his feelings thus: 'The people who are sat in the offices of Sony, who I'm signed to, they're a bunch of fucking cunts, and the rest of 'em in Virgin and all the rest of it, they're fucking killing it [music]. But it's stealthy: they're stealthily taking away extremism and talent.' He had an undeniable point, but there again, which band had so firmly placed plodding balladry at the heart of British rock? Moreover, who had announced rock music's new respectability with his visit to the Prime Minister's residence?

No matter how drab Oasis became, they at least had one bulwark against complete wash-out: Liam Gallagher, who managed to perform even their most middle-of-the-road songs with his trademark flashes of menace. 'All the people the kids look up to now,' said Noel, 'are bland, faceless trainee police officers. Liam should be given a knighthood.' If what often seemed to separate Oasis from their newer contemporaries were the qualities embodied by Liam, one conclusion was inescapable. Perhaps what had taken hold in Britpop's slipstream was best identified as Noelrock.

Such was one explanation of the strange fact that the word 'Indie' – for reasons of historical accident rather than taxonomic accuracy – came to denote the kind of sentimental ballads that played well at outdoor festivals and tended to soundtrack the UK's moments of national doubt. Rock had found a new role in Britpop's wake: providing songs that could be played on TV when princesses died, British tennis players crashed out of Wimbledon and the England soccer team once again returned home early from the World Cup. Far from expressing any kind of dissent in its new tamed state, the music now seemed to be a manifestation of Mr. Blair's beloved inclusivism. This was surely not the kind of future that either the punks, or the 80s counterculturalists who followed in their wake, had envisaged.

There again, five years after Britpop slid into insignificance, it frequently seems that in the UK, the mainstream is all there is. As the likes of Jarvis Cocker could attest, Britpop may have elevated the alumni of the 80s indie milieu to an unforeseen popularity. But it also seemed to pursue a scorched-earth policy – and once the smoke had cleared, it became obvious what had been lost.

Britain's independent sector, once a seething breeding ground for left-field talent, does not really exist anymore. When Alan McGee confirmed that, in the wake of Creation's closure, he was launching a new label called Poptones, his pronouncements implied a revival of indie's maverick ethics. Unfortunately, after a shaky start, Poptones announced in April 2004 that it was effectively being folded into Mercury Records, part of the Universal Music empire. An equally telling development had come when Mute Records – founded in 1978 during punk's do-it-yourself tumult, and credited with pulling off the self-sufficient survival that Rough Trade,* Factory and even Creation could not manage, was sold to EMI. If one of the archetypes

---

* Rough Trade was re-launched in 1999. It is a far smaller operation than it was in its 80s heyday, but between the label (whose roster includes the Strokes) and Rough Trade's long-standing management arm (which sees to the progress of such acts as Pulp, Beth Orton, McAlmont & Butler and Cerys Matthews), the company stands as a rare example of a healthy successor to the indie tradition.

of the early 21st century is the noble small businessmen, squeezed into surrender by the activities of global conglomerates, the modern music industry provides plenty of examples.

Far away from the boardroom, trawling through the racks of any of the UK's remaining 'indie' record shops, one can still get a flavour of the old independent ideal. Self-produced CDs and 7-inch singles seem as abundant as ever, a smattering of fanzines suggests the tradition of countercultural Samizdat remains intact – but the lion's share of such artefacts usually seem to originate in the USA. Britain seems too homogenised and conformist to support any real competition.

The UK's music press, that symbol of British rock's old emphasis on discourse and rhetoric, has been drastically scythed down. The *NME* still appears on Wednesday mornings, though it has the weekly market to itself. *Melody Maker* announced its closure at the end of 2000; *Select,* whose progress had followed Britpop's life cycle, folded at the same time. The halcyon days of 1995, when editors toasted the Blur Vs Oasis war and looked forward to endless sales increases, had never seemed further away.

Had anyone paused for thought, they would perhaps have realised that Britpop was steadily removing any real need for the service their magazines provided. In the 80s and early 90s, the music press had been the only window into an alternative universe – now, with Blur, Oasis, Pulp and Elastica accorded acres of space in the tabloids and broadsheets and abundant airtime on radio and television, it was simply one part of a vast patchwork. Moreover, in the case of the latter media, rock writers had been leapfrogged: why read someone else's account of a record when it is blaring from every radio in earshot? Even when Britpop started to slide, the effect proved irreversible: the BBC was newly attuned to the demands of the youth market; those in charge of gossip columns and newspaper review supplements had discovered that young people with guitars were not nearly as dour – or, sometimes, as scary – as they had once assumed.

As a consequence of all this, there is a new career model for British rock bands. Rather than drafting some borderline ludicrous manifesto, scraping enough money together for a self-financed single and hassling a sympathetic DJ into playing it, they are more likely to look forward to their inaugural MTV appearance and concur with the corporate etiquette whereby each of a band's albums should be aimed at selling more than the last one. Aside from printing the website addresses of NGOs in their CD booklets and ensuring that their records are made using carbon-neutral resources, British musicians seem to have reached unprecedented depths of compliance and timidity.

If one fact confirms all this, it is this: apart from Radiohead, not one high-profile British rock band has yet released a song pointedly about Tony Blair. One would have thought that such trifles as the Iraq War – not to mention the wider political context of globalisation and snow-balling corporate power – might provide some of our rock groups with a fertile source of inspiration. Unfortunately, whereas Margaret Thatcher spawned scores of songs that variously expressed anger, amusement, defiance and ridicule, rock's one acknowledgement of the Blair phenom-enon is You And Whose Army, a rather aimless song on Amnesiac in which Thom Yorke distractedly asks the Prime Minister whether he wants a fight. For most of its duration, Yorke seems about to fall asleep: it suggests a satire on political apathy rather than an irate call to arms.

In the midst of all this, there is at least one cause for celebration. The brief period when New Labour invited musicians for champagne and canapés has long gone. These days, when he is not waging war and seeing to domestic 'delivery', Tony Blair dispenses favours to rock stars who are at least drawn from his own generation, as proved by one of his more maligned acts of patronage. It is perhaps some token of music's passage into old age – and the silliness that still occasionally infects the Blair regime – that, thanks to a knighthood that arrived in 2002, Mick Jagger must now be addressed as 'Sir'. One can only as-sume he was being thanked for his unwittingly provided services to Ugly Rumours.

When *Britpop!* was first published in the UK as *The Last Party*, one aspect of its strap-line seemed likely to attract comment. As it turned out, how-ever, most of its reviewers did not bother to comment on the 'alleged de-mise of English rock', as if the idea that domestic music had fallen into a seemingly endless slumber was worryingly close to being a given.

One year on, not much has changed – which, given the deep changes that have occurred in the UK's society and culture and fed into some of the developments sketched out here, hardly represents much of a surprise. One of the early watchwords of the Labour Gov-ernment was 'inclusivism' – a word that apparently denoted, as much as any item within the Blair lexicon can be traced to anything specific, the idea that all kinds of social divisions could miraculously be healed, and Britain could be tied into a new kind of right-thinking unity. To some extent, the mid-90s saw this hope manifested culturally: sport and music taking on the role of social glue, and Mr. Blair associating himself with both, to give the hint that the unanimity both created could somehow transform politics.

Though that mirage has long since disappeared, what was once known as Youth Culture holds out an example of a once-troublesome part of British life rendered tame and strangely compliant. Such developments as the spread of middle-class affluence, the expansion of higher education and the death of ideology – along with the simple fact that the adult world is no longer as square as it once was – has had one simple upshot: the UK is no longer the kind of society that produces droves of neurotic outsiders. The latter-day appearance of a figure such as Johnny Rotten, or Ian Curtis, or Morrissey – or, indeed, Brett Anderson or Jarvis Cocker – seems pretty much unthinkable; the fires that once fuelled the best British music have, for the moment at least, been snuffed out.

In the summer of 2001, all this was thrown into sharp relief by the arrival of a new generation of American groups, just about all of whom displayed the kind of qualities that were lacking in the UK's rock music. They were led by The Strokes, five young New Yorkers whose records oozed the ambience and musical influences of their home city, but who were also endowed with the kind of poise, economy and artfulness that the likes of Damon Albarn had once claimed to be a uniquely British preserve. At around the same time, The White Stripes were belatedly plucked from their native Detroit and introduced to the wider world: though their music melded a punk rock approach with age-old American music (and the blues in particular), their modus operandi was built around an appreciation of visual aesthetics and conceptual thinking redolent of the British art schools.

In their wake came a slew of bands whose sources were absolutely transparent. In the music of Radio 4, The Rapture, Interpol and Liars, one heard the re-awakening of British post-punk, the music that – in multifarious ways – had combined the late 70s' countercultural ferocity with a cerebral desire to experiment. Their evocation of Joy Division, Gang Of Four, A Certain Ratio et al. suggested a reversal of the age-old British knack of selling the US its own music; moreover, there was something faintly tragic in the fact that no young British musicians had gone there already.

ENDPIECE

All that said, there are occasional glimpses of British rock music's regaining its old strengths. An honourable mention should go to British Sea Power, an admirably ideas-driven band whose records manage to tap into the UK's geography, 20th-century European history, and the kind of bookish romanticism that music's recent bland-out threatened to render obsolete. Similarly, the appearance of the Scotland-based band Franz Ferdinand – whose angular, stiffly funked-up music fitted neatly into the slipstream of the American bands mentioned above – suggested that there might still be cause for hope. Serving notice of their opposition to the rock'n'roll machismo so beloved of the Gallaghers, they aimed to create 'music that girls can dance to'. The Guardian greeted their rise with the headline 'Roll Over Britpop – It's the Rebirth of Art Rock'.

The best example, however, is provided by The Libertines, quite the most promising British group to have emerged since the mid-1990s. Their ragged, stampeding, deeply English music fizzes with ideas, and evokes a London brimming with a downmarket allure unheard since the early days of Suede (poetically, their first single was produced by Bernard Butler). Unfortunately, as if to decisively place them in such a lineage, their first period in the public gaze saw heroin and crack quickly work their deleterious effects: singer and guitarist Pete Doherty endured ejection from the group and a spell in prison (bizarrely, for burgling the flat of his creative partner, Carl Barat), before rejoining the group at the end of 2003. In the wake of that episode, the role of their manager was assumed by Alan McGee, seemingly awarded the job on account of his experience with some of British rock's more accident-prone practitioners.

On their debut album, *Up The Bracket*, there is a song audaciously entitled Time For Heroes. It makes reference to a character named Bill Bones, who 'knows there's fewer more distressing sights than that of an Englishman in a baseball cap'. It's a sentiment that could have been uttered by any one of dozens of musicians, back in the days when bands still came up with manifestos, when awards ceremonies did not cast an irresistible spell, and when the notion that music should be founded on something more substantial than its own popularity had yet to be shoved to the margins.

For all kinds of reasons, however, the kind of British minds that pulse with such thoughts are currently in a woefully small minority. Hold on for tomorrow, as someone once put it . . .

APPENDIX 1 What Happened Next

Tim Abbot fell out with Oasis's management in 1996, when he was asked to sign a confidentiality agreement relating to his dealings with the group. The same year, photographs and video stills of his time with Oasis were collected in a book entitled *Oasis: Definitely*. His management deal with Robbie Williams came to grief around the same time. Abbot soon filed proceedings against Williams claiming £1.2 million in unpaid commission; Williams countered that he had signed the requisite contract while drunk and without proper advice. The two parties settled out of court in an agreement widely believed to have involved the payment of hundreds of thousands of pounds to Abbot. He currently lives in Walsall and works as a freelance marketing consultant; he also runs an independent label called Poolside.

Damon Albarn is still the lead singer and chief songwriter with Blur. Following his split with Justine Frischmann, he began a relationship with the London-based artist Suzi Winstanley: the couple had a daughter, Missy, in October 1999. In the wake of that year's Blur album *13*, he launched Gorillaz, a project whose public identity was based around cartoon characters devised by his sometime flatmate Jamie Hewlett. Gorillaz' self-titled debut album, characterised by some of the most wilfully commercial music Albarn had ever made, sold more than 4 million copies worldwide and brought him his biggest-ever success in the USA. To Albarn's surprise, the record was nominated for a Grammy Award in the Best Rap Performance category. He followed this triumph with *Mali Music*, an album largely recorded in West Africa, and worked on the seventh Blur album, partly put to tape in Morocco. Entitled *Think Tank* and hailed by some – including the band themselves – as the best album Blur had ever recorded, it was released in May 2003. Albarn still lives in West London.

Brett Anderson used the promotional campaign around Suede's 2002 album *A New Morning* to admit to long-term problems with crack and heroin. 'I ended up spending most of my time sat in front of the TV with the sound turned down,' he said. 'Eventually, I took a long hard look at myself and decided: "Either you stop doing this or you're going to do some damage."' His travails had impacted on Suede's unfocused, almost self-parodic fourth album,

1999's *Head Music,* but *A New Morning* – produced by the sometime Blur associate Stephen Street – was not the vast improvement for which many had hoped. In the wake of *Singles,* a Greatest Hits collection released in October 2003, Suede announced their effective dissolution at the tail-end of the same year. Soon after, Anderson was seen in the company of Bernard Butler: the pair have since completed work on around a dozen songs and put together a band, and are aiming at releasing an album in early 2005.

Paul Arthurs left Oasis in August 1999, towards the end of work on their fourth album. Noel Gallagher has repeatedly traced his departure to the fact that, though the rest of the group accompanied the sessions with a spell of tee-totalism, Arthurs caused problems by drinking to excess. Arthurs, however, remains tight-lipped about the reasons for his departure. 'I know the truth,' he says. 'And Liam does. And Noel does.' He lives with his wife, Kate, and their two children in Bowdon, Cheshire, and has worked on a musical project called Moondog One with two former members of The Smiths, Andy Rourke and Mike Joyce. His place in Oasis was taken by Gem Archer, the one-time singer-guitarist with the Creation band Heavy Stereo.

Tony Blair remains the British Prime Minister. He is occasionally photographed either playing a guitar or carrying one into 10 Downing Street, and is rumoured to be in the habit of joining his younger son, Nicky, in playing along to records by the Californian punk rock band Blink-182. On a visit to a London secondary school in November 2003, he spoke – in French – of his fondness for the Foo Fighters, U2, and the tongue-in-cheek British rock band The Darkness.

Bernard Butler's progress since the break-up of Suede has been multi-faceted and fitful. His first single with David McAlmont, Yes, was released in May 1995; unfortunately, by the end of that year, the pair had acrimoniously split, though they reunited seven years later for an album entitled *Bring It Back.* In the meantime, Butler had signed to Creation Records and released two solo albums, *People Move On* and *Friends And Lovers;* unfortunately, the latter suggested that this phase of his progress had quickly reached a dead-end. In 2001, he made overtures to Suede's management about the re-establishment of his songwriting partnership with Brett Anderson. 'I knew they were struggling and I said, "I'll write music for him, no problem,"' he says. Unfortunately, he was rebuffed – though as mentioned above, the pair set off on the path to reconciliation at the end of 2003. Butler lives in North London with his wife and two children.

Jarvis Cocker remains the lead singer with Pulp, though at the time this book was published, their long-term future was unclear: after the release in 2001 of the poor-selling album *We Love Life*, they parted with Island Records the following year, and planned to take 12 months off before considering their options. Having married Camille Bidault-Waddington, a fashion stylist, in 2002, Cocker left Britain for a new life – and fatherhood – in Paris. He made a muted return to music the following year as 'Darren Spooner', one half of a spoof electronic duo called Relaxed Muscle.

Graham Coxon departed from Blur in the summer of 2002, during sessions for the group's seventh album. 'Our manager, Chris Morrison, told me my services weren't required any more,' he said. 'It was something to do with my attitude. Although I felt I was going about my work honestly, and perhaps they mistook honesty for attitude. There's a total problem with honesty and attitude in Blur at times.' In the meantime, he had released three solo albums, *The Sky Is Too High*, *The Golden D* and *Crow Sit On Blood Tree*. His fourth solo work, *The Kiss Of Morning*, was an affectingly confessional, intimate record, made in the wake of treatment at the Priory Clinic. Coxon no longer drinks alcohol, and busies himself with the upbringing of a daughter, Pepper.

Johnny Dean's involvement with the music industry came to an end when, having recorded *Hay Tiempo!*, a second album that was only released in Japan, Menswear split up in 1999. He now works in the Barnet offices of Intec, a company that specialises 'in the after sale support of cellular equipment'. Dean lives with his ex-Menswear colleague Stuart Black in Enfield, and is still in a relationship with the sometime Elastica bassist Sheila Chipperfield.

Justine Frischmann launched the third, six-piece incarnation of Elastica with a performance at the 1999 Reading Festival. Though they were no longer signed to the Geffen label, the group went on to release a scratchy, off-beam album called *The Menace*, released to mixed reviews in April 2000. The group was laid to rest at the end of 2001. Frischmann recently presented a series about modern architecture, *Dream Spaces*, for the BBC's digital TV network, and created the incidental music for an animated Channel 4 programme called *Working It*. She lives in the same West London home she and Damon Albarn shared during the Britpop period, and remains close friends with Brett Anderson.

Liam Gallagher remained married to Patsy Kensit until their divorce in September 2000. One year before, Kensit had given birth to a son, named Lennon. Liam is now the partner of ex–All Saints' singer Nicole Appleton; the couple had a son, named Gene, in July 2001. Liam's role within Oasis has slowly expanded: he contributed one song to 2000's *Standing On The Shoulder Of Giants*, and three to *Heathen Chemistry*, released in 2002. Both albums were the deserved subject of critical hostility, though Liam's bullishness about Oasis's worth remains as indestructible as ever. 'We're not wizards,' he said in 2002. 'We just happen to be the best band in the world.' In late 2003, he and the rest of Oasis began work on a new album with Richard Fearless and Tim Holmes, the two members of the decidedly non-rock Death In Vegas. The two parties subsequently went their separate ways.

Noel Gallagher continues to be the leader of Oasis, though his pre-eminence has been slightly offset by his brother's increased songwriting role. Having piloted the deeply anti-climactic *Standing On The Shoulder Of Giants* to completion in 1999, he joined the new line-up of Oasis in a world tour, but – as in 1994 and 1996 – walked out in May 2000. This time, the group carried on without him, recruiting the guitarist Matt Deighton as a temporary replacement (which meant that Liam was the only original member of Oasis in the line-up). Noel rejoined Oasis later that summer. In the meantime, Meg Mathews had given birth to a daughter, Anäis, though she and Noel split in September 2000. Noel went on to commence a relationship with Sara McDonald, a London-based PR, which came to an end in August 2002. Rumours attributed that break-up to an interview with McDonald in the *Evening Standard*'s *ES* magazine, which allegedly reawakened similar tensions to those that had erupted between Noel and Mathews. The pair have since re-united. During the promotional campaign around that year's *Heathen Chemistry* album, Noel was asked about his plans for the education of his daughter. 'She'll have the best education money can buy,' he said. 'I want her to be Prime Minister, and you have to go to a posh school for that.'

Chris Gentry's activities since Menswear's split have included a spell with Simon White in Finlay Quaye's backing band, TV appearances with Kelly Osbourne and Craig David, and modelling. He is now pursuing songwriting projects, and lives in West London with his partner, Sabina, and their daughter, Lola.

Simon Gilbert was the drummer with Suede until their break-up in 2003. He currently lives in his hometown of Stratford On Avon.

Annie Holland still lives in Brighton. Since the break-up of Elastica, she has played bass in a project called Hi Fi, also featuring her ex-colleagues Justin Welch and Sharon Mew, one of two keyboard players in Elastica's third line-up.

Alex James has continued to be Blur's bass player. In 1998, his friendship with Keith Allen and Damien Hirst was manifested professionally in Vin-Da-Loo, a hugely successful single credited to Fat Les, and aimed at soundtracking England's progress in the 1998 World Cup. James, Hirst and Allen attempted to follow its success with an ill-fated Christmas record entitled Naughty Christmas (Goblin In The Office), and recorded a version of Jerusalem as the official single for England's European Championship bid in 2000. James also makes a habit of publicly keeping abreast of developments in literature and art, though his occasional incongruity in such circles was amply demonstrated when, having smoked between courses at the Royal Academy's summer dinner in 1995 (at which he was seated opposite Cherie Blair), he was not invited back. In 2003, James married Claire Neat, a music video producer. She gave birth to the couple's first child in early 2004.

Darren Kalynuk followed his spell working for Rock The Vote with a role as a Senior Press Officer at the Prince's Trust. In 1999, he became a Senior PR adviser on Marketing and Communications at the BBC. He currently works as a freelancer in the PR field.

Steve Lamacq was the sole host of Radio One's *Evening Session* from 1997 until December 2002. He still hosts the weekly programme *Lamacq Live,* as well as a show on the BBC 6 music channel. His autobiographical book, *Going Deaf For A Living,* was published in 2000.

Tony McCarroll launched legal proceedings against Oasis in 1999, with the aid of Jens Hills, who had previously represented the sometime Beatles drummer Pete Best. Hills aimed at proving that McCarroll had been 'unlawfully expelled from the partnership' and was therefore owed his share of the group's five-album deal with Sony, including royalties for records made after his sacking. McCarroll accepted an out-of-court settlement of £600,000, though his legal fees were estimated at £250,000. He went on to be one of the founders of Potential House, a Mancunian recording studio, and the drummer with a band called Raika. He describes their sound as 'good, honest guitar music'.

Alan McGee followed Creation with a new label called Poptones. After shaky beginnings, the venture was drastically scaled down in 2002, when McGee went into partnership with the Telstar label. His reputation as a discoverer of new talent, however, was given a major fillip by the fact that Poptones' roster included the celebrated Swedish band The Hives. In 2000, McGee funded the abortive London mayoral campaign of Malcolm McLaren and was ejected from the Labour Party. He claimed that a party insider's opinion that he was 'ill' represented a classic New Labour smear, though his ex-associate, Margaret McDonagh, is adamant that the reference was a misinterpreted reference to a bout of 'flu. In the wake of the fall-out, McGee withdrew his support for New Labour in a polemic published by *The Independent.* 'The Labour Party is a joke, and I was conned into helping their cause,' he said. 'I was lied to and used by opportunists, interested only in their careers rather than improving the welfare of the country.' In 2003, in addition continuing his work with Poptones, he took over the management of the acclaimed London band The Libertines.

Paul McGuigan left Oasis soon after Paul Arthurs in August 1999. 'Oasis were not my priority any more,' he later explained. 'They were fourth on the list and that's not fair on the band.' He currently lives on the outskirts of London with his wife, Ruth, and their son. In 2002, he played bass on Lessons Learned From Rocky I to Rocky III, a track from Cornershop's album *Handcream For A Generation*. His place in Oasis was taken by Andy Bell, the one-time singer-guitarist with Creation band Ride.

Meg Mathews was divorced from Noel Gallagher in January 2001. Since then, her once-ubiquitous profile – which arguably peaked with her appointment in April 1999 as the public face of Vladivar Vodka – has noticeably diminished. That said, in 2002, a bronze cast of her breasts was auctioned online in aid of a cancer charity. Two days prior to the auction's close, bids had reached £760.

Donna Matthews returned to London in 1999, and still lives in Kings Cross. She is currently the singer-guitarist and chief creative force in a trio called Klang, who began playing in public in 2002. She does not drink, smoke or take drugs, and has forsworn caffeine.

Richard Oakes was the guitarist with Suede until their split at the end of 2003. He lives in West London, and his current plans are unknown.

Mat Osman ceased his role as Suede's bass player at the same time. His next move remains equally unclear.

Andy Ross put Food Records 'into mothballs' at the end of August 2001, when the label's deal with EMI came to a close, thus ending his professional relationship with Blur. He is now in charge of Bossmusic, a label whose records are independently distributed. 'We've got the right-coloured vans now,' he says, 'just when you don't need vans any more.' Bossmusic is based in Food's former offices in Camden Town.

Dave Rowntree is still the drummer with Blur. His outside interests have included computer animation, flying his own plane, and working with Alex James on fundraising for the Beagle 2 project, which successfully launched a British-made exploration device towards Mars in 2003. Once the mechanism was on the planet's surface, it was intended to transmit a specially composed Blur composition back to earth. Unfortunately, contact with the Beagle lander was lost before it had reached its final destination.

Andy Saunders remains the UK PR representative for Alan McGee, and was integrally involved in Malcolm McLaren's short-lived campaign for London mayoralty. He is the Managing Director of Velocity Communications, a successful capital-based company.

Mike Smith was promoted to Vice President of A&R at EMI Music Publishing in 2000. He still works with Blur. His more recent signings include The White Stripes, Starsailor and Doves.

Adrian Webb was Menswear's manager until their split in 1999. He had spent much of the previous year running Gigi's, a small-scale members' only club on Soho's Dean Street. He eventually relocated to Brighton. In 2000, he established an alternative rock stage at London's Mardi Gras festival, headlined two years later by Suede. He is currently the manager of a Brighton-based rock band called Secret Rulers.

Justin Welch married Sharon Mew in 2002. The couple work together musically, and live in Devon.

Louise Wener called time on Sleeper in 1997, after the disappointing reception to the band's third album, *Pleased To Meet You*. Her first novel, *Goodnight Steve McQueen*, in some part inspired by her life as a musician, was published in 2002, and was followed in 2003 by *The Big Blind*, partly based on similar themes to Sleeper's 1995 hit, Vegas. When sold to an American publisher, it attracted a six-figure advance. She is currently working on her third book.

Alan White was dismissed as Oasis's drummer in January 2004, thus becoming the fourth person to exit the group. According to a baldly worded statement released by the band's management, 'he was asked to leave Oasis by the other band members'. Rumours suggested that his colleagues felt his commitment to the group was in question.

Simon White followed his role in Menswear with a spell as the lead guitarist with Bird Man Ray, a West Coast–esque London rock band. He has also worked with Finley Quaye in addition to pursuing a career in music management. He still lives near Camden Town, and views the saga of Menswear as 'a cautionary tale'.

APPENDIX 2 The musical tastes of Tony Blair

From the *NME*'s Christmas issue, December 1996

My Top Ten singles of 1996 by Tony Blair (In no particular order)

The Ghost Of Tom Joad – Bruce Springsteen
'I've always liked Springsteen – and Steinbeck. Springsteen seems to have made a decision to carry on writing for the audience that's grown up with him, so he probably appears in *NME* about as often as I do.'

Three Lions – The Lightning Seeds featuring David Baddiel and Frank Skinner
'England's football anthem and so good I borrowed it for the Labour Party conference . . .'

Don't Look Back In Anger – Oasis
'I couldn't *not* choose an Oasis song this year. They've all been very vocal in their support – especially Noel.'

Ironic – Alanis Morissette
'She's a stunning live performer. You can't help but admire her confidence. This track stands out from the rest of the album.'

Hallo Spaceboy – David Bowie and the Pet Shop Boys
'The record that Bowie and the Pet Shop Boys performed at the Brits when I presented him with an award. I've always liked both of them so it was good to see them together, though maybe I enjoyed the idea more than the song.'

Say You'll Be There – Spice Girls
'Great pop record. There has been free and frank debate in the Blair household as to our favourite Spice Girl. Why are two of them called Mel?'

Ready Or Not – Fugees
'I love the girl singer's voice. We listened to it a lot when we were driving on holiday this year.'

A Whiter Shade Of Pale – Annie Lennox
'Trying to interpret old songs is notoriously difficult and you have to be an extra confident singer to attempt it and come out on top. Annie Lennox succeeds.'

Angel – Simply Red
'By coincidence, Mick Hucknall is another strong supporter of the Labour Party . . . He's had a good year and this is the best of a good bunch.'

Rotterdam – The Beautiful South
'I heard this on the radio. I just like it.'

Tony Blair's Desert Island Discs from *Desert Island Discs*, broadcast 24 November 1996

1. Ezio, Cancel Today (from *Black Boots On Latin Feet*, Astra)*

2 Debussy, Clair De Lune, performed by Pascal Roge (from *Clair De Lune*, Decca)

3. The Beatles, In My Life (from *1962–66*, Apple)

4. Bruce Springsteen, Fourth Of July, Asbury Park (Sandy) (from *The Wild, The Innocent And The E-Street Shuffle*, Columbia)

5. Samuel Barber, Adagio For Strings (*Cello Concerto/Cello Sonata/Adagio*, Virgin Classics)

6. Robert Johnson, Crossroads Blues (from *The Complete Recordings*, CBS)

7. Free, Wishing Well (from *The Boys Are Back In Town*, Various Artists, Columbia)

8. Francisco Tarrega, Recuerdos de la Alhambra (from *A Portrait Of John Williams*, CBS)

NB For his one allowed book, Blair picked *Ivanhoe* by Walter Scott. His chosen luxury was a 'classical guitar'.

---

* Ezio, a folkish musical enterprise based in Cambridge, and centred around guitarists Ezio Lunedei and Mark Fowell, were the most unlikely inclusion in this list. Since 1996, Blair's endorsement has seemingly found its way into all of the group's promotional material. This, for example, is taken from the programme for the 2002 Cambridge Folk Festival: 'Their first album, *Black Boots On Latin Feet*, was named as one of the albums of the year in Ezio's native Italy, while the song Cancel Today was selected as a Desert Island Disc by none other than Tony Blair.'

APPENDIX 3 The music

Author's note: Most of the records listed below are currently available on CD. For the sake of uniformity, the original labels have been listed. In the case of deleted albums, the worldwide web has made record-buying a surprisingly easy business: I personally recommend Amazon's Z-Shops service.

The pre-Britpop years

The Smiths

The Smiths are crucial to any understanding of the Britpop period: their influence, though manifested in very different ways, was common to nearly all the groups chronicled in this book. Their self-titled debut album (Rough Trade, 1984) is full of brilliant songs, though slightly hampered by buffed-up 80s production; a more satisfying taste of the early Smiths is provided by the invigoratingly raw collection *Hatful Of Hollow* (Rough Trade, 1984). From *Meat Is Murder* (Rough Trade, 1985) onwards, they scraped ever-more dizzying heights. *The Queen Is Dead* (Rough Trade, 1986) is commonly held to be their masterpiece, though two-thirds of their swansong, *Strangeways, Here We Come* (Rough Trade, 1987) is up to a similar standard. In all these albums, one can hear a sardonically-rendered northern grit akin to that later peddled by Pulp (Rusholme Ruffians, Frankly Mr Shankly), along with the sexual/romantic melodrama that was such a huge influence on Suede (Handsome Devil, I Want The One I Can't Have). The Smiths' influence on Blur and Oasis was more diffuse, but undeniable: the former shared The Smiths' overarching sense of place, while, by his own admission, Noel Gallagher was hugely impressed by Johnny Marr's rock classicism.

Morrissey's solo career got off to a commendable start with *Viva Hate* (HMV, 1988), before stalling horrifically thanks to the awfully short weight served up by *Kill Uncle* (His Master's Voice, 1991). Just as the first stirrings of Britpop became audible, he released *Your Arsenal* (HMV, 1992), produced by Mick Ronson and festooned with accomplished songs, though the chances of a unanimously positive response – wider developments were, after all, aligning in his favour – were offset by both the furore surrounding his flag-waving

Finsbury Park performance, and the lyrical ambiguities of National Front Disco and We'll Let You Know (along with the earlier Bengali In Platforms and Asian Rut). A decade after all the outrage, most of it sounds wonderful – as does Vauxhall And I (His Master's Voice, 1994). His subsequent albums have struck a deeply disappointing note – though, after a six-year hiatus, Morrissey's imminent return may yet restore his reputation.

80s indie

Reducing the 80s indie subculture to a handful of records will inevitably attract charges of extreme arbitrariness, but here goes. Joy Division's Unknown Pleasures (Factory, 1979) and Closer (Factory, 1980) cemented the indie world's black-clad outsider pose; after Ian Curtis's suicide, Bernard Sumner, Peter Hook and Stephen Morris went on to explore an altogether more colourful universe with New Order, but their work in laying down the attitudinal bedrock of the 80s counterculture had been crucial. For more of the kind of angular, iconoclastic music that was the Factory label's forte, listen to the early 80s work of A Certain Ratio, collected on Early (Soul Jazz, 2001): its cerebral art-funk represents the kind of approach that both baggy and Britpop wiped from history.

Orange Juice's You Can't Hide Your Love Forever (Postcard, 1982) launched indie's influential anti-macho, shrinking-violet stance in impressive style: in the eyes of many of its adherents, it reached a peak with The Wedding Present's slightly clumsier George Best (Reception, 1987). If curiosity overwhelms you, evidence of the extremes to which this approach could be taken lies with the terrifyingly fey Talulah Gosh – much loved by the student Graham Coxon – and their one album Rock Legends Vol 69 (53rd and 3rd, 1987). For a far more poised, melancholic take on indiedom's bookish wimpiness, Felt are beyond compare: a good starting point is Forever Breathes The Lonely Word (Cherry Red, 1986). By way of a crash course in the listening habits of the archetypal mid-80s indie enthusiast, trawl the web or rummage through junk shops for the NME's cassette-only compilation C86, later issued on vinyl (Strange Fruit, 1990); an exhaustive database of the kind of music it collected is at www.twee.net

The melding of indie and rock'n'roll poses embodied by the Creation label was taken into the album charts by The Jesus And Mary Chain's hugely lauded Psychocandy (Blanco Y Negro, 1985); a much more marketable version of the Creation aesthetic can be heard on The House Of Love's self-titled debut (Creation, 1988). A long line of Creation compilations convey a flavour of the label's pre-90s activities – the best is the long-deleted, vinyl-only Doing It For The Kids (Creation, 1988). In a completely different area, anyone keen to understand Blur's Seymour period should buy the Cardiacs' *Sampler* (Alphabet, 1995), an anthology of their reliably unhinged music that spans the best part of fifteen years.

Agit-pop

To grasp British music's anti-Thatcher period, listen to such Billy Bragg songs as To Have And To Have Not, It Says Here and Between The Wars, collected on *Back To Basics* (Cooking Vinyl, 1993), but bear in mind that his frequently terrific love songs were always better. The Style Council's *Our Favourite Shop* (Polydor, 1985) is tied together by similar themes, and made all the more fascinating by its belief-beggaring contrast to Paul Weller's solo work. The group's most politicised artefact was *Soul Deep* (Polydor, 1985), credited to the Council Collective and issued in support of striking miners; the B-side of the 12-inch finds future Oasis associate Paolo Hewitt interviewing members of the NUM. For left-wing rock in excelsis, try The Redskins, Socialist Worker-ites who were too revolutionary for Red Wedge. *Neither Washington Or Moscow* (Decca, 1986) features titles like Kick Over The Statues and Go Get Organized, and sounds like something from another age.

Baggy and beyond

The late 80s and early 90s saw the superseding of everything outlined above by the culture represented by Happy Mondays and The Stone Roses. The former's end-of-the-pier reformation in 1999 prompted the inevitable *Greatest Hits* (London, 1999), though two other compilations are far more satisfactory: *Loads* (London, 1995), which should be sought out in its limited 2-CD edition, and *Double Easy: The US Singles* (Elektra, 1993). Of the group's four studio albums, the murkily lysergic *Bummed* (Factory, 1988) and the clipped, sun-kissed *Pills'n'Thrills And Bellyaches* (Factory, 1990) are recommended without qualification. See also Black Grape's excellent *It's Great When You're Straight . . . Yeah!* (Radioactive, 1995), whose wonders briefly included Shaun Ryder in the Britpop moment.

The Stone Roses' two albums, separated by their four-year disappearance, were sufficiently different to suggest the work of two different groups. *The Stone Roses* (Silvertone, 1988) is a perfectly realised debut, whose every note and nuance sound like they were pored over for years in advance; the album is also notable for Ian Brown's discovery that the Mancunian accent could sound as well-suited to rock music as American English. *Second Coming* (Geffen, 1994) is a flawed, fascinating document of a group extending its horizons then chasing its own tail, as its myth, in absentia, grew ever larger. The best of both albums was recently collapsed on to one 15-track CD, *The Very Best Of The Stone Roses* (Silvertone, 2002), which also features the superlative Fool's Gold. To instantly ascertain The Roses' influence on Oasis, go to *The Complete Stone Roses* (Silvertone, 1995) and play the Squire/Brown song Standing Here, then move on to Cloudburst, a B-side on the Live Forever single (Creation, 1995): to all intents and purposes, they're the same song. Also, while we're here, Noel Gallagher's brief career as a roadie begs a mention for Inspiral Carpets. *Life* (Mute, 1990) found their fuzzed-up meld of 60s garage and melodic pop reaching its biggest audience, but the best way of sampling their seven-year career is to buy *The Singles* (Mute, 1995).

The immediate pre-Britpop period was hardly the most fertile time, though Creation managed to issue three superlative albums: Primal Scream's multi-faceted *Screamadelica* (Creation, 1991), Teenage Fanclub's gorgeously old-school *Bandwagonesque* (ditto) and My Bloody Valentine's mind-bending *Loveless* (ditto). The latter was a huge influence on *Nowhere* (Creation, 1990) and *Going Blank Again* (Creation, 1992) by Ride, whose line-up included the future Oasis bassist Andy Bell. Their amorphous, wilfully vacant aesthetic, shared by the bands known as 'shoegazers', undoubtedly prompted Britpop's rediscovery of the notion of music with an in-built agenda.

For a fascinatingly fierce example of indie music's last stab at the anti-mainstream approach of yore, the author recommends Huggy Bear's *Taking The Rough With The Smooch* (Wiiija, 1993), a compilation of ragged, dissent-fuelled music by the group who placed themselves at the vanguard of riot grrrl, the small-scale upsurge that would be swamped by the tidal wave of lad culture that arrived in 1994. Their only near-hit single, Her Jazz, still sounds compellingly potent. Huggy Bear's Jo Johnson dated the aforementioned Graham Coxon; some of riot grrrl's pro-female agenda arguably found a new voice with Elastica.

Britpop's key players

Blur

Leisure (Food, 1991) amounts to little more satisfying than transparent proof that the early Blur were a group in search of an idea, although There's No Other Way and She's So High retain a period charm, and the fascinatingly artful, disquieting, quite brilliant Sing is arguably worth the price of the album. The breakthrough came with the following year's Popscene, though its commercial failure so rankled with the group that they have long denied their ungrateful public the chance to own it; it was even excluded from the band's

Best Of (Parlophone, 2000). To own Popscene, either try tracking down the original single, or buy the American version of *Modern Life Is Rubbish* (ERG/ SBK, 1993): it's tacked on to the end.

Modern Life's British release (Food, 1993) represented a key moment in Britpop's early progress – cf For Tomorrow, Star Shaped, Sunday Sunday – before *Parklife* (Food, 1994) took Blur's Anglo-centric aesthetic into the mainstream. The latter remains a wildly diverse, dazzling masterwork, not least on account of the intimate, first-person songs (Badhead, To The End, End Of A Century) that were rather lost in the stampede to acclaim Damon Albarn's rediscovery of Kinks-esque social comment. Most importantly, the album's grand finale is the stunning This Is A Low, which stands comparison with any of Blur's illustrious forebears; even The Beatles. *The Great Escape* (Food, 1995) largely found the *Parklife* approach inflated into something both formulaic and soulless, though Best Days, He Thought Of Cars and the wonderful The Universal are up to 1994's standards. Also, Charmless Man nails the coke-addled ambience of Soho circa 1995: it sounds little short of horrid, but that was probably the whole point. From the same year, Damon Albarn's TV duet with Ray Davies on Waterloo Sunset was belatedly made available on *This Is Where I Belong: The Songs Of Ray Davies & The Kinks* (Rykodisc, 2002).

The sound of Blur in their Britpop pomp is captured on the import-only *Live At Budokan* (EMI Japan, 1996); from there, it was all discord and internal debate, until *Blur* (Food, 1997) announced a rediscovery of their artistic essence. In its own way, it's as good as *Parklife*: home to songs as impressive as Beetlebum, Country Sad Ballad Man, Strange News From Another Star and Essex Dogs – a brilliantly disorientating evocation of the neither-here-nor-there expanse in which Albarn, Coxon and Dave Rowntree grew up. *13* (Food, 1999) is, in part, the document of Albarn's split with Justine Frischmann: Albarn opens his heart to tear-jerking effect on No Distance Left To Run and the divine, gospel-ised Tender, while elsewhere, Blur largely submerge their commercial instincts in favour of the bleary, wee-hours ambience that is impressively realised on Trimm Trabb and 1992.

Blur's B-sides have tended to be either unimpressive studio off-cuts, experimental pieces with little relevance to the group's work proper, or in-jokes. A handful, however, merit attention. The tracks that came with the various formats of Sunday Sunday included five songs by Seymour, and Blur and friends' readings of Daisy Bell and Let's All Go Down The Strand: all are collected on one CD included in the group's limited edition singles box (Food, 2000). Also, All We Want – from the CD single of Tender (Food, 1999) – is a lost gem: a dizzyingly melodic example of Albarn's compositional talents that, had it been issued on an album, would have attracted fulsome praise. The same applies to Young And Lovely, of a piece – aside from its rather slapdash production – with the best *Modern Life* and *Parklife* material, and included on the CD1 format of *Chemical World* (Food, 1993).

As far as Blur's extra-curricular work is concerned, Albarn's talent for mastering any style to which he turns his hand is amply demonstrated by the groovesome pop of *Gorillaz* (Parlophone, 2001); play the album after listening to Graham Coxon's *The Golden D* (Transcopic, 2000), and some of the background to Coxon's exit from Blur is thrown into sharp relief. Coxon's best solo work by far is *The Kiss of Morning* (Transcopic, 2002), written and recorded while he was both undergoing treatment at the Priory and moving through his last days with Blur, though its author insisted that its songs of regret and vituperative hatred were based on his non-professional life. Alex James's Me Me Me never got to make an album, though the rib-tickling Hanging Around (Indolent, 1996), along with its two endearingly whimsical B-sides, Tabitha's Island and Hollywood Wives, is worth hunting down. Fat Les's soccer anthem Vin-Da-Loo (Turtleneck, 1998) sounds like Britpop's absurd last hurrah: it can be found on such compilations as *The Best Unofficial Footie Anthems . . . Ever!* (Virgin TV, 2000), which surely embody one of Britpop's more unfortunate knock-on effects.

Elastica

Some day soon, Elastica's self-titled debut album (Deceptive, 1995) will probably be held aloft as a Velvets-esque totem for a new crop of punk-influenced hopefuls. It has aged remarkably well – as evidenced by both the elegantly commercial likes of Connection, Waking Up and Car Song, and the more splenetic Annie, Stutter and Smile. Suede fans keen to hear Justine Frischmann's side of her relationship with Brett Anderson should study Never Here (which, according to Frischmann, 'sounds like Pat Benatar').

Elastica's B-sides include a few songs that cast illuminating light on the group's history. Rockunroll ('is dead'), which accompanied Line-Up (Deceptive, 1994) sounds like a camped-up summary of the group's iconoclastic intent; See That Animal, from the CD single of Connection (Deceptive, 1994) is a Justine Frischmann/Brett Anderson co-write, salvaged from the early days of Suede; Blue, on the same CD, is a Donna Matthews home demo whose icy ambience makes it sound like a soundtrack to dawn in King's Cross.

The group's protracted lost years are partly captured by *The Radio One Sessions* (Strange Fruit, 2001), which features a wealth of early material, as well as three songs from the 1997 Mk II Line up, two of which – Human and Love Like Ours – attest to the increasing influence of Matthews. *The Menace* (Deceptive, 2000) found Frischmann redirecting the group to music's left-field: devoid of the panache that characterised much of the first album, it's made up of abrasive, off-beam stuff that tends to find the desire to tear up the musical manual getting in the way of much creative achievement. Thankfully, there are exceptions: the almost embarrassingly confessional My Sex, for example, is a wintry, dream-like look back at Frischmann's time with Damon Albarn.

Oasis

Definitely Maybe (Creation, 1994) remains Oasis's best album, not least because Noel Gallagher had a sure grasp of what he was writing about – in essence, the desire to escape – and the music to which his lyrics should be grafted: primal rock'n'roll, alchemised from the most basic ingredients. Aside from Cigarettes And Alcohol, Rock 'n' Roll Star et al, the album contains Married With Children, an acoustic kiss-off founded on a wit which its author quickly seemed to mislay.

(What's The Story) Morning Glory? (Creation, 1995) became so ubiquitous that appreciating it in musical terms alone is almost impossible: for most Britons between twenty and forty, even the wretched Roll With It should prompt a pleasurable Proustian rush. That said, Morning Glory and Champagne Supernova work together to provide a fantastically accomplished portrayal of both sides of the cocaine experience; their combined twelve minutes arguably marks Noel's all-time peak.

Then, of course, comes *Be Here Now* (Creation, 1997), the coke-addled fiasco that Noel recently described as 'offensive'. That might be true, but it also lends itself to the musical equivalent of ambulance-chasing: Magic Pie, Fade In/Out and the absurdly overcooked All Around The World beg, but never quite answer, the question of what exactly they were thinking.

Standing On The Shoulder Of Giants (Big Brother, 2000) attempted to strip things back and thereby stop the rot, but failed: aside from Go Let It Out, its songs are eminently forgettable, though Liam's Little James provides a note of *Be Here Now*-esque ludicrousness. If you don't own it, don't worry: instead, buy the CD single of Go Let It Out (Big Brother, 2000), which features Let's All Make Believe: an impressively bleak bit of lapsed-Catholic atheism that stands as Noel Gallagher's last decent song to date.

Heathen Chemistry (Big Brother, 2002) launched Oasis's new, post-Burnage line-up and was justly dismissed by most of the UK's critics, but found surprising favour with the public, seemingly based on the success of its first two singles. Sales apart, The Hindu Times and Stop Crying Your Heart Out are two sides of a depressingly generic coin: respectively, Roll With It-type rock and Wonderwall-ish balladry, rendered with a plodding efficiency that lies light years from Oasis's early intuitive brilliance.

By way of a reminder of what all the fuss was about, buy *The Masterplan* (Creation, 1998), a B-sides compilation assembled from a commendable archive that might even be their second-best album. It features such highpoints as 1995's exquisite Acquiesce, and their sneering version of I Am The Walrus, along with songs as good as Headshrinker and Stay Young. Thanks to its appearance, there is little need to track down original Oasis singles – although a couple should be highlighted. Whatever (Creation, 1994) is the strange sound of Oasis revealing themselves to be granny-friendly sentimentalists, and is unavailable on any album. Don't Look Back In Anger (Creation, 1995) features both Step Out, Noel Gallagher's most ludicrously plagiaristic song ever, and their cover of Slade's Cum On Feel The Noize; fuel to those who believed – correctly – that comparisons with the Birmingham pop-yobs were a little more apposite than endless references to The Beatles.

Pulp

In the wake of their Britpop-era success, the music Pulp made prior to the mid-90s was reissued, repackaged and re-evaluated. *It* (Red Rhino, 1983), an album characterised by what one critic called 'Brel-flavoured folk', is little more than a fan-only curio; *Freaks* (Fire, 1987) and the retrospective compilation *Masters Of The Universe: Pulp On Fire* (Fire, 1994) betray an increased confidence, but are so steeped in the effete ways of 80s indie-pop that their music gives off the odour of long-confirmed obsolescence. *Separations* (Fire, 1992) was made in the wake of Pulp's relocation to London, and finds them groping towards the approach that would later cohere so successfully – in particular, My Legendary Girlfriend combines Jarvis Cocker's love of discofied camp with glacial eeriness to impressive effect. That song, along with selections from all four of the albums above, is included on *Countdown 1992–1983* (Fire, 1996), which represents the most digestible method of understanding the band's first decade.

The real start of Pulp's career came with three singles released on the Gift label – O.U (Gone Gone), the brilliant Babies, and Razzmatazz – and anthologised, complete with their B-sides, on *Pulpintro* (Island, 1993). Six months later came *His'n'Hers* (Island, 1994), which finds Cocker and his associates gleefully exploring the themes that would frame the following year's *Different Class* (Island, 1995) in almost conceptual terms. On both albums, the low-rent exotica of Pulp's music – once cruelly described as 'disco skiffle' – has rather dated, though the best songs (Joyriders, Lipgloss, Mis-Shapes, I Spy, Sorted For E's And Wizz) still cast an irresistible spell. Special praise must, of course, be heaped on Common People – the Britpop era's only example of a record that fused anger, intelligence and vast commercial appeal.

Though its sales were nigh-on disastrous, Pulp's best album remains *This Is Hardcore* (Island, 1998), Cocker's cold, cathartic treatise on the after-effects of his own celebrity. It is not the kind of record that can be played on either Saturday nights or Sunday mornings – but its title track, The Fear, Party Hard and Help The Aged (among others) prove that for all its woes, the Britpop experience served to sharpen Cocker's talents. Chiefly on account of their lyrics, Pulp's B-sides from this period are worth having: The Professional was a supporting feature with This Is Hardcore (Island, 1998); the admirably timely Cocaine Socialism accompanied A Little Soul (ditto).

We Love Life (Island, 2001) was produced by no less than Scott Walker, though even his presence cannot quite disguise the fact that, lacking the kind of Big Idea that had been the making of both its predecessors, the album finds Pulp occasionally floundering. That said, such pieces as The Trees, Wickerman and Weeds – in which Cocker dares to deal with the travails of asylum seekers – confirm that their light was far from being snuffed out. Finally, after Pulp announced their departure from the Island label, they released *Hits* (Island, 2002), a collection of all their A-sides from 1993 onwards, along with a fantastic new song entitled Last Day Of The Miners Strike. Mapping out some of the history detailed in the early chapters of this book (' '87 – socialism gave way to socialising') against a booming, epic backcloth, it found Pulp sounding more singular than ever.

Suede

Suede's opening trilogy of singles – The Drowners, Metal Mickey and Animal Nitrate – betrayed a talent, confidence and internal bond that, sadly, went awry within eighteen months. Their A-sides are all on their self-titled debut album (Nude, 1993), which speaks in the elegant, outré language of outsiderdom that the success of *Parklife* and *Definitely Maybe* obliterated. The singles' B-sides – the awe-inspiring My Insatiable One and To The Birds, along with such gems as He's Dead and The Big Time – are all included on the 2-CD compilation *Sci-fi Lullabies* (Nude, 1997).

Dog Man Star (Nude, 1994) was recorded as Brett Anderson and Bernard Butler's relationship fell apart, which adds to its air of echo-laden intrigue, though what's most fascinating is how occupants of the same city that played host to Britpop came up with such chunks of doomy ostentation as Introducing The Band, We Are The Pigs and Daddy's Speeding (let alone the Elaine Paige-goes-indie likes of Black Or Blue and Still Life). *Coming Up* (Nude, 1996) marked the debut of Suede Mk II, and dished up a simplified version of their early aesthetic: Brett Anderson's description of it as Suede's 'party album' is not as unlikely as it sounds. *Head Music* (Nude, 1999) found the group embracing electronics, and minting a superficially innovative new approach, but the songs' lyrics were almost self-parodic – witness the borderline preposterous Savoir Faire, Can't Get Enough and She's In Fashion. The first single from this album, Electricity (Nude, 1999) featured Implement Yeah!, the song from Suede's early repertoire performed with Justine Frischmann at Reading '97, on its cassette and minidisc versions: a recording of the Reading performance was released as a fanclub-only CD the previous year.

After a troubled and expensive gestation period, *A New Morning* (Epic, 2002) suggested that the group were moving in ever-decreasing circles: Brett Anderson was still singing about 'the beat of the concrete street' and closed-circuit television, while his group tended to sound like jaded hired hands.

In the meantime, Bernard Butler had fleetingly teamed up with David McAlmont. No deliberately conceived album emerged from the duo's first spell as collaborators, though *The Sound Of McAlmont And Butler* (Hut, 1995) collected the contents of their two singles – including the spectacular Yes – along with a handful of studio off-cuts. Their belated second album, *Bring It Back* (EMI/Chrysalis, 2002) was an altogether more well-rounded record, managing to develop the update of classic pop-soul that had been sketched out seven years before. In the meantime, Butler had briefly been a Creation artist and released two solo albums: *People Move On* (Creation, 1998) and *Friends And Lovers* (Creation, 1999). The former, though it strayed dangerously close to the middle of the road, had enough melodic appeal to make it a qualified success; the follow-up, unfortunately, was an anodyne disappointment.

More Britpop

1990–3

The first stirrings of a new pop-cultural love affair with both London and the totems of British identity can be heard on St Etienne's *Foxbase Alpha* (Heavenly, 1991): London Belongs To Me prophetically begins with the line 'Took a tube to Camden Town.' Hostility to the grunge upsurge found a brief champion in Luke Haines of the Auteurs, fleetingly grouped with Suede as harbingers of a return to the artful ways of English rock, before they slipped free of both the implied generic limitations and the music press's expectations of success. Their debut album, *New Wave* (Hut, 1993) is a frequently thrilling encapsulation of musty-smelling capital bohemia: as an example of how to sound like The Beatles while also oozing intelligence and poise, Showgirl, the opening track, is pretty much perfect. Six years later, the group's chief, Luke Haines, elegantly called time on lad culture with *How I Learned To Love The Bootboys* (Hut, 1999): required listening for anyone who bemoaned the more malign aspects of Oasis's success.

Notice of Britpop's partial footing in a world of spangles, Vimto and crimplene was served by Denim, commanded by Lawrence Hayward, the erstwhile boss of Felt. *Back In Denim* (Boys Own, 1992) is a hilarious conceptual work that evokes the 70s combination of boredom and Day-Glo tackiness; on the equally amusing follow-up, *Denim On Ice* (Echo, 1996), he eruditely bemoans the worst aspects of Britpop in a song called The Pub Rock Revival. From there, Hayward set out on his own doomed equivalent of the Britpop experience. A Denim single optimistically entitled Summer Smash was to have appeared on an EMI subsidiary but was withdrawn after the death of Diana, Princess Of Wales. In 2000, he released *Instant Wigwam And Igloo Mixture* (Cherry Red, 2000), credited to Go-Kart Mozart but a Denim record in all but name. Both bitter and absurd, it contains a morbidly funny piece about heroin addiction entitled Plead With The Man.

The long-lost Mancunian project World Of Twist traded in a multi-textual charity-shop camp very similar to early 90s Pulp. *Quality Street* (Circa, 1991) suggests that an arrival at the time of Britpop may have led to the success that life at the fag-end of baggy denied them. Noel Gallagher was a huge fan: early on in their progress, Oasis considered changing their name to Sons Of The Stage, after a brilliant World Of Twist single that managed to reach number forty-seven.

In a completely different area, Dodgy, the London-based trio who would later enjoy their fifteen minutes in the Britpop sunshine, issued some of their best work when no-one was looking: the use of 60s influences on *The Dodgy Album* (A&M, 1993) achieves far more than the blinkered revivalists of the Noelrock period, as does the lion's share of the following year's *Homegrown* (A&M, 1994), which includes the Britpop staple Staying Out For The Summer. Such were Britpop's distorting effects on musicians that they decided that the creation of such radio fare was their metier, and went on to score a top 5 hit with the cheap and chirpy Good Enough (A&M, 1996). Anyone who understandably has them marked down as perma-grinning lightweights should go straight to *Homegrown*'s transcendent closing track, Grassman.

This period's most impressive nod to the 60s, however, was the only album by The La's (Go! Discs, 1990), a mystical, magical work that, as of 1994, became a Britpop touchstone. They could have returned and made a mint; instead, Lee Mavers, their chief motive force, remained in Liverpool, while his myth grew ever larger. Noel Gallagher claimed that Oasis were 'finishing what the La's had started' – in an unintended sense, he was arguably proved right.

1994

Aside from the raptures prompted by Blur, Oasis et al, 1994 saw the arrival of Supergrass. The pop-punk mini-drama Caught By The Fuzz was released in October: along with the Britpop staple Alright, you'll find it on *I Should Coco* (Parlophone, 1995). It's a particularly interesting album on account of one historical quirk: ten years after Alan McGee had founded Creation with a desire to fuse punk rock and Syd Barrett, the likes of I'd Like To Know and Strange Ones combine both influences to wondrous effect. Two years later came *In It For The Money* (Parlophone, 1997) – less playful, but even better, as proved by Richard III's garage-rock frenzies and Sun Hits The Sky's update of The Who.

Gene arrived sounding alarmingly like The Smiths, though their early singles were better than their reputation as callow impersonators suggested: in their evocation of broken hopes, satellite towns and closing-time violence, For The Dead, Be My Light, Be My Guide and Sleep Well Tonight – all on *As Good As It Gets* (Costermonger, 2001) – conveyed a sophistication lacking in most of their peers, though Gene rather failed to develop it. Shed Seven's name might provoke mirth, but they were as tightly sewn into Britpop as any of their contemporaries. The singles collected on *Going For Gold* (Polydor, 1999) are hardly epochal, but they occasionally capture their moment: Going For Gold (number eight, March 1996) and Chasing Rainbows echo Britpop's fondness for lighter-aloft balladry; 1994's woefully titled Ocean Pie is a surprisingly effective piece that represented Britpop's first grapple with the subject of heroin (for a brief time, Shed Seven singer Rick Witter dated Elastica's Donna Matthews). As of early 1994, Echobelly were similarly buoyed by the Britpop moment and enjoyed eighteen months of mild success. Their first two Smiths-influenced singles, Bellyache and Insomniac, were their best: they're both on *On* (Fauve/Epic, 1994).

1995

The paradigmatic hit of 1995 was The Boo Radleys' Wake Up Boo! (Creation, 1995), the horn-enhanced top 10 hit that duly became an immovable favourite with the UK's breakfast DJs. As an emblem of Britpop's dangerous fixation with the kind of success built on whistling milkmen, it takes some beating: play it after listening to the slightly more visionary music on the group's *Giant Steps* (Creation, 1993) – especially the stunning Lazarus – and you get a Before And After picture of the group's much-praised creative chief, Martin Carr.

Sleeper traded in craftily commercial songs about forlorn suburban lives that were stretched to breaking point on their albums, but made for a run of endearingly throwaway singles: for proof, listen to Inbetweener and Vegas – the latter featuring Graham Coxon on saxophone – on *Smart* (Indolent, 1995), and Nice Guy Eddie from the platinum-selling *The It Girl* (Indolent, 1996). The rise of The Bluetones, by contrast, confirmed Britpop's increasing emphasis on boy-rock craftsmanship: the single Bluetonic (Superior Quality Recordings, 1995) drew on Adrian Mitchell's four-line poem Celia, Celia and suggested a brio and wit that were sadly lacking on their debut album *Expecting To Fly* (ditto, 1996); their early promise was belatedly realised five years later on *Science And Nature* (Superior Quality Recordings, 2001) – see the lushly ambitious The Last Of The Great Navigators and Emily's Pine – but by then, it was rather too late.

Stephen Duffy was the one-time singer with Duran Duran who spent five minutes as an 80s pop star before forming the elegantly folky Lilac Time, who were briefly signed to Creation. In 1994, he had reactivated a solo career; according to his own account, he returned to London from the USA, having heard that record companies were 'giving contracts away', and promptly signed to the same label as Sleeper. He soon released the brilliant album *Duffy* (Indolent, 1995), which contains at least two songs that capture an outsider's perspective of the Britpop experience. Needle Mythology captures the moment at which heroin's outlaw chic snared a new crop of musicians, while London Girls is Britpop's Penny Lane: a fond, filmic evocation of Camden Town, pop stars flopping out of The Good Mixer, and the music weeklies tumbling into the tube station's kiosk on Tuesday lunchtime.

Menswear's first three singles are not exactly great art, but they evoke both the Camden milieu and the group's high velocity rise and fall. I'll Manage Somehow is a serviceable nod to The Jam, Daydreamer uses one chord to pastiche Wire via Elastica and managed to reach a completely unmerited number sixteen, and Stardust has a lightweight poke at Primal Scream's Bobby Gillespie. Along with Sleeping In and the yawn-inducing top 10 ballad Being Brave, they're all on *Nuisance* (Laurel, 1995), but be warned: time has not been kind.

1995 was also the year in which Paul Weller was reluctantly established as Britpop's one elder statesman, a role summed up in the eternally parroted notion that he was 'The Modfather'. *Stanley Road* (Go! Discs) spent endless weeks in the upper reaches of the album charts; it has its moments – The Changingman, the title track, the sublime Out Of The Sinking – and is certainly better than the unfocused, self-important *Heavy Soul* (Go! Discs, 1997), but this author prefers *Wild Wood* (Go! Discs, 1993), the rustic, plaintive record that decisively began Weller's renaissance.

Help (Go! Discs, 1995) was the album that found the united New Swinging London in a moment of philanthropy, and crystallised the confidence and ambition that were coursing around the veins of the UK's musicians. The year ended with Oasis triumphant, and Britpop's first novelty record: The Mike Flowers Pops' version of Wonderwall – included on the album *Groovy Place* (London, 1996) – which was only prevented from reaching number one by Michael Jackson's Earth Song.

1996

The year of Noelrock. Students of the genre, should such people exist, are advised to seek out Cast's *All Change* (Polydor, 1996), made by the band commanded by sometime La's bassist John Power, and Ocean Colour Scene's *Moseley Shoals* (MCA, 1996). The latter became a music press bête noire, a matter hardly helped by their rather oafish belligerence – although the occasionally ornate lyrics of singer Simon Fowler betrayed a substance that was rarely acknowledged. Their best songs – The Circle, The Day We Caught The Train, Travellers Tune – are on the aforementioned album and *Marchin' Already* (MCA, 1997), though it should be noted that their reverence for Marriott, Lennon et al usually gets the better of them. For proof of how awful this strain of music could get, ferret in the bargain bins for Kula Shaker's *K* (Columbia, 1996); if your curiosity about Britpop's fag-end remains unsatisfied, see also Northern Uproar's self-titled debut (Heavenly, 1996), effectively the work of a youth club band with a record contract.

By way of proving that, despite such records, Britpop was now defining the mainstream, 1996 saw two more novelty singles: Star Turn's pub-singer send-up of Parklife and Roll With It (MCA, 1996), and one of the stranger manifestations of Oasis's success: a version of I'd Like To Teach The World To Sing (EMI, 1996) by the tribute band No Way Sis, which seized on Shakermaker's debt to the New Seekers and managed to sneak into the top 30. The Smurfs attempted to turn Wonderwall into Wondersmurf, but Noel Gallagher wasn't having it.

1996 also saw the release of *Trainspotting*. The soundtrack album (EMI, 1996) features Pulp's Mile End, Sleeper covering Blondie's Atomic, Elastica's 2:1, Blur's aforementioned Sing and Closet Romantic, credited to a solo Damon Albarn. It also features Underworld's Born Slippy, a de facto Britpop hit – and dependable provider of yet another Proustian rush – simply by dint of its timing. A second volume (EMI, 1997) has no Britpop aspects at all, aside from Sleeper's lightweight Statuesque.

The Euro '96 tournament also saw a CD spin-off: *The Beautiful Game* (RCA, 1996), which contains the inescapable Three Lions, along with available-elsewhere tracks from Blur, Pulp and Supergrass. Its most noteworthy contribution comes from Black Grape, whose invigoratingly silly England's

Irie tries to be a football song, but can't help dropping the inevitable drug references.

1997

Aside from the release of *Blur*, 1997's most noteworthy Britpop moments were Noel's visit to number 10 and the release of *Be Here Now*. The best records blazed a very different trail, although one song should be mentioned: Adidas World, a song on *I'm Not Following You* (Setanta, 1997), by the ex-Orange Juice singer Edwyn Collins, which seizes on the Britpop generation's love of old-school sportswear and concisely expresses an erstwhile punk rocker's diagnosis of their central problem: 'I heard it once or twice, and unless I got it wrong/You can't defeat the enemy by singing his song.' Fittingly, it features the former Sex Pistol Paul Cook on drums.

The historical context

The sixties

Thanks partly to the Gallaghers, The Beatles' spectral presence hung over the Britpop moment, though the release of the three CD volumes of *Anthology* between 1994 and 1995 undoubtedly helped. *Volume 1* (Apple, 1995) contains Free As A Bird, the single that, for many, will evoke its period as instantly as Live Forever or Girls And Boys. As to the music The Beatles created in the sixties . . .

Revolver (Parlophone, 1966) was a de rigueur album throughout the 90s, though whether one can hear its influence in many records is a moot point. Oasis just about approximate the steely drive of Dr Robert and And Your Bird Can Sing on Up In The Sky from *Definitely Maybe*, and *Setting Sun* (Virgin, 1996) – the Chemical Brothers collaboration with Noel Gallagher – is, to all intents and purposes, a simplified update of Tomorrow Never Knows. The 90s paradigmatic Beatles song, however, is Hey Jude, available on *Past Masters Vol. 2* (Apple, 1988). The following description might sound unnecessarily churlish, but in its nodding-dog meter, non-specific lyrics and elongated sing-along segment, one hears a blueprint that Oasis return to time and again, and the source of a great deal of the lighter-in-the-air ballads that followed in the Gallaghers' wake. If 1997's Beetlebum is anything to go by, Blur – to their credit – preferred the more off-kilter material on *The Beatles* (Apple, 1968), aka *The White Album*.

Both bizarrely illuminating and endlessly hilarious are the infamous Beatles send-ups created to soundtrack the 1978 spoof documentary *All You Need Is Cash*, the tale of The Rutles. They're all collected on a US CD simply entitled *The Rutles* (WEA/Rhino, 1990): Piggy In The Middle and Cheese And Onions sound a little like out-takes from *Be Here Now*; while with a bigger production budget, Let's Be Natural could have taken the place of Who Feels Love on *Standing On The Shoulder Of Giants*. Noel Gallagher shared his credit for 1994's Whatever with chief Rutle Neil Innes: the latter took action on account of the Oasis song's resemblance to his own How Sweet To Be An Idiot – available on *Re-cycled Vinyl Blues* (EMI, 1994) – and was awarded 10 per cent of the songwriting royalties.

The other key 60s name to drop was The Kinks. To varying degrees, *Face To Face* (Pye, 1966), *Something Else By The Kinks* (Pye, 1967), *The Kinks Are The Village Green Preservation Society* (Pye, 1968) and *Arthur (Or The Decline And Fall Of The British Empire)* (Pye, 1969) form the reason why: Ray Davies' withering social comment – cf Sunny Afternoon, Do You Remember Walter, Shangri-La – was a key influence on Damon Albarn. It's also interesting to note that Davies' work on these records attracted similar accusations of haughty snobbishness to those levelled at Albarn circa *The Great Escape*.

Paul Weller's revival ensured that the Britpop period also saw a surge of interest in The Small Faces: for a time, those who aimed at proving they were cooler than the sudden droves of Gallagher-inspired Beatles fans could be heard ill-advisedly claiming that they were the equal of John, Paul, George and Ringo. 1996 saw a lukewarm tribute album, *Long Ago And Worlds Apart* (Nice, 1996), featuring the likes of Dodgy, Gene, Northern Uproar and Ocean Colour Scene, though – with the exception of the latter group, along with Weller – little of the Small Faces' trademark meld of soul, rock and R'n'B seemed to make its way into anyone's original material. It was, however, de rigueur to satirise Britpop's mockney tendencies with a quick rendition of 1968's Lazy Sunday – available, with the cream of the group's post-1965 material, on the 2-CD set *The Darlings Of Wapping Wharf Launderette* (Sequel, 1999).

The Who were a similarly obligatory reference point, though – once again – their audible influence seemed diffuse at best. There is, however, much fun to be had in hearing the handful of Pete Townshend songs that pre-date Britpop's camped-up Englishness: Pictures Of Lily, I'm A Boy, Tattoo, Dogs. The latter in particular is both prescient and delightful, preceding the *Parklife* era's totemic attachment to greyhound racing by twenty-six years, and featuring a chorus that surely predicts the more miserable aspects of lad culture: 'There was nothing in my life/Bigger than beer'. Sadly, it's only currently available on the 4-CD box set *Maximum R'n'B* (Polydor, 1994), though a good 75 per cent of the collection's content is worth the expense.

Though Scott Walker was a native of Ohio, his relocation to the UK saw the creation of music that both evokes 60s-era London, and has long been a touchstone for British musicians who wish to give their songs an epic, expansive aspect: Damon Albarn, for example, self-deprecatingly referred to his vocal on Blur's The Universal as 'my saddo, would-be Scott Walker'. Walker's influence is smeared all over Suede's *Dog Man Star* (cf Black Or Blue, Still Life), and – as evidenced by his production role on 2001's *We Love Life* – he was a central part of Jarvis Cocker's aesthetic universe: for instant proof, play the title track of *This Is Hardcore*. *No Regrets* (Fontana, 2000) gathers up both the best of his work with The Walker Brothers and some of his 60s solo material; a more generous helping of the latter is provided by *Boychild: Best Of 67–70* (Fontana, 1990). For a fuller understanding of what was booming from the stereos of musicians' pads in NW1 and W11, buy *Scott* (Fontana, 1967), *Scott 2* (Fontana, 1968) and *Scott 3* (Fontana, 1969): all showcase the echo-laden melodrama that was so influential twenty-five years later.

While we're here, it's interesting to note that Britpop's debt to The Rolling Stones was negligible. The purple patch that stretches between 1968's *Beggars Banquet* and 1973's *Goat's Head Soup* was so steeped in Americana that – despite the best efforts of Primal Scream circa 1994's *Give Out But Don't Give Up* – such records stood in almost polar opposition to London-based developments. The Stones' brief period as English pop conceptualists – from 66's *Aftermath* to the following year's *Between The Buttons* and *Their Satanic Majesties Request* – could easily have acquired a new clout, but strangely, those records were also confined to the margins. That said, ill-informed journalists were prone to draw comparisons between the Stones and Oasis – though the Gallaghers revealed the misplaced nature of such talk with their truly dreadful cover of Street Fighting Man, tucked away on the B-side of All Around The World (Creation, 1998).

The seventies

David Bowie was a far greater influence on Britpop than any artist of the 60s. Much of the relevant music spans just under five years of Bowie's career, from 1971 to 1975: as of *Young Americans* (RCA, 1975), he strode into areas – funk, soul, the icy experimentalism of 'Heroes' and Low – that were never part of Britpop's vocabulary. To grasp his centrality to the 90s, begin with *Hunky Dory* (RCA, 1971): 'one of the greatest albums ever made,' according to one 1995 Damon Albarn interview. Blur's debt to the album is obvious: lines can be easily drawn between This Is A Low and Life On Mars?, or from Oh! You Pretty Things to End Of A Century.

Elsewhere, the source of much of Suede's early inspiration is revealed: certainly, The Bewlay Brothers – at one time Brett Anderson's favourite Bowie song – finds Bowie falling into a very similar mewl to the one that would later be adopted by Haywards Heath's most celebrated lead vocalist, and Quicksand sounds like a precursor to the more melodramatic songs on *Suede*. That said, the most Suede-ish of Bowie's albums is *The Rise And Fall Of Ziggy Stardust And The Spiders From Mars* (RCA, 1972), as evidenced by the likes of Soul Love, Moonage Daydream and Lady Stardust.

Equally crucial to an understanding of the Britpop period are *The Man Who Sold The World* (Mercury, 1971), *Aladdin Sane* (RCA, 1973) and *Diamond Dogs* (RCA, 1974), though one aspect of Bowie's early 70s music failed to find much of a reflection in the 90s. Throughout all the aforementioned albums, Bowie frequently plunges into knockabout raunch – Queen Bitch, Suffragette City, Rebel Rebel – that was probably never going to find its way into music made by clenched graduates of the 80s indie milieu. Tellingly, it was Britpop's younger purveyors who drew on such songs – most notably Supergrass, whose 1999 single Pumping On Your Stereo – from *Supergrass* (Parlophone, 1999) – is an absolutely see-through pastiche of this side of Bowie's music.

As far as his later work is concerned, two songs in particular attract comparisons with Britpop. Both draw on *Lodger* (RCA, 1979). Blur's M.O.R., from *Blur*, was sufficiently in hock to Boys Keep Swinging to net Bowie a share of the royalties; Party Hard, from Pulp's *This Is Hardcore*, nods – slightly more obliquely but no less deliberately – at the sound minted by Look Back In Anger. It should also be noted that in 1997, Oasis played their role in Britpop's ongoing Bowie-fest by covering 'Heroes', for a B-side of D'You Know What I Mean?. Tellingly, their rendition – sung by Noel Gallagher – was of the edit you'll find on *Bowie: The Singles Collection* (EMI, 1993) rather than the full-length, more lyrically rich version on 'Heroes' (RCA, 1977). They also forgot about the inverted commas.

Two other early 70s names were recurrently mentioned during the Britpop period: Roxy Music and T-Rex. The former had a less pronounced effect on Britpop than Bowie, but on Pulp in particular, the influence of their cavorting art-school camp and parping analogue keyboards – as exemplified by the likes of Do The Strand, Virginia Plain, All I want Is You and The Thrill Of It All – was unquestionable. Within Pulp's oeuvre, one can also hear echoes of more reflective, shadowy Roxy songs like In Every Dream Home A Heartache and A Song For Europe; tellingly, they employed Roxy's 70s producer Chris Thomas for both *Different Class* and *This Is Hardcore*. With perfect timing, a 4-CD Roxy Music box set, *The Thrill Of It All* (Virgin, 1995), was released during Britpop's peak period: three-quarters chimed with the moment, though the material recorded after their 1979 comeback – particularly the airbrushed likes of Dance Away, More Than This and Avalon – was far less relevant. For a cheaper way in, begin with *Roxy Music* (Island, 1972) or *For Your Pleasure* (Island, 1973).

Marc Bolan's calling card was a knowing take on old-school rock'n'roll that frequently placed his songs in the same ballpark as the raunch-based Bowie songs mentioned above; for that reason, his influence on Britpop was not nearly as great as might be supposed. Still, T-Rex's *The Slider* (EMI, 1972) was a reference point for Suede's Coming Up, though it was more a source of the record's broad approach – in keeping with Bolan's abiding philosophy, the album emphasises clipped, economical pop songs – than specific musical ideas. Also, attention must be drawn to Noel Gallagher's brazen cribbing of the central riff from 1971's Get It On (Bang A Gong) for Cigarettes And Alcohol; the former song is available, with Bolan's best work, on *The Essential Collection* (Universal Music TV, 2002).

Finally, a brief word about Slade. Oasis covered 1973's Cum On Feel The Noize on the B-side of Don't Look Back In Anger and arguably improved on the original, though they could probably have delivered Mama Weer All Crazee Now, Gudbuy T'Jane or Far Far Away with equal aplomb: Slade's roughed-up blend of rock dynamics and beat-pop commerciality amounts to an early version of the Gallaghers' aesthetic. Also, simply on account of its brilliance, listen to 1975's How Does It Feel ('one of the greatest songs ever written,' according to Noel), which is collected with the songs referenced above on *Greatest Hits* (Polydor/Universal Music TV, 1999).

Punk and beyond

A love of punk was one of Britpop's leitmotifs: from such adrenalised Blur songs as Popscene and Advert, through Justine Frischmann's fondness for the genre's more angular aspects, to the Gallaghers' frequent tributes to The Sex Pistols (not to mention the reappearance of Rotten et al in 1996), its influence was inescapable. This was partly down to a common generational experience: punk's aftershocks were still audible as the members of the Britpop groups took their first pre-adolescent musical steps.

The Pistols' impact on Noel Gallagher is obvious in the wall-of-sound guitars that have long characterised Oasis's recordings. For proof, play such songs as Headshrinker and Bring It On Down next to the more piledriving moments of *Never Mind The Bollocks Here's The Sex Pistols* (Virgin, 1977). The much-trumpeted similarities between Liam Gallagher and Johnny Rotten/Lydon's vocals can quickly be proved by flipping between Cigarettes And Alcohol and Liar (also from *Bollocks*: compare Liam's pronunciation of 'Imagination'/ 'situation' with the Rotten/Lydon take on 'Suspension'. Flying forward twenty years, the Pistols' Britpop comeback is commemorated on *Filthy Lucre Live* (Virgin, 1996).

The Clash were far too angry, a little too rock'n'roll, and – as of 1979's

London Calling – too fond of the USA to be revived by the Britpop groups. Instead, thanks in part to Paul Weller's reappearance, the 90s saw renewed interest in The Jam. As with The Clash, the abiding tenor of their music was a little too irate and politicised to find its way into Britpop, though the Camden hordes would have happily frugged away to a good two-thirds of the singles collected on *Greatest Hits* (Polydor, 1991) – and besides, a complete understanding of both Blur and Oasis's early musical tastes would be incomplete without knowledge of *All Mod Cons* (Polydor, 1978), *Setting Sons* (Polydor, 1979), *Sound Affects* (Polydor, 1980) and *The Gift* (Polydor, 1982).

Out of all proportion to their punk-era success, Wire were a much more salient Britpop reference point. Their first two albums, *Pink Flag* (Harvest, 1977) and *Chairs Missing* (Harvest, 1978) defined a sizeable part of Elastica's aesthetic universe: cf their fascinatingly angular arrangements, and songs that frequently did their work in well under two minutes. 1995's Connection owed enough to Three Girl Rhumba (from *Pink Flag*) to merit a split songwriting credit; ditto Donna Matthews' Human (on both *The BBC Sessions* and *The Menace*) and *Pink Flag*'s Lowdown. Much was made of Line-Up's similarity to I Am The Fly from *Chairs Missing*, though this boiled down simply to the meter of the former's chorus; hardly enough to bear out charges of plagiarism. Meanwhile, word of Wire's brilliance had spread to Elastica's immediate circle of friends: Menswear's awful Daydreamer owes most of its ideas to I Feel Mysterious Today from *Chairs Missing*.

To sample other parts of Elastica's record library, try the sole studio album by the pre-fame line-up of Adam And The Ants, *Dirk Wears White Sox* (Do It, 1979), and The Stranglers' *No More Heroes* (UA, 1977). Frischmann and co's remoulding of the latter group's music was a particularly inspired move: the fact that three women were paying tribute to such a macho group made a compelling sexual-political point. On one song, however, influence once again teetered into pilfering: Waking Up was sufficiently close to No More Heroes to lead to another royalties pay-out.

As far as Britpop-era Blur are concerned, three further names – all of whom came to prominence in punk's aftermath – spring to mind. XTC's relevance to Blur's Anglo-centric turn in 1993 was confirmed by Andy Partridge's abortive spell as the producer of *Modern Life Is Rubbish*; his lingering influence is proved by the similarities between It Could Be You from *The Great Escape* and the 1981 XTC single Respectable Street from *Black Sea* (Virgin, 1980). For a crash-course, go straight to the *Fossil Fuel* compilation (Virgin, 1996); more curious Blur fans should buy *Black Sea*, along with *Drums And Wires* (Virgin, 1979) and *English Settlement* (Virgin, 1982).

Damon Albarn has long been a fan of The Specials, whose weary, doom-laden take on the English expanse can be heard on Death Of A Party from *Blur*, and *The Great Escape's* less successful Fade Away: for any comprehensive understanding of English music in the 70s and 80s, *The Specials* (2-Tone, 1979) and *More Specials* (2-Tone, 1980) are all but obligatory. Also, the parallels between Blur and Madness are glaring – not just on account of the similarities between the likes of Parklife and Sunday Sunday and Baggy Trousers, House Of Fun, Our House etc., but also because of the qualities shared by Blur's more reflective songs and such oft-overlooked Madness compositions as One Better Day (a portrait of the more hopeless corners of Camden Town circa 1984) and Yesterday's Men. Either could be played after The Universal or Best Days without breaking the mood. Anyone keen to investigate the more cerebral aspect of Madness's music should sample *Keep Moving* (Stiff, 1984) and *Mad Not Mad* (Zarjazz/Virgin, 1985); the requisite *Best Of* compilation is *Divine Madness* (Virgin, 2000).

At least some of the stuff that later cohered as Britpop can be heard in one-off hit singles by bands who appeared in the wake of punk, and had only the smallest bite of the commercial apple. The Regents' 7 Teen (Rialto, 1980), The Vapors' Turning Japanese (UA, 1980), The Members' The Sound Of The Suburbs (Virgin, 1979) and The Leyton Buzzards' Saturday Night (Beneath The Plastic Palm Trees) (Chrysalis, 1979) are all cases in point. As things stand, though the ever-snowballing punk compilations market takes in many such songs, car boot sales and on-line vendors remain the best bet (on Amazon's Z-Shops service, for example, the price of the Regents' single currently hovers between two and five pounds).

Finally, a brief mention for the much-maligned mod revival of 1979: history's first example of the 60s-worship that would become de rigueur fifteen years later. Somewhat inevitably, most of the music was dreck, though a couple of records managed to break from a depressing norm: most notably, The Chords' Jam-apeing Maybe Tomorrow (Polydor, 1980), and Secret Affair's My World (I-Spy, 1980). For a flavour of the surrounding scene, try the CD reissue of *Mods Mayday '79* (Castle, 2002), a multi-band live album recorded at The Bridge House, Canning Town. It brings to mind Britpop with no Blur, and far too many Menswears.

SELECT BIBLIOGRAPHY

Magazines

Melody Maker, Mojo, Loaded, NME, Q, Select, Sounds, Uncut, Rolling Stone, Spin, Vanity Fair. With reference to Oasis, two articles merit special mention: Top Of The World, Mam by Phil Sutcliffe, published in *Q* 113, February 1996; and Titanic! by Paul Lester, published in *Uncut* 34, March 2000. The latter remains Noel Gallagher's most exhaustive account of his career to date. When it came to biographical information about Blur, Andrew Collins's English Music, Art, History, from *Q* 102, March 1995, proved indispensable.

Books

Two books in particular should be singled out: David Cavanagh's brilliant *The Creation Records Story: My Magpie Eyes Are Hungry For The Prize*, (Virgin, 2000), which is recommended for any student of British alternative music; and Stuart Maconie's *Blur: 3862 Days* (Virgin, 1999). In addition, the following proved invaluable:

Abbot, Tim, *Oasis: Definitely*, Pavilion Books, 1996
Aston, Martin, *Pulp*, Pan, 1996
Butler, David and Kavanagh, Dennis: *The British General Election of 1987*, Macmillan, 1988; *The British General Election of 1992*, Macmillan, 1992; *The British General Election of 1997*, Macmillan, 1997
Collin, Matthew and Godfrey, John, *Altered State*, Serpent's Tail, 1997
Denselow, Robin, *When The Music's Over*, Faber And Faber, 1990
Gallagher, Paul and Christian, Terry, *Brothers: From Childhood To Oasis, The Real Story*, Virgin, 1996
Gambaccini, Paul, Rice, Tim and Rice, Jonathan, *The Guinness Book of Top 40 Charts*, Guinness, 1996
Garfield, Simon, *The Nation's Favourite: The True Adventures Of Radio One*, Faber And Faber, 1999
Haslam, Dave, *Manchester, England*, Fourth Estate, 1999

SELECT BIBLIOGRAPHY

Hewitt, Paolo, *Getting High: The Adventures Of Oasis*, Boxtree, 1997; *Forever The People: Six Months On The Road With Oasis*, Boxtree, 1999

Hutton, Chris and Kurt, Richard, *Don't Look Back In Anger: Growing Up With Oasis*, Simon & Schuster, 1997

Kureishi, Hanif and Savage, Jon (eds), *The Faber Book of Pop*, Faber And Faber, 1995

Langdon, Julia, *Mo Mowlam: The Biography*, Warner Books, 2000

Larkin, Colin (ed), *The Virgin Encyclopedia of Popular Music*, Virgin, 1999

Leonard, Mark, *Britain™: Renewing Our Identity*, Demos, 1997

Macintyre, Donald, *Mandelson and the Making of New Labour*, HarperCollins, 1999

Middles, Mick, *From Joy Division To New Order: The Factory Story*, Virgin, 1996

Morgan, Kenneth O., *The People's Peace: British History 1945–1990*, Oxford University Press, 1992

Norman, Philip, *Shout! The True Story of The Beatles*, Penguin, 1993

Rentoul, John, *Tony Blair: Prime Minister*, Little, Brown, 2001

Roach, Martin, *Blur: The Whole Story*, Omnibus Press, 1996

Robertson, Ian, *Oasis: What's The Story?*, Blake, 1996

Rogan, Johnny, *Morrissey and Marr: The Severed Alliance*, Omnibus Press, 1993

Routledge, Paul, *Mandy: The Unauthorised Biography of Peter Mandelson*, Simon & Schuster, 1999

Russell, Dave, *Popular Music In England, 1840–1914*, Manchester University Press, 1997

Seldon, Anthony, *Major: A Political Life*, Phoenix, 1997

Smith, Chris, *Creative Britain*, Faber And Faber, 1998

Strong, Martin C., *The Wee Rock Discography*, Canongate, 1996; *The Great Alternative & Indie Discography*, Canongate, 1999

Taschen, Angelika and Edwards, Jane, *London Interiors*, Taschen, 2000

Weller, Helen (ed), *The Guinness Book of Hit Singles: 11th Edition*, Guinness, 1995

Young, Hugo, *One Of Us*, Pan, 1993

Young, Toby, *How To Lose Friends And Alienate People*, Abacus, 2001

ACKNOWLEDGEMENTS

This book would not even have been begun had it not been for my agent Hannah Griffiths, late of Curtis Brown and now an editor at Faber and Faber Ltd.. She remains an amazing source of advice, motivation, discipline, insight and friendship, and I owe her a debt beyond words. Thanks also to my British editor, Andy Miller, who actually appeared to enjoy conversations about XTC and the more underrated aspects of The Who's back catalogue; and the tireless, eternally gracious Nick Davies at Fourth Estate. When it comes to the American edition, I am especially grateful to Ben Schafer at Da Capo, who provided not only a much-appreciated opinion of the book and its prospects, but also an inspired repackaging job, and my American agent, Sarah Lazin.

I am indebted to everyone who agreed to be interviewed for the book, and particularly grateful to the following: Justine Frischmann, who deserves special thanks not only for four incredible conversations but also for her generous photographic contribution; Alex James, whose courtesy and enthusiasm remained intact even at eight o'clock in the morning; the always-insightful Mike Smith; and Tim Abbot, who repeatedly shone penetrating light on the Gallaghers' progress and trawled through his video and photo archive. Special thanks also to Miranda Sawyer, who generously donated two massively useful interview transcripts.

Thanks to the reliably hospitable editorial staff of *Q* and *Mojo*, who not only didn't mind my rifling through back copies but also asked me how the book was going with sufficient enthusiasm to keep me sane; Cate Jago, Ben Knowles, Karen Walter and Steve Sutherland, who allowed me access to *NME*'s archives; Johnny Cigarettes, aka John Sharp, and Danny Plunkett, who did the same at *Loaded;* and Paul Williams and Martin Talbot at *Music Week*. I also take this opportunity to salute the team at *Select* magazine between 1996 and 1999: I hope some of the inspiration that coursed around the office has found its way into the text.

In addition, I am very grateful to the following: Murray Chalmers at Parlophone, Phill Savidge and Grace Holbrook at Savage & Savidge, John Best at Bestest, Kate Cons at CMO, Mog Yoshihara at Rough Trade, Pippa Hall at

ACKNOWLEDGEMENTS

Monkey Business, Amanda Freeman, all at RMP, Sarah Roberts at the BPI, Katherine Harrison at Big Brother, Terri Hall at Hall Or Nothing, Harry Shapiro at Drugscope, Mo Mowlam, Danny Eccleston, Cila Warncke, Arabella Brooke, Jane Titterington, Steve Peck, Moira Croft, Cheryl Herr at the University of Iowa, and the staff of Kettlewell Village Stores (www.kettlewell.info).

Perhaps most important, I want to express heartfelt gratitude to Shaun Phillips and Steve Lamacq, without whom none of the last ten years would have happened. Thanks also to John Mullen, Polly Birkbeck and, in particular, Steve Lowe, whose interest, knowledge and encouragement were frequently a much-needed tonic; Johnny Dee and Kathy Ball, whose proof-reading was beyond compare; Karl Rhys, a truly great friend; Cerys Matthews for two fantastic trips; Adam Smith and Neil Smith; my mum, who inspires and motivates like no-one else; and Hywel Harris (at www.hywel.biz), for his companionship, brilliant work on the website, portrait photography and Herculean removals assistance. My biggest thanks go to Ginny Luckhurst, whose love, support, patience and home-making genius are truly the stuff of dreams.

John Harris, Hay On Wye, May 2004

Index

411

INDEX

'Labour's coming home' speech 303, 329, 342; Youth Experience Rally 303–4; meets music business representatives 306–7; and *Vanity Fair* 327–8; entertains Noel Gallagher 344–5, 356; at Chequers 357; and Radiohead 372

Blair/Collenette Promotions 154, 155

Blanco Y Negro label 9, 107, 207

Blenheim Crescent, London 7

Blondie 92, 95, 98

Bloor, Charlie 40

Blow Up club-night, The Laurel Tree 98, 204–5

Blue Oyster Cult 129

Blur 321, 324, 348, 369

Blur xiii, xvii, xxi, 98, 123, 135, 205, 234, 279, 357, 368; beginning of 50; alcohol 51, 52, 66–7, 72, 78, 81, 143; Justine on 52; first single 53; first video 54–5; Brit Awards xiv–xv, xix, 192–4, 196, 222, 279; financial problems 66; Popscene 66, 67–8, 77, 78, 79; Morrison starts to manage 66; in America 70–3, 77, 93, 330, 361; compared with Suede 74; Britishness 79–80; and Partridge 81–2; Reading Festival 91; *Top Of The Pops* 143, 197; Glastonbury 167; *Q* magazine award 188; UK tours 237–8, 259–60; official biography (*3682 Days*) 345n

Blur-tigo (EP) 71

BMG group 208

BMX Bandits, The 132

Boardwalk, Manchester 124–8, 132, 337

Boht, Jean 329

Bolan, Marc 105

Bon Jovi 282

Bono 45, 189

Bonzo Dog Doo-Dah Band 328

Boo Radleys, The xvi, 160, 224, 234, 249, 305, 307

Boon, Clint 121–7

Booth, Tim 9

Boston, Massachusetts 70

Bottomley, Virginia 304, 305, 328, 356

Bournemouth International Arena 238, 250

Bournemouth Showbar 238

Bowie, David 27, 32, 36, 64, 75, 85, 96, 105, 135, 222, 263, 273–4, 315, 368

Bowie, Iman 96

BPI (British Phonographic Industry) 84, 273

Bradfield, James Dean 346

Bradford 187–8

Bragg, Billy 4, 22, 151–4, 196

Branson, Richard 357

Brat Awards 138–9

Bratmobile 236

Brewer, Dr Colin 165, 247

Brickell, Edie 109

Bridewell Taxis, The 19

Bright, Graham, MP 13, 22, 109

Brighton 51, 108

Bristol University Anson Rooms 143

Bristow, Virginia 310

Brit Awards xiv–xv, 84–5, 138, 154, 174, 192–5, 216, 222, 223, 271–3, 279, 348, 352, 357

British Council 355–6

British National Party 133

Britpop xv–xxi, 201–4, 366; beginning of xx, 201–2, 321; alcohol 51; high watermark (1995) xv, 222; Albarn's flight from 282–5; debt to the past 367; end of xviii, xx, 343, 348; most potent legacy 369

Britpop Now programme 234

Brixton Academy 67

Brockwell Park, London 10

Brookes, Bruno 137

Brooking, Trevor 162

Brooks, Garth 174

Broudie, Ian 302

Brown, Gordon 343

Brown, Ian 16–19, 124–5, 132

Brown, James 10, 254, 327

Brown, Roy 'Chubby' 234

Browne, Jackson 156

Brownlee, Jason 42

Bull & Gate pub, Kentish Town, London 24, 35

Buller, Ed 171, 172

Bummed 15, 16, 20, 31, 120

Bunce, James 29

Bunce Court, Kent 29

Bunker, The (Creation HQ in Hackney) 109, 111, 112

Burchill, Julie 231

Burgess, Tim 19, 132

Burnage, Manchester 116, 337, 341

Burroughs, William 85, 209

Bush, David 318, 319, 363

Butler, Bernard 36–7, 65, 75, 99, 278, 317, 360; education 32–3; background 33; personality 33, 51; joins Suede 33; composing 34, 63, 134–5; aggressive guitar parts 35; tension within the band 37–8; on the Justine-Brett break-up 61–2; songwriting with Brett 62; leaves Suede 168–72, 186

Butler Education Act 29

Buzzcocks 5–6

Byrds, The 17, 36

Caithness, Lord 150

Cale, John 39

Callaghan, James 151

Camden Falcon, London 24, 50, 64, 94

413

INDEX

INDEX

INDEX

INDEX